Table of Contents

BUFFALO'S DELAWARE AVENUE
Mansions and Families

Second Edition, with Index

By Edward T. Dunn

With Introduction by Cynthia Van Ness and
Index by Amy Miller

First published in 2003 by Canisius College Press
Second Edition published by Buffalo Heritage Press in 2017

Buffalo Heritage Press
266 Elmwood Avenue, Suite 407
Buffalo, NY 14222
www.BuffaloHeritage.com

BUFFALO
HERITAGE
PRESS

1st edition ISBN 0-9740936-4-5
2nd edition ISBN 978-1-942483-32-8

Library of Congress control number available upon request.

Printed in the U.S.A.

10 9 8 7 6 5 4 3 2 1

Introduction to the Second Edition

When Father Edward T. Dunn's history of Delaware Avenue was published by Canisius College Press in 2003, it was the first book-length history of the Avenue and it filled a large gap in Buffalo history scholarship. Until that time, the only other history of Delaware Avenue was written in 1994 by Dr. Frank Kowsky as chapter two of a larger work, *The Grand American Avenue.* When it was released, *Library Journal* called *The Grand American Avenue* ". . . a long-needed book that will appeal to a wide span of readers."

The same is true of Father Dunn's book. Edward T. Dunn, a Jesuit priest and educator, died in 2013. His book went through four printings before he passed away. Perhaps because his mother once worked as a domestic servant, Dunn paid close attention not only to prominent residents but also to their household staff, greatly increasing the genealogical value of the book.

However, the book lacked an index, which hindered access to its encyclopedic content. Knowing how critical an index is to a work of enduring research value, we added it to our project list in the Research Library at The Buffalo History Museum. We hoped to match it up with a library science student in search of an internship. Within librarianship, indexing is a professional specialty and is taught at the graduate level.

In 2014, Buffalo History Museum Assistant Librarian Amy Miller studied Father Dunn's book and decided to take on the project of indexing it herself. It represents about 100 hours of meticulous labor. We planned to make this robust, four-part index available at cost to researchers and fellow librarians. However, when Buffalo Heritage Press, which holds the copyright for Buffalo's Delaware Avenue: Mansions and Families, learned of the existence of the index, it was instead decided to incorporate it into a Second Edition of this important work. You will find it on pages 585-617 complete with use instructions and a valuable table which documents the street numbering changes that took place in 1867.

The Buffalo History Museum is pleased to lend our professional expertise to the new revised edition of *Buffalo's Delaware Avenue: Mansions and Families.*

CYNTHIA VAN NESS
DIRECTOR OF LIBRARY AND ARCHIVES
BUFFALO HISTORY MUSEUM

The decades between the end of the Mexican War and the beginning of World War I revolutionized America's cities and countryside which taken together constituted the largest free trade area in the world. Canals, railroads, and newer modes of lake and ocean transport shrank the nation and enlarged its markets. Industrial growth allied with improved methods aided by science and invention generated an enormous outpouring of goods. One of the most visible results of this astonishing expansion was the rise almost overnight of new classes of men, capitalists and industrialists, who were positioned to garner a disproportionate share of the profits of the process. They had gotten in on the ground floor of America's new industrial prosperity. Dependent on them were concentric rings of professionals: managers, architects, lawyers, brokers, educators, and clergymen. In cities across America, but especially in the Northeast and Midwest, these noveaux riches erected magnificent mansions in the same neighborhood, a largely unconscious cooperative exercise in what Thorstein Veblin termed "conspicuous consumption." The upshot was that, as Sherry C. Birk has noted, virtually every city and town had its "Grand Avenue," demonstrating amid differences a fundamental similarity in rise, growth, and decline. The editors of *The Grand American Avenue, 1850-1920* selected a dozen of these aristocratic residential thoroughfares of which Buffalo's Delaware Avenue was the second. During the last two-thirds of the nineteenth century the Queen City of the Lakes was uniquely placed astride the nation's trade routes to participate in what Mark Twain immortalized as the "The Great Barbecue."

Classic Delaware Avenue ran two and a quarter miles from Niagara Square to Chapin — later Gates — Circle. There were many brave men before Agamemnom, and there were many homes of mansion quality on other Buffalo streets — Swan, Linwood, and West North come to mind — but only on Delaware was there a more or less continuity of wide elm-shaded graciousness. Its original inhabitants were old-stock, transplanted New Englanders almost to a man, usually Protestant, and Whig, later Republican in political allegiance. The clubs along the Avenue, beginning with the Buffalo Club, were splendid settings for the city's power lunches and dinners. In the sixty-two years between 1867 and 1939 Avenue residents held the club's presidency for thirty-five years. Later male clubs, Saturn, University, and for Jews Montifiore, were also located on the Avenue as was the women's Twentieth Century Club. Delaware Avenue Methodist Episcopal, Calvary Presbyterian, Christ Church Episcopal, and Delaware Avenue Baptist attracted fashionable congregations and were in most cases the architectural flagship of their denomination in the city. Later Avenue houses of worship with similar qualifications were Temple Beth Zion (1890) and the ill-starred Saint Joseph's Cathedral (1915).

Four generations, often predating the Civil War, of inter-Avenue marriages created a closely knit complicated cousinry, reminiscent of colonial Virginia. Overall the Avenue aristocrats exhibited a similar life-style. Their homes were well supplied with live-in help, usually Irish or German girls. Most had carriage houses in the back with a resident coachman (later a chauffeur) and family. Many of the boys attended Professor Briggs Classical School on the grounds of Bronson Rumsey's estate and after 1892 the Nichols School. Others went to one of the several quality Northeastern prep schools. The girls favored the Buffalo Female Academy, later Buffalo Seminary, or a fashionable finishing school. Beginning in the 1880s polo was all the rage among Avenue bloods, a sport they pursued avidly despite its obvious dangers. The cult of the horse became as ennobling in nineteenth century America as it had been in the Middle Ages. For less outdoor types the Country Club was organized in 1889 and the Park Club in 1903, both of which were originally located on Delaware Avenue adjoining the Park. For those who could afford it, yachting on the Great Lakes offered another expensive opportunity for their ostentatious expenditure. For the more sedentary, lavish banquets and balls, usually at private homes, provided occasions for genteel relaxation. A handful of the mansions even enjoyed facilities for amateur theatricals. Two further outlets for leisure time activities were foreign, especially European, travel and art collecting. Doctor Walter Cary set the example of the former even before the Civil War, and Seymour H. Knox, Jr.s' acquisitions at the end of the period in the field of modern art were vast. Finally a certain *noblesse oblige* motivated many, women included, to sit on boards of charitable, educational, and health care institutions.

The Avenue's south to north demise promoted by the automobile, the increasing attractiveness of rural or at least suburban life, the first federal income tax ominously enacted in 1913, rising labor costs, and a change in the life styles of the rich and famous was gradual; yet some of Delaware's greatest mansions, many of which have survived but not as residences, were constructed above North Street in the 20th century.

In the late 1970s I wrote a *History of the Park Club*, my introduction to Buffalo's elite. Having completed *Railroads in Western New York* in the mid-1990s, I cast about for a new topic and came up with Delaware Avenue, since most of the research could be done locally. Beginning in the early 1890s, my father's family lived in that part of Milburn, New Jersey, known as Short Hills. It was an upper class community begun by Stewart Hartshorn, inventor of the shade roller, in 1875. The project was to be self-sufficient, with its own post office, coal siding, fire house, Episcopal church, country day school, and living quarters for skilled workmen, one of whom was my grandfather, a plumber, who doubled as fire chief. Hartshorn even built a station and hired a station master to induce the Lackawanna Railroad to stop passenger trains at the new community. Comfortable stone English houses designed by Stanford White were built on large lots of a few acres or more. Roads were laid out without sidewalks to discourage the presence of outsiders and according to the contour of the hills. It was the coachman's job to pick up and post the mail.

From an advertising brochure for Short Hills, n.d., n.p.

Unconsciously my parents oriented me toward a study of Delaware Avenue. On Sunday afternoons in the early 1950s, my father, who had grown up in Short Hills, and I would walk through the Park and he would talk about the houses and families who had lived there. This experience made me big house conscious. My mother, who, though born in New York City, was orphaned early in life and was raised by her grandparents in County Cork. She came to this country at fifteen in 1901 and trained in New York Hospital as a baby's nurse. This solved the problem of food and shelter, since baby nurses were much in demand on a round-the-clock basis in the homes of the wealthy. In New York she belonged for some time to the household of the son of Senator Justin Morrill of Vermont. Later in 1911, when the broker for whose family she worked moved to Short Hills, she went along and lived with them until her marriage in 1924. She was treated almost like one of the family and gave me some insights into a vanishing job category, domestic servants.

Some might object to my including the census data in the body of the book and not relegating them to an appendix. My defense is that I was writing about families and this procedure enables the reader to get a clear picture of just who the families were and what sort of a role domestic servants played on the Avenue. It will also becamc clear to the reader that many houses on the Delaware were not mansions at all, but the mansions gave the Avenue its distinctive cachet. The other houses became mansions by attraction, analogous to the phenomenon in Latin grammar called "subjunctive by attraction" where "a clause depending upon a Subjunctive clause will itself take the Subjunctive [rather than the Indicative] if regarded as an integral part of that clause." (*Allen & Greenough's Latin Grammar*, Boston: 1901.)

EDWARD T. DUNN
BUFFALO, N.Y., 2004

CHAPTER

1 THE WHITE MAN *Cometh*

Before white settlement of Western New York could proceed beginning in the last decade of the eighteenth century, two major obstacles had to be removed, British presence at Fort Niagara and Indian ownership of the area. In the 1783 Treaty of Paris between Great Britain and the United States which ended the Revolutionary War a boundary had been agreed on which placed seven British held forts, including Fort Niagara, within territory ceded to the United States. Citing American failure to permit recovery of pre-Revolutionary debts owed British merchants and of loyalist property confiscated by the states, the British retained these forts until after the Jay Treaty in 1795 when they finally agreed to withdraw from these posts by June 1, 1796. By August the American flag was flying over Fort Niagara. Britain's involvement in war against France since 1791, and General Anthony Wayne's victory over the Indians at Fallen Timbers in August 1794, which ended Anglo-Indian resistance in the Northwest, forced the British government to curtail its New World commitments.

There remained the task of extinguishing Indian title to Central and Western New York. By King Charles I's 1664 grant of what was to become New York to his brother, James Duke of York, the Connecticut River was to be the eastern boundary of that colony, the Delaware the western. But since over half of Connecticut and about a third of Massachusetts lay west of the Connecticut, the Duke yielded to these two colonies all his land east of a line drawn twenty miles east of the Hudson. The western boundary of New York remained the Delaware. But state authorities had bigger ideas:

> New York's [extended] western claims arose from its relations with the Iroquois and the fur trade. In 1686 Governor Thomas Dongan granted the city of Albany a monopoly of the colony's fur trade. Only a few score Albanians, who made up the city's corporation, enjoyed this privilege. Since the Iroquois controlled the fur trade in the area, the city of Albany set up a board of commissioners to deal with them. The Iroquois' only outlet for furs was through Albany, and as a result they began to regard the board of commissioners as the agent of the British Empire.
>
> At this juncture England and France began the first of their series of colonial wars, and the Iroquois, as allies of New York, suffered grievously from the French raids. As the colonial powers, therefore, prepared to renew hostilities in Queen Anne's War, the Iroquois in 1701 sought protection for themselves by conveying all their hunting grounds to the British. Robert Livingston, of the Albany board of commissioners, negotiated the treaty. At the end of the war in 1713, in the Treaty of Utrecht, France recognized British suzerainty over the Iroquois. Under the circumstances it was logical to assume that the New York government, as the voice of the crown in the area, had acquired sovereignty over the

Iroquois country and that the right to exercise this authority rested in the hands of Albany traders.

In subsequent years, New York established Ft. Oswego on Onondaga lands and granted lands to speculators in the Mohawk and Schoharie Valleys and in the plateau country of Otsego County — all Mohawk areas. Informally, these actions seemed to confirm the belief that Iroquois lands were within New York's jurisdiction. Since the Iroquois had conquered the Susquehannas, and held sway over the Illinois, it could be argued that the Ohio country and parts of Pennsylvania were within the limits of New York rule too.[1]

There followed two more wars, ending with final British victory and the exclusion of France from mainland North America east of the Mississippi as provided for in the 1763 Treaty of Paris. Later armed clashes between Indians and colonials on the Northwestern frontier known as Pontiac's Rebellion explain the provision in the Royal Proclamation of 1763 which:

...prohibited colonial acquisition of all land west of a line drawn through the sources of rivers entering into the Atlantic Ocean. In New York this line cut sharply through Iroquois country and supposedly opened to settlement millions of acres in the upper branches of the Susquehanna watershed. The Iroquois, of course, resisted the implications of the Proclamation, and the British, who had no intentions of alienating their Red allies, moved to adjust the territorial dispute. They assembled the Iroquois chiefs at Fort Stanwix (Rome) in 1768 and redrew the Indian property line. Basically the new one accepted the existing settlement patterns as a guide and thus designated the Unadilla River and the Susquehanna Rivers...as the division between New York's white and Red settlements.[2](1.1)

This second treaty is described by John T. Horton:

At Fort Stanwix in 1784 [American] commissioners had treated with the Iroquois and, exploiting the enfeebled condition in which they had been left by the campaigns of 1779 against the Indians through Central New York of General John Sullivan, induced them to accept new boundaries considerably shorter than those which Sir William Johnson had given them at the first Fort Stanwix Treaty. By the second one the Nations ceded their remaining lands in Pennsylvania; in New York they ceded all that lay to the west of a line drawn straight from the mouth of Buffalo Creek to the Pennsylvania border. Thus they lost their old hunting grounds not only in the Chautauqua country but also in the region beyond. Part of a cession they had made to the Crown in Sir William's day they transferred to the United States. That was the Four Mile Strip on the American side of the Niagara. This new Western boundary from Lake Ontario to Pennsylvania, a new Southern boundary coinciding with Pennsylvania's northern one, an Eastern border going from the Delaware northward [via the Susquehanna and Unadilla Rivers to the] vicinity of Fort Stanwix [and thence] to Lake Ontario, now restricted the braves on three sides. On the fourth the Lake completed the circuit of their shrunken domain. (1.2)[3]

In the wake of Sullivan's raid the Senecas had moved west:

The proud and formidable nation fled, panic-stricken, from their 'pleasant valley,' abandoned their villages, and sought British protection under the guns of Fort Niagara. They never as a nation resumed their ancient seats along the Genesee, but sought and found a new home in the secluded banks and among the basswood forests of the Do-sow, or Buffalo Creek, whence they had driven the neutral nation 130 years before.[4]

1 Robert J. Rayback, ed., *Atlas of New York State* (Phoenix, New York: Frank E. Richards, 1957), p. 23.

2 *Ibid.*

3 John T. Horton, *et al.*, *History of Northwestern New York* (New York: Lewis Historical Publishing Co., 1947,) 1:16-17.

4 Henry Wayland Hill, *Municipality of Buffalo, New York: A History, 1720-1923* (New York: Lewis Historical Publishing Co., 1923), 1:49.

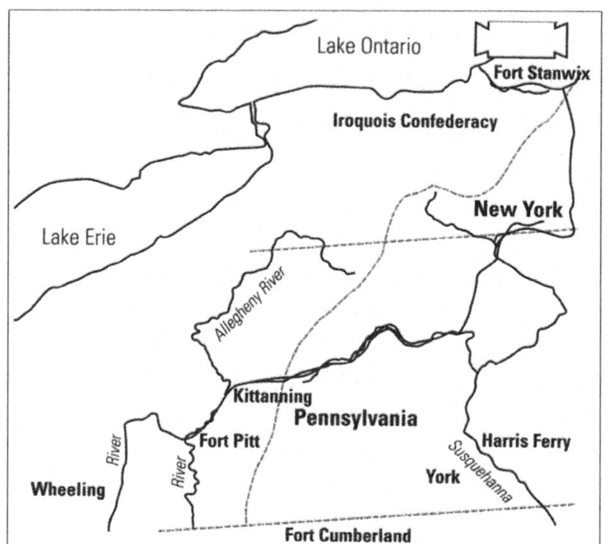

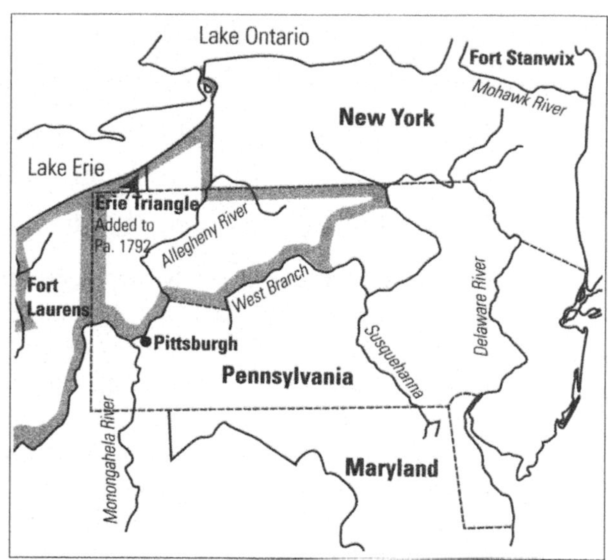

Left 1.1 Proclamation Line of 1763 – – – – and 1st Fort Stanwix Line of 1768 +++++++, James Truslow Adams, ed., *Atlas of American History* (New York: Chalres Scribner's Sons, 1942), p. 61.
Right 1.2 Lands ceded by Iroquois at 2nd Treayy of Fort Stanwix, *ibid.*, p. 90.

Though the outcome of the Revolution had extinguished British claims to Central and Western New York, Massachusetts had claims to the same area and beyond. Relying on a 1620 royal charter a group of noblemen known as the Council for New England had in 1628 granted to the New England Company an area measured from three miles north of the Merrimack to three miles south of the Charles across North America to the Pacific. Doubts as to the validity of this grant were dispelled by the famous charter granted by Charles I on March 4, 1629, to the Governor and Company of the Massachusetts Bay. This was the document John Winthrop and associates carried across the Atlantic in the *Arbella* in 1630. It restated the boundaries of the 1628 document. These provisions were repeated in Massachusetts' second charter of 1691, and included a 126 mile wide swath of land running north from 42-2 to 44-15, embracing all of western New York. New York and Massachusetts had agreed on an eastern boundary, but there remained the disputed land to the west of the Fort Stanwix line. New York took a first step toward resolving this problem by ceding all claims beyond the present boundary of Western New York to the United States in 1780. Massachusetts followed five years later. These cessions contributed to the creation of the Northwest Territories, which consisted of land ceded to the federal government by the states and bounded by Pennsylvania, the Ohio and Mississippi Rivers, and the Great Lakes.

There remained Indian land west of the Second Treaty of Fort Stanwix line, a princely domain of about 19,000 square miles, over twelve million acres. In 1786 Massachusetts and New York sent representatives to Hartford where a compromise was worked out by which New York acknowledged Massachusetts' right of preemption, that is of first purchase from the Indians, of all land in Western

New York west of line drawn north from the eighty-second milestone on the northern boundary of Pennsylvania west of the Delaware, and extending through Seneca Lake to Sodus Bay on Lake Ontario, known as Preemption Line. Excluded was a thirty-five mile long mile wide strip on the east bank of the Niagara from Lake Ontario to Lake Erie known as the New York State Reservation Line. (Richmond Avenue in Buffalo runs along this line.)

> Two years after this treaty, Massachusetts sold all of its land in New York, east and west of the Genesee to two land speculators, Oliver Phelps and Nathaniel Gorham. These men agreed to pay $1 million in three annual installments to Massachusetts for the 6 million acre territory. Before Phelps and Gorham could sell any of the land, however, it was necessary for them to terminate the Indian title to the tract. This they achieved in part. In 1788 Phelps persuaded the Senecas to give up 2.5 million acres east of the Genesee and about 200,000 west of that river in return for $5,000 and an annuity of $500. The Senecas clung to most of the land west of the Genesee because they believed that the "Great Spirit" had fixed that river as the boundary between the Indians and the white man. When it came to meeting the payments to Massachusetts, however, Phelps and Gorham managed to scrape only enough money for the first installment and could not meet the rest of their debt. To settle the financial problem, the Commonwealth of Massachusetts granted to the two men the full title to the land east of the Genesee on the basis of the single payment that had been made, provided that the land west of the river reverted to Massachusetts. Phelps and Gorham accepted the proposal, and this tract has since been known as the "Phelps and Gorham Purchase." [5]

Enter Robert Morris, a prominent speculator, who managed to amass temporarily most of Western New York. From Phelps and Gorham he bought much of the land east of the Genesee, about half of which he quickly sold to English investors. He then bought in five tracts the land west of the Genesee which Phelps and Gorham had surrendered to Massachusetts. He sold the eastern tract of his most recent acquisitions which became known as the Morris Reserve. The remaining four amounting to more than three million acres he sold to Theophile Cazenove, representing six Dutch banking houses — Peter Stadnitski & Son, Nicholaas and Jacob Van Staphorst, P. & C. Van Eeghen, Ten Cate & Vollenhoven, W. J. Willink, and Rutger Jan Schimmelpennick — that later organized the Holland Land Company. Before the sale could be completed Morris had to extinguish Indian title, which his agents did by negotiating the sale at a meeting at Big Tree in the summer of 1797. The Senecas received $100,000. Now the company owned all of Western New York (except some Indian reservations and the New York State Reservation) west of a line the greatest extent of which became known as the Eastern Transit Meridian, drawn a few miles east of the present Batavia. [6](1.3)

It was now incumbent on the company through Cazenove, its Agent-general, to arrange a survey of its holdings to provide for orderly sale. He chose Joseph Ellicott, (1.4) born in 1760 to Jo and Judith Ellicott in Bucks County, Pennsylvania, where Jo had been high sheriff and member of the provincial assembly. Later he migrated to Maryland and founded Ellicott's Mills where the family

5 William Chazanof, *Joseph Ellicott and the Holland Land Company: The Opening of Western New York* (Syracuse: Syracuse University Press, 1970), p. 19.
6 *Ibid.*, p. 20.

raised wheat and the sons opened a flourmill. The oldest son, Andrew, fought in the Revolution, becoming a major and acquiring a competency in science, mathematics, and clock making, and a national reputation as a surveyor. He participated in extending the Mason and Dixon Line, served on a commission to determine the boundary of western and northern Pennsylvania, and was appointed by President Washington to settle the disputed ownership of Erie, Pennsylvania. This Andrew did with the aid of his brothers, Joseph and Benjamin. Andrew also "made the first actual measurements of the entire length of the [Niagara] river and of the falls and rapids from Lake Erie to Lake Ontario,"[7] Soon afterwards, Washington selected him to lay out the national capital, which Major L'Enfant had designed. Andrew began the project in 1791, again bringing Joseph and Benjamin along. In 1793 Washington chose Andrew for his greatest work, identifying the frontier between the United States and the Spanish lands to the south.

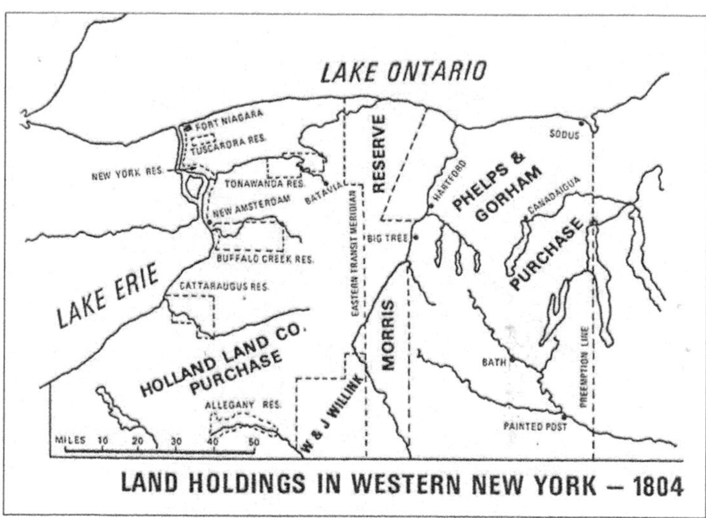

1.3 Chazanof, *op. cit*, p.23.

Cazenove, who had been in America since 1789, had already employed Joseph Ellicott in 1794 to survey and evaluate 1.5 million acres of unpromising mountainous land, which Cazenove had unwisely bought in northwestern Pennsylvania. With the signing of the Treaty of Big Tree, survey of the Holland Land Company's holdings in New York could begin. Ellicott spent the fall of 1797 in an exploration of the boundaries of the Purchase, during which he tramped nearly two hundred miles in the snow. He arranged with the Senecas for boundaries for their reservations which amounted to 200,000 acres.

1.4 **Joseph Ellicott, H. Perry Smith, *History of the City of Buffalo and Erie County* (Syracuse, New York: D. Mason & Co., 1884), facing p. 76.**

The mouth of Buffalo Creek fell within the northwest corner of lands initially earmarked for the Buffalo Creek Indian Reservation, the intended northern boundary of which was the line of the present William Street carried west to Lake Erie. Ellicott, however, arranged for this section to be

7 *Ibid.*, p. 13.

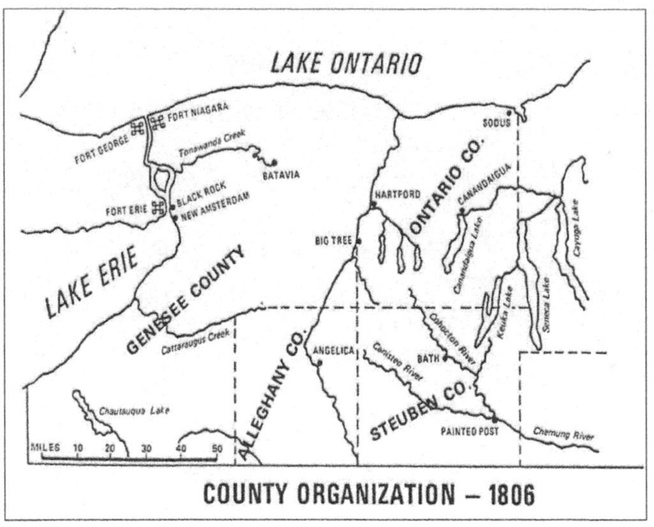

1.5 Chazanof, *op cit.*, p. 107.

kept within the Holland Purchase, since, though a sandbar at the mouth of the creek made it impassible for any but the smallest craft, it afforded the only possibility for a harbor within the Purchase. The protected harbor site at Black Rock was within the New York State Reservation. Ellicott was to subdivide the company lands into ranges of townships of six miles square to be divided not into thirty-six lots of 640 acres (one section) as was the federal practice, but into lots of 360 acres, which were sold in such parcels as buyers desired. In the spring of 1798 Ellicott, with David and Benjamin, headed a party of 130 men into the forest for a survey that would last until October 1800 and cost the company $70,921.69.

Proceeding *pari passu* with sale, survey, and settlement, Central and Western New York were incorporated into the state's political structure. In 1789 everything west of Preemption Line was set off as Ontario county — county seat, Canandaigua — and everything west of the Genesee was erected into the town of Northhampton. Towns were entitled to town meetings and elected supervisors who managed their towns and collectively formed the county legislature. Settlement was continually spreading out, making it difficult for citizens to assemble in meetings, hence the splitting up of large towns.

In 1796 Steuben County — county seat Bath — was marked off from Ontario. Its western boundary was the western boundary of the Phelps Gorham Purchase, and its southern boundary the Pennsylvania line. In 1802 Genesee County was formed from Ontario, embracing all of the state west of the Genesee and a line extending to Pennsylvania from the junction of the Genesee with Canaseraga Creek. Ellicott had pushed this through the legislature by promising to build a courthouse and jail at Batavia, where in 1800 at the junction of several Indian trails he had placed his headquarters as agent of the land company. Land transactions and mortgages had to be registered at county seats, and the trek to Canandaigua had proved tedious to him. The town of Northhampton was at the same time divided into four, of which Batavia comprised all of the state west of the Eastern Transit Meridian, i. e., the entire Purchase. In 1806 Allegany County was set off from Genesee, and in 1808 Chautauqua, Niagara — county seat Buffalo — and Cattaraugus were set off from Genesee.(1.5) Finally, on April 2, 1821, the legislature formed the southern part of Niagara County into a new county to be known as Erie which would contain more than half the area and two thirds of the population of the old as well as the former county seat.

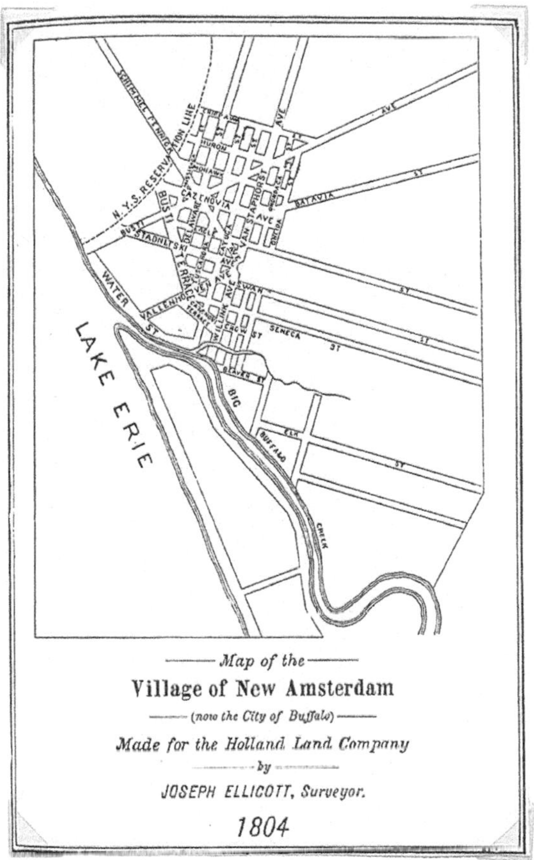

1.6 Inner Lots, Truman C. White, *Our County and its People: A Descriptive Work on Erie County, New York* (Boston History Co., 1898), I, facing p. 140.

To attract settlers Ellicott erected at Batavia a sawmill and gristmill at company expense. He also built roads through the forest, most of them following Indian trails. Of importance to Erie County were the road from Batavia to Buffalo (Route #5), the Middle Road which paralleled the southern boundary of Buffalo Creek Reservation connecting Lake Erie with the Genesee (Route #20), and the Lake Shore Road from Buffalo to Presque Isle in Pennsylvania. These ungraded wagon tracks made the region more accessible, raised the value of real estate, and enabled the settlers to earn real money, which was in short supply.[8]

Horton sketched the antecedents of the first wave of settlers on the Purchase between Cattaraugus and Tonawanda Creeks:

> Some were from Pennsylvania and of these, many were of the German stock that had been settled in that state since the third and fourth decades of the eighteenth century. Others were of the same stock long resident in the Mohawk Valley. Others yet again were Yankees either from the older parts of New York or direct from New England, particularly Vermont. Ellicott had something of a preference for the Pennsylvanians as they were believed to have more money than the rest, but it was with the Yankees that in the main he had to deal, since they constituted the great majority of the pioneers. To his regret he found them poorer than those who were trekking farther West to take up the cheaper land on the Federal domain and in the Connecticut Reserve [in Northern Ohio]. That they were astute and even artful bargainers no doubt contributed to the choler and misanthropy that became marked traits of his character as the years went by.[9] [He committed suicide in 1826.]

In 1804 the village of New Amsterdam, named out of deference to Ellicott's employers, was surveyed by William Peacock, later a judge and prominent resident of Mayville. Villagers ignored Ellicott's designation, preferring Buffalo Creek after the Seneca village on the stream of the same name. Then they dropped "Creek." Ellicott began to sell lots in 1800. The plan of the streets radiating from the square was copied from the survey of Washington of which he had been a part. Most of the streets were named for Indian tribes, including the Delawares, who had some connection to the area, or for officials of the land company. Batavia is Latin for Holland.

8 Horton, *op. cit.*, 1:23.
9 *Ibid.*, p. 24.
10 White, *op.cit.*, 1:148.

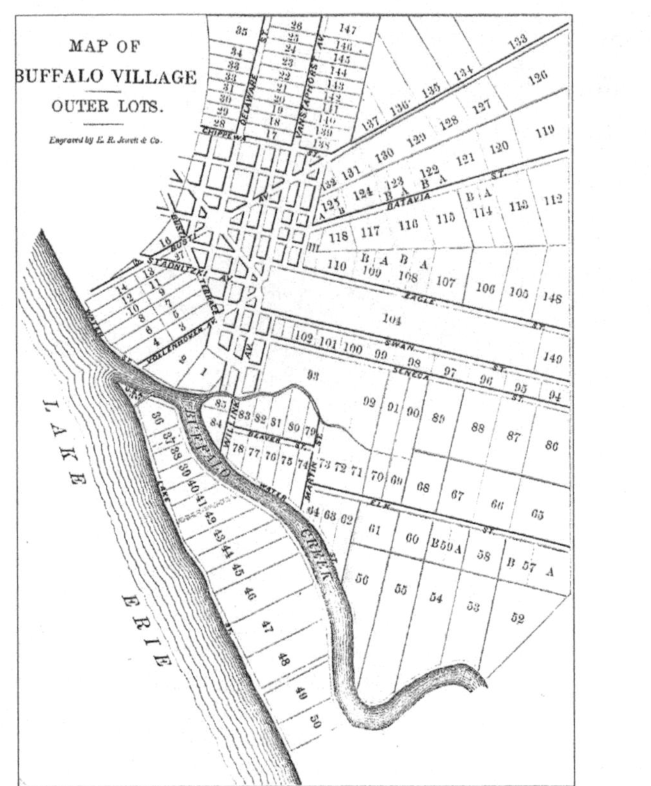

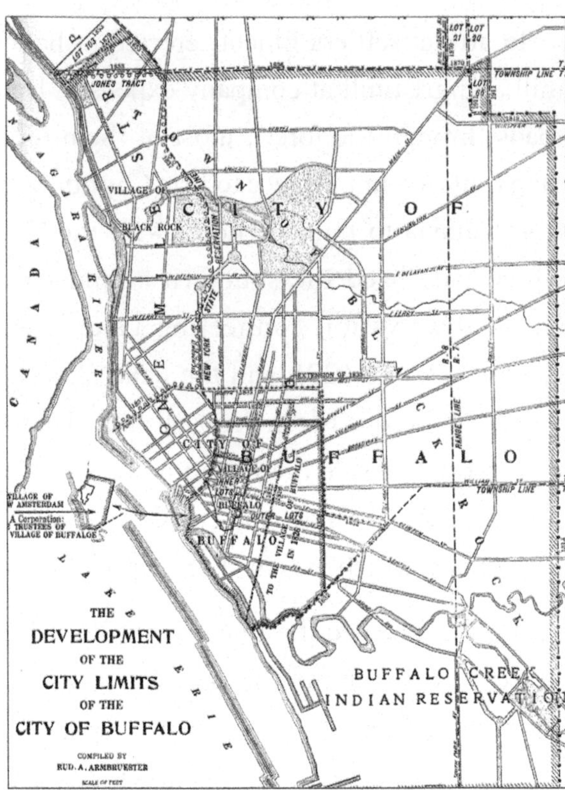

Left 1.7 ❦ Outer Lots, William Ketchum, *An Authentic and Comprehensive History of Buffalo, (Buffalo*, Rockwell Baker & Hill Printers, 1865), II, facing p. 304.
Right 1.8 ❦ Development of Buffalo's city limits, Hill, *Municipality of Buffalo*, I, facing p. 88.

Inner lots were located around the square in an area bounded by Chippewa Street, the New York State Reservation Line, the Terrace, Little Buffalo Creek, and Oneida (later Ellicott) Street. (1.6) Outer lots lay beyond in an area bounded by Virginia, the Reservation Line and the Lake, Buffalo Creek, and Jefferson Street. (1.7) "These [inner lots] were generally about four and a half rods wide and intended for commercial purposes, while the outer lots contained several acres." [10] Many of these inner lots became home sites; beyond them were farm lots.

William Hall of Cleveland, eighty-five in 1863, described the Buffalo he had passed through in 1804:

> At Buffalo there were perhaps twenty houses, of which only three or four were frame, one of which was occupied by a Mr. Pratt, who kept a small store. He had his aged parents with him. Some streets were partially laid out, but the whole were full of stumps, and no fences. We rode up the creek some mile or two, and crossed to see a Mr. Leech who was from Connecticut. Saw no craft, but one or two small boats in one of which we crossed. Leaving Buffalo we went to Black Rock, through woods — small pathway, trodden mostly by Indians, with some appearance of wagons having passed that way. We crossed the river in a scow without horses to the Canada side and found a good road on the bank of the river all the way to Chippewa. [11]

11 Hill, *op. cit.*, 1:106.

This Captain Samuel Pratt had traveled from Connecticut to Detroit to buy furs. Passing through Buffalo on his return, he bought Inner Lot 2 where he built a house, then the largest in the village, and a store where he began a successful business.

Rev. Timothy Dwight, grandson of the sainted Jonathan Edwards (as was also the less saintly Aaron Burr), Calvinist minister and president of Yale, visited Buffalo in 1804 and did not like what he saw. He found the area unhealthy and its people unimpressive. "The inhabitants," he wrote, "are a casual collection of adventurers, and have the usual character of such adventurers thus collected when remote from regular society, retaining but little of the sense of government or religion." After the survey, Buffalo began to fill up. An early settler wrote:

> I settled in Buffalo in 1806. There were then sixteen dwelling houses, principally frame ones; eight of them were scattered along on Main street, three of them on Cayuga street. There were two stores — one of them the 'Contractor's' on the corner of Main and Seneca streets, kept by Vincent Grant, on the east side of Main street. The other was the store of Samuel Pratt, adjoining Crow's Tavern. Mr. Le Couteulx kept a drug store in part of his house on the north side of Crow street. David Reese's Indian blacksmith shop was on Seneca street, and William Robins had a blacksmith shop on Main street. John Crow kept a tavern where the Mansion House now stands and Judge Barker kept one on the site of the Market. [12]

Buffalo became a village on April 5, 1816, an action delayed by the burning of Black Rock and Buffalo by the British in 1813. Black Rock was a rival settlement to Buffalo along the Niagara River. Note in figure 1.6 that the southernmost point of the reservation line reaches Lake Erie at Busti:

> Two miles down the Niagara, farther north along an escarpment was a scattering of dwellings beside a ferry landing. The spot was called Upper Black Rock because of an unusual triangular outcrop of dark stone jutting into the river to form a natural harbor and wharf. Eventually the settlement grew along the river for two miles or so until it joined Lower Black Rock, another small grouping of cabins. A ferry carried passengers across the Niagara to the flourishing village of Fort Erie, which had been established by the British before the Revolutionary War. [13]

The Black Rock at Prospect and Niagara Streets was destroyed during the construction of the Erie Canal. When Buffalo became a city on May 28, 1832, its boundaries were extended to North on the north, Porter on the northwest, Lake Erie on the West, and Buffalo Creek on the south. Thus was Upper Black Rock merged into Buffalo. Upper and Lower reflect the fact that the Niagara flows from south to north. By 1854 the city reached its present configuration by the absorption of both the village and town of Black Rock.(1.8)

12 Hill, *loc. cit.*

13 Wilma Laux, "*The Village of Buffalo: 1800-1832,*" the Adventures in Western New York History, (Buffalo & Erie County Historical Society: 1960), 3:1.

CHAPTER

2 COMMERCE, INDUSTRY, & THE GROWTH OF THE ELITE IN BUFFALO BEFORE & AFTER THE *Civil War*

The Great Surveyor had a vision of the future metropolis of Western New York:

> This plan conceived by Ellicott himself and surveyed in part by him, in part by his assistant, William Peacock, in 1803-1804, was a grid extending from Buffalo Creek up the high bank from which opened the view that Ellicott in 1798 had enthusiastically described to Theophile Cazenove. Around the crest of this bank curved a street called in compliment to the first Agent General Cazenovia Terrace until it was crossed by Vollenhoven Avenue, whence it continued as Busti Terrace to the end. In time the inhabitants would call it simply the Terrace, and Vollenhoven Avenue they would call Erie Street. With other names dear to Ellicott's fancy they would take equal liberties. Cazenovia Avenue, beginning at the end of Busti Terrace and going East through the public square they would call Court; and though they left the musical name Delaware to designate the street that crossed the square from North to South, the names of the diagonals that radiated from its corners they changed from Busti and Schimmelpennick Avenues, respectively to the more euphonious and manageable Genesee and Niagara. Chippewa, Huron and Mohawk [like Delaware itself, Indian names] satisfied them; so did Eagle, Swan and Seneca; but Crow Street, named from an early tavern proprietor, they turned into Exchange, and of Stadnitski Avenue they made Church Street. Of the North-South thoroughfares they converted the heathen Oneida and Onondaga into the Christian Ellicott and Washington; Cayuga they turned into Pearl and Tuscarora into Franklin. The main street they called simply that, though Ellicott had intended it to be called Willink up to Vollenhoven and thence Van Staphorst through the rest of its extent.[1] (1.5)

Ellicott is said to have named Delaware Street after one of the Indian tribes that frequented the portage road around nearby Niagara Falls.[2] Local historian Roy W. Nagle noted that when Ellicott laid out his village of New Amsterdam, he specified that Delaware should be ninety-nine feet wide, "an innovation in those days." Ellicott also intended that the square "be the 'Grand Plaza' for the business of the town and the congregating of its people."[3] David Schuyler adds that, "as had been true of L'Enfant's plan [for Washington], Ellicott's design combined a rectangular gridiron of streets 66 feet wide with a series of radiating avenues." However Schuyler adds:

> Equally important is the differing symbolism of the two plans. L'Enfant envisioned a national capital, not a commercial metropolis, whereas Ellicott reserved the most important space he created, the site of the Public Square (later Niagara Square) formed of the intersection of Busti Avenue and Delaware and Schimmelpennick streets (the modern Genesee Street, Delaware Avenue and Niagara Street), as the location of the headquarters of the Holland Land Company as well as the seat of local government. His plan was a symbolic statement of the primacy of commerce and order in a frontier village.[4]

1 Horton, *op. cit.*, I: 30-32.

2 Francis Kowsky, "Delaware Avenue, Buffalo, New York," in Jan Cigliano and Sara Bradford Landau, eds., *The Grand American Avenue, 1850-1920* (San Francisco: Pomegranate Artbooks, 1994), p. 36.

3 Roy W. Nagle, "Buffalo's Delaware Avenue," Buffalo & Erie County Public Library, Lafayette Square, Buffalo, p. 1.

4 David Schuyler, "Cityscape and Parkscape," in Kowsky, ed., *The Best Planned City: The Olmsted Legacy in Buffalo* (Buffalo: Buffalo State College, 1994), p. 7.

Oddly enough, this statement would not become valid until well into the twentieth century. In a fit of pique, Ellicott himself moved the headquarters of his company to Batavia.

1810	**1,508**	**1910**	**423,715**
1820	**2,095**	**1920**	**506,775**
1830	**8,653**	**1930**	**573,070**
1840	**18,213**	**1940**	**575,150**
1850	**42,261**	**1950**	**580,132**
1860	**81,129**	**1960**	**532,759**
1870	**117,714**	**1970**	**462,768**
1880	**155,134**	**1980**	**357,870**
1890	**255,664**	**1990**	**328,123**
1900	**352,387**	**2000**	**292,648**

2.1 ❦ Population of Buffalo, 1810-2000. *Statistical Abstract of the United States, 1910*, (Washington, D.C.: U. S. Government Printing Office, 1911) covers large cities from 1790-1910. All of Black Rock included within Buffalo by 1860.

In 1821 Delaware was recorded as a street to the north line of the village, Chippewa Street. Five years later it was declared a public highway. In 1827 it was continued to Guide Board Road (North Street.) It was designated Delaware Avenue in 1881, by which time its aristocratic credentials had been long established.[5]

Since the source of the wealth of most of the Delaware families in the Avenue's glory days was originally local, an account of the development of Buffalo's economy, of its population growth, and of its resulting social stratification is indicated.[6] With the completion of the Erie Canal in 1825, Buffalo would soon be seen as "the great natural gateway between East and West." At first, much of its commerce was intrastate, stimulated by the construction of lateral canals tapping the agricultural hinterlands of Central New York. But then came the completion of the Midwestern canals from the interior of Ohio, Indiana, Illinois, and Michigan to Lake Erie. By 1836 Ohio's grain production had surpassed that of New York, and now grain which had hitherto been shipped west from Buffalo began to come east. By 1838, Buffalo's flour and wheat receipts exceeded those of the older port of New Orleans, signaling the predominance of the Lake Erie-Erie Canal-Hudson River route over that of the Ohio and Mississippi rivers. By the mid-1850s, Buffalo was the world's largest grain port.

This development impacted significantly on the city's population growth.(2.1) In 1810, the first time Buffalo appeared in the federal census, its population was 1,508; ten years later it was still only 2,095. But in 1830, five years after the arrival of the canal, it had reached 8,653. Thereafter, population nearly doubled every decade reaching 81,129 in 1860, when Buffalo was the tenth largest city in the United States.[7]

Hence before the 1860s Buffalo's chief economic function was transshipment, with many of its economic activities centered around the development of services linked to this function, e. g. warehousing, forwarding cargoes, commissioning grain and produce for sellers and buyers, breaking down bulk cargoes, brokering in maritime insurance, and providing price and marketing information. The city had also developed a ship and canal boat building industry. What it lacked was an easily available source of fuel to underwrite milling and heavy industry.

5 Nagle, *ibid.*
6 David A. Gerber, *The Making of an American Pluralism: Buffalo, New York, 1825-1860* (Chicago: University of Illinois Press 1989), chapters 1-5.
7 Population of Buffalo, 1810-1920, *Statistical Abstract of the United States, 1910* (Washington, District of Columbia: United States Government Printing Office, 1911) covers large cities 1790-1910.

On the role of commerce in early Buffalo, David Gerber writes:

> The logic by which commerce came to dominate Buffalo was apparent to the eye in the spatial layout of social relations and economic functions. Ellicott envisioned a town in which the use of space was purposefully prioritized. The officials of the Holland Land Company, who saw themselves as an American squirearchy, were to dominate and structure space from their commanding position at the public square, while workaday commerce was to be restricted to the periphery of the inner town. What actually came to happen was the reverse.
>
> After 1825 the city grew around and out from the waterfront — its functional center. Then one of the world's most valuable pieces of land, the central docks, or "inner harbor," were located along the Buffalo River, which joined the canal terminus to Lake Erie via a number of narrow, north-south streets and an ever increasing number of ancillary private slips and public canals and channels. The dock area was a fascinating, congested, battered shambles of scenes and functions. The immediate environs of the docks soon contained elevators, warehouses, wholesale groceries, freight and passenger ticket offices, mercantile yards, dry-docks and small industrial workshops connected with waterborne commerce. The barrel-making, boiler, and engine shops and planning mills were especially heavily concentrated along Mechanic Street, one of the city's first areas of artisanal concentration. So many private slips and canals were eventually placed off the Erie Canal and river that the area was compared by more than one imaginative tourist to Venice. Commercial islands — really warehouses surrounded by shallow, narrow trenches just wide enough for canal boats — were thus formed. By 1845 this Venetian landscape had crossed to the east of Main Street.[8](2.2)

Horton thus describes the growing bustle in the harbor once the canal had established itself as the city's main transportation link to the east:

> As the [canal] barges that brought much of this population drifted into port and as steamboats, schooners, and an occasional full-rigged ship like the *Julia Palmer* sailed out, the Buffalo waterfront along Buffalo Creek came to life. Canallers, dock-hands, steamboat runners, immigrants, travelers, rich and poor, confidence men, ship captains, merchants and merchant's clerks mingled in a noisy and colorful crowd on the dock, on Long Wharf, Central Wharf, and Main Street. On that corner of town forwarding firms throve and increased: Joy and Webster, Sheldon Thompson and Company, Gelson and Evans, Holt, Palmer, Coit, Kimberly and Company, Hunter, Palmer and Company, Townsend and Coit, Kimberly and Pease and a score besides.[9]

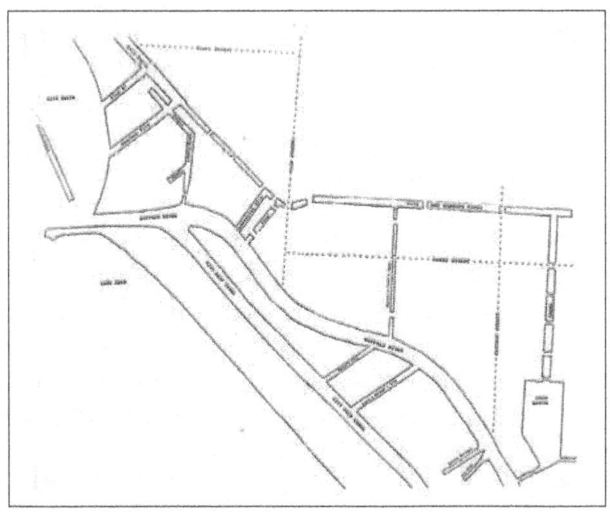

2.2 ❦ Buffalo's Inner Harbor; western terminus of the Erie Canal, from Griffith M. Hopkins, *Atlas of the City of Buffalo, Erie County, New York* (Philadelphia: G. M. Hopkins, 1872).

Buffalo's first businessmen were of New England stock and, though numerically they would soon

8 *Ibid.*, p. 13.
9 Horton, *op, cit.*, 1:72.

be successfully challenged by a flood tide of immigrants from Europe, Yankees would long dominate the local economic and social scene. Gerber thus depicts their geographic and social antecedents:

> The typical bourgeois professional, merchant, or manufacturer of the 1840s and 1850s had come to the city from somewhere else. Approximately 50 to 60 percent of the sample had been born in New York State of parents who were themselves natives of the declining farm country of western New England. In the 1790s this parental generation had migrated to Upstate New York. While often of rural origins, the parents settled in villages in the counties of the Hudson Valley or, in many more cases, of what became the Erie Canal corridor. The higher commercial or professional status of these families is attested to in several ways. Only eight (13 percent) of sixty-three had been apprenticed, while forty (63 percent) were identified as having had some education — fifteen in common schools, eleven at academies, and fourteen at college. Only seven of these biographies are presented in the familiar rags-to-riches mode. Much therefore, points to parental subsidies in the launching of careers. [10]

As will be seen, these traits will be exhibited with great regularity in the case of the heads of older Delaware Street families. The same can be said of what these future leaders accomplished after having attained their majority:

> After leaving school and before settling in Buffalo, most had experienced several types of employment and one or more relocations. They worked commonly as commercial or legal clerks or school teachers in New York State. They came to Buffalo in their twenties or early thirties to take positions as white-collar apprentices. They were clerks in dockside mercantile houses or retail shops, or read law at the invitation of relatives or parents' friends or of men they had met through past employment. A substantial minority (thirteen of the thirty-four whose early career pattern could be discovered) established their own businesses upon arrival. Most ultimately entered businesses. Of the fifty-two who could be said to have distinguished themselves principally at one endeavor over the decades, thirty-eight were in business, almost all of them in commerce, while the rest were lawyers (four), journalists (two), and doctors (eight). The origins of the capital of which mercantile careers were eventually launched suggests the possibilities and limitations of parental support. ...But they were hardly privileged enough not to have to work hard in pursuit of their career goals, which is attested to, for example, by the fact that Buffalo's most successful first-generation commercial firms were not corporations, but for the most part small partnerships and family enterprises. Thus, they could legitimately conceive of themselves as self-made men, for they were more makers than inheritors of their fortunes. Yet what subsidies their careers did enjoy were rooted in family and other primary social networks, and this casts a somewhat ironic light on the much-mythologized individualism of the nineteenth-century bourgeois man of affairs. [11]

The next step for these young men on the way up was acquiring a residence, at first temporary, then permanent. Gerber describes the process:

> With the creation of an economic base came the settling down of familial and other personal roots. The young men working in white-collar occupations often came alone, even when married, which helps to account for the imbalance in the sex ratio in 1855 in

10 Gerber, *op. cit.*, p. 66.
11 *Ibid.*

> the American-born population ages twenty to twenty-five (157) and twenty-six to thirty (139). Men such as Merwin S. Hawley, who at twenty-six began his career as the dockside representative for a firm of Rochester millers, believed that Buffalo was a rather disreputable place to which wives must not be brought until suitable arrangements had been made for lodging and the company of respectable society. Several years would pass before Hawley felt secure enough financially and trusting enough of his living situation to bring his wife to live with him at a lodging house owned by an old school friend. The young couple would live in this homelike setting for five years before building a house on exclusive Niagara Square.[12]

Increased opportunity and the pressure young couples like the Hawleys, now contemplating children, placed on the real estate market widened the area of bourgeois residence:

> Also stimulating this spatial mobility was the expansion of all types of commerce including the growing trade in livestock, into the elite neighborhoods immediately adjacent to the central business district. Now the boundaries of the elite corridor on the West Side were pushed north approximately a mile and a half into one of the city's only remaining forests. Homes on exclusive Delaware Avenue and only slightly less prestigious Pearl, Franklin, and upper Main Street enjoyed large lots, tree-lined streets and stone sidewalks. New, narrower cross-streets, more intimate and cheaper with their smaller lots, developed in between the grand avenues to accommodate the demand among both elite and nonelite Americans for homes and land. The concentration of Whiggish bourgeois householders on Delaware was so evident in 1853 that the *Courier's* editor suggested that the street's name be changed to "Fillmore Avenue."[13]

But a powerful rival to those engaged in the transshipment of waterborne commerce would soon appear. In 1853 the canal's receipts peaked and thereafter they declined. Railroads now dominated east-west passenger traffic because of their speed. The same speed was now available to commercial shippers together with lower insurance rates and the absence of transshipment costs. The weakness in Buffalo's economy was now revealed. It was narrowly developed and seasonal. What milling was done was merely to satisfy local needs; heavy industry was weak. Coal had to be brought by boat from northern Ohio mines. Tanning, the city's third largest industry with 500 employees, faced the depletion of local supplies of hemlock bark. The response to changed conditions is described by Schuyler:

> By mid-century Buffalo's economy faced two pressing challenges: the need to widen the Erie Canal and competition from the recently [1853] merged New York Central Railroad. The railroad effectively made the canal obsolete and threatened the community's port related economic foundations. The city's political leaders, together with representatives of other canal towns, wielded enough power to have the state undertake a major widening of the waterway, but as that work was in progress the railroad continued to attract cargo that formerly had traveled by water. Moreover, large numbers of Irish and German immigrants who established households in Buffalo transformed the city; by 1855 the population, once overwhelmingly native-born, was almost three-fourths immigrant. Civil leaders confronted the task of integrating these newcomers into the economy and the adjusting to a pluralistic society by diversifying the manufacturing capacity of the community, most notable in the

12 *Ibid.*, p. 67.
13 *Ibid.*, p. 69.

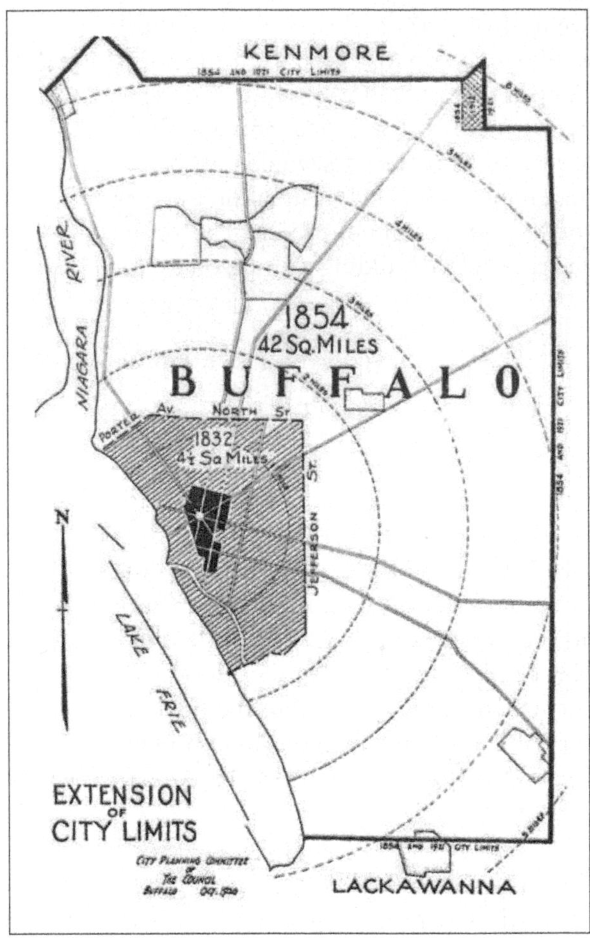

2.3 Map of Buffalo in 1854, Hill, *op. cit.*, I, 299.

emergence of steam-powered grain elevators and several highly capitalized industries, but the vast difference between native and newcomer were evident in political affiliation, church membership, and even social habits. Older residents also attempted to promote orderly urban growth and perhaps to dilute the preponderance of immigrant votes, by annexing in 1854 approximately thirty-seven square miles of surrounding land.[14](2.3)

Buffalo was already famous as a grain center before the Civil War. The conquest of the prairie soil of the Midwest by chilled iron plows unleashed a flood of grain, which in 1880 totaled 112,000,000 bushels. The Court of Appeals noted toward the end of that decade that "a large proportion of the surplus cereals of the country pass through the elevators at Buffalo." Among the most dominant figures in this most distinctive and historic of Buffalo enterprises was Charles W. Evans, who went back to the days of Joseph Dart, promoter of an automated perpendicular conveyor belt which unloaded grain from the hold of a ship and lifted it into a storage house which by metonymy was known as an elevator. Other leading grain elevator proprietors by 1870 were John Wilkeson, Truman G. Avery, and Erastus Seymour of Niagara Square. Commission grain merchants living on Delaware Street that year included Alfred Daw (#42), Nathan Simons (#142), Frank Williams (#163), Ozias Nims (#168), Frank Fiske (#199), George Hazard (#211), John Pease (#217), Henry C. Winslow (#304), Silas Fish (#334), Samuel K. Worthington (#344), Charles Sternberg (#414), Jacob D. Sawyer (#560), and Jason Parker (#661). Dealers in grain were the largest occupational group on the Avenue that year, and by 1880 Charles W. Evans himself had moved to #468 Delaware on the northwest corner of that street and Virginia.

In the 1880s George Urban, Jr., W. C. Urban, and Edwin G. S. Miller formed Urban and Company whose flour, milled at a rate of 400 barrels a day, was sold principally in Buffalo, Albany, and Boston. Older than Urban was the firm of Thomas Thornton and Thomas Chester (#522 Delaware), who had bought the Globe Mill in 1845, to which in 1868 they added the National Mill. Still others were Harvey & Henry's Buffalo City Mill and Jacob F. Schoellkopf's (#553 Delaware) and George B. Mathews'(#830 Delaware) Frontier Mills on Bird Island, and Niagara Falls Mills, with a combined

14 Schuyler, *op. cit.*, p. 9.

capacity of 1,500 barrels a day.

Postbellum attempts to expand and diversify the local commercial and manufacturing sector succeeded. One of the most lucrative commodities to be floated down the Lakes to Buffalo was lumber, a trade which took off with the arrival here of William H. Gratwick (#414, later #776 Delaware), formerly of Albany. As Walter Dunn observes: "Lumber buyers had discovered the possibilities of marketing via the Erie Canal and were also aware of the enormous supplies of fine white pine easily available at Ohio and Michigan ports along the Great Lakes." [15] Besides Gratwick, eight other lumber dealers resided on the Avenue in 1880: Andrew Brown (#303), Harrison Mixer (#311), John N. Scatcherd (#615), William Brown (#758), George Haines (#987), Alfred Haines (#993), and Courtney De Cew (#1205). Meatpacking developed under the leadership of James J. Metcalfe (#672) and Jacob Dold, who took up where livestock shipments from the West ended.

Dunn has noted the "great stimulus to metallurgy created by the discovery of iron ore near Lake Superior in the 1840s." [16] Sherman S. Jewett (#256 Delaware) was the head of a large iron works founded in 1846 that bore his name. Until 1876 he was a partner of Francis H. Root (#221 Delaware) in the manufacture of stoves known nationwide by 1870. John D. Shepard (#38 Delaware) was operating iron works before the Civil War. Pratt and Company set up its first blast furnace in 1864 and by 1870 was operating eight heating and twenty-two puddling furnaces. David Bell (#771 Delaware), a Scotsman, built boats and steam engines including the first iron propeller to cross the Lakes as well as the first locomotive to come out of a Buffalo shop. Chillion Farrar (#506 Delaware) and John Trefts (#735 Delaware) founded a firm in 1864 which came to possess extensive works on Perry Street including machine and blacksmith shops, a pattern shop, and a boiler factory. Other iron and steel mongers flourishing in 1880 and residing on Delaware Avenue were Henry Childs (#141), William H. H. Newman (#157), George Beals (#183), Charles DeLaney (#198), and Rufus Lombard Howard (#251). Owner and manager of the American Glucose Company was Cicero J. Hamlin (#1035 Delaware). The steam plant, which powered his eight-story factory on Scott Street, was consuming 150 tons of coal a day in 1888. [17]

By the turn of the century the two traditional professions of law and medicine were well and almost equally represented on the Avenue. No doctors were listed in the census in 1900 as residing above Allen Street, whereas more lawyers dwelt above than below North Street. Upper Delaware boasted newer and bigger homes, some of them real mansions, while lower Delaware was slipping economically but very gradually, as older homes were being turned into rooming houses. Moreover, most lawyers had offices downtown while the majority of doctors seemed to have practiced out of their homes and hence wished to be more accessible to their patients in an era before the rise of the automobile.

15 Walter S. Dunn, *History of Erie County, 1870-1970* (Buffalo: BHS, 1972), chapter 2, "Industry in the Steam Age," pp. 21-39.
16 *Ibid*, p. 21.
17 Horton, *op. cit.*, 1:225.

LAWYERS		DOCTORS	
184	Thomas Cary	183	Lucius Howe
275	Charles Ribbel	187	Richard H. Satterlee
311	Harrison Mixer	202	George T. Mosley
334	Franklin D. Locke	212	Henry Frost
369	Robert Codd	339	John Coakley
443	Charles B. Sears	340	Charles Cary
560	George W. Parkhurst	341	William Krauss
576	Carlton Chester	369	Floyd S. Crego
641	Ansley Wilcox	382	Cornelius Wykoff
741	Edward Michael	493	Herman Hayd
762	Myron P. Bush	510	Roswell Park
841	William B. Hoyt	516	Joseph Cook
925	Daniel McIntosh	516	Joseph Cook
1069	Wilson S. Bissell	523	Elmer G. Starr
1089	Joseph G. Dudley	525	James W. Putnam
1115	James A. Roberts	564	Charles Jones
1119	George S. Potter	566	Herman Mynter
1131	Charles B. Germain	568	Harvey Gaylord
1168	John G. Millburn		

Not surprisingly, ten residents of Delaware Avenue were bank officials in 1900, as William McKinley, upholder of the gold standard, began campaigning for a second term as president: George Meadway (#169), Laurence Rumsey (#294), Albert Wright (#483), William C. Cornwell (#497), Robert Fryer (#685), Stephen M. Clement (#731), Charles Pardee (#938), Arthur D. Bissell #950), John Wayland (#1032), and Charles A. Sweet (#1040).

The most famous and lasting name on Delaware Avenue and in Buffalo society was Rumsey, concerning which family Horton writes:

> Bronson Case Rumsey [#330 Delaware] and Dexter Phelps Rumsey [#742 Delaware], his brother, heirs of Aaron [#672 Delaware], who was quick and dead in the year 1864, still operated in the '80s the paternal tannery built some forty years previous on the [Hamburg] Canal near Louisiana Street; but since then the establishment had been much enlarged. With about 600 vats, it was approximately the size of the one at Holland. Between them these Rumsey yards had in 1884 a productive capacity of some 200,000 sides a year. Nor was this the limit. The firm was steadily expanding its business until ere the century was out it would be one of the biggest of its kind in the country. Less extensive in their operations, [Myron P.] Bush [#762] and [George] Howard [#806] in the '80s were tanning 75,000 sides a year, hemlock sole leather entirely, and all for the market west of Buffalo. Sheepskin as well as cattle hides went into the [Jacob F.] Schoellkopf [#553] vats at Hudson and Efner streets and at Scott and Mississippi, respectively. Other yards at several different places outside Buffalo boosted their production to goodly figures; though the business was one in which the elder Schoellkopf seems to have been losing interest as he branched out into other fields of enterprise to lay the foundation of one of the really great Buffalo fortunes. [18]

Starting with tanning, (King) Jacob Schoellkopf, the progenitor of the clan in America, moved

18 *Ibid.*, 227.

successively into milling, hydroelectric power at Niagara Falls, and chemicals. He had a large family, and different sons ended up heading up different operations. In 1880 he resided at #553 Delaware and was proprietor of Schoellkopf & Mathews' flourmill. A decade later his son, Alfred P. Schoellkopf, had moved next door and was running the family tannery on Mississippi Street. Jacob had seized upon the potential of Niagara Falls for producing electricity when he purchased a hydraulic canal there in 1877 to supply his flour mill with electric power. Two years later he erected a large plant at Abbott Road and Buffalo Creek for the manufacture of coal tar dyes. He had kept up with developments in science and industry in the Fatherland and sent his sons there for further study and observation. By the end of the 1880s Schoellkopf Aniline and Chemical Company was selling over half a million dollars worth of dyes to eastern manufacturers.

Despite periods of economic downturn occasioned by the panics of 1837 and 1857 and the failure to invest adequately in industrialization, Buffalo continued to grow during the middle years of the nineteenth century. Thus Schuyler writes:

> Fifty years later, Samuel Welch [#271 Delaware] recalled that except along the waterfront there was little economic or residential segregation in the 1830s. Recently, however, historian David Gerber has sketched a much different, more stratified social geography in antebellum Buffalo. Taverns, cheap hotels, and houses of prostitution flourished along with warehouses in the dock area; merchants tended to live in houses on elevated ground between Swan and Seneca Streets a short distance from the port. Churches and homes of the wealthy clustered along Main Street, especially near Niagara Square, while Genesee Street and Delaware Avenue became fashionable residential locations. Buffalo's native-born working classes tended to live northwest of the original city, while the increasing presence of German immigrants was most evident on the east side of the community. Gerber has described their residences as "frame or plank two-story houses or one-story cottages, each with a bit of yard where a vegetable garden or a fruit tree might be tended, and some chickens, pigs, or a dairy cow kept." As was true of other Northeastern cities, urban growth resulted in a community divided by wealth, occupation, and ethnicity.[19]

In connection with Schuyler's remark about flourishing prostitution, R. V. Bruce's observation in his *1877: Year of Violence* that "the Canal Street section of Buffalo was as lawless and depraved as any in the country" should be kept in mind.[20]

Irish immigrants, most of whom lacked job experience and skills, worked chiefly as unskilled laborers on the docks. The most recently arrived in the 1850s lived in the First Ward which ran from Exchange Street to the Buffalo River. Along the canal corridor and near the docks were found the cheapest housing. Even the better off Irish lived in decrepit little dwellings, which had been subdivided to accommodate several families. The poorest often lived in huts no more than twelve feet wide constructed of waste boards or in wrecked canal boats which were regularly decimated by tidal waves.[21]

19 Schuyler, *op. cit.*, p. 9.
20 R. V. Bruce, *1877: Year of Violence* (New York: Bobbs-Merrill, 1959), p. 12.
21 *Gerber, op., cit.,* pp. 123-124.

The story of Buffalo's Germans is more complex than that of the Irish. (Until 1871 there was no unified German nation-state). The Germans were both Catholic and Protestant and among them there was a wider diversity of occupations and a greater range of wealth. Though language may have been thought to hold Germans together, there was then no one German tongue. The east side north of Seneca Street far from the docks and comparatively empty until the 1840s became the heartland of *Das Deutschtum im Buffalo*, and extensive as it was in size, it was less a neighborhood than a German village. [22]

By the last decade of the nineteenth century, Buffalo's Protestant elite, according to Mark Goldman, who seems to dislike them, sensed that their control of things was slipping. Having noted the failure of Grover Cleveland to return to the city at the end of his first term as president, Goldman continues:

> Other members of the city's WASP elite stayed in Buffalo, trying to make the best of the 1890s. It wasn't always easy. Sensing that they were in the crest of a last wave, the WASP gentry strove as the bearers of a noble, yet clearly threatened tradition. For this generation of Buffalo's WASP patricians, the 1890s was a period of intense New England nostalgia. Biographical essays and obituaries of leading citizens were filled with idealized and nostalgic references to New England, describing one person's "hardy and heroic New England ancestors;" another in whom "the blood of New England ran vigorously;" and still another who was recorded as heralding [hailing?] from "ancient, honorable, New England stock, a descendent of good Puritan ancestry who behaved in the usual New England manner." Like the exclusively Protestant clubs and schools that proliferated during the 1890s — the Sons and Daughters of the American Revolution, and the Nichols School, a private preparatory for the sons of the Protestant rich — these sentiments reflected a growing concern that the world — was suddenly changing.
>
> The many chronicles written during the nineties contained nostalgic references not only to New England but also to an earlier time in Buffalo's history, particularly the 1830s, when in fact most everybody in the city was either born in New England or directly descended from New England ancestors. Samuel Welch's Home History, written in 1893, was a fond and misty paean to the Buffalo of those earlier years. In a time, Welch wrote, when "the luxury and abundance of wealth did not stifle them with envious desires," Buffalo women, he said, were far more attractive and its immigrants, "though poor, were composed of the best of their class." But mostly Welch admired and longed for the "sterling and manly New England virtues which planted the grace of civilization and the republicanism of our institutions upon our western frontiers."

Then suddenly Goldman gave away much of his argument, conceding that "these nostalgic references to a lost past, however, should not be taken too seriously. For despite them, the wealthy Protestants continued to dominate far more than any other group the affairs of the city." [23]

Until well into the 1840s Buffalo was ethnically homogeneous, composed as it was chiefly of New England stock. East-to-west patterns of internal migration had been reinforced by the completion of the Erie Canal to Buffalo in 1825. For decades thereafter this ethnic group would continue to

22 *Ibid.*, pp. 163-165.
23 Mark Goldman, *High Hopes: The Rise and Fall of Buffalo*, New York (Buffalo: New York Press, 1983), p. 168.

dominate the economic and social life of the city. Its members had gotten in on the ground floor; they had been present, as Dean Acheson had said in a different context, "at the Creation." New England family names were particularly noticeable on Delaware Street in the federal census of 1860. In fact, of the 102 heads of families listed there from the Terrace to what was later to be Lafayette Street, including Niagara Square, twenty-nine (28.4%) were native New Englanders. Of these fifteen came from Connecticut, six, including Aaron Rumsey, from Vermont, five from Massachusetts, and three from New Hampshire. Ten years later Delaware Street counted 143 households, thirty-two of which (22.3%) were headed by native New Englanders, of whom sixteen were from Connecticut, eight from Massachusetts, three each from Vermont and Rhode Island, and one from Maine.

According to Horton the discovery by Buffalo's elite of the uses of a New England past antedated the 1890s:

> Family reunions no doubt became a custom in consequence of the reminiscent and patriotic spirit of the Centennial era [*circa* 1876] when Americans of Yankee stock in both town and country liked to ruminate upon their personal connection with the nation's past. Reunions were an occasion for ruminating as well as eating; and the experiences and exploits of forefathers figured a good deal in the talk that went on there. In the countryside this was democratic enough, since most country people had the same sort of background and ancestry. Therefore talk of the sort was not calculated to inspire delusions of grandeur as it could easily do in the city where the old stock compassed about with an alien majority was prone to think of itself as patrician in the strict Latin sense of that seductive word. This was especially true of a city like Buffalo; for there the families of wealth and power tended with certain notable German exceptions to belong to the old stock. The result was that pride and riches reinforced each other and mutually encouraged aristocratic pretensions.
>
> In the villages such pretensions were inappropriate, although the people who lived there were by no means all of equal condition. The middling folk predominated. The poor were few. Few also were the rich; and them the majority treated without obsequiousness, calling them by their first names and yet at the same time respecting them for their superior endowment of "git-up-and-git." As for the rich themselves, the relative homogeneity of the population and the intimacy of village life constrained them to keep on democratic and friendly terms with their neighbors. They went to the same festivities, they worshipped in the same churches, attended the same lodges and sent their children to the same schools. These habits distinguished them from the wealthy at the county seat whom otherwise they somewhat resembled.[24]

24 Horton, *op. cit.*, 1:314-315.

CHAPTER 3
FROM TERRACE TO *Square*

Originally, Delaware Street ran from the Terrace through Niagara Square (first called Public Square or simply The Square) to Chippewa Street, the northern boundary of Ellicott's inner lots. (See 3.1 for an 1850 map of this area from the Terrace to Chippewa and 3.2 for an 1872 map of Delaware from the Terrace to Mohawk.) In time this broad straight boulevard was extended far beyond Buffalo. But "the three mile stretch from the Square to Delaware Park (originally The Park), an idyllic pastoral landscape laid out in the late 1860s by Frederick Law Olmsted and Calvert Vaux, became one of the nation's celebrated places of residence."[1] The 1828 *Directory for the Village of Buffalo*, whose northern boundary was Virginia Street, lists the following heads of families on Delaware Street, none of whom qualifies as a member of the elite:

Zephaniah Brewster, carpenter
Elijah Bates, painter
Daniel Bristol, joiner
George Dere, painter
Ezekial Folsom, butcher
Gilman Folsom, Jr.
Calvin Francis, joiner
Simeon Francis, printer
James J. Higley, joiner
Daniel Repsher, joiner
Alfred W. Wilgus, book binder
Charles Yankerman

The preponderance of biblical names suggests a New England origin. Joiner and carpenter are synonymous, while the number engaged in the building trades betokens a growing community.

Number 1 Delaware was still standing in the 1920s, when Alice Evans Bartlett, a devotee of the Avenue's ambiance and residents in its golden age, began gathering material for its history.

> Just at the corner of the Terrace and Delaware Avenue on the easterly side, in early days commanding a beautiful view of Lake Erie, tucked away between the street and the buildings adjacent to the old Roman Catholic Saint Joseph's College, is a square brick house, different from other houses of the city. It is quite evidently of an older generation — a spacious two story brick house; high stone steps with iron railings on either side, long windows, and [a] recessed doorway flanked by stone columns. The fine old wrought-iron fence is intact, and the house looks altogether what it once must have been, a dignified old mansion, although now fallen on poorer days. This was the old Siebold house and is known as #1 Delaware. It stands 80' south of Church Street. The lot, 80' front by 150' depth, was purchased on February 1, 1843, from Thomas E. Davis for $2,000. This would seem to indicate that the house was built somewhat later, most probably by Jacob Siebold himself. He had a grocery store from earliest days, his name appearing in the first Buffalo Directory (1828). City directories of 1848, 1849, 1860, 1862, show him to be living at "#1 Terrace, corner of Church St." or #1 "Delaware."[2]

Siebold had arrived in Buffalo about 1822 from Wurttemberg, the second earliest German to come here. In 1829 he married Adaline, daughter of David Schules of Springville. The Siebolds had

1 Kowsky, "Delaware Avenue," *op. cit*, p. 35.
2 Evans Bartlett Family Papers [hereafter Bartlett Papers] BHS, CC 61-1, vol. 1. Bartlett Family, The Terrace, box 31, folder 1.

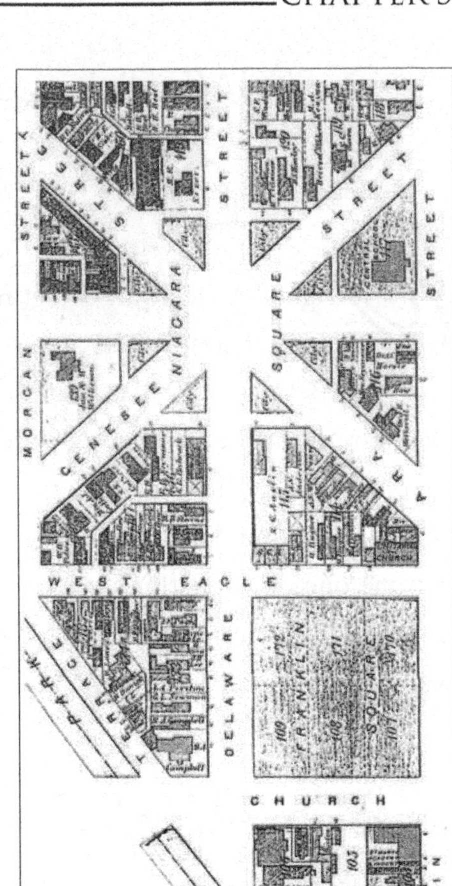

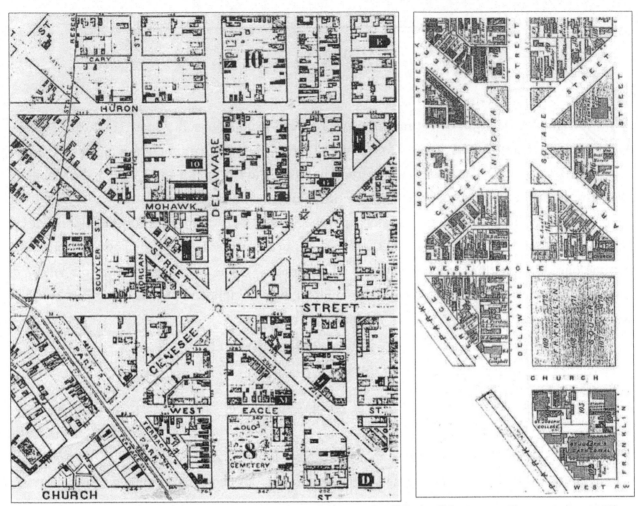

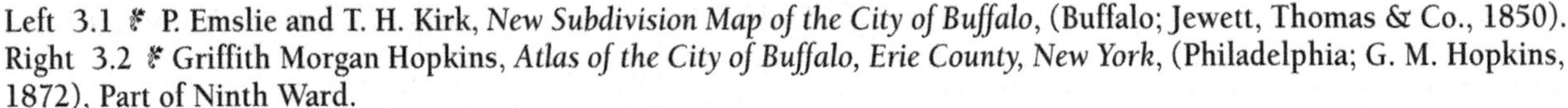
Left 3.1 ❦ P. Emslie and T. H. Kirk, *New Subdivision Map of the City of Buffalo*, (Buffalo; Jewett, Thomas & Co., 1850). Right 3.2 ❦ Griffith Morgan Hopkins, *Atlas of the City of Buffalo, Erie County, New York*, (Philadelphia; G. M. Hopkins, 1872), Part of Ninth Ward.

fourteen children, five of whom survived to adulthood. Gerber accounts Jacob among the five wealthest grocers in Buffalo. He was also a founder of the Board of Trade. One son was named John Quincy Adams, a probable hint of the father's Whig sympathies. According to the federal census there were nine Siebolds at #1 in 1860 and two servants, one of whom was an eighteen-year-old German girl. Jacob died in 1863, and the house was sold in 1865 to Bishop Timon for $15,000. Its site in 1850 can be seen in 3.2 at Delaware and Church.

Eventually the entire block on which the Siebold property was located was acquired by the Catholic Church. Already, in 1850, Timon's vicar general had bought the George B. Webster property on the northwest corner of West Swan and Franklin as a cathedral site.(3.2). About this location Rev. Nelson W. Logal writes: "The Webster Gardens Estate was an idyllic spot. It lay in the heart of Buffalo's loveliest residential district, a beautiful park and rolling terraces stretched in unbroken lines down to the shore of Lake Erie."[3] This bucolic landscape was not to last. A huge cathedral 200 feet long with a tower soaring 202 feet was completed in 1855. The architect was Patrick Keeley, Irish-born student of Augustus Welby Northcote Pugin, father of the gothic revival.[4] The Webster mansion, which had served as Timon's residence, was razed under his successor, Bishop Stephen V. Ryan, and a spacious four story stone mansion, a fit match for the cathedral, was completed in 1874 together with a chapel on the Terrace behind the cathedral.(3.3) Miss Ernestine Nardin and companions of the Religious of the Sacred Heart of Mary (Nardins) purchased property on the northwest corner of the cathedral block in 1863 for Saint Mary's, a girls academy, and a cottage in the rear of their property was made into a free grammar school for the children of the cathedral parish. A building for the academy on the corner of Church and Franklin was opened in 1870 where it remained until 1914, when it was sold to the city as the the site for police headquarters.[5]

3.3 **Old cathedral and episcopal residence, Logal, *op. cit.*, p. 127.**

Meanwhile, in 1861 the Christian Brothers had moved into a three-story building behind the cathedral on the Terrace. Their residence was on the third floor, their academy, Saint Joseph's, on the second, and the cathedral parish's grammar school on the first. In 1863 at Timon's request the name of the academy was changed to Saint Joseph's College, a change looking back to an aborted college Timon had started on Niagara Street in 1851. Title and rights of a college granted then by the state were transferred to the new school on the Terrace. The transfer also looked to the future, since Timon was anxious to establish a bonafide college in his see city.

Timon purchased the Siebold property just north of Church and Delaware in 1865 and turned it over to the brothers who moved their so-called college into the remodeled house, freeing up their former building for the parish free school. In 1871 the brothers purchased the Siebold property from the bishop and built a four story stone structure on the northeast corner of Church and Delaware, strongly reminiscent of the episcopal residence at the opposite end of the block.(3.4) P.S. 8 which

3 Nelson W. Logal, *History of Old Saint Joseph's Cathedral, 1847-1947* (Buffalo: 1947), p. 19.

4 J. David Valaik *et al.*, *Celebrating God's Life in Us: The Catholic Diocese of Buffalo, 1847-1997* (Buffalo: Western New York Heritage Press, 1997), p. 120.

5 Thomas Donohue, *History of the Diocese of Buffalo* (Buffalo: Buffalo Catholic Publication Co.), pp 88-89; *Courier,* May 14, 1922; *Buffalo Evening News* [*hereafter BEN*], January 16, May 16, 1933.

had antedated the coming of the Catholics, having been built in 1838, remained on the block until 1885 when it was demolished. Saint Joseph's College passed out of existence in 1891, but was revived and, after a year at the old site on Church and Delaware in 1897, was moved to a new building at 1238 Main Street north of Bryant and still later to Kenmore Avenue.[6]

3.4 ❦ **Saint Joseph's College, Cynthia Van Ness, *Victorian Buffalo*, (Buffalo: Western New York Wares, Inc. 1999), p. 57.**

The block north of the Cathedral-Saint Joseph's College property on Franklin Street, labeled "old cemetery" in the 1850 map of Buffalo and Franklin Square in the 1872 atlas, was Buffalo's second burial ground.[7](3.1 and 3.2) The first had consisted in a few square rods at Washington and Crow (later Exchange) Streets in what was to be the business center of the city. Burials ceased there with the creation of a burial place on the future Franklin Square. In 1804 two prominent settlers went to Ellicott in Batavia and obtained a deed to the square for a village burying ground. William Hodge wrote in 1879:

> The Franklin Square lot was a central portion of the then beautiful Terrace, on whose grassy surface the Indians used to recline and view the lake in all its pristine beauty; a scene which Judge [William] Peacock described when he first came on the spot (being then nineteen years of age), saying, "It is one of the most beautiful views I ever put my eyes upon."[8]

With the advent of the cholera epidemic in 1832 measures were taken restricting further burials, the last of which occurred in 1836, that of the wife of Samuel Wilkeson. In the 1850s the bodies in Franklin Square were removed to Forest Lawn, which had been first laid out in 1849 on eighty acres purchased from the Granger brothers, Rev. James N. and Warren.

Figure 3.5 is a view of Franklin Square taken from the roof of Saint Paul's Church. By 1872 the house on the northwest corner of Church and Franklin had been razed, since it is not shown in the 1872 atlas.(3.2) Figure 3.6 depicts five of the nine houses across from Franklin Square on the west side of Delaware in 1861. Figure 3.7 is from an 1854 insurance map indicating building facts about the same block. The following is from the 1860 federal census; addresses in brackets are post-1867 when the numbering system was changed. Names are from the 1860 federal census; *ux.* stands for wife, and names below the line indicate live-in domestic help.

6 Donohue, *ibid.*, p. 373; *Buffalo Times*, September 26, 1897; September 19, 1930; *Courier Express* [hereafter *CE*] June 16, 1936; Valaik, *op. cit.*, p. 83.
7 William Hodge, "Buffalo Cemeteries," *PBHS*, 1(1879), 49-52.
8 *Ibid.*, p. 51.

Left 3.5 ❦ Franklin Square, *Proceedings, Buffalo Historical Society*, hereafter *PBHS*, 16 (1912), 212.
Right 3.6 ❦ Numbers 22-38 Delaware Street, *ibid.*, p. 380.

2 [22] Major A. Campbell 59 Vermont lumber
Maria C. Campbell 52 Vermont *ux.*
Henrietta I. Campbell 25 NY
Martha W. Warren 22 NY
George H. Benson 21 Mass.
Sanford A. Tracey clerk
Mary Knight 21 Prussia

6 [26] Mrs. Thaddeus Joy

8 [28] George L. Newman 44 England
ship chandler Lloyd & Prime
Julia Newman 32 NY *ux.*
Jane E Newman 77 England
Mary S. Newman 55 NY
Ada M. Mosier 18 Germany

12 [36] Walter Joy 50 NY coal
180 Main
Jane Ellen Radcliffe Joy 48 NY *ux.*
Louis B Joyce 26 NY oil mfg
Kate Joy 22 NY
June R. Joy 1 NY
Arianda Radcliff 78 Conn.
Rose Conrad 25 Germany

14 [38] John D. Shepard 44 NY Joy &
Webster iron wks
Clarissa Joy Shepard 40 NY *ux.*
Anna Shepard
Charles G. Shepard 10 NY
Walter Shepard 7 NY
Mary O'Neil 19 Ireland

16 [42] Amos D. Ellis 47 NY
commission merchant
Laurette Ellis 39 NY *ux.*
Susan Ellis 9 NY
Ezra D. Ellis 7 NY
Jacob A. Ellis 5 NY
Mary McCory 11

18 [46] William B. Peck 42 Conn.
American Express
Laura E. Peck 40 NY *ux.*
William B. Peck 14 NY
Elizabeth Peck 5 NY
Martha W. Bemis 38 NY
Betsy Craton 43 Ireland
Anna Donohue 15 Ireland

22 [50] Silas Sawin 59 NY builder
Eagle near Main
Elizabeth Sawin 52 NY *ux.*
Carlton F. Sawin 24 NY
Harriet Sawin 23 NY
Jonathan Sawin 18 NY
Charles W. Sawin 21 NY telegrapher
John B. White 28 NY son-in-law
rr agent
Louisa White 28 NY *ux.*
Elizabeth White 6 NY
Charles W. White 5 NY
Dorah Canifier 18 Germany
Catherine Morthyn 24 France
Frank Otionall 21 France

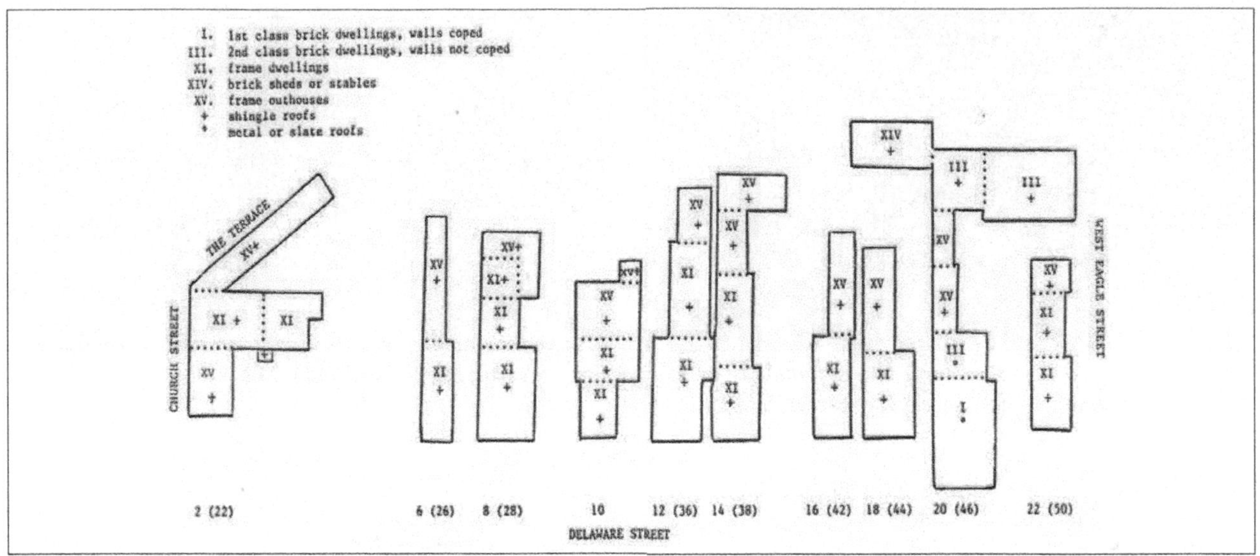

3.7 ❦ Quackenboss & Kennedy, "*Atlas of Buffalo, New York, for the Use of Insurance Companies*," 1854, Plate IV.

Major Campbell had resided at #2 Delaware since 1854. The first owner of this large house was James L. Barton whose annals go back to the origins of Western New York.[9] Only with the withdrawal of British garrisons from Fort Niagara as well as from Lewiston and Schlosser (located above the rapids of the Falls on the American side) in 1796 could Americans engage in transportation between the Hudson Valley and the Great Lakes. Barton recalled that from this time until 1806 traffic was carried on in small bateaux called Schenectady boats, which were poled up the Mohawk and thence via a series of streams and portages to Oswego on Lake Ontario, where cargo was loaded onto lake vessels for Lewiston or Queenstown. Supplies destined for troops at Schlosser and Lewiston were landed at the latter place, while goods for Detroit and other western ports were landed at Queenston, wagoned around the portage over the Falls to Chippewa, and put aboard boats and carried to Fort Erie for distribution to vessels destined for ports up the Lakes.

During 1803-1804 the New York State Reservation was surveyed. On this subject James Barton wrote:

> In 1805 all the surveyed land, farm and village lots, were put up by the surveyor-general for public sale at Albany. Notice was also given that the docks and warehouses at Lewiston and Schlosser, with the Steadman farm at the latter place, would be leased by the State to any responsible party or parties, who would take them for the least number of years, maintain and keep up the storehouses and docks, and at the termination of the lease surrender all the improvements to the State. At the time of the sale, Augustus and Peter B. Porter, my father Benjamin Barton(3.8), and my uncle Joseph Annin, who surveyed the Mile Strip, attended for the purpose of purchasing lands along the river and bidding for the lease. In a conversation among themselves, and finding out each other's views and purposes, they agreed to form a partnership under the name of Porter, Barton & Co., and to bid for the portage lease, and also to make large purchases of lands. They suceeded in

9 James L. Barton, "Early Reminiscences of Buffalo and Vicinity," *ibid.*, 1(1879), 153-178.

obtaining the lease for thirteen years, and purchased the land around the falls, and many other farms and village lots.[10] (For the New York State Reservation within Buffalo, see 1.7.)

3.8 ❦ Benjamin Barton, Turner, *op. cit.*, facing p. 392.

Benjamin Barton had been born in Sussex County, New Jersey. In 1787 at seventeen he accompanied his father driving cattle and sheep to Fort Niagara, then under British control. Next year he moved to a farm near Geneva where he remained until business interests caused his move to Western New York.[11]

Peter Buell Porter was a native of Salisbury, Connecticut, graduated from Yale in 1791, studied law under Judge Tappan Reeve in Litchfield, and moved to Canandaigua in 1795, where he practiced law. In 1797 he was appointed clerk of Ontario County, which embraced most of Western New York. Originally a Federalist, he broke with his party and became a Republican. For supporting Aaron Burr in the 1804 New York gubernatorial election, Porter was stripped of his clerkship, which is why he moved to Black Rock in 1805.[12] His son James provides more details about Porter, Barton & Company:

> In the fall of 1805, Augustus Porter [older brother of Peter] came out from Canandaigua and built a saw-mill at the Falls. He removed with his family in the spring of 1806 to Fort Schlosser, and lived four or five years in the old English mess-house. That summer my father came out (he did not remove his family to Lewiston until the spring of 1807) and assisted in erecting a large grist-mill at the falls...The same year, Porter Barton & Co. commenced the transportation business over the portage, boating up the river to Black Rock, and provided themselves with vessels to carry property on the lakes. This was the beginning of the first regular and connected line of transportation on the American side, that ever did business on these great waters. They were connected with Jonathan Walton & Co. of Schenectady, who sent the property in boats up the Mohawk river, down Wood Creek and other waters to Oswego; Matthew McNair carried it over Lake Ontario, Porter Barton & Co. took it from Lewiston to Black Rock, where they had vessels to carry it over the lakes. I went into my father's warehouse in 1807 to make out way-bills, or slips for the teams carrying salt and other property across the portage.[13]

The company's holdings were destroyed in the War of 1812, during which Peter Porter, who had resigned his seat in Congress to join the army, won distinction as a military leader and emerged from the struggle a major general of militia. Benjamin Barton joined General Porter as quartermaster of the militia and was rewarded at war's end with a commission as quartermaster in the regular army by President Madison. After the war Barton returned to Lewiston where he died in 1842 at seventy-two. This is James Barton's account of post-war business on the portage:

> In 1815, Porter Barton & Co. built a warehouse at Black Rock, nearly opposite the present Queen City Mills...In March, 1816, the forwarding and commission house of Sill

10 *Ibid.*, pp. 162-163.

11 Orsamus Turner, *Pioneer History of the Holland Land Purchase of Western New York.* (Buffalo: Georgr H. Derby & Co., 1858).

12 John C. Fredriksen, "Peter Buell Porter," *American National Biography*, John A. Garrity and Mark C. Carnes (New York: Oxford University Press, 1999) [hereafter *ANB*], 17:707-709.

13 Barton, *ibid.*, pp. 163-164.

> Thompson & Co. of which I was a member, took possession, and occupied it until March, 1821. It furnished ample storage for all the property requiring to be put under shelter, going to or coming from the West, during that time. It would hardly afford sufficient storage room for the business of the present day! The whole business of a season then did not equal in value or quantity what is now done in a single day on our docks during the busy season of the year. To give you an idea how large the business we were doing then appeared to the public, we were called a "monopoly" and an "overgrown monopoly," not satisfied with doing all the commercial business, but trying to control the politics of the county and district. [14]

In 1825 the decision was made to terminate the Erie Canal at Buffalo. Black Rock continued to have a harbor but the lion's share of through traffic would now be handled at Buffalo, so Barton had to change his place of residence and business.

> In the spring of 1827, I left Black Rock, came to Buffalo, and formed a partnership with the late Judge Samuel Wilkeson in the forwarding business. The Judge had been amongst the foremost in the controversy between Buffalo and Black Rock and although many hard things had been said about him in our paper, he remembered with unkindly feelings nothing that occurred in the season of anger and strife. He had a mind of large grasp, quick perception, indomitable energy: never sparing time or money so long as a possibility existed of accomplishing any great object he undertook. ...The partnership lasted two years. The Judge said to me: "This is a poor business, not furnishing sufficient support for two families; I am not acquainted with the business and you have been in it all your life; I will retire; you take the warehouse and dock, pay me two hundred and fifty dollars a year rent, and go on for yourself." I told him I would take the warehouse if he would paint it. He did so and I continued the business alone until the end of the year 1835, at the same rent. While the partnership continued, and afterward when I was alone, we had the agency of a large line of boats on the canal, and vessels on the lake; yet so scarce was western freight that it was difficult to get a full boat load, although the boats were then of light tonnage. A few tons of freight was all that we could furnish each boat to carry to Albany. This they would take in and fill up at Rochester; which place, situated in the heart of the wheat-growing district of Western New York furnished nearly all the down freight that passed on the canal. Thus we lived and struggled on until 1830. [15]

The turning point came in the early 1840s with the completion of the Midwestern canals which began channeling the produce of that region down the lakes to Buffalo and beyond. The 1840 census shows James L. Barton, "clerk combination steamboats" living at Delaware and Church with an office on Prime Street; in 1849-1850 he was deputy postmaster.

Commenting on figure 3.6, Bartlett wrote about the homes on lowest Delaware at mid-century:

> The block from Church to W. Eagle, now site of the jail, was for years before 1876 a pleasant block of residences, back of small door yards and low wooden fences on the sidewalk. The ground was raised above the sidewalk and the area was called "The Bank." The houses were mostly wooden 2 story cottages with porches across the fronts shaded by tall trees. In front of the porches were green plots terraced above the sidewalk, and shrubs were flowering all about. The roadway was smooth dirt, unpaved. All along were stepping

14 *Ibid.*, pp. 164-165.
15 *Ibid.*, pp. 170-171.

stones for carriages and hitching posts for horses. Across Delaware was Franklin Square.

At the extreme left [of the picture] with side and chimneys, #2 Major A. Campbell house; next, hidden by trees, the small house #6 Mrs. Thaddeus Joy; next right the houses of George L. Newman #8, Walter Joy #12, and John D. Shepard #14. Silas Sawin lived at #20 on the corner of Delaware and W. Eagle. [Neither in this picture nor in the 1860 census does #10 appear, only in 3.7. It must have been torn down sometime between 1854 and 1860.]

#2 James L. Barton house, later M. A. Campbell, a lumber dealer in the 1860s. Barton built it about 1835. It was much larger than its neighbors. [See 3.5] He lived there until about 1849. He was the eldest son of Benjamin Barton of Lewiston. James was born in 1795, married Sara Maria Horner in 1818. Postmaster at Black Rock from 1817 until coming to Buffalo in 1827. Partner of Judge Samuel Wilkeson in one of Buffalo's first forwarding businesses, which Barton later continued alone until 1835. He built and owned several large lake vessels. (This was before the coming of the railroads). In 1848 he retired from active business. First secretary of the Western Savings Bank. He died October 6, 1869; his wife had died in December, 1851.

From 1841 to 1844 #6 was the home of Jabez Bull of Jabez Bull & Co., hides and leather. [Actually Bull was still living there in 1847 according to the city directory for that year.] Jabez was the grandfather of Henry Adsit Bull, who would live on upper Delaware Avenue sixty years later. The next occupants were Thaddeus Joy and for years after his death at age sixty eight on June 4, 1853, his wife. Captain and Mrs. Joy came to Buffalo from Le Roy about 1824. Their son Walter married Ellen, the daughter of their neighbor Jerry Radcliffe. Their daughter Clarissa married John Shepard. Their daughter Hanna was the second wife of George B. Webster [whose home at Franklin and Church became for a time the residence of Bishop Timon.] Both Thaddeus and Walter Joy were members of Joy & Webster, forwarders. In 1848 Walter Joy was president of Walter Joy's Bank.

Next to Mrs. Thaddeus Joy lived George L. Newman at #8. Newman had married Julia, daughter of George B. Webster. Later the Newmans moved to Charlottesville, Va.

In the 1830s #10 was the home of Mr. and Mrs. Jerry Radcliffe. They had five daughters, the youngest, Mary, married William Laverack, the parents of George E. Laverack whose home was at 212 Delaware from 1853 on. Jerry Radcliffe was a warden of Trinity from 1818 until his death in 1838.

Mr. and Mrs. Walter Joy (the former Ellen Radcliffe) lived at #12 until 1848. [This is clearly wrong, since Walter Joy is listed as residing there in the 1860 census.] #14 was at one time the home of Walter's sister Clarissa who had married John D. Shepard in 1845. Issue Walter Joy Shepard. [16]

An appreciation of Walter Joy written shortly after his death in 1864 by Oliver G. Steele, bookbinder, bookseller, and first public school superintendent, throws light on Buffalo's forwarding business and lake and canal transportation before the Civil War. Steele prefaces his story with this observation:

When the idea of a harbor capable of accommodating the lake commerce and accessible at all times, became a fixed fact, there arose the class of men whose energies were concen-

> trated upon the development and organization of the great commercial advantages thus opened before them. ...Among the names which should be remembered among the early firms identified with its early history are Townsend & Coit, Johnson & Wilkeson, and Joy & Webster.

The author saw the latter firm as an example of these new men, though as his story goes on, the opposite picture emerges.

Thaddeus Joy was born in Guilford, Vermont, and moved to Fabius, a village near Syracuse in 1800. From there he moved to Le Roy where he was employed as a teamster on the heavy wagons which were the common carriers between Albany and Lake Erie before the coming of the canal in 1825. The year before, he had moved to Buffalo and with George Webster organized Joy & Webster, commission merchants and forwarders on the canal and lakes, which operated the Pilot Line, the first regularly organized through line on the canal, with a warehouse at Canal Street and the waterfront. In 1829 he moved east to Albany where he acted as a general agent for the line's business there. Known as Captain Joy, he died in June 1853.

His son Walter was born in 1810 when the family was still living in Fabius. He too moved to Buffalo with the family when he was thirteen and went to work as a clerk in a store on Main Street. In 1831 Walter entered his father's and George Webster's partnership which already owned four lake schooners. During the next three years Joy & Webster built five more ships, including the 120 ton *Sandusky* and the 156 ton *Florida*, the largest sailing vessels on the lakes. The firm survived the effects of the Panic of 1837 and in 1839 built the *Commodore Perry*, the first steamboat to sail the lakes. The firm continued into the 1840s building and operating ships, including a propeller-powered steamboat, the *Pocahontas*. In 1847 they built the schooner *Petrel* 220 tons and the steamboat *Ohio*, 573 tons. At this point, Steele, without further explanation, notes laconically, "This terminated their connection with vessel and steamboat building, and in 1849 the House, having met with a succession of reverses, was compelled to stop payment and the whole property passed into the hands of an assignee."

Walter Joy's failures were not limited to forwarding and marine transportation. In 1835 Joy & Webster had purchased a lease which obliged them to construct a business block. The firm engaged Benjamin Rathbun to do the work. As Steele writes, "While in process of construction Mr. Rathbun failed and the completion of the block was thrown upon Joy & Webster at a large increase of cost." In 1847 they bought a cotton factory that was being built, introduced new machinery, and saw it fail with heavy losses. Buffalo was ill-situated for cotton factories. They also tried to open coal mines in Ohio and Pennsylvania. In both states they acquired what were thought to be rich coal lands, and even bought expensive equipment. Both venturers went bankrupt in 1849. But Joy was not

16 Bartlett Papers, folder 1.

finished failing:

> In the winter of 1847-8 Mr. Joy was induced by financial parties in Albany to enter into the Banking business which was effected by the organization of the "Walter Joy Bank." The firm of Joy & Webster was not interested in this institution and although the Bank itself was not unsuccessful, yet in its career and closing up it proved to be the most disastrous in its results, both personal and pecuniary, of any of the numerous enterprises with which Mr. Joy was connected. It stopped in 1849 at the same time as the house of Joy & Webster.

Walter Joy was a founder of the Young Men's Association, of which he was later vice president, manager, and in 1840 president. He served several terms on the Common Council and in 1843 was unsuccessful candidate for mayor. He was one of the trustees of the Mutual Insurance Company from its founding, vice president in 1845-1846, and president in 1847, resigning in 1848 due to his financial difficulties. Nonetheless, despite them he was a director of the Attica & Buffalo Railroad in 1848-1849 and vice president in 1849-1850. He was also vestryman of Saint Paul's. His eulogist added that "his habits were simple and unostentatious, shunning rather than seeking fashionable life. He married in 1832 and commenced housekeeping in the unassuming home where he continued through life." His numerous failures better explain than "simple habits" why he did not "increase his domestic establishment." [21] Walter Joy died at fifty-four in 1863. [17]

For the rest of the block there is some contradiction between Bartlett, the censuses, atlases, and city directories. What follows is an attempted reconciliation. At the north corner of the block, #22 old style #50 new, was the home from at least 1840 of Silas Sawin, a builder, who had served as alderman in 1836. In 1860 he presided over an impressive menage, his wife Elizabeth, three unmarried sons, Carlton, Jonathan, and Charles, a son-in-law John B. White, his wife Louise Sawin White, their three children, Elizabeth, Charles, and Lelia, and three live-in-domestics, all foreigners. Silas died at sixty-one in 1863. By 1870 his widow had moved two doors down to #44, and John B. White was head of the household on the corner. Deterioration set in on lower Delaware in the mid-seventies, and by 1900 White, who does not seem to have moved up in the world, and his daughter were living alone in the old homestead, next to a saloon. According to Bartlett, Lelia was still living there in 1921 in the house where she had been born. "Just south of the Sawin house," writes Bartlett, stood an old fashioned house which was one of the later houses on the Bank. William B. Peck [an executive of the American Express Company] lived there in the 1860s and early 1870s. The family came to Buffalo from Canada and later returned ...He was one of the original subscribers to the Buffalo Club in 1867." A friend of Bartlett remarked to her in 1924:

> My memory went wandering to the part of Delaware St. called the Bank where the Jail and Municipal buildings now are. It was so pretty down there with its colony of cunning little cottages set up so high above the street, with flowers and trees all scattered about. [18]

17 O.G. Steele, Esq., *Memorial of the Late Walter Joy*, (Buffalo: Commercial Advertiser, 1864), pp.4-6.
18 Bartlett Papers, folder 2.

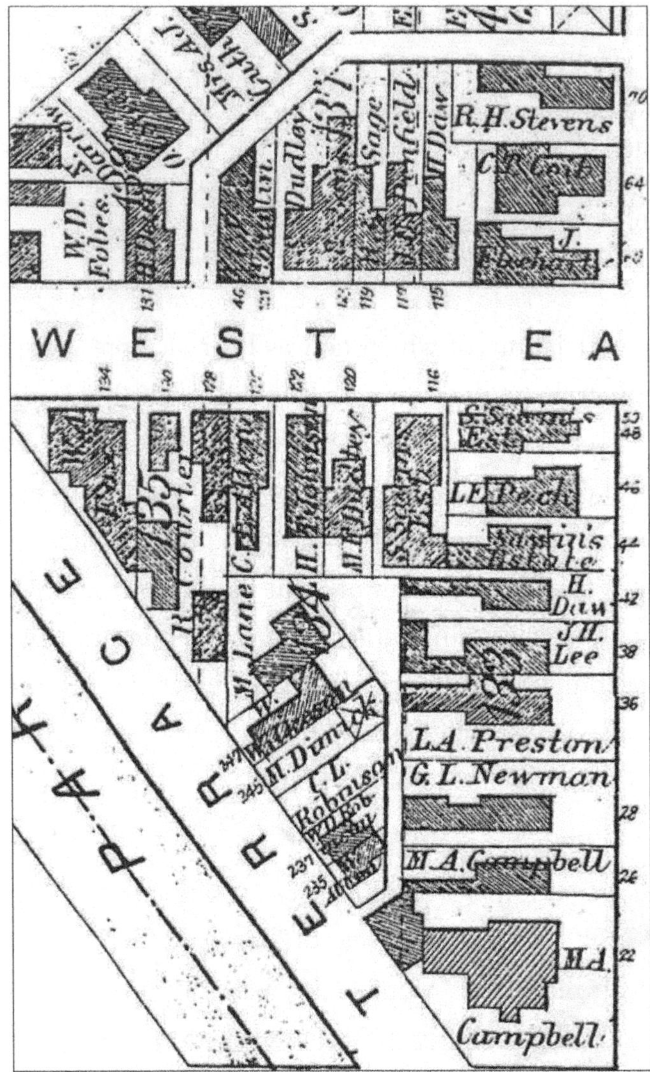

3.9 *Atlas of the City of Buffalo*, 1872, *Ibid.*

For a map of this block and the short one directly north of it in the early 1870s shortly before the neighborhood changed radically see figure 3.9. Number 24 [60] on the corner, Bartlett writes, was occupied as early as 1844 by Philo Durfee, member of the first board of trade and its president in 1848. From then until 1862 it was occupied by John Fleeharty, commission merchant of Fleeharty & Warren, Central Wharf. Figure 3.10 depicts #64 Delaware, a solid commodious residence which during the 1870s was the home of Charles T. Coit, cashier, the equivalent of general manager, of the First National Bank. North of Coit lived Robert H. Stevens, an attorney, at #70 on the corner of Guthrie Alley. While still residing there, both men were counted among the elite of Buffalo according to an 1883 ladies' visiting list.[19]

No houses faced Delaware on the east side of this block (see 3.2), but as Bartlett writes:

> Along the north side of Eagle from Delaware to Franklin was a block of three houses, brick, three stories, high entrance steps built, in the 1830s. (3.11) Before 1868 they were numbered #34, 32, 30; afterwards #93, 91, 89. Owned by the S[tephen] G. Austin estate, inner lot 115, on which the Austin homestead on Delaware Avenue and Niagara Streets was located. The whole block was demolished in 1922 to make way for the Buffalo Athletic Club. It was the very best location in the early days. Many financially and socially prominent families lived there. In #30(90) 1850-1854 lived Henry K. Smith, atty., who married Sara, daughter of Sheldon Thomson, Sr. [1785-1851, pioneer shipbuilder and forwarder.] Their son was Sheldon Thompson Smith. Henry K. Smith had moved to #30 from Cottage Street. In 1854 James Sheldon, Judge of the County Court, came to live at #30. He married Sara E. Carew of Connecticut.
>
> The neighborhood was delightful at that time. Beyond the trees and the [Franklin] Square was a fine view of the harbor, and the shore walk along the lake was not then given over to lumber yards. Charles G. Curtiss lived in #30 in the 1870s. Edward A. Curtenius, atty., lived in #32 in 1850-1859. His wife was an elegant hostess.

19 *The Buffalo Elite Directory or Ladies Visiting List compiled by Sidney G. Sherwood and John Bosche* (Buffalo: Baker Jones & Co., 1883).

Above Left 3.10 ❦ #64 Delaware Street, BHS
Below Left 3.11 ❦ *PBHS*, 26 (1922), np.
Above Right 3.12 ❦ *City Directory of Buffalo* (Buffalo: Courier Co., 1897), facing p. 160.

> In 1851 the corner house, #34 (93) was occupied by Mr. & Mrs. Silas Henry Fish who lived there until 1853 when they moved to their recently built house, #156, now #334 Delaware. In the 1870s #93 was occupied by the Perrine family. [Henry E. Perrine later married Mrs. Folsom whose daughter Frances became Mrs. Grover Cleveland.] At the other end of the block was the Unitarian Church which in 1880 was sold to the Stephen G. Austin Estate and became an office building [still standing today] at #110 Franklin.[20]

This radical change in the neighborhood alluded to above was brought about by three developments during the 1870s, the construction on Franklin Square of a City-County Hall which was completed in 1876, the erection of a jailhouse and exercise yard on property across the street from #22 to #36, and the laying of tracks between the Exchange Street Station east of Main Street and the Michigan Central station near West Genesee.

Buffalo had became the seat of Niagara County in 1808. Two years later, a county court house was erected on the site of the present downtown public library. In 1813 this building was burned by the

20 Bartlett Papers, Folder 2.

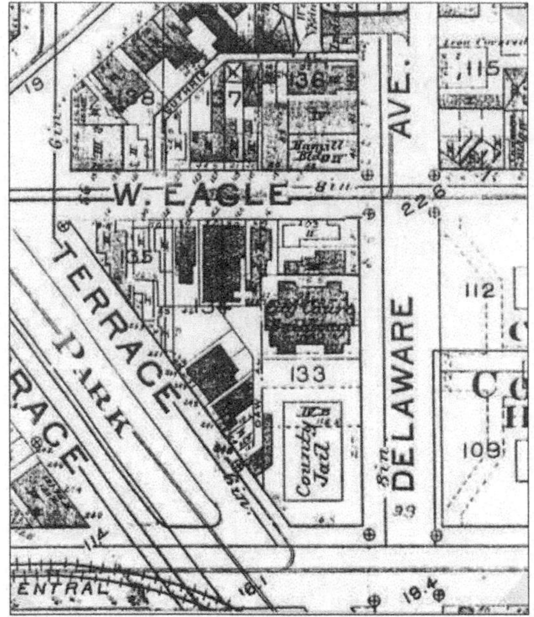

Above 3.13 ❦ *New Century Atlas of Greater Buffalo*, (Philadelphia: Century Atlas Co., 1915), II, Plate 31.
Below 3.14 ❦ Municipal Building, *Buffalo City Directory*, 1897, facing p. 164

British along with the rest of the village but was rebuilt after the War. The third courthouse, a city-county hall, was approved by the Common Council in May 1871, and the cornerstone was laid in March 1876. The structure was 295 feet long and 158 feet wide with a tower the apex of which was 270 feet above the ground.(3.13)[21] A year later the county jail was erected with its exercise yard and adjoining morgue. When the census taker came around in the summer of 1880 he found there the jailer, his wife and family, five live-in employees, and eighteen inmates, fifteen male and three female. Mabel Ganson described her reaction toward the end of the nineteenth century to two of Buffalo's more depressing institutions.

> There were a few public buildings that shed each its own atmosphere over the town. The Insane Asylum was one of these, on the outskirts of the park. We all glanced furtively at this darkened mass over along the horizon whenever we saw it — it really scared "us girls." I think we all conjured up the most dreadful pictures of the life that must go on behind inescapable walls, each of us according to her own fashion. We all knew there were people inside that we had seen among us. And we knew that any one might go there. This was accepted but fought back and out of our thoughts. It was one of the monstrous terrors that we almost knew and harbored.
>
> At the other end of town, below Delaware Avenue, stood the jail. This dark grey stone building with its narrow barred windows was a shadow on life too. Maybe more for the boys than for "us girls." Yet for us too. It was so heavy and so dreary and so dark, and it was always there. Sometimes we saw faces looking out of the windows and tried not to notice. Somewhere in between these two dark guardians were the churches and the theaters, and the Church Home that some of us knew.[22]

During the 1880s another civic structure, the Municipal Building, was built on the lots formerly occupied by #38 to #44, leaving only two of the pre-Civil War houses, #46, site of what Bartlett in 1921 called "a disreputable saloon," and the old Sawin place on the corner in which the unmarried

21 *Buffalo Evening Republican*, March 11, 1876.
22 Mable Dodge Luhan, *Intimate Memories* (London, England: Martin Secker, 1933), pp. 14-15.

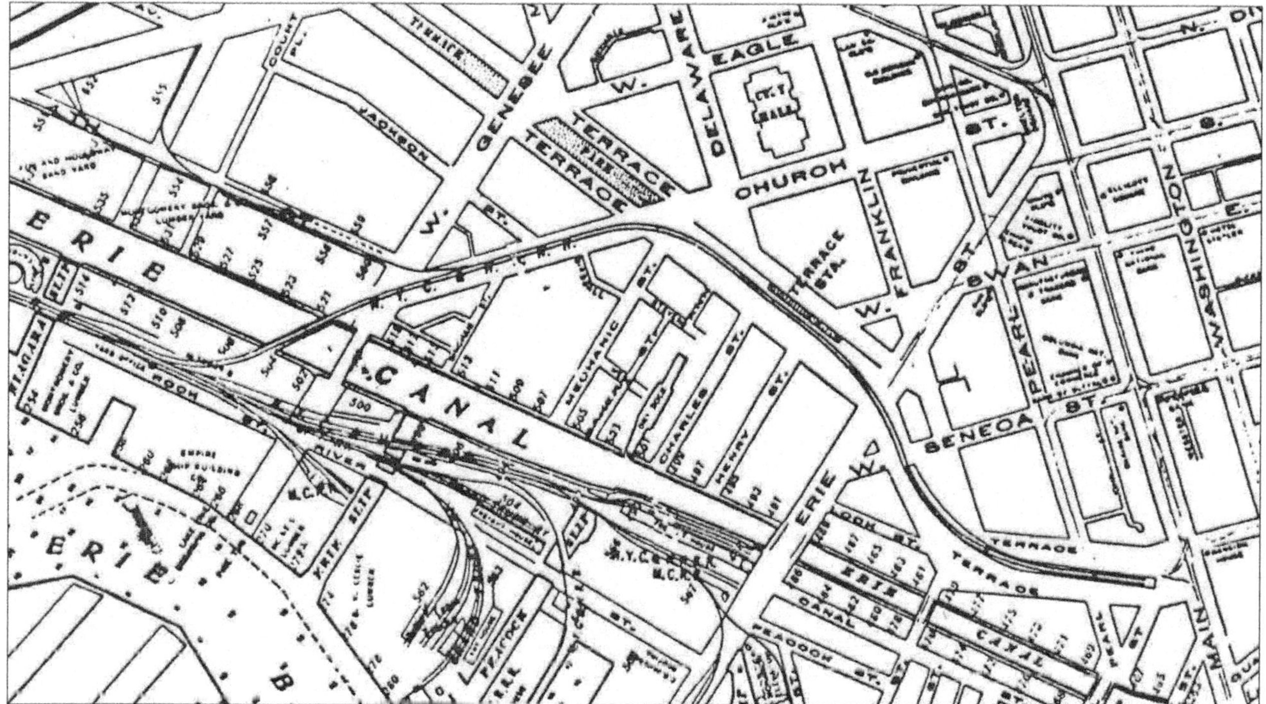

3.15 *Hydrographic Harbor Chart and Railroad Map of Buffalo*, (Buffalo, Charles Green & Co., 1907).

daughter of the original owner lived on. [23](3.13 and 14)

Figure 3.15 shows the 600-yard track connection between the New York Central and the Michigan Central Railroads completed in 1879. The route ran along the Terrace and reached Church and Delaware before turning west. This was no spur but the mainline between Buffalo and Chicago via Canada. The smoke and noise must have unbearable for nearby residents. The Terrace Station also hosted two dozen locals a day on this part of the NYC's Belt Line, which circumnavigated Buffalo. [24] Thus Bishop Ryan moved his mansion to upper Delaware. [25]

23 Bartlett Papers, folder 1.
24 Edward T. Dunn, *A History of 'Railroads in Western New York*, 2nd ed (Buffalo: Canisius College Press, 2000), pp. 99-100.
25 Donohue, *op. cit.*, p. 164.

CHAPTER

4 THE *Square*

Ellicott intended the Square to be the seat of the government of the Holland Purchase,[1] though this objective was not approximated until well into the twentieth century. At least from 1868 it had its own numbering system which began with #3 in the southeast corner and proceeded west to #35 in the southwest corner.(4.1) The west side of the Square ran from #59, the Wilkeson mansion, to #71 at Niagara Street. On the east side of the Square from Niagara to Genesee the Gould house had a Court Street address since it faced that street and the Burt house had none at all. Numeration recommenced at the northeast corner from #42 to #52, and the Sizer mansion across Delaware from #52 had a Delaware Street number since it faced that street.

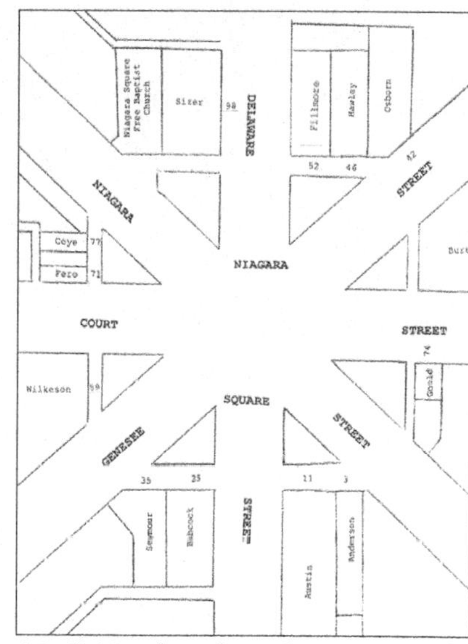

4.1 Numbered residences around the Square, from *1872 Atlas*.

Niagara Square was intended to be the great plaza of a picturesque New Amsterdam for the business of the town and the congregation of its people. In the early days the square was considered far from Niagara Street and the clustering houses of the little hamlet, and there were as yet no settlers there. The pioneer settler and land owner was Henry Lake who bought of the Holland Land Co. lot 116 (3.2) on the east side of the square where the YMCA is today. He paid $40. Even as late as 1828 when the first directory of Buffalo was issued only two names of householders and residents of Public Square were given, William Kaene, deputy sheriff, and Robert Kaene, mason. The old Dutch names were changed in 1826 and probably about that time the public square began to be called Niagara Square, but long before the Public Square became a place of residence it was used for all kinds of general out-of-door meetings of the village, 4th of July celebrations, and other public happenings. The last public execution was held there on June 17, 1825. The three Thayer brothers were hanged for the murder of John Love. The execution was preceded by a procession of dignitaries, a band, cavalry, infantry, and artillery companies. Elder Gleason Fillmore preached the customary sermon.

It is generally known that when this city was laid out Niagara Square was designed as the central point or plaza crossed by four side streets or avenues, two at right angles and two diagonally. The large octagon thus formed was an open space except for eight little fenced in triangular parks around it. The sidewalks between the houses and the parks were connected by cross walks. Crosswalks also traversed the square from the discontinuance of each street to its continuation on the other side. In time the shade trees became something beautiful. The very finest houses in the city were erected here and for awhile it was the most fashionable part of the town...Although alike in shape and equal in size, the

1 See chapter 2, footnote 4.

Above 4.2 ❦ Wilkeson Mansion, *PBHS*, 19 (1915), 387.
Right 4.3 ❦ Samuel Wilkeson, H. Perry Smith, *History of the City of Buffalo and Erie County* (Syracuse: D. Mason & Co., 1884), 2, pt. 2, p. 27.

> eight miniature parks surrounding the square presented a varied appearance. The superintendence of them seemed to belong to no one in particular, and they were utilized in different ways. On a pleasant afternoon in one might be seen a tent and a company of boys in paper caps, in another two or more students lying in the shade with books in hand, or a group of little girls having a play, picnic or tea party. One of them, lawyer [Sylvanus O.] Gould who lived at [#74] Court Street opposite the Central School appropriated as a garden and raised vegetables. [2]

The earliest Niagara Square mansion was #59 on the west side of the Square.(4.2) It had been built for Samuel Wilkeson(4.3) in whom classically minded Buffalonians saw an antitype of Virgil's Aeneas, "urbem condidit," [3] carved on Wilkeson's tombstone at Forest Lawn commemorating his role in having Buffalo, not Black Rock, designated as terminus of the Erie Canal. The house lasted for much of the nineteenth century and for two decades into the twentieth:

> The builder of the 1824-1825 Wilkeson house facing the square was John Hicks. The lot was somewhat raised above the surrounding square. On three sides a substantial brick wall four or five feet high separated it from the sidewalk. The fourth side toward the square was open. There was a wooden fence between the street and the sloping green lawn with many old trees. The style was colonial. The central part of the house dates from 1825. Wide two story wings were added by Samuel Wilkeson's son John around 1860. Four heavily rounded two story columns formed the portal. The house was of wood with clapboards. The whole was painted gray with dark green blinds weathered to harmonize with the lawn and trees.
>
> The uproar of the surrounding area never seems to break in upon or dispel the air of complete repose which surrounds the old mansion. The very dust appears to settle with a certain deference over the garden and through the branches of the elm trees which stand like drowsy sentinel dust within the yard. [4]

2 Bartlett Papers, folder 3.
3 *Aeneid*, bk.1, l.5.
4 Bartlett Papers, *ibid*.

Samuel had been born in Carlisle, Pennsylvania, in 1781, the son of John Wilkeson and his wife, Mary Robinson, who had migrated from Londonderry in Ulster to America in 1760 where they settled in Delaware. Members of this ethnic group fled religious and economic oppression in Scotland in the seventeenth century and in Ulster in the eighteenth. Their New World ports of entry were Baltimore and Philadelphia, whence they penetrated to the fertile lands in the valleys of the mountainous back country. Frontier regions of Pennsylvania and the southern colonies received the largest contingents of this hardy people. [5]

John Wilkeson's family emigrated with twenty others from Carlisle to Western Pennsylvania in April 1784. There were no wagon roads through the mountains so pack horses were used. The route was crisscrossed by swift-flowing streams swollen by melted snow. Reaching the Monongahela the party broke up and families marked out tracts where they embarked on the ancient routine of felling trees, building fences and houses, and planting a crop. John secured a 200 acre tract a few miles south of Pittsburgh. [6]

Samuel Wilkeson, John's son, married Jane Oram, daughter of a Revolutionary War veteran, and moved to Mahoning County, Ohio, near Youngstown, where "he cut down the forest and opened a farm and built a grist mill, the first in the vicinity." [7] But loathing the drudgery of farming he turned to commerce. In 1810 he moved to near Westfield, New York, and with partners in Pittsburgh he conducted the Westfield-Lake Chautauqua-Allegany River link in the tortuous shipment of salt from near Syracuse to Pittsburgh.

> The competition of the Kanawha salt works destroyed this trade, and in 1813 he set out for Detroit to dispose of his remaining stock of salt. Stress of weather drove him into Grand River, Ohio, and while there he undertook the construction of a large number of boats which were urgently required for the transportation of the Army of General Harrison into Canada. The boats were built in a wonderfully short time, when the army crossed the lake and won the battle of the Thames. [8]

Hostilities interrupted commerce on the lakes. During the war Wilkeson served in the militia defending Buffalo from invading redcoats. The militia was defeated, the victors burned down Buffalo and Black Rock at the end of 1813, and the defenders fled. But Wilkeson, recognizing a good commercial site, resolved to return to Buffalo after the war. He walked back to Westfield, collected his wife and four eldest children, and in the spring of 1814 brought them to Buffalo. [9] There he was elected Justice of the Peace and with threats of stiff jail terms ran out of town a turbulent lot of discharged and unattached soldiers. [10]

The judge built his first home on Niagara Street two doors northwest of Main; then the family lived on Main Street, then on Franklin Square, finally moving into the mansion on Niagara Square.

5 R. J. Ferguson, "Scotch-Irish," *Dictionary of American History* (New York: Charles Scribner's Sons, 1927), 4:240-241.

6 "Historical Writings of Judge Samuel Wilkeson," *PBHS*, 5(1902),148-150; *Courier, December 15, 1907.*

7 Rev. John C. Lord, "Samuel Wilkeson," *PBHS*, 4(1896), 75.

8 *Ibid.*, pp. 75-76.

9 *Courier, ibid.*

10 "Historical Writings," *ibid*, p. 140.

He engaged in business with Ebenezer Johnson, Buffalo's first mayor. Their place was originally in the Kremlin Block, and Henry H. Sizer was their principal clerk. Johnson & Wilkeson ran a general retail business, besides engaging in shipping and forwarding.[11] In February 1821 Wilkeson was appointed to a three-year term as First Judge of the Court of Common Pleas. In 1824 he was elected to the state senate and served there and on the Court for the Correction of Errors for six years. In 1836 he was elected mayor of Buffalo.[12]

Black Rock, which lay inside the New York State Reservation (1.7) was the home of the Porter brothers, Peter and Augustus, who had controlled the portage business around Niagara Falls since 1806. For a time their village had seemed the logical terminus for the Erie Canal:

> One major fault marred Black Rock's otherwise preeminent position. Sailing vessels could not move from the harbor up into the lake against the river current and the prevailing westerly winds. They were compelled to rely on the "horn breeze" furnished by Sheldon Thompson, who hitched fourteen oxen to a vessel by a stout hawser and drew it up the river. General Porter's influence had led the national government to make Black Rock the official port of entry in 1811 during the months from April to December, and as plans for the Erie Canal matured, the commercial leadership of Black Rock seemed secure.[13]

But there was an alternative, Buffalo, where Buffalo Creek flowed into Lake Erie and would provide a protected harbor. In fact, it was too well protected, since a sand bar blocked its mouth, allowing only small boats to enter. Wilkeson assembled backers and workers to change the direction of the creek near its mouth, thus forcing the spring floods to flush the sandbar away. The result was the selection of Buffalo as the western terminus of the canal.[14] On October 26, 1825, the *Seneca Chief* with a distinguished passenger list left Buffalo for New York on the first round trip over the entire canal. "When the party returned from New York a grand reception was held at the Wilkeson house, where many guests from other towns and the leading residents of Buffalo met to celebrate the happy occasion."[15]

Samuel Wilkeson also became a major player in the iron industry along the Great Lakes:

> Having secured the canal terminus, Wilkeson's own business grew along with the town. He had begun with a general store, soon added a small fleet of lake boats, and then concentrated on developing industry in Buffalo. Iron was a particular interest, especially cast iron products; pots, kettles, and other cast goods found a ready market on the expanding frontiers of the time. He established the first iron foundry in Buffalo, producing steam engines and stoves. Probably through his knowledge of Lake Erie commerce, Judge Wilkeson learned of good bog ore deposits near Madison in Geauga County, Ohio, owned and worked by the Erie Furnace Company. Erie began working the deposits in 1826 and four years later Wilkeson added the operation to his business interests. He renamed it the Arcole Furnace. Arcole produced simple castings for sale in the lower Lakes region and supplied the pig iron that fed Judge Wilkeson's Arcole foundry in Buffalo.[16]

11 Lord, *loc. cit.*, p. 77.

12 "Historical Writings of Judge Wilkeson," *loc. cit.*, p. 142.

13 Ronald A. Shaw, *Erie Water West: A History of the Erie Canal, 1792-1854*, (Lexington, Kentucky: University of Kentucky Press, 1966), pp. 140-142.

14 *Ibid.*, pp. 146-147.

15 *Courier, ibid.*

16 Marc Harris, "John Wilkeson," *Iron and Steel in the Nineteenth Century*, in ed. William H. Becker, *Encyclopedia of American Business History* (New York: Facts on File, 1989), p. 368.

After his term as mayor was over, Wilkeson embarked upon a non-commercial venture:

> His interest in politics and his conscientiousness and humanity carried him earnestly into the discussions of the problems of American slavery. The tidal wave of abolition was forming. He opposed it. He felt that if the doctrine should obtain, the union of the states would be broken, the negroes in the south would be exterminated by the whites, and an armed struggle would ensue between the North and the South. To save the Union and to save the South, he favored a system of gradual and compensated emancipation. Fearing that a system of slavery could not and would not tolerate the presence of free negroes, he advocated the colonization of blacks on the west coast of Africa. The control of the American Colonization Society was surrendered to him. He removed to Washington, the headquarters and for two years edited its organ, the *African Repository*, governed the colony of Liberia, instituted commerce with it from the ports of Baltimore and Philadelphia, and gathered colonists wherever he could in the South and shipped them to the new Republic. But the flood that was to uproot human bondage in America and overwhelm the slave oligarchy in the slave states, as well as in the free, finally rejected colonization as a remedy and it was abandoned.[17]

Jane, Samuel's first wife and mother of all his children, died in Buffalo in 1819, two years after the birth of her last child. His second wife was Sarah Saint John of Buffalo who died in 1836, and his third wife was Mary Peters (1785-1847) who died a year after her husband. Samuel and Jane had six children who constituted the third generation of Wilkesons in America: (i) Elizabeth (1804-1858) who married Dr. Henry Stagg of Buffalo (+1858); (ii) John (1806-1894) married Mary Louise Wilkes of Portsmouth, England; (iii) Eli (1809-1849), prominent in the Buffalo fire department, devoting time and money to it; (iv) William (1811-1882) who married Mary Swan of Mount Morris, lived all his life on the Square, and operated a foundry on Court Street; (v) Louise (1814-1860) who married Mortimer Johnson and moved South; and (vi) Samuel (1817-1889) who married Catherine Cady, sister of the suffragette, Elizabeth Cady Stanton. He graduated from Union College in 1837, was a staff writer for the *New York Tribune*, and during the Civil War was its correspondent with the Army of the Potomac. Later he became owner and editor of the Buffalo *Democrat* and editor of the *Albany Evening Journal*, having bought out Thurlow Weed. In 1869 he went West to become secretary of the newly organized Northern Pacific Railroad.[18]

Judge Samuel Wilkeson died in 1848 at Kingston, Tennessee, forty miles short of the Tellico Plains home of his daughter Louise and her husband Mortimer Johnson whom he had intended to visit. People said that "a strong rod was broken and withered in Presbyterian Zion when Samuel Wilkeson died." It was also observed by Tennesseans that "his form and appearance strikingly resembled General Jackson [a Tennessean] when he [Wilkeson] rested after nearly 67 years of labor."[19]

John Wilkeson(4.4), the judge's oldest son, was eight when the family came to Buffalo in 1814. He was educated at private schools after which he clerked in a mercantile house in New York. In 1830

17 "Historical Writings of Judge Wilkeson," *loc. cit.*, p. 143.
18 Undated articles, Local Bibliographies, Local History Section, Buffalo & Erie County Public Library, Lafayette Square, 1st series, vol. 3:307-311, 320-324.
19 Lord, *loc. cit.*, p. 84.

4.4 ❦ **John Wilkeson (10/28/1806-4/4/1894),** ***Iron and Steel in the Nineteenth Century*****, p. 367.**

he moved to Ohio to represent his father's interest in the Arcole furnace, selling its products and supervising the company store. Later he moved, probably as a forwarder, to the Mexican State of Tabasco on the Gulf of Campeche. In 1840 he returned to the United States and became secretary to his father at the American Colonization Society. Two years later President John Tyler appointed him consul at the Grand Turk Island, a British colony in the Caribbean. On the voyage out his ship was wrecked, he narrowly escaped drowning, and was picked up by a passing ship which landed him at Newport, Rhode Island. Returning to Buffalo after resigning his consulship, he engaged in iron manufacturing. After his father's death, he became head of the house on the Square. His wife had died at age thirty in 1843 after having presented him with three children, Samuel H. (1836-1915), Louise (1838-1915), and John Wilkes Wilkeson (1835-1862).[20]

John Wilkeson acquired extensive oil and timber lands in Pennsylvania and was intermittently involved in his father's iron business in Ohio:

> Perhaps because coal became cheaply available just as charcoal was running out, John Wilkeson began experimenting in 1840 with raw coal as a furnace fuel. He did not adopt it, however, and the Geauga County iron industry continued to rely on charcoal and local bog ore deposits. By 1850 these resources ran out. In the late 1840s, probably because of his father's death in 1848, Wilkeson sold the Arcole Furnace to the one company left in the county, the Geauga Furnace, which had better access to the lake [via the Pennsylvania & Ohio Canal] and to outside suppliers. Arcole's port had begun salting up, and the creek itself was too small to handle substantial ore shipments. Then too Wilkeson's own experiments with coal eventually helped to make Arcole Furnace unable to compete with emerging firms.
>
> Wilkeson's interests had shifted to the Mahoning Valley even before he sold the Arcole works. In 1845 he and his brother-in-law Frederick Wilkes began as Wilkes Wilkeson & Company to build a new blast furnace in Lowellville. They received financial backing from Judge Wilkeson and from David Tod, a lawyer and politician who owned land and mines at Brier Hill. The furnace was designed to use raw coal as the only fuel. Lowellville was known to have reserves of limestone and was also near Mount Nebo and Brier Hill coal mines. Both mines, along with others, had yielded only a small output until the canal's opening made wider markets available.
>
> Along with the nearly contemporary discovery of black band iron ore in Tod's mine, Wilkeson's furnace inaugurated a new era in midwestern iron production. The Mahoning Valley industry took on new life and expanded even though its charcoal supplies and bog ores played out. Wilkeson gave up control of the furnace in about 1852 [and moved back

20 See above, footnote 4.18.
21 Marc Harris, *ibid.*, pp. 368-369.

to Buffalo where he lived until his death.] [21]

Back in Buffalo John Wilkeson in 1858 established on the harbor at the end of Washington Street a grain elevator which bore the family name well into the twentieth century. For years he was also chairman of the Western Elevator Company and a familiar figure along the docks. [22] Horton describes Buffalo's preeminence in this area in 1855:

> As its traffic in that commodity exceeded Chicago's, Buffalo now ranked as the first grain port and the first grain market on the Continent. As Chicago's traffic exceeded that of Danzig, Riga and St. Petersburg on the Baltic, of Odessa on the Black Sea and of Archangel on the White, Buffalo ranked as the first grain port of the world. [23]

As of 1860, residents at the Niagara Square mansion were:

John Wilkeson 51 Ohio grain elevator operator
William Wilkeson 48 N.Y.
Mary Swan Wilkeson 38 [wife of William]
John Wilkes Wilkeson 25 N.Y. [son of William]law student
Louisa M. Wilkeson 20 N.Y.[daughter of John]
Sara M. Stagg 20 N.Y. [niece of John]
Margaret Coffey 25 Ireland servant
Barney Neeson 20 Ireland servant

During the Civil War John Wilkeson devoted his knowledge of metallurgy to improving military armaments. He accompanied the army in the field and was present at Gettysburg and other important engagements. After the war he accompanied his neighbor across the Square, ex-President Millard Fillmore, on a journey through Europe. His later years were occupied with grain storage and transshipment. He died in Buffalo in 1894. [24]

John Wilkes Wilkeson graduated from Union College, and was a law student when the Civil War broke out. He enlisted on September 23, 1861, and became First Lieutenant in the 100th Regiment, New York Volunteers and was killed May 31, 1862, at Fair Oaks during the disastrous Peninsula Campaign. [25] His younger brother Samuel graduated from Phillips Andover and from Yale's engineering course, and had a more distinguished military career:

> With the outbreak of the Civil War he enlisted in the 21st New York Volunteer Infantry, as first Lieutenant of Company H. On February 22, 1862, he was mustered into the 11th New York Cavalry (Scott's 900) as Captain of Company C. He was promoted to Major June 24, 1862, Lieut. Colonel December 24, 1862, and Colonel March 15, 1865, and was discharged March 27, 1865, at Memphis, Tenn. [26]

In the course of the war the Scott's 900 functioned as unattached partisan raiders behind the lines, imitating the guerrilla tactics of Confederate generals, Nathan Bedford Forrest and John Mosby, traversing long stretches of hostile country in Louisiana, Mississippi, and Tennessee, capturing soldiers and horses, and devastating the countryside. [27]

22 "Old Homestead on Niagara Square," Local Biographies, *ibid.*, p. 320.
23 Horton, *op., cit.*, 1:102.
24 See above, footnote 4.18.
25 Frederick Phisterer, *New York in the War of the Rebellion, 1861-1865*, 3rd ed. (Albany: J. B. Lyon Co. 1912, 6 Vols.), 1:493.
26 *Memorial and Family History of Erie County, New York* [hereafer *M&FH*] (New York: the Genealogical Publishing Co., 1906-1908),
27 See above, footnote 4.18.

After the war, Colonel Wilkeson lived for a year at the mansion and in 1868 married Matilda Franks of Mackinac Island, whose father was agent for John Jacob Astor's American Fur Company. The newlyweds moved to an estate in nearby Cheektowaga where they had six children who survived childhood. All except Mary Juana Wilkeson married and moved away.[28] With the death of his father in 1894, Samuel moved back to Buffalo to manage the extensive Wilkeson estate. His wife died in 1903, at fifty-three, followed a month later by Samuel's sister Maria Louise who had lived her whole life in the mansion:

> For many years she occupied a brilliant and distinctive position in the social world of Buffalo. Miss Wilkeson was keenly interested in the fine arts, of which she was a liberal patron. Her collection of paintings, bric-a-brac and other articles of vertu was a notable one.[29]

Maria's estate was valued at in excess of $500,000 ($8,350,000 in 1997 dollars). She left legacies of $10,000 each to seven female relatives, and $1,000 each to long-time domestic servants, Annie Ryan and Patrick McGuire. The residue of the estate was left to her lawyer for twenty years, Henry Ware Sprague, in trust for her brother Samuel, the interest of which was to be paid to him during his lifetime. After his death it was to be equally divided among his children. Should Samuel not reside at the Square, the house was to be razed, since Maria "could not bear the thought of its being transformed into a rooming or boarding house, a fate that has come to so many of the fine old-time residences of the city." Samuel was not happy about the provisions of the will and argued that he was a co-executor with Sprague. The judge discovered that this was not so:

> The brother, Samuel H. Wilkeson, who is an old man, sat in court throughout the proceeding and made several interruptions [though his own lawyer was present]. After announcing the decision, Justice Lambert added that he would not appoint Wilkeson anyhow. "He's an old, feeble man, and it strikes me he himself is in need of a guardian."[30]

Actually, Samuel was only sixty-seven at the time, though he had failed since his glory days galloping through the South with Scott's 900. He died of pneumonia at seventy-eight in January 1915. His funeral was held at his home on the Square, his wife's pastor, Rev. George F. Williams of Saint Mary's Episcopal Church officiating. Only family members and a few intimate friends were invited. Burial was in the family plot in Forest Lawn. The only military presence was provided by six honorary pallbearers from the G.A.R. and six privates from Fort Porter who were actual pallbearers.[31] Eight of Judge Samuel Wilkeson's descendants had fought in the Civil War, of whom John Wilkes Wilkeson, the colonel's older brother, was killed at Seven Pines in 1862, and his cousin Bayard, was killed at Gettysburg in 1863.

At Colonel Wilkeson's death the *Courier* remarked that "the site [of the mansion] has been frequently mentioned as favorable for the location of a municipal or state building in harmony with

28 *Buffalo Courier*, January 9, 1903.
29 *M&FH*, 1:15.
30 *Buffalo Courier*, January 12, 1915.
31 *Ibid.*, January 13, 1915.

Left 4.5 ❦ John H. Conlin, *Buffalo City Hall: Americanesque Masterpiece* (Buffalo: Landmark Society of the Niagara Frontier, 1993), p. 12.
Above 4.6 ❦ Niagara Square Baptist Church, *PBHS*, 24 (1920), np.

the movement to create a civic center at the point." [32] Designs for a city hall were submitted during the 1920s; meanwhile the site was occupied by a gas station. Finally, groundbreaking was held in September 1929. The thirty-two-story-high structure was built on two triangular lots, blocking Court Street. It was an elongated octagon, 315 feet on the north-south axis and 164 feet on the east-west axis and 375 feet high. Completed on November 10, 1931, at a cost of $6,851,547, it contained 566,313 square feet of space. Its chronicler considers it "a world class example of civic architecture in the Art Deco style." [33](4.5)

Across Niagara Street on the northwest corner of the Square there was located in 1872 the Niagara Square Baptist Church.(4.1,6) Baptist ministers had preached the word in Western New York as early as 1801, and the First Baptist Church was organized in 1822. A frame structure was erected in 1829 on the northeast corner of Washington and Seneca Streets, which the federal government later took over for a post office. A second church was built further north on Washington which served until 1894 when a third structure was secured which was dedicated in September 1900 on Pearl and North Streets. [34]

> The edifice now [1889] used by the Congregational Society on Niagara Square was originally a fold for a Baptist church. Back in the forties the cottage Baptist church [a branch from the Washington-street Baptist church] which owned the French church on Washington street, began to pine for larger pastures; so the lot on Niagara Square was bought and the church built. It was dedicated in 1851. Its first pastor was the Rev. C. P. Sheldon. After moving into their new quarters the cottage Baptists were confronted with a large debt which they had contracted in building the church, and within a few years the property was sold under the foreclosure of a mortgage. The mortgagee bid it in, and in 1861 it was taken off his hands by the First Free Baptist Church under the Rev. Dr. George

32 *Ibid.*, March 26, 1915.
33 John Conlin, *Buffalo City Hall: Americanesque Masterpiece* (Buffalo: Landmark Society of the Niagara Frontier, 1993), p. 13.
34 Hill, *op. cit.*, 2:603.

Left 4.7 ❦ Niagara Square, looking northwest, *PBHS*, 16 (1912), 220.
Right 4.8 ❦ 98 Delaware, Sizer-Barnard Mansion, Hill, *op. cit.*, II, facing p. 688.

> W. Ball. In 1880 the [Baptist] society bought the Hudson-street property and the church on the square was bought by the Congregationalists. [35]

Though most New Englanders were originally Congregationalists, as they moved west they joined Presbyterian congregations, since the two bodies differed not on doctrine but only on the question of church government. Therefore this Niagara Square Congregational Church was the sect's first church in Buffalo. Seventy-three of its early members had belonged to the Lafayette Avenue Presbyterian Church. [36] Figure 4.7 is an 1870 view of Niagara Square from the southwest. The Square's church can be seen clearly with its twin steeples that were later removed.

Next to the church was another grand old mansion of the 1830s (4.8), the story of whose residents is told by Bartlett:

> The house at 98 Delaware on the northwest corner of Delaware and Court was built around 1838 by Benjamin Rathbun. Henry Huntington Sizer its original owner came to Buffalo in 1814. He was the principal clerk of Judge Wilkeson [of the forwarding firm of Johnson and Wilkeson, first in the Kremlin block on Main Street and then on the docks]. Colonel Sizer bought the unfinished house when Rathbun went bankrupt [in the summer of 1836 for fiscal crimes which disrupted the city's economy and for which he was sent to the penitentiary at Auburn for five years.] Sizer had married Mary Whiting of Herkimer who with her sister had come to visit Sizer on the Square. The sister (Harriet) married Col. David Burt who also lived on Niagara Square.
>
> Sizer's five children were all born at Niagara Square. Between the church and the Sizer house was an alley which was originally the carriage drive. Flower beds, fruit trees, out-houses, and every comfort of the country gentleman surrounded the family. For many years glorious elms grew on the lawns. The brick and stone house was of square colonial design and was reached by stone steps leading to a platform edged with balustrades, one on the Square, the other on Delaware Street. Vines draped the outside walls and the rooms inside were lofty and spacious and finished in old mahogany.

35 *Buffalo Express*, May 5, 1889.

H. H. Sizer died of smallpox in June, 1849, his wife died in August, 1874. Their daughter Clara had married Albert J. Barnard. The Barnards moved into the house and continued to live there after Sizer's widow died. The house had always been a center for social hospitality. Evelyn, another daughter of the Sizers married Richard Hilliard of a prominent Cleveland family in one of the largest weddings Buffalo had ever seen. The Sizer mansion was the first in Buffalo to be lit by gas, an illumination which was used at the wedding though it took place at noon. The first time Poppenburg's band played in America upon its arrival from Germany was at Evelyn's wedding. Hilliard died in 1905. [37]

To Buffalonians of the 1830s the Sizer mansion provided a grand vision:

When Mr. Sizer built his home, it was the second house west of Main St. Across the avenue lay an open field, later to be occupied successively by the home of President Millard Fillmore and the Hotel Statler. The Sizer home was surrounded by beautiful lawns and gardens. The tall trees that provided cooling shade were survivors from primeval forests cleared only a few years before the house was built. In the garden grew fruit trees of many varieties. A favorite haunt of the Sizer children and grandchildren was the extensive grape arbor.

Mr. Sizer was proud of his fine cattle and horses. He kept them a short distance from his home on a farm that extended along Delaware Ave. from Huron to Chippewa St. Mr. Sizer, a partner of Ebenezer Johnson, first Mayor of Buffalo, and Samuel Wilkeson, also an early holder of that office, included lumber among his business interests. For the doors and all interior woodwork of his home he imported fine mahogany from San Domingo.

The broad doors opening on Delaware Ave. and Niagara Sq. are identical. The exterior of each is adorned with a large, hand-carved wreath of leaves and flowers and a silver escutcheon. The knobs and hinges of the doors were of silver. From a large reception hall rose a graceful mahogany circular stairway with treads painted ivory white. The tops of the newel posts were of silver. When Mr. Sizer saw them he thought them too plain. Taking from his pocket silver dollars, he slapped one down on each post. "There's a suitable top for my newel posts," he declared and sent for a silversmith to fasten the dollars in place. These post tops are preserved by Mr. Sizer's descendants.

In every room of the house was a large fireplace, many of them with marble mantels. In the 1830s those fireplaces provided the only means of heating the rooms. The rooms were large. Ceilings were so high that the four-poster beds had to be cut down when moved into modern homes. The mahogany dining table was so large that it has been divided into three sections, each used by a great-granddaughter of Henry Sizer. The spacious drawing-room looking out on the square was decorated in blue. The walls were covered with blue damask, the floor with blue velvet carpet. The furniture was upholstered in blue velvet. In this room the Sizers received many callers and invited guests. The family preferred to use the back parlor. From its windows they could see the garden. The two parlors, connected by sliding doors could become one room for large social functions.

The second hostess of Buffalo to invite friends to afternoon tea, Mrs. Sizer sent invitations each adorned with an engraved teapot. Every New Years's Day hundreds of guests gathered in the two parlors to extend the seasons good wishes to the Sizers. On those occasions a wide variety of delicacies were served to visitors. A favorite still remembered was pickled oysters.

36 Hill, *op. cit.*, 2:631-632.
37 Bartlett Papers, *ibid.* See also Horton, *op. cit.*, 1:75-76; Phisterer, *op. cit.*, 5:3363.

4.9 ❦ 98 Delaware, Spencer Kellogg offices, BHS.

Originally, kitchen and dining room were in the basement. In the 40s the house was remodeled and they formed a part of the first floor of the added wing. At that time a bathroom and the most modern heating available were installed, and the entire house was lighted with gas. The ornate bronze and crystal gas chandelier from the drawing room is preserved by a member of the family. It had to be cut down for use in her home.[38]

The youngest daughter, Clara, married Albert J. Barnard, and the couple lived at #98 Delaware until 1910. Albert, the son of Albert and Eliza Barnard of Buffalo, was born in 1841, attended local public schools, and became general manager of the United Express Company. Later he was a partner in Plum Burdict & Barnard, a Tonawanda-based manufacturer of bolts. In 1862 he enlisted as captain in the 116th New York Volunteers and stayed on after the war until 1877, becoming colonel on the staff of General O. O. Howard, Commissioner of the Freedman's Bureau, eponym and president of Howard University, and an Indian fighter.[39] Spencer Kellogg & Sons, manufacturers of linseed oil, bought the Barnard property in 1910 and enlarged it, keeping the original colonial design.(4.9) Kellogg & Sons was the first business to move to Niagara Square. The building was razed and replaced by a parking lot in January 1960.[40]

An early inhabitant of the site directly across Delaware was Albert H. Tracy who had been born in Norwich, Connecticut, in 1793. In 1811 he migrated to New York where he abandoned a projected career in medicine and came to Buffalo where he studied law and was admitted to the bar in 1815. He represented Buffalo in Congress from 1816 to 1824 and from 1830 until 1837 served as state senator. He was an unsuccessful Whig candidate for the United States Senate in 1839 and died in Buffalo in 1859.[41] Tracy was succeeded there by James Hollister:

> In 1843-44 the frame house on the northeast corner of Delaware Avenue and Niagara Square was occupied by James Hollister who lived there 1848-49. His son, Frank M. Hollister, remembers: "In those days swine and cattle were allowed to roam for forage in the streets of this and other American cities greatly to the surprise and disgust of Mrs. Trollope, Charles Dickens, and other fastidious travelers." The frame house was moved down Niagara Street in 1848 (and converted into a Parsonage of the Unitarian Society for

38 H. Katherine Smith, "Landmark Since 1835," *CE*, June 15, 1952.
39 *Commercial Advertiser*,(hereafter *CA*), January 11, 1916.
40 Bartlett Papers, *ibid*. *CE*, April 4, 1960.
41 *Biographical Directory of the United States Congress, 1774-1989* (Washington, D.C. United States Congress, Government Printing Office, 1989), p. 1951.

the use of the Rev. Geo. W. Hosmer), and James Hollister built the house on its site and lived there until the Panic of 1857 and the failure of his own Hollister Bank.

There were six Hollister brothers, all of whom were prominent in the social and business life of the nation. They established a series of chicken stores from Utica to the interior of Ohio. This unique mode of advertising by painting their stores in varied colored chickens became widely known throughout the west. They took up other pursuits; they did a business in pot and pearl ashes which was a source of profit in a timbered new country. They built the first two Ericson propellers, the *Hercules* and the *Samson*, and the Hollister Elevator was one of their enterprises. James was president of the bank on Main and East Seneca Street; his brother Robert was vice-president, his son Edward P., was teller. His house was bought by [Millard] Fillmore.[42]

4.10 ❦ Millard Fillmore, White, *op. cit.*, I, facing p. 469.

Fillmore had been born in Locke in Central New York's Military Tract in 1800, son of Nathaniel Fillmore and Phoebe Millard, tenant farmers.(4.10) Apprenticed to a textile mill, he began to educate himself and to attend school when the mill shut down. Later, by clerking for a local judge and teaching school, Fillmore bought out his indenture. Following his family west, he continued to read law and teach in Buffalo where he was admitted to the bar at twenty-three. He opened a law office in East Aurora and married Abigail Powers. They had two children, Millard Powers and Mary Abigail.

Fillmore joined the anti-Masonic Party, originally a widespread protest movement against the rural establishment, and was elected to three terms in the legislature, where he played an important role in legislation abolishing imprisonment for debt. In 1834, having moved to Buffalo, he was elected to Congress, where he became one of the founders of the Whig Party, which espoused the protective tariff and federal support for internal improvements. In 1836, 1838, and 1840 he was elected to Congress where he became prominent as chairman of the powerful Ways and Means Committee. In 1844 he was the Whig candidate for governor but lost to Democrat Silas Wright. Continuing active in public life, he opposed the Democrats' incitement of war with Mexico. The Mexican Cession consequent on the war raised the issue of slavery in the territories that split both major parties. Most New York Whigs, under the leadership of Thurlow Weed and William H. Seward, adopted an anti-slavery stance, whereas Fillmore was a nationalist and a friend of the South, though personally opposed to its Peculiar Institution. He was elected state comptroller in 1847 by a wide margin, and next year was selected as Zachary Taylor's running mate. With Taylor's victory Fillmore became vice president in March 1849.[43] His chief claim to fame and notoriety was his role in the adoption of the Compromise of 1850.

42 Bartlett Papers, folder 3.
43 Anbinder, Tyler, "Millard Fillmore," *ANB*, 7:910-912.

After the Mexican War the United States had acquired an immense amount of land in what became the Southwest. This raised the sectional question of whether slavery should be extended to the area. Henry Clay had a plan which included "the admission of California as a free state, organization of the Utah and New Mexico territories without prohibiting slavery, settlement of the Texas-New Mexico boundary dispute, outlawing the slave trade but not slavery in the District of Columbia, and a more rigorous fugitive slave law." Taylor opposed the law and it stalled in Congress but he died on July 9, 1850, and was succeeded by Fillmore who supported it and by accepting Senator Stephen A. Douglas's strategy of separating the compromise into several smaller bills, secured its passage. This won Fillmore many enemies within his own Whig Party and he was not nominated for President in 1852. But he was nominated by the American (Know-Nothing) Party which sought to reduce the political clout of immigrants and Catholics. The Americans were also unionists, an element in their platform that Fillmore, no bigot, admired. In the end he carried only Maryland and twenty-two percent of the popular vote. Thus ended his political career.[44]

Fillmore's wife died three weeks after he left office. After his failed run for president, he toured Europe for a year and, back in Buffalo, married the wealthy Caroline C. McIntosh, the fifty-two-year-old, childless widow of a Troy merchant:

> Fragile, with a tragic air about her — almost giving the appearance of a Mona Lisa grown old — she quickly won acceptance amid Fillmore's wide circle of friends and effortlessly became one of Buffalo's leading ladies. Her finishing-school training and her dilettante achievements enhanced a native graciousness.
>
> Mrs. Fillmore, of course, had no desire to hoard her money and willingly joined her husband in purchasing John Hollister's huge mansion(4.11) on Niagara Square [the year after the Panic of 1857]. Alone, Fillmore's savings were too small to undertake both purchase and maintenance. This mammoth structure became their home for the remainder of their lives. Its gothic style, with parapets, balustrades, and simulated towers, decorated in the elegant taste of the Victorian era, sharply contrasted with the "plain, white, two-story house with green blinds and a little yard in the front" at 180 Franklin Street that had been Fillmore's home for twenty-six years. In front of the house [on the Square]...was one of the small triangular parks fenced off containing trees and grass.
>
> In another way the Niagara Square home differed from the old house. The new one was ideally suited to the kind of life that circumstances had created for the Fillmores. In the past both had paid punctilious attention to social requirements. And now, with little else to occupy their time, they turned their home on Niagara Square into one of society's most gracious centers. Hardy a distinguished person of America or other lands who visited Buffalo failed to experience the Fillmore's hospitality. Besides a long list of political celebrities, they shared in entertaining a Japanese ambassador, Tommomi Iwakuar, and H. R. H. Prince Arthur of England.[45]

44 Robert J. Rayback, *Millard Fillmore: Biography of a President*, vol. 40, *PBHS* (Henry Steward, 1959), pp. 416-418.
45 *Ibid.*, pp. 424-430.

4.11 ❦ Victorian mansion, Rayback, *op. cit.*, following p. 116.

4.12 ❦ Fillmore as Commander of the Union Continentals, *ibid*, facing p. 303.

The Fillmore household in 1860 was as follows:

Millard Fillmore 60 NY atty 7 Court St
Caroline Fillmore 44(!) NY wife
Millard P Fillmore 32 son NY attorney
Ann Lawler 24 Ireland servant
Julia Lawler 24 Ireland servant
John Dooley 25 Ireland servant
John Nash 25 Ireland servant

Ten years later at what was now #52 Niagara Square were:

Hon. Millard Fillmore 70 retired attorney
Caroline C. Fillmore 56 wife
Millard Fillmore 42 NY son clerk in US District Court
Mary Heinlich 21 NY servant
Kate Ryan 19 NY servant

Fillmore had been chancellor of the University of Buffalo since its founding in 1846. This was an honorary position which involved merely conferring degrees at commencements. For decades the university conducted only a medical school and a law school. His favorite civic cause was the Buffalo Historical Society whose origins he had presided over in 1862 and of which he was first president. After the outbreak of the Civil War he organized the Union Continentals, of which he went from captain to commander.(4.12) The unit was composed of men too old to be drafted but ready to act in a local emergency. Members wore

4.13 ❦ Hotel Fillmore, Niagara Square, *PBHS*, 25 (1921), np.

colorful uniforms and were drilled to act as an escort guard. Whenever an affair needed a show of pomp and patriotism, the Union Continentals supplied it. Nevertheless, Fillmore criticized Lincoln's conduct of the war and supported George B. McClellan for president in 1864, thereby becoming a favorite whipping boy for local Republicans. [46]

Because of his support of the Compromise of 1850, especially the Fugitive Slave Act, and running on the nativist ticket in 1856, Fillmore has been denigrated by most liberal historians. However the Compromise postponed the Civil War for a decade during which the North progressed materially far more than the South and hence was in a better position to wage a successful war. This is his recent biographer's assessment of the man:

> As I began my research for this book, I expected to find that Millard Fillmore was a weak and pompous President, for tradition had painted that portrait of him. When, instead, my investigations revealed that he possessed extraordinary strength of character and an enviable tenacity of purpose — as well as an admirable personality — I was startled.
>
> For a while this discrepancy between the man I had encountered and his historical image caused me no end of concern. Eventually it became clear that until now the picture of Fillmore which is found in most history books was a product of the reports of his enemies, just as Hamilton's and Hoover's were of theirs.
>
> What was disparagingly reported as Fillmore's overweening, personal ambition, upon investigation turned into self-sacrifice; his fatal vanity, moreover, became simple dignity. True, he was not a clever politician or an inspiring orator. But more important, if promo-

46 *Ibid.*, Preface.

tion and preservation of the nation are the criteria, he was a statesman with only a handful of White House rivals. Even after retiring from a lifetime of public service, his actions for civic improvement on the local level were nearly boundless, and his personal life was impeccable. Instead of a self-serving politician, the person who emerged from the sources was a quiet, almost modest, man, who had no desire for power and who wanted to do good and make good according to the best conventions of the day. And he succeeded.[47]

Fillmore died on March 8, 1875. Caroline followed him in 1881, after which the mansion was merged with the Hawley house next door and became the Hotel Fillmore.(4.13) After reconversion, the name was changed to the Castle Inn in time for the Pan-American Exposition.(4.14, 15, 16) In May 1921 E. M. Statler broke ground for his hotel which was opened two years later in April 1923.[48](4.17)

Above 4.14 ❦ Castle Inn, *ibid.*
Middle 4.15 ❦ Entrance hall, Castle Inn, *ibid.*
Below 4.16 ❦ Drawing room, Castle Inn, *PBHS*, *ibid.*

The completed caravansary had cost $8,000,000 and covered an entire block. Two hundred and sixty five feet high, it contained thirteen guest room floors with a capacity of 2,500 guests, and

47 Bartlett Papers, *ibid.*
48 *Courier*, April 17, 1923.

4.17 ❦ Hotel Statler, BHS.

employed a work force of 900. Lower floors contained Turkish baths, barbershops, beauty parlors, a drug store, haberdashery, and a women's shop. There were six different eateries, besides private dining rooms, and a ballroom seating 1,500.[48]

Statler was a giant among hoteliers. Born in rural Pennsylvania, he moved with his family as a boy to a town across the Ohio from Wheeling. At thirteen he got a job as a bellboy in a Wheeling hotel. Head bellboy at fifteen, night clerk at seventeen, he then leased the billiard room, added a ticket agency, and purchased a bowling club, to which he added a barbershop and lunchroom. By 1894 he was making $10,000 a year. In 1895 he opened a 500-seat restaurant in the Ellicott Square Building in Buffalo. During the 1901 Pan American Exposition he built a temporary hotel to serve 2,084 people, which offered meals and rooms at a flat rate. A similar operation at the Louisiana Purchase Exposition in 1903 in Saint Louis netted a profit of $361,000. In 1908 he erected the 200-room Hotel Statler (later renamed the Buffalo) on the southeast corner of Washington and Swan Streets. Statler balanced an appeal to the wealthy with an emphasis on the traveling public and offered amenities at a reasonable price. These included innovations like baths, radios, closets, full length mirrors, medical and laundry services, and a free newspaper delivered to each room.[49] Diagonally across from the hotel on the northwest corner of Delaware and Mohawk was the six-story Statler Garage with a 690-car capacity. It opened at the same time as the hotel with a facade that matched the hotel and spaces for eight stores on Delaware. Entrance and exit were on Mohawk, and ramps rather than elevators brought cars to the upper floors.[50]

It had been Statler's original intention to erect a legitimate theatre directly across from the hotel at the same time as the parking garage, but the city had not yet decided on the location of the city hall. One proposed site was the block between Delaware and Genesee on the Square. By 1926, however, the present site on the west side of the Square had been decided upon, and bids were let for a four-story building with shop and office space above the theater entrance, and a theatre with 1,600 seats, to be leased to A. L. Erlanger, operator of a nationwide chain of theaters.[51] It opened in August 1927

49 Spoonholt, Lloyd, " Ellsworth Milton Statler," *ANB*, 29:581.
50 *Times*, May 4, 1923.
51 *Express*, April 5, 1926.

and closed in June 1956, when local interests bought it, demolished the theatre section, and used the front for offices. Its sad story was told by Ardis Smith, drama critic of the *Buffalo Evening News*, in an article entitled "Erlanger's Fatal Affliction-From First, Nobody Loved It." In fact many actively despised it, accusing it of an acoustical dead spot, spreading from about the middle of row J. Then came the Depression and the introduction of talkies. [52]

Nevertheless, during its unhappy tenure, the Erlanger's audiences were treated to such classics as Eugene O'Neil's *Mourning Becomes Electra,* and *Ah! Wilderness*, Tallulah Bankhead in *The Little Foxes*, Katherine Hepburn in *The Philadelphia Story*, Catherine Cornell in *Saint Joan*, Helen Hayes in *Victoria Regina,* and George M. Cohan in *I'd Rather be Right*. Dunn in his history of Erie County analyzes the decline of theaters like the Erlanger:

> Beginning in the 1920s the road show — and with it the commercial theatre in all inland cities — went into a long and gradual decline, brought on by rising costs and competition from the movies ...The standards and techniques of the movies improved until they were a competitive art form of unlimited possibilities. They added dialogue; they added color; they added size; they added a third dimension. [53]

Forty-six Niagara Square was built around the same time and in the same domestic gothic style as the Fillmore house for Merwin S. Hawley, commission merchant on Central Wharf. His daughter Ellen married Jerome I. Prints, and both families lived there till the place was sold to Castle Inn. [54]

Long-time Buffalo resident Samuel M. Welch, writing in 1891, continues the story eastward:

> At the northeast corner of the Square [#42] resided Stephen Osborn (Government Agent for the Seneca Tribe of Indians) and Hezekiah A. Salisbury, one of the original proprietors of the *Buffalo Commercial*; the old house is still standing in that very central location. Where is now our "Free Collegiate High School" [across Genesee Street] lived General David Burt (father of Henry W. Burt, cashier of the German American Bank); the house forms a part of the present school building. At this house General Burt entertained the venerable John Quincy Adams, "the old man eloquent," when here in a late year of his life. [55]

Burt, Indian agent at Buffalo, brigadier general in the 47th Brigade of the state militia, and once a director of Buffalo's branch of the Second Bank of the United States, saw service during the Upper Canadian Rebellion in 1837. New York authorities were determined to check the enthusiasm of Americans to help dissident Canadian refugees who had fled when their pathetic uprising had been checked on a single day in Toronto. Fort Poinsett, further up Delaware Street, had been established by the federal government for the same purpose. Burt died in 1848 and four years later his house(4.18) was sold to the city for its first Central High School. Its early years were rocky, but a wing was added in 1870 fronting on Franklin Street. In 1885 the old Burt building fronting on Court Street was demolished and a new three-story brick structure was built adjoining the Franklin Street wing, which

52 *BEN*, September 26, 1956.
53 Dunn, *op. cit.*, p. 395.
54 Bartlett Papers, *ibid*.
55 Samuel M. Welch, *Home History. Recollections of Buffalo During the Decade from 1830-1840* (Buffalo: Peter Paul & Bro., 1891), p. 55.

Above 4.18 ❦ Niagara Square east, 1870, *PBHS*, 16 (1912), 221.
Middle 4.19 ❦ Old Central High School, *PBHS*, 29 (1927), 332.
Below 4.20 ❦ *PBHS*, 30 (1930), np.

served as Central High(4.19) until Hutchinson Central High was erected on Elmwood north of Chippewa.[56] Old Central High was demolished in 1926 and today is the site of the New York State Building.

Mention has been made above(4.2) of Sylvanus Gould, a Vermont-born attorney, who lived across Court Street from General Burt. Gould's house lot can be seen in figure 3.1. On it in 1889 was built at a cost of $55,000 a five-story residence for the Women's Christian Association (after 1904 the Young Women's Christian Association).[57](4.20) It was demolished in 1930 and replaced by a two-story office building with shops on the first floor popularly known as the Rumsey Building. After a long debate going back to 1926 about the location of a new federal building (the previous one on south Division Street, now the city campus of Erie County Community College, having become hopelessly overcrowded), the Rumsey location was chosen. Since the Depression was on, funding to the amount of $2,230,000 fell to the Public Works Administration. Considerations of economy scaled down the original twelve stories to seven, and the United States Courthouse opened on May 29, 1936.[58] Together with City Hall, these state and federal buildings represent a partial fulfillment of Ellicott's wish that the Square be a seat of government:

> The Center was also realized with disastrous consequences albeit in a much altered form. By the end of the twentieth century Niagara Square, with the exception of the Statler Hotel [and the Buffalo Athletic Club and the parking lot on the site of the demolished Spencer-Kellogg building], was given

56 Hill, *op. cit.*, 2:507.
57 Ibid., 2:690-704.
58 *Buffalo Times*, August 11, 1929; September 11, 1932; *BEN*, May 26, 1936.

over completely to government uses. The heart of it was the Civic Center, a series of public buildings grouped around the center of Buffalo and already dignified in City Beautiful terms by the placement there of an obelisk dedicated to the memory of William McKinley.(4.17) The gigantic hulking City Hall, a grotesque Gothic Revival structure, a monumental classic portico for an entrance way, was the centerpiece of the Civic Center. On both its flanks were to be two large but neo-classical government buildings. [59]

4.21 ❦ H. H. Richardson's proposed ceremonial arch for Niagara Square, Kowsky, *Best Planned City*, p. 53.

Another monument was projected for the Square:

> On the 4th of July 1876, ground had been broken in Niagara Square for a memorial arch to the founders and defenders of the Union. The never completed monument was part of the scheme that Olmsted had prepared in 1874 for giving Joseph Ellicott's square an urban character commensurate with its role as the city's principal civic space. However, in place of Vaux, Olmsted asked H. H. Richardson, whose office at the time was in New York City to prepare the design for the arch.
>
> Richardson's arch, which appears in one of the eight watercolor drawings of Buffalo that Olmsted exhibited at the Centennial Exhibition in Philadelphia, was to have been built of white stone and to have stood seventy feet high.(4.21) Reminiscent of the Arch of Triumph in Paris (where Richardson had spent the war years), the arch was to have displayed reliefs commemorating heroes of the Revolution, the War of 1812, and the Civil War. It would have formed a commanding frontispiece to Delaware Avenue as it began its three mile course to the Park. [60]

Across Niagara Street on the south of the Square were two grand old mansions that lasted well into the twentieth century, #3 and #11.(4.1, 22) Number 3 was the home of the eponym of Anderson Place, Alexander S. Anderson, an Irish-born wholesale grocer and liquor dealer who had bought the lot from Samuel Wilkeson, the original purchaser from Ellicott. On it in the 1850s Anderson built a house "of brick with brown sandstone facing quite in the style of the old-fashioned brownstone fronts of New York City." [61] In 1860 Anderson lived there with his mother, sister, niece, and a nineteen year-old Canadian servant girl. He sold it in 1874 to William H. Greene(4.23) who had been born in Shrewsbury, Massachusetts, in 1812. He attended Ashfield Academy in his native village before moving west to Skaneateles, New York, where he read law and was admitted to the bar in 1838, upon which, at age twenty-five, he came to Buffalo, becoming a law partner of Thomas Sherwood. Hailed by some as "one of the ablest and most successful members of the bar of Western New York," he was almost wholly engaged in litigation. He entertained literary pretentions, delivering lectures to members of the Young Men's Association on Milton, Burke, and Cicero. He died in 1882 and was survived by his wife, the former Helen Bull, and a daughter, both of whom continued to live at the Square until 1889 when they moved to New York. Then the mansion became a rooming house with offices on the first floor. [62]

59 Goldman, *op. cit.*, p. 194.
60 Kowsky, "Calvert Vaux and the Architecture of Buffalo's Parks," pp. 50-54, in Kowsky, ed., *Best Planned City*, pp. 50-54.
61 Bartlett Papers, *ibid.*
62 Smith, *op. cit.*, 2, pt. 2, p. 27.

Next eastward on the Square to was Stephen Godwin Austin's solid, imposing mansion. Austin(4.24) was born in Goshen, Connecticut, in 1791. He attended the academy at Westfield, Massachusetts, and graduated in 1815 during the presidency of Rev. Timothy Dwight whose influence on his students was said to have been "incalculable." [63] After graduation, Austin moved to Geneva, New York, where he read law in the offices of Daniel W. Lewis and passed the bar. In 1819 he came to Buffalo, reckoning correctly that the village would be designated the terminus of the Erie Canal. Growing up with the city he became president of the National Savings Bank. In later life he spent much of his time managing the large estate he had accumulated. There lived in the mansion on the Square according to the census of 1870 Austin, his wife Lavinia, their daughter Delia and her husband Truman Gardner Avery, a grain elevator manager, together with two Irish serving girls in their twenties. Stephen Austin died in 1872, after which #11 became the home of his widow, his daughter, her husband, and the Averys' daughter Lavinia Austin, age four. The Averys at this time employed six live-in servants including a nurse for Lavinia Senior, a coachman, and a seamstress. Later Avery built an artistic mansion on The Circle at North Street and Richmond Avenue. Both the Austin and the Greene mansions were demolished in 1922 together with homes on the north side of Eagle Street pictured in Figure 3.2 to make way for the Buffalo Athletic Club. [64] Figure 4.25 shows Niagara Square in the early twentieth century, but before 1922 since both the Greene and the Austin houses are still standing, as is the Y.W.C.A. building. The view is from Niagara Street looking southeast. The streetcar is a #5 which ran from Shelton Square along Niagara Street to the city line at Vulcan Street, the tracks transcribing an arc as they passed around the Square. [65]

Above 4.22 ❦ Numbers 3 and 11 Niagara Square, *PBHS*, 26 (1922), np. Below 4.23 ❦ William H. Greene, Smith, *op. cit.*, II, facing p. 474.

The Ellicott Club had been a dinner club, chartered in 1895, with quarters on the tenth floor of the Ellicott Square Building. Membership consisted of outstanding business and professional men, some of whom, after World War I, called for the addition of health facilities. A thousand members signed on for a new organization to be known as the Buffalo Athletic Club, to which each pledged $1,000.

63 William C. Dowling, "Timothy Dwight," *ANB*, 7:193.
64 Smith, *op. cit.*, 2:pt. 2, pp. 27-30.
65 William R. Gordon, *90 Years of Buffalo Railways, 1840-1950* (Buffalo: 1970), p. 130.

Left 4.24 ❦ Stephen G. Austin, *ibid*, II, facing p. 460.
Above 4.25 ❦ Niagara Square from Niagara Street, circa 1920, *Buffalo Gazette*, vol 1, #7.

With this the Ellicott Club became the Ellicott Club Association, a holding corporation for the B.A.C. In 1922 work was begun on a twelve-story home for the club on Niagara Square.(4.26) Formal opening was on October 29, 1923. The new facility contained 156 sleeping rooms for bachelor members and visiting guests, a main dining room, a ladies dining room, a stone tiled grill, and a floor of private dining rooms. The seventy-five foot long pool was the largest in the city and a gymnasium, sun lamp room, Turkish baths, three squash courts, eight bowling alleys, and a billiard room with fourteen tables provided justification for the name change. [66]

Above 4.26 ❦ Buffalo Athletic Club, BHS.
Below 4.27 ❦ Number 25 Niagara Square, Potter-Babcock house, *PBHS*, 16 (1912), 381

Number twenty-five, the next house west across Delaware (4.27), was built by Heman B. Potter, an attorney who had come to Buffalo in 1811 and was allegedly "less assertive than the majority of successful pioneers yet he continued so long in active life that he was more than any other man the connecting link between the forest shaded hamlet and the swarming metropolis." In 1819 he became Erie County's first district attor-

66 *Buffalo Times*, March 1, 1935.

Left 4.28 ❦ 86 Delaware, Women's Educational & Industrial Union, *PBHS*, 22 (1918), facing p. 147. The entrance was on Delaware.
Above 4.29 ❦ Seymour-Hammond house, *PBHS*, 18 (1914), 362.

ney, a post he held for ten years. By the 1830s he was living in the house he had built on Niagara Square and was brigadier general of the 47th Brigade, New York State Militia. His daughter Mary married her father's law partner, George Babcock; the other daughter married Abraham Phineas Grant, Congressman from Oswego. Potter died in 1854 at sixty-eight.[67] He was followed at #25 Niagara Square by George Babcock. One of fifteen children, Babcock had been born in Gorham, Ontario County, New York, in 1806. He attended public school and the academy at Gorham and at seventeen was teaching there himself. In 1824 he came to Buffalo where he read law in Potter's office, passed the bar in 1829, and became Potter's partner. Like most lawyers of the time and place they combined land speculation with the practice of law. A clerk for Potter & Babcock was Elbridge Gerry Spaulding who eventually became a partner, and when the firm dissolved in 1844 took over its business, enjoying a busy legal practice thereafter. Spaulding was congressman from Buffalo 1859-1863 during which time he sponsored legislation calling for the issuance by the government of paper money to serve as legal tender, a move which earned him the sobriquet "Father of the Greenbacks."[68] Babcock was elected assemblyman in 1843, state senator in 1850 and again in 1852. From this vantage point he served as emissary to his friend and fellow-Whig, Millard Fillmore, during the latter's presidency (1850-1853). He was also Fillmore's unsuccessful campaign manager for the Whig nomination for president in

4.30 ❦ William W. Hammond, Smith, *op. cit.*, II, facing p. 484.

67 Bartlett Papers, *ibid.*
68 Williams, Patrick G., "Elbridge Gerry Spaulding," *ANB*, 20:224-225.

Left 4.31 ❦ Century Atlas Co., *Century Atlas of Greater Buffalo* (Philadelphia: Century Atlas Co., 1915), II, plate 30.
Right 4.32 ❦ Middle Class housing on the Square, BHS.

1852. A political conservative, he favored "the policy which would most speedily restore kindly relations between the states after the Civil War." Babcock died at his Niagara Square mansion in 1876, survived by his wife, who died there a year later, and two children, one of whom, Dr. Heman Potter Babcock, had moved to California.[69] After the death of Babcock's widow #25 was purchased by the Women's Educational Union and some alterations were made. But by 1893 activities had outgrown the house which was accordingly demolished and replaced by a more ample brick structure.(4.28) By 1914 the Union had outlived its usefulness, and the facility was donated to U.B.[70]

The last mansion to be covered in this tour of the Square was #35 into which Erastus B. Seymour moved at the beginning of the 1850s.(4.29) Born in 1805, Erastus was a descendant of Richard Seymour of Devon, England, who settled in Hartford in 1640 and a cousin of Horatio Seymour, governor of New York 1853-1855 and 1863-1865 and Democratic candidate for president against Ulysses S. Grant in 1868. A grain merchant, he migrated to Buffalo by way of Batavia in 1845 and formed a partnership with Chandler Wells which later branched out into lake boats and grain elevators. In 1860 Seymour, probably a widower by then, headed up a household of five daughters and a bank clerk son, waited on by three Irish-born females. He sold his place on the Square to William Wallace Hammond in 1877, moved to Franklin Street, and died in 1888.[71]

Hammond(4.30) had been born in Brant in 1831 of pioneer farmers on the Holland Purchase. He attended the district school, an academy in Irving, and another in Fredonia. At sixteen he began teaching school in Columbus, Pennsylvania, and then near Louisville, Kentucky. After a tour of the southern states, he returned home where he mixed teaching, running a general store, and practicing in lower courts. At twenty-nine he came to Buffalo, read law in the office of Albert Sawin and Judge

69 *CA*, September 22, 1876; Rayback, *op. cit.*, pp. 283, 285, 286, 335, 358.
70 Bartlett Papers, *ibid.*
71 *CA*, June 7, 1888.

Stephen Lockwood, and was admitted to the bar in 1861. During the Civil War, the volunteer regiment in which he had enlisted, the 65th New York National Guard, was ordered out to defend Harrisburg from Lee's invasion which ended ingloriously on the 3rd of July 1863 at Gettysburg. Mustered out shortly thereafter, Hammond moved to Farnham where he farmed and ran a lumber business and a general store. A term as justice of the peace followed, and twelve years as supervisor. In 1877 he came to Niagara Square and was elected county judge, serving 1878-1890. Losing the Republican nomination that year, he retired from politics and returned to law. He remained at the Square until 1888 when he sold the place for a Catholic working boys' home and moved to Franklin Street.[72] In 1897 a new home was erected where boys were admitted for nominal rates and some for free.[73] The Square was fast losing its distinctive cachet.

A final segment of homes on the Square, the block between Court and Niagara Streets, eluded gentrification. The four houses, #71, #73, #77 and #79,(4.31 and 32), were demolished with the rest of the block to make way for the new city hall at the end of the 1920s. They were townhouses, small by comparison with the mansions on the rest of the Square, and their occupants followed middle class pursuits, with few or no servants.

Thus did Niagara Square in its salad days bear out Bartlett's claim at the start of this chapter that "the very finest houses in the city were erected here and for awhile it was the most fashionable part of the town."

72 *Express*, September 28, 1915.
73 Hill, *op. cit.*, 2:693.

CHAPTER

5

FROM THE SQUARE TO *Chippewa Street* (5.1)

Niagara Square and Delaware Avenue to the south were the first segments of the thoroughfare to be commercialized or institutionalized. Since this is primarily a study of the Avenue's golden age, later chapters will deal chiefly with private homes north of the Square. Square and Avenue played a role in Frederick Law Olmsted's master plan for a Buffalo park system. William Dorsheimer, prominent German-American attorney and politician, was an ardent park promoter. He invited Olmsted to Buffalo in 1868 to make suggestions. By 1869 the legislature had created a park commission in Buffalo which appointed Olmsted, Vaux & Company its landscape architects. Olmsted called for three parks, the Park, the Front overlooking the lake and river, and the Parade on the East Side in a working-class German-American neighborhood.(5.2)

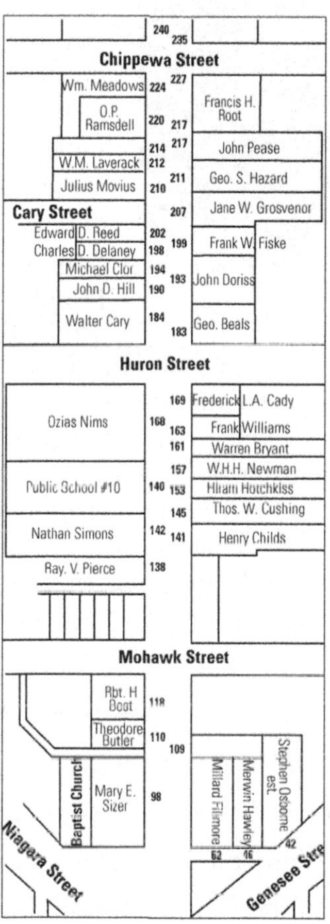

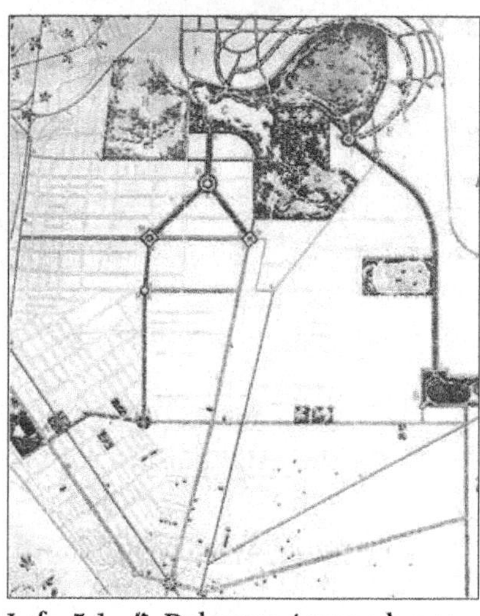

Left 5.1 ❦ Delaware Avenue house lots from Niagara Square to Chippewa Street drawn by author relying on *Atlas of Buffalo, 1915*, II, plate 10. Names are from census of 1870.
Above 5.2 ❦ Delaware Avenue as part of Olmsted's system of parkways for Buffalo. Kowsky, *Best Planned City*, p. 18.

These parks were to be joined by parkways and boulevards:

> The parkways too followed the general framework Olmsted had suggested in August 1868, as did the widening of the streets that connected the older city to the new improvements. Following his plans the park commissioners constructed Humboldt Parkway, which extends some three miles east and south from the Park to the Parade, as well as Lincoln, Bidwell, and Chapin Parkways south from the Park to the city. To connect these new avenues with the built areas of Buffalo, Delaware Avenue was widened from Niagara Square north to Chapin Square where it linked with the parkway system leading to the Park.[1]

1 Schuyler, "Cityscape and Parkscape," op. cit., p. 11.

5.3 ❦ **Bristol Cottage, *PBHS*, 25(1921), np.**

About the east side of Delaware between the Square and Mohawk local historian Frank Severance wrote in the 1920s:

> The oldest house in this block for very many years was at the northeast corner of Delaware and Mohawk Street. It was torn down two or three years ago. It was built in 1816, by Daniel Bristol, who had come to Buffalo in 1811, fled with his family when the village was burned, and then came back to help rebuild it. So far as is known to the writer, there were no buildings in this block prior to the burning of Buffalo in December 1813. Daniel Bristol's house, built [facing Mohawk] a little more than two years after the destruction of the village, was the first in the neighborhood. In the decade of the 30s Mr. Bristol built for his son Cyrenius C., to the south of his garden, a cottage which was distinguished by a pillared portico.(5.3) This cottage was torn down when the block was cleared for the new [Statler] hotel. C. C. Bristol was a druggist, long famous for his preparation of "Bristol's Sarsaparilla," and for the equally famous "Sarsaparilla Almanac" which he published annually for many years. Later occupants or owners of the Bristol cottage included Thomas C. Welch, father of the late Gen. Samuel M. Welch, a Mr. Groesbeck and family, Dr. Walter Kenyon, and Thomas Sizer, a well known attorney.[2]

Samuel Welch recalled in the 1890s that in the 1830s there "were very few houses on Delaware Street above the Square." He recalled the house on the northwest corner of Delaware and Chippewa, later #240, which had been built in 1835 by Philander Hodge, as "a costly house, finished elaborately with rosewood doors and highly ornamented stuccoed ceilings." Later occupants included Aaron D. Patchin, John S. Ganson, and the Buffalo Club. Across the street at #235 was the English basement house built for Alexander A. Eustaphieve in 1836, later the home of Ebenezer Carleton Sprague.[3]

The centerpiece of Welch's recollections of Delaware Street in the 1830s was the Johnson cottage(5.4) and its builder, Ebenezer Johnson.(5.5) Born in Connecticut, in 1786, son of a veteran of the Revolution, Johnson migrated to Cherry Valley, New York, where he studied medicine. He came to Buffalo in 1809, and practiced until the War of 1812. His affability won him a large clientele. When the British burned Buffalo the Johnsons fled to Williamsville where their services were welcomed by the wounded soldiers. After the war Johnson returned to Buffalo, opened a drugstore, invested in real estate, established a bank, built a grain elevator, and became a very rich man. In 1832 Buffalo was made a city, and Johnson was chosen its first mayor:

> In the same year the cottage was completed. Few houses were ever more stoutly built, for its massive walls of gray sandstone are today as solid as when first put up, and the

2 Frank Severance, "The Changing Town," *PBHS*, 25(1921), following p. 412.

5.4 ❦ Johnson Cottage, Welch, *op. cit.*, p. 58.

5.5 ❦ Ebenezer Johnson. Smith, *op. cit.*, I, facing p. 122.

mortar is as hard as the stone. In its early days, a glass dome and the white Doric pillars of its spacious verandas added greatly to the pompous dignity of the old mansion. The interior was fashioned with reference to providing of ample room for entertainment. Four large reception rooms clustered around a spacious rotunda, and might be opened together for evening companies. The room in the northeast corner was Dr. Johnson's office, for he was still a practicing physician, while the corresponding one on the Park-Place side contained the doctor's library and a cabinet well stocked with Indian curiosities.

The house was finished throughout in the most magnificent style — walls tinted in peach-blow colors; doors of solid mahogany with silver-plated door-knobs; windows hung with costly satin draperies and provided with rich cushioned window seats; splendid mirrors, each with a luxurious divan beneath it; sturdy, hardwood mantelpieces that upheld glittering candelabra; carpets and furniture, the finest that could be procured, all combined to produce an effect which those who enjoyed the hospitality of the house remember with enthusiasm to this day. Balconied windows, daintily curtained, looked down from the second story into the rotunda, where the old-fashioned piano stood, and in these balconies musicians were posted when social festivals were in progress. A spiral staircase led from the second floor to the top of the rotunda, which in those days was considered as fine a point of observation as the City Hall tower is today.

Handsome services of solid silver (even to the drinking cups) which were used by Dr. Johnson, are still in existence, as is also much of the furniture of this residence. An

3 Samuel Welch, *Home History: recollections of Buffalo during the decade from 1830 to 1840, or Fifty years since* (Buffalo: Peter Paul & Bro., 1890), p. 56-59.

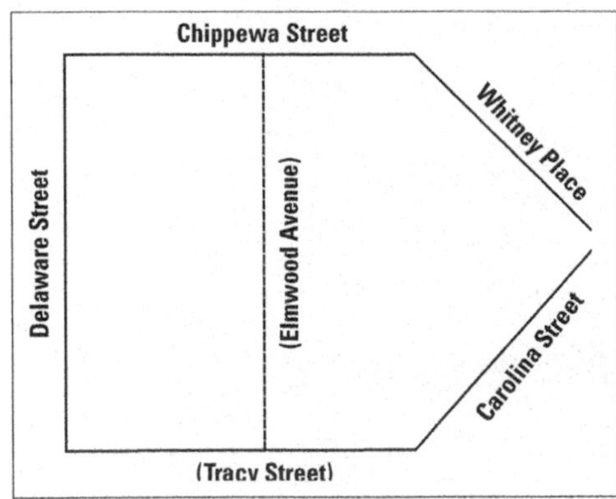

5.6 Dimensions of the Johnson estate.

elegantly carved sofa and a solid mahogany sideboard 150 years old are still preserved in the family.

> Splendid as was the cottage, its spacious grounds were not out of keeping with it. They were bounded by Delaware Avenue, Chippewa Street, Whitney Place, Carolina Street, and Tracy Street.(5.6) Near where the Chapter House now stands there was an artificial lake where the doctor kept a boat and allowed the good little boys of the town to come every Saturday afternoon to play. The little white cottage in Johnson Place that looks so like a Greek temple in embryo was then the bath-house and the residence of Prof. Briggs in Park Place was also standing. Near the lake was quite a flourishing deer park, the wonder of many an old citizen's boyhood. Besides deer there were rabbits innumerable, and their mounds formed a conspicuous feature of the landscape. On the corner of Tracy Street and Delaware Avenue was a fine orchard, where Dr. Johnson had a great variety of choice fruit trees.

> Directly in front of the cottage was a wide gate with a giant willow on either side. These veterans remained till uprooted by the hurricane that did so much damage to Buffalo in the summer of 1866. Broad gravel paths led up to the porch, and outlined in their graceful curves a great heart-shaped green, with its apex at the gate. In front of the piazza is still a semi-circular area, which was then occupied by the conservatory. It was stocked with plants especially rare at that day — the rubber plant, sensitive plant, great palms, and choice roses without number. The first magnolia trees ever brought to Buffalo stood on either side of the greenhouse. The lane or drive-way entered a high gate near where Mr. Sherman S. Jewett's house is now; passed a pretty little cottage where the Mayor's aged parents lived; left the quaint old flower garden on its right; took a curve so as to pass between the sites of Mr. Depew's and Mr. Marshall's houses; passed the rear of the cottage and made a second curve toward the barns. The stables were of wood, painted yellow, and stood about where the fountain in the park now is.

> Dr. Johnson employed no less than 25 servants about his house and grounds. He was frequently obliged to import "help" from New-York, and there is a tradition in the family of a laundress who came from Gotham whose valuable services could only be secured upon the promise that she should be furnished with a constant supply of light reading.

On the evening of Washington's Birthday, 1840, the cottage caught fire and only the outer walls survived. The interior was rebuilt on a less grand style, since the effects of the Panic of 1837 had swept away much of Johnson's wealth. Three years later, he sold out and went to Tellico Valley in Tennessee to try his luck at mining, taking along $83,000, all that remained of his fortune. There he died in 1849 at sixty-three.[4]

Johnson Park did not long remain vacant:

> Buffalo Seminary began in 1851 when a few gentlemen met at the house of Stephen G. Austin [on Niagara Square] to consider the need of an academy for girls. The trustees chosen at that meeting elected as its president Samuel F. Pratt, later succeeded by Horatio

4 *Express*, August 28, 1887.

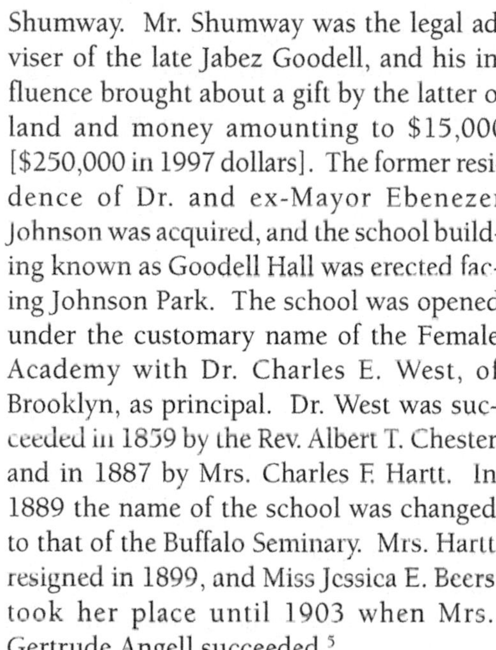
Shumway. Mr. Shumway was the legal adviser of the late Jabez Goodell, and his influence brought about a gift by the latter of land and money amounting to $15,000 [$250,000 in 1997 dollars]. The former residence of Dr. and ex-Mayor Ebenezer Johnson was acquired, and the school building known as Goodell Hall was erected facing Johnson Park. The school was opened under the customary name of the Female Academy with Dr. Charles E. West, of Brooklyn, as principal. Dr. West was succeeded in 1859 by the Rev. Albert T. Chester and in 1887 by Mrs. Charles F. Hartt. In 1889 the name of the school was changed to that of the Buffalo Seminary. Mrs. Hartt resigned in 1899, and Miss Jessica E. Beers took her place until 1903 when Mrs. Gertrude Angell succeeded.[5]

Above Left 5.7 ❦ Johnson Park, site of the Buffalo Female Academy, Emslie & Kirk, *Subdivision Map of Buffalo*, 1850.
Above Right 5.8 ❦ Goodell Hall, #284 Delaware, Dunn, *op. cit.*, p. 143.
Middle 5.9 ❦ Johnson Cottage in winter, *PBHS*, 22 (1918), np.
Below 5.10 ❦ Johnson Cottage in winter, *PBHS*, 16 (1912), 412.

Albert T. Chester had been born in 1812 in Norwich, Connecticut and graduated from Union College, Schenectady, in 1834. He became a minister in parishes in Ballston Spa and Saratoga Springs. In 1849 he became pastor at North Presbyterian in Buffalo, on Main Street between Huron and Chippewa.

Figure 5.7 shows the diminished dimensions of Johnson Park by the time of the Female Academy. Figure 5.8 depicts Goodell Hall facing the park with houses on Johnson Place to the south; figure 5.9 shows the cottage in winter with the top of Goodell Hall in the rear; figure 5.10 is the same cottage in summer.

5 Hill, *op. cit.*, 2:534.

> In 1870 it was a complete school from elementary grades through college and it accepted boarding pupils as well as those from the city. The principal, the Rev. Albert T. Chester, who gave up the pastorate of the North Presbyterian Church to serve, received some boarders in his home and others were cared for in neighboring houses. He remained in charge for thirty years. There was every need for devotion and diligence since so large a span of work was attempted, and it may be doubted whether in this case, as in others, the grasp was equal to the reach, which was most ambitious for a small faculty. The original catalog's list of subjects and texts included on the secondary and collegiate level many standard scholarly works of the period, which even for the students to have read would constitute something of a triumph. With the close of his principalship in 1887, the collegiate work was ended, and ten years later the elementary grades were transferred to the Elmwood School, which for two years was united with the seminary… In 1909 the present building in Bidwell Parkway [itself an extension of Delaware Avenue] was occupied, which was expanded in 1930.[6]

Residing at #284 in 1870 were Chester, his wife, and four children, aged twelve to twenty-eight. A second household was that of the janitor and his Irish-born wife and three children. Ten years later, Chester and wife were still there with two daughters who taught at the school and four domestics. Mrs. Hartt lived there in the 1890s, but by 1905, four years before the move to Bidwell Parkway, the cottage was housing thirteen roomers serviced by five domestics.

Welch's recollections of Buffalo in the 1830s continue:

> Nothing to the north of this cottage until you came to the large old mansion, built in 1835, and in which lived Sixtus Shearer. This was the end of Delaware Street, beyond which was a straggling country road but very little used. On the road near the Ferry Road (now Ferry Street) lived a well-known Buffalonian, Henry P. Russell. The Shearer house stands on the corner of Allen street; in the thirties Mr. Shearer was an enterprising hardware merchant, did business on Main Street, below the bridge at No. 84 (old number). He moved from here to St. Louis and after he was sixty studied law, was admitted to and practiced at the bar. Since Mr. Shearer lived there it has undergone many changes and owners; it was at one time the Catholic Seminary of the "Sacred Heart." The daughter of President Fillmore was a student at this school. The place has been owned at different times by Joseph Christopher, Hiram Niles, S. N. Derrick, Stephen D. Caldwell, and more recently by George B. Gates, where his widow and their daughter now reside.[7]

The 1860s, 1870s, and 1880s were the golden age of lower Delaware above the Square. Thereafter the former private homes became rooming houses, or were commercialized, and often demolished. The 1920s were a bad time for lower Delaware:

> The Delaware Avenue Association [boosters of commercialization] succeeded in 1924 in having the city widen the avenue from Niagara Square almost up to North Street. The widening of the roadway from forty feet to sixty feet was accompanied by the laying of new sewer lines, the placement of traffic signals, and the installation at one-hundred-foot intervals of 1500-candle-power electric light standards. The modernization of the avenue, however, occasioned the destruction of most of the splendid elm trees that had lined the

6 W. Dunn, op. cit., pp. 352-353.
7 Welch, *loc. cit.*

Left 5.11 ❦ Numbers 116 and 118 Delaware Avenue, *PBHS*, 29 (1927), 347.
Above 5.12 ❦ *Courier-Express*, July 9, 1927. Pomander: "A mixture of aromatic substances, usually made into a ball and carried in a small box or bag in the hands or pocket, or suspended by a chain from the neck or waist, esp. as a preventive against infection." It came to mean "something scented or having a sweet odor." J. A. Simpson and E. S. C. Weiner, eds. *The Oxford English Dictionary*, 2nd ed., (Oxford: Clarendon Press, 1989), 12: 81-82.

> thoroughfare, two rows on each side, since even before Olmsted's day. The effort by many citizens both on and off the avenue — including artist Charles Burchfield, who had come to town in 1923 to work in the Birge wallpaper factory — to stay the massacre of the trees was to no avail. "A platoon of the city's oldest residents went under the executioner's ax yesterday," wrote the *Buffalo Courier*. "They were in the way."

The Avenue was widened, and one row of trees on each side removed from the Square to Allen Street in 1924 and from Allen to North in 1931. Kowsky notes the long-run failure of the designs of the philistines: "But what the realtors and city fathers could not recognize at the time was that Delaware Avenue was only a stopping place for business on its migration to the suburbs."[8]

The south side of the double house, #110, across Delaware from the Fillmore mansion is shown in figure 4.11. In the 1880s it was the home of Oscar T. Flint, long the representative of the Aetna Insurance Company in Buffalo.[9] In figure 4.31 the alley which began south of #110 and ran to Mohawk is called Flint Alley. Flint died in 1899 and was followed by his son Charles, but by 1900 #110 had become a boarding house.

An official of the Buffalo Creek Railroad, Charles S. Cutler, resided at #112 during the 1880s. He was succeeded there during the 1890s by Carl T. Chester, who had been born in Norwich, Connecticut, attended the Norwich Free Academy, graduated from Yale in 1875 and Columbia Law School in 1877. He practiced law and joined the Buffalo, Saturn, and University Clubs.

Number 118, a two and a half story brown brick house on Mohawk and Delaware, and #116 to the south, are shown in figure 5.11. Robert H. Best, a long-time resident who had been born in Melrose, Pennsylvania, in 1808 and had built #118 in the early 1850s. His father William moved his family to Black Rock in 1810. They fled the during the War of 1812 but returned afterwards. Robert began as

8 Kowsky, "Delaware Avenue," in *Grand American Avenue*, p. 59.
9 *Express*, June 7, 1899.

Left 5.13 ❦ Numbers 169-137 Delaware, *PBHS*, 30(1930), following page 289.
Right 5.14 ❦ Numbers 157-145 Delaware, BHS.

a constable, served as police chief, 1858-1861, and sheriff, 1862-1864. Thereafter he was a detective for American Express until his death in 1891, when it was noted that "he traveled over all parts of the United States on important, sometimes dangerous missions, and was concerned in some of the most famous cases in the annals of crime."[10]

Number 116 was a large brick house owned by Theodore H. Butler, stationer and bookseller. Kate Burr, a descendant of Aaron, wrote a column on Buffalo's elite in the *Courier Express*, "The Duchess Strolls Pomander Walk," which often described breathlessly her vision of an earlier Delaware Avenue. It was usually headed by illustrations, of which figure 5.12 is an example, showing a flapper walking her Borzoi presumably through Central Park. Her job on the Butlers is vintage Burr.

> Next door to the Best home was a substantial brick house that was once the home of a charming, refined family prominent in civic, social, and church circles. Theodore H. Butler built this residence [in 1858] and lived there many years [until his death in 1879.] He was associated with his brother Hunt Butler who owned the Butler bookstore, which enjoyed the patronage of the literary set of Buffalo's early residents. Theodore Butler was a man of high integrity and courtesy of manner. Mrs. Butler was a sweet and gracious lady, a gentlewoman of a type not in vogue nowadays. This was a day when the breeding, simplicity of manners, gentility and good family were the credentials demanded by society of that time.
>
> [Their daughter,] Sara Denison Butler was a tall, dignified brunette, with the most charming manners and the merriest kind of a laugh. She was a great favorite in social circles, although she never married. She continued to reside with her father and brother until the death of her father, after which she moved with her brother, Theodore H. Butler [II], to Chicago… She was honored and beloved to the end, and many Buffalonians still remember the Butler family, one of the prominent ones in the early history of the First Presbyterian Church.[11]

Numbers #110 to #118 had been demolished to make way for the Erlanger in 1926. Long before they had become rooming houses.

10 *Men of New York* (Buffalo: G.E. Matthews & Co., 1898), 2:46-46D.
11 *CE*, April 12, 1926; July 9, 1927. The above is a conflation of these two articles.

Figures 5.13 and 5.14 represent the same houses on the east side of Delaware from Mohawk to Huron, but from opposite vantage points; figure 5.13 looks from north to south and pictures #169, #163, #161, #157, #153-#151 (a double house) #145, and #137; figure 5.14 goes from south to north and catches only numbers #145, #151-153, #157, and part of #161. Figure 5.13 was taken in 1923 or later, since the Statler in the background was finished that year; figure 5.14 is earlier since the cars are older. These houses antedated the Civil War, with the exception of #153, which was built in the mid-1860s. Number 145 is probably the oldest since frame buildings were banned in 1833 south of Mohawk Street between the east side of Pearl and the west side of Washington Streets.[12] The following lists are from the federal censuses for 1860, 1870, 1880, 1900, and 1920. The census for 1890 burned years ago in Washington, hence the subsitution of the *City Directory* for 1891. The censuses of 1905 and 1915 were state counts. Lots in the south of the block had Mohawk Street numbers and are not indicated here.

1860

WEST MOHAWK STREET

47 [141] Peter H. Devinny 39 NJ carpenter
Clarissa Devinny 39 *ux.* NJ
Francis Devinny 15 NY
George H. Devinny 10 NY
Florence J. Devinny 1 NY
Cordelia Tuttle 18 NY

James Mings 28 *ux.* England hostler
Mary Mings 22 Ireland
John W Mings 7 NY
Sarah J. Mings 4 NY
Alice Mings 10 mos NY

49 [145] William Lovering Jr. Grosvenor & Brown insurance Franklin near Allen

53 [157] William H. H. Newman 34 NY rubber belting dealer
Jerusha Burrows Newman 34 NY *ux.*
Emily Newman 6 NY
John B. Newman 2 NY
Sarah Burrows

1870

WEST MOHAWK STREET

141 Henry Childs 51 Mass. oper. steam forge works
Elizabeth Childs 51 Mass. *ux.*
Catherine W. Childs 14 Ohio school
Elizabeth Childs 19 Ohio
Harry K. Childs 7 NY
William H. Stebbings 21 Mass. bank clerk
Sarah Tremmer 21 England
Martha Tremmer 16 England
Winfield Scott black Virginia

145 Thomas W. Cushing 31 Mass. cattle dealer
Helen E. Cushing 26 NY *ux.*
Mary L. Cushing 9 NY school
Francis Cushing 6 NY school
Alice M. Cushing 1 NY

153 Hiram Hotchkiss 49 Conn. jeweller

157 William H. H. Newman 44 NY dealer in metals
Jerusha Newman 44 NY *ux.*
Emily Newman 16 NY school
John B. Newman 12 NY school
Euphemia Hume 18 NY
Margaret Bateman 28 Ireland
Mamre Hotchkiss 46 Conn.
William Pease 20 Conn. clerk in store

12 *PBHS*, 16(1912), 347.

55 [161] John Newman 62 NY boiler manufacturer
James M. Newman NY MD
Ellen Newman 36 Conn.
Erastus Scoville 36 Conn. ship chandler
Esther A. Scoville 33 NY
Barbara Wuenst 20 Germany

57 [163] Mrs. John R. (Louisa) Williams
56 Mass. widow
Frank Williams 32 Conn. civil engineer
Olive Williams 32 Conn. *ux.*
John Williams 6 NY
Frank Williams 4 NY
Robert Williams 3 NY
Bernard Williams 26 Conn.
Amelia Williams 20 NY

WEST HURON STREET ❦ End of Block

1880

WEST MOHAWK STREET

141 Henry Childs 60 Mass. steam forge proprietor
Elizabeth H. Childs 50 Mass. *ux.*
Katherine W. Childs 24 Ohio daughter
Elizabeth H. Childs 22 Ohio daughter
Henry K. Childs 17 NY son school
Ellen Brown 26 NY
Fannie Finnegan 45 Ireland

145 Thomas W. Cushing 42 Mass. live stock dealer
Helen E. Cushing 36 NY *ux.*
Francis Cushing 16 NY son bank clerk
Mary L. Cushing 7 NY daughter
Alice M. Cushing 11 NY daughter
Maude H. Cushing 7 NY daughter
Eliza Stevens 28 England

153 Hiram Hotchkiss 59 Conn. jeweler
Mamre Hotchkiss 56 Conn. *ux.*
Mamre E. Dodge 7 NY granddaughter
Mary Brackhouse 27 NY

157 William H. H. Newman 54 NY iron merchant
Jerusha Newman 54 NY *ux.*
John B. Newman 22 NY son iron merchant

Harry Wallbridge 28 NY son-in-law iron merchant
Emily Wallbridge 26 NY daughter
Grace Wallbridge 1 month granddaughter
Mary J. Gilhooley 24 NY
Kittie Culligan 23 England
Mary A. Murdock 26 Cape Colony

161 Warren Bryant 69 NY bank president
Amelia Bryant 60 NY *ux.*
Warren W. Bryant 24 NY son bank teller
James Bryant 29 NY son
Annie Collins 25 NY
Bridet Garven 25 NY

161 Warren Bryant 57 NY bank president
Amelia Bryant 49 NY *ux.*
Warren W. Bryant 26 NY bank clerk
Joseph Bryant 19 NY bank clerk
Mary S. Bryant 14 NY school
Mary Royal 25 Ireland

163 Frank Williams 42 Conn. commission merchant
Olive Williams 41 Conn. *ux.*
John R. Williams 16 NY school
Frank A. Williams 14 NY school
Robert J. Williams 12 Pa. school
Arthur H. Williams 8 NY school
Hurburt Williams 3 NY
Elizabeth Williams 10 months NY
Mary A. Burch 18 NY
Mary Appenheimer 17 NY

WEST HURON STREET ❦ End of Block

1891

WEST MOHAWK STREET

141 Mrs. Henry Childs

153 Thomas Lothrop MD
Jacob Walter coachman

157 John B. Newman WHHN&Co. iron and tin 70 Main

161 Warren Bryant president
Buffalo Savings Bank
Joseph S. Bryant clerk
Buffalo Savings Bank

163 Frank Williams 53 Conn. coal dealer
Olive Williams 51 Conn. *ux.*
John R. Williams 26 NY son
Frank F. Williams 24 NY attorney
Robert H. Williams Pa. son coal dealer
Grace Williams 20 NY daughter
Arthur J. Williams 17 NY son school
Herbert V. Williams 17 NY school
Elizabeth Williams 10 NY daughter school
Katie Kraft 44 Ireland

169 Sarah Baker 65 NJ widow
Kathleen Baker 28 NY daughter
Mary O'Connor 23 Ireland

WEST HURON STREET ❦ End of Block

1900

WEST MOHAWK STREET

141 Joseph Fowler 53 NY MD
Cornelia Fowler 52 NY *ux.*
Estella Fowler 29 daughter
Christina Hetzler 56 Canada
Albert Barry 32 boarder MD
Tilly Mabel Nagle 19 Cnada

145 Thomas W. Cushing 62 Mass. slaughter house
Helen Cushing 56 NY *ux.*
Elizabeth Cushing 10 NY daughter
Helen Maud Cushing 37 NY daughter
Albert Berry 32 MD boarder
Christina Hetzler 56 Canada
Tilly Mabel Nagle 19 Canada

153 Thomas Lothrop 64 Mass. MD
Earl Lathrop 29 NY son MD
Arletta Lathrop 40 Mass. niece
Catherine Schwartz 25 NY
Emma Schwartz 24 NY

157 William H. H. Newman 74 NY retired
Jerusha Newman 74 *ux.* NY
Jane McKee 43 Ireland
Anna Walls 39 Canada

161 Warren W. Bryant 30 NY
Mary S. Bryant 33 NY sister
Florence Matthewson 20 NY
Sarah Beatie 40 NY

163 James Lannie Canada 65 retired farmer
Jessie Lannie 63 Scotland *ux.*
Anne Ferguson 32 Scotland

163 Robert H. Williams
John R. Williams Frank Williams & Co coal
Herbert W. Williams MD

169 George Meadway Bank of Buffalo

WEST HURON STREET ❦ End of Block

1905

WEST MOHAWK STREET

141 Joseph Fowler 58 NY MD
Cornelia Fowler 56 NY *ux.*
Estella Fowler 32 NY daughter
Tilly Mabel Nagle 26 Canada

145 Joseph C. Windsor 61 NY livestock broker
Ella C. Chaflin 64 sister
Nellie Mahoney 27

153 Earl Lothrop 34 MD
Ella Lothrop 33 *ux.*
Ella Lothrop 3 daughter
Emma Schwartz 29 NY
Mary Schurz 20

157 William H. H. Newman 79 NY capitalist
Jeanette Newman 70 *ux.*
Jane McKee 40 Ireland
Carrie Eberhardt 33 Germany

161 Warren W. Bryant 35 capitalist
Mary S. Bryant 38 sister
Mary Donovan 31 Ireland
Anna Seal 33 Germany

163 Jessie Lannie 65 Scotland housekeeper
Jessie Snow 44 daughter
Andrew Snow 40 son-in-law
Lillian Snow 20 daughter
9 lodgers

169 George Meadway 50 England assistant cashier Bank of Buffalo
Kathleen Meadway 45 NY *ux.*
Helen Willard 27 German

WEST HURON STREET ❦ End of Block

169 George Meadway 52 England banker
Kathleen Meadway 48 *ux.*
Helen Willard 42 Germany

WEST HURON STREET ❦ End of Block

1915

WEST MOHAWK STREET

141 rooming house
1 landlady 8 lodgers
Elizabeth Williams 63 Canada

153 Earl Lothrop 45 MD
Ella Lothrop 44 *ux.*
Ellen Lothrop 13 daughter school
Bridget McMullan 50 Ireland cook

157 Charles Harrison 54 England janitor
Eliza Harrison 47 England *ux.*
2 lodgers

163 Basel Hillman 28 England printer
Bertha Hillman 28 England *ux.*
6 lodgers

169 George Meadway 65 England cashier
Kathleen Meadway 60 *ux.*

WEST HURON STREET ❦ End of Block

1920

WEST MOHAWK STREET

141 Arthur Williams 56 Maine garage manager
16 boarders

145 Wilhelmina Rodems 37 NY housekeeper
3 lodgers

153 Anna Winters

163 Josephine Bonno 40 Pa housekeeper
3 lodgers

169 George Meadway 70 England banker
Kathleen Meadway 65 NY *ux.*

WEST HURON STREET ❦ End of Block

Sometimes they are contradicted by city directories and Bartlett, but the censuses have been let speak for themselves.

Rev. George W. Hosmer wrote in 1880:

> I remember when the face of Buffalo was rather rough, and parts of the city were too dirty for washing to do any good. Main Street was as broad as Mr. Ellicott laid it out, but its mud was said to have no bottom. I have seen teams sloughed on Mohawk Street near Delaware and one team I remember sunk so deep that it seemed to be going through until another team was brought to drag it out and rescue the sinkers.[13]

Bartlett's description of the area in its heyday reinvests the drab structures in 5.13 and 5.14 with their former lusture:

> The east side of Delaware from Mohawk to Huron comprised a series of comfortable and once handsome houses, homes of several of the early families of the city and the scene of much pleasant hospitality. The houses of mostly diversified design were mostly of vine-clad red brick with stone trimmings. A verandah with tiny lawns and shrubbery was in front of each, sometimes separated from the sidewalk by an iron fence and gate, and all

13 George W. Hosmer, "The Physiognomy of *Buffalo*," *PBHS*, 2(1880), 5.

> along a double row of trees, a few of them beautiful elms which later made Delaware Avenue famous all over the country.[14]

5.15 William H. H. Newman, *PBHS* 17(1913), p. 416.

Prominent among the 1860 residents of the block were John Newman and his son, William H. H. Newman(5.15), at #55 and #53. John came to Buffalo in 1833 from New York where he had been born *circa* 1798. A boilermaker, he built #55 in 1850 and later built #53 next door for his son. Also residing at #55 in 1860 were John Newman's daughter Esther and her husband, Erastus Scoville, a ship chandler and Newman's business partner. John died 1859. William became sole owner and continued to live on Delaware, collecting rare medieval books and manuscripts.

> His interest in the history of Buffalo and the relics and records of his home city led him to associate himself with the Historical Society soon after its organization. He became a life member in 1872 and was elected President of the society in 1879 and 1885.

He belonged to the Saturn Club for years, was a founder of Cherry Hill, and a member of the Ellicott Club. His wife was Jerusha Avery Burrows, sister of Judge Roswell Lester Burrows, a lawyer who came to Buffalo in 1847 where he practiced with Ebenezer Sprague. Burrows had been city clerk 1854-1855, member of the legislature 1866-1867, and county judge 1869-1870. A son of William and Jerusha, John Burrows Newman, born in 1858, attended Professor Brigg's school and at twenty went to work with his father who died at eighty-six in 1912. John took over his father's company until stricken by illness in 1929. He died at his home on #685 West Ferry Street in 1933.[15]

5.16 Dr. Thomas Lothrop, *Men of Buffalo* (Chicago: A. N. Marquis & Co., 1902), p. 379.

Succeeding John Newman I at #161 by 1870 was Warren Bryant who had been born in Woburn, Massachusetts, in 1811. He came to Buffalo in 1837 with a supply of toys and notions and set up shop on Main Street. Frugal and hardworking, he prospered and in 1846 was among the incorporators of the Buffalo Savings Bank, the first of its kind in the city, of which he later became president. In 1859 he bought the Niagara Street Railroad, a horsecar line from downtown to Black Rock, of which he was also president. President Buchanan made him Collector of Customs for Buffalo, a post he held for two years. He was a founder of the Unitarian Church and a charter member of the Young Men's Association. After his death in 1893, his son Warren, Jr., lived on at #161, listing himself as a "capitalist."[16]

14 Bartlett Papers, box 31, folder 4, p. 4.
15 *Ibid*; Hill, *op. cit.*, 3:69; *Express*, April 13, 1890; *PBHS*, 17(1913), 416; *CE*, April 4, 1935.
16 *Courier*, August 5, 1892.

Hiram Hotchkiss, a Connecticut-born jeweler was the first resident of #153 — which incredibly is still (2004) standing. He was followed by Doctor Thomas Lothrop(5.16) who had been born in Provincetown, Massachsetts, in 1836, a descendant of Rev. John Lothrop, an emigrant from England to Scituate in 1634. Thomas Lothrop obtained his M.D. from the University of Michigan in 1858 and came to Buffalo where he took over the practice of Dr. John Hill while the latter was in Europe. On Hill's return Lothrop spent eleven years in practice at Black Rock. He was professor at Niagara medical college, superintendent of Buffalo's public schools 1869-1872, president of the Erie County Medical Society in 1874, editor of the *Buffalo Medical Journal*, founder and chief physician of the Buffalo Women's Hospital, president of the Buffalo Academy of Medicine 1893-1894, and fellow of the American Association of Obstetrics and Gynecologists. Governor Benjamin Odell appointed him visitor to the Buffalo Hospital for the Insane. A member of Saint Paul's Episcopal Church, he died in 1902.[17]

Dr. Lathrop never married but adopted Earl Lathrop and Earl's sister Arletta and brought them up. Earl also became an obstetrician, married, and lived at #153 with his wife Ella and daughter Ellen.[18] They were still there in 1915. It was not until 1913 that the American Medical Association ruled that all medical schools wishing to remain in Class A must require one year of college as an entrance requirement.[19]

About the house at Delaware and Huron Bartlett wrote:

> As early as 1851 [it was] the home of Judge and Mrs. Albert L. Baker, parents of Julia Baker (later Mrs. F. W. Abbott) and Kathleen Baker (later Mrs. George Meadway) and home of Mr. and Mrs. George Meadway until sold in 1920 when they retired to apartments on Oakland Place.
>
> The house, of brick painted brown, was older than the others on the block of this design. High outside steps admitted to the main floor over a basement, dining room, and kitchen. The rooms were high and spacious and the outlook from the corner windows to the life of the avenue was delightful. On the Huron St. side were pleasant trees and beds of lilies of the valley and on the south side was a lawn and shrubs.
>
> A. L. Baker came to Buffalo from Washington County in 1835. He studied law with Stephen G. Austin, [was] admitted to the bar in 1838, returned to Washington County, [was] elected Judge of the Court of Common pleas, [and] a delegate to the [state constitutional] convention of 1846. In 1848 he returned to Buffalo where he practiced law until his death in 1873. [He] was an alderman and promoter of a plan to found Central High School.[20]

Judge Baker and family were residing at #63 (later #169) in 1850 but moved in the 1860s, though his wife returned to their former home after the judge died and was living there with her twenty-eight year old daughter Kathleen and a maid from Ireland in 1880. After her mother's death, Kathleen married George Meadway from London, England, who came to America in 1883, worked for the

17 Hill, *op. cit.*, 2:394; *M&FH*, 1:151-153. "An act of the legislature elevated the [Niagara] college to university status on Aug. 7, 1883. On the following Oct. 10 Niagara medical school opened in the city of Buffalo, followed by the establishment of a law school in the same city. Both schools have since become amalgamated into the University of Buffalo." Frank Mogavero, "Niagara University," *New Catholic Encyclopedia* (New York: McGraw-Hill Book Co., 15 Vols., 1967), 10:430.
18 Bartlett Papers, folder 4.
19 Hill, *op. cit.* 2:529.
20 Bartlett Papers, *ibid.*

Bank of Buffalo, and headed the marketing branch of Marine Midland. At their house "the old Browning Club met to discuss Browning's poetry." When the Meadways moved in 1920, the block was completely given over to rooming houses. George died in the Park Lane at eighty-five in 1933.[21]

5.17 ❦ Ray V. Pierce, Ray V. Pierce M. D., *The People's Common Sense Medical Adviser in Plain English; or, Medicine Simplified*, 95th edition (Buffalo: World's Dispensary Medical Association, 1918), frontispiece.

The west side of Delaware from Mohawk to Huron began with eight brick row houses — a rarity in Buffalo — called the Kissan Block after the builder and numbered #105 to #125 Mohawk. Built in the 1830s, they appeared to Bartlett a century later as very "old-fashioned...expensive, inconvenient, and unlighted." They had three stories and high basements. Their front doors were reached by high stone steps.[22]

North of these houses at #138 in 1870 was the home of a well known charlatan, Dr. Ray Vaughn Pierce.(5.17) Born in Stark, Herkimer County, in 1840, he graduated in February 1865 after a five-month course at the Eclectic Medical Institute at Cincinnati. He first practiced as a specialist in "private" and female diseases in Hydetown, Pennsylvania, on Oil Creek north of Titusville where the first successful oil well had been drilled in 1859. He soon relocated, acquiring in the process a phony medical degree from the Philadelphia University of Medicine and Surgery, which he used in his advertising. He began distributing a free pamphlet for the masses, *The Medical Gazette*. In 1866 he sold his first bottle of The Golden Medical Discovery and left Titusville for Buffalo.

By 1874 Pierce had moved his office to Main Street, opened The World's Dispensary, where his golden tonic was concocted, and dazzled the opposition by a campaign of nationwide ads in *Harper's Weekly*. In 1875 his golden book appeared, *The People's Common Sense Medical Adviser in Plain English: or Medicine Simplified*, which ran to 100 editions, selling over four million copies between 1875 and 1935. Luella S. Allen writes:

> Pierce had a keen sense of his audience, which dictated the revisions (and lack of them) in successive editions. He was a master strategist and, as he was to prove in his many court room battles, an expert at stealing his enemy's fire. He was also clever with his pen and quick to both use and abuse the power of the press. Many small newspapers at this time (1870-1890) were dependent on the revenue from patent medicine advertising. Pierce was an early and effective user of the advertising medium. He used his literary, persuasive, and medical talents in creating the *Adviser*: the medium through which he dosed his readers with tincture of basic science, decoctions of basic hygiene, drachims of sexual titillation, and liberal spoonfuls of quotes from the classics. He also used the *Adviser* to attack his detractors (the Buffalo Medical and Surgical Society) when it suited his purpose.

21 *CE*, October 30, 1933.
22 Bartlett Papers, folder 3.

Above 5.18 ❦ Pierce's Invalids Hotel Before, *PBHS* 16 (1912), p. 292.
Below 5.19 ❦ Same After, *ibid.*, p. 293.

In 1876 he built Pierce's Invalids' Hotel, *alias* Pierce's Palace, the first luxury hotel in Buffalo.(5.18) Of French Renaissance style, it was located where D'Youville is now. Its 250 rooms had fireplaces, fifteen foot ceilings, Brussels carpets, air shafts and windows, a billiard room, gymnasium, bowling alley, tiled murals, the city's first elevator and one of its first telephones. His colleagues may have scoffed at him but local businessmen loved him. He joined the Buffalo Club and was asked to run for the state senate in 1876. Though successful, he resigned to enter Congress to which he had been elected in 1878. Illness forced him to resign in September 1880. Next year his palace burned down.(5.19) Though this had hurt him financially, that he had recently taken out a large fire insurance policy gave rise to unproven charges of arson.

A smaller Invalids' Hotel was built near the Dispensary at #663 Main Street the year of the fire. By 1880 Pierce had moved up Delaware to #1040. There he dwelt with wife Mary Jane, two boys, Matthew and Clay, a daughter, Ida Bell, and two female domestics. Presiding over the stable out back was Charley Cassidy, his wife, two young boys, and a mother-in-law. Unlike domestics, coachmen tended to have their own families and separate residences. Pierce was an officer in the Association of Manufacturers and Dealers in Proprietary Articles of the United State, successfully lobbying against laws to force manufacturers to disclose the ingredients of their potions. Losing ventures in gold and coal mining darkened his later years. By the turn of the century, he was living with his son, Van Mott Pierce, next door to the Dispensary on Main Street. In 1904 *The Ladies Home Journal* attacked the *Golden Medical Discovery* as a fraud; and, though Pierce sued and technically won the case, the damage had been done. In 1905 he actually lost money. In 1906 the Federal Pure Food and Drug Act was passed, reforming patent medicine advertising; and shortly thereafter the American Medical Association took aim at patent medicines. Sensing that his style had become passé, Pierce retired and spent his last days on his nature preserve on Saint Vincent's Island off the coast of Florida where he died in 1914.[23]

The house Pierce left to move up the Avenue had been built in 1856. Dr. Augustus C. Hoxsie purchased it and built a new house of unusual design there in 1881. He had been born in Skaneateles in 1839. He studied medicine as a boy under local physicians and when he came to Buffalo at twenty-three in 1862 he chose Dr. A. A. Wright as his mentor. Two years later Hoxsie graduated from the Cleveland Homeopathic College. In 1868 he married Anna Poole, set up an office on Franklin Street, built up a large practice, and moved to the residence he had just built at #138 Delaware Avenue.[24]

Homeopathic medicine was based on the theory that the way to treat a disease is by drugs or other agents that produce the symptoms of the diseases in healthy persons. Its promoter was the eighteenth-century German physician Christian Friedrich Samuel Hahnemann, who had been repelled by the crude medical treatments of his time, which included bleedings and purges. The first great cholera epidemic that swept through Europe in 1831 and reached the United States gave impetus to homeopathy because it seemed an improvement. By 1900 there were thirty-two schools of homeopathy in the United States. With advances in medicine, its popularity declined, and even homeopaths abandoned it. At least it had done less harm to patients than the brutal methods it supplanted.[25]

Doctor Hoxsie died on May 24, 1885. Next day the lead editorial in the *Commercial Advertiser* was his obituary plus an unusual encomium:

> When all his resources had failed, and he [Dr. Hoxsie] had spent himself in vain, he seemed to feel crushed and humiliated. But while there was a spark of life remaining, he never gave up the fight and never spared himself. During the last ten years Doctor Hoxsie burned the candle at both ends faster than any other man we know of. There was no sacrifice of rest, strength, comfort, or pleasure he was not ready to make in response to any call from the four quarters of the city. In the early years of his practice he had a large percentage of poor people on the east side of the city. When his fame spread and he had the largest practice in Buffalo, he never refused to answer a call from his old patients in that quarter or to send relief of some sort, though from much of this practice he received no pecuniary return.[26]

Hoxsie's widow married Dr. Joseph Tottenham Cook, an associate of Hoxsie, and the couple lived at #138 Delaware until 1893 when they moved up the Avenue to a new house at #536. They were

23 *Biographical Directory of Congress*, p. 1647; Luella S. Allen, "Golden Discoverer," *Buffalo Physician*, 7(May 1983), pp. 9-11.

24 *CA*, May 25, 1885.

25 Miriam G. Hill, "Homeopathy," *Encyclopedia Americana* (Danbury, Connecticut: Grolier Inc., 1988), 14:325.

26 *CA*, *ibid.*

5.20 ❦ **Public School #10, *Buffalo City Directory*, *1897*.**

there in 1900 with three children and two domestics, and an Irish-born coachman and his wife and family over the stable. After the Cooks moved, #138 became a rooming house and was demolished in 1923 together with the Kissan Block to make way for the Statler Garage.[27]

These are Bartlett's thoughts on the next building north:

> Public School #10(5.20) north of the Hoxsie house was built in 1847. The present structure was built later. When it was first built Ephraim Cook was the principal. Later he became superintendent of schools. …I liked him with much affection and little fear. There was little strictness of discipline in the school and not much teaching in his system. But he did interest his classes in many matters of knowledge outside of as well as inside of textbooks and gave a supereducational influx to their minds. Cook was good at chemistry and bookkeeping. Miss Abbie Fillmore was the daughter of the president and a graduate of the Normal School. She taught French for one term. Most of the boys went to work on the docks, the girls married young.[28]

The lot from P.S. 10 to Huron Street was long vacant and used by traveling circuses. Finally in 1869 Ozias Nims built a house there. Nims and son Charles were forwarding merchants on Central Wharf. Their house, as befitted the home of three marriageable daughters, Clara, Frances, and Mary, "was the scene of pleasant hospitality." Clara married W. Eugene Richmond and by 1880 was living at #1008, a big house on the corner of Delaware and Utica, with five young children and six servants.[29]

Nims left Buffalo in 1878, and his house was purchased by John Blocher, whose father, of Pennsylvania Dutch ancestry, had migrated to Scipio, Cayuga County, New York, in 1823, where John was born in 1825. Next year the family moved to Erie County where the father died, leaving a widow and three children of whom John was the youngest. His only formal education was a winter term in a log school. After a year working for a neighboring farmer at $4 a month, he was apprenticed at twelve to a tailor and began tailoring on his own at eighteen. In 1845 he married Elizabeth Neff of Williamsville. In 1861 he answered the call to the colors and enlisted in the 74th Regiment, NYNG, but was discharged as a Second Lieutenant after a year because of a disability. He bought a farm in Clarence and spent a year in the lumber business. He then moved to Buffalo and opened a boot and shoe manufac-

27 Bartlett Papers, *ibid.*
28 *Ibid.*
29 *Ibid.*

Left 5.21 ❦ Church of Our Father and the Blocher house, Olga Lindberg, *Buffalo in the Gilded Age* (Buffalo, BHS, nd), p. 3.
Right 5.22 ❦ *PBHS*, 29(1927), following p. 349.

turing business on Wells Street, where he was soon employing 200 men. His only son, Nelson W. Blocher, died at thirty-seven after a long illness in 1884. The statuary his father provided for him in Forest Lawn cost $100,000 ($1,743,174 in 1997 dollars) plus $5,000 annually for maintenance. John Blocher died in 1911 on Delaware Avenue where he had been living with a niece, his wife having died in 1904. The chief beneficiary of his large estate was the Blocher Homes in Williamsville which he had established for the aged in 1905 under the aegis of the Methodist Church of which he was a devout communicant.[30]

Between Blocher's on the corner and P.S. 10 stood the Unitarian Church of Our Father. An offshoot of Congregationalism, the established church in colonial New England outside Rhode Island, Unitarianism appealed to the more educated and affluent offspring of New England Puritans,[31] showing its greatest vitality in the early nineteenth century. The First Unitarian Church of Buffalo was organized in 1831. The popular and learned George Hosmer became pastor in 1836 and remained for thirty years. A church was built on the northwest corner of Franklin and Eagle Streets, which served until 1880 when the Church of Our Father was erected on Delaware next to the Blocher place. Figure 5.21 depicts the southwest corner of Delaware and Huron in Blocher's time. In 1906, again under the name of the First Unitarian Church of Buffalo, the former Church of Our Father was moved to its present location on the northeast corner of Elmwood and Lafayette on land donated by John J. Albright.[32]

The old church became a cathedral of the Ancient and Accepted Scottish Rite of the Masonic Order. Masonry in Buffalo dates from 1867. Many lodges sprang up, but as Hill writes:

> The two higher bodies of Scottish Rite masonry were organized in 1892-1893, and in 1904 movement was begun to seek a new home for the order. The edifice of the Unitarian Church in the 100 block of Delaware Avenue was purchased and became the cathedral of

30 Bartlett Papers, *ibid; CA*, June 30, 1911, White, *op. cit.*, 2:14; Phisterer, *op. cit.*, 4:2833, 2835.

31 John M. Blum *et al., The National Experience: A History of the United States to 1877* (New York: Harcourt, Brace & World, Inc., 2nd ed., 1968), p. 252.

32 Hill, *op. cit.*, 2:617-618.

the consistory. The first meeting of Palmoni Lodge in the Delaware Avenue cathedral was on April 23, 1906. In 1912 the Blocher mansion adjoining the cathedral was acquired and adapted to the purposes of a Masonic home for Scottish Rite bodies.(5.22) It is more generally known as Consistory House, and has been the scene of many pleasurable social functions. The cathedral and consistory house were estimated to be worth $218,624.43 in 1915.[33]

These addresses for the block from Huron to Chippewa are from the federal censuses for 1860, 1870, 1880, and 1900. For 1891 the city directory is used, and for 1905 the state census.

1860

WEST HURON

68 [184] Walter Cary 41 NY MD
Julia Cary 31 NY *ux.*
Trumbull Cary 11 NY
Thomas Cary 10 NY
Charles Cary 8 NY
Jennie Cary 6 NY
George Cary 2 NY
Mary Murphy 22 NY
Christine Clori 37 Germany
Susan Togler 30 Canada West seamstress
Elizabeth O'Brien 18 Ireland nurse

70 [190] John D. Hill NY MD
Esther Hill 38 NY *ux.*
Ella S. Hill 4 NY
Frances Hill 4 NY
Thomas Hill 2 NY
Baby Hill 1 NY
Ellen Brennan 25 Ireland
Christine Hiefenger 19 Baden
Christopher Dedman 17 Baden stableboy

72 [194] Michael Clor 42 France boot & shoe dealer
Minewa Clor *ux.* 30 NY
Kate Clor 1 NY
Kate Levegler 20 NY
Jane Johnson 15 Ireland
Mary Johnson 10 Ireland

74 [198] Charles D. Delaney

CARY STREET End of Block

1870

WEST HURON

184 Walter Cary 50 NY land owner
Julia Cary 38 NY *ux.*
Trumbull Cary 20 NY school
Thomas Cary 19 NY school
Charles Cary 17 NY school
Jennie Cary 15 NY school
Walter Cary 13 NY school
Seward Cary 8 NY school
Maria Love 25 NY
Elizabeth Love 24 NY
Mary Meyers 22 NY
illeg. Meyers 22 NY
Ellen Meyers 20 NY
Elizabeth Wall 22 NY
Elizabeth Holbrook 30 Ireland

Alexander Seacrist 38 France coachman
Barbara Seacrist 38 *ux.*
Barbara Seacrist 12 NY school
Henry Seacrist 12 NY school
Augustus Seacrist 10 NY school
George Seacrist 9 NY school
Rose E. Seacrist 33 NY
Charles Seacrist 1 NY

190 John D. Hill 47 NY MD
Esther Hill 45 NY *ux.*
Essie Hill 5 NY
Hattie Clor 6 NY

194 Michael Clor 57 France leather merchant
Kate M. Clor 38 NY housekeeper
Bella Clor 11 NY school
Hettie Clor 11 NY school
Libby Clor 8 NY school
Jennie Clor 5 NY school
Stephen Clor 4 NY
Anna Neale 21 Maryland

CARY STREET End of Block

76 [202] James M. Ganson 42 NY banker
Nancy S. Ganson 34 NY *ux.*
Charles Ganson 9 NY
Mary Rennora 21 NY

78 [210] Julius Movius 47 Germany
railroad agent (LS&MS)
Mary Movius 38 NY *ux.*
Edward Movius 11 Michigan
Sarah E. Movius 9 NY
John Van Cleve 18 NY clerk
Susan Havell 24 Pennsylvania
Mary E. Howell 24 Missouri

80 [212] William Laverack 45 England
drugs wholesale grocer
Mary Laverack 40 NY *ux.*
Belinda Laverack 17 NY
William Laverack 16 NY
Alice Laverack 11 NY
George Laverack 14 NY

82 [214] Edward P. Beals 38 NY
Pratt & Co. hardware
Mary Beals 33 Tennessee
Kate Beals 11 NY
Pascal P. Beals 10 NY
Mary Beals 6 NY
Julia Beals 4 NY
Edward P. Beals 10 months NY
Sarah Morrisey 24 Ireland
Sarah Beals 25 NY
Margaret McGee 28 Ireland
Mary Kane 29 Ireland nurse

84 [220] Orrin P. Ramsdell 50 Conn.
OPR&C. wholesale shoes
Anna C. Ramsdell 50 NY
Albert Ramsdell 7 NY
Thomas Ramsdell 6 NY
Baby Ramsdell 2 months NY
Kate Shaw 24 Bavaria
Latitia Mentena 46 England
Catherine Roebling 18 NY

86 [222] John S. Buell 49 NY
commission merchant
Ellen Buell 41 NY
Franklin Buell 16 NY
Nelly Buell 14 NY
Alice Buell 12 NY
Carrie Buell 7 NY

88 [224] Elijah Ford 46 NY attorney
Louisa Ford 45 NY
James E. Ford 22 NY attorney
June L. Ford 19 NY
Flavia Ford 16 NY
Isaac N. Ford 12 NY
Fanny Klaus 17 Bavaria
Deborah White 62 NY
Caroline White 30 NY

210 Julius Movius 57 Hanover
retired railroad official
Sarah Movius 19 NY
Edward H. Movius 21 NY traveling in Europe
John Berry 40 England coachman
James Jackson 22 black Virginia waiter
Mrs. Howell 60 NY cook
Rose Hamilton 24 Ireland
Catherine Felber 28 Prussia

212 William Laverack 56 England grocer
Mary Laverack 49 NY *ux.*
Alice Laverack 21 NY
Sarah O'Reilly
Lizzie Schmidt 19 NY

214 Edward P. Beals 49 NY hardware merchant
Mary Beals 43 Pa *ux.*
Kate Beals 21 NY
Mary Beals 16 NY
Julia Beals 14 NY
Grace Beals 10 months
Eliza *illegible* 40 Ireland
Kate *illegible* 13 NY
Julia Brennan 18 Ireland

220 Orrin P. Ramsdell 59 Conn. shoe manufacturer
Anna Ramsdell 42 NY *ux.*
Albert M. Ramsdell 17 NY clerk in store
Thomas T. Ramsdell 15 NY school
Annabella Ramsdell 12 NY school
Annie Ramsdell 7 NY school
Clarissa Ramsdell 4 NY
Evelyn Ramsdell 2 NY
Ellen Sheridan 24 Ireland
Ellen McAvery 67 Ireland
Rose Wagner 17 NY
Mary A. O'Neill 38 Ireland

224 Elijah Ford 65 NY attorney
Flavia Ford 25 NY housekeeper
Isaac Ford 22 NY
Mrs. H. White boarder
Caroline White 35 NY boarder
Sarah McGuiness 25 Ireland
Bridget Maury 40 Ireland

WEST CHIPPEWA STREET ❦ End of Block

1915

WEST HURON STREET

184 Walter Cary 61 NY MD
Julia Cary 52 NY *ux.*
Thomas Cary 29 NY son attorney
Walter Cary 23 NY son student
George Cary 21 NY son student
Seward Cary 18 NY son school
Maria M. Love 40 NY
Margaret Corcoran 31 Ireland
Betsy Sloan 60 Ireland
Caesar DuBois 28 Belgium
Philomena Flynn 25 Ireland

Michael Secrist 35 Alsace coachman
Eugenie Secrist 32 Alsace *ux.*
Justin Secrist 13 Alsace son school
Michael Secrist 11 Alsace school
Eugenie Secrist 4 NY daughter school

190 John D. Hill 58 NY MD
Esther A. Hill 58 NY *ux.*
Essie Hill 15 daughter
Sophia Chittenden 22 Ireland
Kate Riley 22 Ireland

Joseph Supple 23 NY coachman
Mary Supple 21 NY *ux.*
James K. Supple 3 NY son

194 Peter Emslie 65 Scotland civil engineer
Gertrude Emslie NY 40 *ux.*
Imogene Emslie NY 27 daughter
Rosa Conrad 35 Germany
Susan Conlson 50 Germany

198 Charles A. DeLaney 68 Pennsylvania iron founder
Amanda A. DeLaney 56 Maine
Charles DeLaney 33 NY son foundry
Louise DeLaney 30 NY daughter-in-law
Florence L. DeLaney 5 NY granddaughter
Jerusha Jenkins 68 Mass. boarder
Fanny Dole 50 Ohio boarder
Kate Verel 40 Ireland
Emily Ronsselat 21 France
Jane Bourne 17 England

202 Samuel M. Brayton 41 MD
Francis A. Brayton 38 NY *ux.*
Jane Brayton 63 NY mother
Helen Higlslov 50 NY mother-in law
Jay J. Brayton 50 NY clergyman
Maggie Coburn 28 Scotland
Jennie Fleming 29 Scotland

CARY STREET ❦ End of Block

WEST CHIPPEWA STREET ❦ End of Block

1920

WEST HURON STREET

184 Julia Cary 75 NY
Walter Cary 48 NY
George Cary 41 NY architect
Maria Love 64 NY sister
Elizabeth Cary 62 NY sister
Mary C. Cody 32 Ireland
Katie Cody 26 Ireland
Katherine A. Fitzgerald 25
Mary J. Mills 37 cook

[119 West Huron] Frank Kaniery coachman

190 Robert Fulton 50 NY promoter
Linda Fulton 56 NY *ux.* artist

192 Elizabeth Forbes 36 NY housekeeper
Hattie Adams 69 Germany mother
14 roomers

194 Catherine Powers 36 NY housekeeper
Ella Powers 18 NY daughter milliner
Margaret Powers 16 NY daughter school
Joseph Powers 13 NY son school
16 roomers

198 Louise DeLaney 50 NY
Louise Delaney 30 daughter
6 roomers

CARY STREET ❦ End of Block

210 Charles Cary 27 NY MD
Evelyn Rumsey Cary 25 NY *ux.*
Johanna O'Leary 32 Ireland

212 William Lavarack 65 England
wholesale groceries
Mary Laverack 60 NY *ux.*
Nellie McCall NY 17
Maggie Mannan 36 Ireland
Elizabeth Welch 22 NY

214 Edward P. Beals 59 NY hardware
Mary L. Beals 53 NY *ux.*
Kate L. Beals 30 NY daughter
Pascal P. Beals 29 NY son clerk
Mary Beals 25 daughter
Julia Beals 24 NY daughter
Mary McCarthy 23 NY
Bridget Gleason 23 Ireland

220 Orrin P. Ramsdell 59 Conn.
boot & shoe manufacturer
Anna T. Ramsdell 51 NY *ux.*
Thomas T. Ramsdell 25 NY son boots & shoes
Anna K. Ramsdell 22 NY daughter
Clara C. Ramsdell 18 NY daughter
Evaline Ramsdell 12 NY daughter school
Jennie Miller 18 Canada
Katie Schaffer 27 Wurtemburg
Rosa Saegor 23 Wurtemburg

224 [114 W. Chippeawa] William J. Meadows
commission grain merchant

WEST CHIPPEWA STREET ❦ End of Block

210 Joseph Bork Bork & Voght real estate
& insurance
George Bork Jr. Grand Island Steamboat Co.

212 Henry C. Frost MD

214 Edward P. Beals Beals & Brown hardware
Pascal Beals electrical engineer

220 Mrs. Orrin P. Ramsdell
Anthony Trenck butler

224 [114 W. Chippewa] William J. Meadows
commission grain merchant

WEST CHIPPEWA STREET ❦ End of Block

1900

WEST HURON STREET

184 Julia Cary 70 NY widow
Thomas L. Cary 49 NY son attorney
George W. Cary 41 NY son architect
Walter Cary 43 NY son electrician
Maria Love 60 NY sister
Elizabeth Cary 55 NY sister
Jennie Williams 26 NY lodger
William Williams 3 NY lodger
Mary Cody 29 Ireland
Catherine Cody 23 Ireland
Ellen Walsh 32 NY
Delia O'Rourke 26 Ireland
Michael Seagrist 59 NY

190 William Henderson 34 NY MD
Isabel Henderson 34 NY *ux.*
Dorothy Henderson 10 NY daughter school
Duncan T. Henderson 5 NY son
Hannah Sullivan 23 Ireland
Nellie Goodman 41 Rhode Island
Isabel Gibson 50 NY

1905

WEST HURON STREET

184 Julia Cary 75 NY
Walter Cary 48 NY
George Cary 41 NY architect
Maria Love 64 NY sister
Elizabeth Cary 62 NY sister
Mary C. Cody 32 Ireland
Katie Cody 26 Ireland
Katherine A. Fitzgerald 25
Mary J. Mills 37 cook

[119 West Huron] Frank Kaniery coachman

190 Robert Fulton 50 NY promoter
Linda Fulton 56 NY *ux.* artist

194 Madelene Hood 27 NY housekeeper
16 boarders

198 Charles A. DeLaney 53 New York
Louise DeLaney 57 NY *ux.*
Louise DeLaney 25 NY daughter
Frances DeLaney 21 NY daughter
James Buno 74 Spain boarder music teacher
Kate Buno 45 Ohio
James F. Buno 26 NY real estate agent
Christine Buno 17 NY school

202 Samuel Brayton 59 NY
George T. Mosley 36 NY MD boarder
J. H. Radford 44 NY
Marian Smith 25 England

CARY STREET ❦ End of Block

210 Charles Williamson 31 NY clerk
Isabella Williamson 31 NY *ux.*
Olive Williamson 31 NY daughter school
Ethel Williamson 7 NY daughter school
Bridget McCruden 42 NY daughter-in-law

212 Henry C. Frost 40 New Hampshire MD
Mary A. Frost 52 NY *ux.*
Mary A. Frost 19 NY daughter
Loring L. Frost 17 NY son school
Herbert Frost 16 NY son school
William H. Frost 12 NY son school
Margaret Cooney 5 Ireland

214 Edward Beals 79 NY hardware
Mary L. Beals 45 NY sister
Julia L. Beals 43 NY sister
Grace Beals 70 NY sister
Margie Miller 33 Canada
Amy Beck 21 NY

220 Anna T. Ramsdell 72 NY
Clara Lawrence Allen 34 NY daughter
Constance Allen 8 NY granddaughter
Libby Balsa 66 Germany
Amelia Fairbanks 19 Canada

WEST CHIPPEWA STREET ❦ End of Block

192 Elizabeth Forbes 36 NY housekeeper
Hattie Adams 69 Germany mother
14 roomers

194 Catherine Powers 36 NY housekeeper
Ella Powers 18 NY daughter milliner
Margaret Powers 16 NY daughter school
Joseph Powers 13 NY son school
16 roomers

198 Louise DeLaney 50 NY
Louise Delaney 30 daughter
6 roomers

CARY STREET ❦ End of Block

210 William H. Granger 55 NY wholesale grocer
Anna Lathrop 38 NY guest
Anna Harris 19 NY guest
Catherine Misco 24 Ireland
Emily Fisher 36 NY

212 Jean Donaldson Forbes housekeeper
17 boarders

214 Katherine L. Beals 56 NY
Mary L. Beals 51 NY sister
Julia Beals 49 NY sister
Grace Beals 36 sister
5 roomers
Amy Beck 25 NY
Nellie Sweeney 38 NY

WEST CHIPPEWA STREET ❦ End of Block

1915

WEST HURON STREET

184 Julia L. Cary 87
Thomas Cary 64 son attorney
Walter Cary 59 son
Maria M. Love 75 sister
Elizabeth M. L. Cary 72 sister
Therese Bangnies 22 Belgium guest
Louise Bangnies 21 Belgium guest
Edmes Bangnies 18 Belgium guest
Kate Doohen 48 cook
Elizabeth Doohen 14 daughter school
Martha Oberringer 23 Germany
Mattie Murea 35
Ellen Nichert 23

192 Florence Ford 40 landlady
15 lodgers

194 Melissa Guy 67 landlady

202 George F. Mosley 54 MD
Joyce Remington 22
Anna Swift 46 cook

CARY STREET ❦ End of Block

210 Cora Gilman 42
Richter Gilman 20 son machinist

212 Katherine Roders 45
Howard Roders 18 son school
Ethel Roders 20 daughter
Edna Roders 16 daughter school
4 lodgers

214 Katherine Beals 40 landlady
Mary Beals 50 sister
Julia Beals 55 sister
Grace Beals 40 sister
Katherine Nolan 22 Ireland
Anna Hartt 35 Germany

220 Julia Blackman 40 landlady
Emma Blackman daughter
Blanche Baron

WEST CHIPPEWA STREET ❦ End of Block

1920

WEST HURON STREET

184 Thomas Cary 68 NY attorney
Walter Cary 62 NY brother
Elizabeth M. L. Cary 72 widow sister-in-law
Maria Love 80 NY sister-in-law
Susan Kelly 29 Ireland
Charlotte Talty 56 Germany widow
Hattie *illegible* 47 NY

192 Solomon Weinberg president
Weinberg Furniture
8 lodgers
1 maid

194 Edward W. Biant 50 NY carpenter
Lois Biant 48 NY *ux.*
Merritt Biant 17 NY son

CARY STREET ❦ End of Block

210 Joseph L. Eddy 53 Pennsylvania
Hettie Eddy 52 Pensylvania *ux.*
21 boarders

214 Mary Duggan 31 Canada widow housekeeper

220 Helene D. Clyde 42 NY arts & crafts teacher
Matthew M. Snow 24 NY lodger drawing teacher

222 William J. Winsor 38 Newfoundland electrician
Catherine Winsor 24 England *ux.*

WEST CHIPPEWA STREET ❦ End of Block

5.23 ❦ Cary mansion, #184 Delaware, BHS.

On the corner of Delaware and Huron at #184 stood the mansion of one of the most famous families of Buffalo in the nineteenth and early twentieth centuries.(5.23) "The house was irregular in plan, had projecting bays with wooden detailing, a mansard roof with pointed-arch dormer windows, and exterior window label moldings — all accented by a three-story octagonal entrance tower topped by an octagonal cupola with crenellated wooden parapet." Originally the adjacent land covered the entire block from Delaware to Chippewa. Stables stood behind the house at #119 West Huron. In 1870 the mansion was raised one story and the French roof was added.[34]

Number 184 (until 1867 #68) had been built for Dr. Walter Cary and his wife, Julia Love, in 1852-1853. Because of its castellated exterior it was called Cary Castle. Cary had been born in Batavia in 1818, son of Trumbull Cary, formerly an agent for the Holland Land Company. Trumbull, a native of Mansfield, Connecticut, came to Batavia in 1815 and married Margaret Brisbane. The land company had failed to show a profit, and by 1835 was disposing of its holdings. All its land in Chautauqua County, 365,000 acres, was sold for $919,175 to Trumbull Cary and two associates. Glyndon Van Deusen describes the sequel:

34 Historic American Buildings Survey, No. NY-5613, 15-Buf 1, Cary House, Office of Archeology and Historic Preservation, National Park Service, Department of the Interior, Washington D.C., 20240; *Times*, June, 3, 1930.

> The Holland Land Company had been lenient, if not generous with the settlers, and they were disturbed by this sale to native landlords. Grumblings changed to wrath and violence when it became apparent that the latter were determined to collect compound interest on old debts, and were raising the price of land to those asking renewal of contracts. Early in 1836, encouraged by rumors that the Holland Company had no title and that they could avoid all further payments, the settlers sacked the Mayville, Chautauqua County, land office. The new owners, distraught at this turn of affairs, began looking for an agent who had no connection with their rigorous policies and who might calm the settlers' wrath. They asked [William Henry] Seward to take the position.[35]

Seward, erstwhile state senator and future governor of New York, United States Senator, and Abraham Lincoln's Secretary of State, mediated the disputes between the farmers and the successors to the land company including Trumbull Cary and so laid the basis for the Cary family's wealth. This won Seward the life-long friendship of Trumbull Cary, whose only son Walter named his youngest son after his benefactor. Horton saw Trumbull as "the great landlord against whom in the old days the farmers of Chautauqua County had rioted like raging *sans culottes*."[36]

Walter Cary studied medicine at the University of Pennsylvania and traveled widely in Europe and Africa. Then he came to Buffalo and practiced medicine. Horton tells of Cary's impact on local medicine:

> Meanwhile younger physicians were bringing in new and more scientific ideas. It augured well for the future of medicine in Erie County when in 1847 Dr. Walter Cary, adorned with a medical degree from the University of Pennsylvania, began to practice in the county town. Dr. Cary might well have distinguished himself in his calling; but the happy augury of his advent in Buffalo was not followed by a realization of all the hopes that it had inspired. The son of a great landowner, Trumbull Cary of Batavia, he was a man of wealth, a man of the world, a man of taste, in short, a gentleman even according to the stiff standards of Europe. Marrying Julia, daughter of Thomas Cutting Love, [in 1848] he established a house that became the very court and center of fashionable life. Thus he reflected a certain worldly luster upon the medical profession; but otherwise he advanced it less than his talents and training had led his colleagues to expect. Yet he was sage and proficient and when he wished to apply himself to professional matters he acquitted himself with credit.[37]

Thomas Love, a soldier in the War of 1812, was taken prisoner at Fort Erie, and after the war returned to Batavia. Later he came to Buffalo where he became a judge in 1828, member of Congress in 1834, and surrogate of Erie County in 1841. He gave his daughter three houses on Franklin Street for a wedding present and Trumbull Cary

5.24 ❦ *PBHS* 16(1912), "Picture Book of Earlier Buffalo," p. 184.

35 Glyndon G. Van Deusen, *William Henry Seward* (New York: Oxford University Press, 1967), p. 38.
36 Horton, *op. cit.*, 2:286.
37 *Ibid.*, 1:111.

gave his son the Genesee House(5.24) on Main and West Genesee Streets on the same occasion. There were six boys, Trumbull (1849), Thomas (1851), Charles (1852), Walter (1857), George (1858), and Seward (1863), and a girl, Jennie (1856). The three oldest boys were born in one of the Franklin Street houses. When the Carys moved into #184 in 1853, Mrs. Cary's mother and her two younger sisters, Maria Maltby Love and Elizabeth Love, came along. Elizabeth married and lived briefly in Latin America, but returned to her sister's home and lived there until her death in 1924 at eighty-two.[38]

5.25 ❦ **Interior view of #184, BHS. The picture in the foreground over the bookcase with the coat of arms in the upper left hand corner is that of Trumbull Cary, Dr. Walter Cary's father and progenitor of the family in Western New York.**

Mabel Ganson, who was to marry an Indian, had known the Carys in her youth. She wrote in her memoirs in 1933:

> Old Mrs. Cary, who was the daughter of William Love and came from Batavia, was said to have been adopted into the Iroquois tribe when a girl and made a princess, whatever that means, because the Indians said she had their blood in her veins and was one of them. Surely she did look like an old Indian man — and she had their endurance and cheerfulness, and complete absence of made-up emotions. All her sons except Walter looked like Indians, dark-skinned and clear cut and having that certain constant glow of life in them.[39]

From figure 5.30 it will be seen that her judgment about the likeness was accurate at least in the case of George Cary.

Family, travel, and society were the father's chief interests, and, relieved of the need to earn a living, he indulged in them extensively. In 1870 he described himself as "land owner." That year his ménage counted eight Carys, two Loves, and five domestics in the big house, and a coachman, his wife, and five relatives quartered over the stables, for a total of twenty three persons. In 1852, as narrated by Burr, Dr. Cary embarked on a four-month tour of the American South, accompanied by his parents, his wife, her sister, Maria Love, Trumbull, aged three, three-month old Charles, and his nurse. The party entrained for Albany, put up at the Delevan House, then it was on to the New York Hotel on Broadway. After a week they moved on to Charleston, Jacksonville, and St. Augustine, Florida. Crossing the Gulf States by stage to New Orleans, they stayed at the St. Charles Hotel. Sailing up the Mississippi they came to Cinicnnati where they visited before returning to Buffalo.

38 *Biographical Directory of Congress*, p. 1393; Bartlett Papers, folder 8.
39 Luhan, *op. cit.*, p. 120.

Cary travel was just beginning:

> In 1861 Dr. and Mrs. Cary, Trumbull, Charles and Miss Maria Love sailed on January 5th for six months abroad. They landed at Queenstown after a stormy voyage. The ship (six thousand tons burthen) struck on a rock in the fog but the captain of the Inman line brought her to shore. Then began the wandering through Ireland and England, over to Paris, through the south of France into Italy, stopping in Rome and Naples. The Carys came back with a load of Southerners and as war feeling was high relations were somewhat strained.
>
> Meanwhile, this family of growing children included Tom, George, Walter, Jennie, and Seward. Dr. Cary sent the boys to school in Paris and took them again in 1866-7-8, when the Franco-Prussian War broke out and altered the plans. This took him to Brussels, where he took a house for a year, sending the boys to day school and placing Jennie Cary in the Convent of the Sacred Heart.
>
> Always resourceful and progressive with a long look ahead, Dr. Cary went to London where he had a coach practically rebuilt, and strengthened to stand severe strain. He bought the horses in Belgium, and the family — Dr. and Mrs. Cary, six sons, the daughter, and his wife's sisters, Misses Maria and Elizabeth Love — started away from Brussels to Naples.
>
> The old Roman roads were helpful to this journey. But the family gypsied, stopping where night overtook them, staying sometimes a week, sometimes a day as the occasion warranted. Dr. Cary usually handled the ribbons [reins], alternating with Trumbull, Charles and Tom, the three elder boys. They took along two saddle horses in addition to their coach and four. The route brought them to the Rhine, through Wiesbaden, Baden Baden, into Switzerland and through the Italian lakes, visiting Milan, Genoa, and Florence where they spent a month. They soon were rich in experiences: one of them that of seeing a devilfish caught in a net in the Mediterranean. They traversed the line of the hill cities to Rome where they stayed for six weeks.
>
> Back in the seventies stories were rife of Italy being infested with banditti and it was considered unsafe to travel in the mountains. But never a bandit did the family see. General Sherman and Fred Grant [General Grant's son] were in Naples upon the Cary arrival. Dr. Cary took them in charge and showed them Naples. There was a special discovery in the Pompeiian excavations during their sojourn in Italy. This delightful trip lasted over a year. While in Brussels the children renewed acquaintance with many of the masters they had studied under at Paris. In Naples they all studied Italian.
>
> Dr. and Mrs. Cary assembled many choice spirits around them...Men of affairs and beautiful women have dined around the hospitable board during three quarters of a century. William H. Seward...often brought foreign diplomats and housed them at No. 184 Delaware Avenue. At least three Presidents have dined in state in the high-ceilinged dining room.[40]

Other guests at #184 over the years included Fillmore and his law partners, Nathan K. Hall and Solomon G. Havens. President and Mrs. Charles W. Eliot of Harvard twice spent a week here. Other guests were President Lowell of Harvard, Mrs. Julia Ward Howe, William Dean Howells, Henry H.

40 Kate Burr, "This World Traveler took his Family Along," Local Biographies, series, 3, vol. i, pp. 108-116. Buffalo Public Library, Lafayette Square.

Richardson, the dean of American architects, Stanford White, the architect, and his father Richard Grant White, music critic and Shakespearean scholar, William Dean Howells, the novelist, Governor Reuben E. Fenton of New York, and Albert Brisbane, the Batavia-born social reformer, and his newspaperman son, Arthur. Bartlett recalls that "during the childhood of the Cary children, fortnightly musicals were given on Friday evenings where the children with their friends played the piano, sang songs, recited poems, followed by dancing, cooking and apples. 10:00 PM home."[41]

Mabel Ganson remembered the Cary house as a rare instance of the happy convergence of home, inhabitants, and furnishings:

> It was not inevitable for people to move, for some families have stood solidly in the houses in which I first knew them until today [1933], when I look back over forty and more years. The Carys' house way down on Delaware Avenue is one of these. Their house was a tall mass, tower-like and ending in a cupola. It stood near the street and was covered with ivy. Nearly all Buffalo houses were covered with ampelopsis, a rapidly growing, small-leaved vine, but there was ivy on the Cary house. Its rooms were dark and stately. From earliest days its appearance and its odours, its deeply lived-into atmosphere, have been the same. A small vestibule opening on a hall — not a large hall, but one with a lofty ceiling and a very shining dark floor. A large, high-ceilinged reception room with paintings in carved gold frames, many mirrors, and — what else? I do not remember the individual things in that house at all. I only know it attracted me from the first time I saw it, and I knew that it was distinguished and alive. The feeling there was of a gracious, well-bred, appreciative family life where everyone was unfolding his scroll as God had written it. The bitter irony and caustic, stinging, tonic with what went on in that house were good for me from the first day I ever entered there.
>
> I was hardened and shaped a good deal by that house and the people in it in later years, as I shall relate in other volumes. Sitting-room…dining room…comfortable furniture… a piano…many plants and shelves of books, open fires, and family portraits. All these things combined in the needed daily accompaniment and comprised the baggage those people carried with them on their way. In that house "things" were not superfluous in any way. They were not there to make anything. They were not so beautiful that you would notice them, nor so ugly that you would be hurt. They were just all together, making, in a simple organic manner, a live and comfortable interior.[42]

Mabel did not find this happy convergence in Buffalo's other fine old or grander new mansions, especially in her own. She was an extremely sensitive only child in a dysfunctional family headed by two totally unsuitable parents.

5.26 ❦ Genesee Hotel, *PBHS*, 24(1912), following p. 422.

41 Bartlett Papers, folder 3.
42 Luhan, *op. cit.*, p. 26.

For an interior view of Castle Cary see figure 5.25.

Dr. Walter Cary died in 1881 in Marseilles where he had gone with his wife to regain his health. Sensing the end was near, he had a family member promise that he would be cremated. This was done in Milan, and the family funded the Buffalo Crematory on West Delavan where a memorial window is dedicated to Dr. Cary.[43] Most of his offspring were cremated there.

His wife, *nee* Julia Love, was a force to be reckoned with:

> In the Buffalo Society of the Gilded Age [she] held a position equivalent to that of Mrs. Stuyvesant Fish in the Society of New York. From her castle-like house in Delaware Avenue she rode abroad in the town in an equipage that makes the handsomest automobiles look tinny. This equipage was a D'Orsay with the Cary arms emblazoned on the door and the Cary crest in relief around the top. When the coachman reined in the prancing pair to a stop, a liveried footman nimbly leaped down to open the door and draw the step for the great lady to descend. Sitting one day in her carriage to watch the young men play polo, Mrs. Cary observed that a mishap had caused the game to pause. Summoning a bystander to inquire the reason, she was told that one of the Cary boys had been hurt. "What!" exclaimed the lady, "are there not enough other Cary boys to get on with the game?" Thereupon she turned to one of her sons who happened not to have been playing on this occasion and bade him put on his injured brother's boots and take the field.[44]

Trumbull, Dr. Cary's oldest son had been born in Batavia but grew up at #184. He attended the universities of Heidelberg in Germany and Liege in Belgium, which boasted an advanced technical program. He also took special studies at Harvard. Back in Batavia, he married and moved into the family homestead on Main Street. At his death in 1913 he was president of the Bank of Geneseo; but, it was noted in his obituary:

> ...he was chiefly famous as a lover of horses, a breeder of and dealer in blooded riding horses, and as a founder of the Genesee Valley Hunt Club. He was acknowledged as one of the best four-in-hand drivers of green horses in the country and he had acted as a judge in horse shows at Madison Square Garden, New York, and in Boston, Massachusetts, and other cities. Many years ago he was given considerable publicity when he drove a fine four in hand across Europe. [45]

Thomas, the second son of Walter and Julia Cary, was a Harvard graduate and an attorney. Most of his practice, however, consisted in managing the family estate, especially the Genesee Hotel at Main and Genesee,(5.26) an earlier version of which grandfather Cary had given Walter's mother as a wedding present in 1848. Thomas was, like his brothers, an expert polo player. He never married and his lifelong interest was the Charity Organization Society for which he arranged its first fund-raising ball. In 1900 President McKinley appointed him to the Taft Commission to establish civil government in the Philippines after the Spanish-American War and the following oddly named Philippine Insurrection. He died at seventy in 1921.[46]

43 *Times*, August 9, 1929.
44 Horton, *op. cit.*, 1:289.
45 *BEN*, April 9, 1913.

Dr. Cary's third son Charles,(5.27) after public and private schools, attended Professor Briggs' classical school, on the estate of its sponsor, Bronson C. Rumsey. It was a select school, which prospered for a quarter of a century under Horace Briggs, a fine classicist, responsible for the secondary education of many of the leaders of the generation then rising.[47] Charles studied medicine at U.B., receiving his M.D. in 1875. After a year of medical study in France and eighteen months in Belgium, probably at Liege, he did more post-graduate work in New York at the College of Physicians and Surgeons and at Bellevue.

Above 5.27 ❦ Dr. Charles Cary, *Men of Buffalo*, p. 382.
Below 5.28 ❦ #210 Delaware, Rupert Warren, *The Buffalo Club — 1867-1992* (Buffalo: Buffalo Club, 1992), p. 14.

Unlike his father, Charles did something with his medical degree. In 1879, the year he returned to Buffalo, he was appointed attending physician at Buffalo General and joined the medical faculty at U.B. There he was Professor of Anatomy, Materia Medica, Therapeutics, and Clinical Medicine until 1911. Until retirement in 1921, he remained on the staff of Buffalo General. In 1879 he had married Evelyn Rumsey, daughter of Bronson C. Rumsey of #330 Delaware. A women's suffragist, artist, and patroness of the arts, she painted *The Spirit of Niagara*, official emblem of the Pan American Exposition in 1901, and the portrait of Charlotte Mulligan in the Twentieth Century Club, which Charlotte founded. Charles and Evelyn first resided at #210 Delaware, former home of Julius Movius, and 1867-1870 the first site of the Buffalo Club, a few doors north of Castle Cary.(5.28) By the 1890s they were at #340 Delaware next to where Evelyn had been born and raised.

Charles Cary was not only a first rate-physician but one of America's leading sportsmen. With brother Thomas and brothers-in-law Laurence D. and Bronson Rumsey, and John M. Scatcherd, he played against the first polo team in America at Newport, Rhode Island. Buffalo lost the first match and won the second, which took place at Driving Park on East Ferry Street. He also promoted golf in America and was an organizer of the Aeronautical Club of America, the second oldest aviation club

46 *Courier*, July 6, 7, 1921.
47 Horton, *op. cit.*, 1:257.

in the world. He died at Delaware Avenue in 1931 at seventy-nine. His wife predeceased him, having died there in 1924.[48]

The only daughter of Dr. Walter Cary was Jennie who in 1876 married Laurence D. Rumsey.(5.29) Laurence's younger sister Evelyn married Jennie's older brother Charles. Laurence attended Professor Briggs' school and graduated from Harvard in 1872. He entered the family's tanning business and worked there until 1893 when the firm was sold to United States Leather. He spent the rest of his life managing the estate of his father, Bronson Rumsey. He was president of the Buffalo Club in 1908.

5.29 ❦ Laurence Dana Rumsey, *ibid.*, p. 53.

The Laurence Rumseys lived at #1 Park Place, on the corner of that street and Delaware where his father had lived from 1850 to 1862. After Bronson died in 1902, Laurence moved again into his father's house, this time at #330 Delaware where he died in 1917. Laurence and Jennie had five children: Evelyn, who married Rev. Walter R. Lord, rector of St. John's Episcopal Church in Buffalo; Charles, the sculptor, who married Mary Harriman; Gertrude, who attended Buffalo Seminary and married Carlton M. Smith of Buffalo; Grace, who married Charles W. Goodyear, Jr; and Laurence D. Rumsey, Jr., Harvard 1908, who joined the Lafayette Escadrille when World War I began.[49] He died at his summer home in Lewiston in 1967.

Walter Cary, Jr., died in 1933, in his apartment at #172 Linwood:

> In excellent health, Mr. Cary only a week ago took several of his nieces and nephews to Chicago to view the World's Fair. While there he contracted a cold. Shortly after his return early this week he developed pneumonia. Son of the late Dr. and Mrs. Walter Cary, Mr. Cary was born in the famous Cary homestead at 184 Delaware Avenue February 26, 1857. For 74 years he lived there except for intervals of study in this country and abroad and a subsequent brief excursion into the field of journalism. When his aunt, Miss Maria Love, died two years ago, he moved to the Linwood avenue address.
>
> At an early age, Mr. Cary went to Europe to devote himself to literary studies, attending the University of Brussels in Belgium and the University of Bonn in Germany during a three-year sojourn. Returning to this country, he studied for a short time at Hamilton College before matriculating at Harvard University. At Cambridge he majored in English literature, winning the degree of A. B. in 1879. Returning the following year, he received his master's degree.

48 *Courier*, April 21, 1924; *CE*, December 9, 1931.
49 Merton M. Wilner, *Niagara Frontier: A Narrative and Documentary History*, [hereafter Wilner] (Chicago: S. J. Clarke Publishing Co., 1931), 3:599; Rupert Warren, *The Buffalo Club: 1867-1992* (Buffalo: The Buffalo Club, 1992), pp. 53-54.

> Upon leaving college, Mr. Cary devoted himself for a time to the journalistic field. After a brief stay in Denver, Colorado, he went to New York, where he was associated with Arthur Brisbane on the World. [A niece, the daughter of Walter's brother Seward, was Brisbane's wife.] After a short time he returned to Buffalo, from time to time contributing literary articles to the old Courier. Unlike other members of his famous family, Mr. Cary shunned a business career, choosing to devote himself to literary pursuits. To a close circle of friends he was a delightful host or guest, a charming conversationalist. Mr. Cary never married.
>
> Mr. Cary was a member of Alpha Delta Phi fraternity of Harvard University, the Harvard clubs of Buffalo and New York. He was a communicant of Trinity Episcopal Church.[50]

Walter had joined no clubs. Oddly enough, he had described himself to the census taker in 1900 as "electrician."

5.30 ❦ George Cary, *PBHS*, 30(1930), following p. 22.

After schooling at home and in Europe, George, the fifth of the Cary boys, graduated from Harvard, and received a Masters of Philosophy at Columbia in 1885.(5.30) He attended L'Ecole des Beaux Arts in Paris from 1886 to 1889. His interest explains the presence of H. H. Richardson and Stanford White as guests at #184, since Cary continued living there as a practicing architect until he married Allithea Birge, the last day of 1908, by which time he was fifty. Allithea was the daughter of George K. Birge, president of the Pierce Arrow Motor Car Company on Elmwood. Cary was the architect of the Ethnology Building and the New York State Building at the exposition, of Buffalo General, of U.B. medical school on High Street at the head of Washington, the New York State Hospital for Malignant Diseases, and of numerous homes throughout Buffalo. His memberships included Park, Saturn, Country, and Genesee Valley.[51] He died in 1945, at eighty-six.

The last Cary of his generation was Seward who graduated from Harvard in 1886, and married Emily, daughter of James N. Scatcherd, a wealthy lumberman. Seward and Emily had two daughters who survived childhood, the younger of whom, Phoebe, married Arthur Brisbane, yellow journalist and lieutenant of publisher William Randolph Hearst. On the deaths of James Scatcherd and his wife, their home at #615 Delaware became that of the Seward Carys, who remained there several years before moving to Hempstead, Long Island. Seward died at eighty-five in September 1948 at which time his residence was #277 Park Avenue, New York. His wife had died in 1934.[52]

50 *CE*, October 13, 1933.
51 Hill, *op. cit.*, 4:249-250.
52 CE, October 30, 1934; *BEN*, September 9, 1948.

His wife and children excepted, life for Seward meant horses, a family fixation he carried to the limit. He seems never to have held a job. When the census taker came to #615 Delaware in 1900, Seward identified himself as a capitalist, and when another came five years later, Seward, though only forty-three, described himself as retired. That year he, his wife, and four children were waited on by five domestics, three of them Irish girls, and a coachman, though one suspects that Seward, more often than not, was his own coachman.

Even before Seward's move to Hempstead in the heart of the Long Island's polo country, he was a horseman:

> Seward Cary started playing polo before the now famous Westchester International Cup was placed in competition in 1886. In fact he had been at the game for half a dozen years before the United States and England decided to test their skills. His early experience was in Buffalo where his elder brothers and the Rumseys and Hamlins organized the sport in that section. Back in 1884 the sport was organized at Harvard with Seward Cary and Raymond Belmont doing the missionary work and forming the backbone of a team that invaded and defeated what was then regarded as a stellar Meadow Brook four. Polo was the first love of Seward Cary, and he remained faithful to it throughout the years. But horses had been as much of the attraction as anything else. Consequently it is not surprising that he has spent much of his time in fox hunting, exhibiting hunters and saddle horses, and in driving. Furthermore it has always been his pleasure to break and train his own horses. Even today, when the risk of mounting green horses is much greater than it was in the past, the grand old veteran still takes great delight schooling his mounts.[53]

The unwary, reading that Seward ran a stagecoach line between Buffalo and Niagara Falls, might conclude that he had a job. Involved here actually was a late nineteenth century sport that aristocratic Americans had adopted, like so much else including polo, from the English gentry:

> The driving of coaches with four horses was a task in which a considerable amount of skill was required, and English literature is full of the difficulties and humors of "the road" in old days. A form of sport thus arose for enterprising members of the nobility and gentry; and after the introduction of railways [had] made the mail coach obsolete as a matter of necessity, the old sport of coaching for pleasure still survived though only to a limited extent. The Four-in-hand Club was started in England in 1856 and the Coaching Club in 1870, as the successors of the old Bensington Driving Club (1807-1852) and the Four-Horse Club (1808-1829); and in America the New York Coaching Club was founded in 1875. But coaching remains the sport of the wealthier classes.[54]

Under the heading "ROAD COACHING," Establishment of the new Boulevard Route Between Buffalo and Niagara Falls — Society Ties up Coaching," the *Express* for May 26, 1895, announced:

> The last Sunday in May, 1895, will go into history as the date of the informal opening of a route between Buffalo and Niagara Falls. The establishment of such a route is due to the coaching propensities of Mr. Seward Cary, one of the best whips in the country, and society in the two cities has already shown a readiness to add this old English past time to its other social pleasures.

53 *Brooklyn Eagle*, April 12, 1931.
54 "Coach," *Encyclopedia Britannica*, 11th ed. (Cambridge: University Press, 1910-1911), 6:574.

> This first round trip of the coach has been chartered by Mr. Henry Brunn of this city who has invited a party of 20 friends to dine with him at the Cataract House. As the coach will only accommodate 12 persons, the remainder will travel in Mr. Cary's break [*sic*]. [A brake was a vehicle built high in the air so that the passengers would be above the dirt cloud which followed it.] Teams will be changed six times, requiring for this occasion the use of 20 horses. Monday, May 27 a dozen newspaper men will be invited to ride over the route and Tuesday the initial trip of the two-months program will be made when Mr. George Bleistein [#438 Delaware] will entertain a party of Buffalo, New York, and English friends. Miss Martha Williams has engaged the coach for Wednesday, and the *Red Jacket* will belong to Mr. George E. Laverack [#519 Delaware] and his friends on Decoration Day. On Friday Mr. J. A. Butler will entertain a party of friends in a similar manner. Mr. Joseph L. Hunsicker has engaged the coach for Saturday and the Sunday party will be invited friends of Mr. Robert K. Root [#650 Delaware].
>
> The coach, which is pictured in today's *Express* with Mr. Seward Cary on the box [5.26] is the well-known Brewster coach *Vivid*, which took first prize at the [Chicago] World's Fair [in 1893], and ran between New York and Philadelphia in the spring of 1894. It has been rechristened *Red Jacket*, and will be conducted as a public road coach on the Buffalo and Niagara Falls route during pleasant weather.
>
> The route will be down Genesee Street to Niagara Square, up Delaware Avenue, along the edge of North Park, and over the Buffalo-Tonawanda boulevard to the Lumber City, eight miles away, where the first change of horses will be made. Owing to the unfavorable condition of the River Road between Gratwick and La Salle, which is now torn up for the construction of the new electric railway, the route for the present will be diverted by the way of Johnsburg and Bergholtz village, returning to the River Road at La Salle, where the second change of horses will be made. From La Salle the six-mile drive is especially delightful, part of it lying in the Niagara Falls Reservation close by the grandest rapids in the world. The route is 23 miles long, 12 of it over smooth brick and asphalt pavements. From the time occupied in making the trip on Monday, the time-table will be covered with three relays in two hours. It is proposed to leave Buffalo at 10 a. m., reaching Niagara Falls at 12 o'clock. The coach will remain at the Falls four hours and will be due in Buffalo again at 6 p. m.[55]

This was hardly a profit-making venture for Cary. It enabled him to drive four spirited horses at a fast clip to dine at a fine restaurant with members of his class. Dinner was not an essential part of coaching, however. In a nostalgic vein a writer for the *News* the year after World War II ended discussed Buffalo's love affair with horses "in coaching days:"

> Forty-five years ago this Summer, all Buffalo was discussing the latest innovation in family carriages with the same zest the exploits of Bob Feller and Ted Williams now receive. For Buffalo was crazy over horses both before and after the turn of the century. Every home of some size had its stable in the rear.
>
> Even today, the old guard in dozens of Western New York stables are making preparations for the fall horse shows, county fairs, and harness meets in the old tradition. They don't care much whether an outboard motor should be stored for the Winter in a horizontal or a vertical position or whether they'll be able to get a new car before next spring.
>
> And as they shine their gear in preparation for the big days ahead, their talk sometimes turns to the old days when Delaware, Linwood and Richmond Aves. were the show places

55 *Express*, June 16, 1895.

of the equine world. They remember stables maintained by Seymour H. Knox Sr.[#1045 Delaware], the Cary Family [#184 Delaware], Frank A. Babcock and hundreds of others in all stages of wealth and affluence. Perhaps some speak once in a while of Mambrino King, the "handsomest horse in the world,"

The King was owned by Cicero Jabez Hamlin [#1035 Delaware], grandfather of Chauncey J. Hamlin [#1014 Delaware], president of the Buffalo Museum of Science. On May 1, 1855, Mr. Hamlin founded the Village Farm in East Aurora. As the years progressed the farm became famed as the world's greatest trotting nursery, breeding more world's champions than any other single farm in either hemisphere.

Mambrino King was the farm's museum piece. In 1882 Cicero Hamlin bought the 10-year old for $17,000 — not a bad price for a horse even in these days. Two years later, the King had attracted no less than 16,000 visitors who went "all the way to East Aurora" just to see him.

Indicative of the Hamlin farm's importance in the equine world was the fact that in 1892 Cicero and his son the late Harry Hamlin [#1008 Delaware], signed Edward F. (Pop) Geers, to a ten-year contract at $10,000 a year as chief executive of the farm's racing department. Pop Geers, one of the greatest drivers in racing history, was killed Sept. 3, 1924, when a wheel of his sulky locked with another during a race at Wheeling.

All the racing didn't take place on formal tracks. One old resident recalls that on cold winter avenues "stern-faced men" invaded Delaware Ave. They drove fast horses hitched to light sleighs and staged races to decide tavern wagers. The races continued until the lamp-lighters appeared, hurrying from gas light to gas light with their long wands. As the shades were pulled down and the candles and gas mantels were lighted in the homes along the avenue in preparation for the evening meal, the racers disappeared only to come back the next day. [See Luhan, *op. cit.*, p. 13.]

The more staid citizens owned coaches of many kinds. They took vast pride in their turnouts. Form in appointments and gear was as important as form now is to a golf or a tennis star. In judging contestants at horse shows the shape of a buckle on a harness might be a factor.

Samuel Waiter Taylor, editor of the *Rider & Driver*, still the horseman's bible, in collaboration with President Burton Mansfield of the New York Tandem Club, formulated a code which is rigidly observed. The accepted code for buckles was square for Victorias, Broughams, George IV ladies' Phaetons, and other town vehicles. The horseshoe-shaped buckle was acceptable for road work.

Form extended to the drivers, whether groom or owner. Most of the grooms and coachmen were European-trained and were men of the world, having traveled as cavalrymen or family retainers over the highways of many countries before coming to Buffalo. Frank A. Babcock Jr., now a resident of New York, recalls how his father followed the accepted form while driving. "What a picture father made on the box seat of his coach," says Mr. Babcock. "Stalwart, bearded and immaculately groomed, he knew just what pressure to put on the lines he held so gracefully yet stoutly in his hands. His long-leashed whip, of trout-rod proportions, was carried at just the right angle, with the lath twisted until there was a loop at the end. Rarely was the whip used except for effect."[56]

Horses were everywhere in Victorian and Edwardian Buffalo:

56 *BEN*, August 10, 1946.
57 Horton, *op. cit.*, 1:297.

> Winter or summer, horses were a major interest of the people of that time as perforce they had to be. They served a practical purpose even for persons of the *beau monde*. The ladies of Franklin Street and Linwood Avenue, of the precincts of the Fargos and the Thompsons on the far West Side and of the Circle, the ladies of Delaware Avenue, and Summer, North and Bryant Streets seldom, if ever, used Stephen Van Rensselaer Watson's street railway. They went to and fro upon their various occasions in victorias or other carriages or, indeed, sometimes they dispensed with their coachmen and taking the reins into their own hands drove buggies. The clop of their horse's hooves on the asphalt was a distinctive sound of summer time along the streets of quality and fashion as the ladies made their calls or turned toward downtown to go shopping to William H. Glenny's for china and pottery, to Denton-Cottier's for music or to Flint & Kent's.[57]

Mabel Ganson situated Flint & Kent on Buffalo's social ladder:

> Farther down on Main Street there stood Flint & Kent's, a large refined drygoods store. We knew Ed Kent and his sisters. He built houses; he was an architect, the only one in those early days until George Cary studied abroad and began to practice there. But Ed Kent was the first one I remember, and he had a leaning towards beauty and lovely colours and Flint & Kent's store was like him. It had attractive things in it; all our ribbons and ginghams for summer dresses came from there, and when people bought some new furniture coverings or things for their houses they bought them upstairs in that store.
>
> Still farther down Main Street were other larger department stores — Jay & Adams [*sic*], and Adam's & Meldrum's — but these were not pleasant stores to go to. One met fewer people one knew there. These stores were full of people we didn't know and never would know, and the air was close and had a disagreeable common smell we always associated with common people.[58]

Horton continues on the horse and Buffalo society:

> Some ladies there were who like Mrs. Lucien Howe [#183 Delaware] had a more noble use for horses than as mere means of locomotion for shopping tours; though prior to 1889 not many of them could have qualified as horsewomen. As the *Express* in that year observed, a woman on horseback would have attracted as much attention as "an electric trolley would today." But, said the *Express*, the Buffalo Riding Club had changed all that. This club, incorporated in 1888, had its headquarters in Utica Street near Elmwood Avenue. Its sponsors included young Frederick Pratt [#690 Delaware], son of Pascal Paoli Pratt, Jewett M. Richmond [#844 Delaware], John J. Albright, Thomas Guilford Smith [#489 Delaware], John Satterfield [#1022 Delaware], William H. Gratwick [#414, #776], Delaware and Edmund Hayes. Of the women members Mrs. Jewett M. Richmond [#844 Delaware], according to the *Express,* was the most accomplished rider, but many others no doubt came close to equaling her and some would have considered that they excelled her.[59]

As feudal society was based upon the horse, so too was the social life of *fin de siecle* Buffalo. Hunts, horse races, horse shows, and polo matches were accompanied by extravagant parties, dinners, and dances which gave men and women the opportunity to dress up to their best. On the second floor of the Buffalo Club hangs the picture *Hunt Supper*.(5.31) Like portraits by John Singer Sargent, it

58 Luhan, *op. cit.*, pp. 15-16.
59 Horton, *op. cit.*, 1:298.

depicts the members of the *haute monde* as they liked to imagine themselves. Horton adds:

> Prominent among the Buffalonians who indulged this aristocratic taste [in horses] were Thomas Cary [#184 Delaware], the Charles Carys [#340 Delaware], the George Carys, the Seward Carys [#615 Delaware], the George P. Sawyers, the Ansley Wilcoxes [#641 Delaware], the John N. Scatcherds [#615 Delaware], and the Harry Hamlins [#1008 Delaware]. The Hamlins had a country seat, the North Place, in the Genesee [country], not far from the Homestead, the seat of William Austin Wadsworth [the Wadsworths were the leading family of Livingston County.] In the same general neighborhood stood the Hermitage, the country house of the Seward Carys. All these houses were full of guests during October and November, when the Genesee Valley Hunt met thrice a week. Besides the hunt was the Genesee Valley Horse Show held at Mount Morris in S. S. Howland's stud grounds at Belwood. Here the Buffalonians annually awarded the Buffalo Cup, one of the coveted trophies of the show.[60]

Above 5.31 ❦ *Buffalo Club*, p. 66.
Below 5.32 ❦ Maria Maltby Love as a young woman.

The last of the family at #184 was Dr. Walter's sister-in-law, Maria Love, who had been born on a farm in Clarence in 1840.(5.32) She attended P.S. 10 and Central High and completed her education at Farmington School for Girls in Connecticut. After her father, Thomas C. Love, died in 1853, thirteen-year old Maria and her younger sister Elizabeth moved into #184 Delaware from the former Love home at Mohawk and Franklin Streets. Maria starred in the productions of an amateur group of local thespians, sang in the choir at Central Presbyterian and Trinity, and crossed the Atlantic fourteen times. After Julia, her widowed sister, died in 1917, Julia's place in society and as mistress of #184 was taken by Maria. The primary beneficiary of Maria's time and money was the Red Cross and the Fitch Creche, a four-story home on Swan Street built in 1880 for the infants of mothers who worked during the day, possibly on Delaware Avenue.

Maria's major interest was also that of the Carys:

> Perhaps I feel differently about horses than most people. We always had horses. Before I stopped playing with dolls I could catch and saddle my own horse and ride anywhere. One day I remember, there was a great deal of work to be done on the farm — my father's

60 *Ibid.*, pp. 298-299.

farm in Clarence. My father came to where my sister and I were playing in the garden and asked if we would go to the pasture and bring up the horse. "Five men have tried to catch him," said he but they cannot get near to him." So we went down to the field and Bill came trotting toward us just as he always did, and we brought him up to the barn, just walking along between us, our arms reaching away up so we could reach to pat his nose. Horses have always meant so much to me; it seems sad that we can no longer enjoy having them.

Maria had kept her horse and carriage(5.23) and sleigh until 1929, but even she had to give them up:

But it is quite impossible. Never before in all my experience do I remember a winter when it was told me that the horse could not go out because of the icy pavement. They are sent to the blacksmith to be sharpshod and it only lasts 48 hours; and they are back again in the very real danger of slipping.

In other days there was heavy snow and the sleigh jingled along merrily, or perhaps there was mud, but at all events, there was a pavement that gave sure footing to the patient beasts. But with the oil from the automobiles on the road all the time and the melting snow, it is just a sheet of ice. The heavier traffic is dangerous too.[61]

Two years later she had accepted the change:

"No, it's not for speed that I am glad I made the change," she said. "It's because a car is so comfortable and convenient. I always had to worry about the coachman and the horses when they were out in the rain or snow, for fear they'd catch pneumonia. The automobile is almost like the inside of a house. No matter what the weather, those within are warm and protected."

She was less happy about other modern developments:

But Miss Love does not accept the other foibles of this era of jazz, as readily as she had the motorcar. She's afraid of airplanes. And then there's the new status of women, for example. There are many things wrong about that in her opinion: their smoking, their pursuit of careers, their restlessness.

"When I was a young woman it was considered disgusting for my sex to smoke," declares this delightful, loved, old person. "Nor did men smoke in the presence of ladies. If a gentleman was smoking indoors, he threw his cigar or cigarette away when he reached the carriage in which his lady was sitting."

Miss Love believes that the new regime in which so many women are working outside their homes means destruction of family life. And anything tending to disintegrate the home is bad for the community, she declares.[62]

With emancipation won, many former abolitionists and their descendants moved on to another reform, prohibition. Maria favored prohibition but not another reform, women suffrage:

Although most of her friends favored women suffrage, Miss Love was opposed to it. In 1914 when a large group of New York State women was working to obtain the representation of women at the constitutional convention in opposing it she said, "I am interested in all questions of human welfare, but I do not recognize the necessity for women's participa-

61 *BEN*, July 20, 1931.
62 *Times*, July 16, 1926.
63 *Courier*, January 20, 1931.

tion in reconstructing the provisions of the constitution, and firmly believe that the deterioration of the family, the home, the children, the working women, and of all men will follow the entrance of women into politics."

"It is a sad day for womanhood when votes are given to women, and because I respect my sex, and because I realize how vast her domain today, how heavy is her responsibility, how much is left undone by her. I call upon every man in this community to see that no further burden is laid on her, and that the men of the State of New York take charge of its politics.[63]

Above 5.33 ❦ Last days of #184, Historic Buildings Survey, *loc. cit.*
Middle 5.34 ❦ North of 184 to Cary St., BHS.
Below 5.35 ❦ *PBHS*, 25(1921), following p. 412.

Maria Love died in 1931. Her estate was valued at $120,000, much less than it would have been before the Crash of 1929. A trust fund was settled on nephew Walter who lived with her, but other relatives were mentioned along with three domestics. Cary Castle became a rooming house and later the *Normandy*, a steak house.(5.33) The Carys sold it to the federal government in 1964, and a General Services Administration Building was erected on Delaware between Huron and Cary Streets.[64]

There were four houses north of the Cary mansion below Cary Street(5.34) and from there to Chippewa five more.(5.35) All were solid brick structures, many with mansard roofs. Number 70 old style, #190 new, was Dr. John Davidson Hill's office with its own entrance to Delaware and #192 was his home. Hill had been born in Manchester, Ontario County, New York, in 1822, studied at Lima Seminary and Geneva Medical College, and graduated from the medical department of U.B. He interned at the county almshouse. His experience there with typhoid fever, brought to Buffalo by recent immigrants, enabled him to revolutionize treatment of the blind. In May 1850

64 Times, July 23, 1931; Historic Buildings Survey.

he married Esther Lapham of Macedon, Wayne County, New York, and soon after built the house in which the couple spent their entire married life. It was a tall, brick edifice, with two stories, a basement, and a mansard-roofed attic. Seven children were born here, six of whom died early. The sole survivor was Esther Lapham Hill who in the winter of 1887 at #192 married William Ballard Hoyt, of Humphrey Lockwood & Hoyt, an attorney who had been admitted to the bar in 1883. The Hoyts lived with the Hills for several years.

In 1852 cholera and smallpox struck Buffalo, and Hill was made City Health Physician. He treated over 1,000 victims of cholera and cured many. He then attended medical lectures in London and Paris and learned to use the ophthalmometer, an instrument invented in 1851 by the German scientist, Hermann von Helmholtz, which enabled an examiner, using a hand-held light, to see magnified images of structures at the back of the eye. Hill was for long the only physician in Buffalo who had one and understood its use. He performed the first successful cataract extraction in the city.

For twenty-five years Hill was a trustee of the Buffalo Ophthalmologic Society and its president for six. Governor Cornell appointed him a trustee of the State Institute for the Blind at Batavia, a post he held until appointed to the board of managers of the Buffalo State Asylum for the Insane, to which he was reappointed by Governor Cleveland. Hill was vice-president and director of the Third National Bank of Buffalo, a director of the M&T, and for over fifteen years a trustee of the Buffalo Savings Bank. From his youth he had been a devout Methodist Episcopalian and was a long-time president of the Young Men's Christian Association. In his library at #192 the meeting was held in 1870 at which the Delaware Avenue Methodist Episcopal Church, which opened in 1876, was organized. Hill was also a founder of the Buffalo Orphan Asylum and its president 1876-1878 and again 1879-1893. A popular physician with a large practice, he died at seventy in 1892 at #192, where his wife resided for five more years until her death.[65] In 1900 another doctor, William Henderson, with wife, two children, and three domestics were living there, but five years later an artist and her husband who described himself as a "promoter," were living at #190, and the much larger #192 was providing quarters for sixteen roomers. It was all demolished in 1925.

At #72 old style, #194 new, through the 1860s and 1870s lived Michael Clor, a French-born dealer in boots and shoes, his wife, and five children, with a single domestic from an old Maryland family, Anna Neale. Clor had been born in Alsace in 1813 and at sixteen came to Buffalo where he learned shoemaking. He opened his own shop on Main Street in 1843 where he worked until his death at sixty in 1873. He once represented the 10th Ward on the City Council and served on the Board of Health. He was a staunch Unionist and Republican and left behind a wife and five daughters.[66] He

65 Bartlett Papers, folder 9.
66 *CA*, January 17, 1873.

5.36 ❦ Charles D. DeLaney, *CA*, September 24, 1883.

was followed at #194 in the 1880s by Peter Emslie, a native of Aberdeen, Scotland, where he was born in 1814. A graduate of the engineering school there, he came to America at eighteen. Settling at Mount Morris, he was chief draughtsman on the Genesee Valley Canal. In 1849 he came to Buffalo and he became a partner of Henry Lovejoy who had surveyed the city for the Holland Land Company. Their firm laid out the eastside of Buffalo (where Emslie Street was named for him) and a large portion of Black Rock. In 1871 Emslie & Lovejoy was dissolved, and Emslie was successively civil engineer for the New York Central, the Erie, and the Lake Shore Railroads. He was city surveyor 1850-1861, and Governor Robinson appointed him to superintend construction of the Buffalo Insane Asylum. Emslie married (1) Imogene Dole in 1851 and (2) Mary Gertrude Bullen in 1855. He died at seventy-two at #194 in 1887.[67] His widow resided there into the 1890s but then #194 too became a boarding house.

Residing at #74 old style, #198 new, was Charles D. DeLaney, a pioneer in heavy industry in Buffalo.(5.36) Born in Westmorland County, Pennsylvania, in 1811, he was apprenticed at eighteen to an iron worker, left and went to Cincinnati and then to a machine shop in Pittsburgh where by twenty he had mastered his trade and demanded and secured journeyman's wages. He was sent to Black Rock to oversee the installation of marine engines into lake steamers. By 1833 he was responsible for the ironwork in a large dry dock at Niagara Falls, Ontario. He spent two years as manager of an iron foundry, saved his money, and returned to Buffalo where he purchased a machine shop for building marine engines. Fire destroyed his shop in 1841 but he bounced back next year and formed the Fulton Foundry, later Vulcan Ironworks, on Water Street. For the Attica & Buffalo Railroad, which went into operation in 1842, he constructed the first railroad cars in Buffalo and what is believed to be the first locomotive, the *Tecumseh*. Once again his business failed, but, nothing daunted, he built on Perry Street the Delaney Forge & Iron Works, boasting the first steam forge in Buffalo and the first successful steam hammer in the United States. Soon he had a backlog of orders. During the Civil War the DeLaney Works received contracts for six monitor turrets for the Union Navy's ironclads, the success of which gave his firm a national reputation. Some of the best smiths and hammersmen in the nation were trained at DeLaney which at its peak employed 150 workers.[68] He died at seventy-two in 1883.[69] His role at the forge and at #198 was taken over by his son, Charles A. DeLaney, who died in 1902 at fifty-five, having disposed of the family business four years before.[70] As late as 1905

67 *Ibid.*, May 9, 1887.
68 *Sunday Times*, May 7, 1882.
69 *CA*, September 24, 1883.
70 *Ibid.*, April 25, 1902.

there were still DeLaneys at #198. Charles A. Delaney's widow and daughter were both named Louisa and had been reduced to taking in half a dozen borders.

Number 76 old style, #202 new, on the southwest corner of Delaware and Cary was occupied in 1859 by James M. Ganson, Batavia-born banker, and his wife Nancy, Mabel's grandparents:

> Grandma Ganson, then, as a girl used to walk past the bank in Batavia on her way to school and James Ganson, a stern young man of thirty-five, saw her pass and said to himself that she was the girl he would marry. And he did. James Ganson was a severe, humourless man — with a square white beard when he came into my life. He was in his bank all day until the middle of the afternoon, the Marine Bank of Buffalo.[71]

Mabel also noted a pattern among homeowners on the Avenue:

> Now the houses of the people we knew - houses that stood on Delaware Avenue or on Linwood Avenue, on North Street or Ferry Street or Franklin Street, and of course so many others that I cannot name them all — these houses were all big, solid houses, each standing on its own lawn and having flowers about it in the summer. Buffalo always grew northwards and people beginning life down on lower Delaware Avenue or Franklin street where my grandparents first lived in Buffalo and where I was born in 1879, people living already in comfortable brick or stone houses, following some urge, from time to time would build new and larger houses farther uptown.[72]

James Ganson was a founder of the Marine Bank in 1850 and was cashier there for eight years before seeking to improve his lot in New York. He soon returned and became president of the Bank of Attica in the early 1860s. He retired in 1873. He died at sixty-six in his mansion at #396 Delaware in 1883[73] where his wife lived until her death in 1918 at ninety-two. Edward D. Reed, who followed James Ganson at #202 in 1870, was a lumber dealer with a yard on the Erie Basin.

5.37 ❦ **Samuel Nelson Brayton, Smith, *op. cit.*, 2, facing p. 6.**

During the 1880s and 1890s #202 was the home of Dr. Samuel Nelson Brayton, scion of seventeenth century emigrants to New England.(5.37) He was born on a farm in Queensbury, Warren County, New York, in 1839, received a classical education at high school in Lawrence, Massachusetts, and graduated from the College of Physicians and Surgeons at Columbia in 1861. While there, he also practiced medicine in a hospital on 65th Street. During the Civil War he served as a surgeon at the Boston Navy Yard, on the ironclad *Montauk* during the siege of Forts Moultrie and Sumter off Charleston Harbor, and on frigates on the Pacific for two years. Later he practiced homeopathic medicine at

71 Luhan, *op. cit.*, pp. 120-121.
72 *Ibid*, pp. 22-23.
73 *CA*, March 19, 1883.

Honeoye Falls, Monroe County, where he married Frances Hyslop in 1868. Coming to Buffalo, he was an incorporator of the Buffalo College of Physicians and Surgeons in 1879, a member of the faculty, and in 1881 dean of the college. He also edited *Physicians and Surgeon's Investigator*, a monthly.[74]

Succeeding Brayton at #202 by the late 1890s was another doctor, Buffalo-born George T. Mosley, who had attended P.S. 10, Central High, the homeopathic college attached to Columbia, as had Dr. Brayton, and Flower Hospital in New York. Thereafter, he studied medicine at Edinburgh, Heidelberg, and Munich. A vigorous outdoorsman, Mosley made frequent hunting trips to the Adirondacks and Canada. He belonged to the Saturn Club, and died in 1935.[75]

The house north across Cary at #78 old style, #210 new(5.35), was in 1860 occupied by Julius Movius, his wife, two children, an employee of Julius, and two domestics. Movius had been born in 1811 at Liebenau, Hanover, in Germany. As a young man he emigrated to America, landing at Baltimore, moving to Pennsylvania, and thence to Ypsilanti, Michigan, where he entered the hardware business. In 1841 he married Mary Leonard Virbard. They had two children, Edward Hallam and Sarah. Movius, Sr., formed a close association with Erastus Corning, a major hardware merchant of his day. Corning was president of the Utica & Schenectady Railroad and built his fortune on selling ironware to his own road. In 1853 he was the prime mover behind the Great Consolidation of lines across Central New York from Albany to Buffalo to form the New York Central. Ypsilanti was near Ann Arbor on what was to become the Michigan Central, a subsidiary of the Central, linking Buffalo with Chicago via Detroit.[76] Corning extended Movius a line of credit enabling him to secure employment with the Michigan Central at Detroit in 1849. In 1852 he became general agent of a steamship line running between Buffalo and Detroit in connection with the railroad. Thereafter, he became general agent of Canada's Great Western, the Detroit & Milwaukee, and finally, when he moved to Buffalo, the Michigan Central. Movius retired from the railroad in 1866, "having accumulated a handsome competency, the result mainly, of judicious investment in railway stock." He planned to take his family for a prolonged tour of Europe. Since his mansion would be vacant, he rented it for three years at $1,500 a month to the fathers of the Buffalo Club who were looking for a clubhouse.

Men's clubs, such as the Buffalo and the Saturn, are the descendents of the British clubs of the eighteenth and nineteenth centuries. English clubs appeared first in Elizabethan times and were literary in character. Later they became more social. In 1693 an Italian, Francis White, founded White's Chocolate House, which began as a restaurant, degenerated into the greatest gambling center in London, then, as the quirks of the eighteenth century and the Regency passed, became a club where members were chosen according to position and sociability. Their distinctive note became the payment of a fee to exclude undesirables. The British clubs of the eighteenth and nineteenth centu-

74 Smith, *op. cit.*, 2:6.
75 Local Biographies, *ibid.*, Series 3, 2:103-104.
76 E. Dunn, *op. cit.*, pp. 22-25.

ries were the crystallization of the elite that had conquered half the world, built the British Empire, and ruled it for over two hundred years. That elite was composed of the aristocracy and landed gentry, the sons of ministers, officers, industrialists, and civil servants. They were a homogeneous and able class of leaders. The heyday of these clubs came in the decades after the defeat of Napoleon, when the country had reached the pinnacle of world power. London then had more than two hundred clubs. Whole streets — Pall Mall, Regent Street, and St. James's — were lined with club buildings.[77]

Movius's decision to spend three years abroad proved disastrous. He and his wife returned broken in health and both soon died, she in February 1870, he in October 1871.[78] Their son Edward Hallam Movius, born in Ypsilanti in 1848, attended private schools in Buffalo, graduated from Phillips Exeter in New Hampshire in 1867, and from Heidelberg with a Ph.D. in 1869. He returned to study law at Hamilton College and spent several years working for the New York Central. In 1877 he married Mary Lovering Rumsey, daughter of Bronson Rumsey. The newlyweds moved into #334 Delaware in what was becoming a Rumsey family compound next to Bronson's mansion at #330. During the early 1880s Movius practiced law in partnership with Richard Crowley of Lockport, Federal Attorney for the Northern District of New York 1871-1879 and Congressman from Lockport 1879-1883. Later the firm became Allen, Movius & Wilcox. Its principal work was bringing the 1882-1884 New York West Shore & Buffalo Railroad into Buffalo. Movius examined the land titles and Ansley Wilcox tried the cases. Later Movius handled successfully the affairs of the bankrupt First National Bank of Buffalo. President Cleveland appointed him to a commission examining land claims in the Helena, Montana, District. He was a member of the University Clubs of New York and of Buffalo and of the Buffalo Club. When his law firm was dissolved, he moved to Cincinnati and entered the law department of the Baltimore & Ohio Southwestern Railroad. Later he moved to New York and entered the same department of the Central Railroad of New Jersey. He died in New York in December 1917. His widow long outlived him, alternating between sunny Pasadena, California, in winter and a mansion on Nottingham Terrace in Buffalo in summer. She died there in her nineties in September 1948.[79]

After the Buffalo Club moved to #240 in 1870, Dr. Charles Cary lived at #210 for a time, followed by Joseph Bork, a real estate and insurance broker; near the end of the century, by John Boardman, a doctor; and in 1905-1910 by William H. Granger, a wholesale grocer, director of the Columbia National Bank, and the Buffalo Club,[80] who lived at #210 with two female guests and two domestics. Thereafter decline set in.

Number 80 old style, #212 new, was the home of William Laverack, one of Buffalo's pioneer merchants. The family, Scottish in origin, had migrated to Yorkshire in England. Edward Laverack was

77 Paul Porzelt, *The Metropolitan Club of New York* (Milan, Italy: Rizzoli International Publications Inc.. 1982.), pp. 1-2.
78 *CA*, February 10, 1870; October 14, 16, 1871.
79 *Biographical Directory of Congress*, p. 851; *Express*, December 31, 1917; *BEN*, September 9, 1948.
80 *CA*, October 17, 1910.

5.38 ❦ Edward Preble Beals, *Memorial and Family History*, I, facing p. 43.

a ship owner and timber merchant in Hull who imported lumber from the Baltic. His son William, born in Hull in 1815, worked with his father until eighteen when he emigrated to America. He was employed by a woolen manufacturing firm in Pittsfield, Massachusetts, until 1833 when he came to Buffalo and clerked in the drug store of Robert Hollister at Main and Seneca. They formed a partnership, Hollister & Laverack, groceries and drugs. In 1840 Laverack married Mary Radcliffe, daughter of Jerry Radcliffe and his wife, the former Ariadne Webster, who was the sister of Robert Hollister's wife and of Mrs. Walter Joy. In the early years of the firm Laverack was wont to tour the Midwest annually soliciting orders. In 1854 the store was rebuilt, Hollister established his bank there, and the drug and grocery business was moved to Washington Street. Hollister retired in 1861. Laverack had no interests outside business and family until the Buffalo Club was organized in 1867 at #210 next to his own house, when he signed up, becoming a charter member. He was a life member of the Young Men's Association, the Fine Arts Academy, and the Society of Natural Sciences. He was an organizer of Trinity Church in 1836 of which he was a vestryman and in 1840 warden. He died in 1888 and the firm was dissolved. His house was taken over by Dr. Henry C. Frost who had married Laverack's daughter Mary.[81] The Frosts were still at #212 in 1900, but five years later seventeen boarders had moved in.

Number 82 old style, #214 new, was a three story brick house similar to the Laverack house. For many years it was the home of the Edward Preble Beals.(5.38) It had a verandah across the front, with a door-yard, and wrought iron fence between steps and sidewalk. Charles Ramsdell, brother of Orrin P. Ramsdell, had built it in the early 1850s but never lived there. In the spring of 1853 he sold it to a Pittsburgh banker who bought it for his daughter Mary Lorenz who had married Edward P. Beals. Beals had been born in Canandaigua in 1821, but at five moved with his parents to Buffalo where he was educated at a military school and at Canandaigua Academy:

> Edward P. Beals was for half a century associated with the firm of Pratt & Co., the famous old iron and hardware company on the Terrace. The firm was begun by Samuel F. Pratt, the elder brother of Pascal P. Pratt, and the later had joined it in 1842. Four years later (1846), Edward P. Beals entered the firm which then became Pratt & Co., a business title which continued for nearly forty years unchanged amid all the commercial vicissitudes of the times. Pratt & Co. dissolved in 1886, Pascal Pratt withdrawing to assume the presidency of the Manufacturers and Traders Bank. A new partnership was formed, suc-

81 *M&FH*, 1:191-193.

cessors to the celebrated firm of Pratt & Co., which for fifty years was the leading house in their line in Western New York as wholesale and retail dealers in iron, steel, and general hardware. The new firm was Beals & Brown — E. P. Beals and David E. Brown. The former was the partner of Pascal Paoli Pratt in the firm of Pratt & Co. for more than half a century. Brown was for many years principal manager of the old firm. They continued business at the old stand on the Terrace.[82]

Four children of Edward and Mary Beals survived infancy, Pascal Pratt Beals, Catherine Lorenz Beals, Julia Lorenz Beals, and Grace Romney Beals. Edward died in 1903.[83] In 1905 his four daughters still lived together at #214, but, though their needs were attended to by two domestics, they also had taken in five roomers. Pascal Pratt Beals followed his father as head of Beals & Company. He had attended Professor Briggs' school and graduated from Yale in 1872. He served in the NYNG 1879-1892, rising to Lieutenant Colonel. In 1893 he married Cornelia Shepard Angle of Grand Rapids, and they built a house on Nottingham. Pascal was a member of North Presbyterian, the Society of Natural Science, the Fine Arts, the Young Men's Association, and the Y.M.C.A. His clubs were City, Saturn, and Ellicott.

Above 5.39 ❦ Orrin P. Ramsdell, Smith, *op. cit.*, II, facing p. 264.
Below 5.40 ❦ Nos. 225-227 Delaware. *PBHS*, 26(1922) np. Note that the corner house actually opened on to Huron Street and that the Ramsdell house, like that of Dr. J. D. Hill's, had two entrances.

Orrin P. Ramsdell(5.39), born in Mansfield, Connecticut, came to Buffalo in 1837 where he opened a boot and shoe store on #168 Main Street. In 1851 he married Anna C. Titus of Brooklyn, by whom he had one son, Thomas Titus Ramsdell, and four daughters. Orrin built his house, #86 old style, #214 new, in 1860, incorporating into it an earlier house which in 1851 had been the home of Deacon Amos Callander, practically the only building in that part of the city at the time:

> Callander died in 1859 by which time the block had been built up and was a desirable space for residences. Callander was born in Vermont in 1807 or 1808. In Buffalo he was a bookkeeper and taught school at night. Tradition says he carried the town records in an oxcart out Seneca Street to the Red Jacket Mission during the burning of Buffalo. He was surrogate in 1813 and an elder of the First Presbyterian church when it was organized in 1811.[84]

82 Bartlett Papers, folder 5.
83 *M&FH*, 1:43.
84 Bartlett Papers, folder 5.

Ramsdell was one of the original stockholders of M&T Trust and in 1861 invested in the construction of a grain elevator on the Erie Basin. He died in 1889,[85] his widow in 1902, after which #214 stood vacant for years. Their son merged the business with another boot and shoe firm and moved up the Avenue.

The situation at Delaware and Chippewa in 1922 is depicted in figure 5.40 and explained in the same issue of the *PBHS:*

> One of our pictures shows the house at the southwest corner of Delaware and Chippewa [#88 old style, #224 new] which was built as far back as 1860 or thereabouts for Elijah Ford and was his home for many years. It was better known to the present generation as the William H. Meadows House. In its last days it was Service Club #1, War Camp Community Service of the Buffalo Commission affiliated with the Army and Navy Departments' commission on training camp activities. Thousands of soldiers, sailors, and other service men used its facilities. Our picture was taken after demolition had begun. It shows the former residence of Mr. O. P. Ramsdell adjoining and beyond the steel frame of the Ford Hotel. The site of the old residence is now covered by the six-story Jackson building.[86]

Richard T. Ford of Rochester began his twelve-story Ford Hotel in 1922 as a low cost alternative to the Statler. It was imploded in 2000 to furnish a parking lot for the Hampton Suites Hotel, which occupies the site of the ex-Jackson Building.

Elijah Ford was born in Columbia County, New York, in 1805. His grandfather had fought in the Revolution in the campaign that ended with Burgoyne's defeat at Saratoga in October 1777. One of nine children, Elijah worked on the family farm until he was nineteen, teaching school for two years during the winter. Resolved on a college education, he prepared by attending a local academy and entered sophomore year at Union College graduating in 1828. He then headed for Buffalo, read law in a local law office, married Louisa Merrick in 1833, and was admitted to the bar in 1834. He was alderman of the 4th Ward 1834-1835, ran unsuccessfully for mayor in 1848, sat in the Assembly in 1850, and ran unsuccessfully for lieutenant governor in 1848. From 1850 to 1857 he was attorney for the New York Central, working on legal matters connected with its direct line between Batavia and Buffalo.[87] He also administered the Samuel DeVeaux estate in the interests of DeVeaux College. Louisa died in 1866, and Elijah in 1879, at seventy-four.[88]

William H. Meadows had been born in Wilberstone near Kettering, England, in 1837. Brought to Kingston, Ontario, at three by his parents, he later moved on to Chicago, but after the great fire of 1871, settled in Buffalo where he joined Trinity Church, became a successful grain merchant, a director of the Merchants Exchange, and a power in the commercial life of the city. After his death in 1899, his wife Susan lived on at #226 but by 1905 it too had become a rooming house.[89] This is a nostalgic picture by the block just covered:

85 *Times*, July 16, 1889.
86 *PBHS*, 26(1922), 414.
87 E. Dunn, *op. cit.*, p. 9.
88 *CA*, March 10, 1879.
89 *Times*, March 2, 1899.

The west side of Delaware between Chippewa and Huron was a block of handsome homes shaded by beautiful old trees. During the 1870s, 1880s, and early 1890s the sidewalk past these homes was a favorite promenade. The period was one of verandah parties, and during summer afternoons the porches of the homes were crowded with girls sitting and doing fancy work and entertaining their many visiting friends. The many colors of the girls' gowns against the green vines and shrubs gave the impression of blazing flower beds, a pretty sight, one which passed away with the growth of the city.[90]

1860

WEST HURON STREET

71 George S. Hazard 50 Conn merchant 25 Central Wharf
Sarah M. Hazard 45 *ux.*
John R. Hazard 22 Ohio clerk
Archibald Hazard 15 Ohio
Bridget Anderson 35 Ireland
Johanna Powers 26 Ireland

73 John Pease 49 Conn commission merchant foot of Lloyd
Sarah Pease 49 NY *ux.*
John Pease 17 NY clerk
James L. Pease 13 NY
Thomas Dugan 31 NY freight agt
Sarah Brennan 40 Michigan
Polly Kimberly 79 Conn
Mary Kimberly 28 Ireland

WEST CHIPPEWA STREET ❦ End of Block

1870

WEST HURON STREET

183 George A. Beals treas Union Iron Wks
Herbert J. Beals MD

193 John Dorris

199 Frank W. Fiske 36 NY grain commission merchant
Charlotte M. Fiske 36 Conn *ux.*
Evelyn Fiske 6. NY school
Frank W. Fiske Jr. 4 NY school
Charlotte M Fiske 2 NY
Bridget O'Shea 25 Ireland
Mary Donovan 20 Ireland
Elizabeth Kileen 40 Ireland

207 Mrs. Seth Grosvenor 51 NY
Jane W. Grosvenor 21 NY
William S. Grosvenor 16 NY school
Lucretia S. Grosvenor 13 NY school
Anna O'Hearne 22 Ireland
Bridget Fitzpatrick 26 Ireland
Ellen McMahon 26 Ireland

211 George S. Hazard 59 Conn. grain commission merchant
Sarah M. Hazard 65 Conn. *ux.*
Archibald M. Hazard 25 Ohio bookkeeper

217 John Pease 59 Conn. grain merchant
Sarah E Pease 52 NY *ux.*
James L. Pease 22 NY clerk
Eugene Farrell 22 Ireland school
James Demarest 44 NY money & land broker boarder
Agnes Demarest 38 NY boarder
Catherine T. Gold 51 Conn. boarder
Charles A. Gold 19 NY clerk
Thomas Gold 17 NY clerk

WEST CHIPPEWA STREET ❦ End of Block

1880 (3)

WEST HURON STREET

1891

WEST HURON STREET

90 Bartlett Papers, folder 8.

183 George Beals
Herbert Beals MD

193 Levi Allen 78 NY retired
Kate Allen 46 *ux.*
Maria Kennedy 21 Canada

199 Frank W. Fiske 46 Mass grain merchant
Charlotte M. Fiske 46 Conn. *ux.*
Susan Fiske 23 NY daughter
Evelyn Fiske 16 NY daughter
Merrick Fiske 14 NY daughter school
Charlotte Fiske 11 NY daughter school
Manson L. Fiske 4 NY son
Mary McDonald 18 NY
Katie O'Rourke 23 NY

207 Mrs Seth Grosvenor 63 NY
Mary Caroline Grosvenor 84 mother
Abby W. Grosvenor 23 NY daughter
Sarah Minehan 24 NY
Mary Gervan 24 NY

211 George S. Hazard 70 Conn. retired
Sarah M. Hazard 35 Conn *ux.*
Archibald Hazard 35 Ohio son grain merchant
John R. Hazard 42 Ohio son bookkeeper
Sarah M. Hazard 17 NY granddaughter school
______ Hazard 15 NY granddaughter school
Jennie Holland 25 NY
Ellen Holland 12 NY

217 Sherman Petrie 66 grain inspector
Lucy A. Petri 46 NY *ux.*
Sherman Petrie 12 NY son school
11 boarders

221 Walter J. Sheppard 27 NY hardware manufacturer
Mary S. Sheppard 24 Ohio *ux.*
Jennie Whelan Canada

227 Emily Hall 69 NY

WEST CHIPPEWA STREET End of Block

183 Lucien Howe MD 87 West Huron

199 Frank W. Fiske 57 Mass cashier
Merchants Bank

207 Mrs Seth Grosvenor 74 NY
Abby W. Grosvenor 44 NY
Wilson S. Bissell 44 NY attorney

211 George S. Hazard 81 Conn. retired
Archibald M. Hazard 46 Ohio
Calvin Hazard planing mill

217 6 boarders

227 Jane Hall teacher School #1

WEST CHIPPEWA STREET End of Block

1900

WEST HURON STREET

183 Lucien Howe 51 Maine oculist
Elizabeth Howe 42 Virginia *ux.*
Katherine Flynn 18 Canada cook
Alice Strode 33 Canada waitress
Mary Flotron 31 Switzerland nurse
Edith Legg 25 Canada laundress
William Legg 25 England coachman

1905

WEST HURON STREET

183 Lucien Howe 56 Maine surgeon
Elizabeth M. Howe 45 Virginia *ux.*
Mary Norah Clancy 22 Ireland

187 Richard H. Satterlee 38 NY oculist
Clara Satterlee 41 NY *ux.*
Charles Cunningham 30 NY real estate broker boarder
Carrie Ostwein 23 Canada

189 Alice A. Halladay 43 NY
Frank F. Halladay 18 Michigan bookkeeper
Joanna Kearney 39 NY lodger

191 Arthur G Bennett MD 38 England
Alice Bennett 33 England *ux.*
Alice E Bennett 3 NY daughter
Arthur L. Bennett 1 NY son
Sarah Ross 60 Ireland mother-in-law

193 George Theobald 52 NY
Francis Theobald 50 NY *ux.*
Abigail Theobald 23 NY daughter
George Theobald 21 NY son
Walter Theobald 19 NY son musician
Lena Harder 17 NY servant
19 boarders

199 Frank W. Fiske 66 NY banker
Charlotte M. Fiske 65 Conn. *ux.*
Evelyn Fiske 34 NY daughter
Manson Fiske 24 NY son insurance
Rachael Orr 19 NY

207 Emma Hersey 23 Nebraska housekeeper
9 boarders

211 George Hazard 90 Conn. retired
Archibald Hazard 53 Ohio son
Sarah Hazard 34 NY granddaughter
Della Garvey 40 Ireland
Mary Kane 44 Pennsylvania

217 *The Delaware*
Priscilla Strong 49 Canada housekeeper
Arthur Strong 29 Pa. bookkeeper
Nellie Strong 27 NY daughter-in-law
Orrin Strong 1 NY grandson
Celia Howard 19 NY waitress
Ellen Bunker 32 Canada cook
Jennie Christie 40 Scotland Chambermaid
Julia Dailey 29 NY

WEST CHIPPEWA STREET ❦ End of Block

187 Richard H. Satterlee 43 NY oculist
Clara Satterlee 47 *ux.*
Charles A. Cunningham 36 lodger
Theresa Scharf 21

189 Alice F. Halladay 48 NY
Frank A. Halladay 23 son clerk

191 Henry C. Houghton 53 superintendent of mails
Mary B. Houghton 43 England *ux.*
Winifed D. Houghton 19 Canada daughter
4 lodgers

193 Elizabeth Lyman 22
Florence Lyman 20 sister
7 lodgers

199 Frank W. Fiske 70 NY
Charlotte Fiske 70 *ux.*
Manson Fiske 28 NY son insurance
Evelyn Fiske 38 NY daughter
Emma Dale 23
Anna Conrad 27

WEST CHIPPEWA STREET ❦ End of Block

1915

WEST HURON STREET

183 Emma Howland 40 landlady

187 Richard H. Satterlee 63 NY oculist
Clara Satterlee 67

1920

WEST HURON STREET

183 George Fox 35 NY carpenter
Emma Howland 45 NY housekeper
8 lodgers

187 Richard H. Satterlee 68 NY oculist
Clara Satterlee 72 NY *ux.*
Helen Drieling 18 NY

189	Stephen Jewett MD 30 Caroline Jewett 30 *ux.* Stephen Jewett 4 son George Cable lodger	189	Grace A. Hopkins 34 NY dressmaker housekeeper 7 lodgers
191	Charles A. Landy 60 insurance Sahara E. Landy 58 *ux.* Francis Landy 23 daughter actress Masie Landy 20 daughter school teacher	191	Rooming house 7 lodgers
193	Benjamin Monroe 78 Helen Monroe 72 *ux.* Arthur Monroe 22 son chauffeur Leola Monroe 28 daughter manicurist Grace Bedford 32 daughter Arthur Bedford son-in-law sales	193	James L. Sweeney 48 NY salesman Mary Sweeney 28 *ux.* 14 lodgers
		195	August Mosler 54 Germany fireman Emma Mosler 49 Switzerland 19 lodgers
		197	John Burns 60 NY Cary Burns 47 NY housekeeper 14 lodgers
199	Rooming house 1 landlady 3 lodgers	199	Sidney Smith 65 NY engineer DL&W RR Alice A. Smith 62 NY *ux.* 7 lodgers
207	Rose F. Sartwech 72 Germany Stephen Sartwech 38 Germany son Anna C. Sartwech 39 Germany daughter Helen D. Sartwech 9 granddaughter school Grace Sartwech 4 granddaughter	207	Anne Sartwell 43 Germany widow Nellie R. Sartwell 14 Canada daughter Grace Sartwell 8 Canada daughter 10 lodgers
211	Elks clubhouse	211	Elks clubhouse
217	Rooming house 1 landlady 5 lodgers	217	Ida E. Hallen 37 Canada widow housekeeper 23 lodgers
		227	Nellie Jones 47 NY restaurant
	WEST CHIPPEWA STREET ❦ End of Block		WEST CHIPPEWA STREET ❦ End of Block

This block, inner lot #129 in Ellicott's survey, had been set off to Jonathan Sidway in 1826. Several frame cottages were erected here at an early date. In 1841 Benjamin H. Austin of the law firm of Austin and Thompson, the father of Harriet Austin Townsend, foundress of the Women's Union on Niagara Square, resided on the northeast corner of Huron and Delaware, across from the Cary mansion. About 1861 the lot was purchased by George A. Beals, brother of Edward P. Beals, who lived across the street. (Their father, John W. Beals, was a partner in Wilkeson Beals & Co., proprietors of the Orazaba Iron Works.) Several cottages were joined together and partially rebuilt, and the structure was occupied by George Beals and family until 1875 when he built a double brick house on the

5.41 ❦ Lucien Howe, M. D. *Men of Buffalo*, p. 387.

corner at #183 and lived there until 1890. The cottage in the rear, #85 West Huron, was sold in 1875 to Dr. Bradley Goodyear, progenitor of one of Delaware Avenue's most prominent families. Beals sold the brick house to Dr. Lucien Howe(5.41) in 1890 and moved to East Aurora where he died in 1907.[91]

Howe had been born in Standish, Maine, in 1848, and raised in New Mexico where his father, an army officer, was stationed. Later Lucien was placed under the tutelage of a Unitarian minister at Topsham, Maine. He graduated from Bowdoin College in 1870 and, after studying medicine at Harvard and at Bellevue Hospital, went to the great medical centers of Europe for more study. At Edinburgh he met Lister who was then inaugurating the antiseptic era in surgery. Completing his studies with Helmholtz, Howe specialized in ophthalmology and in 1856 founded the Buffalo Eye and Ear Infirmary which he dominated for forty years. In 1879 he was made professor of ophthalmology at U.B. and in 1885 became ophthalmic surgeon at Buffalo General.

> In 1890, after ten years working to reduce widespread infant blindness, Howe was instrumental in securing the passage by the New York legislature of the Howe Bill, a first in America, requiring attendants at childbirth to apply prophylactic to the eyes of newborn children. Other states followed and soon the scourge of *ophthalmia neonatorum* was almost completely eliminated from America. In 1896 he was invited to explain his work to *the Societe Francaise d'Ophthalmologie* in Paris. On this occasion he became the first American to be made honorary president of the organization. His final medical achievement was the foundation in 1926 of a laboratory at Harvard for research on diseases of the eye. He contributed $250,000 [$4,357,000 in 1997 dollars] towards its endowment, while the General Education Board added enough to raise the total to $500,000.[92]

By 1891 Howe was living with his wife Elizabeth, one of the earliest graduates of Vassar, at #183 Delaware with an attached office around the corner at #87 Huron. His domicile in 1900 consisted in a Canadian-born cook, a "dining room girl," a laundress, a Swiss-born nurse, (perhaps the doctor's assistant), and an English-born coachman. Here the Howes "gave handsome entertainments to their friends and acquaintances."[93] In 1912 they moved into a mansion at #522 Delaware between Virginia and Allen Street designed by architects the Doctor imported from Europe.

Howe was famous locally long after his death in 1928:

> Through half a century in Buffalo, Dr. Howe was the horseman most frequently seen on this city's bridle paths and in the parks. Still remembered is the distinguished figure of

91 *Ibid; Express*, February 17, 1907.
92 J. Herbert Waite, "Howe, Lucien," *Dictionary of American Biography* [hereafter DAB], Dumas Malone, ed. (New York: Charles Scribner's Sons, 1932), 9:293.
93 Bartlett Papers, *ibid.*
94 *CE*, May, 25, 1952.
95 Bartlett Papers, folder 4.
96 *Ibid.*

this man, white haired and with white mustache, seated upon his coal black mount. When well past 70, Dr. Howe rode with head erect and with hand steady and sure.[94]

5.42 ❦ Reformed Protestant Dutch Church. *PBHS*, 16(1912), 456.

By the end of the century Dr. Richard Satterlee, also an oculist, had set up his home and office at #187 (with #189 it constituted a double house) north of Dr. Howe and remained there until the early 1920s. It is probable that this move was influenced by the presence next door of Dr. Howe.[95]

At #193 in 1880 lived one of Buffalo's earliest residents:

> #193 was the home of Captain Levi Allen who died there in 1893, *aet*. 91. He had come to Buffalo from Herkimer County in 1806. When he was eleven, Buffalo was burned by the British in December, 1813. Allen fled out Seneca Street with his mother. The greater part of his life was spent navigating the lakes. He was a member of the crew of *Walk-in-the Water*, which started on its first trip August 21, 1818. He worked for Reed's Passenger Line whose ships were the *Buffalo* and the *James Madison* of which he was the captain. In 1848 he represented the 3rd Ward on the Common Council. Allen was Collector of the Port under President [Zachary] Taylor. He was a founder of the First National Bank and first president of the Buffalo Steam Engine Company. He also built several of the older Delaware Avenue houses, including Dexter Rumsey's on the southwest corner of Delaware and Summer. In fact, he lived there till he sold it to Rumsey in 1860.[96]

Allen does not shine in Rayback's *Fillmore*. A split had developed in the Whig party between Seward and Thurlow Weed:

> In May 1849 Weed delivered the *coup de grace*. He invaded western New York and Buffalo itself. In Fillmore's political fortress, Weed found a partially illiterate political hack, Levi Allen, whom [William H.] Meredith [Taylor's Secretary of the Treasury] appointed collector of the port of Buffalo over Fillmore's candidate, William Ketchum.[97]

After Fillmore became president in July 1850, however, the situation had changed:

> In the first months of his administration Fillmore withdrew only a single Weed appointment. The one removal was balm to the president's dignity; he fired Levi Allen, Weed's appointee to the Buffalo collectorship and the symbol of Fillmore's former undoing.[98]

The future #199 Delaware was from 1855 to 1860 the site of the Second Reformed Protestant Dutch Church.(5.42) Communicants were a small band led by Rev. John L. See, aided by the mother church in New York. The project failed and the chapel closed in 1860. Next year See returned to New York.[99]

For the next half century #199 would be the home of the Frank W. Fiske family. Frank's father, William Manson Fiske, had brought his family to Buffalo from Framingham, Massachusetts, in 1838

97 Rayback, *op. cit.*, p. 204.
98 *Ibid.*, p. 257.
99 Bartlett Papers, folder 9.

when Frank was three. William ran a grocery business at #5 Webster Block. Frank graduated from Harvard and in 1856 married the girl next door (#207 had yet to be built), Charlotte Hazard, daughter of George Starr Hazard, in whose house at #211 the couple lived for a while before moving into their new house at #199 in 1861. It was a big square brick house with a verandah across the front. There they entertained their guests handsomely. Fiske was a produce and commission merchant in partnership with his father-in-law. Fiske was also a charter member of the Buffalo Club and attended Trinity. By the 1890s he had moved into banking and in 1893 was cashier of the Merchants' Bank. Frank and Charlotte had six children: Susan, who married Dexter Rumsey, Evelyn, Frank, Jr., Merrick, Charlotte, and Manson. In 1912 the Fiskes sold #199 to the family of the late Charles H. Burnett, and with daughter Evelyn moved up Delaware to #610 where Frank died in 1914. His widow Charlotte continued there until her death in 1922.[100]

Abel Grosvenor, a native of Pomfret, Connecticut, had opened a mercantile house in Buffalo before the War of 1812. He was killed during the war in a case of mistaken identity. His younger brother Seth came to Buffalo to reestablish Abel's business, but in 1815 returned to New York where he prospered but maintained ties with Buffalo. He died in 1857. In his will he provided $40,000 for land and a building in Buffalo to house "books not to be lent out nor rented and only used for reading in the building." Thirty-eight years later the Grosvenor Library opened at Franklin and Edward Streets.[101]

A nephew of Abel and Seth, Seth Hancock Grosvenor, and his wife Jane had a house built just north of Fiske's into which they moved in 1863. Jane was the niece by marriage of Lucretia Stanley Grosvenor Shelton, second wife of Rev. William Shelton, rector of Saint Paul's (1829-1882). Lucretia's first husband had been Stephen K. Grosvenor, a brother of Abel. In fact, the Seth H. Grosvenors had lived with the Sheltons in the rectory at #198 Pearl before moving into #207. In May 1864 Seth unexpectedly died. He and Jane had four children: the eldest, Jane, married William Glenny and died in 1898; the only son, William Shelton Grosvenor, married and moved to Kansas where he died in 1915; Lucretia and Abby, who were twins, never married and continued to live with their mother.[102]

Though he died young, Seth had left Jane well fixed. Number 207 was a fine brick house with brownstone copings, a verandah, and high ceilinged rooms. Here Jane and the twins, when not traveling, entertained their friends. During a trip to Europe in 1889 they rented the house to Wilson S. Bissell, Grover Cleveland's future Postmaster General (1893-1895). Mrs. Bissell (Louise Fowler Sturges of Boston) had married Bissell that February, and they began their married life with a big wedding reception at #207. After they returned to Buffalo, Mrs. Grosvenor and the twins reoccupied the house until her death at seventy-nine in 1897.[103] Thereafter it became a boarding house.

100 *Ibid; CA*, February 15, 1922; *PBHS*, 19(1915), 360.
101 Wilner, *op. cit.*, 2:1037-1039.
102 *Courier*, February 10, 1924.
103 Bartlett Papers, folder 6.

5.43 ❦ George S. Hazard, *PBHS*, 13(1909), facing p. 307. He was thought to be a Henry Wadsworth Longfellow look-alike.

Number 211 new style, old style #71, was from 1850 until 1903 the home of that quintessential nineteenth century Buffalo merchant George Starr Hazard.(5.43) He had been born in New London, Connecticut, in 1809, a direct descendant of The Settler (the traditional name for the New England founder of a family in America), Thomas Hazard, who emigrated to Narragansett, Rhode Island, in 1683. Orphaned as a young boy, George began clerking in a general store at fifteen, earning a partnership within five years. In 1835 at twenty-six he went west to Maumee, Ohio, as a fur trader and pushed on to Indiana where frontier conditions prevailed until about 1850. In 1847 he came back east to Buffalo and began a grain commission business on Central Wharf, and became in the process "one of the most successful grain handlers and vessel owners on the Great Lakes," and proprietor of a block on the foot of Main Street.(5.44) In 1848 he bought the land for his house from Henry Sizer. The house was built during 1849, and Hazard moved in in 1850 and lived there for the rest of his long life. It was a square brick two-story building with a drawing room and windows facing the street with a side verandah, an entrance porch, and high ceilings and tall windows. "When built," Bartlett wrote, "it was considered far out in the country, but the neighborhood soon filled up with handsome houses of prominent citizens."[104]

Above 5.44 ❦ *PBHS*, 16(1912), 54
Left 5.45 ❦ Elks Lodge. *Truth*, October 21, 1925.

Hazard was president of the Buffalo Board of Trade, 1857-1858 and 1862-1865. Under his presidency the Board adopted the 100th Regiment, New York Volunteers, which had left Buffalo early in 1862, 900 men strong, only to be reduced to 451 May 31-June 1, 1862, at Fair Oakes, Virginia, during the Peninsula Campaign. Lest its remnants be incorporated into other regiments, the Board raised a liberal fund to spur recruiting with bounties and other premiums and thus preserve the good name of the city. Thereafter the unit was known as the Board of Trade Regiment.[105]

In July 1886 Hazard was elected president of the Bank of Attica; three years later his wife died. He was counted

104 *Ibid.*

among the founders and promoters of many local institutions: Buffalo General, U.B., the Young Men's Association, the Fine Arts Academy, of which he became president, the Society of Natural Sciences, and the Buffalo Club. He loved books, pictures, and travel and was successively prominent in Saint John's, Saint Paul's, and Trinity Episcopal churches. The Hazards had three children. Their eldest son Frank died early, leaving two daughters who for years lived with their grandparents. Charlotte, the only daughter of the George Hazards, married the boy next door, Frank W. Fiske. George Hazard died in 1903 at ninety-five. He had retired from active business thirty years before. His younger son, Archibald, was living at #211 in 1905 with his wife, the former Alice McLuren of Saint Louis, three boarders, and three domestics, but by 1910 it was a boarding house, *The Kenyon*. After Archibald moved, the Elks purchased it and made it their clubhouse. In 1923 they bought the place next door, demolished both houses, and erected a lodge, which opened in 1925.(5.45) They lost it during the Depression.[106]

The house at old style #73, new #217, was built *circa* 1850 by John Pease on what had been Henry Sizer's farm which comprised the north part of the block from Delaware to Franklin. Pease was born in 1811, son of Isaac and Sarah Thompson Pease, in Derby, Connecticut, on the Housatonic River near New Haven. His uncle was Sheldon Thompson, who with Benjamin Barton transported freight from tidewater through Lake Ontario to Lewiston and around the Falls to points on Lake Erie. In 1826 Pease met Thompson in New York who sent Pease to Buffalo as supercargo on a canal boat. Arriving in Black Rock, he was met by another uncle, Harry Thompson, who got him a job with a forwarding firm, Coit, Kimberly & Company, in which the Thompson brothers were interested and whose office was on the dock at Prince Street. Three years later Pease made partner in the firm, which became Kimberly & Pease. In 1839 John Pease married Sarah Barton, daughter of James Barton of #2 Delaware Street, Benjamin's son. About 1850 the Peases built a brick mansion on Delaware. George Hazard was building his square house next door and said to Pease, "Why are you building such a deep house? It's like a ropewalk." Pease smiled when Hazard later lengthened his own house. "The neighborhood," Bartlett recalled, "was ideal with great forest trees all about and the lots extended half the way to Franklin with lawns and shrubs and garden plots." Sara Barton Pease died in 1873.

The Peases had five children, two of whom died in childhood, leaving John, Jr., Sarah Marie, and James L. In the 1870s young John owned and operated a line of boats on the Erie Canal. In winter the barn behind his parents' house housed many of the canal mules, whose presence cannot have elevated the tone of the neighborhood. Sara and James, lived with him until the late 1870s when the house was sold and the family moved to 14th Street. John Pease died at ninety-seven in 1908. A

105 Frank H. Severance, "Historical Sketch of the Buffalo Board of Trade," *PBHS*, 13(1909), 271-279.
106 Bartlett Papers, *ibid.*

Left 5.46 ❦ Southeast corner, Delaware & Chippewa Streets, *PBHS*, 1(1912), 403.
Right 5.47 ❦ Same corner later, *PBHS*, 30(1930), following p. 289.

staunch Connecticut churchman, he was a vestryman of Saint Paul's for thirty-four years. Bartlett wrote that the house was renovated and became first a boarding and then a rooming house.[107] In 1920 Ida E. Hallen, a widow, managed to pack twenty-three lodgers into the place.

During the 1880s #221 Delaware was the home of Walter Joy Shepard, the son of John D. Shepard of the Webster Iron Works who had lived at #12 Delaware in 1860, where Walter grew up. His grandfather was Walter Joy, whose career is narrated in chapter 3. Walter Shepard was the proprietor of a hardware manufacturing concern on Chicago Street.

Figures 5.46 and 5.47 are two views of the southeast corner of Delaware and Chippewa. The first is older, since Stone's Delaware Tailor Shop opened in 1907, while the cars and structures depicted in the latter are from the late 1920s. The seedy, frame tenement house in 5.46 was the first building on the tract. Stone's shop was listed as at #94 Chippewa, and the Francis H. Root estate owned all the buildings along the south side of that street as far as Franklin. The corner building must have clashed loudly with the other high-class dwellings of the period 1860-1900. Commenting on figure 5.46 Alice Bartlett wrote that "it was taken while the building was still being used for residences. Later the ground floor was divided for shops."[108]

107 *Ibid.*
108 *Ibid.*

CHAPTER

6 FROM CHIPPEWA TO 

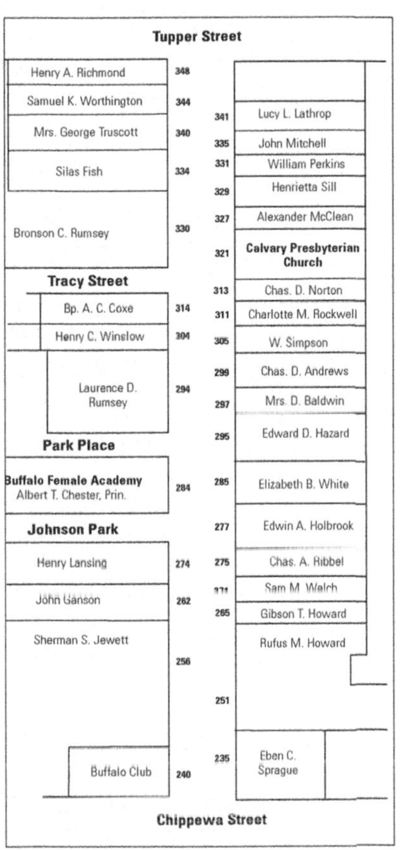

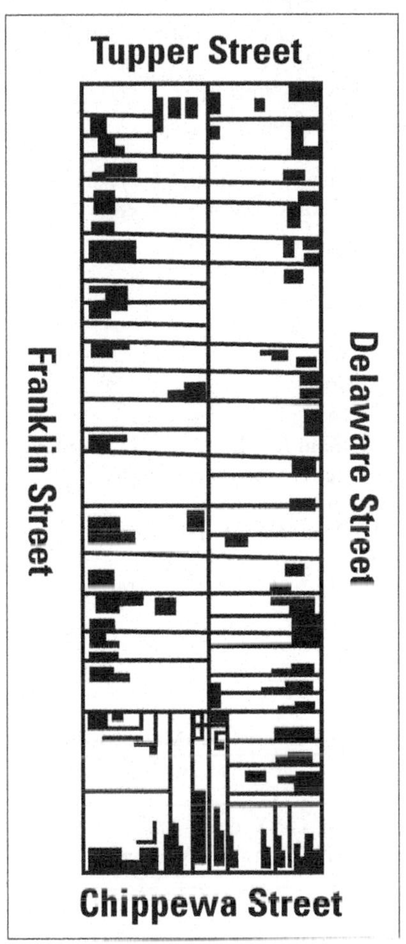

Left 6.1 ❦ Chippewa to Edward Streets. See figure 5.1.
Right 6.2 ❦ Emslie and Kirk, *op. cit.*

Homes had been built on eighteen building lots on the 275 foot long block on the eastside of Delaware from Chippewa to Tupper as early as 1850.(6.2)

1860

WEST CHIPPEWA STREET

[235] Samuel Strong 40 Virginia gentleman
Marion Strong 35 NY *ux.*
Marion Strong 15 NY
Mary L. Strong 9 NY
Isabella P. Strong 7 NY
Samuel Strong 5 NY
Bridget Loftus 21 Ireland
Anna Conway 25 Ireland
Margaret Scott 15 Ireland

1870 (2)

WEST CHIPPEWA STREET

235 Eben Carlton Sprague 46 New Hampshire attorney
Elizabeth Sprague 39 Conn. *ux.* housekeeper
Louise Sprague 16 NY school
Henry Sprague 14 NY school
Carlton Sprague 11 NY
Amelia Williams 30 NY
Mary Carney 21 Ireland
Clara Hayes 15 NY

99	[251] Rufus Lombard Howard 42 NY Ketchum reapers Chicago & canal Maria L. Howard 37 Virginia *ux* Gibson F. Howard 16 NY Harriet C. Howard 6 NY James E. Field 30 NY reapers manufacturer Emily Field 26 NY Hannah Ray 46 Ireland Ellen Ray 24 Ireland	251	Rufus Lombard Howard 53 NY iron works proprietor Maria Howard 47 NY housekeeper *ux.* Harriet C. Howard 15 NY school Mrs. Phillips 42 England Jennie Phillips 15 NY school Sadie Phillips NY school Kate Schmit 30 NY
107	[265] Serena McClennan 57 NY lady Elizabeth George 59 Hesse-Cassel	265	Gibson F. Howard 25 NY tobacconist Georgiana Howard 24 NY housekeeper Gibson Howard 3 NY
		267	Silas Parsons 60 Connecticut wholesale flour merchant Lucy Parsons 60 NY ux Mary Thompson 19 NY
109	[271] William Ketchum 61 NY gentleman Lamira Ketchum 56 Vermont *ux.* Lang Ketchum 12 NY Victor D. Reed 45 NY minister	271	Samuel M. Welch 44 Conn. leather & wool merchant Elizabeth P. Welch 34 Ohio *ux.* Deshler Welch 16 NY school Lucia Welch 14 NY school Bessie Welch 11 NY school Emily Welch 10 NY school Mary Nye 20 NY Gertrude Schmitt 22 Austria
111	[275] George C. Coit 57 Mass. cashier Int Bank Sophrina Coit 50 Mass. *ux.* Edgar Coit 24 NY Alfred Coit 21 NY clerk Magdelene Bachman 33 Belgium	275	Charles A. Ribbel 38 Mass. tailor Mary Ribbel 40 NY housekeeper *ux.* Edward Ribbel 13 NY school Julius Ribbel 9 NY school Emma Ribbel 9 NY school Frank Ribbel 6 NY school Susan Heimerle 16 NY Elizabeth Marbach 18 Hesse Darmstadt
113	[277] George W. Sweet 26 NY Pettit Sweet & Co. wholesale boots & shoes Fanny Sweet 20 NY *ux.* Anna Sweet 1 NY Clara Ramsdell 16 Conn. Martha Weber 15 NY Mary Shaeffer 14 Baden Bridget Hickey 17 Ireland William B. Pettit 35 Conn. Pettit Sweet & Co. Sara W. Pettit 30 Conn. *ux.* Grace G. Pettit 2 NY Allen F. Pettit 1 NY	277	Edwin A. Holbrook 46 Mass. retired bookseller Elizabeth Holbrook 41 Conn. *ux.* housekeeper Mary A. Murphy 32 Ireland
119	[285] George L. Hubbard 46 Conn. insurance 5 Spaulding's Exchange Juliana Hubbard 39 Conn. *ux.* Robert Hubbard 15 NY Ophelia Hubbard 50 Conn. Mary Lawson 26 Ireland James Ross 20 Scotland Barbara Orr NY nurse	285	Elizabeth B. White

		295	Edward D. Hazard commission merchant elevator owner
121	[297] Daniel Baldwin 50 NY lumber dealer Niagara & Carolina Ann M. Baldwin 36 NY *ux.* Frederick Baldwin 19 NY clerk Adella Baldwin 11 NY Alice Baldwin 7 NY Horace Baldwin 5 NY Gordon Baldwin 3 NY Frank Baldwin 1 NY Catherine Eagan 18 Ireland Johanna Reedy 26 Ireland Sara McVane 18 Canada West	297	Ann N. Baldwin 47 NY housekeeper Alice G. Baldwin 17 NY Horace Baldwin 15 NY clerk Frank Baldwin 11 NY school Anna Mills 20 Scotland
		299	Charles Andrews 36 NY pork merchant August Andrews 28 NY housekeeper *ux.* Alice Ryan 21 NY Julia Spice NY
129	[305] William Stimpson 49 commission merchant Eliza W. Stimpson 49 NY *ux.* James M. Stimpson 13 NY Henry C. Stimpson 11 NY Hannah Grinsell 29 Mass.	305	William Stimpson
		311	John M. Rockwell Schoellhorn & Rockwell boot and shoe manufacturer
139	[313] Lucretia Norton 73 Conn. Fanny Norton 40 Conn. Mary Norton 36 Conn. Sophia Kane 26 Germany	313	Samuel Garland tailor
145	[321] *Calvary Presbyterian Church*	321	*Calvary Presbyterian Church*
149	[329] Mark B. Moore 36 New Hampshire Babcock & Moore attorneys Matilda Moore 29 Ohio *ux.* Maria Barlow 13 Conn. Margaret Kelch 25 Germany	327	Rev. Alexander McLean 36 Scotland clergyman Sophia McLean 29 Conn. housekeeper *ux.* Jeannette Russell 35 Canada West
	[331] J. Morris Gwinn teller New York & Erie Bank	329	Henrieta Sill 45 NY widow Fanny Sill 27 NY Henry S. Sill 23 NY life insurance agent Charles Sill 25 NY court clerk Mary Sill 18 NY Mary McLaughlin 24 Ireland
155	[335] James D. Mitchell 52 Ireland fish rod manufacturer Mary Mitchell 40 England *ux.* Ann Mitchell 22 NY John Mitchell 18 NY Mary Mitchell 14 NY Jenny Mitchell 12 NY	331	William Perkins 38 Ohio treasurer iron works Jennie Perkins 28 NY housekeeper *ux.* William H. Perkins 10 NY school Mary Perkins 6 mos. NY Mena Meyer 19 NY

157 [339] John Crossman 39 Vermont
ticket agent MCRR

WEST TUPPER STREET End of Block

335 John Mitchell 32 NY detective
Jennie Mitchell 20 NY housekeeper *ux.*
Edward Hemmenway 32 NY clerk
Anna Hemmenway 29 NY boarder
Mary Hennemway 6 NY school
Sarah Dickson 27 NY boarder
Hattie Dickson 6 NY school

341 Lucy L. Lathrop 50 Conn. housekeeper
Ferdinand A. Lathrop 24 Conn. clerk

WEST TUPPER STREET End of Block

1880

WEST CHIPPEWA STREET

235 Eben Carlton Sprague 57
New Hampshire attorney
Elizabeth Sprague 49 Conn. *ux.* housekeeper
Henry W. Sprague 24 NY son attorney
Amelia 29 NY
Nora Fain 27 Canada

239 John M. Horton NY 38 Pratt & Co.
Catherine P. Horton 28 NY *ux.*
Minna 20 NY
Rosa 25 NY

251 Rufus Lombard Howard 60 NY
iron manufacturer
Maud Howard 57 NY *ux.* housekeeper
Gibson F. Howard 13 NY grandson school
Maria Howard 36 NY daughter-in-law
Georgiana Howard 5 NY granddaughter
Leonard Gibbs 41 Mass.
Anna Smith 46 Ireland

265 Ralph H. Plumb 35 NY nut & bolt manufacturer
Millie Plumb 34 NY *ux.* housekeeper
George Plumb 18 NY brother
Ralph Plumb 4 NY son
Mary O'Brien 30 Ireland
Lizzie Brown 17 Canada

271 Samuel M. Welch 56 Conn. wool & hides dealer
Elizabeth D. Welch 46 Ohio *ux.* housekeeper
Lucia Welch 26 NY daughter
Bessie Welch 22 NY daughter
Emily Welch 19 NY daughter
Mary Beekman 13 Germany
John R. Neale 21 Maryland

275 Charles A Ribbel 57 France merchant tailor
Magdelena Ribbel 52 France *ux.* housekeeper
George E. Ribbel 26 NY son clerk
Julius Ribbel 25 NY son clerk
Frank E. Ribbel 16 NY son
Anna Ribbel 18 NY daughter
Louise Drons 20 NY

1891

WEST CHIPPEWA STREET

235 Eben Carlton Sprague attorney
Morey & Sprague

239 Mrs. S.A. Meredith
Grace E. Meredith
Julian F. Meredith
Mabel E. Meredith

247 William Talmage

251 Rufus Lombard Howard 71 NY

265 Gibson F. Howard Howard Iron Works
287 Chicago St.

269 Charles A. Slater real estate 404 Main
S. S. Todd teacher College of Commerce
327 Main

275 George E. Ribbel
Julius A. Ribbel Ribbel Bros. tailor
13 North Division
Mrs. Charles A. Ribbel

277 Edwin A. Holbrook 66 Mass. retired
Elizabeth Holbrook 50 Conn. *ux.* housekeeper
Anna Holbrook 25 daughter
Martha Gilroy 21 England

285 Elizabeth B. White 62 Conn. housekeeper
James Fero 66 Conn. brother real estate agent
Myra Comestock 20 cousin
Mary Hackett 42 Ireland
Henry Rut 32 NY
Francis Hoffman 34 Germany
James Walsh 21 NY coachman

295 James N. Matthews 51 England
proprietor *Morning Express*
Harriett W. Matthews 42 NY *ux.* housekeeper
George E. Matthews 25 NY son Matthews Press
Frances Matthews 13 daughter school
Elizabeth Bachman 26 NY
Katrina Conrad 30 Ireland
Louise 24 NY

297 Mary Shumway 88 Mass. housekeeper
Mary H. Lee 44 NY daughter
Horatio Lee 12 NY grandson school
Mary McFee 27 NY

299 Andrew Brown 41 England lumber merchant
Maria A. Brown 26 NY *ux.* housekeeper
Mary Brown 16 NY daughter school
Henry F. Brown 4 NY son
Maria Carmody 28 Ireland
Teresa Burns 22 NY
Mary Slattery 21 Ireland

305 Patrick Smith 71 Ireland gun dealer
Bridget Smith 69 Ireland *ux.* housekeeper
Mary Gall 39 NY daughter
Anna Gall 13 NY granddaughter school
Bertha Glance 18 NY

311 Harrison B. Mixer 59 NY
lumber merchant
Carrie S. Mixer 43 NY *ux.* housekeeper
Mary L. Mixer 18 NY daughter

313 Mary Thompson 50 NY housekeeper
Charles Thompson 14 NY
Nora Pettibone 20 NY boarder
Lucy Lathrop 62 Conn. boarder
Mary Smith 23 Bavaria

321 *Calvary Presbyterian Church*

277 Charles Pugsley

285 Mrs. Elizabeth B. White
Mrs. George C. White
Richard Piper coachman

297 E. J. Tribble 42 fisherman river
J. Phillip Tribble *same*
Walter F. Tribble

299 Mrs. Peter A. Porter
George M. Porter
Miss S. Morris

305 F. Whitehill Hinkel MD

311 George W. Lewis MD

313 Mrs. L. L. Lathrop

321 *Calvary Presbyterian Church*

327 William Reed 33 NY clergyman
Jerusa Reed 33 NY *ux.* housekeeper
Ruth D. Reed 5 NY daughter school
Edward N. Reed 1 NY daughter
Lizzie O'Hara 22 NY
Minnie Kerscher 12 Pa.

329 Henry S. Sill 33 NY maritime insurance
Harriet Sill 59 NY mother housekeeper
Fanny Sill 37 NY sister
Louise 28 Germany

331 Harriet A. Perkins 65 Conn. housekeeper
Thomas G. Perkins 33 NY son marine insurance
George H. Perkins 21 NY son clerk
Dora 25 NY

335 Leonard Chester 54 Conn. retired
Lucy Chester 28 Conn. *ux.* housekeeper
Carl T. Chester 26 Conn. son attorney
Margaret Quince NY 25
Anna Ganroy 28 France

337 Augustus M. Westfall 48 NY force pump manufacturer
Elizabeth Westfall 48 NY *ux.* housekeeper
Mabel A. Westfall NY 6 daughter

347 *Delaware Avenue Methodist Episcopal Church*

WEST TUPPER STREET End of Block

329 Henry S. Sill Worthington & Sill insurance agents 10 Board of Trade

331 Mrs. Elizabeth Dellebaugh

335 Mrs. George Truscott

339 John B. Coakley MD

347 *Delaware Avenue Methodist Episcopal Church*

WEST TUPPER STREET End of Block

1900

WEST CHIPPEWA STREET

247 Mr. & Mrs. Gibson F. Howard
(*Buffalo Address Book 1901*)

265 Georgiana Howard
(*Buffalo Address Book 1901*)

1905

WEST CHIPPEWA STREET

239 Jennie Quirk 38 Canada
Freda Quirk 21 Canada daughter
Myrtle Quirk 17 Canada daughter
Frank Quirk 42 Canada brother-in-law
Isabella Quirk 40 Canada sister-in-law
4 lodgers
1 servant

245 Elizabeth Harry 37
Glen Harry 17 son school
10 lodgers

251 Mrs. George Theobold 30
Abby Wright 26 sister
Harry Wright 31 brother-in-law clerk
George Theobold 57 father
Francis Theobold 55 uncle
4 lodgers
Mary Siegfried 20 Canada

265 Charles W. Lowes 58 Canada RR clerk
Louise J. Lowes 48 Canada *ux.*
George W. Lowes 23 son traveling salesman
5 lodgers
1 servant

267	Duncan Creighton 45 Mass. machinist Emma Creighton 44 England *ux.* James A. P. Creighton 18 NY son Cecilia Creighton 14 NY daughter school Raymond Creighton 11 NY son school Nellie Drew 22 NY lodger John D. Squier 20 NY tool maker lodger	267	John Nagal 38 Germany saloon keeper Nellie Nagal 37 *ux.* Isabelle Nagal 5 daughter school 2 lodgers
269	Elizabeth Allen 36 Canada Emma Robertson 28 Michigan milliner boarder Frances Purdy 69 NY healer	269	Julia McK. Houlihan 45 dressmaker 2 lodgers
271	Samuel Welch 76 Conn. merchant Elizabeth D. Welch 66 Ohio *ux.* Dashler Welch 45 NY journalist Elizabeth D. Whiting 41 daughter Mildred Welch 15 granddaughter Dashler Whiting Welch 17 granddaughter	271	6 lodgers
275	Magdelene Ribbel 69 France Charles Ribbel 48 NY son attorney George Ribbel 44 NY son tailor Frank Ribbel 33 NY son Emma Ribbel 34 NY daughter Sarah Rafferty 40 Ireland	275	Magdelene Ribbel 74 Germany George Ribbel 50 son tailor Frank Ribbel 39 real estate agent 7 lodgers 2 servants
277	Charles E. Puglsey 49 NY Clara Pugsley 49 NY *ux.* Edwin Pugsley 14 California Margaret McDonald 39 Pennsylvania May McDonald 19 NY	277	Charles Pugsley 55 civil engneer Clare E. Pugsley 54 *ux.* Edwin Pugsley 19 son school Margaret O'Brien 38 Ireland Margaret *illegible* 20 Germany
285	Elizabeth White 82 Conn. Elizabeth M. Otis 24 Conn. niece Kate Welch 36 Germany Hannah Dailey 24 NY George Van Valkenburg 33 NY coachman		
295	Stephen Mitchell 31 NY steward Michael Mitchell 27 NY assistant steward 5 boarders Margaret Murphy 30 Canada cook Kate Deane 25 Michigan	295	Harry W. Smith 40 Rose Smith 37 *ux.* Ella M. Sawyer 60 mother-in-law
297	J. Phillip Trible 55 NY president Empire Company Ellen Trible 48 Ohio *ux.* Grace Trible 24 NY daughter Anna Bihi 48 NY	297	John B. Sears 46 salesman Helen M. Sears 48 *ux.* Wilbur Williams 18 son school 7 lodgers 2 servants
299	John Preston NY 48 bookkeeper Ida Preston 33 NY *ux.* Howard Preston 2 NY 7 boarders	299	Amelia B. Vogel 46 Lewis Vogel 28 son traveling salesman 8 lodgers
305	John Sears 40 Mississippi bookkeeper Helen Sears 44 Wisconsin *ux.* 12 boarders Bertha Oswald 31 NY cook	305	Charlotte Jones 64 9 lodgers

311	George W. Lewis 36 NY MD Mary Lewis 33 NY *ux.* Geraldine Lewis 1 NY daughter Edward E. Lewis 27 NY brother attorney Marian Harcourt 60 England Mary Laur 20 NY William Bergman 50 Germany coachman	311	Charles Pendill 55 traveling salesman Mary K. Pendill 43 *ux.* 5 lodgers 2 servants
313	Mary Thompson 77 Conn. Hugh A. Sloan 37 NY pharmacist lodger Matilda Sloan 30 NY *ux* Catherine Becker 35 NY	313	Mary E. Mixer 75 Frederick K. Mixer 45 son teacher Hugh A. Sloan 42 druggist Matilda Sloan 35 *ux.* David Wilcox 32 artist Annie Wilcox 29 *ux.* Ethel Wilcox 1 month daughter
321	*Calvary Presbyterian Church*	321	*Calvary Presbyterian Church*
327	Louis Burton Crane pastor Calvary	327	Richard E. Locke 37 pastor Calvary Maud S. Locke 33 *ux.* Mary M. Locke 3 daughter Margaret Locke 2 daughter Jennie Lex 19 Germany
329	Henry S. Sill 52 NY insurance agent Francis Sill 58 NY sister Laura Webster 37 NY cousin Delia Tansey 19 Ireland	329	Henry S. Sill 58 insurance agent Fanny Sill 63 sister Bertha Logan 16 Canada Louise Kelch 28 cook
331	Wilhelm Kotting 41 Bohemia teacher Mary Nesbitt 19 Canada	331	John P. Trible 60 Ellen Trible 53 *ux.* Reese P. Risley 34 land commissioner Tropical Development Mary V. Risley 36 *ux.*
335	Sarah Truscott 71 Mass. Sarah L. Truscott 44 NY daughter Lena Glanz 32 NY	335	Sarah Truscott 76 Sarah L. Truscott 49 daughter
339	John Coakley MD 62 Virginia Sarah Coakley 47 Conn. *ux.* Morgan Coakley 21 Virginia son school Elizabeth Coakley 20 Virginia daughter Gilbertine Coakley 16 NY daughter school Henrietta Hall 52 Canada	339	John J. Coakley MD 67 Virginia Sarah T. Coakley 52 *ux.* Morgan T. Coakley 26 son RR clerk
347	*Delaware Avenue Methodist Episcopal Church*	347	*Delaware Avenue Methodist Episcopal Church*
	WEST TUPPER STREET ❦ End of Block		WEST TUPPER STREET ❦ End of Block

1915

WEST CHIPPEWA STREET

247 Nina Tucker 28 Canada landlady
Bonnie Tucker 7 daughter school
10 lodgers

251 Magdelene Lambrix 75 Germany
Isabelle Lambrix 42 daughter hotel work
5 lodgers

257 rooming house 5 residents

261 Children's Welfare Association
William Cleaver 42 superintendent
Ella Cleaver *ux.*
7 employees
65 inmates

267 Catherine Ganger 55 Canada landlady
2 lodgers

269 Albert Bernhardt 31 singing waiter
Nellie Bernhardt 27 *ux*

271 N. J. Stratton 47 landlady
Nellie Nobleman 23 daughter
illegible Nobleman son-in-law
5 lodgers

275 Charles H. Ribbel 62 attorney
Julius Ribbel 59 brother
Frank Ribbel 51 brother
Bertha B. Ribbel 55 sister
housekeeper
Mary Roche 56 Canada
Helen Smart 23

277 Emma Heldmeyer 55 landlady
5 lodgers

285 John H McLean 50 Canada salesman
Katherine McLean 44 Canada *ux.*
Mary Butner 22 sister-in-law
Gladdis McLean 20 daughter stenographer
John C. McLean 18 son school
Wilbert McLean 12 son school
Ruth McLean 10 daughter school
Dorothy McLean 7 daughter school
3 boarders

297 Delia McCann 60 landlady
Mary McCann 70 sister

1920

WEST CHIPPEWA STREET

241 George Alexandra 42 California furrier
Alice Alexandra 43 England *ux.*

251 Delaware Avenue Garage

261 Children's Aid Society
Elizabeth Ancker matron
14 resident employees
57 inmates ages 1-20

275 Walter E. Green 59 NY painter
Matilda Green 49 NY *ux.*
Harold R. Chandler son-in-law caskets
Gladys Chandler 24 NY daughter
13 lodgers

277 Emma Heldmeyer 60 NY landlady
18 lodgers

285 John H. McLean 55 Canada oil refiner
Katherine McLean 48 Canada *ux.* housekeeper
Ruth McLean 14 NY daughter
Dorothy McLean 11 NY daughter
11 lodgers

295 Joseph W. Short 54 NY
Florence Short 40 NY
housekeeper
12 lodgers

297 Delia McCann 65 NY widow
housekeeper
lodgers

299	apartment house 40 residents	299	Margaret B. Kieth 45 NY widow housekeeper Edna Kieth 19 NY daughter 12 lodgers
305	John Marchese 34 Italy barber Lena Marchese 33 *ux.* James Marchese 11 son school 5 lodgers	305	Charles E. Reed 54 NY furniture store salesman Edith Raymond 47 Florida housekeeper 5 lodgers
311	Nellie D. Swift 46 school teacher John Swift 7 son school Jeanette Swift 12 daughter school Alice Swift 9 daughter school Eugene Stacy 34 salesman Myrtle Stacy 35 *ux.* Merrill Stacy 3 son 6 lodgers	311	Paul Wagner 54 Germany salesman in machine shop Mary R. Wagner 49 Germany *ux.* housekeeper Paul Wagner Jr. 24 NY son machinist Rudolph Wagner 21 NY son salesman in feed store
313	Hugh Sloan 52 pharmacist Matilda M. Sloan 45 *ux.* Edward B. Herrick 45 MD Ella Herrick 38 *ux.*	313	William J Brewer 24 NY church janitor
321	*Calvary Presbyterian Church*	321	*Calvary Presbyterian Church*
327	Apartment house 18 residents	327	8 lodgers
329	Katherine Powers 60 Joseph Powers 22 son salesman Margaret Powers 25 daughter stenographer Ella Kelsey 27 daughter Charles Kelsey 28 son-in-law assistant superintendent rubber works Katherine Golden 27 Canada daughter-in-law	329	Emma Taft 51 NY 7 lodgers
331	William Wrightman 32 commercial teacher Mary Wrightman 45 *ux.* Bruce Wrightman 14 son school William Koehler 25 streetcar conductor May Koehler 25 *ux.*	331	Warren Butcher 25 NY salesman in shoe store Elizabeth Butcher 20 NY *ux.* housekeeper Grenville Buther 2 mos. NY 14 lodgers
335	Sarah Truscott 85 Sarah L. Truscott 59 daughter real estate agent	335	Ralph D. Schwartz 35 California orchestra musician Elizabeth Schwartz 35 NY *ux.* housekeeper 6 lodgers
339	John B. Coakley 76 MD Sarah Coakley 62 *ux.* (illegible) son 37 electrical engineer Henrietta Hll 70		
349	*Delaware Avenue Methodist Episcopal Church*	349	*Delaware Avenue Methodist Episcopal Church*
	WEST TUPPER STREET ❦ End of Block		WEST TUPPER STREET ❦ End of Block

6.3 ❦ Ebenezer Carleton Sprague. *Buffalo Club*, p. 36.

The house on the northeast corner of Delaware and Chippewa was built in 1836 for Alexander Eustaphieve. Welch described it as an "English basement house." In figure 5.47 it appears to be Jacksonian American. Eustaphieve was born in Boston, Massachusetts, in 1812. His father was Russian consul in New York. About 1832 Alexander came to Buffalo and got a job as a teller in the Bank of Buffalo and then in the brokerage office of Henry Sizer. Later he became cashier of the Bank of Commerce. In 1837 Eustaphieve enlisted in the militia and served during the Patriots' War (a Canadian, not an American phenomenon) at Black Rock. Next he appears as a broker and receiver of an insurance company in New York. In 1848 he returned to Buffalo and opened his own insurance company, Walker & Eustaphieve. He died on Georgia Street in 1866.[1]

In 1860 the corner house was home to Samuel Strong, a self-styled "Virginia gentleman." Three Irish girls, the youngest of whom was fifteen, ministered to Strong, his wife, and four children. By 1870 the owner was Ebenezer Carleton Sprague, one of the city's leading attorneys.(6.3) The first Sprague in America, Francis, landed at Plymouth in 1623. His son married Ruth Alden, granddaughter of John Alden. Ebenezer was born in Bath, New Hampshire, in 1822. He came with his family to Buffalo four years later, attended Phillips Exeter, graduated from Harvard in 1843, read law in the offices of [Millard] Fillmore, Hall & Haven, passed the bar in 1846, and practiced law for fifty years. Among his clients were the Erie County Savings Bank, the Great Western Railway, and the Erie. He eschewed politics but consented to fill a vacancy in the state senate for a year. An incorrigible joiner, he belonged to the Fine Arts Academy, the Society of Natural Sciences, the Civil Service Reform Association, and the Saturn Club. He also served as Chancellor of U.B., president of the Young Men's Association, the Harvard Club, and the Buffalo Club, director of the Children's Aid Society, secretary of the Buffalo Orphan Asylum, and vice-president of the Unitarian Association. He was widely read in history, philosophy, and religion. He read French and German, and his favorite authors were Saint Paul, Plato, Homer, Virgil, Dante, Goethe, and Milton. For this he received an honorary L.L.D. from his alma mater in 1892.[2]

1 *Express*, October 21, 1866.
2 *M&FH*, 1:110-112; Warren, *op. cit.*, p. 36.

In 1849 Sprague married Elizabeth Williams of Buffalo. He died in 1895 and was survived by four children — Carleton and Henry Ware, and two girls. The girls married and moved away. Carleton, whose education was a repeat of his father's, began reading law with him, but soon deserted the law in favor of the Buffalo Pitts Company, one of the largest producers of agricultural and road building machinery in the country. He assured his rise in the company, in which he later became vice-president, by marrying a Pitts. Henry Ware Sprague graduated from the University of Leipzig, read law in his father's office, passed the bar in 1878, and two years later became a partner in Sprague, Melbum & Sprague. He was a founder of the Saturn Club. [3]

Above 6.4 ❦ #99-#251 Delaware, BHS.
Below 6.5 ❦ Rufus Lombard Howard, Smith, *op. cit.*, II, facing p. 238.

The next house north was #99 old style, #251 new(6.4):

> The Rufus L. Howard(6.5) house at 251 Delaware, however, displayed the most flamboyant ornament of any of its Italianate neighbors, indicating a date in the later 1850s. [Actually the 1847-1848 *City Directory* shows Howard already living there.] The exterior was festooned with ornate labels over the windows, long pendants beneath the eaves, and flagrant finials on the roof. Howard, who had made his fortune by perfecting and marketing the first mechanized lawn mowers, owned his own iron works. The exuberant ornament on his house, however, appears to have come from Buffalo's Eagle Iron Works; the vase-crowned labels above the round-headed windows on the second floor as well as the bracketed pediment over the large central window repeat patterns illustrated in the firm's catalogue of cast-iron architectural elements. [4]

The history of the Buffalo Club of which he was president for two terms sketches the owner's career:

> Howard was born in the town of Litchfield, Herkimer County, New York, October 30, 1818. He first saw the Buffalo waterfront on May 6, 1839, and went to work for a ship chandler, salary $200 a year. In two years he was offered a quarter interest in the business to be paid for at his convenience. Twelve years later, he sold this interest and invested in the Ketchum mowing machine. [William] Ketchum, discouraged after years of experimentation, was glad to work for Howard, who not only laid his money on the line but gave

3 *M&FH, ibid.*; Hill, *op. cit.*, 4:355-356; Dunn, *op. cit.*, p. 26.
4 *Grand American Avenue*, p. 44.

the project his personal attention. In the summer of 1851, five mowers were sold and won approval. Sales soon zoomed to 128,000 a year. After the mowing machine era [and after the Ketchum patents had run out], the business long continued as the Howard Iron Works.(6.6)

Besides being an entrepreneur of extraordinary ability, Howard was also a great humanitarian. Long interested in the Young Men's Association, he was one of nine men in 1840 who subscribed $3,000 each to purchase St. James Hall for it. He gave a like amount to the Trinity Church building fund, was one of twelve who started the Buffalo park system, helped found the Buffalo General Hospital, and was president of St. Margaret's School for Young Women. At one point he bought 200 acres of timber at $95 an acre in Buffalo's 13th Ward and during a hard-time winter employed more than 100 jobless men to cut the timber. He developed a farm there, was the first to introduce Jersey cattle in this area, took up horse breeding, [and] helped organize the driving park association. [5]

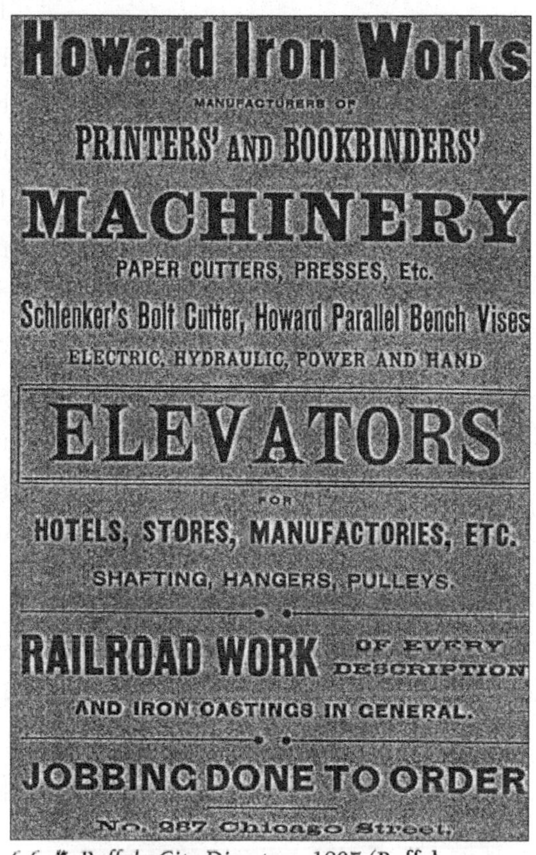

6.6 ❦ *Buffalo City Directory, 1897* (Buffalo:

He had another interest not mentioned here. He "always had a decided taste for military life" — though, only forty-two when Fort Sumter was fired on, he passed on the Civil War. But his rise in the local military was rapid. He was appointed as Major to the staff of the Major General of the Western New York Division, NYNG. He soon made Chief of Staff and Colonel. In 1865 Governor Fenton appointed him Major General of that division. During his command, Buffalo underwent a nasty strike amid railroad upheavals that rocked the nation in 1877 and were widely seen as an uprising of labor against capital. [6] Howard may well have felt that this was just what the NYNG was all about.

Howard had married Maria Louisa Field in 1842 and they had six children, all of whom predeceased their father who died in 1896. A son, Gibson Field Howard, born in 1844, resided next to his father at #265 Delaware, a house which had been built for George Hubbard. Gibson became a partner at the Howard Iron Works. His father appointed him chief of artillery in the Eighth Division, but he died at age twenty-nine in 1875, leaving a wife and eight-year old Gibson, Jr. [7] The latter grew up at #251, married, moved into #247 next to his grandfather, and became president of the Hungerford Water Company. After his grandfather's death, Gibson assumed the presidency of the family firm, which he sold to Otis Elevator in 1910 and moved to Los Angeles, where he died at fifty-nine in

5 Warren, *op. cit.*, p. 29.
6 Smith, *op. cit.*, 2:36; E. Dunn, *op. cit.*, p. 63-64.
7 *CA*, April 13, 1875.

Above 6.7 #295 Delaware. *PBHS*, 22 (1922) np
Below 6.8 *M&FH*, 1:75.

1926, survived by his wife Charlotte. The widow of Rufus Howard lived on at #251 Delaware, a house which must have seemed increasingly antique, until 1900, when she sold it and left to live with a niece in Illinois, where she died in 1907.[8] By 1905 Ebenezer Sprague's former home at #235, a newer neighbor at #239, the old Rufus Howard mansion at #251, and #265, the southern end of the block, had become rooming houses. The nine-story Hotel Touraine across the street at #264 and its annex at #262, with combined accommodations for 130 guests, had been completed. By 1915 the Howard mansion had been incorporated into the Delaware Avenue Garage.

Most of the remaining houses on the east side of the block were solid brick structures, inhabited chiefly by prosperous burghers, provided employment to a few domestic servants each, but were not mansions. The lots on which they were built were too small for that. Samuel Welch, who lived at #271 from 1868 until he died in 1902, had been born in Windom, Connecticut, came to Buffalo in 1830 and clerked in stores there and in Milwaukee before returning to Buffalo where he remained until his death. He dealt in hides, leather, and real estate, and built the Welch block on Washington Street above the Hamburg Canal. He was not a rich man, but penned a 432-page sketch of early Buffalo.[9]

Number 295 was also typical of the houses on this block. (6.7) It was built about 1870 by Edward Hazard. During the late 1870s and until his death in 1888 it was the home of James N. Matthews(6.8), saluted as the bearer of "an historic name in Buffalo Journalism." He was born in Suffolk County, England, in 1828 and was apprenticed to a printer. Coming to Buffalo in 1846 he secured a job with the *Commercial Advertiser* and soon became foreman of its printing plant. In 1850 he was made foreman of the printing office of the *Express,* and at year's end was admitted to partnership. Under his management Clapp, Matthews & Company became known as the best railroad printing firm in the country. In 1862 he formed a partnership with James D. Warren to publish the *Commercial Advertiser,* and became editor. He stayed with the *Advertiser* for fourteen years, resigned in 1877, and became sole owner of the rival *Express*. Matthews

8 *Ibid.*, August 5, 1907.
9 *Ibid.*, November 14, 1902.

aligned his paper with the Republican Party and was a delegate to the National Convention which renominated Ulysses S. Grant in 1872 and nominated Rutherford B. Hayes in 1876. Matthews married Harriet Wells of Westfield in 1851 and had one son, George Edward Matthews, born in 1855. No apprenticeship in printing for George, who attended local schools and graduated from Harvard in 1877. Next year he began his ascent to editor-in-chief of the paper and president of its printing operations, Matthews, Northrup & Company.[10]

In 1872 Elizabeth White lived at #285 with her husband George. As a widow she was there in 1880 with her brother, a cousin, three servant girls, and a coachman, and she was there at eighty-two in 1900 with two domestics and a coachman. Wilson Bissell moved to #295 after he left the Grosvenor home at #207 as mentioned in chapter 5. He was Postmaster General during the first two years of Cleveland's second administration. Bissell moved to #1069 when the University Club acquired #295 in 1897.

Number139 old style, #313 new, from 1855 until 1867 was the home of a niece of a Signer of the Declaration of Independence and grandmother of a chancellor of U.B., Lucretia Huntington Norton. Born in 1787, she was the mother of Joseph G. Norton, a shipping merchant of Hartford, Connecticut, who with his family, including his son, Charles Davis Norton, born in 1820, had come to Black Rock in 1827 where he entered the dry goods business. Lucretia's father, Joseph Huntington, a Yale alumnus, had been a Congregational minister. His brother Samuel was the Signer and later governor of Connecticut; Joseph's son Samuel became the second governor of Ohio and later chief justice of that state. In 1830 Joseph Norton moved to Buffalo, where he prospered enough to send his son to Union College from which he graduated in 1839. Charles read law in the office of Horatio Shumway, and became a Whig during the controversies arising from the annexation of Texas and the Mexican War. Meanwhile, his father died in 1844. Charles was elected city attorney in 1849 and surrogate in 1851, the year he married Jeanette Phelps of Canandaigua. They had two children, Porter Huntington and Charles Phelps Norton. In 1865 Charles Norton, the father, was appointed by the embattled President Johnson Collector of Customs for the Port of Buffalo, which he held until his sudden death at forty-six in 1867.[11] His mother Lucretia died that same year at eighty-nine.

Porter Norton became a lawyer and built a mansion on Gates Circle. Charles Norton, born in 1858, graduated from Harvard in 1880, read law, and began to practice in 1885. Two years later, he began twenty-one years of teaching at the U.B. law school. He was elected vice-chancellor of the university in 1905 and chancellor in 1909. In these positions he enlarged the institution, building up the college of arts and sciences and the professional schools and securing a site on upper Main Street where these operations could be centralized. He died in 1922.[12]

10 *M&FH*, 1:75-79.
11 Smith, *op. cit.*, p. 26.
12 *Express*, July 13, 1923; "Charles Phelps Norton," *Who Was Who in America, 1897-1942* (Chicago: A. N. Marquis Co., 1942), p, 905.

Delaware between Chippewa and Tupper boasted two churches, Calvary Presbyterian and Delaware Avenue Methodist Episcopal. A First Congregational and Presbyterian Church Society was organized in 1812. Meetings were held in the courthouse, schoolhouses, and private homes, but any impulse to build a church was aborted by the War of 1812. In December 1815 the First Presbyterian Church was organized, and five years later received from Ellicott a triangular plot of land bounded by Main, Pearl, Church, and Niagara Streets.(6.9 #8) A frame building was erected in 1823, but four years later was replaced by a permanent brick structure which lasted until 1891 when the congregation moved to grander quarters on the Circle on Richmond Avenue. First Presbyterian was the mother of eight, the grandmother of two, and the great grandmother of one of the city's Presbyterian churches. [13]

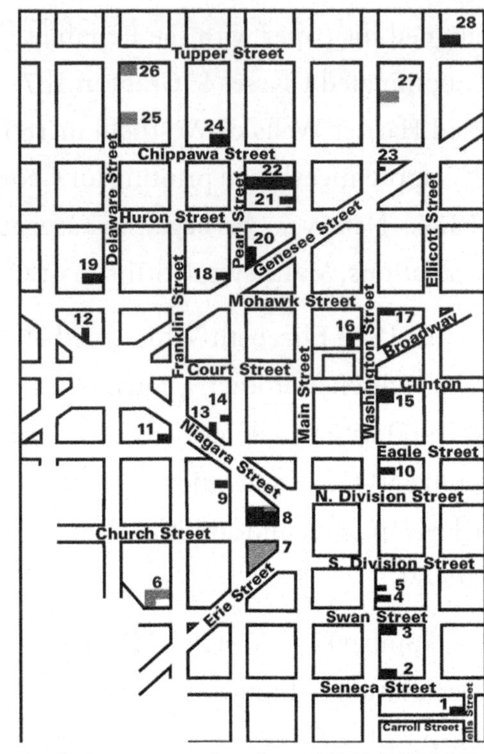

6.9 ❦ Downtown churches. *PBHS*, 16(1912), p. 104.

Central Presbyterian was organized by members of First Presbyterian in 1835 on the corner of Pearl and Genesee Streets.(6.9 #18) Later it moved to more commodious quarters but was still known as Central Presbyterian.(6.9 #20) Its members seem to have been Old Side Presbyterians, as opposed to the New Side members of First Church. The distinction went back to a split in the denomination in the eighteenth century, the New Side favoring enthusiastic revivals, the Old Side a more restrained approach to God. By the next century the terms were more a matter of emphasis rather than formal affiliation. [14] The first pastor of Central Presbyterian, Rev. John C. Lord, was Old Side. He was a forceful personality, and the church soon became known as Dr. Lord's Church. He hated revivals and denounced abolitionists, a rarity among his colleagues. [15] Calvary Presbyterian began with an 1854 exodus from Central. Lord's stand on slavery, a desire to enjoy the surroundings of a higher toned neighborhood, or a dispute over pew rents may have influenced the move. The new group called itself the Delaware Street Congregation and held services in Goodell Hall in Johnson Park.(5.8) The first minister was Rev. E. A. Huntington, followed in 1856-1857 by Rev. Everard Kempshall. For the next two years the congregation was without a minister and worshipped at North Presbyterian on Main below Chippewa, but the organization remained intact. By 1860 meetings were being held in a chapel erected by a wealthy member, George Palmer, on Delaware in the rear of the site of the future church. He was an iron monger, president of one of the railroads that merged into the Lake Shore &

13 Hill, op. cit., 1:576-583.
14 Ibid., 581; John Dall, "Presbyterianism," *Encyclopedia of Religion and Ethics* (New York: Charles Scribner's Sons, 1962), 10:196.
15 Horton, *op. cit.*, 1:127-128.

Michigan Southern, and a founder of Marine Bank. Functioning in lieu of a regular pastor from 1860 to 1866 were Rev. V. D. Reed and Rev. A. T. Chester. Reed lived with William Ketchum at #109 Delaware and listed himself in the census of 1860 as "OSP minister," ("Old Side Presbyterian minister.") Chester was principal of the Female Academy. A full-time pastor was Scottish-born Alexander McLean whose term lasted from 1866 to 1874. At this time Palmer at his own expense built a large gothic church costing $85,000 which was dedicated in 1872.(6.9 #25) The architect was John H. Selkirk. Palmer also built a parsonage at #327 which housed McLean and his successors at least until 1910.

George W. Fisher who had acted in lieu of a pastor during the church's final years told the story of its demise in 1931:

> It's a rather sad thing to see the beautiful church, once surrounded by beautiful residences, being left isolated by the encroachment of business houses. During the closing years of the last century and the first 15 of the present one, Calvary was strong and prosperous and a leading church in Buffalo. The Sunday school under the leadership of Marc W. Comstock grew to an enrollment of more than 600 pupils. Arthur McArthur established a Sunday school library. Missionary zeal led to the establishment of Lebanon church, Northampton street, and Bethany church, later merged with Bethesda and Bethlehem.
>
> But progress was halted about 15 years ago and the church slowly began to retrogress as members moved one by one from the crowded city section to the residential districts. Now there are but a handful of loyal members attending this large and historic church, which has an 800 seating capacity, plenty of Sunday school space, and equipment for social or welfare work.
>
> Every arrangement has been made to perpetuate the fine name and reputation of Calvary church. As soon as the building in Delaware avenue can be sold, the name and funds will be transferred to the Parkside United Presbyterian Church on Parkside avenue near Hertel. Deeds have been signed, approval given, and as soon as the downtown church is sold, the name will be moved out North Park way. Parkside United Presbyterian Church is growing rapidly in a thriving community. Already it is over crowded, especially in the Sunday school where it is necessary to hold three classes daily to accommodate everybody. That's where we plan to spend some of the funds from the sale of the old church in building Sunday school additions. [16]

Delaware Avenue Methodist and Calvary shared a somewhat similar history. The earliest local Methodist churches were: on Niagara between Pearl and Franklin founded in 1819(6.9 #13), Grace Church on Swan and Michigan founded about 1840, and Asbury on the northwest corner of Chippewa and Pearl.(6.9 #24) [17]

> Meanwhile in 1870, a group of Methodists, many of whom had been connected with Grace Church, moved uptown from the Swan Street section, which was gradually losing favor as a residential district. Under the leadership of Mr. Francis H. Root, property was purchased at the corner of Delaware Avenue and Tupper Street. Many people thought that the location was altogether too far out from the center of the city to prosper. Bishop

16 *Times*, July 11, 1931.
17 Hill, *op. cit.*, 2:595-597.

6.10 ❦ **Delaware Avenue Methodist Episcopal Church.** *Express*, May 16, 1886.

Simpson looked carefully into the whole matter, and decided that a church there would be a success.

The plans for the new church were by far the most pretentious that Buffalo Methodism had yet seen. The plans for the building were drawn by John H. Selkirk, one of the most celebrated architects of Buffalo. The style of architecture is Gothic.(6.10) The material is Medina sandstone, with Connecticut stone for trimmings. The interior finish is plain, but of fine workmanship and of the most beautiful material. The altar and the trimmings of both wainscotting and pews are of solid rosewood. The windows, while filled with rather plain glass, show a delicate and varied tracery. Back of the church is the chapel, containing in addition to the chapel proper, a large parlor, the pastor's study, the church offices, and rooms for various classes and departments of the Sunday school. The chapel was the first unit built, being completed in 1871.

Within three years the rapidly growing congregation was ready to proceed with the building of the church itself which was dedicated in 1876 by Bishop Simpson, who had had such a large part in the founding of the church. [18]

The most prominent pastor of Delaware Avenue Methodist, James Whitford Bashford, served there only two years. Born in Fayette, Wisconsin, 1849, he received an A.B. from Wisconsin in 1873, an A.M. from there in 1876, an S.T.B. in oratory from Boston University in 1876, and a Ph.D. in 1881. He was ordained in 1878 and held pastorates at Jamaica Plain, and Auburndale, Massachusetts, Portland, Maine, and finally in Buffalo 1887-1889. Thereafter he began fifteen years as president of Ohio Wesleyan. Finally he became bishop of China and was the author of numerous published sermons and lectures and several books. [19]

The status of lower Delaware posed a problem for Buffalo's Methodists as it had for other Protestant sects:

> By 1910 both Ashbury [*sic*] and Delaware Avenue Church began to be seriously affected by the up-town tide of population. [Asbury had featured evangelical fervor, Delaware distinguished, cultural preaching.] A large proportion of the membership of both churches now lived miles from their place of worship, and other churches were face to face with the problem of decreased financial support and a floating constituency. The usual method when such a problem confronts a congregation is to sell the downtown property, now become valuable, for a large sum, move out into the residential section, and with the proceeds of the sale put up a handsome church building. The Asbury and Delaware churches resolved to take a different course. They said, "Why not unite our forces, take the magnificent Delaware Avenue property for our church home, sell the Asbury property, so desirable for business purposes, hold the principal of the sale intact, using only the income to help in the maintenance of a strong downtown church." This was done. The two congregations were legally merged under the incorporated name of the "Asbury Delaware Methodist Episcopal Church of Buffalo." In July of 1917 the Asbury congregation

18 *Times*, November 15, 1924.
19 "James Whitford Bashford," *Who Was Who, 1897-1942*, p. 66.

6.11 ❦ **Delaware Avenue north of Chippewa before and after the Elms were cut down and the avenue widened.** ***Truth*, October 31, 1925.**

> left the old church at the corner of Chippewa and Pearl and united with the Delaware Avenue congregation, thereby assuring for all time, as far as human foresight can judge, that there will be a strong aggressive church in the downtown section represented by the lower Delaware Avenue territory.[20]

Methodists would remain at Delaware and Tupper for many more years. During the 1920s nearly twenty church-connected groups met regularly in the parish's ample meeting rooms. "A splendid parsonage" was acquired at #501 Delaware. In 1944 in an exercise of defensive buying the church acquired #339 Delaware, formerly the office and residence of Doctor John A. Coakley. But decline continued, and the church disbanded in 1989.[21]

Figure 6.11 contains two views of this block before and after the Avenue had been widened and the trees cut down. The first steeple visible after the removal is Calvary Presbyterian whose congregation would soon be departing for North Buffalo. The second steeple was that of the Methodist Church on Tupper.

1860

WEST CHIPPEWA STREET

[240] John S. Ganson 57 NY
president NY & Erie Bank
Sophrona Ganson NY 55 *ux*
James Sweeney 27 NY cashier
Kate Sweeney 24 NY
Helen S. Ganson 18 NY
Margaret McCall 22 Ireland
Mary Kele 20 Baden
Frances Kele 21 Baden
Lawrence Smith 27 Germany
Sarah Smith 25 Ireland
Mary Smith 4 NY
Baby Smith 2 months

1870

WEST CHIPPEWA STREET

240 Buffalo Club

20 *Times., ibid.*

21 *Ibid; CE*, May 14, 1944; James Napora, Houses of Worship: A guide to the religious architecture of Buffalo, New York , M.A. thesis submitted to the faculty of the State University of New York at Buffalo, 1995, p. 42.

100 [256] Sherman S. Jewett 52 NY
Jewett & Root stoves
Deborah Jewett 35 NY *ux.*
Henry C. Jewett 19 NY clerk
Josiah Jewett 17 NY
Emma Jewett 16 NY
Jenny Jewett 11 NY
Sherman Jewett 5 months NY
Mary Greenan 24 NY
Ann McGovern 16 Canada nurse
Anna Munchen 22 Hesse-Cassel
Edward Hanson 20 England coachman

102 [262] John H. Ganson 41 NY attorney
18 Spaulding's Exchange
Mary S. Ganson 37 NY *ux.*
Emily Ganson 7 NY
Mary Ganson 3 NY
Catherine Quinlan 50 Scotland
Jennie Quinlan 27 Scotland
Agnes Quinlan 19 Scotland

104 John C. Sibley 29 NY attorney
Mary G. Sibley 29 NY *ux.*
Mark H. Sibley 2 NY
Ellen Parker 28 Scotland

106 [274] Henry Lansing 42 NY treasurer
Lake Shore & Michigan Southern RR
Catherine O. Lansing 40 NY *ux.*
Henry G. Lansing 20 NY clerk
Livingston Lansing 18 NY
Charles M. Lansing 16 NY
Sarah Lansing 14 NY
Walter S. Lansing 9 NY
Elizabeth McManus 17 Ireland
Mary Feeney 30 Ireland cook
Elizabeth Conway 20 Ireland cook
Valentine Wolf 27 France coachman

JOHNSON PLACE ❦ End of Block

[284] Buffalo Female Academy

PARK PLACE ❦ End of Block

256 Sherman S. Jewett 62 NY iron
founder
Deborah Jewett 48 NY *ux.*
Anna Haven 14 NY school
Caroline Meyers 32 Prussia
Jane Neathercot 34 England

262 John H. Ganson 51 NY attorney
Mary Ganson 47 NY *ux.*
Emily Ganson 17 NY
Mark K. Sibley 12 NY school
Mariah H. Sibley 65 NY boarder
Catherine Quinlan 60 Scotland
Agnes Quinlan 35 Canada West
Sarah Crosley 55 England
Mary Walsh 50 Ireland

274 Henry Lansing 52 NY treasurer
Lake Shore & Michigan Southern RR
Catherine Lansing 50 NY *ux.*
Livingston Lansing 27 NY law student
Grace C. Lansing 26 NY
Charles M. Lansing 26 NY
Eliza G. Lansing 31 NY boarder
Henry L. Lansing 11 months NY
Francis Lynch 30 Ireland coachman
Frances Lynch 30 Ireland
Ellen Gillen 28 Ireland
Bridget Henson 28 Ireland
Hettie Schultz 24 Switzerland
Albertine Leak 15 Bavaria
Mary White 45 England
Kate Kelley 21 Ireland nurse

JOHNSON PLACE ❦ End of Block

284 Albert T. Chester 57 Conn.
principal of Buffalo Female Academy
Elizabeth Chester 55 Conn. *ux.*
Walter T. Chester 28 NY editor daily paper
Catherine Chester 19 NY
Ellen Chester 17 NY school
Walworth Chester 12 NY school

George W. Jones 44 Pa. Janitor
Susan Jones 35 Ireland *ux.*
Sarah L. Jones 7 NY school
Mary Jones 5 NY
Theresa Jones 2 NY
George Jones 4 NY
Minerva Havens 45 NY boarder

PARK PLACE ❦ End of Block

1 Park Place [300] Bronson C. Rumsey 37 NY leather dealer
Evelyn Rumsey 37 NY *ux.*
Laurence Rumsey 11 NY
Mary L. Rumsey 9 NY
Evelyn Rumsey 5 NY
Panthea Hall 55 NY
Sarah Forbes 31 Michigan
Louisa Forbes 14 NY
Rose Meyers 33 Germany
Philopen France 22
William Horton 25 England coachman

304 Henry C. Winslow 30 Ohio grain dealer
Josephine Winslow 25 NY *ux.*
Kate Winslow 5 NY
Howard Winslow 3 NY
Mary Winslow 1 NY
Josephine Winslow 11 months NY
Eliza Baltz 33 Bavaria
Joanna *illeg.* 20 Ireland
Eliza Burns 38 Ireland

130 [314] Henry W. Rogers 54 NY attorney Rogers & Bowen
Kezia Rogers 49 Conn. *ux.*
Ellicott Evans 42 NY language teacher
Jennie Evans 24 NY
Martha Evans 18 NY
Julia Evans 18 NY
Margaret Lutz 25 Baden
Margaret Grisell 18 Ireland
Magdelene Rhein 16 Bavaria

TRACY STREET ❦ End of Block

TRACY STREET ❦ End of Block

330 Bronson Case Rumsey 45 NY leather
Evelyn Rumsey 42 NY *ux.*
Mary Rumsey 19 NY
Bronson Rumsey 16 NY school
Evelyn Rumsey 15 NY school
Bridget Maddigan 22 Ireland
Louisa Weinman 21 Wurtemberg
Emma Gumpert 20 Switzerland
Belle Campbell 20 Canada West
Mary Quinn 40 Ireland
Maggie Graham Ireland

156 [334] Silas H. Fish 40 Conn. Fish & Avery commission merchants
Emily Fish 35 NY *ux.*
Henry H. Fish 17 NY
Edmund Fish 15 NY
Julia A. Fish 2 NY
Mary J. Fish 2 months
Mary Morgan 20 Canada
Margaret O'Connor 8 Ireland
Marcia Madden 20 Ireland

334 Silas H. Fish 53 Conn. grain commission merchant
Emily A. Fish 49 Conn. *ux.*
Edmund P. Fish 25 NY life insurance agent
Mary Flynn 35 Ireland
Maggie Murphy 21 Ireland

158 [340] Christopher L. Avery 34 Conn. Fish & Avery produce
Sarah E. Avery 30 NY *ux.*
Latham Avery 7 NY
Mary L. Avery 5 NY
Bessie W. Avery 2 months NY
Helen Fox 19 NY
Mary Bamberg 25 Bavaria
Ann Kennedy 15 Ireland nurse

340 George Truscott 443 England file manager
Sarah Trucott 40 NY *ux.*
Grace Truscott 17 NY school
Lovering Truscott 13 NY school
Fred Truscott 7 NY school
Jane Saunders 22 England
Charlotte Phillips 24 England
Mary Mahar 25 Ireland

WEST TUPPER STREET ❦ End of Block

344 Samuel K. Worthington 47 NY grain commission merchant
Rachael W. Worthington 35 Ohio *ux*
Robert Worthington 13 NY school
Arthur Worthington 12 NY school
Florence Worthington 10 NY school
Louise Worthington 8 NY school
Ann Livintston 31 Scotland
Rachael Cowden 25 Ireland
Elizabeth Cowden 20 Ireland

WEST TUPPER STREET ❦ End of Block

1880

WEST CHIPPEWA STREET

240 Buffalo Club

256 Sherman S. Jewett 62 NY stove manufacturer
Deborah Jewett 58 NY *ux*
Henry C. Jewett 32 NY stove manufacturer
Lucy Jewett 32 NY his *ux*
Mary Gorman 38 Ireland
Minnie McDuff 21 NY
Louis White (negro)

262 Mary S. Ganson 58 NY
Emily Ganson 28 NY daughter
Catherine Quinlan 65 Scotland
Agnes Quinlan 45 Scotland
Sarah Crosley 65 England
Mary Barnall 26 Ireland

274 Henry M. Kent 56 NH Flynt & Kent dry goods
Harriett Kent 48 Maine *ux*
Charlotte Kent 16 Maine daughter school
Nora Kent 12 NY school
Adelaide Bain 40 West Indies
Emily Gallop 32 England

JOHNSON PLACE ❦ End of Block

284 Buffalo Female Academy
Albert T. Chester 54 NY principal
Cordelia Chester 54 NY *ux.*
Kittie Chester 25 NY daughter teacher
Nellie Chester 27 NY daughter teacher
Sallie O'Brien 40 Ireland
Ellen Doyle 30 Ireland
Annie Shannon 21 Illinois
Elizabeth Armstrong 28 Ireland

George W. Jones 58 NY janitor
Susan Jones 44 Ireland *ux.*
George W. Jones 6 NY son

PARK PLACE ❦ End of Block

1891

WEST CHIPPEWA STREET

240 Francis Root Keating

256 Sherman S. Jewett S. S. Jewett & Co. stoves president Bank of Buffalo

262 Mrs. John Ganson

JOHNSON PLACE ❦ End of Block

284 Buffalo Female Academy
Mrs. Charles L. Hartt principal
F. L. Ansley teacher
A. L. Linde

PARK PLACE ❦ End of Block

1	Park Place [300 Delaware] Laurence D. Rumsey 30 NY leather merchant Jennie Cary Rumsey 25 NY *ux.* Evelyn Rumsey 2 NY daughter Charles Cary Rumsey 2 months NY son Anna Morgan 22 NY Mary Carroll 28 Ireland Ellen Kearns 32 Ireland	300	Laurence Dana Rumsey
304	Washington Bullard 55 NY manager Union Steamboat Line Fidelia Bullard 51 NY *ux.* Paul W. Bullard 18 NY son school Kate Cody 32 Ireland Mary Toher 28 Ireland Kate Downey 17 Ireland	304	N. Howard Winslow Lehigh Valley Transportation Co. Mrs. Henry C. Winslow Joseph W. Winslow Kate W. Winslow Loren C. Winslow
314	Arthur Cleveland Coxe 62 NJ Episcopal bishop Catherine Coxe 59 NY *ux.* Reginald Coxe 25 Maryland son art student Hanson Coxe 21 Maryland son college student Martha Williams 62 NY Mary Jutter 24 Wisconsin	314	Arthur Cleveland Coxe Episcopal bishop of WNY
	TRACY STREET ❦ End of Block		TRACY STREET ❦ End of Block
330	Bronson Case Rumsey 56 NY leather dealer Evelyn Rumsey 51 Michigan *ux.* Bridget O'Brien 40 NY Jane Bowen 15 NY Mary Quinn 46 Ireland Abby Barrett 44 Ireland Kate Powers 18 NY	330	Bronson C. Rumsey Aaron Rumsey & Co. leather dealers 78 Erie St.
334	Edward H. Movius 31 Michigan attorney Mary L. Movius 28 NY *ux.* Evelyn H. Movius 2 NY Julia Strachan 18 NY Elizabeth Boltz 46 Hesse-Darmstadt Anna Specisz NY	334	Edward H. Movius attorney Allen Movius & Wilcox 39 White Bldg.
340	George Truscott 54 England water commissioner Sarah Truscott 51 Michigan *ux.* Frederick Truscott 17 NY son school Sarah Truscott 23 NY daughter Bridget Cronin 26 NY Maggie Kane 23 NY	340	Charles Cary MD
344	Samuel K. Worthington 57 NY grain merchant Rachael Worthington 43 Ohio *ux.* Robert H. Worthington 23 NY son law student Florence Worthington 20 NY daughter Louise Worthington 18 NY daughter school S. Frances Worthington 13 NY daughter school Edith Worthington 8 NY daughter Maggie Leonard 26 Ireland Mary Davis 17 Ireland	344	Samuel K. Worthington water commissioner coal 5 Hayen Bldg
348	Henry Richmond 45 NY lithographer Mary Duffy 58 Ireland housekeeper	348	Henry A. Richmond lithographer 61 Carroll
	WEST TUPPER STREET ❦ End of Block		WEST TUPPER STREET ❦ End of Block

1905

WEST CHIPPEWA STREET

256 Frank X. Lambrecht livery stable proprietor
Elizabeth Lambrecht 42 *ux.*
Alice Lambrecht 19 daughter
Margaret Hay 72 mother-in-law
18 roomers
3 employees

262 *Hotel Touraine* Annex
48 residents

274 *Hotel Touraine*
83 residents

JOHNSON'S PARK ❦ End of Block

284 Delia McCann 35 proprietor
Mary McCann 40 sister
13 roomers
5 employees

JOHNSON'S PARK ❦ End of Block

304 Miss Cordelia Burtis proprietor
Emma B. Terry 58 sister
4 roomers

314 William D. Walker Episcopal bishop

TRACY STREET ❦ End of Block

330 Laurence D. Rumsey 56
Jennie Cary Rumsey 51 *ux.*
Charles Cary Rumsey 24 son
Grace Rumsey 21 daughter
Laurence D. Rumsey Jr 19 son college
Ellie Davis 28 England maid
Bridget O'Brian 58 maid

340 Charles Cary 52 MD
Evelyn Rumsey Cary 49 *ux.*
Sarah Holleran 36
Kate Collins 58 Ireland
Annie Sullivan 23 Ireland
Mary McDermott 45

1915

WEST CHIPPEWA STREET

256 Henry Betts 65
Mary A. Betts 53 *ux.*
Lenora Betts 18 daughter
Loretta Hawthorne 31 daughter
Henry N. Hawthorne 9 grandson school
3 lodgers

Robert B. Morris 36 salesman
Irene Morris 30 *ux.*
Vera Morris 10 daughter school
Mary A. Morris 7 school
Ethel Morris 4

262 *Hotel Touraine* Annex
69 residents

274 *Hotel Touraine*
36 residents

JOHNSON'S PARK SOUTH ❦ End of Block

284 Apartment house
33 residents

JOHNSON'S PARK NORTH ❦ End of Block

304 Rooming house
15 residents

TRACY STREET ❦ End of Block

330 Laurence D. Rumsey 65 NY
Jennie Cary Rumsey 60 *ux.*
Laurence D. Rumsey Jr. 27 NY soldier
Maria Driscoll 39 Ireland
Rose Walters 35 England
Nora Concannon 28 Ireland
Nellie M. Kelly 23 Ireland

334 George B. Beals 53 rr superintendent
Mary Beals 46 *ux.*
Lillian Richardson 60
Bertha Dean 37

340 Charles Cary 62 MD
Evelyn Rumsey Cary 59 *ux.*
Gertrude Knottley 25 England
Mary Joyce 22 Ireland
Marian Morrison 28 Scotland
Sarah Dunn 56

344 Franklin Locke 60 attorney
Edward Mills 30 son-in-law attorney
Clara Mills 24 daughter
Elizabeth Mills 6 granddaughter
Sarah Mills 2 granddaughter
Bridget Bar 35 Ireland
Albertine Hoover 30 Germany nurse

348 Henry Richmond 64
Kate Hopper 44 Canada housekeeper
Margaret Hopper 18 daughter
Harry Hopper 17 son driver

WEST TUPPER STREET ❦ End of Block

344 Franklin D. Locke 72 attorney
Agnes Lynch 27 Ireland
Emma Dale 27

348 Neal Johnson 50 Norway tailor
Katherine L. Johnson 36 *ux.*
Mary Heyer 45 sister
Audrey E. Johnson daughter 2

WEST TUPPER STREET ❦ End of Block

6.12 ❦ #240 Delaware, *PBHS*, 16(1912), p. 404.

The two-story building with the curved corner in the left foreground of 6.11 is the Delaware Court Building erected in 1917 on the site of the house built by Philander Hodge in 1835, and occupied successively by Aaron Patchin, John S. Ganson, and the Buffalo Club. (6.12) Patchin was a orphan boy born in Hoosick, New York, who came to Buffalo in 1841 where he made good, for a time anyway, as a banker. As president of the Patchin Bank he was living on Delaware and Chippewa in 1844 and later became president of the Buffalo & New York Railroad, an Attica to Hornellsville line completed in 1852. It defaulted on its bonds in 1855, and the Patchin Bank also went under, probably in the depression following the Panic of 1857. Patchin's 1864 obituary lamented his "lack of success due to circumstances beyond his control" and "the struggles of his business life." [22] Anyway, he could no longer maintain a grand house on Delaware. His successor as early as 1855 was John S. Ganson, who had been born in LeRoy in December 1802, son of one of the earliest settlers of Western New York, Major John Ganson, an officer on General Sullivan's raid during the Revolution. Like others in that expedition the major liked what he saw, returned, and settled near Avon in 1790. At twelve his son, John S. Ganson, moved to Canandaigua to clerk in a dry goods store. He read law for a few months in the office of James Hosmer at Avon, but Blackstone bored him, so he headed for Batavia where he formed a partnership with John Foote, a storeowner, under the name Foote & Ganson. This venture did not last, since Ganson was soon engaged in winding up the affairs of the Holland Land Company whose main offices were in Batavia.

22 Dunn, E., *op. cit.*, pp. 16, 20; *CA*, July 29, 1864.

In 1832 when he was twenty, Ganson was appointed cashier of the Bank of Genesee in Batavia. Later he transferred to the Farmers & Mechanics Bank of Batavia. In 1850, with eighteen years of banking experience, Ganson came to Buffalo as cashier of the Bank of Buffalo, a position he held until 1856 when, now a major stockholder, he became president of the New York & Erie Bank. Now a wealthy man, he had invested in real estate, owned a block containing a planing mill, and was a large stockholder in the bridge completed across the gorge below the Falls in 1855. In 1860 Ganson, wife, Sophronia Sweeney Ganson, Helen, their eighteen year old daughter (who would marry William B. Depew, the father of Ganson Depew), their daughter Kate Ganson Sweeney, and her husband James Sweeney, who was a bank cashier, lived in the mansion. It was a big operation and required the services of three German and two Irish young women. After selling his home to the Buffalo Club in 1869 for $65,000 ($1,132,950 in 1997 dollars), Ganson moved to nearby Johnson Place where he died in 1875. The Panic of 1873 had struck the nation in September and Ganson's bank, a delayed casualty, failed in September 1875.[23]

Above 6.13 ❦ Francis Root Keating. *M&FH*, 2, facing p. 371.
Below 6.14 ❦ #256 and #262 Delaware Avenue. *PBHS*, 22(1918), np. #262 remodeled and the Hotel Touraine are to the right and in the rear is Hutch Tech.

From 1870 to 1887 #240 was the second home of the Buffalo Club. On the corner in 6.12 is a temporary lock-up for drunk and disorderly awaiting the police wagon. In 1887 the house was acquired by Francis Root Keating,(6.13) before it became a rooming house early in the twentieth century, and in 1917 the site of the Delaware Court Building. Keating was born in Buffalo in 1862, the son of Francis Keating, and graduated from Central High. Thereafter, he secured employment with Root & Keating, a leather company, with headquarters in Buffalo and tanneries in Olean. He soon became a partner in the firm, but retired after ten years to manage the implement department of the Buffalo Pitts Company of which he became a stockholder and trustee. In 1893 he married Grace, daughter of James Brayley, a founder of Pitts. Like Rufus Howard, his hobby was the military, and he spent fifteen years in the NYNG, rising to the staff of the commanding general of the signal corps. He died in 1901 at thirty-nine.[24]

23 *CA*, August 30, 1875; Warren, *op. cit.*, p. 21; E. Dunn, *op. cit.*, pp. 31-32; Horton, *op. cit.*, 1:554; Hill, *op. cit.*, 1:432.
24 *M&FH*, 2:371-372.

At #100 old style, #256 new (6.14), above John Ganson's, lived Sherman Skinner Jewett, having moved there in 1858 from East Swan Street. Grandfather Nathan Skinner from Rowley, Massachusetts, was killed during the Revolution at the battle of Long Island in August 1776. Nathan's great grandfather and family had migrated from Rowley, in Yorkshire, England, to Massachusetts in 1638, where they were among the founders of Rowley. Nathan's son Joseph was born in Lyme, Connecticut, and moved to Cayuga County, New York, in 1814. There in January 1818, Sherman Jewett was born.(6.15) His boyhood was spent on his father's farm, and winters he attended the district school. At sixteen he came to Buffalo where his uncle, Isaac Watts Skinner, owned a foundry where Sherman learned the iron moulder's trade. Beginning in 1836 he engaged a series of brief partnerships with other iron mongers until 1843 when he and Francis H. Root formed the firm of Jewett & Root which lasted thirty-five years. Finally in 1878 Sherman S. Jewett & Company was formed, composed of Sherman and his sons, Henry Clay and Josiah Jewett:[25]

6.15 **Sherman Skinner Jewett.** ***M&FH*, 2, facing p. 371.**

> Sherman Jewett helped organize the Bank of Buffalo and was president of it until 1892. One of the founders of the Manufacturers and Traders Bank, he was a director of it for more than thirty years as well as being a director of the Marine Bank for over twenty years. He was a director of the Columbia National Bank from its founding until his death and also a director of the Buffalo New York & Philadelphia Railroad and was its president in 1867. He fought for Buffalo harbor improvements, served on the Buffalo Common Council for three years, supported the Young Men's Association, helped found the Fine Arts Academy, and contributed liberally to Buffalo's Baptist churches.[26]

6.16 **Number 102 old style, #262 new.** ***PBHS*, 16(1912), 499.**

Jewett was president of the Buffalo Club in 1878 and a member of Saturn and Wanakah. He died in 1897. Within three years, a barber and his family were living in #256 which now housed nine families. It was demolished during World War I.

As can be seen from figure 6.16 north of Jewett's place was a dwelling celebrated by Kowsky:

> Another beautiful Gothic dwelling was that built at 262 by attorney John H. Ganson in 1866 [better 1850] as a double residence. Entrances to each house (the other half

25 *Ibid.*, 1:69-71.
26 Warren, *op. cit.*, p. 28.

> was owned by lawyer John Sibley) were on the sides; the street façade was given over to a series of tall windows fronted by lacey iron balconies. The delicate and strict lines of the house, the proportions, which paid a lingering debt to the Federal style, made it one of the most distinguished designs of the period. [27]

John H. Ganson and family lived in the south wing, old style #102, from about 1850 until his death. A cousin of John S., he was born in LeRoy in 1818. Educated at public schools and the LeRoy Academy, he graduated from Harvard in 1839, read law and was admitted to the bar in Canandaigua in 1846, but left that year for the brighter lights of Buffalo where he became a law partner of Ebenezer Spaulding for as long as Spaulding practiced. In 1860 Ganson resided at #102 with his wife, the former Mary Sibley, two daughters, and three domestics, all Scottish women. In the north end of the house at #104 lived Ganson's brother-in-law, John C. Sibley, his wife, and one son, Mark. The Sibleys had no servants so it would seem that they shared those of the Gansons. Ten years later both elder Sibleys had died, and Mark was being brought up by the Gansons. Ganson was a life-long Democrat who before the Civil War followed the state boss, Dean Richmond, in advocating free trade and opposing abolitionism. A handsome man, Ganson was elected to the state senate as a Democrat in 1862 and 1863 and to the Thirty-Eighth Congress, which sat 1863-1865. He was a War Democrat, supporting the Emancipation Proclamation in 1862 and breaking with Richmond who at the National Convention in 1864 endorsed George B. McClellan as candidate for president. Ganson feared that the general would not prosecute the war vigorously. After that, Ganson failed of renomination for Congress. His grandniece Mabel wrote of him:

> He was large and clean-shaven and knew things. I mean he knew about life. Even a child felt that. He looked with his heavy bones like noble hound. He was a friend of Lincoln's and sometimes his lawyer, and the family brought me up hearing the rumor that he would have been President had not — something, I've forgotten what. [28]

Mabel may have been anticipating her later experimentation with drugs, since she was born five years after her granduncle died. Ganson returned to Buffalo from Washington, cemented

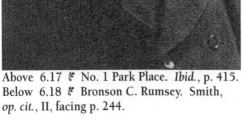

Above 6.17 ❦ No. 1 Park Place. *Ibid.*, p. 415.
Below 6.18 ❦ Bronson C. Rumsey. Smith, *op. cit.*, II, facing p. 244.

27 Kowsky , "Delaware Avenue," in *Grand American Avenue*, p. 41.
28 Luhan, *op. cit.*, p. 121.

his reputation as "the leading member of the Erie County bar," and died in 1874.[29] His widow lived on at #262 until the early 1890s, but by 1897 it had become a rooming house, *The Livingston,* with fourteen residents. Remodeled #262 can be espied on the right of figure 6.14. Mary Ganson, the ex-congressman's widow, died 1906.

The north part of #274, the Lansing-Kent home directly above the Ganson mansion, is depicted in figure 5.9. It became the site of the *Hotel Touraine.* By 1905 *The Livingston* had been demolished and replaced with the four-story *Touraine* Annex. At #1 Park Place where it joins Delaware was the rambling residence(6.17) from 1850 to 1862 of Bronson Rumsey(6.18) and from 1862 to 1902 of his son Laurence Rumsey(5.29) and his wife Jennie Cary. Since the Rumseys and their in-laws were socially prominent on the Avenue in its glory days (the Carys and the Rumseys have been called the Lowells and the Cabots of Buffalo),[30] a genealogy of the clan is provided through four generations of those with Avenue connections.(6.19)

1st Generation

Aaron Rumsey 1797-1844 m.1819 Sophia Phelps 1796-1870

2nd Generation Issue of Aaron Rumsey & Sophia Phelps #672 Del.

Bronson Case Rumsey I 1823-1902 m.1848 Eveline Hall 1822-1900

Dexter Phelps Rumsey 1827-1906 m. Mary Coburn +1859
Mary Bissell 1839-1884
Susan Fiske 1857-1941

3rd Generation Issue of Bronson C. Rumsey I & Eveline Hall #300 #330 Del.

Laurence Dana Rumsey 1849-1917 m. 1876 Jennie Cary 1854-1943

Mary Lovering Rumsey 1851-1948 m.1877 Edward H. Movius 1848-1917

Bronson (Bert) Rumsey II 1854-1946 m. Mary Coxe
Elizabeth Lockwood
Edna Lewis 1885-1974

Evelyn Rumsey 1855-1924 m.1879 Charles Cary 1852-1931

3rd Generation Issue of Dexter Phelps Rumsey & Mary Coburn #742

Cornelia Coburn Rumsey 1854-1880 m.1878
Ansley Wilcox 1856-1930

Mary Grace Rumsey 1855-1933 m.1883

3rd Generation Issue of Dexter Phelps Rumsey & Susan Fiske #742

Ruth Rumsey 1891-1977 m.1914 William Donovan 1883-1959

Dexter P. Rumsey Jr. 1893-1966 m.1916 Margaret A. Ramsdell 1895-1975

4th Generation Issue of Laurence Dana Rumsey & Jennie Cary #300 #330

Evelyn Rumsey 1877-1961 m.1932 Rev. Walter R. Lord 1873-1952

Charles Cary Rumsey 1878-1922 m.1910 Mary Harriman 1881-1934

Gertrude Rumsey 1880- m. Carlton Smith +1925

Grace Rumsey 1883-1963 m.1908 Charles W. Goodyear Jr. 1883-1967

Laurence Dana Rumsey, Jr. 1885-1967

4th Generation Issue of Bronson (Bert) Rumsey II & Mary Coxe #132 W. Tupper #133 Chapin

Bronson (Bob) Case Rumsey III m.1928 Elizabeth Beckwith Lynch

Mildred Cleveland Rumsey 1879-1940 m. Arthur C. Hawes

Dexter Cleveland Rumsey

4th Generation Issue of Bronson (Bert) Rumsey & Elizabeth Lockwood #132 W. Tupper #133 Chapin

Rosamonde Rumsey +5/24/1966

Daniel Lockwood Rumsey 1900-1956 m. Luella Hitterdeur

Sarah Rumsey m. Edward B. Archbald

Polly Rumsey m Milton G. Wolfe

4th Generation Issue of Mary L. Rumsey & Edward H. Movius #334

Evelyn Hallam Movius 1878-1952 m. James Parker Hall

Hallam Leonard Movius 1880-1942

4th Generation Issue of Cornelia Rumsey & Ansley Wilcox #641

Nina Wilcox +1968 m. (1) Putnam (2) Henry Adsit Bull

4th Generation Issue of Mary Grace Rumsey & Ansley Wilcox #641

Frances Wilcox m. Thomas F. Cooke

4th Generation Issue of Ruth Rumsey & William Donovan #742

David Donovan 1915- m. 1939 Mary Grandin

Patricia Donovan 1918-1941

4th Generation Issue of Dexter Rumsey Jr. & Margaret A. Ramsdell #742

Dexter P. Rumsey III 1917-1980 m. Kathryn H. Skinner 1915-1978

Douglas Rumsey

Donald Scott Rumsey 1923-1990

Margaret Rumsey m. Milton Mugler

6.19 ❦ Rumsey Genealogy.

The home (6.20) of Aaron,(6.21) progenitor of the Buffalo Rumseys, was on the northwest corner of Delaware and North, and that of his younger son, Dexter Phelps Rumsey(6.22), a block north on the southwest corner of Delaware and Summer.(6.23) When they were built in the 1850s they were both way up the Avenue. Nevertheless, geography must yield to genealogy, and these two residences and their owners will be discussed ahead of Rumsey Park on Delaware and Tracy.

Aaron Rumsey was born in Hubbardstown, Vermont, in 1797. His brother Calvin had left home and settled in Warsaw where he set up and operated a tannery. Aaron walked all the way across the state to join him. In Warsaw Aaron married Sophia Phelps in 1819. They had two sons, Bronson Case, born in 1823, in Warsaw, and Dexter Phelps, born in 1827 in Westfield. The family came to Buffalo in 1832 and lived on the west side of Ellicott north of Seneca. By now Aaron had built several tanneries throughout Western New York. Of this industry Walter Dunn writes: "Railroads had made

29 *CA*, September 28, 1874; *Biographical Directory of Congress*, p. 1041.

30 And this is good old Boston, The land of the bean and the cod, Where the Lowells speak only to the Cabots, And the Cabots speak only to God. John C. Bossidy, Toast, Holy Cross Alumni Dinner, 1901.

Above Left 6.20 ❦ *PBHS*, 16(1912), 424..
Middle 6.21 ❦ Aaron Rumsey. White, *op. cit.*, I, facing p. 240.
Below 6.22 ❦ Hill, *op. cit.*, III, facing p. 31.
Above Right 6.23 ❦ Dexter Phelps Rumsey house, southwest corner of Summer & Delaware, BHS.

Buffalo a cattle mart as well [as a milling center], a fact taken advantage of by Jacob Dold and Christian Klink to set up packing firms. ...Slaughter of animals inevitably set tanneries going, George Palmer's and Aaron Rumsey's among the earliest:"

> Hides shipped down Lake Erie from the West sold cheap in the Buffalo market. Heavy stands of hemlock in the vicinity provided cheap bark. As a consequence tanneries multiplied, the manufacture of leather throve. By 1835 at least every town in the county [Erie] had a tannery, some two or three. Notable were those in [East] Aurora and Holland built by Aaron Rumsey in 1843 and 1850; notable also the one opened in 1849 in Lancaster by Myron P. Bush and George Howard. Less extensive was Jacob Schoellkopf's Hamburg tannery of 1843; but Schoellkopf's enterprise was not limited to Hamburg. Like Howard, Bush and Rumsey, he developed his most ambitious concerns in Buffalo, where by the middle fifties about a dozen tanneries fumed profitably, representing a capital of $1,000,000 and employing about 500 workmen, the auspicious start of an industry that would expand to large proportions in the years to come.[31]

In 1838 Rumsey took on as a partner George Howard. The result was Rumsey & Howard; in 1842 Howard left and formed a partnership with John Bush, forming Bush & Howard. In 1847 Aaron took on his sons, Bronson and Dexter, who had been clerking for him, as partners in Aaron

31 Dunn, W. *op, cit.*, p. 21; Horton, *op. cit.*, 1197-1198.

Rumsey & Company. Its Buffalo operation was on Exchange Street across from the Central Station. [32]

From Ellicott Street Aaron moved in 1853 to #53 East Swan, since Ellicott, Washington, and Exchange Streets were going commercial. Swan at the time was judged a desirable residential location, but it too was succumbing to commercialization, and Aaron moved again, this time two and a half miles north to Delaware and North. In 1856 he bought "a large tract of land between what is now North and Summer Streets, facing and extending west from Delaware Avenue," upon which he built the red-brick mansion into which he moved in 1856. The barn matched the main house and the glass conservatory on North was the most unique structure ever seen by most Buffalonians. The land purchase was not merely for a home. Aaron was investing his profits in real estate around the city. With its rapid growth during the nineteenth and early twentieth century (2.1), his heirs would be most grateful for his choice. He died in 1864, and his widow in 1870. Aaron's younger son Dexter, who *circa* 1852 had married Mary, the daughter of his landlady, lived after his marriage in his father's former house on Swan Street. In 1857 he built a house on the southwest corner of Delaware and Summer, the northeastern most point of the tract his father had bought in 1856. In 1954, the *Courier-Express* featured a history of this house:

> Probably the oldest house in Delaware Ave. is the yellow brick mansion of Gothic architecture at the southwest corner of the avenue and Summer St., owned and occupied since 1945 by the University Post No. 2647, Veterans of Foreign Wars.
>
> For 88 years — from 1857 to 1945 — that was the home of the late Dexter P. Rumsey I, his widow, their children and grandchildren. During that period, its gracious hospitality was known and appreciated not only here but internationally. Guests it sheltered included eminent statesmen, writers, concert artists and leaders in important women's and girls' organizations such as women's suffrage and Girl Scouts of America.
>
> Incredible as it seems, this mansion began its existence nearly a century and a quarter ago, as a two-room bungalow. Erected for Capt. Allen back in the 1830s it was built to last. The substantial beams supporting the original ceiling are admired today. The Rose brothers [architectural gardeners], second owners of the property, enlarged the cottage into a story-and-a-half farmhouse. In their day, this house, now centrally located, was in the country, well beyond the North St. burying ground which marked Buffalo's northern city line for decades. [Better: from 1832 to 1853.(1.8)] It is believed that the Rose brothers built on the property the small house at 148 Summer St. now occupied by Douglas Rumsey, grandson of the late Dexter P.
>
> In the [18]50s and 60s, the late Dexter P. Rumsey kept cows. He pastured them and let his spirited horses graze on land occupied by the parking lot of Westminster Presbyterian Church. His ample stables now are that church's junior parish house.
>
> Yet Mr. Rumsey did not buy his house for a country home. Such was his faith in Buffalo's growth that he was certain he would see the city's expansion far beyond his house. Impelled by that faith, he bought extensive tracts of land, then woodland, in the vicinity of Delaware Park. After his death, the late Mrs. Rumsey gave the city seven acres between

33 *Times*, March 17, 1911.

Lincoln Pkwy and Rumsey Rd. now included in Delaware Park.

The house was enlarged, first by the late Dexter P. Rumsey, and later by his widow. It was one of the earliest Buffalo homes equipped with an elevator. The original elevator was operated manually, by means of ropes. For years after it ceased to be used, the pump that once supplied water for the house was left standing in the garden. A memento of former days, that pump graces the lawn of the home of Donald Rumsey, grandson of the late Dexter P.

6.24 ❦ D. P. Rumsey house, interior, circa 1920. BHS.

Most familiar to Buffalonians is the music room now occupied by the bar of the V.F.W. Post. Its floor and mantel of Italian design are of marble, while the white, marble-like walls are of Caenstone. The late Mrs. Dexter P. Rumsey added color to this white room with furniture upholstered in crimson brocade. In that music room, Gertrude Watson, Buffalo-born pianist, and the Coolidge quartet were heard. Probably the most famous concert artist to be a house guest in the mansion was the internationally known pianist Myra Hess.

The music room was made available by Mrs. Rumsey for meetings of several organizations and embryo movements. An early exponent of women's suffrage, she opened her home to groups furthering the cause. A frequent guest and close friend of Mrs. Rumsey was the late leader of the women's suffrage movement Carrie Chapman Cott. A director of the Girl Scouts of America, Mrs. Rumsey opened her home to early Girl Scout meetings. Juliet Lowe, founder of the organization, and other prominent Scout leaders knew the hospitality of the mansion. Margaret Sanger also visited Mrs. Rumsey in whose home some of the first birth control meetings were held.

For parties, including the debuts of Ruth Rumsey Donovan, daughter of the late Mr. and Mrs. Dexter P. Rumsey, their granddaughter Margaret (Mugler) and Susan Kimberly Warren, Mrs. Rumsey's niece, the orchestra was stationed in the conservatory off the music room, and young people danced from one to another of the beautiful first floor rooms.(6.24)

Perhaps the most unusual room of the house is the Gothic drawing room, now a banquet room of the post. The dark oak panels of its walls are carved to suggest a Gothic cathedral. Because of the late Dexter P. Rumsey's predilection for fishing, the fish motif is seen in every panel. As one enters the house, the Gothic drawing room is on the right, with the spacious dining room behind it. On the left is the library, one of the oldest rooms of the house, with the billiard room in its rear.

In addition to rooms mentioned, the first floor comprises a large kitchen, pantry, and a round tower room. Nearly every room in the house has an ample open fireplace to contribute to both warmth and an inviting aspect. Except for the library, now the VFW director's room, first floor rooms are dining rooms, with the drawing room used as a ballroom on occasion. Second story sleeping rooms, each with its own bath, now are offices or rooms for small private parties.

When members of the Rumsey family lived in the mansion, it was elegant with rich Oriental rugs, Chinese tapestries, Italian primitive paintings, gold candelabra and Italian and Spanish furniture carved and inlaid with rare artistry. Among objects of art from the old home treasured by Mr. and Mrs. Dexter P. Rumsey, Jr., is an ebony Spanish chest inlaid with ivory and tortoise shell. In addition to those mentioned, distinguished visitors in the house included Gilbert K. Chesterton, Katherine Cornell, Hugh Walpole, author; Alice Doerr Miller, poet; Marshal Badoglio of Italy, members of an Italian peace commission to the U.S., the pianist, Gabrilovich, and his wife, Sarah, daughter of Samuel Clemens, known and loved as Mark Twain; Mrs. Joyce Kilmer, widow of the poet; Vincent Sheehan, Dorothy Thompson, Sen. Bankhead, and several leaders of the Republican party.

While Mr. and Mrs. Dexter P. Rumsey, Jr., lived in the mansion, prominent guests included Joseph Grew, U.S. ambassador to Japan preceeding and until the Pearl Harbor attack and Congressman Walter G. Andrews with his entire Congressional Armed Services Committee.

The late Dexter P. Rumsey was identified with tanneries, real estate and banking in Western New York. He was president of the Buffalo Club and the wide range of his interests included business, civic activities, cultural and social organization. Mrs. Rumsey also was a leader for decades in civil, cultural and social activities, intensely interested in the development of her home city. She was a member of the City Planning Association. She was president of the Twentieth Century Club and the Chamber Music Society, a trustee of the University of Buffalo and a prominent supporter of the Albright Art Orchestra, Millard Fillmore Hospital and the League of Women Voters. [33]

After Aaron's death Bronson and Dexter took over his booming tanning and leather business, which they managed with continuing success until it was absorbed by the United States Leather Company. Thereafter, both brothers managed their investments from the former offices on Exchange Street. As can be seen from figure 6.19 Dexter was married three times. His first marriage to Mary Coburn ended with her death in 1859 but produced two children, Cornelia who married Ansley Wilcox in 1878 but died two years later, and Mary Grace, who married Ansley in 1883. Dexter's second marriage was to Mary Bissell, but seems to have been childless, and she died in 1886. His third wife, whom he married in 1889, was Susan Fiske, born in 1867, the daughter of Frank and Charlotte Hazard Fiske of #199 Delaware Avenue. Susan, who was thirty years younger than her husband, presented him with two children, Ruth Rumsey, born in 1891, and Dexter P. Rumsey, Jr., born in 1893. As mistress of #742 she outlived her husband by thirty-five years. She is the doyenne in the foregoing sketch, promoting the arts, music, women's suffrage, birth control, Girl Scouts, and other activities then popular with her class. [34]

On July 15, 1914, Ruth Rumsey took an unusual step for a Delaware Avenue girl. She married William Joseph Donovan(6.25), son of a first-generation Irish-American and sometime New York Central yardmaster. The Donovans lived on lower Michigan Avenue in the First Ward. In 1915 two of the three domestics at #742 were Irish-born Mary McMahon and Agnes Mahaney. By then the

33 *CE*, January 27, 1952.
34 *Times*, June 24, 1924; *Courier*, June 5, 1926.

6.25 ❦ William J. Donovan, looking very much the general. Donlop, *op. cit.*, facing title page.

Donovans had moved to Prospect Avenue where Tim Donovan, Bill's father, could be closer to Saint Joseph's Cathedral(3.3) where he had become secretary of Holy Cross Cemetery. After attending Saint Bridget's School, Saint Joseph's Collegiate Institute, and Nardin Academy, Bill enrolled in Niagara intending to study for the priesthood, but was dissuaded by a priest there, and transferred to Columbia from which he graduated in 1905, and from which he received a law degree in 1907. He began practice with a small firm in Buffalo; but in 1912 he and Bradley Goodyear, scion of a wealthy Delaware family, formed a partnership that merged with the city's leading law firm, O'Brian, Hamlin, Donovan & Goodyear. Donovan had successfully engineered a social switchover:

> The mansions of the well–to-do-and-privileged lined Delaware Avenue, and Donovan made every effort to win friends among them and gain access to their drawing rooms. Donovan, a strong oarsman, rowed for the Celtic Rowing Club, pride of the First Ward Irish, for which his father had once rowed, and on occasion he stroked the team to victory over a Canadian club in a 15-man war canoe event. Then Donovan changed his allegiance and became captain of a war canoe crew at the Buffalo Canoe Club at Crystal Beach, Ontario, some 25 miles away from Buffalo by road, but in plain sight of Buffalo's downtown towers across Lake Erie. The Buffalo Canoe Club, then and now a haunt of Buffalo's blue bloods, still keeps one of the old war canoes in its boathouse, although the club no longer enters a team in war events.

Like sports, the military was another access to the Avenue:

> Theodore Roosevelt had ridden to fame as a Rough Rider, and Bill Donovan was delighted to hear early in 1912 that the State of New York had decided to increase the cavalry units of the National Guard. When Col. Oliver B. Bridgman of the First Cavalry of the New York National Guard and Capt. Lincoln G. Andrews of the Second Cavalry, U.S. Army, called a meeting of interested young men from the Buffalo area at the University Club on Delaware Avenue, Donovan was among them. So were many other members of the Buffalo Canoe Club who, listening to Donovan's enthusiastic talk about military service had decided to come along. [35]

Donovan had never ridden a horse, but with his usual determination he rose early every morning and cantered through rain or sunshine along Humboldt Parkway, every day becoming surer of himself, until he could ride as well as any of the young aristocrats whom he had induced to sign on with Troop I. Evenings he studied cavalry tactics and strategy. His company elected him captain in October 1912, after their first encampment. In the summer of 1913 he organized a week's march

35 Richard Dunlop, Donovan, *America's Master Spy* (New York: Rand McNally & Company, 1982), pp. 27-28. My entire treatment of Donovan is based on this work.

from Buffalo to Orchard Park, Springville, Lake View, and back to Buffalo. Troop I was recognized as one of the top cavalry units in the state.

Donovan also spoke at Republican gatherings and attended amateur theatricals, an activity favored by the local gentry:

> There he met Ruth Rumsey, a tall girl with blue eyes who was counted among the most beautiful of Delaware Avenue's young women. The daughter of the city's first citizen, the late Dexter Rumsey, she had an air of assurance that might have been a trifle overpowering, except that it was lightened by a certain genial charm and wit. Being fond of riding and fox hunting, she had an outdoorswoman's complexion. Bill Donovan was drawn to this girl, who was not only beautiful but had both intellect and his zest for the active life. [36]

The Donovans, who would live apart much of their married life, lived with the Laurence Rumseys in 1915. Bill and Ruth had two children, David, born in 1915, and Patricia in 1917. Bill was called for duty on the Mexican border in 1916. Returning, he joined the Guard's "Fighting Irish" 69th Regiment which became the 165th Regiment in the Rainbow Division of the American Expeditionary Force during World War I. He was several times wounded and showed such leadership that he became a national hero under the sobriquet "Wild Bill," the antithesis of his character, and was decorated with the *Croix de Guerre*, the Distinguished Service Cross, the Bronze Oak Leaf Cluster to be worn with it, the Italian War Cross, and the highest American military decoration, the Congressional Medal of Honor. After the war, Ruth expected a return to a normal family life, but Bill left her in Tokyo on what was to have been a second honeymoon and set out to investigate conditions in Siberia, suggesting she wait for him in Japan. Frustrated, she returned to Buffalo and her children. In 1920 the Donovans resided with Ruth's mother at #742.

President Harding appointed Donovan U. S. District Attorney for Western New York in 1922. He was fierce in his prosecution of bootleggers, drug runners, and Mayor Frank Schwab, who continued to run a brewery. However Donovan's raids on the Saturn and the Country Clubs, which consisted in breaking into members' lockers searching for forbidden liquor and giving the press a list of the lawbreakers, which read like a *Who's Who* of Buffalo, permanently hurt his standing with both Delaware Avenue and the First Ward. "What kind of a man would raid his own club?" asked his erstwhile friend, Bradley Goodyear, who broke up their partnership and never spoke to Donovan again. Ruth's brother, Dexter Rumsey, II, explained that the raid was just what might be expected from a moralistic Irishman with no sense of the proprieties. Ruth never forgave Bill for embarrassing her family and friends. He seemed a traitor to the class he had so arduously sought to enter. Other enemies spread the story that he wasn't moralistic after all but a philanderer. When the gossip reached his wife, "her embarrassment and anger increased. She was left with a lasting wound when it became clear that there was more than a little truth to the rumors." [37]

36 *Ibid.*, p. 30.
37 *Ibid.*, p. 149-150.

In 1924 Donovan moved to Washington when he joined the Justice Department as assistant attorney general. He ran the Criminal Division for a year and the Anti-Trust Division until 1928. He had hoped to be appointed attorney general when Herbert Hoover became president, but did not get the job. Disappointed, he moved to New York and formed a law firm, Donovan, Leisure, Newton, Lumbard and Irvine. In October 1932 he received the Republican nomination for governor at the Broadway Armory. At a parade in support of his candidacy he received the greatest ovation in the city's history. The previous afternoon Ruth and Susan gave a tea at #742 for the convention delegates and stood two hours shaking hands. But 1932 was not a Republican year. Donovan lost, dragged down by Hoover's lackluster campaign and the Depression. After World War II broke out, Frank Knox, a Republican whom Roosevelt had made Secretary of the Navy, sent Donovan, now an ardent anglophile, to England to assess its survivability. But the Buffalo connection lasted as long as Susan Rumsey lived:

> Throughout these hectic years of public service and private law practice in Washington and New York, Donovan continued to think of himself as a Buffalonian. He gave the Buffalo Club as his voting address, and stayed there when he returned to the city without Ruth. "He had a room on the top floor," said Phil Impelliteri, the clubmanager. "He would have breakfast at the club and then be gone all day, return for dinner and then go for a long walk."
>
> Bill Donovan would walk up Delaware Avenue past the big Rumsey house, where he had courted Ruth, or down to the waterfront and the grain elevators that he had known as a boy. At Christmastime Ruth and Bill and their children would arrive in Buffalo for the holidays. They stayed in the house on Delaware Avenue, and there was much good cheer and singing around the piano. Then the children would return to school, Ruth would go back to New York, and Bill more often than not would go to Washington. [38]

The death of their daughter Patricia in an automobile accident in 1940 and of Susan at seventy-four in 1941, after which #742 was closed, changed even this. As Dunlop noted:

> Donovan had always liked his mother-in-law, but he had little time for grief. Since Patricia's death, he had given less and less time to his family. Now he scarcely saw Ruth, who stayed either in the New York duplex or on the Massachusetts coast. Even when Donovan found it necessary to go to Manhattan, he now occupied a suite that he kept at the St. Regis Hotel. [39]

After America had entered the war, Donovan planned with the assistance of British intelligence the Office of Strategic Services (OSS) to carry out research and analysis, sabotage, subversion, economic warfare, propaganda broadcasts, and commando operations. President Truman, ever ready to shoot from the hip, shut it down abruptly after the war, but Donovan's brainchild was the blueprint for the Central Intelligence Agency (CIA) in 1947. [40] His last mission was ambassador to Thailand at age seventy. Ill health forced him to retire after a year, but all was not lost:

38 *Ibid.*, p. 176.
39 *Ibid.*, p. 340.
40 Thomas F. Troy, "Donovan, William Joseph," *ANB*, 6:736-737.

6.26 ❦ Dexter Phelps Rumsey Jr., Wilner, *op. cit.*, IV, facing p. 130.

Ruth Donovan, who in these last years of Donovan's life had drawn close to him again, was with him in Bangkok, and he now showed her the courtly attention and concern that had never failed to win a woman. They enjoyed their time together and this was to remain so after their return to New York. [41]

Donovan had come a long way from the First Ward, though he went by way of Delaware Avenue to do it. A hero in two world wars, he died at Walter Reed Army Hospital in Washington on February 8, 1959, at seventy-six. He was buried at Arlington Cemetery, after a requiem mass at Saint Matthew's Cathedral celebrated by his brother, Rev. Vincent Donovan, O. P., a chaplain at Sing Sing. Ruth died at eighty-six in 1977.

Ruth's brother, Dexter Phelps Rumsey, II,(6.26) attended Nichols, Saint Marks in Southborough, Massachusetts, and Harvard from which he received a B.A. in 1915. He spent a year at U.B. law school, but war clouds made his future uncertain. With other area bluebloods, he had joined his brother-in-law's Troop I, now headquartered in the new armory on #1015 Delavan Avenue and in May 1916 married Margaret Adam Ramsdell, a expert horsewoman, daughter of a former publisher of the *Express* and niece of Robert B. Adam of #448 Delaware, president of AM&A's department store. On June 19 came orders for Troop I to join General John J. Pershing's expedition to the Mexican Border. President Wilson's meddling in Mexican politics to teach Mexicans "to elect good men" had produced a crisis at the very time the situation in war torn Europe was worsening.

Most units called to the border thought the experience tedious, but Captain Donovan put the elite of Buffalo, Dexter Rumsey, Jr., included, through their paces, with dismounted hikes, long horseback rides, and maneuvers. Troop I was recalled to Buffalo and mustered out in March 1917. There followed a civic celebration with Donovan and his men on horseback parading down Main Street while the crowds cheered. Afterwards, he provided the inevitable dinner for the officers at the Buffalo Club. [42]

Cavalry would not play a significant role for Americans in World War I. Troop I was converted into the 102nd Trench Mortar Battery, and Dexter Rumsey rose from first lieutenant to artillery captain in the 85th Division. After the war he entered the investment and security business. In 1926 he formed Dexter P. Rumsey & Company, real estate and insurance, a field he abandoned for banking in 1931. He became vice president of Erie County Savings Bank in 1940, president 1943-1960, and in

41 Dunlop, *ibid.*, p. 502.[A former associate remembered Donovan, a staunch anti-Communist to the end, lying on his bed in his Sutton Place apartment "looking out over Queensborough Bridge. His clouded mind imagined Russian tanks advancing over the bridge to take Manhattan." *Ibid.*, p. 506.]
42 *Ibid.*, pp. 44-47.

Above 6.27 ❦ #330 Delaware, (exterior), BHS.
Below 6.28 ❦ #330 Delaware, (interior), *ibid.* The figurine in the left lower corner is a miniature of *The Centaur* by Bronson C. Rumsey's sculptor grandson, Charles Cary Rumsey.

1960 chairman of the board, following his father, Dexter Rumsey, and his maternal grandfather, Frank Fiske. He was also president of the Forest Lawn Cemetery and Crematorium, a director of Marine Midland, and of AM&A's. His children were Dexter Phelps, III, Douglas, Donald, and Margaret. The oldest boy, born in 1918, graduated from the Berkshire School in Massachusetts and Rensselaer Polytechnic Institute. In the mid-1950s he and his wife, the former Kathryn S. Skinner, a Buffalo Seminary and Vassar girl, moved to Boothbay Harbor in Maine, where Dexter worked as a boat designer and builder. In the best tradition of the Rumseys, he was an avid sailor and skier, as well as an architect, pianist, and composer. He died in 1980 at sixty-three. His widow, an art fancier, had died two years earlier. During the 1920s and 1930s his father, Dexter Rumsey, Jr., lived at #60 Middlesex Road; later he moved to Faraway Farms on Old Lake Shore Road, Derby. He also resided for a time at Daytona Beach, Florida. Doctor Johnson would have called him "clubbable," belonging to the Buffalo, Buffalo Athletic, Buffalo Country, Wanakah, Saturn, Buffalo Yacht, Buffalo Tennis and Squash, and Harvard clubs. He died at Derby in 1966.[43]

Bronson, Aaron Rumsey's elder son, married Evelyn Hall in 1848, a year after he and Dexter had become partners in Aaron's tanning enterprise. The Bronson Rumseys had four children, Laurence Dana born in 1849, Mary Lovering born in 1851, Bronson (Bert) born in 1854, and Evelyn born in 1855. Two years after their marriage, Bronson and Evelyn moved into the house at #1 Park Place.(6.17) Grander quarters were soon to take shape:

> In the late [eighteen] fifties, a brick and lumber yard conducted by Hodge & Baldwin occupied many acres, beginning at Delaware and Tracy Place. A brook ran through the yard, where the feeding spring kept the water fresh and cold, and where brook trout once abounded. In 1861 the lumber yard disappeared. In its stead rose a stately mansion, and the little stream became a forest-bound lake, and far back behind the mansion was a sylvan scene of enchantment.[44]

43 *BEN*, April 25, 1980; Horton, *op. cit.*, 4:237; *BEN*, August 6, 1966; Wilner, *op. cit.*, 4:130-134.
44 *Times*, January 22, 1927.

In 1862 Bronson Senior completed the palatial vine-covered mansard-roofed mansion surrounded by extensive flower gardens and grape vines at what was to become #330 Delaware, his home for the rest of his life.(6.27, 28) Burr recalled:

> If one sweeps up the driveway under the broad port-cochere at the side, one enters a vestibule leading into the great hall, planned for splendid entertaining. On one side is the Gothic library, on the other the large dining-room; there are other rooms too, but life centers on the morning room with its side windows on the garden. One looks over the terrace into the shrubberies and winding paths, and before Elmwood Ave. was lengthened, one glanced down through a park of birds and squirrels to a pergola [trellis]beside a park. [45]

A week later she added:

> Rumsey mansion was always a place for imagination to conjure with. Its splendid hall opening into drawing rooms, library, music and living rooms, the walnut cases fitted into Gothic hand-carved niches, the rare pictures brought from the salons in Paris, the bronzes, the Cloissonne and all the articles of virtu and objects of art give the interior an old-word atmosphere. [46]

Severance relates the origin of Rumsey Park:

> Before Mr. Rumsey built his residence on Delaware avenue, the ample grounds to the westward were practically in a state of nature. Emily street, [planned] to run from Delaware to Carolina, between Tupper and Tracy street, was discontinued as a street in 1854. This area, included in Mr. Rumsey's purchase, also included a fine natural spring which was utilized in beautifying the grounds. In Mr. Rumsey's employ were Henry and Edward Rose, brothers, both architects, who had come to Buffalo from England. The principal features of Rumsey Park were of their designing. The abundant spring made possible a pretty lake of clear water. The topography of the lot was carefully studied, and the native forest trees were augmented by spacious planting. A boat house, a tiny Swiss chalet, was set at the water-side, and a little Grecian temple, now destroyed, bespoke the taste of the owner. The gardens near the house were terraced, set with flowers and fountains. For half a century this beauty spot in the heart of the city was the joy of its owner and his friends. It was the ideal setting for many festivities and social gatherings, and in the skating season no place was so poplar for those privileged to use it as Rumsey Park. Surrounded, except on the house side, by a very high tight-board fence, it naturally aroused the curiosity and perhaps the envy of strangers and "outsiders" generally. At the present hour, some of the buildings are gone and Elmwood avenue traffic cuts through this charming demesne. The spring still flows, and some fine old trees guard the lake; but what its future will be is beyond the ken or the province of the present chronicle. [47]

Burr remembered some of the joys of life in the Park:

> In the bygone days when ice-skating was the fashionable pastime of winter, tickets were issued to the public during the cold season and anybody who liked could come into the charmed realm and skate. Many a gray-haired man in today's Buffalo had his hockey practice on the lake and almost every boy who played hockey there made his team in college. Among them were the Rumsey boys, the Wheeler and Goodyear youngsters, Gerry and "Rennie" Spaulding, Parke Wright, the Laveracks, Joseph Dart, Charles Cary, the Milburns and many others.

45 *Ibid.*
46 *Ibid.*, January 30, 1937.
47 Frank Severance, ed., "Picture Book of Earlier Buffalo," *PBHS*, 16(1912), p. 416-417.

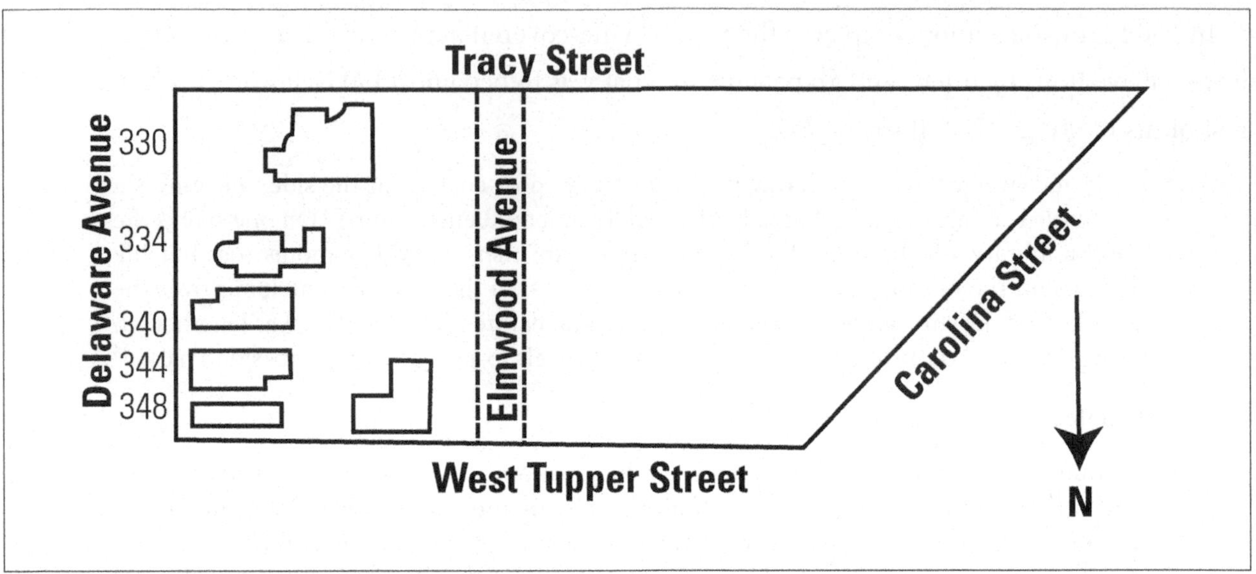

6.29 Ground plan for Rumsey Park.

> There were ice-Carnivals and costume parties, toboggan meets in winter, gymnastics with all kinds of stunts, Easter parties with egg-rolling and prizes, tennis tournaments, boating parties, the *fete champetre*, and little plays, with the guests seated on the terrace and the players acting on an improvised stage below
>
> One summer "Midsummer Night's Dream" was given against the fountain in the background. Colored lights were thrown on the players, producing a lovely picture. Mrs. Irving Snow and Miss Edwine Noye were among the actors in this booking of Shakespeare's delightful fantasy. Queen Titania and her fairy train elicited much admiration and the singing of women's voices hidden in the shrubbery enhanced the effect. [48]

Figure 6.29 is the ground plan of Rumsey Park, a family compound since besides Bronson Senior in the big house at #330, at one time or another in the last quarter of the nineteenth century Edward Movius and his wife, Mary Lovering Rumsey Movius, resided at #334, Doctor and Mrs. Charles Cary resided at #340, and Bronson (Bert) Rumsey at #132 West Tupper. Old man Rumsey's eldest son, Laurence, still lived at #1 Park Place

Bert Rumsey, fourth of the Rumsey Park quartette, attended local schools and graduated from Oxford. On his return to Buffalo he joined his father and uncle in the leather and later in the real estate business. Two of his children by Mary Coxe who will figure in this story were Bronson Case Rumsey, III, nicknamed Bob, and Mildred Cleveland Rumsey. An ardent equestrian Bert participated in one of the first polo matches in America. By the early 1900s he was living at #133 Chapin Parkway, part of the irredenta of Delaware Avenue. He died at ninety-two at his summer home at Niagara-on-the-Lake in Ontario in 1946. [49]

48 *Times*, January 30, 1927.
49 *NYT*, August 20, 1946.

Wealthy nineteenth century Buffalo families entertained sumptuously at home. Their exemplar was Gotham society, where the wives of rich men competed in parties, dinners, soirees, and costume balls. Mrs. William Vanderbilt launched an assault on the city's entrenched inner circle, presided over by Caroline Astor, with an affair to end all affairs in March 1883 that newspapers called the grandest social event in the city's history. The rooms of her mansion on Fifth Avenue had been transformed into a tropical wonderland. The Louis XV salon was resplendent with tapestries and wainscotting from an old French chateau. The hostess, dressed as a Renaissance princess, welcomed an array of Mary Stuarts, Marie Antoinettes, and Queen Elizabeths, with properly costumed escorts.[50]

In the winters of 1872 and 1888 and the spring of 1898 the anglophilic Bronson Rumseys responded with Waverly Balls, pageants from the pages of Sir Walter Scott. With his tongue-in-cheek style, Horton described the 1888 ball:

> In mid-January the *Commercial Advertiser*, the paper most favored by the *beau monde*, remarked that the invitations had been sent out and that the hosts and hostesses would be Mr. and Mrs. Laurence D. Rumsey, Mr. and Mrs. Edward Movius, Mr. and Mr. Bronson Rumsey, Jr., and Dr. and Mrs. Charles Cary. On Tuesday evening, February 7th, the guests assembled in the Rumsey mansion; and at the appointed time they began to descend the stately stairs into the great hall, a more debonair and picturesque throng by far than the angels on the ladder in Jacob's dream. The flunky with suitable pomp announced Sir Vernon Lee in the person of Truman Avery and in that of Mrs. Avery, Her Grace the Duchess of Rutland. The Right Honorable the Earl of Leicester was announced; he turned out to be Harry Hamlin; Mrs. Hamlin was the Duchess of Derby; ...Mrs. Glenny was Lady Penelope Penfeather; Mrs. Wadsworth, Princess Anne. Sir Walter Raleigh doubled for the occasion: he came in the person of Dr. Roswell Park, Mrs. Park being Catherine Seyton. Mrs. S. S. Spaulding passed for Lady Peveril. Sherman S. Rogers was the Lawyer in *Guy Mannering*; Samuel Welch, Rob Roy; Robert Adam was Old Morality. Young Carleton Sprague played Quentin Durward; Walter Cary, Sir Percy Shafton; Thomas Cary, Edmund Tresillian; Seward Cary, Roland Graeme. Mrs. Walter Cary was the Lady of Lochleven; Miss Ivy Love, Evelyn Berenger. Miss Maria Maltby Love should have been announced with the sound of hautboys, a flourish of silver trumpets and a ruffle of drums, but she needed not the flunky's bland and sonorous voice to tell the gathering multitude that she was Queen Elizabeth.
>
> In a supper room whither the company now casually began to drift the guests were regaled at a beautiful board in the midst of which grew an enormous bed of callas. Their palates titillated and their spirits refreshed, lords and ladies, squires and dames, palmers, monks, beauties and gallants reassembled in the great hall to see a Scotch reel performed by half a dozen nimble young men in kilts. Two of these may be presumed to have come by the dance and the costume through ancient inheritance: their names were Dunbar and Stuart. The others, unless perhaps through title on the distaff side, footed it in borrowed tartans; for their father's names at least smacked more of Yankeedom than of Lone Glen Artney or the Trossachs. These four young pageant-Scots were Charles North, George Coit, John Dorr and Ansley Wilcox.

50 Edwin G. Burrows and Mike Wallace, *Gotham: A History of New York City to 1898* (New York: Oxford University Press, 1999), pp. 1071-1072.

> When the reel ended, the hands of the clock pointed to near four in the morning; but the ball was far from over. In a swirl of color and a glister of gems the company took their places around the room for a cotillion which lasted until seven. Then the lively strains of music gave way to slower, more majestic rhythms as the court proceeded in a final march after which Queen Henrietta Maria, Queen Berengaria, the Queen of Scots and the Princess Anna Comnena resumed their stations on the dais. The couriers and their ladies formed in line, passed leisurely by the throne and with bow and curtsey bade adieu. Soon their coachmen were whisking them home through the dingy gray light of a February morning. [51]

A week later the *Maine* blew up in Havana harbor.

Bronson's enormous wealth depended on the tanning business he and Dexter had inherited from their father which they sold in 1893 and on their real estate holdings "in Buffalo, in counties nearby, and in property in other cities." Bronson was also a founder of the M&T Bank.

> He was at one time, a good many years ago, a member of the park board, and the city profited immensely by his service in that capacity. The establishment of a park system had become almost a hobby with him; he had given the subject a great deal of thought and attention, and had offered in many ways to do all that it was in his power to do. Thirty-five years ago [i. e., in 1867], associated with such men as Dennis Bowen, who was the founder of the present firm of Rogers Locke & Millburn, and William Dorsheimer, who was lieutenant-governor of New York, and a prominent figure in state affairs, he formulated a plan for the broadening out of the city's park system. To these three men, and to others not quite so well known, perhaps, the city is indebted for its present park system, which is envied by a great many cities, and the board itself is indebted largely for its conceptions and ideas to Bronson Case Rumsey. [52]

Be that as it may, the only mention of him in Kowsky's *Best Planned City* is this reference to the North Park area: "He [Olmsted] planned this region [the future Central Park] for Samuel S. Jewett and Bronson C. Rumsey and others, primarily involving property of the Villa Park Land Company and Hyde Park Land Company." [53] The author of a 1961 master's thesis at Canisius raises the question whether undue influences were involved in rejecting the first choice of experts for locating the 1901 Pan-American Exposition at The Front on the Niagara shore in favor of a less desirable spot, the Rumsey tract on Forest Avenue. [54] While Bronson never involved himself in politics nor in many other businesses than the tannery and his investments, he served as president of the ambitiously named Buffalo & Washington, a railroad that joined the Pennsylvania at Emporium, Pennsylvania, in 1873. The B&W was backed by Buffalo capitalists and industrialists but never fulfilled the dreams of its founders, generated inadequate on-line traffic, went through two reorganizations, and was taken over by the Pennsylvania in 1900. Horton, in an attempt at humor, suggested that Bronson "ought to have been president of a road connecting Buffalo with the western cattle range whither he often traveled, whence he brought back exciting mementos for the adornment of his house." Horton asserts that "in 1903 Bronson Case Rumsey and Dexter Phelps Rumsey gave to the Society of Natural

51 Horton, *op. cit.*, 1:304-306

52 *Courier*, March 3, 1902.

53 Charles Beveridge, "Frederick Law Olmsted's Vision for Buffalo," Kowsky, ed., *Best Planned City*, p. 23.

54 James Anthony Farley, History of the Pan-American Exposition, May 1, 1901-November 1, 1901. Master's Thesis, Department of History, Canisius College, June, 1961.

Sciences a site on Elmwood Avenue adjacent to Delaware Park" which later became the site of the Albright Art Gallery.[55] Actually Bronson had died in 1902. Obsequies were conducted at the family residence. His wife, the queen of the Waverly Balls, had died in 1900.[56] Their eldest son, Laurence D. Rumsey, born in 1849, received his early education at Professor Horace Briggs' classical school. He graduated from Harvard in 1872, married Jennie Cary in 1876, and entered the family leather business. Bronson and Evelyn's second son, born in 1854, was also named Bronson but nicknamed Bert. Bert was to be wed three times, his first wife being Mary Coxe, the bishop's daughter, his second Elizabeth Lockwood, and his third, younger than Bert by thirty years, was Edna Lewis. The girls of the family were Mary Lovering, born in 1851, and Evelyn, born in 1855, who married respectively Edward Movius and Dr. Charles Cary, and resided respectively at #334 and #340.

Mabel Ganson described the Rumsey Park of her childhood:

> A little later than this time, I learned to go with the other girls and boys to play in the Rumsey garden. Old Bronson Rumsey had bought a block of the City street — a whole square of it — and he built a large and impressive red-brick house on the lower corner of Delaware avenue out of money made from traffic in hides. ...Mr. Rumsey's house was large and gloomy and had a strange, sinister dignity inside and out. To each of his sons and daughters he gave a house and a piece of land — an interest in the whole. Their back doors all opened on the garden, in the centre of which was a lake with a little boathouse. His oldest son, Lawrence, a hard-faced man with the red cheeks and cold blue eyes of his granite father, married [in 1876] Jennie Cary, the only sister of "the Cary boys." His son Bert or Bronson, the second, married Mary Cox, the daughter of Bishop Cox, and a mysterious woman she certainly was.
>
> Now Lawrence had three girls — Eva always remained childless — and Bert had two boys and a daughter. All these children grew up in the garden, where their little friends came and played with them, in rowboats in the summer and skating in the winter, and all manner of games that a group of children think up to play when they have a whole grand piece of land to themselves, with water on it and big old trees and few grown-ups to interfere with them.
>
> Mildred was Bert Rumsey's daughter, a stout, jolly girl with bold brown eyes and golden hair, and she was my friend...
>
> ...Her brother Bob, Bronson III, was quite different. He was a very handsome little boy with big brown eyes and an olive skin. He had a fine retrousse nose and a thin-lipped mouth that was nervous-looking and sensitive. He was two or three years older than Mildred and a hero to the other boys and girls. He was the best skater and the most daring hockey player of all. A real athlete. His little Brother Dexter, named for Dexter Rumsey, the brother of Bronson, was a cameo-faced child, weak and beautiful and unlikely to succeed.
>
> I liked Mildred Rumsey's home [#132 West Tupper], though it hadn't much comfort in it. Her mother was mysterious. She was tall and slim and she wore long white muslin gowns with long black taffeta mantles over them flowing and sweeping. Her hair was a

55 Horton, *op. cit.*, 1:218, 324, 371; E. Dunn, *op. cit.*, pp. 162-163.
56 *Courier*, March 3, 1902.

> crinkly, dusky brown and it parted in the middle and rolled about her head. Her eyes were huge and dark and her face was white. She always had an exasperated expression on her thin lips. Bob looked like her. Mr. Rumsey and she didn't get on. They scarcely spoke to each other. She stayed up in her room all day until late afternoon, and when it grew dark she put on a dark cloak and a low hat with a long curling feather and she went out. It was then that she did her shopping. She never would go downtown when the other women did. She hated to meet them. She was like a rarer, stranger clay than they. She laughed and gibed at them and kept to herself. What she did all day alone in her room over the garden, one never knew.
>
> There was a huge living-room with a deep recess in one end of it that held the great fireplace where logs burned all winter ling. And from a trapdoor carved into a seat at one side of the chimney Bert Rumsey would go down to a workroom below, where he carved all kinds of furniture and things. He had decorated the whole room with strange plants and animals. He made seats and chairs and tables; he was always down there when he was in the house. All around the oak walls of that low — ceilinged room were the mounted heads of deer and elk and mountain sheep, for old Mr. Rumsey owned a lot of land out in Cody, Wyoming, and his sons went out there to hunt every year. Buffalo Bill and the Rumseys were like one family in the days before the former became a world figure.
>
> So that household held romance in it. Bert Rumsey was a handsome, taciturn man with gleaming eyes that had steel in them. He hated his wife and she hated him. Once when Dexter was sick and Mrs. Rumsey had taken care of him all day, she asked her husband to go and give Decky his medicine while she lingered resting at the dinner table. "I'm not going to give him his pap," replied the father savagely, almost in a jealous voice. She raised her eyebrows and smiled her exasperated smile. "You needn't be a boor, Bert," she said in her disciplined voice. [57]

George Goodyear gives another view of the young aristocrats disporting themselves in Rumsey Park in the 1880s and 1890s:

> The friends of the early years were the Laverack brothers, Howard C. and William H. (Jummy), Hallam L. (Hal) Movius and the Rumsey boys. There were three Rumseys, Charles Cary (Pad) and his brother, Laurence Dana (Red), and their cousin, Bronson Case, 3rd (Bob). Hal Movius was a cousin of the three Rumsey boys, his mother being a Rumsey. This group, with Conger [Goodyear, George's father], was what would today be called a gang. Female adherents were the Rumsey sisters, particularly Evelyn, who later married the Rev. Walter Lord, and Mabel Ganson, of whom I shall have more to say later. Younger members were Conger's brother Charley, and the Spaulding brothers, Elbridge G. (Gerry) and Stephen V[an] R[ensselaer].
>
> Headquarters of the gang was the Rumsey garden, stretching back of the big house on the corner of Delaware Avenue and Tracy Street. It was a beautiful place, and ideal for the gang, winter and summer. There was a pond on which they rowed in summer, and skated and played hockey in the winter. The wooded paths were fine for Indian games and the lawn was ample for football and one-old-cat. Unquestioned leader of the gang was Bob Rumsey, handsome and athletic and loved by all the girls. Later in life he somewhat went to seed — married several times and was a poor father and husband. He eventually bought a ranch near Cody, Wyoming, where I spent several weeks, at about age 14, on a trip out west. I disliked him intensely. [58]

57 Ganson, *op. cit.*, pp. 105-109.
58 George Goodyear, *Goodyear Family History* (Buffalo: privately printed, 1976-1977), pp. 138-139.

As after his marriage Laurence moved into his father's former house on Park Place, so after Bronson's death in 1902, Laurence moved into #330 and remained there until his death. He was vice president of the Bank of Buffalo and director of the Erie County Savings Bank. [59]

Laurence and his wife, Jennie Cary, had five children. The eldest, Evelyn, was born in 1877 and educated at Miss Hoffman's in Buffalo and at the Chateau Dieudonne near Paris, completing her education at Miss Porter's School, Farmington, Connecticut. She lived at #330 for forty-five years, but from 1914 on she painted in her studio at #18 Tracy Street, site formerly of the Rumsey stables. Her inspiration was her aunt, Evelyn Rumsey Cary, who had painted the Spirit of Niagara, official emblem of the Pan-American Exposition, and the picture of Charlotte Mulligan which hangs in the Twentieth Century Club. A home was added to the studio after Evelyn married Dr. Walter Russell Lord, rector of Saint John's on Colonial Circle, but as late as 1925 the Lords were living with Evelyn's mother at #330. Thereafter they moved to #18 Tracy. Evelyn's earlier paintings were "chiefly of women, well-bred with aristocratic features and family names that are still prominent in the city's social and cultural life," subjects with whom she would have been well acquainted. She and her brother, Charles Cary Rumsey the sculptor, were the only Buffalonians invited to exhibit at the historic 1913 International Exposition of Modern Art at the 69th Regiment Armory in New York, which signified a definite break in the hold over the arts exerted by the academic school. [60]

Walter Lord was a fit helpmate for an artistic Delaware Avenue girl. The first Lord in America, Thomas, came from Yorkshire and settled in Connecticut where in 1635 he was among the founders of Hartford. The father of Walter R., Walter D., had fought in the Civil War. His minister son was born in Lisle, Broome County, in 1873, attended high schools in Detroit and Buffalo, graduated from Harvard in 1896 and from General Theological in New York in 1898, and was ordained that year. After five years as assistant in parishes in Buffalo and New York, he returned to Buffalo in 1907 as rector of Saint John's. He belonged to the Saturn, Rotary, and Thursday Clubs and to the Harvard Club of New York. He retired in 1944 after thirty-seven years as rector and died in November 1952. His wife died at eighty-five in June 1963. The Lords were childless. [61]

The second child of the Laurence Rumseys was Charles Cary Rumsey, born in Buffalo in 1879, who was educated in grammar schools and Central High, graduated from Harvard with a B.A. in 1902, and studied art in Paris for four years. In August 1910 at Saint John's Episcopal Church on the Arden estate of the late E. H. Harriman, Rumsey married Harriman's daughter Mary. Harriman is becoming increasingly recognized not as the robber baron of popular mythology but as America's greatest railroader. [63] After marriage, the Rumseys settled on a 500-acre farm in the Blue Ridge Mountains of Virginia where they rode and hunted together, for, like many of his Delaware Avenue

59 *HNF*, 4:599.
60 *BEN*, June 26, 1930; March 25, 1959; *CE*, May 26, 1963; Richard B. Morris, *Encyclopedia of American History* (New York: Harper & Row, 1965), p. 639.
61 *HNF*, 4:617-619; *BEN*, October 28, 1944; *CE*, May 5, 1963.

contemporaries, Charles was an accomplished horseman:

> He was known as Tad Rumsey among polo players. While in college he played as a member of the Myopia Hunt Club of Hamilton Mass. In this city he played with the Buffalo Country club and was rated as a four-goal man. Last year [1921] he was rated as an eight-goal man, only two below the highest rating known in modern polo. He went abroad as a substitute on the American team which won back the international polo challenge cup at Hurlingham, England. His presence as substitute, with Earl Hopping, gave him the reputation of being the best available man in the United States outside of the Big Four. [63]

During World War I Rumsey rose to captain with the 77th Division and the 40th Engineers. Before and after the war, he exhibited his sculptures in museums throughout the country. Among his creations were a frieze on the Manhattan Bridge in New York, the Soldiers and Sailors' Monument in Brooklyn, a statue of Francisco Pizzaro the conqueror of Peru, a muscle-bound nude dubbed by his critics *The Bolshevik Woman*, *The Centaur* in front of the Buffalo Historical Society Building on Nottingham, and *The Three Graces* in Forest Lawn. His masterpieces were, not by accident, sculptures of polo ponies and their riders. He was killed in a car crash on Long Island in 1922. His wife, who had become an ardent New Dealer, died from injuries sustained when her mount fell with her at a hunt near Middleburg, Virginia, in 1934. [64] Gertrude, a third child of Laurence and Jennie, born in 1880, married Carlton M. Smith. The scion of an old Buffalo family, most of his business career was identified with Smith Fassett, a North Tonawanda lumber company founded by his father. He was also involved, in banking, steam and electric railroads, power development, construction, and manufacturing. The couple lived on #304 West North Street, where Gertrude continued to reside after her husband died in 1925. [65]

Grace Rumsey, born in 1883, the fourth child of Laurence and Jennie, married and was divorced from Charles W. Goodyear, Jr. Laurence Dana Rumsey, Jr., born in 1885, the youngest child of Laurence and Jennie, never married and lived for years with his mother at #330. His big moment came during World War I when he joined the Lafayette Escadrille, a voluntary squadron of American aviators who fought for France before the United States entered the war. Formed in April 1916, it numbered 267 recruits, of whom 180 saw combat. Many flew in French units but all were deemed members of the Lafayette Flying Corps. At the start of 1918 the squadron was incorporated into the United States Air Service. Fifty-one of its members were killed in action. [66]

After the war Laurence, Jr., returned to his now widowed mother's home. The census for 1920 listed him as an insurance agent. In 1925 he was still there but unemployed. Though it was the height of the prosperous 1920s, Laurence had no need to work. In September 1965 on his eightieth birthday a lady reporter for the *Courier-Express* interviewed him at his home on River Road in Young-

62 Maury Klein, *The Life and Legend of E. H. Harriman* (Chapel, Hill, N.C: University of North Carolina Press, 2000), *passim*.
63 *Express*, September 9, 1922.
64 *BEN*, December 20, 1934.
65 *Times*, May 19, 1925.
66 "Lafayette Escadrille," *Dictionary of American History*, 4:83.

stown about his experiences with the Escadrille. He was the sole living member of his squadron.[67]

The oldest son of Bert Rumsey and his first wife, Mary Coxe was Bronson Case Rumsey, III, who spent much of his time on his ranch at Cody, Wyoming. Bert and Mary's second child was Mildred Rumsey, the stout and jolly friend of young Mabel Ganson. Born in 1878, Mildred married Arthur Hawes, moved to La Jolla, California, and died in 1948. Her younger brother, Dexter Cleveland Rumsey, also moved to La Jolla. Bert's second wife was Elizabeth Lockwood, daughter of Daniel Lockwood, who made the nominating speech for Grover Cleveland for mayor of Buffalo in 1881, for governor of New York in 1882, and for president of the United States in 1884.[68] Bert had four children by Elizabeth, Daniel Lockwood Rumsey, a sculptor like his cousin Charles Cary Rumsey, Sarah Rumsey who married Edward Archbald and moved to Delaware, Polly Rumsey who married Milton Wolfe of Buffalo, and Rosamunde who did not marry. Though Bert left the compound when he moved to #133 Chapin, his children had grown up next to Rumsey Park. Bert spent his declining years at Daytona Beach, Florida, where he dabbled in real estate, a family standby. Jennie Rumsey, Laurence Senior's widow, died in 1943 and #330 was sold to the Children's Aid Society, after which commercialization proceeded apace.

The point has been reached to return to moving up Delaware from where that movement stopped, at #274, the house of Bronson, then of his son Laurence Rumsey. Numbers 304 and 314 constituted a double house. In 1872 the southern part was the home of Henry C. Winslow, a commission merchant and vessel owner and member of Winslow & Sill, insurance agents. Henry Sill lived across the street at #329 Delaware. Winslow's widow continued there until the end of the century, but by 1905 the place had become a rooming house. The northern half of the house in 1860 (then #130) on the corner of Tracy Street was inhabited by Henry W. Rogers, who had been born in Unadilla, New York, in 1806 to parents of New England ancestry, educated in the common school, moved to Bath in 1824 where he read law and taught school, and was admitted to practice before the Court of Common Pleas of Steuben County in 1827. In 1829 Rogers married Kezia Adams; the couple had no children. In 1836 they moved to Buffalo, where he was recognized as a fine lawyer, and within a year was appointed district attorney, a post he held until 1843. For Rogers' services to the Democracy, James K. Polk, successful candidate for president in 1844, appointed him Collector of the Port of Buffalo. Four years later when his term was up, Rogers resumed his practice as a partner in Rogers & Bowen. Having inherited a fortune, he retired in 1863 and devoted himself to travel. In 1870, "deeming the climate of this city in the winter and spring too rigorous for his health, he removed to Ann Arbor, Michigan, where he purchased and fitted up a charming rural home, and in the society of cultivated and congenial friends, he passed the remainder of his days." He died there in 1881.[69]

67 *CE*, September, 1965.
68 Alan Nevins, *Grover Cleveland: A Study in Courage* (New York: Dodd, Mead & Company, 1948), p. 811.
69 Smith, *op. cit.*, 2:77-79.

6.30 ❦ Views of Rumsey Park. *PBHS* 16(1912), 418-423.

Rogers was followed at #314 by Arthur Cleveland Coxe, second bishop of the Episcopal diocese of Western New York. If central casting had existed in the nineteenth century, Coxe would have been the odds-on choice to play an Anglican bishop.(6.31) He was born in 1818, at Mendham, New Jersey, the son of Samuel H. Cox, a Presbyterian minister. While still a youth, Arthur went to live with his uncle, a physician and an Episcopalian, under whose tutelage the nephew became an Episcopalian in 1828. At this time Arthur appended a final *e* to the family name, alleging that that this was the original English spelling. He graduated from N.Y.U. in 1838 and from General Theological

6.31 ❦ Arthur Cleveland Coxe, two views. (1) Mixer, *op. cit.*, facing p. 51; (2) White, *op. cit.*, I, facing 263.

Seminary in New York in 1841. Ordained a priest in 1842, he served in several parishes at New York, Hartford, and Baltimore, before coming to Buffalo in succession to a churchman with an old New York name, William Heathcote De Lancy, in April 1865.

Since seminary Coxe had been a leader of the Anglo-Catholic revival in the Church of England, an outcome of the Tractarian phase of the Oxford Movement, which began in 1833. It aimed to restore the practice and belief of Catholicism in the Church of England by renewed sacramental life and enriched liturgies. The movement also focused on cities rather than the countryside, which may explain why Coxe rejected an offer from Texas in favor of Buffalo. Arrived there, he incorporated these themes into his administration. He moved the seat of the diocese from Batavia to Buffalo and made Saint Paul's with the largest congregation in the city a cathedral where he promoted vivid worship, focusing on weekly celebration of the Eucharist. Another principle of the Oxford Movement was "Back to the Fathers." In this spirit Coxe organized the Christian Literature Company in 1885, which produced *The Ante Nicene Fathers*, a volume of church writers before the Council of Nicea in 325. Thus far the *American National Biography* on Coxe.[70] There follows a different but not necessarily contradictory view:

> The new bishop lacked the superb balance and judgment of his predecessor but he was a much more colorful figure. He had graduated from the General Theological Seminary in 1841, at the time when the Tracts for the Times were making their greatest impact on the boys in the Seminary. While therefore Bishop De Lancy represented the old high churchmanship of [John Henry] Hobart and [Samuel] Seabury, Coxe rather belonged to the same school of churchmanship as modified by Tractarianism. But the ecclesiastical storms of the 1840s had left him with a violent anti-Roman complex which manifested itself on numerous occasions.[71]

Horton rode several hobbyhorses in naming chapters and selecting material for his history. In "Capitalists Promote Piety and Learning," he cited this from a Coxe sermon:

70 Thomas L. Purvis, "Coxe, Arthur Cleveland," *ANB*, 5:633-635.
71 George E. DeMille, *Saint Paul's Cathedral, Buffalo: A Brief History* (Buffalo: Hoffman Printing Company, 1960), p. 52.

> The possession of wealth is a glorious heritage when properly used, for such a use gives the possessor enjoyment in this world and eternal felicity in the next — nor is the state of the poor unenviable for they are relieved of the fearful responsibilities which the possession of riches entails. They are representatives of Christ and are unclogged by the temptations of wealth in the performance of their religious duties. [72]

Later in the same chapter Horton, wrote:

> Shortly after the American Association for the Advancement of Science had adjourned its Buffalo meeting in 1876, the Episcopal diocesan convention met at Saint Paul's. Bishop Coxe took advantage of the occasion to rebuke the scientists who accepted Darwinism and to assert that without the clergy the world would sink to the level of these animals "which a suicidal philosophy claims we have descended from." [73]

In a chapter with the socialist title, "Appeasement with a Dinner Pail," Horton, on the 1896 Bryan-McKinley campaign, quotes Dr. Thomas Slicer, a Unitarian pastor and Avenue resident:

> I openly state that the principles of the Chicago [Democratic] platform ethically considered, should lead every man to protest against them. They are the result of the relaxed loins of immorality." Whether this climax could have been caped by Bishop Coxe is a question that cannot be answered. That prelate had died in July; and as his successor, Bishop William D. Walker, would not be enthroned until December, the widowed church had no spokesman of Episcopal rank to voice its views on Bryan and the social revolt of which he was the symbol. As for the rectors of churches, they either held their peace or spoke in such guarded language that the public prints took little interest in their observations. It is probable, however, that they deplored Bryanism; quite possible too that some of them even marched with the others in the great anti-Bryan parade that took place at the end of October. [74]

About 35,000 marchers in fifteen divisions according to profession or trade, headed up by bands, and carrying Republican slogans marched up Main Street on October 31. Bankers S. M. Clement, Robert L. Fryer, Bronson Rumsey, General George S. Field, C. J. Hamlin, George V. Forman, and Robert K. Root led the second division. Leading the doctors were Lucien Howe, Roswell Park, Floyd S. Crego, and Ray V. Pierce, while the lawyers were marshaled by John G. Milburn, Sherman S. Rogers, and Harlow Curtiss. Harry Altman mobilized the tailors, and oil men marched behind Joseph P. Dudley. All these leaders lived on Delaware Avenue. Erie County gave the G.O.P. a sizeable majority, 45,555 to 29,857. Horton's conclusion was:

> The majority better understood the interests of their section; they better understood also that though the discontents which were made manifest in the Bryan vote may have been justified, the Bryan panacea, viewed in relation to the practice of the world at large, could only have made bad matters worse. [75]

Coxe's thinking was strictly conservative. "It was sometimes said during his lifetime that his antagonism to Puritanism on the one side and to Roman Catholicism on the other was too pronounced... Novelties in religion he detested whether they came from Rome, from Geneva, or from the Oxford he loved so well."

72 Horton, *op. cit.*, 1:259.
73 *Ibid.*, p. 271.
74 *Ibid.*, p. 332.
75 *Ibid.*

Coxe was first elected as coadjutor to Bishop DeLancy who lived in Geneva but that prelate died July 20, 1896. Coxe quickly moved into a house provided by the diocese at Delaware and Tracy costing $20,000 ($388,000 in 1997 dollars). He enjoyed being a bishop but was less happy with his quarters:

> He questioned the location of the house and its fitness for a Bishop's residence. The first objection, that it was "too far out of the way," has long since been removed by the growth of the city beyond it; the second, that it was wanting in space and dignity — being only half a double house — remains in increasing force, the Bishop himself declaring to the Council in 1892 that "it was not such as should be provided by the diocese for its Bishop," and, while for himself he was content to spend his days under its roof, "the Diocese owed something to itself, and its Bishop should have an official homestead adapted to his office. There should be a wing or side office for the Library, and this should be so arranged that visiting Clergy and students might use it freely. There should be a chapel where the Bishop with the Clergy could freely meet for devotion. In other respects he thinks the house is sufficient for "a plain and primitive bishop, in a republican state of society."[76]

Coxe died at Clifton Springs, New York, and was succeeded by Bishop William D. Walker(6.32), born in New York in 1839. He was educated at Trinity School, Columbia, and the General Theological Seminary, and was ordained in 1862:

> For more than thirteen years Bishop Walker had charge of congregations in the frontier district, and in that time organized and erected three churches, two of them exclusively for Indians. To the study of the various tribes he devoted much of his time, and because of his uplift work among them he was appointed in 1887 by President Cleveland to the Board of Indian Commissioners. During his Western service he conceived the idea of his famous "cathedral car," a railway vehicle fitted with sanctuary appointments and equipped with seats for seventy-five persons. Since that time this deal has been in vogue in all parts of the world where missionary work is done.[77]

6.32 ❦ **Bishop David Walker, *PBHS* 24 (1920), facing p. 183.**

For services to the Indians he was made bishop of North Dakota in 1883. In 1900 Governor Theodore Roosevelt appointed him to a commission on living conditions among the Indians of New York. Among his writings were *Reports to the President and Congress on the Sioux and Chippewa Tribes of Indians in North Dakota,* and *God's Providence in Life.* Walker lived at #314 and never married but by 1905 he had moved to Elmwood, and the former See House had become a rooming house. He died in 1917. A history of Saint Paul's

76 Charles Wells Hayes, *The Diocese of Western New York* (Rochester: Scrantom Whetmore & Co., 1904), p. 257.
77 *NYT*, May 3, 1917.

contains a sketch of Walker based on a sanitized vision of Coxe:

> By contrast with his two great predecessors, Bishop Walker necessarily appears something of an anti-climax. And yet he was no nonentity. Six feet tall, of a rugged masculinity, he was very much of an authoritarian. By contrast with the versatility [?] of Bishop Coxe, the chief note of his character is a rigid inflexibility. Belonging to the old high church school, he leaned neither to the right nor to the left. He had use for neither Roman Catholicism nor Protestantism and turned his back on all attempts at inter-church cooperation. He was completely unresponsive to the intellectual currents of his day, unaffected by post-Darwinian science and biblical criticism which was sweeping through the church. He was primarily a chief pastor who delighted to meet and counsel with the laity, and was indefatigable in parish visitations. [78]

Silas Fish, who lived just north of Bronson's Rumsey at #330 during the 1860s and 1870s until his son-in law, Edward Movius, moved into Rumsey Park, was an insurance agent. Fish's neighbor to the north, George Truscott, was born in Exeter, England, in 1825. He went to California via Cape Horn, in the 1840s. Back in Buffalo, he read law in the office of William Greene of Niagara Square and passed the bar. He was President of the Young Men's Association in 1867 and for several years sat on the Board of Water Commissioners. He retired from his law practice at fifty and lived until 1884. [79] His widow, Sarah Loring Truscott, whom he had married in 1851, moved across the Avenue to #335 where she died in 1910, having been president of the Women's Board of Buffalo General and president of the governing board of Buffalo General and of Children's Hospital. Loring Avenue in Buffalo is named after her. [80] Number 340 which she vacated became the home of another Rumsey in-law, Doctor Charles Cary.

Samuel K. Worthington resided at #344 from the 1870s to the 1890s. He had been born in Richfield, New York, in 1822 and died in the Trubee Hotel on Delaware and Edward in 1912. At twenty-three he came to Buffalo and engaged in the grain business. Later he switched to coal and served a term as Water Commissioner. Cleveland asked him to become a member of the Buffalo Club when it began, and Worthington and Cleveland were long its only honorary members. He was a director of the Society of Natural Sciences and the Fine Arts Academy. Two sons and four daughters survived him. [81] Burr had fond memories of #344:

> It seems not such a long time ago that the Samuel K. Worthington home on the west side of Delaware below Tracy street housed a family of beautiful girls who on summer evenings grouped themselves on the front steps of the spacious brown brick mansion, which had a hall that ran straight through the center and overlooked gardens, the gardens with intriguing glimpses of other gardens behind. Mr. Worthington was a somewhat autocratic man who represented the old aristocracy and who conducted himself with dignity and a certain aloofness, but he was a generous host and gave many wonderful diners. [82]

By the late 1890s Worthington had moved to smaller quarters on Johnson's Park, and #344 was occupied by Franklin Day Locke(6.33), one of the city's leading lawyers. Born in Gowanda of New

78 DeMile, *op. cit.*, pp. 94-95.
79 *Express*, March 4, 1884.
80 *Courier*, July 23, 1910.
81 *Express*, August 27, 1912.
82 *Courier*, October 6, 1928.

England ancestry, Locke came to Buffalo soon after graduating from Hamilton College in 1864 and two years later married Frances Ellen Cooper. His law firm, Locke, Babcock, Hollister & Brown, traced its origins to a partnership which had included his friend Grover Cleveland. The only political office Locke ever sought was consul at London, and his friend denied him that. In 1892 Locke led a thousand-man protest march from Buffalo to the state nominating convention at Syracuse which was packed with supporters of Cleveland's rival for the presidential nomination, David B. Hill. Large personal and corporate interests sought Locke's services. At his summer estate at Idlewild hard by Eighteen Mile Creek in Evans the Erie County Bar Association was organized in the summer of 1886. In 1899 he and John G. Milburn brought together the principals from Scranton and Buffalo to create the Lackawanna Steel Company. He was among the band of men who built up the M&T Bank from a small financial institution to the mighty M&T-Peoples Trust Company. He was president of Buffalo Abstract & Title, trustee of Hamilton College, a Presbyterian, and a Mason. In 1905 when he was sixty, his daughter Clara, her attorney husband Edward M. Mills, and their two young children lived at #344 with an Irish maid and a German baby nurse. Locke does not appear to have fancied the big dinners that many of his class enjoyed and his domestic staff was sparse. At seventy-two he lived alone with two young domestics and rarely appeared in court, concentrating on finance. Leisure time he spent reading and had no club memberships, which he may have considered a waste of time. He died at #344 at eighty-three in 1927. His son, Rev. Charles A. Locke, president of Union College, conducted the obsequies and the remains were cremated and returned to Franklin's birthplace, Gowanda.[83] The fifty-five honorary pallbearers at his funeral, including Elihu Root, former Secretary of War and Senator from New York, comprised the elite of the state. Soon thereafter #344 became the site of the four-story Vars Building.

6.33 ❦ **Franklin D. Locke, *Men of Buffalo*, p. 324.**

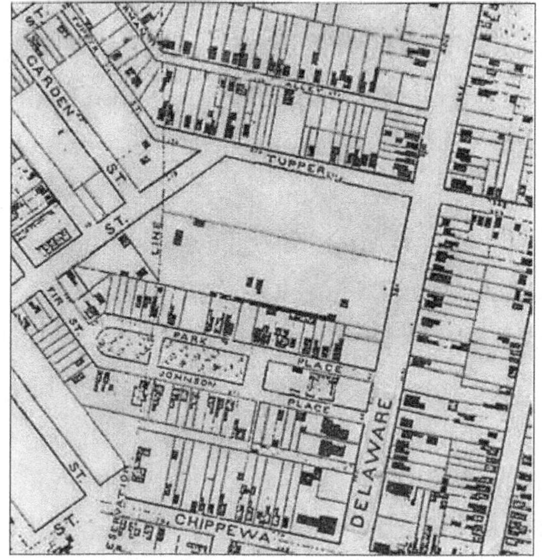

6.34 ❦ **Emslie & Kirk, *op. cit.***

Figure 6.34 depicts the situation at the northwest corner of Tupper and Delaware in 1850. Tracy Street and

83 *Who Was Who in America*, 2:738; *Truth*, May 28, 1927; *Times*, May 25, 1927, *BEN*, May 25, 1927.

6.35 Henry A. Richmond, *PBHS*, 17(1913), following p. 317.

Elmwood Avenue have not yet been cut through, so that the scene was set for Rumsey Park. There are no houses between Park Place and Tupper, though this stretch was filled up by 1860, so any houses there were built during the fifties. Residing at #162 in 1860 was Harriet Sill, widow of Seth Ely Sill who had died at forty-three in 1851. He had been born in Moreau in Saratoga County, came to Buffalo where he studied in the law offices of Sherwood & Hawley, was admitted to the bar in 1836, and practiced with several partners until his election to the Supreme Court for the Eighth Judicial District. In 1840 he married Harriet E. Allen from Batavia. They had two boys and two girls. [84]

The next occupant of #348, Henry Augustus Richmond(6.35), was the son of Dean Richmond, a powerbroker in New York business and politics. Richmond *pere* was born in Vermont in 1804. In 1816 the family moved to Syracuse where Dean learned how to manufacture salt. In 1833 he married Mary Mead, by whom he had eight children. In 1842, by then a successful businessman, he moved to Buffalo and entered the grain transportation business. Buffalo's winters were too much for his wife, so he built a mansion on East State Street in Batavia, but lived and worked in Buffalo during the week. The Batavia house was a large, gray-painted brick building with a pedimented portico of four Greek Ionic columns. Inside was a dining room famous for its yellow-damasked walls and yellow velvet carpets.

Richmond was a founder and director of the Buffalo & Batavia Railroad, which bypassing Attica shortened the route from Buffalo to Rochester, and was president of the Buffalo & State Line, which ran along Lake Erie to Pennsylvania. In politics he was a Democrat believing that party more favorable to railroads than the Whigs. But he belonged to the "Barnburner" faction of the party, which opposed the spread of slavery but advocated compromise with proslavery southerners. In 1848 he was a delegate to the Barnburner state presidential nominating convention in Utica and to the Free Soil convention in Buffalo. Both endorsed ex-president Martin Van Buren, who lost to the Whig, Zachary Taylor. By adroit maneuvering, Richmond became leader of the Albany Regency, one of the most powerful agencies of the New York Democracy, becoming chairman in 1850. This enabled him to have enacted an 1853 consolidation of ten railroads across the state into the New York Central of which he became vice-president, and president in 1864 with the death of Erastus Corning. Richmond's politics were railroads. The Civil War was a bad time for him but he kept his party together by backing the war but attacking Lincoln's policies of emancipation and reconstruction. Richmond

84 *M&FH*, 1:248.

died in the home of Samuel J. Tilden in Yonkers, on the eve of the National Union Convention on August 27, 1866, which supported President Johnson's policies.[85]

Henry Augustus Richmond was born in Syracuse in 1839. He came to Buffalo in the winter of 1860-1861 and studied law but neither practiced it nor entered into politics. By 1880 he was living at #348 diagonally opposite the administrator of his late father's estate. Spared the necessity of earning a living, Henry became a clubman, an art connoisseur, and an intrepid world traveler. After the Civil War civil service reform much exercised men of Richmond's class, whom Theodore Roosevelt called "Goo-goos." Henry had the leisure to work for reform and was once elected president of the National Civil Service Reform Association. He was also very active in the Buffalo Historical Society. His home was the scene of brilliant parties fondly recalled by Burr who attributed his bachelorhood to his having been turned down by a society belle. He died in 1913 in Los Angeles where he had gone for his health. His brothers, Alfred and Eugene, resided in succession at Delaware and Utica. After Henry's death, his house was sold to Neal Johnson, a Norwegian tailor, who lived and had his shop there as late as 1925.[86]

85 "Richmond, Dean," *ANB*, 18:464-465; *New York: A Guide to the Empire State* (New York: Oxford University Press, 1940), p. 473; E.T. Dunn, *op. cit.*, p. 9.

86 *Express*, June 6, 1909; May 30, 1926; *Courier*, September 12, 1926; *PBHS*, 17(1920), p. 316.

CHAPTER

7

FROM TUPPER TO *Virginia Street*

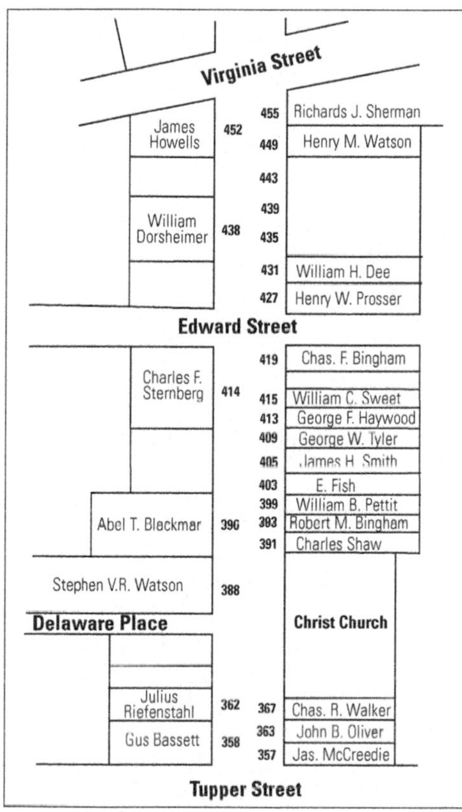

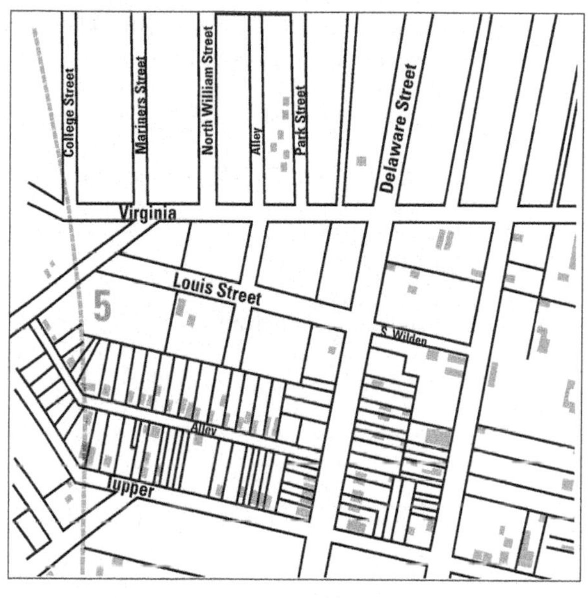

Left 7.1 ❦ Drawn from *Atlas of Buffalo, 1872, ibid.*
Above 7.2 ❦ Emslie & Kirk, 1854, *ibid.*

As can be seen from figure 7.2, an 1854 map, the 648 feet long east block of Delaware between Tupper Street and Walden Alley (later Edward Street) was settled then, while the two blocks on the west side, Tupper to German Alley (later Delaware Place, later still Trinity Street) and German Alley to Louis Street (later also called Edward), were less so. North of Edward on both sides of Delaware there were almost no habitations in 1850. During the 1860s houses this far north were not assigned numbers. Figure 7.1 is based on the 1870 census as were figures 5.1 and 6.1, but supplemented by the *1872 City Directory* and *Atlas*:

1860

WEST TUPPER STREET

170 [358] Reuben E. Sage 52 Vermont
Sage & Allison architects
Ann E. Sage 46 NY *ux.*
Theodore Sage 46 NY
Mary L. Sage 19 NY
Isaac E. Sage 6 NY
Caroline Heuser 19 NY

1870 (2)

WEST TUPPER STREET

358 Gustavus Bassett 56 Mass.
Helen M. Bassett 26 Mass. housekeeper
Susie Bassett 24 NY
Abbie F. Bassett 23 NY
Mary Haggerty 27 Ireland

172 Henry W. Faxon 23 NY ed. *The Republic*
Eunice Faxon 24 NY *ux.*
Frank Faxon 4 NY
Charles Faxon 2 NY
Mary Wood 48 Vermont
Harriet Smith 18 Bavaria

174 [368] George Smith 28 England bookkeeper
Emily Smith 26 England *ux.*
Henry Smith 2 NY
Minnie Smith 8 months NY

176 William Campbell 27 NY lake captain
Sarah Camphell 31 NY *ux.*
Edgar Campbell 9 NY
John Campbell 7 NY
William Campbell 5 NY
Ann Godwin 23 England

DELAWARE PLACE ❦ End of Block

184 [396] William B. Bishop 53 England gentleman
Anna L. Bishop 59 NY
John Corlz 27 NY
George S. Cary 25 NY dry goods merchant
William H. Bishop 15 NY
Thomas Bishop 20 Ohio bookkeeper
Jenny Bishop 19 NY
Josephine Shaw 20 NY
Mary Welch 23 Ireland

EDWARD STREET ❦ End of Block

234 [430] Michael Kingsley 50 Vermont
Margaret Kingsley

362 Julius Rieffenstahl Brunswick
Anna Rieffenstahl 36 NY *ux.*
Amelia Rieffenstahl 8 NY school
Julia Rieffenstahl 6 NY school
Anne Hoffinager 21 Bavaria

DELAWARE PLACE ❦ End of Block

388 Stephen V. R. Watson 62 NY
street railroad president
Charlotte Watson 40 NY *ux.*
Anna Watson 17 NY
Jennie Watson 14 NY
Gertrude Watson 12 NY
G. Van Delfson 55 NY
Marian Campbell 28 Scotland
Katie Forbes 26 Scotland
Margaret McBean 26 Scotland

396 Abel T. Blackmar 56 NY maltester
Lucy Blackmar 57 NY *ux.*
William C. Blackmar 27 NY boarer
Charles V. D. Blackmar 27 NY boarder
Isabella Blackmar 28 NY boarder
Harry Blackmar 1 NY
Kate Murphy 22 Ireland
Mary Sullivan 24 NY
Bridget O'Neil 26 Ireland

414 Charles F. Sternberg 31 NY grain merchant
Mary Sternberg 29 NY *ux.*
Natalie Sternberg 7 NY
Pearl Sternberg 5 NY school
Mary Richard 25 NY
Agnes Wright 30 NY
William Hornsby 24 NY coachman

EDWARD STREET ❦ End of Block

434 William Dorsheimer

1880	1891
[442] John C. Smith contractor	
[452] James S. Howells stone dealer	452 James Howells 55 England stone merchant Rosetta Howells 47 NY *ux.* Angelina Howells 22 NY Carrie Brunner
VIRGINIA STREET End of Block	VIRGINIA STREET End of Block

1880 / 1891

1880	1891
WEST TUPPER STREET	WEST TUPPER STREET
	358 William H. Walker WHW&Co. boots & shoes 210 Main
362 Julius Rieffenstahl 52 Brunswick Anna Rieffenstahl 41 NY *ux.* Amelia Rieffenstahl 18 NY daughter Julia Rieffenstahl 16 NY daughter school Louise Rieffenstahl 9 NY	
366 Irving Chamberlain 45 NY veternarian Carrie Chamberlain 37 Michigan *ux.* Willard Chamberlain 17 NY son clerk Frederick Chamberlain 15 NY school Elton Chamberlain 13 NY school Arthur Chamberlain 4 NY school Earle Chamberlain 1 NY Libbie Laner 20 NY	366 John C. Glenny
368 Lucus Westover decorator	
374 Thomas Jebb 46 Canada capitalist Frances Jebb 42 NY *ux.* William Jebb 23 NY son Mary O'Connell 36 Ireland Bridget McGrath 26 Ireland Mary Smith 38 NY	374 Mills W. Barse banker Olean Mrs. C. V. Barse
DELAWARE PLACE End of Block	DELAWARE PLACE End of Block
388 Mary J. Pratt 62 Mass. Samuel King 17 NY grandson school William King 15 NY grandson Daisy King 8 NY granddaughter school Mary Bringle 50 Ireland Annie Nikels 26 NY Mary Smith 38 NY	388 The Buffalo Club
396 James M. Ganson 62 NY retired banker Nancy Ganson 52 NY *ux.* Charles F. Ganson 26 NY daughter- in-law Mabel Ganson 1 NY granddaughter David Thompson 32 Scotland coachman Margaret Bateman 40 Ireland Elizabeth Thomas 35 NY Mary Thomas 13 NY Illegible Kavanaugh 22 NY	396 Mrs. James M. Ganson

414 William Gratwick 40 NY lumber dealer
Martha Gratwick 39 NY *ux.*
Harry Gratwick 10 NY son school
Freddie Gratwick 7 NY son school
Mildred Gratwick 2 NY daughter
John McKrink 50 Ireland coachman
Sarah McKrink 45 Ireland *ux.*
Rosa Smith 26 Ireland
Maregaret Smith 28 Ireland
Nancy Morgan 30 NY
Mary Reany 20 Ireland

EDWARD STREET ❦ End of Block

438 Charles W. McCune 48 Vermont
proprietor *Morning Courier*
Ellen McCune NY daughter
Kate Healey 23 NY
Mary Neville 30 Ireland
Mary Lawson 35 Ireland

448 Robert B. Adam 48 Scotland AM&A
Grace Adam 47 Scotland *ux.*
Robert B. Adam Jr. 17 Scotland son school
Margaret Adam 13 Scotland daughter school
Mary A. Sharp 26 NY
Jennie Consline 33 NY

452 Robert B. Bement 31 NY
manufacturer steel hammers
Mary E. Bement 30 NY *ux.*
Lansing Bement 6 NY son
Cornelius Lansing 74 NY father-in-law
Mary Lansing 71 NY *ux.*
Anna Curry 24 NY
Matilda Burns 20 NY
Ellen Russell 20 NY

VIRGINIA STREET ❦ End of Block

410 James Foster cashier
Shepard Sidney & Co sheet metal
James G. Forsythe boarder
Mrs. J. D. Foster

414 The Trubee boarding house
S. Curtis Trubee proprietor

EDWARD STREET ❦ End of Block

432 Thomas T. Ramsdell
boots & shoes 215 Washington

438 George Bleistein president
Courier Corporation 197 Main
Patrick De Lacy coachman

448 Robert B. Adam AM&A 400 Main
Robert B. Adam Jr.

452 George S. Field Union Bridge Co

VIRGINIA STREET ❦ End of Block

1900

WEST TUPPER STREET

1905

WEST TUPPER STREET

358 John H. Walker 30 boots & shoes
Evelyn Walker 25 sister
Nellie Farmer 62 cousin
Mary Condon 34 Ireland
Rose Redding 37
Caroline Howard 82
Emily McIntosh 30 nurse
Nora Enright 50 cook
Mary Howard 40 maid

TRINITY STREET End of Block

388 The Buffalo Club

396 Mrs. James Ganson 72 NY
Margaret Bateman 50 Ireland
Catherine Nebelhoer 28 NY

410 James G. Forsythe 68 NY merchant
James F. Foster 38 Wisconsin nephew capitalist
Ellen W. Foster 32 NY niece
James F. Foster Jr. 35 NY grandnephew
Mary Foster 6 NY grandniece
Dorothy Dettman 27 NY
Cornelia Dettman 22 NY
Frances Hoffman 54 Germany

414 The Trubee Hotel
Harry Phillips manager
12 boarders
5 domestics

EDWARD STREET End of Block

430 Edwin Bell 48 NY broker
Annabelle R. Bell 43 NY *ux.*
Madelene Bell 18 NY daughter
Evelyn Bell 14 NY daughter
Nellie E. Leman 24 Canada
Marian Grant 30 Canada

432 Thomas Ramsdell 46 NY shoe manufacturer
Louise Ramsdell 40 Illinois *ux.*
Orrin P. Ramsdell 17 NY son school
Alice M. Ramsdell 11 NY school
Thomas Ramsdell 11 NY school
Christine Campbell 30 Canada
Alice Hellen 61 Canada

438 George Bleistein

366 Mrs. Ethan Howard

374 Francis B. LeFevre 55
Clara A. LeFevre
Mills W. Barse
Isabel Harris 2 England
Hattie Dalton 19

TRINITY STREET End of Block

388 The Buffalo Club

396 Nancy S. Ganson 70
Mary Strasser Germany
Ella Kane Ireland

410 James F. Foster 43
Sidney Shepherd Co.
Catherine O'Connor 36
Kate Smith 30 Ireland

414 The Trubee S. Curtis Trubee proprietor
21 roomers
6 servants

EDWARD STREET End of Block

430 Edwin A. Bell broker
Annabelle Bell 48 *ux.*
Madeline P. Bell 23 daughter
Evelyn Bell 19 daughter

432 Thomas T. Ramsdell 51
vice president Bell Telephone
Louise M. Ramsdell 45 *ux.*
Orrin Ramsdell 22 son
Alice Ramsdell 18 daughter
Thomas Ramsdell 16 son school
Mary Schurn 21

438 George Bleistein 47 president Courier Co.
Elizabeth Bleistein 37 *ux.*
George Bleistein Jr. 18 son school
Chandler W. Bleistein Jr. 18 son school
Barbara Bleistein 13 daughter school
Ellen McFee 56
Ada Chandler 33 England
Nellie Dauberthein 30 Canada
Jane Haggerty 32 Scotland

448	Robert B. Adam 67 Scotland dry goods merchant Robert Adam Jr. 36 England dry goods merchant Deborah H. Clifford 25 Ireland Josephine Somersby 25 Ireland	448	Robert B. Adam 72 Scotland dry goods merchant
452	George S. Field 56 NY civil engineer Margaret C. Field 60 NY *ux.* George H. Field 16 NY son Fred B. Ussher 36 Canada stepson builder Eleanor Ussher 35 Canada stepdaughter Mary B. Conley 49 N Helen Busch 30 NY Ellen Corcoran 20 NY	452	George S. Field 69 NY civil engineer Margaret C. Field 55 Canda *ux.* George Field 22 son college Eleanor Ussher 35 daughter Henry Clipstone 38 England builder Alice McKinnon 28 Canada Margaret Sheehan 25 Ireland Agnes Winters 18
	VIRGINIA STREET ❦ End of Block		VIRGINIA STREET ❦ End of Block

	1915		1920
	WEST TUPPER STREET		WEST TUPPER STREET
358	Perry Wood Mrs. Perry Wood 10 boarders	358	Charles C. Keller 59 NY manager rooming house Elizabeth Keller 52 NY *ux.* 9 lodgers
374	boarding house 27 boarders	374	Jennie Canfield 50 NJ widow manager rooming house 9 lodgers
	TRINITY STREET ❦ End of Block		TRINITY STREET ❦ End of Block
388	The Buffalo Club 5 lodgers	388	The Buffalo Club
396	Nancy Ganson 89 NY niece servant		
414	Trubee Hotel	414	Trubee Hotel Curtis S. Trubee president Frank Trubee 49 bank manager 37 lodgers 6 employees
	EDWARD STREET ❦ End of Block		EDWARD STREET ❦ End of Block
430	Andrew Baker manager 9 roomers	430	Fred Shoemaker 40 NY paint salesman Maude Shoemaker 39 Canada *ux.* Raymond Shoemaker 16 NY son 9 lodgers Magdalene Wildan
436	Edgar McGuire MD 38 Mary Gibboney 45	436	Anna Pratt 23 Illinois 3 lodgers
438	George Bleistein 56 collector of customs Elizabeth Bleistein 50 *ux.* Barbara Bleistein 22 daughter Clara Diebold 31 Mary Rogers 38	438	Walter A. Mack 43 Pa. dress designer Lillian Mack 46 Ohio *ux.* 10 boarders

448 James McLeod 41 MD
Charlotte McLeod 48 sister housekeeper
Charles McLeod 73 father
Charles K. McLeod 38 brother
Belle McLeod 45 sister
Mary Lyons 28 Ireland
Hattie Finbreon 26 England

452 George S. Field 69
Margaret Field 75 *ux.*
George H. Field 32 son attorney
Eleanor Ussher 56 stepdaughter
Lucie Dein 35
James Klipstone 54 England butler
Alice McKenna 45 Canada
Catherine Leinehan 55
Esther Forman 23 Canada
Lena Eicholz 38 Canada

VIRGINIA STREET ❦ End of Block

448 James A. MacLeod MD 45 Canada
Billie McLeod 34 Minnesota
Charles A. MacLeod 42 brother
shoe polish manufacturer
Sue Baker MacLeod 12 California daughter
Rixie Baker MacLeod 11 California daughter
Kathleen McIntosh 48 NY
Emma Gruber 62 NY

452 General George S. Field 74 Pa.
Margaret Field 79 Canada
Eleanor Ussher 58 Canada stepdaughter
Henry Klipstone 51 England butler
Alice McKenna 50 Canada chambermaid
Elizabeth Turnull 36 Pa. parlor maid
Jean Thompson 32 England chambermaid
Ernestine de Wein 36 NY cook
Sarah Quinn 32 Ireland assistant cook

VIRGINIA STREET ❦ End of Block

7.3 ❦ **Number 358 Delaware, *Grand American Avenue*, p. 60.**

The short block on the west side from Tupper to German Alley in 1850 boasted five houses but that on the corner of Tupper was a double house.(7.2) In 1860 there were four houses on the block. The double house had been supplanted by a single house, shown in figure 7.3, a picture from the next century after commercialization had occurred, and the mongrelized structure had been christened the Parsons Building. The four houses were occupied south to north in 1870 by an architect, the editor of *The Republic*, a bookkeeper, and a lake captain. In 1870 only two families, one headed by a German-born druggist, Julius Reiffenstahl, answered the census-taker's questions. Julius was still around in 1880 at #362, while next door at #366 Irving Chamberlain, a veterinarian, lived with his wife, five children, and one young maid. On the corner of Delaware Place a forty-six year old self-described capitalist, Thomas A. Jebb, lived with his wife and twenty-three year old son. The requirements of the three Jebbs were met by three domestics, two of them Irish girls. About 1890 John C. Glenny moved into #366. He was a son of William H. Glenny, who had come to Buffalo in 1835 and became an importer and retailer of fine pottery and glassware. After his death his three sons, William H., Jr., John C., and Bryant, continued the business until it closed in the late 1890s.[1] Following Glenny at #366 in the late

1 *Times*, February 11, 1929.

7.4 ❦ **The Buffalo Club in the nineteenth century, BHS.**

1890s was Ethan Howard. He had been born in Vermont to parents whose ancestors were early settlers of Boston. He came to Buffalo in 1830 and clerked in a dry goods store before going into business on his own in 1836. He retired in 1865 when his business merged into Flynt & Kent, and was later associated with Joseph Warren in the Courier Printing Company. Howard was a trustee of the Erie County Savings Bank, treasurer of the *Courier*, and director of Buffalo Gaslight and the Bank of Niagara Falls. He died in 1898, survived by his second wife, the former Caroline Cogswell of Peterborough, New Hampshire, who lived on at #366 until after 1910, by which time the entire block was given over to rooming houses. During the 1920s it was the site of the Parsons and Huyler buildings with stores on the ground floor. His obituary hailed Ethan as "one of the old guard of businessmen who laid the foundation of Buffalo's greatness."[2]

Commercializing lower Delaware did not just happen; interests with an agenda promoted it. The following failed prophecy exemplifies the babbitry of the 1920's. The gods must have been smiling:

> The rerouting of [street] cars through Franklin street started its development for business about 1911, with new buildings increasing until 1914 when the war began and put a stop to this kind of enterprise. A little later attention began to be attracted toward Delaware by reason of high rentals on Main street and because it was so clearly evident that the street was ideally located for business and that the property was held at very moderate prices.
>
> Development commenced at Chippewa street, because of its connection with Main street, it being the only cross street built up with business blocks. Since that time, especially in the last two or three years, Delaware has progressed very rapidly, as its advantages became apparent and the high rentals on Main street made it difficult for certain classes of business to remain there.
>
> The success of Delaware as a business street has not been interrupted, and so far as I know, no merchant who started business on the street has moved to any other location. Many people who started in a small way have moved into larger quarters. Rentals have kept pace with increased valuations. That this will continue is practically assured, basing this opinion on what is happening on streets similarly located in other cities.
>
> This development is most important for the merchant who wishes to remain in the downtown section and cannot afford to pay Main street rental. Before the opening to business on Delaware and Franklin streets such merchants moved to some neighborhood business section such as Grant, Ferry, Hertel, North Main, Kensington or some smaller neighborhood, and our downtown business district was hurt to that extent.

2 *Express*, March 3, 1898.

> After lower Delaware had started on its way as a business street a number of owners got together to plan for a high-grade street and not have buildings erected in a haphazard way. To that end they brought the president of the Fifth Avenue Association to Buffalo and he gave the benefit of his advice, and informed us how the problem had been handled on Fifth avenue. Rules and regulations of that association, which were applicable to Buffalo, were adopted and the members of the Delaware Association have loyally stood by and worked for the best development of the street.
>
> Buffalo will be as proud of Delaware avenue as a high-grade business street, in the business section, as it has been boastful of it as a residence street. The idea of building it up as a dignified shopping street, without obstructions such as stands, overhanging signs, etc., is one of the main objects of the Association. Bus service has already done a great deal in the way of making it convenient for shoppers and has also given pleasure to those people not familiar with the beauties of the avenue. Widening and better lighting transform the street in the old section from a narrow roadway filled with residences which had degenerated into boarding houses, into an up-to-date business thoroughfare...Main street will be the Broadway of Buffalo and Delaware its Fifth avenue.[3]

This sweeping agenda had its opponents:

> Meanwhile, the Association had obtained from the Council a resolution directing the widening of the roadway from its original width of 40 feet to a width of 60 feet as far north as Allen Street, which would take advantage of the 100-foot width of the thoroughfare for traffic purposes, would permit the installation of an adequate new sewer, and would be followed, the decision having been reached as to the permanent width of the roadway, by the installation of a modern lighting and signal system. This meant the end of the century-old phase of the Avenue in which it had been famous for its four rows of fine elms, and the fight to "save the trees," backed by many sincere sentimentalists but turned into a burlesque by the adherence of sectionalists from various parts of the City who mistakenly feared that the business development of the Avenue would hurt their sections, became a matter of acute social and political strife. The Association was called upon to spend large sums of money in explaining the needs of the Avenue in the press, and for legal services, before the opposition was routed and it was possible to proceed with the work. Such of the trees [two of four rows] as were in the way were removed in the midwinter of 1924-1925, and the widened roadway, new-lined with luminous arc lamps of about 1,400 candlepower at 80-foot intervals was opened to traffic in July, 1925.[4]

In 1930 the Avenue was widened to North and more trees removed.[5]

The Buffalo Club's third and final site was #388 Delaware at Delaware Place. The site was a lot 100' by 284' with a stable to the rear on another 100' square lot. Total cost was $63,000 ($1,098,090 in 1997 dollars). The old clubhouse on Buffalo and Chippewa was sold to Mrs. Mary A. Brayley for $25,000:[6]

> The Buffalo Club was built for a home, not a clubhouse. In the large brick building at Delaware and Trinity remodeled four times to meet the demands of increasing membership and expanding activities, the trained eye can detect the brick mansion of architecture suggestive of French Renaissance design, once one of the city's most elegant homes. (7.4-7)

3 Richard W. Goode, "Delaware Avenue as a High-Grade Business Street," *Truth*, October 31, 1925.
4 H. B. Saunders, "Delaware Avenue Today and Tomorrow," *ibid.*
5 *Courier*, February 15, 1930.
6 Warren, *op. cit.*, p. 37-38.

> In 1870, the mansion was completed and occupied by the late S[tephen] V. R. Watson (7.8), his wife, and their three daughters. Mr. Watson was a founder of three institutions that have played an important role in the development and life of Buffalo for three quarters of a century — the street railway system with cars drawn by horses while he was president, the Erie County Savings Bank, and the Buffalo Public Library. In 1860, Mr. Watson represented this city's interests in the State Legislative Assembly...

This man's interests included the Watson Grain Elevator, extensive local real estate [on the East Side where he sold house lots particularly to German immigrants], and Great Lakes shipping. He enjoyed thoroughly every phase of living, among them organizing and developing business enterprises, heading civic projects and planning original entertainment for his family and friends.

The entire third floor of S. V. R. Watson's mansion was given over to recreation. The ballroom on that floor was the scene of some of the most beautiful balls ever given for Buffalo society. The theater was complete with stage, curtain, scenery and footlights. Its seating capacity was 300. Mr. and Mrs. Watson were hosts at three theater parties in their home each year.

Plays were presented by the well-remembered Buffalo Amateurs. The night after Christmas 1872, the play "Look Before You Leap" was presented in the Watson home. Maria Love read the prologue which was written by E. Carleton Sprague. The cast included Tom Viele, Trumbull and Charles Cary, Jennie Cary,

Above Left 7.5 ❦ The Buffalo Club in 1908, BHS.
Above Right 7.6 ❦ Buffalo Club, late twentieth century, Dr. V. Roger Lalli, *Watercolor Series*, GJK Enterprises, Buffalo, NY, 1993.
Middle 7.7 ❦ Buffalo Club, interior, Warren, *op. cit.*, p. 68 (2).
Below 7.8 ❦ Stephen Van Rennsselaer Watson, Smith, *op. cit.*, II, facing p. 530.

who became Mrs. Lawrence D. Rumsey, and Annie Watson, later the wife of Samuel S. Spaulding. The play was directed by S. Douglas Cornell, grandfather of Katherine Cornell. Following the performance, guests visited the mirror-paneled drawing room. Its exquisite crystal chandeliers shed soft light on a Christmas tree and other holiday greens. Red holly berries added to the festive atmosphere while mistletoe hung from doorways. In the building of his home, S. V. R. Watson spared no expense. The woodwork of the drawing room was rich English walnut inlaid with walnut burls. The latter odd pieces of wood are attractive with natural swirls.

The two daughters of Watson, besides Annie, were Jennie, who became the wife of Porter Norton, and Gertrude. Gertrude did not marry. Music and philanthropy were the interests most important in her life. She was an accomplished pianist whose recitals delighted her friends in Buffalo and Pittsfield, Mass., later her home, and won praise from music critics. At Pittsfield, Gertrude Watson established Camp Onota, one of the first vacation resorts made available for low cost to working girls of New York City.

Descendants of S. V. R. Watson living here include Daniel Barton Streeter, Porter Norton Streeter, Mrs. Robert Lowell Putnam, Jr., Edward R. Spaulding, Mrs. Albert Gurney, Samuel S. Spaulding, S. V. R. Spaulding, Jr., Allen Spaulding, Mrs. George Foreman Goodyear, Mrs. William Meadows, William Gregory Meadows, Jr., Rufus Meadows, Mrs. Albert Dold, Mrs. Langdon Albright, Jr., Miss Charlotte Albright, and Watson Albright.[7]

Watson died in 1880, and his mansion was sold to the widow of Samuel F. Pratt. No Buffalo families had better Yankee credentials than the Pratts, the first of whom, John, had come to America in 1639. Samuel Pratt, born in Townsend, Vermont, in 1787, was the son of a veteran of the Revolution, Captain Samuel Pratt, who had come to Buffalo early in the 1800s and died there shortly after the outbreak of the War of 1812. His widow fled to Vermont after the burning of Buffalo, but returned and died in 1830. The captain's son, Samuel, Jr., had not accompanied his family to Buffalo but came out in 1807 with his wife, Sophia Fletcher, daughter of a veteran of both the French and Indian War and the Revolution. In Buffalo Samuel, Jr., engaged in mercantile pursuits with his father, was appointed sheriff of Niagara County in 1810, served as adjutant to General Peter Porter during the War of 1812, and died at Buffalo in 1822. Samuel Fletcher Pratt was born to Samuel, Jr. and Sophia 1807, just before the family moved here. In 1819 he began three years clerking in a general store in Canada, returned to Buffalo, and in 1828 got a job in the hardware store of George and Thaddeus Weed, later known as Weed & Pratt. In 1836 Pratt purchased the Weed interest and in 1842 with his brother, Pascal Paoli Pratt, and Edward P. Beals, formed Samuel Fletcher Pratt & Company, which dealt in hardware, bar iron, sheet iron, tools, contractors' and railroad supplies, and coach and saddlery ware. In 1848, with Pratt & Company continuing in its old line, a new firm, Pratt & Letchworth, was organized to deal exclusively in carriages and saddles. Partners were the Pratt brothers and William P. Letchworth from Auburn, where he had used convict labor in a like enterprise. Manufacturing was done at #165 Main where inmates of the nearby jail did the work. It was also in 1848 that Samuel F. Pratt bought into Buffalo Gas Light, of which he became president until

7 *CE*, March,23, 1952.
8 *M&FH*, 1:5-6; Horton, *op. cit.*, 1:98-99.

his death. He was the first president and long-time trustee of the Buffalo Female Academy.[8] He died in 1872. His widow, Mary Jane, bought the Watson home and was living there in 1880 with three grandchildren. In 1887 she sold it to the club, whose doings occasionally made the national news:

> In the Autumn of 1901, the year of the Pan-American Exposition, while President McKinley lay battling for his life in the home of John Milburn, several members of the Presidential Cabinet were lodged in the Buffalo Club. The directors' room was reserved for their use. A private telegraph line connected this room with the White House in Washington. During that anxious period the Buffalo Club was the center from which the nation's business was conducted.[9]

Earlier, during the switchmen's strike of 1892, when freight cars were being derailed and burned, passenger trains uncoupled and stoned, strikebreakers terrorized, and more violence threatened, the club had played a minor role in forcing a solution. As Horton wrote with populist exaggeration:

> At this juncture the seat of government in city and county shifted to the Buffalo Club. There the railroad lawyers, Daniel H. MacMillan, Frank Brundage, Wilson Shannon Bissell and Eben Carleton Sprague met with Sheriff Beck and Mayor Charles Bishop and after a long consultation succeeded in overcoming the Sheriff's reluctance to request Governor Flower to send the entire National Guard of the State of New York to Buffalo. The telegram to effect this had been already prepared by the lawyers. Mayor and Sheriff had but to sign it. Their signatures brought a military force of about 8,000 men to the city. The force was smaller than had been requested, but it was sufficient to give the lawyers and persons of property in general a sense of security.[10]

The downtown men's club completed and strengthened the socialization of America's late nineteenth century elite. As an unfriendly observer of the process writes:

> When the gilded youths at Harvard, Yale, and Princeton finally left the protected world of the "Gold Coast" to seek their fortunes in the Wall Streets and executive suites of the nation, they naturally joined one or another exclusive men's club. Here they dined with others of their kind, helped each other to secure jobs and promotions, and made friends with influential older members who might some day be of help to them in their paths to the top. Proper club affiliation was, after all, the final and most important stage in an exclusive socializing process.

But more than socialization was involved in the process:

> In the 1900s the metropolitan club became far more important than the country club, the private school and college, or the exclusive neighborhood as the crucial variable in the recruitment of America's new corporate aristocracy. Family position and prestige built up as a result of several generations of leadership and service in some provincial city or town, were gradually replaced by an aristocracy by ballot [new members were voted in by old members], in the hierarchy of metropolitan clubdom.[11]

Changes to the Buffalo Club occurred over the years. In 1889 an addition was made to the rear for a billiard room, dining rooms, kitchen, and servants quarters, paid for partially by selling the stable and lot to the Buffalo Widows' Asylum. The board approved a gymnasium annex with six sleeping

9 *CE*, March 23, 1952.
10 Horton, *op. cit.*, I, 327.
11 E. Digby Baltzell, "The Social Defenses of the Rich," in *The Private Side of American History: Readings in Everyday Life* (Orlando, Florida: Harcourt Brace Jovanovich, 1975), 2:97-99.

rooms in June 1898. In 1907 a wing was built on Trinity Place. The property next to the club at #396 Delaware was acquired in 1919. In 1925 part of this was sold for $136,000 to reduce the club's debt. However in 1929 at the start of the Depression the purchaser defaulted. In 1947 the Club bought the infant asylum at Elmwood and Edward and promptly sold much of it, retaining only the part next to the parking lot. In 1958 a north wing was added with an entrance on the ground floor. In August 1966, "the Club purchased, for cash, the adjacent property to the north on [#410] Delaware Avenue and razed the building thereon to provide additional parking space and for future protection against undesirable neighbors."[12]

7.9 ❦ Numbers 396, 410, and 414 Delaware, BHS. The section of Delaware Avenue in front of this block was probably asphalted in 1889. Warren, *op. cit.*, p. 39.

Figure 7.9 exhibits the lineup of three old mansions north of the club, #396, #410, and #414 in the 1920s. An article in the local press written in 1931 on the occasion of the razing of #396 recapitulated its history:

> Another of Buffalo's beautiful old homes is being demolished — the James Ganson residence, on the west side of Delaware avenue. The handsome edifice, a smart, brown brick house with bay windows on either side, and ornamental designs over the top of the plate glass windows, has witnessed many changes during the years of existence. It was once the Blackmer [read Blackmar] home in the early 60's. Mr. [Abel T.] Blackmer [a brewmaster] was a prominent and wealthy citizen and his daughter married Charles Sternberg, who at that time was considered the handsomest young bachelor in Buffalo. He was the son of Pearl Sternberg, another wealthy resident, and he built the splendid red brick mansion at the southwest corner of Delaware avenue and Edward. Following Mr. Blackmer's death, his residence was sold to Edward Stevenson(7.10), who occupied it for some years before purchasing the Jason Parker mansion at the southeast corner of Delaware avenue and North street. The property then took on a new owner, James Ganson, a leading financier, who with his wife and his only son, Charles Ganson, were its last occupants. Since that

7.10 ❦ Edward L. Stevenson, Smith, *op. cit.*, II, facing 284.

12 Warren, *op. cit.*, pp. 39, 47, 53, 83, 108, 121, 129.

> time this historic home has been a center of Red Cross activities and church work, but it has finished its course and must make way for a new era. Many fine entertainments have taken place within its walls, and it was one of the very few left of those imposing homes which once graced Delaware avenue as far back as when it had the peaceful serenity of a dirt road and asphalt was unheard of.[13]

He lived until 1891, but Stevenson's career was over by the time of the coming of the railroads. He represents an earlier Buffalo, as is seen in this Horatio Alger account of his life:

> Edward L. Stevenson. — The subject of this notice was born in Auburn, Cayuga county, N. Y., on the 31st day of March, 1806. His father was Edward Stevenson and his mother was Ann Lockwood; they came westward from Massachusetts, the former being a native of Greenwich, and the latter of Pittsfield. The family remained in Auburn until Edward L. was seventeen years old, during the most of which period, after he had reached a suitable age, he attended the common schools of that village, at the same time applying himself in his leisure hours to the acquirement of such education as was obtainable with his limited advantages.
>
> During the last years of his life in Auburn Mr. Stevenson was in the employ of Chauncey H. Coe, who then kept a hotel there and had charge of that division of the great stage route running from Buffalo to Albany. In the stage office the young man made himself thoroughly conversant with the details of that business; and so well did he please his employer that when Mr. Coe sold out his business in Auburn and came to Buffalo, he brought his assistant with him. Mr. Stevenson arrived in Buffalo on the 18th of October, 1823. His employer purchased the western division of the stage route from Sylvanus Marvin, a brother of the late Mrs. Judge Walden and Mr. Stevenson was at once placed in the office. In 1825 Mr. Coe exchanged the stage business with his brother, Bella D. Coe, then of Canandaigua, who came to Buffalo and took charge of the stage line, still retaining Mr. Stevenson in the office.
>
> The stage route from Buffalo to Albany constituted in those days an enterprise of very considerable magnitude. At one time four regular lines of coaches left Buffalo — the "Telegraph" line which limited the number of its passengers to six and in seasons of good roads made the distance to Albany in forty-eight hours, charging fifteen dollars fare; the "Pilot" line, the "Diligence," and the regular mail and accommodation line. The three latter charged about ten dollars fare. Old residents tell many amusing and interesting experiences while bowling along in the old days of stage travel.
>
> Immediately upon the arrival of Mr. Stevenson in Buffalo he entered upon the duties in the stage office, which was then located in the old Mansion House, but after about six months was removed to the building in which was located the old and long popular Eagle tavern, where it permanently remained. This division of the stage line was operated by Mr. Coe for a number of years, a large share of the management of which devolved upon Mr. Stevenson. It was finally sold to Benjamin Rathbun a short time previous to his disastrous bankruptcy, Mr. Stevenson's continued service being a stipulation in the bargain. Upon the occurrence of that memorable event, the assignees (Messrs. Lewis F. Allen, Joseph Clary, Millard Fillmore, and David E. Evans) placed the stage business in the sole charge of Mr. Stevenson pending the settlement of the estate; and it is said that at the time they closed up the wrecked affairs of the famous speculator, the stage business was the only portion of his property that was found to be paying a profit.

13 *CE*, December 8, 1931.

> Mr. Stevenson continued in the stage office until the spring of 1842, at which time the Buffalo & Attica Railroad was completed, forming the last link in the line from Buffalo to Albany and practically ending the stage business over that route forever. During the period since Mr. Stevenson's arrival in Buffalo and the date just mentioned, he made numerous investments under the advice of his friend, the late Hon. Albert H. Tracy, and his employer, Mr. Coe. Their real estate operations, being carefully and judiciously conducted, yielded handsome profits and laid the foundation of his present large fortune. He is one of the comparatively few men whose wisdom, prudence and foresight carried him safely through the panic of 1836 and other financial revulsions, in which such a large portion of the business men of the country were overwhelmed.
>
> Mr. Stevenson was for nearly twenty-five years engaged with his brother, the late George Stevenson, in conducting a livery business in this city. At one period they kept in stable sixty horses and practically controlled that business in the community.
>
> In 1837 Mr. Stevenson was elected Alderman of the Third Ward of Buffalo, and was again elected to the same office in 1839. The duties of this office he discharged to the eminent satisfaction of his constituents and for the best good of the city. He is now a trustee of the Buffalo Savings Bank; a director in the bank of Buffalo; was at one time a real estate commissioner of the Young Men's Association, in which he has always felt a warm interest, and a director of the Buffalo Insurance Company. He is an attendant at St. Paul's Church, of which he has been one of the vestrymen. In person Mr. Stevenson is naturally of a retiring disposition, never courting the notice of the public and devoting himself quietly to the management of his own affairs. For many years past he has devoted his attention almost entirely to the care of his large real estate interests, and now, having accumulated a competence and won the unqualified respect and friendship of all with whom he has come in contact with during his long life in Buffalo, he may look back upon a long career of honor and usefulness. It is his pride to say that he has transacted business within a circle of one hundred feet from his present office on Main street for a period of sixty years.
>
> Mr. Stevenson was married in 1832 to Miss Amelia S. Geer, of Shelburne, Chittenden county, Vt. She was a daughter of William and Sally Geer, of that State. They have had two children, Edward Henry, born October 23, 1838, died May 5, 1850; and George P. Stevenson, born May 9, 1849, and died May 23, 1878. The latter was one of the most promising and respected young men of Buffalo, and his loss was a terrible blow to his fond parents.[14]

In the 1860s James M. Ganson, third resident at #396, lived at Delaware and Cary Streets. His son Charles was Mabel Ganson's father, who married Sarah Cook and lived at #675 Delaware in the 1880s and 1890s. Mabel has left published impressions of growing up unhappy in Buffalo, entitling an entire chapter "Grandma Ganson and Her House," the source of these excerpts:

> Grandma Ganson lived on Delaware avenue in a large square brick house with a cupola on top of it with windows to the four corners. The house was painted with what they called dun-colour, a fawn-grey tone. It had an iron fence, and two large iron vases set in the lawn on both sides of the front steps. In the summer these vases always had "ornamental grasses," geraniums, and fuchsias growing in them. Some people had iron deer on their lawns.

14 Smith, *op. cit.*, 2:89-92.

On the left side of Grandma's house, the lawns running together, was the Buffalo Club, the club of the middle-aged and elderly gentleman. Right opposite, close to the street, stood Trinity Church — "our church." At the corner of the block on Edward Street was the cosy-looking Saturn Club of red brick, the young men's club, that bore on its inner walls the device: "Where the women cease from troubling and the wicked are at rest!" I am sure the new edifice of the Saturn Club, grown prosperous, far up on Delaware Avenue, all plate glass and Gothic arches, has no such gay, light touch about it.

Grandma loved her neighbourhood. In winter she used to sit in her bay window that was projected out into the world with its glass panes reaching to the floor. She sat in a fine, light, shining cane rocking-chair and knitted cotton washcloths. As she knitted she peered over her spectacles toward the Buffalo Club or the Saturn Club, or towards the church. She knew all the men who frequented all these places, and she was open and earnestly interested in them all. She knew them personally, most of them — their houses and their businesses and their families. And besides that she knew their club habits. And all the men knew her and always looked towards her bay window, and lifted their hats whether they saw her there or not, which depended on the year and the time of day.

Grandpa Ganson did not plant many memories with me. I remember he was cross with my grandmother, and very amiable when he sat out in the large warm kitchen in the rocking-chair, with Maggie Donnelly. Old Maggie, the cook was older than my grandmother or him. She had come from Batavia with them. She had a small round head and beautiful silver hair parted in the middle and brushed back in waves like a sand pattern. She was always giving sage advice to everyone, even to grandpa Ganson that always began with "Faith an' ..." Up in her little bedroom there was a mystery very entrancing. She kept her window shade down and on sneaking into her room one saw at first only a dull glitter and shimmer in the corner. And it never fully revealed itself. But a closer look showed a complicated altar created on her high mahogany dressing-bureau. Virgins, infant Jesuses, little shining candlesticks and crucifixions, silvery lace and imitation white alabaster — the Virgin's blue, and shining tin ornaments — who knows what it all was? But it made an atmosphere! A holy, mysterious atmosphere very delicious to absorb.

At the back of the house was a space of green grass and a grape arbour and a stable. In the stable were the two carriage horses, a coupe, a victoria, and David. David was truly the blackest-natured man I have ever seen, except my father. He had black hair mixed with grey and smoke-black eyes and a black expression. Awful. He never spoke except to snarl. He would come blackly in from the stable and through the back hall to the back sitting-room, in the morning, and he'd stand by the door with his queer cap in his hand, and snarl: "Orders?" And my grandparents wouldn't notice he was snarling. Grandma would reply pleasantly: "Yes, David, we'll want the closed carriage at half-past two" - and out he'd go without a word. In those days people didn't bother to analyse other people - they just let them be, more. To my grandmother, David was just himself, and he had a right to be so, as a plum has a right to be purple, or an apple to be red. David was just a dark thing. All right. That was David. He had a right to be whatever he was. He did his work faithfully and took good care of the horses and drove carefully. But I must say children hated him. Even if one didn't analyse him. But then one kept out of his dark shadow.

As I grew older Grandma seemed to grow younger. I remember hearing my mother and father and other people grumbling about her — and even speaking with some kind of apprehension in their voices.

For Grandma began to get interested in young men. She always took Cousin Carrie with her for their usual summer trip to the White Mountains where they stayed at the Profile House, or to Lake George or Richfield Springs. And when they came back from one of these visits Aunt Carrie was looking rather worried. She was my grandmother's niece and lived with her, and it was understood that grandma had left her a lot of money in her will, to compensate her for giving up her life. Well, Cousin Carrie said that Grandma had put on white duck dresses and a leghorn [fine plaited straw] hat and had gone out on the lake with a young man. This very plainly alarmed everybody. I can remember the alarm very well. It had an element of shame in it, and a kind of queer, half-humorous concern. But no one did anything about it.

From that time, for many years, Grandma worried the family. There were always curates from our church calling on her. She got a great deal out of church. It was like a wing of her own house to her. It became incorporated in the housed life she always lived — maybe that was why in her will she left her house to be Trinity Rectory. That and the curates. Trinity Church was not one of those "Holy! Holy! Holy!" churches. It was large and light, with light oak pews and a red carpet a good deal like Grandma's hall carpet. It had large stained-glass windows of high light colours, not the dark, rich, mysterious small-paned kind. Everybody in it knew every one else, and it had a drawing-room atmosphere, with a smell of cut flowers and candles.[15]

Grandma Ganson outlived her husband by thirty-five years, dying at #396 in 1918. Difficult he may have been, but he left her well situated for the rest of her life. She left her house to Trinity as a rectory, but the church sold it to the Buffalo Club for $35,000 and used the proceeds to buy a smaller rectory. The surplus was invested for its upkeep.[16]

The Queen Ann mansion at #410 was built for James G. Forsythe, an industrialist. Born in Wisconsin in 1832, he received a common schooling at Kenosha where he was then apprenticed to a tinsmith. He came to Buffalo at twenty in 1832 and went to work for Pratt & Company, wholesale hardware. In 1836 he transferred to Sidney Shepard & Company, sheet metal goods, in which he became a top executive. He never married and his household consisted in a nephew, James Foster, also a Sidney Shepard executive, and family. Forsythe retired in 1897 and spent the rest of his days as a world traveler. He died at #410 Delaware in 1903. In his will the Buffalo Parks Department and the Fine Arts received $200,000 each.[17] The Fosters stayed at #410 for several years, but by the mid-1920s it was a rooming house, *The Edward*, with eighteen guests. It was bought and razed by the Buffalo Club in 1966.

7.11 ❦ Second Empire at its best, #414 Delaware Avenue. *Buffalo News*, June 28, 1997.

The Second Empire (after Napoleon, III, Emperor of the French 1852-1870) masterpiece at Delaware and Edward(7.11), recently restored to its original

15 Luhan, *op. cit.*, pp. 118-136.
16 *Times*, January 10, 1925.
17 *Express*, March 29, 1903.

splendor, was built 1869-1870 by Charles F. Sternberg, a grain elevator owner, for his bride, Mary Blackmar, for $200,000 ($3,486,000 in 1997 dollars).

> Sternberg apparently desired an abundance of light in his new house, for [architect George M.] Alliston's elevations are distinguished by many graceful, wide-arched openings. In all, there are twelve bay windows. The center piece of the façade is the elegant entrance porch, elevated several feet above the street, approached by two curved flights of marble steps and trimmed with delicate iron cresting; it is supported by cast-iron Corinthian columns from which spring small pointed arches."[18]

7.12 William H. Gratwick, J. N. Larned, *A History of Buffalo* (New York: Progress of Empire State Co., 1911), I, facing p. 228.

Interior features included fourteen-foot high ceilings on the first floor, and oak and mahogany wainscotting and molding throughout. In the late 1870s #414 became the residence of lumber baron William H. Gratwick(7.12), born in Albany in 1839 and educated at the Boys Academy there, of whom Horton writes:

> Along the channel of that [Great Lakes] navigation there floated into Lake Erie commodities of which Buffalo, not Cleveland, took the lion's share. Of these one of the most lucrative was lumber. This traffic, unlike that in ore, had been well developed in *ante bellum* days; but in the '70s and '80s it grew beyond all previous bounds as the lumber kings and the lumber-jacks denuded the lands of Wisconsin, Michigan and Minnesota of their ancient stands of pine and hemlock. Timber of all kinds, hard as well as soft, came into Buffalo from up the Lakes in ever mounting volume: 119,146,000 feet in 1876; by 1884 the volume had more than doubled. Cumbrous and bulky, this product was well suited to canal transportation and it helped in some measure to compensate the Erie Canal for the dwindling volume of grain borne over its sluggish waters. In 1876, 57,213,584 feet of lumber moved over the Canal to the Eastward; 107,144,819 feet moved in 1879, though by '84 the amount had gone down to less than 50,000,000. But even this was enough to make the port of Tonawanda a busy place. There it was that the transfer from the Lake to the Canal was for the most part effected. The business, despite its ups and downs, was already on its way to making Tonawanda the greatest lumber port in the world, though most of the product there piled and thence transshipped was owned by interests located in New York, Buffalo, and Albany. From the last mentioned place, about 1880 came William H. Gatwick to identify himself with the lumber interest of Buffalo. In the yards of that city every foot represented an investment of local capital which Gratwick's arrival helped enlarge and reenforce.[19]

Gratwick did not stay long at #414. In the early '80s he hired architect H. H. Richardson to design a more spectacular mansion at #776 Delaware.[20] He was followed briefly at #414 by Civil War

18 Francis R. Kowsky, *et. al.*, *Buffalo Architecture: A Guide* (Cambridge, Mass., MIT Press, 1981), p. 128.
19 Horton, *op. cit.*, 1:220.
20 Kowsky, "Delaware Avenue," *Great American Avenue*, p. 41.

veteran John Condit Smith, a native of Troy, Morris County, New Jersey, who joined his uncle's construction company and built thousands of miles of railroad. During the Civil War Smith served on the staff of General Sherman whom he accompanied on the notorious march through Georgia. Smith died in 1883.[21]

> In 1883, Samuel Curtis Trubee took ownership and converted the home into a family hotel. Sometime in the 1890s, an addition was built at the rear of the building, expanding the structure to include 40 rooms. By the 1930s rumors circulated that the family atmosphere had long-since evaporated and the hotel had turned into a bordello.
>
> Hugo DiGiulio bought the place in 1947 and transformed it into Victor Hugo's Wine Cellar, a name synonymous with excellent French and Continental cuisine. DiGiulio also maintained apartments in the building that often were rented to celebrities who were performing in Buffalo. The guest list included actor Howard Keel and piano virtuoso Liberace. For a time the building also housed a theater run by the Catholic Actors Guild.
>
> The restaurant closed in July 1977. The building continued its life as an apartment hotel for several more years. A handful of unsuccessful attempts were made to convert the structure to an office complex, dating back to the mid-1980s.[22]

The west side of Delaware from Edward to Virginia was unimproved in 1850.(7.2) During the next decade, a mansion was built on the corner of Delaware and Virginia by James S. Howells, an English-born stone merchant and paving contractor, who lived there with his family into the 1870s. He died in 1880. Second owner was James C. Harrison, son of Jonas Harrison, a pioneer settler. Born in 1818, young Harrison started out in the office of General Charles Reed. During the 1840s, a decade of vast migration westward, Harrison supervised shipbuilding for Reed's extensive fleet on the Great Lakes and managed his passenger and cargo business. In 1873 he built Reed's grain elevator on the lakefront. A founder of the Erie County Savings Bank, he was its president for several years, and his directorships included the International Bank and the Buffalo & Erie Railroad.[23] He served a term as alderman, was a vestryman of Trinity, and curator of the Fine Arts Academy. He was followed on the Avenue in the late 1870s by Robert B. Bement of Kip & Bement, steel hammers. However the glory days of #452 were during its ownership by General George S. Field(7.13) beginning in 1883:

7.13 ❦ Gen. George Spencer Field, Warren, *op. cit.*, p. 41.

> To the original mansion...General Field added a living room 40 feet square, with a large inviting fireplace surmounted by a carved mantel. Beneath this room, he built a completely equipped Turkish bath. His favorite

21 *Courier*, November 10, 1883.
22 *BN*, June 6, 1997.
23 Dave McLellan and Bill Warrick, *The Lake Shore & Michigan Southern Railway* (Polo, Illinois: Transportation Trails, 1989), p. 23.

boast was that his parties were followed by no ill effects. He delighted to play host to a large group of prominent men, among them Gen. Hayes, John J. Albright and Grover Cleveland.

In General Field's day, the house was the last word in luxury, fashion, and gracious living. One entered into a long hall leading to a broad graceful mahogany stairway. On the right was a somber room known as the formal drawing room. Decorated in the mode of the '80s, that room had an atmosphere of gloom. It would have offered an ideal setting for the most depressing tales penned by Edgar Allen Poe. The entire interior of the room was in black, from the heavy ebony woodwork to the furniture of matching wood, upholstered in black. Across from the black drawing room was the library in mahogany woodwork.

Passing through the library one arrived in the great square living room, planned by Gen. Field to accommodate comfortably the many friends he invited so frequently into his home. Dark blue was the predominating color of the walls, furniture, upholstery, drapes and the Oriental rug that nearly covered the 40-foot square floor.

Toward the rear of the house were General Field's office, its walls lined with engineering books, the commodious dining room, maid's dining room, pantries and spacious kitchen. The great round mahogany table that once centered the Field living room continued to be used, though built to order nearly 70 years ago. Cut into two semicircular tables, it stands in the dining room of the YWCA residence on North St.

The general may never have heard a shot fired in anger:

He came by his military appellation through his close personal friendship with the late President Grover Cleveland. He was made a general on Cleveland's personal staff when the latter was Governor of New York State, and the title remained with him during the remainder of his life.

Nor did he have any formal training in engineering:

Born in Springfield, N. Y., February 26, 1846, General Field was educated in the rural schools and helped his father on the farm. His education was more or less practical, and while still very young he taught in the rural schools, many times having pupils in his care who were several years his senior.

It was shortly after he reached the age of 20 that he joined a railroad surveying crew and began studying engineering. So successful did he become that he went to New York City and became active in railroad construction. He centered his attention on bridge building and while still a comparatively young man he formed a company of his own to erect bridges.

Though his experience had not been that of a military man, his avocation certainly was:

Horses were Gen. Field's pastime. On Trinity Pl., around the corner from his home, were the stables in which he kept his carriage horses, so finely bred that they were awarded several prizes in shows at Madison Square Garden in New York. Gen. Field, who lived in this city a full half century, was a charter member of the Buffalo Club. He also was prominently identified with the Union League Club of New York City.[24]

24 Homes in Buffalo and Vicinity, Buffalo Public Library, local history section, Lafayette Square, F129, B8B86925, pp. 60-61.

However, Field's 1929 obituary notices exaggerated his accomplishments, leaving the reader with the impression that his company had built the cantilever bridge in Niagara Falls, the Hawkesbury Bridge in Australia, and the famous bridge over the Ohio River at Cairo, Illinois. However "in Buffalo, his associates were Gen. [Edwin] Hayes and John J. Albright." This refers to the Union Bridge Company of which Field was listed as a member in the city directory of 1891 and of which Horton writes:

> One of the most imperative needs of the railroads was for bridges. In the Union Bridge Company, said to be the largest concern of its kind in the world of the '80s, Buffalo supplied that need on a colossal scale. This company, represented in the city by Edmund Hayes, arose out of a combination of lesser firms in 1884. With an office in New York, and a plant at Athens, Pennsylvania, the enterprise had its principal works at Buffalo, where they sprawled over about eight acres at the foot of Hamburg Street, employing between two and three hundred skilled workers and turning out each year some 15,000 tons of material for bridges all over the world. Nearest home was the Michigan Central's Cantilever Bridge at Niagara Falls. Building in 1888, another cantilever structure for railways by the same firm would soon span the Hudson at Poughkeepsie. For the New York, Providence and Boston Railroad a bridge already spanned the Thames at New London, Connecticut; another the Ohio at Cairo, Illinois, for the Illinois Central; another the Missouri at Sioux City, Iowa, for the Chicago and Northwestern. At Nebraska City, the company had thrown still another bridge over the Missouri. Besides these, it had built bridges in Mexico, South America, and Japan. In 1888 it was at work on a $2,000,000 contract for a bridge across the mouth of the Hawkesbury River at Hawkesbury, New South Wales.[25]

In the mid-1920s General Field and his second wife, Margaret Catherine Warren, abandoned #452 and moved to Chapin Parkway.

> The general was six feet tall. His heavy hair was snow white, and his brown eyes were bright and kind. Mrs. Field was a woman of exceptional elegance and charm. Her gowns, from Paris, were far in advance of those worn by other well-dressed Buffalonians.[26]

7.14 #452 Delaware, BHS.

George died at eighty-four in May 1929, following an appendectomy. Rev. Cameron Davis of Trinity conducted the funeral from Field's home. Afterwards #452 was occupied by an insurance company.(7.14) In 1933, at the nadir of the Depression, it was bought by the Edward M. Daly Post of the American Legion.

In the late 1860s William Dorsheimer asked H. H. Richardson to design a house for #438:

> The scheme that Richardson drew up was a pure example of the type of house being built in the suburbs of Paris during the years

25 Horton, *op. cit.*, 1:225.
26 Homes in Buffalo, *ibid.*

7.15 ❦ #438 Delaware, BHS.

that Richardson studied at the Ecole des Beaux-Arts.(7.15) Lacking the heavy ornamentation and inflated proportions of other Second Empire houses such as the Altman and Sternberg residences [#767 and #414 Delaware], the Dorsheimer house conveyed restraint and Neo-Grec rationalism, while at the same time recalling, especially in is materials, the seventeenth-century architecture of Louis XIII. The elegant dwelling, in appearance so unlike Richardson's later work, must have pleased its owner...that it represented the latest in contemporary design.[27]

William Edward Dorsheimer was born of German immigrants at Lyons in 1832. After attending Phillips Andover, he entered Harvard in 1849, but left after two years because of ill health. Admitted to the bar in 1854, he began to practice law at Buffalo and became active in the Democratic Party, though his father was a founder of the state Republican Party and William himself supported it in 1856 and 1860. His power base was Buffalo's sizeable German community on the East Side. He was one of the few Avenue residents not of WASP extraction. After serving on General Fremont's staff in Missouri in 1861, Dorsheimer returned to Buffalo and partnership with Spencer Clinton. President Johnson appointed him United States District Attorney for the Northern District of New York in 1867, a post he resigned in 1871 to campaign for Horace Greeley. He was a delegate to the Liberal Republican convention at Cincinnati in 1872. Returning to the Democratic Party, he was elected lieutenant-governor on the ticket with Samuel J. Tilden in 1874, and with Lucius C. Robinson in 1876. In 1876 Dorsheimer attended the Democratic convention at Saint Louis, which nominated Tilden for president. Dorsheimer reported the platform, which he had saved from an inflationist plank. During the campaign he made many speeches and wrote articles on behalf of Tilden. But he felt that "The Sage of Greystone" had prevented his being nominated for governor and therefore supported "Honest John" Kelly, Tammany's candidate, not Robinson, the regular nominee. This division within the ranks insured the election of the Republican Alonzo B. Cornell. That year the Democrats in the legislature vainly supported Dorsheimer for United States Senator against Roscoe Conkling. Dorsheimer was elected to Congress in 1882 where he sat on the judiciary committee. He also promoted Cleveland's candidacy and wrote the 1884 campaign biography, *Life and Public Services of the Honorable Grover Cleveland.* For this Cleveland made him United States District Attorney for the Southern District of New York in 1885. He resigned to direct the New York *Star*, which he had bought. Worries over the paper's losses took him to Savannah in late 1887 in a vain quest for health. He died there in March 1888.[28]

Involvement in Albany, New York, and Washington had caused Dorsheimer to leave Buffalo, and by 1880 #438 was the abode of Charles W. McCune, thus described by Horton in connection with

27 Kowsky, *Great American Avenue*, p. 47.
28 *Ibid.*; Milledge L. Bonham, Jr., "Dorsheimer, William Edward," *DAB*, 5:387-388.

Buffalo newspapers and politics in the 1880s:

> James D. Warren and James N. Matthews were still the great Republican journalists; the corresponding place on the Democratic side had been held until 1876 by the scholarly Joseph Warren. Editor and chief owner of the *Courier*, he had succeeded Dean Richmond in 1866 as the boss of the local Democratic organization. Dying ten years later, Joseph Warren was succeeded in control of the paper by William G. Fargo, who gave way in 1880 to the genial Vermont Irishman, Charles W. McCune. To great political influence this personage added business ability of a high order. No economic theorist, he had been trained in as practical a school for free trade as any iron foundry or blast furnace could have provided for the training of a protectionist. He had been a successful importer in New York City; had retired in 1867 and while traveling in Europe had been prevailed upon to come to settle in Buffalo.
>
> McCune's *Courier*, four years before McCune had joined its staff, had been preparing the way for the reemergence of free trade doctrine as a practical factor once again in national counsels. The work it had done had been unwittingly done; but it was fateful, nevertheless. In 1870 when William Williams, the railroad magnate, had been elected to the Congress on the Democratic ticket, the *Courier* had of course supported him; but more significantly, as it turned out later, that journal had supported a thirty-three year old lawyer for the office of Sheriff of Erie County. The name of the *Courier's* candidate for the post was Grover Cleveland.[29]

Upon McCune's death in 1885 he was followed both in the executive offices of the *Courier* and at #438 by his protégé, George Bleistein, who had been born in Buffalo in 1861. Educated at P.S. 15 and at Saint John's German School, George began his career as an office boy at the *Courier*, where his industry caught the eye of McCune who promoted him to superintendent of the Courier Printing Company, a large show-business printing house which brought him into contact with producers like P. T. Barnum, George Ringling, and Colonel William Cody, and theatrical celebrities. In the tradition of McCune, Bleistein supported the reformist Cleveland and became a power in the Democratic party. In 1893 he was chosen head of the Erie County Home Rule Democracy, a clean-government revolt against the rule of Boss William F. ("Blue-Eyed Billy") Sheehan, whose base was the First Ward.[30] Concerning Billy, Horton writes:

> Prominent among those who followed other precepts than Cleveland's was the Democratic boss, William F. Sheehan [1850-1917], who from the middle '80s for about a decade had kept a firm grip on the local Democracy, notwithstanding the efforts of such notables as John G. Milburn and Wilson S. Bissell to break it. These gentlemen considered Sheehan a stone of reproach to their party. Along with Republicans, they denounced him as a corruptionist. Be that as it may, he was a Tammany Democrat and after displaying an excessive zeal in guiding voters in certain wards in the local elections of 1893, he departed for New York, where he could take a more intimate part in Tammany councils.[31]

In 1886 Bleistein married Elizabeth Wells McCune, daughter of the Chandler Wells McCunes; the pair had three children. Bleistein sold the *Courier* in 1897 to William J. Connors; and in 1914, for

29 Horton, *op. cit.*, 1:235-236.
30 *Courier*, April 22, 1918.
31 Horton, *op. cit.*, 1:348

7.16 ❦ Robert Borthwick Adam, *M&FH*, I, facing p. 151.

having been such a good Democrat, was appointed Collector of Customs for the Port of Buffalo by President Wilson. The former editor was also two-term president of the New York State Press Association and a member of the executive committee of the Buffalo Savings Bank. Along with the Carys and other Buffalo bluebloods, Bleistein rode to hounds in Genesee Valley where he had a summer home near the Wadsworths. He presented a splendid jumper to Theodore Roosevelt which the president named Bleistein. With his friend Monty Gerrans and the Rumseys he promoted Cody, Wyoming, and gave antlers and other trophies to the Country Club of which he had been a president and to the Buffalo Club. He belonged to the Manhattan Club and to the Jekyll Island Club, a gated-community for the very rich off the coast of Georgia. Still residing at #438, he died at fifty-six in 1918.[32] By 1920 a dress designer and wife had moved in and had taken on ten roomers.

At #448, between McCune and Field, John C. Smith, a contractor, first appears in the 1872 city directory. However the substantial dwelling soon became the residence of a businesslike Scotsman, Robert Borthwick Adam(7.16), born in 1833, at Peebles on the River Tweed, son of Thomas Adam, Presbyterian pastor there, and his wife, Isabella Borthwick. When only ten Robert moved to Edinburgh to avail himself of its opportunities for education and business experience. He married Grace Harriet Michie in 1855 and two years later emigrated to the United States. He settled in Boston where he spent a decade learning the importing business. In 1867 he came to Buffalo and, with two young men with whom he had worked in Boston, organized Adam, Meldrum & Whiting, a dry goods concern which soon became Adam, Meldrum & Anderson, *alias* AM&As, which the fastidious Mable Ganson found "common." His favorite charity was the Young Men's Christian Association of which he became a director in 1879, serving until 1886, when he was made trustee. In 1891 he was again elected director and in 1897 president, continuing in these roles until his death in 1904. In 1883 and again in 1903 he was

7.17 ❦ Edwin A. Bell. *Men of Buffalo*, p. 50.

32 *Courier, ibid.*

Above 7.18 ❦ Thomas T. Ramsell, *ibid.*, p. 215.
Below 7.19 ❦ Looking south on Delaware from the Buffalo Club. The steeples belong to the Methodist Church on Tupper Street and to Calvary Presbyterian. W. Dunn, *op. cit.*, np.

chairman of the building committee which erected the association's first two buildings in Buffalo.[33]

As president of the Merchants Exchange, Adam was the natural choice for chairman of the Grade Crossings Commission, established by the legislature in 1888. These crossings had become killers, and Adam's energetic work on their elimination carried the project successfully through.[34] Robert B. Adam, II, succeeded him at #448 and lived there until 1915 when James McLeod, a Canadian-born doctor, took over, but by 1925 the it was housing an embalmer and shortly afterwards had became a rooming house.

There were four large brick houses on the west side of Delaware between Edward and Virginia, but from the early 1880s five households were listed as residing there. The reason is that #430 and #432, the building on the corner of Edward and Delaware, was a double house. At #430 there lived from about 1880 to 1905 Edwin A. Bell(7.17), a stockbroker who made the 1892 illustrated *Men of Buffalo,* followed by Doctor Edgar McGuire, after whom the place had become by 1920 a rooming house. Thomas T. Ramsdell (7.18) of #432 was born in 1854, and had grown up at #220 Delaware, home of his father, Orrin P. Ramsdell. Thomas attended public school and graduated from the technical course in Professor Briggs' Classical School in 1871. In 1873 he entered the wholesale boot and shoe business of Orrin P. Ramsdell & Company, established by his father in 1837. At the time the company was being run by Orrin Ramsdell and William H. Walker. In 1877 Walker retired, and Thomas became a partner along with W. C. Walker and Sidney. M. Sweet to produce Orrin P. Ramsdell, Sweet & Company. With Orrin's death in 1885, Thomas became senior partner, a position he retained until 1902 when he resigned to become vice president of Bell Telephone of Buffalo which in 1910 was merged with New York Telephone. By then Ramsdell and his wife, the former Louise Miller of Stirling, Illinois, whom he had married in 1881, had joined the migration of wealthy Buffalonians to the Lake Shore Road in Lakeview, now easily accessible by automobile, to an estate they christened "Shore Acres." For many years Thomas Ramsdell served as

33 *M&FH*, 1:11-154; *Express*, September, 1888.
34 Robert B. Adam, "History of the Abolition of Railroad Grade Crossings in the City of Buffalo," *PBHS*, 8:151-254.

a director of the Buffalo Public Library, Buffalo General, the Erie County Savings Bank, New York Telephone, and the company which built and managed the Ellicott Square Building. He was a member of the Fine Arts, the Buffalo Historical, and the Society of Natural Sciences. Mayor Jewett appointed him to an advisory board when electric power first came to Buffalo. A member of Westminster and a Republican, his clubs were Park, Buffalo, and Saturn. He died in 1931.[35]

1860

WEST TUPPER

167 [357] William Tweedy 57 NY
Tweedy & Smith hats & caps
Harriet Tweedy 28 NY
Jennie Tweedy 5 NY
William Tweedy 1 NY
Mary Tweedy 55 NY
Christine Meyer 18 Scotland
Hannah Ganson 21 Bavaria

169 [363] John N. Oliver 49 NY joiner
Elizabeth Oliver 49 NY
Hettie Oliver 22 NY
Margaret Oliver 21 NY
Charles Oliver 8 NY

173 [367] Stephen Walker 67 NY master carpenter
Sally Walker 70 NY
William H. Walker 34 NY
with O. P. Ramsdell
Mary E. Walker 17 NY
Catherine Moriarty 45 Ireland

177 [371] Louis A. Majot 35 France wigs
Mary A. Majot 22 France
Louis M. Majot 3 NY
Paul Majot 2 NY
Dona Smith 19 Wurttemberg

181 [381] Amos L. Matthews 43 NY
druggist 220 Main
Mary B. Matthews 44 NY
Edward I. Matthews 12 NY
Eliza B. Matthews 10 NY
Elizabeth Talmadge 17 NY
Anna Coyle 23 Ireland

185 [387] John Locke 49 England mason
Harriet Locke 59 England
John Locke 20 NY
James Locke 17 NY
Edward Locke 10 NY

1870

WEST TUPPER

357 James McCreedie 54 NY clerk
Caroline McCreedie 52 NY
Mary Irish boarder
Minnie Fraiser 15 NY

363 John B. Oliver 69 NY builder in wood
Elizabeth Oliver 38 NY
Hettie Oliver 33 NY
Charles Oliver 18 NY clerk

367 Charles R. Walker 46 NY retired drug merchant
Angeline Walker 43 NY
Stephen Walker 15 NY school
Angeline Walker 8 NY school
Mary E. Walker 26 NY
Lizzie Mang 18 NY

35 Hill, *op. cit.*, 3:22-23; *Courier*, March 12, 1931.

187 [391] Charles A. Shaw 39 New Hampshire
clerk C. Bull
Amelia Shaw 43 Mass.
Mary F. Shaw 14 NY
Martha P. Shaw 12 NY

391 Charles Shaw 49 New Hampshire clerk
Amelia Shaw 53 Mass.
Mary Shaw 24 NY public school teacher
Martha Shaw 21 NY

189 [393] Robert M. Bingham 52 England
Eddy & Bingham iron foundry
Mary Bingham 42 England
Matilda Bingham 18 NY
Charles Bingham 16 NY
Minnie Bingham 12 NY
Kate Bingham 7 NY
Fred Bingham 4 months NY
Jared W. Walker 23 Mass. clerk
Ann Reilly 18 Ireland

393 Robert M. Bingham 59 Wales iron founder
Mary Bingham 51 England
Katie Bingham 19 NY

191 [399] George Langdon 33 England Langdon
& Sears pork dealers 22 Hanover
Harriet Langdon 29 Ohio
George S. Langdon 3 NY
Mary C. Langdon 36 England
Bridget Cassidy 22 Ireland

399 William B Pettit 45 Conn.
shoe manufacturer
Sarah M. Pettit 40 Conn.
illegible, female 12 NY school
Allen Pettit 11 NY school
Louise Pettit 4 NY
Harry H. Pettit 2 months NY
Margaret Doyle 19 Ireland
Mary Deibold 18 Prussia

193 [405] James McCredie 40 NY manager
Dean Richmond estate
Caroline McCredie 39 NY
Carrie McCredie 18 NY
William McCredie 3 NY
Wilhelmina Hophner Germany

405 James H. Smith 35 Bush & Howard
Jemima Smith 30 *ux.*
Annie Smith 8 school
Albert W. Smith 7 school
Maggie B. Smith 5
Howard Smith 4
Mary McCollum
Lizzie Hideuck 15

207 [409] Aaron R. Vail 47 Vermont G. O.
Vail marble & slate Chicago & Ohio
Carrie Vail 23 Vermont
M. Henry Vail 20 Vermont
Helen Vail 15 Vermont
Libby Vail 12 Vermont
Camilla Vail 60 NY

409 Mrs. George W. Tyler

209 [413] Thomas Toy Hardiker & Toy plumbers
Main & Eagle

413 George F. Haywood 29 England realtor
Jennie E. Haywood 29
Mary Moore 42

227 [415] John W. Annin 48 NY
commission merchant 9 Central Wharf
Sarah Annin 21 NY
Julia Annin 59
Ann Annin 13 NY
Sophia Machenvor 17 Germany

415 William C. Sweet 33 NY boot & shoe merchant
Harriet Sweet 42 Conn.
Sidney Sweet 17 NY school
Lizzie Sweet 14 NY school
George W. Sweet 36 NY retired shoe merchant
Fanny Sweet 30 NY boarder
Bessie Sweet 8 NY
Clara Sweet
Louise Sweet 32 NY boarder
Frances A. Ramsdell 64 Conn.
Kate O'Melia 30 Ireland

417 Amos W. Morgan
Bingham & Morgan iron works

419 Charles F. Bingham 25 NY iron founder
Maggie Bingham 20 NY
Belle Bingham 1 NY
Mary Bauer 20 NY

EDWARD STREET ❦ End of Block

231 [427] Gilbert Cameron 44 NY railroad treasurer
Elizabeth Cameron 19 NY
Hannah Cameron 19 NY
William Cameron 17 clerk
Margaret Cameron 12 NY
Mary Cameron 9 NY
Gilbert Cameron 5
James Cameron 1

[445] Noyes Darrow 60 Connecticut gentleman
Mary Darrow 58 Vermont
Charles B. Darrow 23 NY
Nelly S. Darrow 19 NY
Elizabeth Quinlan 18 NY
William Ernst 16 NY

[455] Richard Sherman 53 NY dry goods
Julia Sherman 32 Conn.
John Hudson 45 NY attorney
Archibald Hudson 18 NY

VIRGINIA STREET ❦ End of Block

EDWARD STREET ❦ End of Block

427 Henry W. Prosser 30 NY envelope manufacturer
Anna Prosser 30 NY
Hattie Prosser 6 NY
illegible, male 3 NY
Mary G. Fay 59 NY boarder
Minnie Lilga 24 Prussia
Susan Pollock 17 Canada West

431 William H. Dee 49 Canada West
dry goods merchant
Lucinda Dee 30 Indiana
William H. Dee 9 NY school
Julia Dee 7 NY school
Charlotte Dee 5 NY school
Annie Dee 3 NY
Arthur Dee 8 months NY
Mary Webster Scotland
Mary Schneider 17 NY

435 J. D. Dudley

445 Noyes Darrow 70 Conn. gentleman
Mary Darrow 68 Vermont

449 Henry M. Watson 36 NY street railways
Ellen Watson 28 Ohio *ux.*

455 Richard J Sherman 63 NY
Julia Sherman 42

VIRGINIA STREET ❦ End of Block

1880

WEST TUPPER STREET

359 James McCready 60 NY agent for
Richmond estate
Caroline McCready 57 NY *ux.*
William McCready 24 NY son bank teller
Anna M. McCready 82 NY
Mary McCready 57 NY sister
Maggie Reichat 17 Canada
Mary McB___ 25 Canada

1891

WEST TUPPER STREET

357 Rev. Francis Lobdell rector of
Trinity Church

363 Willis M. Meads 24 NY attorney
Louise Meads 26 NY *ux.*
Rose 19 NY

363 George S. Hubbell civil engineer 174 Pearl
Nathan Hubbell *ditto*

367 Angeline Walker 52 NY
Stephen Walker 25 NY son clerk
Angeline Walker NY 17 daughter
Edmund Walker 32 Michigan cousin clerk
Samuel Walker 38 Michigan cousin clerk
Mary Walker 37 Michigan cousin clerk

369 Abigail Codd 75 NY
Robert M. Codd 30 NY son bank clerk
Maggie Codd 31 NY daughter school
Bessie Codd 26 NY daughter
Robert Codd 5 NY grandson

369 Robert M. Codd attorney 41
7 Coit Block
Mrs. Robert Codd
Murray A. Verner

389 *Christ Church*

371 Joseph E. Hadcock commission merchant
4 Board of Trade

Trinity Episcopal Church and Chapel

391 Charles A. Shaw 57 NY coal merchant
Amelia Shaw *ux.* 63 NY
Frances Mott daughter 34
New Hampshire housekeeper
Illegible Mott grandson 6
Mattie Cass 31 Massachusetts daughter
William Cass 31 England son-in-law
Maud Cass 2 NY granddaughter
Nellie Boyd 30 Massachusetts dressmaker
Lizzie Kersten 21

391 William H. Cass pattern maker
Buffalo Car Manufacturing Co.
Charles A. Shaw

393 Robert M. Bingham 66 England retired
Mary Bingham 61 England *ux.*
grandson 6 school
Elizabeth Burge 25 Michigan niece boarder
Kate Dunn 20
Illegible Schultz 40

393 Jessie Shepard MD
Kate Palmer Joy

397 Joseph Monroe 31 Massachusetts
manager powder mills
Sarah Monroe 30 Massachusetts *ux.*
Willis Monroe 6 Massachusetts son
Charles D. Monroe 5 NY son
Anna Holland 24 Ireland
Anna *Illegible* 24 Ireland

399 Robert Palmer 70 NY retired
Joanna Palmer 39 NY *ux.*
Robert J. Palmer 14 NY school

399 William Bowman Moore US Claims
attorney 360 Main
Harry M. Dixon

401 Andrew J. Packard 42 Ohio
Elaine Packard 24 Maine *ux.*
Mark Packard 18 Ohio son school
Lizzie Packard 17 Ohio daughter
Lucy Packard 17 Ohio daughter
Mary Millen 21 England
Kate *Illegible* 13 NY

401 Seth S. Spencer manager R. Ovens
Bakery 159 Ellicott

405 James H. Smith 44 NY leather merchant
Harriet Smith 35 NY *ux.*
Anna C. Smith 18 NY daughter clerk
Albert W. Smith 17 NY son school
Maggie B. Smith 15 NY daughter school
Howard Smith 14 NY son
Hyatt W. Smith 4 NY son
Louise Smith 26 NY
Carrie Smith 25 NY

413 George F. Haywood 38 England title searcher
Winnie Haywood 34 NY *ux.*
George Haywood NY 2 son
Mary Brennan 20 NY

415 William C. Sweet 52 NY leather merchant
Harriet Sweet 52 Conn. *ux.*
Sidney M. Sweet 27 NY son clerk
Lizzie Sweet 24 NY
Maggie Brunett 22 Ireland
Kate O'Malia 58 NY

EDWARD STREET ❦ End of Block

427 Inez Whitmarsh 32 Halifax
Mary Hammond 58 Canada mother
Susan Brewster 22 Missouri cousin

431 William E. Foster 40 Conn.
proprietor *Commercial Advertiser*
Sara Foster 38 NY *ux.*
Flora B. Foster 7 NY daughter school
Loren H. Foster 7 NY son
Lettie Shanks 28 Michigan
Mary Brick 20 NY
Minnie Bunse 15 NY

445 Joseph Hadcock 41 NY J. C. Jacus & Co.
Lucy Hadcock 38 NY *ux.*
Katy F. Hadcock 10 NY daughter
Joseph E. Hadcock 7 NY son
Ava Hadcock 5 NY daughter
Maggie Smith 25 NY

449 Henry M. Watson 46 NY street railways
Ellen Watson 38 Ohio *ux.*
Arnold B. Watson 3 NY son
William Watson NY 30 clerk
Mary Buell 27 England
Sarah Nolan 24 NY
Barbara Flail 22 NY

453 Richard J. Sherman 60 NY retired
Julia Sherman 50 Conn. *ux.*
Margaret Keane 26 NY
Drew 36

VIRGINIA STREET ❦ End of Block

405 John B. Sage lithographer

413 William E. Foster editor *Buffalo Commercial*
George F. Haywood general manager
Buffalo Abstract Guarantee

415 Mrs. S. S. Mulford

423 The Saturn Club
William J. Hanley steward

EDWARD STREET ❦ End of Block

427 Warren P. King Lehigh Valley Coal Co. 223 Main
Knowlton Mixer
Mrs. M. E. Mixer

443 Charles W. Hamlin attorney 110 Franklin

445 Harrison B. Mixer Mixer & Co. lumber 287 Elk

455 Mr. Emily Fish
Mrs. Richard J. Sherman

VIRGINIA STREET ❦ End of Block

1900

WEST TUPPER STREET

357 4 lodgers 4 servants

363 Ida Parsons 40 NY

367 Walter Trible 29 NY lounge manager
Louise Trible 28 NY *ux.*
Anna Rieffenstahl 61 NY mother in-law
Mary Duggan 26 Canada

369 Abigail Codd 65 NY
Robert Codd 50 son attorney
Robert Codd Jr. 26 NY grandson attorney
Bessie Codd 43 NY .daughter
Margaret Codd 36 NY daughter

371 William Krauss MD 36 NY
Clara Krauss 36 NY *ux.*
Magdelene Krauss 8 NY daughter
Alma Krauss 6 NY daughter
Martha Kossio 19 Germany
Tillie Smith 22 NY

389 *Trinity Episcopal Church*

391 Charles Shaw 77 New Hampshire
Arthur Froats 40 Canada son-in-law builder
Martha Washburn 69 NY lodger

393 William Morgan 34 NY capitalist
Clara Morgan 29 Illinois *ux.*
Ella Martin 25 Sweden

399

401 The Colonial Apartments
Charles Huber 34 NY dentist manager
27 lodgers

405 Nellie Jones 35 England
Jennie Jones 29 England sister
10 boarders

413 George F. Haywood 54 England
abstract company manager

1905

WEST TUPPER STREET

357 Jane Phillips 60
Bessie M. Phillips 27 daughter
Florence Reets 23 niece stenographer
17 boarders
4 servants

363 Margaret Montague 45
Agnes Arnold 23 lodger clothing store
Gertrude Cunningham 30 lodger dressmaker
Thomas J. Gilmore 35 lodger tailor
Henry Karl 26 France cook

367 Walter P. Trible 35 manages lounges
Louisa T. Trible 35 *ux.*
Anna Rieffenstahl 66 mother-in-law

369 Abigail J. Codd 73
Margaret J. Codd 43 daughter
Robert M. Codd 55 son attorney
Elizabeth A. Codd 43 daughter
Robert M. Codd Jr. 31 grandson attorney
Illegible Adams 18

389 *Trinity Episcopal Church*

391 Arthur S. Froats 31 Canada
Frances S. Froats 45 Canada *ux.*
Martha G. Semow 80 Canada aunt

393 Herbert A. Smith 24 medical student
6 lodgers

401 The Colonial Apartments
40 residents

405 Nellie Jones 40 England
Jean Jones 24 England partner
10 lodgers

413 George Haywood 60
Bridget McManus

415 Harriet Barnard NY
Seymour Barnard 24 NY son insurance agent
Josephine Barnard 31 NY daughter student
Elizabeth Barnard 29 NY daughter registrar
Anna Wolf 33 NY

423 The Saturn Club

EDWARD STREET ❦ End of Block

427 Mary E. Mixer 73 NY
Frederick K. Mixer 40 NY son scientist
Veronica Ess 25 NY

431 William E. Foster 60 Conn.
editor *Commercial*
Sarah E. Foster 59 NY *ux.*
Louise N. Foster 25 NY daughter
Louisa Crick 25 NY
Helen Cressy 18 NY

435 Louisa Germain 51 NY
Mary H. Germain 55 NY sister
Elizabeth Griffin 72 NY boarder
Fannie Steele 52 Michigan boarder
Caroline Kunka 22 Germany

443 Charles B. Sears 29 NY attorney
Florence Sears 27 Conn. *ux.*
Leona B. Sears 60 Ohio mother
Margaret Durkin 30 Ireland
Anna Durkin 23 Ireland

445 Minnie Jenkins 38 Ohio
Horace Jenkins 22 Ohio son
manufactures bicycles
Charles W. Jenkins 21 Ohio bookkeeper
Anna B. Jenkins 18 Ohio daughter
Edward Jenkins 15 Ohio clerk

455 Julia Sherman 68 Conn.
Agnes Honan 32 Ireland
Annie Connolly 24 NY
Harriet McCarthy 24 NY

VIRGINIA STREET ❦ End of Block

415 R. Walker Niak 28 milliner
Lillian R. Niak 32 ux.
Georgia Ranndall 30 sister-in-law milliner

423 The Saturn Club

EDWARD STREET ❦ End of Block

427 Mary Almy 82
Helen W. Almy 58 daughter
Francis Almy 47 business
Frederick Almy 47 attorney
Susan Murray 33 Ireland
Minnie Loughlin 33 Ireland

431 William E. Foster editor *Commercial*
Sarah E. Foster 63 *ux.*
Louise F. Thompson 27 daughter
Albert S. Thompson 30 son-in-law
National Lead Co.

435 Charles B. Germain 60 attorney
Mary B. Germain 53 *ux.*
Annie E. Germain 19 daughter
Edward B. Germain 15 son

439 Frederick B. Usher 40 cement
Mary L. Usher 30 *ux.*
Pauline Usher 2 daughter
Elizabeth Walsh 29 Ireland
Julia Webber 28

443 Charles W. Hamlin 68 retired
Carrie L. Hamlin 48 *ux.*
Ruth Hamlin 18 daughter school
Charles Hamlin 16 son school
Margaret Ward

445 Alfred W. Thorn 42 England Portland
Cement Co.
Katherine Thorn 33 *ux.*
Alfred G. Thorn 20 son Buffalo Asphalt Co.
Louise Smith 24
Ida Follett 29

449 Rev. Cameron J. Davis 31 N.Y. rector of Trinity
Elizabeth S.Davis 28 *ux.*
Elizabeth S. Davis 4 daughter
Frances H. Davis 2 months daughter
Frances Schneider 35
Winnie Alexander 21
Winifred Duffy 21

455 Julia Sherman 73
Nellie Scanlon 28
Agnes Honan 35

VIRGINIA STREET ❦ End of Block

1915

WEST TUPPER STREET

357 Louis Cherner 41
Alice Cherner 45 *ux.*
Ruth Cherner 22 daughter
3 roomers

363 Elizabeth Bodine 38
Albert Orr 40 brother plumbers supply co.
Anna Austin 72 mother

369 Robert M. Codd 41 attorney
Margaret Codd 60 mother
Robert M. Codd 65 uncle attorney
Elizabeth Codd 50 aunt housekeeper

371 Trinity Parish House
Ralph Crum 28 minister
Ralph Ball 25 roomer office assistant

389 *Trinity Episcopal Church*

391 Van Cleve Mott 41 England
Bell Telephone Co.
Mary Mott 43 *ux.*
Lawrence Mott 12 son school
Mabel Mott 10 daughter school

393 Lila Gottwals 60
Kitty Roesser daughter
Julia Frank 65 niece
Louise Krap

401 The Colonial Apartments
26 boarders

413

423 The Saturn Club

EDWARD STREET ❦ End of Block

1920

WEST TUPPER STREET

357 The Delano House
Henry Glor manager
27 lodgers

363 Eugene Greaney 30 Vermont
restaurant manager
Annie Greaney 27 NY *ux.*
Timothy Greaney 6 NY son
William Greaney 2 NY son
John Greaney 32 Mass. brother
6 lodgers

367 Morris Peterson 36 Denmark laborer
Florence Peterson 40 Pa. *ux.*
Viola Kane 22 Pa. stepdaughter
Loretta Kane 20 Pa. stepdaughter
Arthur Kane 17 Pa. stepson
3 lodgers

369 Robert M. Codd 70 NY attorney
Elizabeth A. Codd 55 NY sister
Robert M. Codd Jr. 56 NY attorney

371 Trinity Parish House
Percival Nichols 37 NY sexton

389 *Trinity Episcopal Church*

391 Van Cleve Mott 46 NY NY Telephone Co.
Mary E. Mott 48 NY *ux.*
Laurence V. Mott 17 NY son
Mabel E. Mott 14 NY daughter
Alice H Banfield NY lodger dressmaker

393 Kate B. Roesser 68 NY widow
Lisa B. Evans 68 NY boarder
Eleanor Schaffer 23 NY

401 The Colonial Apartments
26 tenants

405 Nancy Stratton 52 NY widow
10 lodgers

413 *(illegible)*

423 The Saturn Club

EDWARD STREET ❦ End of Block

427 Helen Almy 68
2 brothers
2 maids

431 William E. Foster
Louise F. Thompson 37 daughter
Albert S. Thompson 40 son-in-law
1 maid

435 Charles Germain 70 attorney
Louise Germain 62 *ux.*
Mary McConnell 24 Ireland

439 Edward Hawley 63 president insurance co.
Carnos Hawley 50 *ux.*
Victoria Bremmer 24 Hungary

445 Alfred Thorn 52 president
Lehigh Portland Cement Co.
Catherine Thorn 43 *ux.*
Alfred Thorn 26 son cement co.
Alice Allin 34 England

449 Rev. Cameron J. Davis 41 N.Y. rector of Trinity
Elizabeth Davis 36 *ux.*
Frances Davis 10 daughter school
Mary Fleming 30
Elsie Shaw 22

455 Julia Sherman 76
2 maids
1 nurse

VIRGINIA STREET ❦ End of Block

427 Helen Almy 72 Mass. widow
Francis Almy 61 Mass.
brother estate manager
Frederick Almy 61 Mass.
Charity Organization Society
Martha Luesne 19 Germany
Hannah Glavin 34 Ireland

431 Sarah Foster 79 NY widow
Albert S. Thompson 45 son-in-law
Louise F. Thompson 42 daughter
Albert F. Thompson 15 NY grandson
Elliott P. Thompson 13 NY grandson

435 Charles B. Germain 78 NY attorney
Mary B Germain 60 Ohio *ux.*
Abbie Heaney 48 NY

439 Edward S. Hawley 70 NY insurance
Jane A. Hawley 65 NY *ux.*
Victoria Bremmer 29 Hungary

443 Etlinda Staub 36 NY rooming house proprietor
Sylvia Staub 10 NY daughter
Elwood Staub 6 NY son
13 roomers

445 Alfred Thorn 56 England cement manufacturer
Kate Thorn 36 NY
Alfred Thorn Jr. 39 Missouri sales
Katherine Hartigan 33 Ireland
Eva Begin 40 Maine

449 Louis J. Beyer MD 43 NY
Sarah Beyer 32 Canada *ux.*
June D. Beyer 5 NY daughter
Caroline Sachenminger 60 Canada
Mary Tush 59 NY

455 Julia Sherman 92 Conn. widow
Agnes Honan 57 Ireland
Lizzie Havene 52 Canada nurse

VIRGINIA STREET ❦ End of Block

7.20 ❦ Number 367 Delaware. *PBHS*, 29(1927), np.

The lots on the east side of Delaware between Tupper and Virginia were smaller than those across the Avenue and so not mansion-friendly.(7.1) The few dwellings that remain confirm this. Also many of the occupations of the heads of households are unremarkable. Many houses had no servants and some only one or two. Figure 7.19 views the Avenue looking south from the Buffalo Club across from Trinity Church. It appears to date from the first decade of the twentieth century. However eight of those pictured in the 1902 *Men of Buffalo* lived on this block, 1860-1900.

Residing at #167 in 1860 was William Tweedy, proprietor of Tweedy & Smith, hats and caps, on Main Street. He was born in 1804, in Danbury, Connecticut, seat of the hat industry. At twenty-one in 1825 he married Mary Taylor and next year moved to Buffalo where he plied his trade in partnership with William Ketchum. In 1831 Tweedy built a modest home on Tupper and Delaware.(7.2) For thirty years he belonged to Dr. Lord's Church. He was a founder and director of the Buffalo Savings Bank. Before the Civil War he had been a Whig but thereafter a Republican. In 1865 he moved to Lewiston where he died in 1881. Purchaser of his Delaware Street home was James McCredie who tore it down and built the mansion with a mansard roof in 7.20.[36] He had been born in 1817 in New York; later he moved to Canandaigua where he became assistant postmaster. About 1843 he came to Buffalo, married Caroline Irish, and set up a crockery store. His bookkeeping skills caught the eye of Dean Richmond who made him his accountant and by will appointed him sole manager of his estate. McCredie died in 1889 and his wife Caroline in 1891, willing #357 to Trinity. It became the residence of the third rector, Rev. Francis Lobdell.(7.22) She also left the church $30,000 ($522,900 in 1997 dollars) as an endowment fund.[37]

Number #363 was occupied during the 1860s by John N. Oliver, a carpenter, who was succeeded in the 1870s by another Oliver of the same calling. By 1880 it had become the home of Willis Howard Meads, born in South Limington, Maine, in 1846 and a graduate of Bowdoin College. He came to Buffalo where he became a teacher and principal of P.S. 13. He studied law and passed the bar in 1880. His clubs were University, Buffalo, and Acacia. His work as Commissioner of Jurors merited him inclusion in the 1898 *Men of New York*.[38] He died in 1910 and his former home became a rooming house.

The Stephen Walkers lived at #367 from the 1860s into the 1880s. Stephen, a carpenter, died in 1869, but his wife Angeline stayed on, and her home sheltered several relatives and their children.

36 *BEN*, May 18, 1918.
37 *Express*, May 22, 1888; Mary E. Mixer, *History of Trinity Church* (Buffalo: The Peter Paul Book Company, 1897), *op. cit.*, p. 98.

During the 1890s and as late as 1905 it was the home of Walter Trible, who worked for the Buffalo Lounge Company, which not surprisingly, manufactured lounges. His picture appeared in *Men of Buffalo*.(7.22) By 1920 it was a rooming house.

Above Left 7.21 ❦ Rev. Francis Lobdell, Mixer, *op. cit.*, facing p. 87.
Above Right 7.22 ❦ Walter P. Trible, *ibid.*, p. 144.
Below 7.23 ❦ Christ Church as originally designed, Mixer, *op. cit.*, facing title page.

By 1872 a house had been erected at #369 for Abigail, widow of Robert Codd, an immigrant from County Meath, Ireland, and a founder of the Exchange Bank of Buffalo. Abigail had three children, Margaret born in 1849, Robert M. in 1850, and Elizabeth in 1854. In 1880 a five-year old grandson of Abigail, always referred later to as Robert M. Codd, Jr., and as nephew of the older Robert, was also listed as at #369, though it was not clear who his father was. After eighteen years working in a bank, the elder Robert M. Codd read law in the office of General Samuel M. Welch, #514 Delaware, and was admitted to the bar in 1883. His nephew attended local schools, graduated from Cornell in 1897, and from U.B. Law in 1900. He and his uncle formed a famous legal team. Robert M. Codd, Jr., was highly trusted by the Indian tribes of Western New York. He represented the Six Nations in their border controversy with the United States Government and won. As a result Indians could cross and recross the border with Canada without submitting to immigration restriction or regulations. He belonged to the University, Buffalo, and Canoe clubs, but in September 1940 was disbarred for commingling his clients' funds with his own. He died in 1954.[39] Miss Elizabeth Codd was one of the founders of the Women's Educational and

38 *Men of New York*, 1:167-168.
39 Wilner, 3:247-249.

Industrial Union where she taught classes in business and domestic science and in Americanism for the foreign-born. A Daughter of the American Revolution and a Colonial Dame, she lived for seventy-five years at #369 Delaware Avenue where during the grand parade which was the finale of the 31st Annual Encampment of the G.A.R. in August 1897 she held open house. Since the line of march was up Main to Chippewa, over Chippewa, to Delaware, up Delaware to North, and over North to the Circle, she served lunch throughout the day to wavering veterans. She died there at eighty-six in 1940.[40]

The principle of rule by councils in the 1708 Saybrook Platform goes a long way to explain why Congregationalism, the established church in much of colonial New England, yielded to Presbyterianism in frontier regions like Western New York, whose first settlers were mostly Yankees.[41] But how explain Horton's claim that "in Buffalo as distinguished from the rest of the county, the Episcopal influence vied in potency with the Presbyterian?"[42] The answer is the fact that so many of Buffalo's early settlers came from Connecticut. There only one Anglican parish existed, founded in Stratford in 1707, but without a church and usually without clergy:

> 1722 became memorable, however, as the year of the "great apostasy" in the New Haven area. The leader of this defection was Timothy Cutler, sometime Congregational minister in Stratford but since 1719 rector of Yale College, who seems to have been somewhat influenced by [John] Checkley's polemics in Massachusetts. In close contact with him was a group of Yale graduates, including Daniel Brown, the college's one tutor, Samuel Johnson, a former tutor now minister in West Haven, James Wetmore, minister in North Haven, and three somewhat less avid ministers in nearby towns. These men during a period of several years had been reading and discussing many works of Anglican divinity and recent philosophy that had been given to the Yale library by various English donors. They were fascinated by these broader, more urbane attitudes, and became correspondingly less committed to the stricter doctrines of New England theology. They also began to have serious doubts as to the validity of "presbyterial" (i.e. non Episcopal) ordination. Finally, after stating their doubts to the college trustees, they were asked by the Reverend Gurdon Saltonstall, a trustee who was then also governor of Connecticut, to discuss their problems with a group of Congregational ministers. On the day after commencement historic colloquy was held in the college library. But to no effect other than to strengthen the resolve of the incipient Anglicans, who very soon thereafter proceeded to England for ordination.
>
> They returned within a year to New England. Cutler, now with an honorary doctorate from Oxford, began his long ministry in Boston; Johnson went to Stratford where he completed the first Anglican Church building in Connecticut and for two decades acted as "dean" of the small but slowly growing group of SPG [Society for the Propagation of the Gospel] missionaries serving congregations in Connecticut; Wetmore was sent to Rye (New York). By 1742 there were fourteen churches and seven clergymen in the colony; by 1760, thirty churches and fourteen ministers. By 1775 there were twenty ministers and perhaps twice as many parishes or missions.[43]

40 *BEN*, October 12, 1940.

41 "Saybrook Platform," *Concise Dictionary of American History*, (New York: Charles Scribners's Sons, 1962), 858.

42 Horton, *op. cit.*, 1:121.

43 Sydney E. Ahlstrom, *A Religious History of the American People* (New Haven: Yale University Press, 1972), pp. 224-25.

Above 7.24 ❦ Libertus Van Bokkelen, Mixer, *op. cit.*, facing p. 69.
Below 7.25 ❦ New Trinity and Christ Chapel, *ibid.*, p. 65.

The first Episcopal Church in Buffalo, Saint Paul's, was founded in 1817. A building was erected in 1819 on a lot donated by the Holland Land Company and bounded by Main, Pearl, Erie, and Church Streets,(6.9 #7) where Saint Paul's still stands. Three settled pastors served from 1819 to 1828. In 1829 William Shelton, eponym of Shelton Square, began his pastorate of over fifty years until 1881. Of him Horton wrote: "The gruff rector of St. Paul's, the Reverend William Shelton, no doubt inclined to the view that religion need not burst the restraints of the Book of Common Prayer in order to be effective. Revivals the rubric did not prescribe."[44] The growth of the town made the seating capacity inadequate, and in 1836 Trinity Church was organized. Rev. Cicero Stephens Hawks became pastor and began his six-year ministry in 1837. A permanent church on the southeast corner of Mohawk and Washington(6.9 #17) was completed in 1842. Hawkes was followed by Rev. Edward Ingersoll, rector 1844-1874.

A third Episcopal church, Saint John's, was organized in 1845. It sprang from Trinity and was called "a Young Men's Church," the first rector, wardens, vestrymen, and most of the members being young men:

> The institution of Doctor Ingersoll was an important era in the history of Trinity. The church had become very popular, and the seating capacity was already too small. So at the annual sale and renting of pews, certain square pews accommodating eight or ten people in separate sitting were sold for the occupancy of families. One of these had been rented to a party of bachelors, who were thus sold out, and had to accept the hospitality of friends which was not an agreeable arrangement.
>
> ...Soon after Easter they met at a convivial supper in a popular restaurant called the Pantheon. One topic of discussion was "what shall we do for sittings in Trinity?" Finally the suggestion was offered that then and there they should organize a new parish.[45]

And so it was done. Their church, on the southeast corner of Swan and Washington built in 1846-1847 of gray stone, "was considered the finest specimen of pure Gothic architecture in the country." But a Fourth of July 1868 skyrocket lodged in the steeple and set it on fire, causing a loss of $23,000.[46]

44 Horton, *op. cit.*, 1:121.
45 Mixer, *op. cit.*, p. 30.
46 Hill, *op. cit.*, 2:589.

Owing to this accident, a part of the congregation determined to leave the old site and erect a building on Delaware. Three lots were purchased at a cost of $40,000 on which were to be erected a church, a chapel and a rectory. The parish was to be known as Christ Church, and the rector of Saint John's, the Rev. Orlando Witherspoon, was to be rector. Plans for the edifice were obtained and preparations were begun for the buildings.(7.23) The foundation for the church was laid, but the rectory was not even begun. Only the beautiful little building now known as Christ Chapel was finished. It was begun in 1869 and was substantially completed in 1871. The new parish went on for a time but passed out of existence in 1875 in debt. The lots were mortgaged and the parish owed over $100,000. The chapel, its furniture, and the lot on which it stood was to be sold at sheriff's sale. At this crisis some faithful women who had accumulated a few hundred dollars for church purposes, stepped in and saved the furniture, while the building and lot were rescued by Bishop Coxe who bought them for $10,000, giving his own bond and mortgage for that sum, and taking title to the property in his own hands. The lot on which the foundation of the church was laid came into the hands of William G. Fargo, and the rectory lot reverted finally to its original owner.[47]

Above 7.26 ❦ Trinity Church interior, BHS. Below 7.27 ❦ Rev. Cameron J. Davis, *Men of Buffalo*, p. 396.

As early as 1852 proposals to sell Trinity and move up town had been made. Money had been raised and land at Park Place and Delaware had been bought, but many contributors disliked the location. Christ Chapel's troubles suggested merger of the two parishes, opposition to which caused Doctor Ingersoll to resign in 1873. He was followed by Libertus Van Bokkelen(7.24), rector 1874-1886, who presided over the shift of Trinity from Mohawk and Washington to Delaware and the consolidation of Trinity and Christ Chapel. Van Bokkelen was born in New York in 1815. His grandfather came from Holland in 1796, exiled by the revolutionary French government, which had invaded Holland and exiled adherents of the House of Orange. From age nine he was educated at boarding schools, the last of which was Muhlenberg's Flushing Institute. In 1842 he was ordained and in 1845 founded Saint Timothy's Hall, Catonsville, Maryland. His unionist and abolitionist

47 Smith, *op. cit.*, 2:86-87
48 Mixer, *op. cit.*, p. 69-70.

views made his life in the Free State uneasy, and he moved to Mount Morris until called to be rector of Trinity.[48]

Meanwhile the chapel on Delaware had risen from the ashes, where services were conducted 1875-1879 by Rev. M. C. Hyde without a vestry but under the supervision of Bishop Coxe. On April 14, 1879, a new parish, Christ Church, was organized by chapel worshippers. A vestry was elected which invited Rev. A. Sidney Dealey to be rector. On February 16, 1882, the bishop's mortgage having been paid off and title delivered to the congregation, Christ Church was consecrated.[49]

Pressure was increasing on rector and parishioners of Saint John's to move out of an increasingly commercial area and to join Christ Church on Delaware, many of whose members were attached to their little church which was now free from debt, thanks to their sacrifices. They wished to retain their institutional identity. Even the local press got in on the act. But the influence of the bishop told in favor of merger and on June 14, 1884, Judge Loran Lewis granted a decree of consolidation, the new corporation to be known as Trinity Church. It was agreed that in the erection of a new church "no encumbrance of any kind shall be placed upon the present property of Christ Church." Of the seven laymen on the building committee four lived on Delaware. To save money it was decided to build on the 1869 foundation. For the same reason plans for a clerestory were omitted and the tower was left for further determination. (It was never built.) The plans for this church, made in 1869 by Arthur Gilman of New York, were adapted by a local architect, Cyrus K. Porter. The corner stone was laid on July 22, 1884.[50]

> On Easter 1886 was dedicated Cyrus K. Porter's local masterpiece adapted from the original plans of Arthur Gilman of New York.(7.25, 26) This was the new Trinity Episcopal church on Delaware just north of the Methodists.(7.19) There is nothing hesitant about the Gothic of Trinity. Fittingly enough inspired from English rather than from German sources it yet resembled St. Louis' Roman Catholic Church in being one of the few beautiful churches raised in that period.[51]

A guide to Buffalo enthuses about the building's interior:

> Trinity Church possesses some of the finest stained glass in America. The five magnificent scenes in the apse and the rose window are by John La Farge, who also did several others, along with Tiffany, in the nave and transept. Especially important is his so-called Watson Window over the altar on the north transept. The subject, drawn from Revelations 7, is "The Sealing of the Twelve Tribes," a mystical event depicted in an otherworldly atmosphere of blue opalescence. The client for the window was Stephen Van Rensselaer Watson, founder of the Erie County Savings Bank, who lived across the street from Trinity in the commodious Second Empire house (1870) that is today the Buffalo Club. La Farge required that Watson allow him to exhibit the window, before sending it to Buffalo, at the 1889 Exposition Universale in Paris, where, he hoped, it would establish his international reputation as a modern master of glass. Greatly impressed by the beauty and originality of

49 Smith, *op. cit.*, 87.
50 Mixer, *op. cit.*, pp. 66-67.
51 Horton, *op. cit.*, 1:249-250.
52 *Buffalo Architecture, op. cit.*, p. 127.

the work, the French government awarded La Farge the insignia of the Legion of Honor, the highest honor bestowed upon a foreigner.[52]

The site of old Trinity had been sold and the money used to buy land next to Christ Church. On the Washington and Swan block the first Statler Hotel was later erected. During Lobdell's rectorship the number of communicants rose from 200 to 900, though some of the former members of Christ Church groused that they had "been swallowed by Trinity and not digested." A debt of $50,000 had been extinguished, and the McCredie house acquired for a rectory. Lobdell died in 1899, after which it was determined that the house was too big. It was sold and the proceeds used to buy land for a parish house adjoining Christ Chapel. In 1897 Lobdell had called for assistance from Cameron J. Davis(7.27), who served as a curate at Trinity before becoming rector at Lobdell's death. [53] Davis moved into #449 Delaware, the former home of Henry Watson. Davis had been born in 1873, at Watkins, New York. He attended DeVeaux School, and Trinity College in Hartford, from which he received a B.A. in 1894 and an M.A. in 1897. From the New York's General Theological Seminary he received a B. D. also in 1897. He resigned as rector of Trinity in 1929 to become coadjutor Bishop of Western New York. Consecrated bishop in 1930, he headed the diocese a year later when it was divided. For many years he was a trustee and member of the executive committee of the church pension fund, and later president of the fund and of the Church Life Insurance Corporation. He retired as a bishop in 1945 when he reached seventy-two. He was Phi Beta Kappa and an honorary member of the Buffalo, Saturn, and Country clubs. He was twice married and died in 1952.[54] In the mid-1920s he moved to Oakland Place, a tonier neighborhood, and as bishop lived on Summer Street.

Under Davis membership rolls climbed to more than 1,400. In 1904 a three-story Oxford gothic brownstone parish house on Delaware was completed(7.19), committing Trinity to downtown. The basement had a kitchen, coal bin, hot air furnace, bowling alley, lavatories, lockers, and a coatroom. The first floor contained a suite of three rooms, a choir room, a vesting room for the choir, an administration room, and a parlor-library. On the second floor were an assembly room with a stage, a kindergarten, and a room for teaching domestic science. The third floor had two living suites, each with a sleeping room and a study, one for a curate, the other for visitors. Total cost was $75,000.[55]

Though the exterior of Christ Chapel was attractive, its interior was merely a large carpeted room, with a platform. In 1913 Charles Clifton and his wife offered to redo the interior in memory of their daughter. Bertram Goodhue, a New York architect, and Ralph Adams Cram, who had designed the Trinity parish house, did the planning, features of which included stone pillars, a chancel arch, exquisitely carved choir stalls, an organ case, an altar rail, a triptich reredos (an ornamental screen) with a painting of the Boy Jesus in the Temple in the center and the apostles on the sides, and an

53 Mixer, *op. cit.*, pp. 72-73, 83.
54 *NYT*, June 8, 1952.
55 *Times*, January 10, 1925.
56 *Times*, December 20, 1920.

enlarged and richly decorated gothic ceiling.[56]

Davis was succeeded as rector by Rev. Elmore McKee, ex-chaplain at Yale, a graduate of the Taft School in 1914, Yale in 1919, and graduate studies in Edinburgh. He had been ordained in 1922 and made pastor of the Church of Christ in New Haven in 1927. He had been born in Ridgewood, New Jersey, and as a boy had attended schools in Germany, England, China, and Japan.[57]

The lot acquired *circa* 1903 for the Trinity parish house was #371, site of the residence in 1860 of Louis Majot, a French-born wig maker. In 1891 Joseph E. Hadcock, a commission merchant, was living there, and in 1900 it was the home and office of William Krauss, a physician. Number 319 was the home of Charles A. Shaw, a New Hampshire-born clerk and later coal merchant from 1860 until the 1890s. One son-in-law, William H. Case, a pattern maker with the Buffalo Car Manufacturing Company had moved in by 1880, and another, Arthur Froats, in construction, had located there by the end of the century. The place remained in the family with Van Cleve Mott, a grandson of Shaw and a New York Telephone executive, until the early 1920s when it joined the growing list of Avenue rooming houses. Proprietor of an iron foundry, Welsh-born Robert M. Bingham, resided with his wife and five children at #393 from the 1860s to the 1880s. In 1891 it was the office and residence of a female physician, Jessie Shepard, a doctor's daughter, who had studied under Dr. Hoxsie at #183 Delaware. She later studied at Cleveland's homeopathic hospital and at the medical department of U.B. For some years she practiced with Hoxsie's partner, Dr. Joseph T. Cook, who had married Hoxsie's widow. Jessie also spent a year in the General Hospital in Vienna. Self-described capitalist, William Morgan, followed the doctor at #138 in 1900, but by 1905 it had become a lodging house run by an enterprising twenty-four year old medical student.

A succession of households followed each other at #399 from 1860 until 1900: George Langdon, proprietor of a pork packing concern; William B. Pettit, a Connecticut-born shoe manufacturer, who died in 1876; Robert Palmer, a seventy-year old retired business man, his thirty-nine year old wife, and fourteen year old daughter; and William B. Moore, a United States claims attorney.

Number 401 first appeared in the census in 1880 when it was the home of Andrew J. Packard, an executive of Hamilton Coal & Iron. By the mid-1890s Seth Spencer, a bakery manager, had taken up residence there, but later in the decade as the *Colonial Apartments* it was home to as many as forty lodgers. Before building his mansion at Tupper and Delaware in 1865, James McCredie had resided at #405, old style #193. Thereafter it became the residence of James H. Smith, a Bush & Howard executive, until the mid-1880s when it became the home of John B. Sage, a lithographer. In 1860 #409 was the home of Aaron Vail, proprietor of a marble and slate business, from Vermont. In 1870 it was the home of Mrs. George W. Tyler. From the 1870s until the 1890s #413 was the residence of George Haywood, an English-born realtor who worked his way up to general manager of Buffalo

57 *Forty Years*, p. 17.

Abstract Guarantee, a position he held until his death in 1893.

Commission merchant, John W. Annin, lived at #415 new style in 1860, but within ten years William C. Sweet, a boot and shoe manufacturer, was there with his wife, two children, and five other Sweets, the relation between whom is hard to determine. With a smaller family, William was still there in 1880, but died in 1893. He was followed by Harriet Barnard and son Seymour, an insurance agent. In 1870 Amos W. Morgan and Charles Bingham, owners of the Bingham & Morgan Iron Works, were neighbors at #417 and #419 at Delaware and Edward. Bingham was the son of Robert Bingham, an iron monger who had lived at #393 in 1860.

7.28 ❦ The first five homes of Saturn, *Forty Years, 1885-1925* (Buffalo: The Saturn Club, 1925), p. 17.

In 1890 that corner lot became the site of the first permanent club house of Saturn(7.28) whose founding fathers included Carleton Sprague, son of Ebenezer, William F. Kip, and Francis Almy, #427 Delaware. They and the other charter members were college graduates from wealthy Buffalo families and in their twenties or early thirties — second or third generation elite. Sprague arranged that meetings be held at his grandfather's temporarily vacant house on Johnson Park. Since meetings were to be held on Saturday, Saturn's day, Almy suggested the club's name. He also suggested titles of officers derived from prospective members' college experience: dean, registrar, bursar, and faculty. The annual meeting was to be called a Saturnalia, which was quickly dropped since the word meant an orgy. The original membership limit of thirty-one, was raised within a year to 100, and dues were $100 a year.[58]

In April 1886 the club moved from Johnson Park to rooms specifically built for it in the back of an apartment house at #640 Main between Chippewa and Tupper, owned by member William Kip. Next year the club rented for $700 a year a tiny frame house on #331 Delaware. Mrs. George Truscott, who lived next door said that she "knew what trumps were all night long." In the spring of 1889 a larger building at #393 Delaware was rented while plans were laid for "a large and well-appointed club," since "there was room in Buffalo" for such a club. Photos of #331 and #339 reveal that many homes on the eastside of Delaware between Chippewa and Edward were not mansions.[59]

Since Saint Patrick had been made patron saint of the club "in order to keep the snakes away," a

58 *Ibid.*, pp. 16, 22.
59 *Ibid.*, p. 23.

Saint Patrick's dinner was held that year and sporadically thereafter. Indicative of the contempt the largely WASP membership held for the Irish and their patron was the fact that at this Saint Patrick's celebration:

7.29 ❦ **Enlarged Saturn Club, 1896, *ibid.*, p. 82.**

> ...the dinner was served on rough boards with whiskey kegs for seats; the lights were green candles in beer bottles; everything possible, from the water to the bread and mashed potato, was colored with green dye, the costumes were Irish; Rev. Thomas R. Slicer [of #487 Delaware, pastor of the Unitarian Church of Our Father] and others wore green halos; a goat with green ribbons on its horns wandered at large; a snake charmer with snakes was introduced; and Saint Patrick entered with an acolyte and exorcised the snakes, driving them across to the Buffalo Club.[60]

Father Patrick Cronin, fiery editor of the *Catholic Union*, denounced these affairs as "an affront to Ireland," but his objections were overruled amid an outpouring of sophomoronic verse and songs composed by Almy and Charles P. Norton in honor of Saint Patrick as if he were the patron saint of hard liquor. The Saturn 1925 history abounds in the sort of high-jinks and doggerel usually associated with a college fraternity. Mabel Ganson's depiction of the Buffalo Club as peopled by "middleaged and elderly gentlemen," and Saturn as "a young man's club" was true only the first decade or so, since dozens of Buffalonians belonged to both clubs, but a certain playfulness characterized Saturn as long as it was located on Edward Street.[61]

In February 1890 the club voted to buy a lot on Delaware and Edward and to build a clubhouse to cost about $17,500. When finished the building cost $15,236 and the furnishings $3,225. The house was opened on December 13, 1890. It was enlarged in 1896 when a shed for bicycles and an extension along Edward was built for a billiard room below and a cafe above, the old billiard room being turned into a library for the more literary.(7.29) A second enlargement costing about $40,000 was approved in April 1905. The new facilities were opened April 21, 1906.

> The old club house has been added to in two ways. It has been built out towards Delaware Avenue, and an extension of thirty feet has been built upon the south side, so that it is now about twice as large as it was. The old main room, or lounging room, has been extended and is now T-shaped, the stem running out towards Delaware Avenue. The stem is sixty feet long and the crossbar fifty feet in length. This room is two stories in height, and the old balcony effect, with its loges, has been carried out around the new portion of the room. The same color scheme, dark red, has been retained. A stage has been provided at the Delaware Avenue end of the room.
>
> The new gymnasium is in the southern addition to the house. It is thirty feet by eighty in dimensions. The old gymnasium, which was located in the basement, has been con-

60 *Ibid.*, pp. 22, 31-32.
61 *Ibid.*, p. 82.
62 *Ibid.*, pp-102-103.

Left 7.30 ❦ Interior of the Saturn Club, 1896, *ibid.*, p. 83.
Above Right 7.31 ❦ Proposed seven story clubhouse, 1917, *ibid.*, p. 102.

> verted into a plunge room and provided with Russian and Turkish baths and spacious rubbing rooms. Space has been provided for a bowling alley, but it has not yet been equipped. New card and dining rooms have been added on the second floor, and the third floor is equipped with suites for transient and permanent guests. The new kitchen is in the rear of the third floor.[62]

Figures 7.29 and 7.30 are exterior and interior views of the 1896 clubhouse.

As war clouds gathered over Europe some Saturnians were calling for a yet bigger clubhouse. This was not to be:

> In January 1914 a building committee recommended the purchase of additional land on Edward Street for an enlargement, and an increase of dues from $60 to $75. Both propositions were voted down by the club, but in April the membership limit was raised from 325 to 350. In April 1915 another building committee proposed an addition, but the Faculty later voted that the dean appoint a committee with reference to an entirely new building. No further action appears until January 12, 1917, when the Faculty voted that Dean Crane "appoint a committee of which he shall be chairman to have plans prepared for a new club house." Ex-dean Dudley was made chairman of a Committee on Preparation of Plans, and soon after a book was sent to the club members showing plans in full for an entirely new building of seven stories, besides a mezzanine floor and a story for a roof garden and bowling alleys.(7.31) This was to be on the old site, on the Corner of Delaware and Edward 81.2 by 115 feet, with the entrance again on Edward street, as it was from

> 1890 to 1906. This book proposed an increase of membership from 350 to 375 and of dues from $60 to $100; but nothing was to be effective until after the war. The club vote in June was merely to increase the dues from #60 to $80 and defer all further action until the war was over. This inaction caused great discouragement and some of the leaders of the club predicted that it would soon cease to exist.[63]

But even wars end:

> After the war the club action was almost unanimous. In November 1919 authority was given to sell the club house at Delaware and Edward [at the time there was no other] without any plan for moving, and in January 1920 the dues were raised to $100 by a practically unanimous vote of 111 to 1. A combination with the Tennis and Squash Club was considered. In May 1920 the house was sold to the Montefiore Club, composed of members of the B'nai B'rith.[64]

A lot had been purchased on Delaware south of Utica, and on it a Tudor structure of brick and stone was erected. The facility was opened on October 21, 1922. Concerning the new landlord of #417 Adler wrote in 1960:

> Dating also from the Harding-Coolidge Era is the Montefiore Club, the latest and most successful organization of its type in Buffalo's Jewish history. We have already noticed the present tendency of American Jews to found clubs of their own. This tendency accelerated as the present century matured, for there were greater numbers of Jews who desired and could afford club membership. While at the same time they were excluded from many non-Jewish social organizations. Precisely at the point of success where other immigrant groups could join the Old-Anglo-Saxon elite, the Jew of prominence and wealth was excluded. A representative club under Jewish auspices was, therefore, a virtual necessity if the Jewish community was to participate in this area of ordinary American life.
>
> The Montefiore was the successor of the Standard, Phoenix, and Apollo Clubs, all of which had been founded for similar purposes. It, in turn, has existed longer than any of its predecessors, but it was founded somewhat accidentally. About 1920, Montefiore Lodge of B'nai B'rith had grown to the point where its members thought that they could afford a permanent meeting place. David Rodenberg, president of the Lodge, heard that the old Saturn Club on Delaware Avenue and Edward Street was for sale; but when he tried to buy, he found that the Apollo Club had already been given an option on the Saturn property. Rodenberg then visited August Keiser and other Apollo members and they released their option hoping that a new all-community club would unite Buffalo Jewry. The idea of putting the new club under B'nai B'rith auspices was dropped, for the chief aim of the group was to draw together, for social purposes, all segments of the male Jewish population. So the Montefiore Club was opened to all men of good character who could afford the dues, and for almost forty years it has been a chief center of Jewish social activity in Buffalo.[65]

$550,000 FIRE DESTROYS MONTEFIORE CLUB HERE was the headline that greeted readers of the *Courier-Express* the beginning of the workweek on December 29, 1969:

> More than 100 club members fled to safety Sunday morning when a 4-Alarm Inferno swept through the Montefiore Club of Buffalo at 417 Delaware Ave. leaving the three-story

63 *Ibid*, p. 103.

64 Selig Adler and Thomas E. Connolly, *From Ararat to Suburbia: The History of the Jewish Community of Buffalo* (Philadelphia: The Jewish Publication Society of America, 1960), p. 339-340.

65 *CE*, December 29, 1969.

> brick structure a mere shell. Fed by natural gas from a broken gas main for more than an hour, flames spread throughout the entire structure, causing the first floor and roof to collapse.
>
> Commissioner Robert B. Howard, Jr., estimated damage at $350,000 to the building and $200,000 to the contents. "Part of the structure had recently been refurbished at a considerable expense," the commissioner said. The Montefiore Club is a private club for men. The building did not house any resident guests.
>
> The first alarm was sounded at 11:21 a.m., the second at 11:27 a.m., and the third at 11:37 a.m. Howard said he ordered the fourth alarm at 1:11 p.m. when the structure suddenly burst into flames again.
>
> Heavy smoke permeated the area, and for a time fire officials feared an explosion might occur. Captain Carrol E. Lymas of the Franklin Station ordered a detail of 20 uniformed policemen to shut off traffic and move onlookers a block away from the structure when word spread that an explosion might take place.
>
> "We could have saved the structure from destruction had the gas supply been shut off promptly," Howard said. "When a crew from the Iroquois Gas Co. arrived, it had difficulty locating the main shut off valve. Finally, it was located near the entrance of the building but buried two feet beneath the sidewalk surface."
>
> Meanwhile, Howard said, no attempt was made to extinguish the gas-fed flames. He explained that had fire fighters put out the gas fed flames before the gas was turned off, fumes would not only permeate the building but the immediate area as well. A mere spark could then have blown the structure as far as Elmwood Ave., he said.[66]

Though reports circulated that the a new building would be erected *in situ*, the club in the end moved to the magnificent former residence of Seymour H. Knox on #806 Delaware north of Summer where athletic facilities were added. The club had sued Iroquois Gas for $2.1 million in 1972 but had to settle for $1.2 million four years later.[67]

7. 32 ❦ Numbers 427, 431, 435, 439, and 443 Delaware, 1930, *PBHS*, 30 (1930), following p. 289.

Five of the eight homes on the east side of Delaware between Edward and Virginia are shown on the eve of their demolition in 1930.(7.32) None could have been called mansions even in their prime; though in 1880 the six employed ten domestics. The cars are reminiscent of Prohibition Era gangsters. (The second from the left is a Buffalo-built Pierce Arrow.) There was only one home on this block in 1850(7.2), that of Noyes Darrow, a builder of luxury apartments. By 1860 there were three houses there. One on the corner at #427, old style #231, was the home of Gilbert Cameron, a

66 *BEN*, June 27, 1972; January 27, 1976.
67 *Times*, November 25, 1928.

7.33 ❦ Knowlton Mixer, *Men of Buffalo*, p. 103.

treasurer for the New York & Erie Railroad. The second was that of Noyes Darrow, who would soon move to a new house he had built at #841 at Delaware and Barker. At the third, on the corner of Virginia at old number #233, resided Richard J. Sherman, a dry goods merchant, and his wife *nee* Julia Avery. She had been born in Groton, Connecticut, in 1828. An ancestor had come over with John Winthrop to Massachusetts in 1630. She married Sherman in 1854. He and a brother, Robert D. Sherman, organized a dry goods firm which evolved into the William Hengerer & Company. R.D. & R.J. Sherman was the quality house of Buffalo, since the brothers were jobbers and importers of fine laces, linens, silks, velvets, jet and crystal garnitures, organdies, and mousselines which adorned chic party dresses before the Civil War. Richard died in 1888. Julia, a member of First Presbyterian and a Daughter of the American Revolution, died at ninety-eight in 1925 at #455 Delaware. She left her maid $6,000 and the same ($104,580 in 1997 dollars) to her houseman.[68]

Number 427 in 1870 was the home of Henry W. Prosser, an envelope manufacturer. A decade later it was the home of Mary Hammond, a fifty-eight year old Haligonian, her daughter, and a cousin. They managed without servants and survived on Delaware until the end of the 1880's when Knowlton Mixer(7.33), a lumberman, and his mother, Mary E. Mixer, historian of Trinity, had moved in. By 1900, Mary's son, Frederick K. Mixer, a graduate of the Sheffield Scientific School and curator of the Buffalo Museum of Natural Science, had joined her. Another matriarch, the eighty-two year old Mary Almy, with three children, Helen, Francis, and Frederick, was residing at #427 in 1905. The era from 1900 until World War I is often referred to as the Progressive Era, when urban governments (like "Blue Eyed Billy" Sheehan's Buffalo) and institutions (like Buffalo's Bell Telephone Company) were being subjected to increasing scrutiny. Frederick Almy was the quintessential progressive. Born in New Bedford in 1858, he graduated from Harvard in 1880 with an A.B. and in 1881 with an A.M. He spent two years at Harvard Law, passed the bar in 1885, and came to Buffalo to practice. He never married. He was secretary of the Buffalo Civil Service Reform Association, 1886-1911, and 1894-1921 of the Charity Organization Society which had been founded in 1877 to coordinate the efforts of Buffalo's private charities and to eliminate waste and fraud. He was also a member of the council of the National Civil Service Reform League 1905-1907 and of the executive committee of the National Municipal League. He and brother Francis, also apparently unmarried, were charter

68 "Almy, Frederick," *Who Was Who in America, 1897-1942*, p. 20; Dunn, *op. cit.*, p. 20; George E. Mowry, *The Era of Theodore Roosevelt and the Birth of Modern America , 1900-1912* (New York: Harper & Row, 1958), p. 61; "The Changing Town," *PBHS*, 30(1930), 285-286.

Above 7.34 ❦ Number 443, BHS.
Below 7.35 ❦ Henry M. Watson, *Men of Buffalo*, p. 46.

members of Saturn and took part in amateur theatricals at the Studio Club. Frederick, Francis, and Helen Almy were still at #427 in 1920, but by 1930 all houses on the block were razed to make way for stores and apartments. Frederick died in August 1935.[69]

In 1870 the house next door, #431, was home to a manufacturer of envelopes, William H. Dee and family, and two servants. About 1877 it was bought by William Edward Foster, a newspaper man, who lived there until his death in 1915. In 1862 James N. Matthews had formed a partnership with James D. Warren to publish the *Commercial Advocate*, lineal descendant of Buffalo's first newspaper. Matthews was editor-in-chief and Foster associate editor, an arrangement which lasted until 1877 when Matthews retired and bought the *Express*. Thereupon, Foster became editor-in-chief of the *Commercial,* which he remained until his retirement in 1911. Under him the paper became a power in Republican circles.[70] Foster died in 1915, but his widow continued at #431 until the early 1920s. Her brother, Albert Thompson, was there in 1925, on the eve of the great demolition.

Number 435 was in the early 1880s the home of two sisters in their sixties, Clarissa and Mary Hill, who conducted The Misses Hills' School for Young Ladies. In 1897 sixty-two year old Elizabeth Griffin resided there with Louisa Germain and her sister Mary. Since no occupations were listed, the ladies probably lived on inherited wealth. In 1905 attorney Edward B. Germain appeared as Mary's husband and with two teen-aged children. They were still there in 1910 but by 1915 they had been supplanted by Charles Germain, a seventy-year old attorney and wife Louisa, probably the Louisa who was living there in 1897. Charles stayed on after #435 had become a rooming house in 1920.

The earliest resident at #439 was Dr. Edward C. W. O'Brien in 1897. Frederick Usher, a cement company executive, with his wife, two children, two domestics were there in 1905. Portland Cement was not produced in America until 1872, but it soon rivaled steel as a structural material. By 1915

69 Hill, *op. cit.*, 1:473.
70 Horton, *op. cit.*, 1:350.

#439 had become the home of Edwin Hawley, an insurance company president. He was still there in 1926, a widower, with one Hungarian domestic.

The big house to the left in figure 7.34 was #443, probably Noyes Darrow's house in 1850. It was occupied by Charles W. Hamlin, a lawyer, through the 1890s down to at least 1910. Arthur Halmes, an attorney, and his father were living there in 1915, but by 1920 Etlinda Staub was putting up thirteen roomers there. Harrison B. Mixer, owner of the Mixer Lumber and a relative of the Mixers at #427, was resident at #445 in 1891. He was followed in 1900 by Charles B. Sears, fresh from Harvard Law, who quickly moved up the Avenue to #848. Next came Alfred W. Thorn, English-born head of the Portland Cement Company, whose son, lived at #445 and worked for the Buffalo Asphalt Company. The Thorns remained there until the early 1920s. For a partial view of #443 and frontal of #445 see figure 7.34.

In the early 1870s #449 was the residence of Henry M. Watson(7.35), son of Arnold Watson of Albany and nephew of Stephen V. R. Watson of #388 Delaware, who had been identified with Buffalo's street railways since their origin in 1869. Henry Watson was born in Unadilla, Otsego County, in 1839. He moved to Albany in 1857 and engaged in banking for nine years before becoming general passenger agent for the Albany & Susquehanna Railroad. Two years later, he came to Buffalo where his uncle made him secretary and treasurer of the Buffalo Street Railroad Company. By the 1890s he had moved up the Avenue to #622. In 1871 he was also made secretary-treasurer of the Buffalo East Side Railway Company. With Stephen Watson's death in 1881, he became president of the Buffalo Street Railroad which merged with other lines in 1890 to become the Buffalo Railway Company. Electrification of all lines, hitherto horse drawn, proceeded rapidly. He had been a founder of the American Street Railway Association in 1882 and was elected president in 1890. Bell Telephone had been formed in 1879 with Henry Watson as president. He served until its take-over by New York Telephone in 1910. The presidency enabled him to make his brother William, who also lived at #622, treasurer, and his son, Arnold Watson, manager. Arnold was married to Esther Goodyear, daughter of Charles W. of #888 Delaware. The conduct of Bell Telephone on Watson's watch, thought typical of public utilities, led to a national outcry for trust busting associated with Theodore Roosevelt.[69] Watson was trustee of the Erie County Savings Bank and of Union Fire Insurance. He was vice president of Fidelity Loan and Trust, vice dean of Saturn, and a vestryman. He died in 1911 at a sanitarium in Watkins, New York, at seventy-one.[71]

71 White, *op. cit.*, 2:509-510.

CHAPTER

8 VIRGINIA TO NORTH: *West Side*

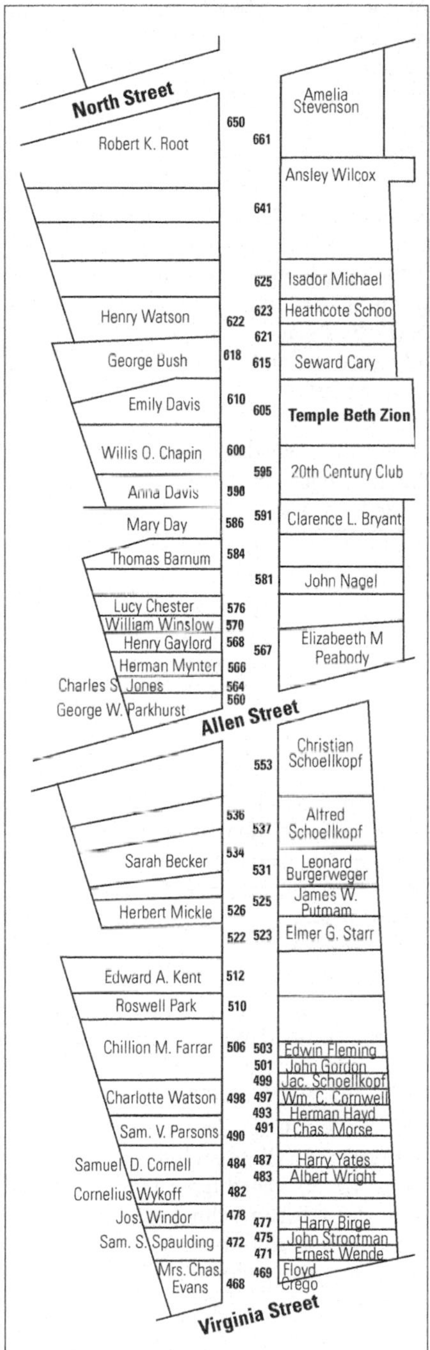

Left 8.1 ❦
Above 8.2 ❦ *PBHS*, 16(1912), 304.

Unlike previous Avenue maps, figure 8.1 reflects the situation Virginia-North in 1900. Settlement in 1860 was so sparse as to be ignored. Inhabitants in 1870 are from the census and the atlas for 1872. Settlement had been moving north, but not until 1889 was the Cornell White Lead Company(8.2), which since 1865 occupied over two acres on the northeast corner of Delaware and Virginia, demolished. The southwest corner of North and Delaware, moreover, contained a five acre cemetery dating from about 1820, which was abandoned, the bodies moved, and the tract made available for homes during the 1890s.

1870

VIRGINIA STREET

468 James Lyon L. Baker & Co. land office real estate insurance
Henry L. Lyon Sherman & Lyon surveyors

472 Samuel Clemens 30 Missouri
Olivia Clemens 24 NY housekeeper
Patrick McFey 26 Ireland
Margaret Brown 23 NY
Ellen White 29 Ireland

478 W. E. Story

482 Cornelius Wykoff 47 NY physician
George Wykoff 20 NY son
Cornelius Wykoff 11 NY school
Fanny W. Hall Mass. boarder
Ann Valentine 40 Ireland
Robert Dargavel 16 Canada West

484 C. Young

490 P. Parsons

498 John Locke 62 England builder
Susan Locke 62 England housekeeper
James Locke 29 NY letter carrier
Margaret Locke 29 NY boarder
Edward W. Locke 19 NY mason
M. A. Stouter 54 England boarder

1880

VIRGINIA STREET

468 Charles Worthington Evans 68 Maryland elevator owner
Mary Evans 59 NY *ux.* housekeeper
Alice M. Gorham 21 NY daughter
Virginia Gorham 17 NY daughter school
Kate Oswald 20 NY
Kate Zumbein 21 NY

472 Samuel Spaulding 33 NY assistant bank cashier
Anna W. Spaulding 27 NY *ux.* housekeeper
Marion Spaulding 4 NY daughter
Charlotte Spaulding 6 mos. daughter
Bridget Conroy 42 Ireland
Maggie Ahern 26 Ireland
Charles Culver 16 Ireland
Eliza Gorham 22 NY

478 Henry S. Larned 37 Canada government storekeeper
Emma F. Larned 33 Mass. *ux.* housekeeper
Alice Larned 7 NY daughter school
Amelia Roth 22 NY

484 William J. Dunlap 49 clerk AM&A
Jane Dunlap 47 NY *ux.* housekeeper
Lydia Dunlap 18 NY daughter
Emma Sheppard 33 daughter
Ira T. Sheppard 7 West Virginia grandson

486 David Davies 55 England printer
Mary E. Davies 27 England daughter housekeeper
Isabella McCabe 38 Scotland

490 Samuel Parsons 57 Newfoundland ship carpenter
Sarah Parsons 47 Conn. *ux.* housekeeper
R. Grover Parsons 23 NY son clerk
Lillian Parsons 15 NY daughter school
Frank Parsons 13 NY son school
R. H. Hopkins 28 NY son-in-law clerk
Annabelle Parsons 50 Newfoundland sister at home
Maggie Hamilton 28 Canada
Sarah Rush 18 NY

498 John Locke 69 England house builder
William Locke 43 NY son house builder
James Locke 36 NY son produce dealer
Margaret Locke 38 NY daughter-in-law at home
John Locke 18 NY grandson clerk
Hattie Locke 10 NY granddaughter school
Mary Streeter 65 England sister

506 Chillion M. Farrar Farrar & Trefts
steam engines 54 Perry

506 Chillion M. Farrar 51 Michigan foundry owner
Alvira Farrar 50 NY *ux.* housekeeper
John Holloway 30 NY contractor
Anna M. Holloway 23 NY daughter
Stacia McKay 19 NY
Lousia Paul 20 NY
Margaret McDonald 45 Ireland
Henry Dunham 34 NY

514 Maria M. Welch 41 Maine housekeeper
Samuel M. Welch Jr. 19 NY clerk in office
James Welch 16 NY school
Wilfred Welch 16 NY
Thomas C. Welch 5 NY

514 Maria M. Welch 51 Maine housekeeper
Samuel M. Welch Jr. 29 NY son attorney
Jennie Welch 25 NY daughter
Thomas C. Welch 15 son school
Jane G. Mead 77 Maine mother

522 Thomas Chester Thornton & Chester
flour milling

522 Thomas Chester 69 England flour mill owner
Mary Chester 59 England *ux.* housekeeper
George J. Chester 22 England clerk
Helena Richard 22 NY
Carrie Hoover 26 NY

526 William B Sirret 44 France county treasurer
Amelia Sirret 33 NY *ux.* housekeeper
Marie Sirret 18 daughter
Ada Sirret 12 NY daughter
Isabella 25

528 H. Chandler

528 Moses Robertson 39 Virginia real estate
Anna Robertson 48 Virginia *ux.* housekeeper
Mary Robertson 28 Virginia daughter
Anna D. Robertson 18 Virginia
Edward Robertson 14 England school
William Robertson 11 England
Anna Connors 23 Ireland
Matilda Watson 16 NY

546 Seth D. Caldwell president Union
Steamboat Co. 1 Main St.

546 George B. Gates 67 NY banker
Sarah Gates 61 NY *ux.* housekeeper
Elizabeth A. Gates 40 NY daughter
Ann Ballentine 45 Ireland
Kate Neu 26 NY

ALLEN STREET ❦ End of Block

ALLEN STREET ❦ End of Block

560 Jacob D. Sawyer 57 NY grain
merchant 9 Central Wharf
Charlotte Sawyer 52 NY housekeeper
Elizabeth Sawyer 22 NY
Ida Sawyer 14 NY school
William B. Sawyer 14 NY school
Mary Dorst 16 NY
Emily Kopplein 22 Prussia

560 James D. Sawyer 66 NY
Elizabeth Sawyer 33 NY daughter
Ida Sawyer 26 NY
Nellie McDermott 19 NY
Thomas Hackett 37 Ireland

564 Francis C. King commission merchant

564 Joseph Dudley 60 New Hampshire oil refiner
Carrie Dudley NY *ux.* housekeeper
Clara Dudley 23 NY daughter
Mary Shields 20 Pa
Mary Henderson 28 NY

568 Stephen M. Clement cashier Marine Bank

570 Cornelia Bentley 62 NY housekeeper
William Sage Jr. 30 NY boarder
Cornelia Sage 3 NY boarder
Sabena Knowlton 70 NY boarder
Ellen Milvin 22 Ireland

576 William G. Boardman 69 NY lithographer
Amanda Boardman 69 NY housekeeper
Mary Boardman 24 NY
Sarah Boardman 20 NY
Mary Mill 25 NY

578 John W. Dickson 33 NJ life insurance agent
Josephine Dickson 28 NY housekeeper
Hamilton Dickson 4 NY
William Dickson 1 NY
Kate Sandendel 20 NY
Theresa Walter 17 NY

584 Stephen O. Barnum 54 NY variety merchant
Elizabeth Barnum 52 NY housekeeper
Theodore Barnum 28 NY variety merchant
Sarah Barnum 27 NY boarder
Fanny Barnum 3 NY
Henry Barnum 23 NY clerk in store
Frank Barnum 15 NY school
Sarah Stoddard 53 NY
Mary Doster 20 Wittemberg
Annie Gallan NY

586 James M. Willett Laning Folsom & Willett 160 East Seneca St.

568 Samuel A. Wheeler 43 Ohio
banker and oil producer
Mary C. Wheeler Ohio *ux.* housekeeper
Fred R. Wheeler 18 Ohio son school
Carrie W. Wheeler 9 Ohio daughter school
Letta Clare 18 Ohio daughter
Mary Letts 55 Conn.

570 Cornelia Bentley 72 NY housekeeper
William Sage 45 son-in-law retired lithographer
Josephine Sage 39 NY daughter
Cornelia B. Sage 13 NY granddaughter school
James R. Bentley 20 NY grandson clerk
Katie Donnelly 35 Ireland
Maggie Fondes 24 NY

576 Theodore D. Barnum 38 NY
fancy goods merchant
Jennie Barnum 37 Ohio *ux.* housekeeper
Fannie Barnum 12 NY daughter school
Kate Stelen 18 NY
Mary Jacoby 23 NY

578 Josephine Dickson 38 NY housekeeper
Hamilton Dickson 13 NY son school
John W. Dickson 11 NY son school
Josephine Dickson 4 NY daughter school
Marian Thompson 17 NY
Bridget Collins 23 Ireland

584 Stephen O. Barnum 64 NY
fancy goods merchant
Elizabeth Barnum 62 *ux.* housekeeper
Frederick Barnum 34 NY son clerk
Edward J. Chatfield Jr. 51 Conn.
brother-in-law fancy goods merchant
Mary Sampson 23 Scotland
Lana Keller 19 NY

586 Helen Willett 43 NY housekeeper
Pauline R. Willett 18 NY daughter school
Porter G. Willett 15 NY son school
Nora Mooney 20 Ireland

596 Townsend Davis 40 Pa. fire insurance agent
Annie Davis 39 NY *ux.* housekeeper
Millie Davis 12 daughter school
Harry Davis 12 NY son school
Willie Davis 8 NY son school
Minnie Feshing 26 NY

Buffalo Cemetery Association

NORTH STREET ❦ End of Block

600 Edward W. Eames 38 NY
grain commission merchant
Adelaide Eames 35 Conn. *ux.* housekeeper
Hattie D. Eames 12 NY daughter school
Mary Eames 10 NY daughter school
Milo D. Eames 4 NY son
Edward A. Eames 7 NY son
Olive R. Eames 2 NY
Daniel D. Eames 6 mos. son
Rebecca Gissens 30 Canada

Buffalo Cemetery Association

NORTH STREET ❦ End of Block

1891

VIRGINIA STREET

468 Mrs. Charles W. Evans

472 Samuel S. Spaulding

478 Joseph C. Windsor Pfeiffer & Windsor
livestock 936 William St.
Mrs. Ellen C. Chapin

482 Cornelius C. Wyckoff M.D.

484 James B. Parke Jr. reporter *Buffalo Enquirer*

486 Mrs. L. J. Barnard

490 Samuel V. Parsons marine surveyor
Frank V. Parsons

1900

VIRGINIA STREET

468 Mrs. Charles Evans 79 NY widow
Walter Devereux 45 son-in-law insurance agent
Virginia Devereux 37 NY daughter
Walter Devereux Jr. 2 NY grandson
Mary Maney 29 NY
Mary Friedham 30 NY
Nellie House 23 England

472 Samuel Strong Spaulding 51 NY
Annie Watson Spaulding 46 NY
Elbridge Gerry Spaulding
Stephen R. V. Spaulding
Charlotte Spaulding

478 Joseph C. Windsor 42 NY livestock dealer
Ellen P. Chapin 60 NY sister
Ella Lothrop 21 NY niece
Emma Draper 30 Canada

482 Cornelius Wyckoff M.D. 77 NY
Alice Wykoff 57 Washington D.C. *ux.*
Aurelia Ramsey 75 NY boarder
August Carlson 37 Sweden boarder
Delia Mack 20 Ireland

484 Samuel D. Cornell 60 Conn. capitalist
Lydia H. Cornell 32 NY daughter
Douglas Cornell 31 NY son civil engineer
Mary H. Selby 22 England
Bridget Smith 35 Ireland
Nora Burns 27 Canada

490 Samuel Parsons 78 Conn. capitalist
Sarah Parsons 67 Conn. *ux.*
Lillia B. Parsons 35 NY daughter
Frank A. Parsons 28 NY secretary
Mary Newman 21 Germany

498	Mrs. Stephen V. R. Watson Marianne W. Pease		
506	Chillion M. Farrar Farrar & Trefts engines and boilers 54 Perry John A. Holloway paving contractor 101 Franklin	506	Chillion M. Farrar 70 Michigan iron works proprietor Alvirah Farrar 71 NY *ux.* Maria F. Holloway 19 NY granddaughter Evadne Holloway 14 NY granddaughter Martha J. Pirwan 33 Canada Bertha C. Benning 18 NY Charles Heirch 22 NY coachman
510	Roswell Park M.D.	510	Roswell Park
522	Mary P. Chester widow of Thomas		
526	Henry Altman Altman & Co men's wear 72 Seneca	526	Herbert Mickle 40 Canada M.D. Susette Mickle NY *ux.* Catherine Weber 23 Germany
528	Edward P. Hollister		
534	Phillip Becker PB&Co.	534	Sarah Becker 68 Germany widow Christine Goetz 43 NY niece Elizabeth Gates 22 NY
		536	Joseph Cook 44 NY M.D. Anna Cook 61 NY *ux.* Martha Poole 22 NY daughter student Maud Poole 30 NY daughter-in-law Margaret Wall 60 England Kate Collins 40 NY James Borum 49 Ireland coachman Laura Borum 50 Ireland *ux.* Mary J. Borum 24 NY daughter James W. Borum 18 NY son school
546	Mrs. George Gates		
	ALLEN STREET ❦ End of Block		ALLEN STREET ❦ End of Block
		560	George W. Parkhurst 63 Vermont attorney Elizabeth Parkhurst 52 NY *ux.* George Parkhurst 18 NY son college Margaret Heaney 29 Canada Alice Murphy 60 Ireland
564	Margart Beemer 40 Morgan Bldg. Belle Beemer	564	Charles Jones 41 NY M.D. Emma P. Jones 41 NY *ux.* Pascal P. Jones 5 NY son school Mary Kelly 40 Canada Julia A. Cullinan 40 Ireland Mary Moran 55 Ireland
		566	Herman Mynter M.D 54 Denmark Harriet Mynter 49 NY *ux.* Agnes Mynter 22 NY daughter student Emily Mynter 19 NY daughter Mary Dugan 25 Ireland

		568	Henry Gaylord M.D. 27 Michigan Bertha Gaylord 26 Michigan *ux.* Bradley Gaylord 4 Austria son Margaret Memiock 27 Canada
570	William G. Winslow	570	William Winslow 54 Ohio capitalist Helen Winslow 28 NY daughter Pauline M. Winslow 24 NY daughter Henry C. Winslow 21 NY son stenographer William Winslow Jr. 17 NY son Margaret Barton 23 Ireland Esther McCafferty 28 NY Carrie Wells 28 NY
576	William Dickson Mrs. J. W. Dickson	576	Lucy Chester 75 Conn. Carlton Chester 46 Conn. son attorney Elizabeth O'Connor 27 Ireland Wilhelmina Burkhard 42 Germany
578	William Dickson Mrs. J. W. Dickson		
584	Stephen O. Barnum SOB & Son notions 265 Main St. Theodore D. Barnum *ibid.*	584	Theodore D. Barnum 57 NY fancy goods merchant Sarah A. Barnum 57 Ohio *ux.* Stephen Barnum 18 NY son Fanny Keating 33 NY Theodore B. Keating 6 NY son of above Margaret Mechan 26 Ireland Anna Neville 37 Ireland
586	Clarence L. Bryant Bryant & Stratton business college Main & Lafayette Square	586	Mary Day 60 NY Ida Havens 52 NY sis Lizzie Spaulding 37 Ireland Norah Fitzgibbons 47 Ireland
596	Townsend Davis Smith Davis & Co. marine insurance 200 Main St. H. Townsend Davis clerk *ibid.*	596	Anna Davis 63 Ohio widow H. Townsend Davis 33 NY son insurance agent William H. Davis 27 NY son insurance agent Henrietta P. Davis 25 NY daughter–in-law Elizabeth Buckley 27 NY Mary McKinnon 46 Canada *illegible* Good 34 England
600	Willis O. Chapin attorney Viele & Chapin 71 White Bldg. Mrs. William B. Flint	600	Willis O. Chapin 39 NY attorney Abby Chapin 35 NY *ux.* Janet Chapin 9 NY daughter school William Chapin 7 NY son Mary Carney 29 Ireland Mary *illegible* 26 NY Kate Bannister 53 Ireland Margaret Hayes 24 Ireland
610	Mrs. William H. Davis	610	Emily Davis 86 NY Helen McLane 20 Scotland
		618	George Bush 38 NY Anne W. Bush 38 NY *ux.* Hannah Fitzgerald 24 Ireland Hannah Corcoran 45 Ireland

622 Henry M. Watson president Buffalo Railway Co. 346 Main St.
William H. Watson

NORTH STREET End of Block

622 Henry Watson NY 61 president telephone company
Ella Watson 60 NY *ux.*
Arnold Watson 22 NY son
William Watson 50 NY brother
Margaret Griffin 37 Ireland
Mary McGillicudy 31 Ireland
Ellen McGee 19 Ireland

628 Henry W. Box 63 England capitalist
Mary P. Box Conn. *ux.*
Mary E. Box 25 NY daughter
Agnes McKenzie 57 Ireland
Katie Flynn 26 Ireland

NORTH STREET End of Block

1905

VIRGINIA STREET

468 Mrs. Mary Evans 84
Walter Devereux 50 son-in-law insurance agent
Virginia Devereux 42 daughter
Walter Devereux Jr. 7 grandson
Mary Friedman 30
Margaret Griffin 25 Ireland
Clara Perry 21 England

478 Harvey R. Gaylord M.D. 24
Bessie Gaylord 11 *ux.*
Bradley Gaylord 9 son school
Harvey Gaylord 1 son
Florence Goering 20
Kate Lehane 17 Ireland

482 Mrs. Alice Wyckoff 61
Harry R. Frank M.D. boarder
Mrs. Sarah W. Davidson 62 boarder
Ethel W. Davidson 24 daughter boarder
Eliza Claire 22

484 Albert J. Wright 49 banker
Gertrude B. Wright 46 *ux.*
Agnes Wright 15 daughter school
S. Kurata 21 Japan
Mary Sheehan 49 servant
Lillie Abram 24 Ireland
Edith Ruferal 20 Canada
Celeste Quinn 43 France

1915

VIRGINIA STREET

472 Alfred W. Bayliss 62 M.D.
Mary L. Bayliss 58 *ux.*
Jacob W. Bayliss M.D. son
Albert Schneider 25 Germany nephew mechanical engineer

478 Floyd C. Crego M.D. 59
A. R. Johnson 45 M.D.
Elizabeth Daley 40 Ireland

482 Alice Wyckoff 72
Fanny Hall 63 sister
Michael Conboy 42 M.D.
Maude Kuhn 29

484 Robert O. King 40 Canada mechanical engineer
Frances King 35 Canada
Florence King 11 daughter school
Sarah King 8 daughter school
Frank King 7 school
George King 6 son school
Jennie King 5 daughter kindergarten
Donald King 4 son
Marie King 4 mos.

William Warren 30 England coachman
Reginold Warren 10 daughter
Rennie Warren 5 daughter
Arthur Weichman 30 England coachman
Mary Weichman 28 England *ux.*
Arthur Weichman 2 England son

490 Samuel M. Parsons 83 Newfoundland
Sarah Parsons 72 *ux.*
Lillian B. Parsons 33 daughter
Anna Meigan 23 Ireland

498 Arthur E. Hedstrom 50 coal dealer
Katherine Hedstrom 46 *ux.*
Erick Hedstrom 6 son
Brenda Hedstrom 2 daughter
Clemline Kaufer 24 Germany
Ethel Green 18 Canada
Elizabeeth Dickson 45 Canada
Rosanna O'Connor 25 Ireland

506 Chillion M. Farrar 75 manufacturer steam engines
Alvira Farrar 75 *ux.*
Margaret Howard 83 boarder
Evadne Holloway 20 granddaughter
Martha Piernam 44
Rose Ludwig 19

510 Roswell Park M.D. 53
Roswell Park Jr. 19 son college
Julian Park 17 son military school Pottstown, Pa.
Mary Park 66 sister
Killianwald 40

512 Harriet Kent 73
Edward Kent 58 son architect
Charlotte N. Kent 40 daughter
Alice E. Hoffman 59 boarder school teacher
Mary W. Hoffman boarder school teacher
May Malloy 22

522 Edward H. Butler 55 editor *Buffalo Evening News*
Edward H. Butler Jr. 21 son Yale
Ada Butler 26 daughter
Josephine Barber 28 niece
Catherine Clark 38
Ana Peliscoro 32
Anna Sticht 32

August Gerhardt 33 coachman
Nellie E. Gerhardt 32 *ux.*

490 James J. Mooney 48 M.D.
Ellen Mooney 50 sister
Anna McKenna 35 maid

498 Charles McCulloch 48 vice president Lackawanna Company
Jessie McCulloch 37 *ux.*
Eleanor McCulloch 13 daughter school
Anna Ryan 38
Julia Busch 51 cook
Delia Hunt 27 Ireland

510 Clayton M. Brown 43 M.D.
Evelyn M. Brown 33 Canada *ux.*
Clayton M. Brown 5 son
Margaret E. Brown 1 daughter
John E. Hansen 50 Denmark gardener
Katherine Stevens 20

512 Albert J. Wright 53 banker & broker
Ellie Bottger 40 Germany housekeeper
Beatrice Stearson 22 Ireland
Katherine Callan 37
Nellie Normayle 30 Ireland cook

520 Lucien Howe 66 M.D.
Elizabeth Howe 55 *ux.*
2 lodgers
Hanna Sullivan 70 Ireland cook
Hannah Wienscheimer 62 Germany launderess
Jennie Colson 22 Sweden

526 Frank W. Talbot 40 roofer
Margaret A. Talbot 36 *ux.*
Ruth Graham 32 Scotland boarder

534 Mrs. Sara Becker 70 Germany
Christine Goetz 49 niece
Elizabeth A. Goetz 25 niece

James Brown 53 Canada coachman
Nora M. Brown 52 Ireland *ux.*
Mary Brown 29 daughter school teacher

546 University Club 30 residents
10 employees

ALLEN STREET End of Block

560 Elizabeth Parkhurst 59
George W. Parkhurst 22 son
Buffalo Car Wheel Company
Minnie Clancy 28 Canada

564 David E. Wheeler 32 M.D.
Mabel B. Wheeler 31 *ux.*
E. Wheeler 4 son
Caroline Conway 35

566 Harriet B. Mynter 58
Agnes Mynter 28 daughter music teacher
Emily Mynter 24 daughter school teacher
Elizabeth Eagan 38

568 Stephen Clark 65
Anna Clark 60 *ux.*
Julia Standast 26

570 William G. Winslow 61 retired
Pauline Winslow 32 daughter
William G. Winslow Jr. 23
Eliza Ellias 22
Clara Fletcher 19

526 Harry Thomas 37 hotel manager
10 lodgers

528 Robena Bennie 41 landlady
Harry Bennie 12 son school
10 lodgers

534 Sarah Becker 81 Alsace
Elizabeth Goetz 37 niece
Charlotte Niess 42

546 University Club T. S. Henerelway 35 manager
35 lodgers
4 employees
Michael Keller 35 steward
Amerlia Keller 27 *ux.*
Emil M. Keller 9 son school
Michael M. Keller 7 son school
Wengel C. Keller 7 son school
Dorothy Keller 4 daughter

ALLEN STREET End of Block

560 John Murphy 25 clerk
Rachael Murphy 23 *ux.* nurse

564 Alice Clark 44 manager gown shop
Sarah Sayre 19 lodger
Anna Taheney 58

566 Mrs. Herman Myntner 65
Agnes Mynter 38 daughter piano teacher
Mary Gallagher 15 Ireland

568 Edward H. Round 57 assistant
treasurer Pierce Arrow Company
Edith C. Round 46 *ux.*
George C. Round 17 son school
Elizabeth D. Round 13 daughter school
Catherine Sheehan 30 Ireland
Julia Donovan 55 Ireland

570 Burt J. McGrath 48 Maryland
Louise McGrath 48 *ux.*
Joseph T. McGrath 14 son school
Burt F. McGrath 13 son school

576 James How 31 Hartford Rubber Works
bicycle tires 22 West Chippewa
Franny How 37 *ux.*
Theodore B. Keating 11 son school
Theresa Atkinson 31 Ireland
Augusta Olday 27

582 George H. Selkirk 74 secretary
Park Commission
Emma S. Selkirk 58 *ux.*
John E. Selkirk 33 son title searcher
Henry B. Selkirk 31 son attorney
Grace H. Selkirk 21 daughter
Rose Thureck 18

584 Sarah O. Barnum 60
Stephana O. Barnum 23 daughter
Dora Conlon 39
Clara J. Wiebman 31
Barbara Eason 36 Scotland
Thomas S. Reeves 26 England coachman

586 Mary H Day 61
Ida Havens 57 sister
Nora Fitzgerald 55 Ireland
Elizabeth Koester 28

600 Willis O. Chapin 41 attorney
Abby Chapin 40 *ux.*
Janet Chapin 14 daughter school
William B. Chapin 12 son school
Ida Doran 29 Ireland
Mary Coleran 25 Ireland
Grace Osborne 23 Ireland

618 Anna Bush 40
Catherine Sheehan 21 Ireland
Hannah Cochrane 30 Ireland

622 Henry M. Watson 30
president Bell Telephone Company
Ellen Watson 60 *ux.*
William Watson 56 brother retired
Arnold Watson 29 son manager
Bell Telephone Company
Margaret Needam 50
Rose Raff 35
Ellen McGee 24 Ireland
Nora Murphy 60 Ireland

628 W. Carl Ely 49 attorney
Carrie Ely 43 *ux.*
Marion Ely 18 daughter school
Mary Koerner 45
Katherine McMahon 22

James Foxall 39 England coachman
Mary Foxall 38 England *ux.*
Martha Foxall 11 Canada daughter
Francis L. Foxall 2 son

576 James How 39 president of general store
Fanny How 47 *ux.*
Theodore Keating 21 son college
Anna Summer 31
Clara Pawlowicz 38 Germany

582 George Selkirk 80 secretary Park Commission
Emily H. Selkirk 69 *ux.*
John E. Selkirk 44 son attorney
Grace Selkirk 30 daughter
Stephanie Dombach, 24 Austria

584 Frank Henry 45 miller
Grace Henry 40 *ux.*
James Henry 2 son
Elizabeth Ziegler 40
Dorothy Gast 40
Nettie Wrieths 20 Germany

586 Ida Havens 67
Mary H. Day 75
Nellie Ryan 23 Ireland
Norah Fitzgibbons 56 Ireland

600 George A. Forman 35
Lucy Forman 26 *ux.*
George Forman 3 son
Lena Weber 35 France nurse
Margaret Jost 20 Germany
Nora Sheehan 32 Ireland
Margaret Scanlon 30 Ireland

618 Harry Taylor 30 England chauffeur
Ada Taylor 26 *ux.*
Anabelle E. Taylor 7 daughter
Marjorie Taylor 2 mos.

622 John Woodward 55 judge supreme court
Mary B. Woodward 54 *ux.*
Frances Woodward 20 daughter
Albertine Hanson 27 Sweden
Julia Johnson 30 Sweden

636 Joseph T. Cook MD 49
Anna Cook 66 *ux.*
Anna M. Hoxsie 35 daughter
Margaret Will 65 England seamstress
Elizabeth O'Connor 40 Ireland
Mary Powers 38

Charles Johncox 51 England coachman
Bertha Johncox 37 England *ux.*
Laura Johncox 7 daughter school
Ernest Johncox 12 son school

650 Robert K. Root 39
Emily D. Root 49 *ux.*
Ellen Wilson 40
Elizabeth Davies 30 England
Della N. ? 31 Ireland

NORTH STREET End of Block

636 Mrs. Joseph T. Cook 75
Maude Hoxsie 45 daughter
Abby J. Cone 48 housekeeper
Isabella Walter 33 Canada

650 Robert K. Root 48 real estate
Emily D.Root 50 *ux.*
Mary Niblet 38 England
Ella R. Wilson 35 housekeeper
Margaret Scanlon 28 Ireland

Albert Zemina 37 chauffeur
Ann Zemina 33 *ux.*

NORTH STREET End of Block

1920

EDWARD STREET

468 Virginia Devereux 56 NY
Walter E Devereux 32 NY son real estate agent
Ferdinand Shepherd 69 Conn. librarian
Ellie Shepherd 65 Mass. *ux.*
Martha Morrison 47 Canada
Ella Conley 57 Canada
John Conley 58 Canada husband mechanic

472 Jacob W. Bayliss M. D. 38 NY
Teresa Bayliss 30 Canada *ux.*
Alfred W. Bayliss M.D. 62 NY
Mary Bayliss 62 NY *ux.*

478 Nellie Bloomer 61 NY proprietor
rooming house
6 lodgers

482 Edgar E. Joraleman 66 NY architect
Elizabeth Joraleman 48 NY *ux.*
Michael A. Conboy M.D. 43 NY
lodger
Elizabeth Jones 59 Illinois

484 Emma Tunney 32 Ohio proprietress
1 boarder 1 servant

490 James Mooney M.D. 53 NY widower
Ellen Mooney 56 NY sister
Anna McKenna 42 Pennsylvania

1925

EDWARD STREET

468 Rooming house 2 roomers

470 Nellie Newhall 35 insurance

472 Jacob W. Bayliss M.D. 43
Theresa Bayliss 35 *ux.*
Frederick McMasters 27 insurance
Helen McMasters 28 *ux.*
Margaret Theis 33 Germany cook

484 Rooming house 5 roomers

490 James J. Mooney M.D. 59
Ellen Mooney 62 sister
Ana McKenna 47 cook

498 Boarding house 3 boarders

506 Knights of Columbus
Buffalo Council #184

510 Clayton Brown M.D. 48 NY
Evelyn M. Brown 35 Canada *ux.*
Margaret Brown 5 NY daughter

512 Albert Wright 60 NY broker
Josephine Jackson 43 Tenn. housekeeper
Anna Farkus 50 Scotland
Jennie Kelley 44 Wisconsin
Gertrude Grimach 21 Mass.
Masachite Erypahara 42 Japan butler
? Yai Japan waitress
Kato Kintara 43 Japan

522 Lucien Howe 76 M.D. Maine
Elizabeth Howe 59 Virginia *ux.*
Elizabeth Thompson 44 NY
Robert Thompson 19 NY son of maid
Josephine McDonald 43 NY
Fraser McDonald 43 NY husband of maid
Hannah Wenig 64 Germany

526 Robena Bennie 45 Pa. widow
proprietress of boarding house
Henry J. Bennie 15 NY son
16 boarders

528 Jean Jones 48 NY single
proprietress of boarding house
9 boarders

534 Sarah Becker 88 Alsace
Elizabeth A. Gates 41 NY niece
Pearl Michalski 15 NY

546 University Club
29 male boarders
6 employees

ALLEN STREET ❦ End of Block

566 Harriet B. Mynter 70 NY widow
Agnes Mynter 42 NY daughter
teacher Buffalo Seminary
Hilda Elang

498 Ray A. Edson 34 eye specialist
Elmer Feltz chauffeur

506 Knights of Columbus Buffalo Council
#184 50 roomers

510 Helen Caffrey 40
Irwin C. Caffery 16 son school

512 Albert J. Wright 67 stock broker
Elsa Gardner 26 secretary
Annie Evans 32
John H. Warner 28 England valet
Andrew Forbes 54 Scotland chef
Masikide Jrjehara 45 Japan butler
Yai Ujehara 32 Japan

522 Lucien Howe 77 M.D.
Elizabeth Howe 50 *ux.*
John M. Murray 13 ward school
Russell Sicard 39 Italy doctor's assistant
Rose Schindler 33 Germany nurse
Anne Armstrong 57 Canada

526 William Hughes 44 sales
Leona Hughes 49 *ux.*
Elizabeth Merigold 57 Canada
2 lodgers

528 David Bromberg M.D. 40
Inez Bromberg 33 *ux.* pathologist
Elsie Curley 17 daughter school

534 Rose M. Horgan 52
Edward J. Horgan 23 son sales
Rose M. Horan 19 daughter secretary
7 lodgers

546 University Club 19 boarders

ALLEN STREET ❦ End of Block

560 Rooming house 6 residents

564 Boarding house 9 residents

566 Charles L. Tenney 35 sales
Ethel D. Tenney 43 *ux.*
Olive Tenney 14 daughter school
George F. McClintock sales

568 Edward H. Rounds 62 Conn. assistant
manager Pierce Arrow Company
Edith D. Rounds 52 NY *ux.*
George Clarke Rounds 22 NY son bank clerk
Elizabeth D. Rounds 18 NY
Julia Donovan 56 Ireland
Nellie Gallagher 24 Ireland

570 Burt G. Maycock NY 52 M.D.
Louise Mycock 45 NY *ux.*
Farwell Maycock 18 NY son
Burt Maycock 17 NY son
Joseph Maycock 76 England father
Anna Nelson 30 Sweden

576 James How 44 NY dry goods store
Fanny How 52 NY *ux.*
Theodore D. Keating stepson
Elizabeth Harte 28 Ireland
Clara Pawlowicz 38 Germany

578 George J. Selkirk 74 NY secretary
public parks commission
Emily Selkirk 73 Conn. *ux.*
John E. Selkirk 46 NY attorney
Grace Selkirk 34 NY daughter

584 Charles L. Couch 49 NY
president Weaver Coal Company
Ethel Couch 40 NY *ux.*
Leonard H. Couch 17 NY son
Grace Fenstate 19 NY
Mary Conolly 45 Ireland

586 Ida Haven 72 NY
Helen M. Madden 48 NY nurse
Anna Reaume 65 Canada cook
Bridget Ryan 27 Ireland

596 Frederick B. Usher 55 Canada
Louise Usher 43 NY *ux.*
Margaret B. Usher 25 NY daughter
Pauline Usher 17 NY daughter
Catherine F. Usher 17 NY
Delia J. Keating 23 Ireland
Margaret O'Day 25 Ireland cook
Mary McKinnon 28 Michigan

610 Charlotte M. Fiske 85 Conn. widow
Evelyn J. Fiske 50 NY daughter
Julia Fiske 60 NY daughter-in-law
Florence Conrad 50 NY
Lena Cronmeyer 35 NY
Christine Pfeiffer 21 NY

576 James How 48 sales
Fannie B. How 48 ux.
Mary O'Gorman 32 Ireland
Emily Berkstrum 62 Sweden cook

578 Emily Selkirk 79
John E. Selkirk 54 son attorney
Grace H. Selkirk 41 daughter housekeeper

584 Ralph H. Sidway 40 retired
Stephana B. Sidway 42 *ux.*
Ralph H. Sidway Jr. 12 son school
Alice A. Higgins 65 nurse
Mary Ellison 50 Canada
Augusta Rapp 38 Sweden

586 Ida Haven 77
Helen Madden 52 nurse
Nellie Ryan 31 Ireland
Delia Scanlon 35 Ireland cook

596 Fred B. Ussher 60 Canada retired
Louise W. Ussher 50 *ux.*
Catherine F. Ussher 20 daughter

600 Fred Dempsey 42 retired
May Dempsey 38 *ux.*
Louise Dempsey 2 daughter

610 Manson Fiske 47 sales
Fanny Fiske 43 Germany *ux.*
Susan Fiske 6 daughter
Marie Schriener 20 Germany

618 Thomas F. Cooke M.D. 36
Francs W. Cooke 33 *ux.*
Christian Wilcox 11 school nephew
Catherine O'Connor 43 NY
Evelyn Barnnwell 21 England
Kate Barnwell 21 England

Harry Taylor 39 England chauffeur
Ada Taylor 31 Conn. *ux.*
Annabelle Taylor 11 Conn. daughter
Marjorie Taylor 4 NY daughter

622 Edgar McGuire M.D. 42 Canada widower
Angeline Burkhardt 27 NY
Bertha Burkhardt 23 NY
Jack Farrington 22 England chauffeur

628 Charles H. Wood 51 Rhode Island
treasurer factory
Sadie Fraser Wood 50 Rhode Island *ux.*
Luther Edward Wood 28 Conn. son clerk
Kenneth A. Wood 25 Conn.
Alton Wood 23 Conn. clerk
Margaret Halleran 29 Ireland
Maeve Dunworthy 32 Maryland
Fannie Dunnigan 36 Ireland

Arthur A. Koch 32 NY chauffeur
Lee Ann Koch 30 NY *ux.*
Doris Elizabeth Koch 2 NY daughter

636 Francis Masten Lee M.D. 42 Pa.
Ethel W. Lee 39 Colorado *ux.*
Francis Masten Lee Jr. 12 NY son
Sarah Mae Du Passa 38 Indiana cook

650 Robert Keating Root 53 NY widower
bank president
Ella Wilcox 47 NY housekeeper
Mary Niblett 44 England
Josephine McCarthy 53 Canada

Albert Zimmerman 41 NY chauffeur
Anna Zimmerman 37 NY *ux.*
Anna C. Dade 71 NY mother-in-law

NORTH STREET ❦ End of Block

618 Thomas F. Cooke M.D. 40
Frances W. Cooke 38 *ux.*
Christian Cooke 16 son school

Harry Taylor 40 chauffeur England
Ada Taylor 38 Conn. *ux.*
Annabelle Taylor 15 daughter school
Margery Cook 10 daughter school

622 Edgar R. McGuire M.D. 40 Canada
Mildred McGuire 27 *ux.*
Edgar R. McGuire Jr. 3
Annette McGuire 21
Rose Wagner 21
Eve Morris 31 nurse

628 Charles H. Wood 56 manufacturer
Sarah F. Lee 52 *ux.*
Jennie Coughlin 42

Arthur Koch 37 chauffeur
Leonora Koch 37 *ux.*
Doris Koch 8 daughter school
Marian Koch 4 daughter

636 Francis M. Lee 40 M.D.
Ethel Lee 38 *ux.*
Francis M. Lee Jr. 18 son school
Frances Lee 12 daughter
Allen Pierce 28 black cook

650 William A. Morgan 53 sales
Marian Morgan 53 *ux.*
Marian D. Morgan daughter school
Harriet E. Grader 40 sales
Christine Binderwin 35 sales

NORTH STREET ❦ End of Block

Residents of the house on the northwest corner of Delaware and Virginia which dates from the 1860s were Henry Lyon and his brother James who ran a land office and surveying operation. Henry had been born in Buffalo in 1842 and attended Central High and Cornell where he studied engineering. He then worked as an engineer laying out Delaware Park in the early 1870s. He also practiced his profession in Utah. He became a wealthy man and a member of the Idlewood Club, a group of Buffalonians with summer homes on Lake Shore Road. A 32nd Degree Mason and a communicant of Westminster, Henry Lyon died at eighty-six in 1938.[1]

In the mid-1870s James Lyon had been convicted of receiving an unauthorized $2,200 in 1875 from Joseph Bork, city treasurer. The case ended up in the Court of Appeals, which in 1883 reversed two lower courts and, on a technicality, freed Lyon from all liability.[2] James died in 1892.

The Lyons resided at Delaware and Virginia only a few years. H. Katherine Smith wrote in the *Courier* in October 1956:

> The original residence at 468 Delaware Ave. was bought by [Walter E.] Devereux's grandfather, the late Charles Worthington Evans, from Henry Lyon. Lyon chose for his home massive bronze doorknobs, each ornamented with a lion's head, to remind all the visitors of the family name, Lyon. When the house was remodeled, Devereux returned the lion head knobs to the descendants of Henry Lyon.
>
> The original brick house was surmounted by a mansard roof topped by a cupola. The drawing-room, spacious and inviting, was furnished in accord with the taste of the later years of the last century. Its massive black walnut furniture was upholstered in rich brocades. Simplicity and soft colors characterized the decoration and furnishings of the house, due, doubtless, to the Quaker background of the family.[3]

The house was purchased late in the decade by Charles Worthington Evans whose ancestry goes back to Joseph Ellicott of the Holland Land Company who had six sisters, three of whom married Evanses. The issue of one of these unions, that between Latitia Ellicott and John Evans, was William Evans, who married Margaret Cary Randall. Their third son was Charles W. Evans, born in Baltimore in 1812.

> In early life he was connected with the Fireman's Insurance Co. and the Farmers' & Merchants' Bank in that city. He first visited Buffalo in 1829, and determining to make this city his future home during a second visit in 1834, came here permanently on the 28th of June, 1835. The following year he built a warehouse on the Evans Ship Canal(8.3), and in October 1836 entered into partnership with his brother, William A., in the produce and commission business, the firm being C. W. and W. A. Evans. They continued in business till January 1846, when the firm was dissolved and Charles carried on the business alone till May 1st, 1847, when he entered into partnership with Robert Dunbar, under the firm name of Evans & Dunbar, in the storage and elevating business. Their warehouse was made into a grain elevator, elevating the grain by steam. The business was profitable and the firm acquired 160 feet front on the Evans Ship Canal. The firm of Evans & Dunbar was dissolved August 9th, 1853, and Mr. Evans became sole owner of the elevator, also

1 CE, May 29, 1938.
2 Courier, June 3, 1883.
3 CE, March 4, 1952.

8.3 ❦ On the Evans Ship Canal, two views, *PBHS*, 16(1912).

adding to it the coal business. September 19th, 1862, the Evans elevator was destroyed by fire, in the midst of a very busy season, and Mr. Evans built a new and substantial one in 1863 at a cost of $60,000. In 1864 he sold one half of it to George W. Tifft which interest is still held by the heirs of the Tifft estate. It was again destroyed by fire in that year, and was rebuilt in 1865.

During the 53 years of his business life in Buffalo, he was established on the Evans Ship Canal(2.2), which was constructed in 1833 by his father, Wm. Evans, through part of outer lot No. 3 deeded by the Holland Land Company to Benjamin Ellicott, brother of Joseph Ellicott who laid out Buffalo in 1804. On the death of Benjamin Ellicott this property was set off to his sister Letitia Ellicott Evans, the mother of William Evans...Charles W. Evans was the oldest surviving elevator owner in the city, having operated the Evans Elevator for more than 41 years. He was also one of the oldest members of St. Paul's in this city having been connected with the parish for more than 43 years. He had been honored by his fellow-parishioners with all the offices in the parish and was one of the wardens for the past 25 years. In 1857 he married Miss Mary Peacock of Mayville, Chautauqua County, niece of the Hon. William Peacock. Throughout Mr. Evans's long life many large estates were entrusted to him for settlement; probably the most delicate and difficult task of this nature was his successful partition and settlement of the extensive Peacock estate in this city about ten years ago.

Mr. Evans was a studious man and a lover of good books and of literary work. In 1882 he published a history of the "Fox, Ellicott and Evans families," compiled from data which he had accumulated since his 20th year. It is probably one of the most elaborate and comprehensive family histories ever published in this country and is illustrated with family portraits and reproductions of valuable old maps and plates. It is much used as a standard book of reference. He had also completed, in manuscript, a history of St. Paul's parish from its beginning to the present time, and was probably more familiar with all matters relating to that parish than any other person.[4]

Charles Evans died at seventy-six in 1889. His widow Mary lived at #468 until her death in 1912. Their younger daughter, Virginia, and her husband, Walter E. Devereux, lived there until 1921 when he turned it into an office building. A Buffalo native, he was educated at Nichols and Hobart. He divided his time between Buffalo and Denver and was trustee for vast tracts of land in Western New York.[5] Alice Evans, the older daughter, married G. Hunter Bartlett. She and her husband published

4 Express, February 17, 1889.

5 *Buffalo Truth*, October 31, 1925; *Courier-Express*, March 4, 1956.

her father's history of Saint Paul's 1817-1888 and updated to 1903.

The next house north, #473(8.4), was briefly the home of Samuel Langhorne Clemens(8.5) and his bride, Olivia, daughter of Elmira coal baron, Jervis Langdon. In the judgment of the *Encyclopedia Americana*, Clemens, (pseudonym Mark Twain), was "America's greatest humorist and one of her greatest writers." He was born in Florida, Missouri, in 1875. When he was five, his father moved the family to Hannibal, Missouri, on the Mississippi, where Sam grew up amid river sights and sounds. By eighteen he had served as an apprentice printer, written some juvenile articles, and learned how to pilot riverboats. After two weeks in the Confederate army, he deserted and headed to Nevada with his abolitionist brother who was secretary to the territorial governor. There Sam tried prospecting and writing for the Virginia City newspaper. His humor, like that of most frontier writers, was a form of literary violence, like gun-slinging. He fled Nevada to avoid a duel with a rival journalist and reached San Francisco where his attacks on the city government embroiled him in a feud with the police and forced him, once again, to leave town. In California he wrote *The Celebrated Jumping Frog of Calaveras County*, a humorous piece which, published in a New York paper, won him fame back East. In 1867 he joined a junket to the Holy Land which he described in dispatches to a San Francisco paper, gaining further fame and fortune.

Above 8.4 ❦ Number 472 Delaware, BHS. Below 8.5 ❦ Mark Twain, from a 1995 Guinness ad. Shelley Fisher Fiskin, *Lighting out for the Territory: Reflections on Mark Twain and American Culture*, (New York: Oxford

Olivia Langdon's brother Charles was on this junket, and Twain, seeing her miniature in her brother's stateroom, determined to marry her. He used the time during which she rejected his suit to compose *Innocents Abroad* and hundreds of love letters. When the book was finished he had won Olivia's heart and during their engagement he submitted the book's proofs to her censorship, actually expurgation, setting a custom for the rest of their life together.[6] Tom Reigstad, a Twain scholar, takes up the story:

6 James M. Cox, "Twain, Mark," *The Encyclopedia Americana*, 27:291-291.

> In the summer of 1869, Twain accepted his prospective father-in-law's offer of $20,000 to buy a one-third interest in the Buffalo Express, the forerunner of the now defunct Buffalo Courier-Express. When he arrived in early August, he took a room at Mrs. Randall's boarding house at 39 E. Swan St. and eagerly began his editorial duties at the Express, just a few doors down at 14 E. Swan St.
>
> In his first few months in Buffalo as a bachelor journalist, Twain was very busy. He often worked 14-hour days, advising his reporters, scanning news exchanges, improving the paper's layout, and writing feature stories and brief, gossipy items in a column called "People and Things."
>
> In his first three months at the Express, he contributed about 20 stories in addition to his editorial and layout responsibilities. However, Twain was worried about the upcoming expenses of married life. So from October 1869 to February, 1870, he hit the lecture trail and mailed in his weekly Express stories.
>
> While Twain was on the road, Olivia and her father were busy making secret plans in Buffalo. In November, Jervis Langdon paid $20,000 [another source says $43,000] for a lovely house at 472 Delaware Ave. Olivia and her mother then went to New York City to pick out furniture and decorations. By the time Twain completed his lecture tour in time to be married in Elmira in February [2,] 1870, the Buffalo house had been furnished and refitted as a surprise wedding gift.[7]

The marital residence had been built six years before:(8.5)

> Henry M. Kinne and his wife, Elizabeth owned the home from 1864 to 1869 before Clemens moved in. That was the period in which the Second Empire, or "high style," of Victorian architecture flourished. Kinne had built nine stores on Main Street, three on Prime Street, three grain elevators and four private dwellings, so it's a safe guess he built the Delaware Avenue mansion.
>
> In addition to being a builder, Kinne was a commercial pioneer in other Buffalo enterprises in the mid-19th century. He primarily was in the grain business, building, buying and operating sailing vessels and steamers. The grain stored in Joseph Dart's first steam elevator in Buffalo in 1842 came from one of Kinne's schooners.[8]

The day after the wedding, the couple with a large party of family and friends traveled by private car on the Erie to Buffalo. They were met at the station by two agents of Jervis Langdon in Russian sleighs, since it was winter in Buffalo and snow had fallen. The sleigh with the newlyweds was driven through the slums of the city. Sam had previously requested the driver to locate a boarding house suitable for Olivia, and as they passed rows of wretched houses the couple's spirits sank. Finally they reached a brightly lit mansion at #272 Delaware Avenue, where they were greeted at the door by Langdon, who handed the deed to the house to an astonished groom, who expressed his thanks to his benefactor: "Whenever you're in Buffalo, even if it's twice a year, come right here and stay overnight if you want to. It won't cost you a cent."[9]

> It was a $2^1/_2$ story, stately house...with a mansard roof, arched windows, arched doorways and a porch along the south side. Inside, the front entrance led to a long hall. A grand staircase led directly to the third floor. On the north side was a large parlor with the

7 Tom Reigstad, "Mark Twain and Buffalo", *Western New York Heritage Magazine*, Hereafter *WNYHM*, 4 (Fall 2000), 4-22, 48.
8 *Ibid.*
9 *CE*, April 13, 1952.

dining room behind it. The dining room featured a massive chandelier and a full-length mirror. The south side of the house had a huge living room with a bay window.

Throughout the house were lovely marble fireplaces and polished woodwork of black walnut or curly maple, the 15 or so rooms had wainscoating and high ceilings with beveled corners. Wooden cornices above the windows were ornamented with hand-carved heads and faces.

The large brick carriage house had six stalls in the stable section and a high passageway into the buggy room. A circular stairway led upstairs where hay was stored on sturdy floors of white pine 2 $^1/_2$ inches thick. The carriage house walls were 2 feet thick

Facing the prestigious avenue in front of the house were towering elm trees. When spring arrived, Langdon arranged for junipers and a variety of colorful plants to grace the grounds. He also hired a cook, maid and coachman. All in all, his wedding gift came close to $50,000.[10]

Patricia Biederman reports on their early days at #472:

The young couple were blissfully happy in that house, for a time. Twain, whom Livy affectionately tagged "Youth," now wrote warm letter to his in-laws, letters in which he recounts their honeymoon pleasures, playing in that wonderful big house. Twain teasingly reveals to her parents Livy's problems in balancing her cash account and making a turkey last a week [in 1870 she had the assistance of three domestics, two of then young Irish girls], then reports mock heroically that he has mastered the domestic art of carving so well that he no longer needs to take the bird's leg in his hand. "We entirely enjoy these glad days," he wrote. We sit alone in the loveliest of libraries, in the evening, and I read poetry — and every now and then I come to a passage that brings tears to my eyes, and I look up to her for loving sympathy, and she inquires whether they sell sirloin steaks by the pound or by the yard."

The glow was short-lived:

Sam and Livy would never be that happy again. By early summer her father, their mutual benefactor, discovered that he had stomach cancer. Jervis Langdon died August 6, [1870]. A school friend of Livy's who had come to stay with the grieving newlyweds, developed typhoid fever and died in their canopied bed on September 29. Livy, who had never enjoyed blooming health, was pregnant through this awful summer. She delivered prematurely on November 7, their only son, a sickly child who never learned to walk and who died of diphtheria in 1872.

Only a little more than a year after their marriage Twain wrote bitterly to a friend, "You do not know what it is to be in a state of absolute frenzy – desperation. I had rather die twice over than repeat the last six months of my life." As Twain biographer Justin Kaplan writes, "He loathed Buffalo. What he remembered now was not the night he was tricked into entering the gaslit fairyland on Delaware Avenue but instead months of illness, death, drudgery, failure. On March 2 [1871] he put up for sale his interest in the *Express*. Livy was still so ill that she was carried to Elmira on a mattress.[11]

Even absent the difficulties he experienced here, Twain might not have enjoyed his stay in Buffalo. Concerning the Young Men's Association to which many of the city's elite belonged, he wrote, "I mortally hate that society."

10 Reigstad, *ibid.*
11 Patricia Ward Biederman, "Mark Twain in Buffalo," *Western New York Heritage* (Summer, 2001), 73-88.

The Hartford years that followed were Twain's most creative: *The Gilded Age* (1873), *Roughing it* (1875), *Old Times on the Mississippi* (1875), *The Adventures of Tom Sawyer* (1876), his masterpiece *Adventures of Huckleberry Finn,* (1884), and *A Connecticut Yankee in King Arthur's Court* 1889). But foolish investments, the death of a beloved daughter, and the spectre of bankruptcy left him in a black mood from 1896 until 1904. Ravaged by age and bad health, he died in Redding, Connecticut, in 1910.[12] Richard Alleva has recently entered a demurer against the opinion that Twain was a populist or even a progressive:

> But a political progressive has a vision of society as a thing that can be brought to perfection or, at least, significant improvement by political change and social activism. Twain had no such vision in the long run. He mistrusted humanity's capacity to save or significantly improve itself, and was pretty certain that our civilization would self-destruct. He mistrusted democracy and the jury system and organized religion and sometimes reality.
>
> Twain's several *pronunciamentos* in favor of causes most of us now find noble were not gestures toward Utopia. They were efforts to disconnect himself from the stupidities of the rest of "the damned human race." [Compare Augustine's *massa damnata.*] Surely that is the meaning of the physical image Twain took such pains to cultivate: The Man in the White Suit. "I prefer to be clean in the matter of raiment — clean in a dirty world." Exactly. And his disgust with this "dirty world" peeks out at us even in his early, cheerful writings and becomes savagely explicit in the later ones.[13]

Next owner of #472 was J. Condit Smith, a Civil War veteran, who had made his fortune as a railroad builder and executive. The Smiths lived there for two and a half years before moving to another Second Empire mansion at #414 at Delaware and Tupper in 1874.[14] Number 472's next householder, Samuel Strong Spaulding, was the son of a distinguished Buffalonian whose life straddled much of the nineteenth century, Elbridge Gerry Spaulding, who was born in Cayuga County, educated at Auburn Academy, read law in Batavia and Attica, was admitted to the bar in 1834 and went to Buffalo to clerk in the offices of Potter & Babcock. Spaulding was city clerk in 1836, alderman in 1841, mayor in 1847, assemblyman in 1848, and was elected to Congress the same year. As the Whig party broke up, he became a Republican and again was Congressman 1859-1863, where his Ways and Means Committee sponsored the Legal Tender Act of 1862, which legalized fiat money despite the constitutional ban on it. He did not seek reelection and returned to Buffalo to concentrate on the Farmers' & Merchants' Bank and after 1875 on Buffalo's horsecar business, in the course of which he became a director of Buffalo Street Railroads, and died in 1897.[15]

Elbridge's son, Samuel Strong Spaulding, was born in 1849, attended prep schools in Andover and New Haven but did not go to college. Instead he went to work as cashier in his father's bank and later became president of the M&T Trust Company. He also interested himself in his father's other operation, the Buffalo Street Railway, of which he became president until it was absorbed into the I.R.C. in

12 Cox , "Mark Twain," *loc. cit.*
13 Richard Alleva, "Missing the Dark Side," *Commonweal*, 1:129,4, February 22, 2002.
14 Reigstad, *loc cit.*
15 *ANB*, 424-425;Hill, *op. cit.*, 3:59-160.

8.6 Alfred William Bayliss, MD, Hill, *op. cit.*, III, facing p. 4.

1902. Over all, he seems to have coasted on his father's reputation. In 1875 he married Annie Watson, daughter of Stephen V. R. Watson. They had two sons and two daughters: Marion, Charlotte, Elbridge Gerry, and Stephen Van Rensselaer. At the end of the nineteenth century Samuel and Annie moved up the Avenue to the former residence of Sherman S. Rogers at #698, next to the Westminster parish house. Samuel Spaulding died at eighty-four at his summer home in Cooperstown in 1933, the oldest member of the Buffalo Club. His estate was appraised at $400,000 ($6,972,000 in 1997 dollars.)[16]

Following Spaulding at #472 was Alfred William Bayliss:(8.6)

> The road to eminence was a long and hard one for Dr. Bayliss, radiographer and electro-therapist, leading from an Erie county farm through county school rooms were he studied and taught, and in this manner earned the wherewithal to finance a medical education, and post graduate study abroad, until finally the goal was reached and his rightful place taken among the eminent men of his profession.
>
> Alfred William Bayliss was born at the home farm at Colden, Erie county, New York, August 23, 1854, son of William and Ann (Smith) Bayliss, his father a farmer with whom life was a struggle to maintain his position and properly provide for his large family. Alfred Bayliss began his education in the district public school and in his spare time worked on a farm. Later he attended the academy at Aurora, New York, there fitting himself for a teacher. For several years he taught in the district schools, some of his pupils being now prominent in Buffalo's legal fraternity. He had been self-supporting from the age of fifteen and had paid for the course at the academy from his own funds. He taught and farmed for several years, then gave up teaching but continued farming until 1885, then at the age of thirty-three he entered the medical department of the University of Niagara (see chapter 5, note #19), and for four years studied and worked at the carpenter's trade, supporting himself and paying for his education while acquiring it...In 1889 he received his M.D. from the university and for about a decade he was engaged as a general practitioner in Buffalo, building up a good practice and gaining his reputation as a skilled reliable physician.
>
> But Dr. Bayliss, a born student, at the age of forty-four embarked on a new line of study, beginning in 1898 courses in electro-therapy and a little later added courses in radiology [which dates from the work of Wilhelm C Rontgen, a physicist, in 1895]. He pursued study in these branches of medical science in New York City, Philadelphia, Pennsylvania, London, England, Heidelberg, Germany, and Paris, France, then returned to Buffalo to engage in special practice, but continuing as a general practitioner also until 1912, when he retired from the latter to devote himself entirely to electrotherapy and radiology.[17]

Bayliss had married Mary L. Snyder of Marilla in 1880, and they had three children, one of whom, Jacob William Bayliss, after graduating from Masten Park, entered the medical department of U.B.,

16 *Times*, August 23, September 26, 1933.
17 Hill, *op. cit.*, 3:4-5.

graduating in 1906. Like his father, he did post-graduate study in electrotherapy and radiology. Father and son lived at #472 where the first floor was remodeled for their specialties, and the second floor turned into a living room-dining room-kitchen complex.[18] Bayliss died in 1937; and during the 1950s the house became an office building.

> Despite an intensive last-ditch effort by a few civic leaders, the house at 472 Delaware Ave. fell to the wrecker's ball in 1963, joining the ranks of important buildings lost to Buffalo. For the final seven years that it stood, though, the house was frequently in the headlines. That would have delighted Mark Twain.
>
> The house was first threatened with demolition in 1956. The owners wanted to replace it with a $150,000 office building. Buffalo attorney Roland Benzow proposed the house be used to display Twain manuscripts owned by the Buffalo and Erie County Pubic Library and suggested that the county purchase it for a library annex.
>
> Unfortunately, the library's special Gluck collection, which includes the invaluable handwritten manuscript of Twain's "Adventures of Huckleberry Finn," was bound by stipulations that it be maintained in a room in the library at the corner of Washington and Clinton streets. If any of the rare manuscripts were moved, the entire collection would become the property of Cornell University.
>
> Preservation fever was particularly high when the Buffalo Mark Twain Society Inc. was formed in February 1958 under the leadership of Benzow. Consisting of more than 20 local leaders in business, industry and education, the society aimed to raise more than $40,000 to acquire the Twain house for a museum. However, little, if any money was raised and the status of the house once again was in limbo. By November 1962, a new owner announced plans to raze the Twain house and replace it with a parking lot, or sell it to one of 20 interested parties for a restaurant, beauty shop, nightclub or apartments.
>
> Seven years of riding a roller coaster of high and dashed hopes came to an abrupt, disastrous halt when the building was partially destroyed by a fire on Feb. 7, 1963. What was left of the house was demolished. The Cloister restaurant was built on the site using the carriage house and original foundation of Twain's house.
>
> In August 1966, the Buffalo and Erie County Historical Society and the Buffalo Courier-Express sponsored a marker to be placed in front of the spot where Mark Twain's house formerly stood: "*Mark Twain lived in a house here as a newlywed editor of the Express 1870-1871.*"[19]

8.7 ❦ Floyd C. Crego, *Men of Buffalo*, p. 393.

Several turnovers in residency leading to two doctors also marked the home at #478. In 1880 Henry Larned a "government storekeeper," resided there with a small family and a single live-in girl. In 1880 through the 1890s Joseph C. Windsor, a Canadian-born livestock dealer, lived there with his sister, her daughter, and a single domestic. Harvey Gaylord, a twenty-four year old physician, was there in 1905, followed by Floyd C. Crego(8.7), who

18 *Ibid*; *CE*., April 13, 1952.
19 Riegstad, *ibid*.

had earlier lived across the street at #469 on the Midway. Crego was an alienist (a specialist in diseases of the mind), from about 1905 until his death at sixty-three in 1919. Thereupon #478 became a rooming house. In the 1930s Grever's Flower Shop occupied the first floor.

Crego was born in Trumansburg, New York, and educated at Cincinnati University and for four years in Europe:

Above 8.8 ❦ Numbers 482, 484, 490, 498, 506 Delaware, BHS.

Left 8.9 ❦ Dr. Cornelius C. Wyckoff, Smith, *op. cit.*, II, facing p. 440.

> Dr. Crego was one of the greatest nerve specialists in the country and he figured in some of the most prominent cases testifying not only in criminal actions but also in civil law suits for damages for injuries. His opinion was sought by some of the most prominent people of the country as well as leading lawyers who depended upon his knowledge of the nervous system to aid them.
>
> Dr. Crego was the first nerve specialist to occupy the chair of nervous diseases at the Niagara University medical department back in the eighties. He at that time was prominent as a neurologist. Under his direction the study of the nervous system became one of the leading branches of the medical training. Dr. Crego was connected with all of the hospitals of the city as a specialist in his chosen line and his success gave him a world-wide reputation.
>
> He practiced his profession and among his patients he numbered some of the wealthiest people of the country. He traveled around the world on several occasions with his patients, it being reported that he received the highest fees ever recorded for this nature of work. In Buffalo criminal cases he often had been retained off and on by the district attorney and frequently by the defense where insanity was the plea of the defendant. His most recent case was one of the biggest and most sensational trials in New Jersey. His last case was the examination of Samuel Kingsbury, [accused] wife murderer, now in county jail.
>
> Dr. Crego is survived by Mrs. [Kate] Crego and two sons. He was prominent in Catholic societies as he became a convert to that faith several years ago. He was a devout Catholic and attended the Church of Our Lady of Lourdes. He was a member of the Knights of Columbus and other societies.[20]

Figure 8.8 exhibits the status of four Delaware Avenue houses north of Cregos's from #482 to #506. The solitary auto suggests a date between the mid-1920s and the mid-1930s. From 1869 until

20 *Times*, April 23, 1919.

his death in 1903 #482 was the residence of Doctor Cornelius Wyckoff (8.9), born in 1822 in Romulus, New York, of Pennsylvania-Dutch ancestry. He was a farm boy who attended local common schools, completed his classical education at Genesee Wesleyan, studied medicine at Geneva Medical College, and finally received his M.D. from Buffalo Medical College in 1848. He was attending physician at Buffalo General from 1858 on, president of the Erie County Medical Society that year, and president of the Buffalo Medical Association in 1876. By his first wife, Frances Hall Hastings, whom he married in 1849, he had two sons, George S. Wyckoff, M.D., of Bradford, Pennsylvania, and Cornelius Hastings Wyckoff, who became a dry goods merchant in Buffalo. Frances died in 1869, whereupon he married Alice Lindsley Hall of Washington, D.C. He was a vestryman at Saint Paul's and then at Ascension at the head of Franklin Street.[21] After his death, his wife remained at #482 until about 1915. In 1920 Edgar Jorlamenon, an architect, and his wife together with a doctor-boarder resided there. Thereafter no further residents are recorded.

On #484 and #486 two wooden cottages had stood for years opposite the Cornell Lead Works. In 1894, however, S. Douglas Cornell had them torn down and erected on the site a four-story French Renaissance Revival mansion(8.10) of gracefully curving, light-colored limestone, the architect of which was Edward Kent of #514 Delaware. The house was approached by a circular porch of stone steps with gothic pillars. On the southeast corner was a large bay window. The entire woodwork of the room behind was finished in cherry. The fourth floor was a theater, complete with stage, footlights, curtain, scenery, and seating. There the Buffalo Amateurs, including prominent gentry like Maria Love, Porter Norton, Charles Clifton, Townsend Davis, Lars and Eva Sellstedt, Walter, Thomas, and Doctor Charles Cary and their sister Jennie, Carleton Sprague, Cornell himself, his sons Peter and Douglas and daughter Lydia, put on four plays a year in the 1890s and in the early years of the twentieth century.[22]

8.10 ❦ S. Douglas Cornell house, #484 Delaware, built 1894, BHS.

Cornell belonged to the eighth generation of Cornells in America, the first being Thomas Cornell of Essex County, England, born about 1595, who came Boston in the 1630s and moved to Portsmouth, Rhode Island, with Roger Williams, where he died about 1655. Samuel G. Cornell was born in 1808 in Glenville, Connecticut. There he and brothers Peter and Isaac formed the Union White Lead Company, makers of lead pipe, which in 1852 moved to Buffalo as the Cornell White Lead Company. He was a

21 Smith, *op. cit.*, 2:122; *CA*, February 19, 1884; *ibid.*, November 9, 1903.
22 *CE*, May 18, 1952.

trustee of Hobart and De Vaux and a warden of Saint Paul's. He married Sarah Douglas and they had three children, the first of whom was S. Douglas, born in Fairfield County, Connecticut, in 1839.

S. Douglas came to Buffalo with his father and graduated from Hobart in 1860. There he excelled in oratory and dramatics, talents he exercised later as stage manager of the Buffalo Amateurs. In 1862 he married Lydia Hadfield and they had three children, Peter Cortelyou, Lydia, and Douglas. S. Douglas was also prominent in the National Guard, having enlisted in the 74th Regiment as a private and rising to colonel, serving on the staff of General William F. Rogers for fifteen years. S. Douglas was associated with his father in the lead works of which he was vice-president for many years, before retiring from the company in 1888. S. Douglas it was for whom the mansion at #484 was built in 1894. He died in 1910 but had already moved from #484 after his wife's death.[23]

Peter C. Cornell, son of S. Douglas, studied medicine and married Alice Gardner Plimpton. They resided in Berlin, Germany, while Peter pursued graduate studies in medicine, and their daughter, Katherine, was born there in 1893.(8.11) Six months later the family returned to Buffalo where they resided on Mariner Street. At thirty-six Peter abandoned his medical practice to manage the Star Theatre. Neither Katherine nor her father had ever lived at #484, but the plays on the fourth floor of the mansion played a part in shaping her career. She wrote in 1938:

8.11 ❦ Katherine Cornell, *I Wanted to Be an Actress*, after p. 93.

> Acting is in my blood. The feeling for it was absolutely born in me. My first memories, however, are not of actors but of the theatre — a stage; the curve of a proscenium; a curtain with something wonderful behind it, which might lift at any moment. That was in my grandfather Cornell's house in Buffalo. I never got to act there, of course, I was just a very small child sitting on the steps watching rehearsals. My grandfather was a gifted amateur actor, a brilliant director. John Drew, his good friend, always considered him one of the best. I can't remember his acting. In my day he was always directing. My father was an exceptionally fine amateur player — my aunt was too. Even at our summer home in Cobourg, Ontario — a grand old-fashioned house built round a rotunda like a state capital — there was a long gallery at the back near the garden where they used to put on plays. I did too.
>
> I think it was the advent of Maude Adams' *Peter Pan* in my father's theatre [in 1907] that first made me know that I wanted to devote my life to the stage. I had looked forward to Maude Adams with such eagerness that, when the time came, it was sheer agony. At first I hid my face in the curtains of the box because I couldn't bear to look. Then, afterward, utter enchantment; particularly the flying part.[24]

23 Hill, *op. cit.*, 4:353-354.
24 Katherine Cornell, *I Wanted to Be an Actress* (New York: Random House, 1938), pp. 3-4.

She lived in Buffalo long enough to graduate from St. Margaret's School, dismissed by Horton as a foundation under Episcopal auspices for genteel young ladies of Protestant faith at North and Franklin Streets opened in 1884 which flourished for three decades then faded away. Her childhood was unhappy. A tyrannical father, an alcoholic mother, and awareness that she was not beautiful contributed to her feelings of inadequacy. After St. Margaret's, she was sent to Oaksmere, a finishing school in Westchester, from which she graduated in 1911. Her first success was in the role of Jo in the London production of *Little Women*. Her first big hit in the United States was Clemence Dane's *Bill of Divorcement* (1921) followed by *Candida* (1924), *The Green Hat* (1925), *The Barretts of Wimpole Street* (1931), *Romeo and Juliet* (1934), and *Antigone* (1946). She was one of the great actresses of her day.[25]

After his wife's death, Katherine's grandfather moved out of #484 and rented it to Frances Wolcott who in the brief time she was there welcomed into it many celebrities, Ann Morgan, Ethel Barrymore, Walter Damrosch, Rachel Crothers, and members of the British aristocracy. At eighty, asked to write an article on the society of her youth, she wrote instead a book, *Heritage of Years: Kaleidoscopic Memories, 1851-1889*, published in 1932. The author was best known to her friends as the mistress of Hill Crest, her estate in the Genesee Valley.[26]

Frances was followed at #484 by Albert Jay Wright, who had been born in Oswego in 1858. He had previously lived across the Avenue at #483. His ancestors had come to New England during colonial days, and a forebear was Silas Wright, United States Senator and later Governor of New York. At eight Albert came with his parents to Buffalo where he attended P.S. 14 and Horace Briggs' Academy. He majored in science at Wesleyan, where he suffered an injury in a baseball game which cost him his sight. Returning to Buffalo in 1878, having married Gertrude Bent of Middletown, Connecticut, he went to work at his father's grain handling firm, Preston & Wright, which became Alfred P. Wright & Son two years later. In 1884 at twenty-six Albert was elected president of the Merchants' Exchange. Though blind, he was regarded as the dean of Buffalo stockbrokers. He was for years the only Buffalonian member of the New York Stock Exchange. As a result, his firm had the largest clientele of any brokerage house in Buffalo. It also had branches in Rochester, Syracuse, Niagara Falls, Bradford, Pennsylvania, and Toronto. He was a world traveler, an art enthusiast, and an authority on matters monetary, which led him to publish in 1933 a novel entitled *Red Demon*, actually a treatise on the gold standard.[27] In 1905 Wright, Gertrude, and their fifteen year old daughter enjoyed the services of an ethnically diverse staff of servants, two Japanese, two Irish girls, a Canadian girl, and a forty-year old French woman. In the stables lived two English coachmen with their families. Albert Wright was an incorporator of the Country Club of Buffalo in 1889 and belonged to the Buffalo, Ellicott, and Yacht clubs of Buffalo and the Chicago Club. By 1915 he had

25 "Cornell, Katherine," *ANB*, 5:522-523; Horton, *op. cit.*, 1:257; Dunn, *op. cit.*, 1:396.
26 H. Katherine Smith, "Cornell Mansion," *CE*, May 18, 1952.
27 *Men of New York*, 1:463-464; Wilner, *op. cit.*, 4:628-630.

8.12 ❦ Samuel V. Parsons, *M&FH*, 2:308.

moved up the Avenue to #512. In 1931 Wright, by then over seventy and a widower, his wife having died in 1925, married in London Tatina Moslova, a young woman in her early thirties whose aristocratic family had fled Russia during the Revolution. The dramatis personae included the Lord Bishop of Norwich, the Earl of Albemarle, and the youthful and beautiful Princess Marie-Helene of Reuss. The wedding party then headed across town to a Russian church where an Orthodox ceremony was performed by Archbishop Seraphim of Paris, brought over for the occasion, before a second cast of supporting actors.[28] Wright died in 1940 at eighty-one at his summer home at Cazenovia.[29] As for #484 it had become a rooming house in the '30s and a nightclub in the '40s. It housed the Green Door Antique shop in the '50s, Ziegler Medical Supplies in the '60s and '70s, and a photography studio in the '80s. Attorney Thomas J. Eoannou bought it in 1994 and extensively restored it.

From the 1870s until 1906, #490 Delaware was the home of Samuel V. Parsons, one of Buffalo's premier's shipbuilders.(8.12) Born and raised in St. Johns, Newfoundland, in 1821, he migrated to New York where he worked on the People's Line of steamers plying between that city and Albany. In 1852 he was sent by L.& H. Crampton to Buffalo to take charge of shipbuilding contracts there. Later he engaged in shipbuilding on his own in Buffalo and became a large employer of labor. He then set up a yard at Tonawanda where he built and repaired ships 1866-1878. A Republican, he campaigned for Lincoln in 1860 and 1864. He was elected alderman of the 10th Ward in 1882, the only time he campaigned for office. Meanwhile, he paved a city street with asphalt as an experiment. He was a trustee of Delaware Avenue Methodist and a generous contributor to its causes. In 1854 he married Sarah Thompson and they had eight children, six of whom survived into adulthood.[30] Parsons died 1906.

He was succeeded at #490 by Dr. James J. Mooney, a nose, ear, and throat specialist, chief of the nose ear and throat staff at Sisters' for years, and one of the most active laymen in the Buffalo Catholic diocese. He was born in Buffalo in 1866, graduated from St. Joseph's Collegiate Institute, and received his M.D. from Niagara. Later he graduated from the American College of Nose and Throat Specialists in Philadelphia. For over fifty years he sang tenor in the choir of St. Joseph's Cathedral. He also managed the Buffalo section of John McCormack's American tour at the Broadway Auditorium. In 1902 he married Mary Cronin, a fellow parishioner, and about 1906 they moved into #490 where he lived and practiced until the late 1920s. She died in 1910 and Mooney married Estelle

28 *CE*, July 14, 1931
29 *NYT*, July 3, 1940.
30 *M&FH*, 2:308-309.

O'Leary, his sole survivor when he died at sixty-eight in 1934.[31]

8.13 ❦ Chillion M. Farrar, *Ibid.*, I, facing p. 223.

A succession of families occupied #498, the least impressive of the residences in figure 8.8, during a half century. In the 1870s and 1880s the family of John Locke, an English-born house builder lived there. The Lockes were middle class, had no servants, and would occasionally take in boarders. In 1890 Charlotte Watson, widow of Stephen V. R. Watson, street railroad company president, resided there with one companion. During the first decade of the twentieth century #498 was the residence of Arthur E. Hedstrom, a coal dealer. Son of Swedish immigrants, he was born in Buffalo in 1868. His father, Erick Hedstrom, founded a coal firm, and the son succeeded him as president in 1927 by which time Arthur had moved up the Avenue.[32] However as early as 1905 the fifty-year old Arthur had a wife, two children, and four female domestics. In 1915 Charles McCulloch, vice president of Lackawanna Coal was there, enjoying the ministrations of three domestics. By 1920 #498 had become a boarding house.

The last of the four houses in figure 8.8 is #506, built in 1870 by Chillion M. Farrar(8.13), who had been born in Detroit in 1829. He came to Buffalo in the 1840s and found employment in the Sidney Shepard Iron Works. In 1871 Shepard sold out to William King who changed the name of the plant to his own and began to specialize in stationary and marine steam engines. Farrar moved up to manager. At the same time John Trefts, a native of Pittsburgh who arrived in Buffalo in 1845, took a similar position with the George Tifft foundry. Farrar and Trefts together with Theodore C. Knight, the father of ex-Mayor Erastus C. Knight, formed a partnership, Farrar Trefts & Knight, until 1869 when, with the departure of Knight, it became Farrar & Trefts. For forty years they turned out excellent metal work in the form of locomotive and stationary boilers, metal tanks, stocks, and stills. They produced aluminum, iron, and brass castings, pattern work, gas engines, grade bars, and propellers.(8.14) With the growth of the oil industry, they began making boilers and engines for oil producers, selling nearly 20,000 of these not only at home but in Europe and India. The foundry on Perry Street — #47 to #61 — covered an acre on both sides of the street with 200,000 square feet of floor space. A second plant in East Buffalo employed about 600 men engaged in blacksmithing, forging, and repairing gas engines.[33]

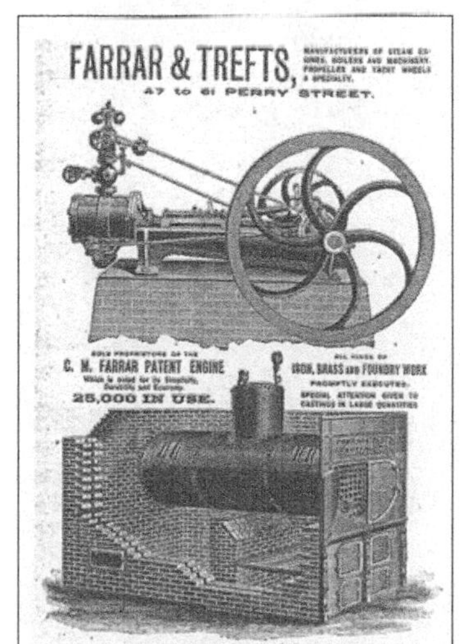

8.14 ❦ *Buffalo City Directory, 1880*, p. 126.

31 *BEN*, September 5, 1934.
32 *BEN*, February 25, 1946.
33 *Times*, December 16, 1909.

A visitor to the Farrar home, which unlike the other Delaware Avenue homes met with thus far was longer along the Avenue than wide, entered a large hall. On the left was a parlor with an open fireplace. Another long room opened onto the spacious porch where, during his ill-stared visit to Buffalo in 1901, President McKinley paused for a chat with Farrar. A third living room larger than the others ran the width of the house and contained an ample fireplace and one large mirror with a walnut frame. Also on the first floor was a "dining room designed for hospitality," a breakfast nook, and two conservatories with great palms, aspidistra, and flowers. Throughout the mansion, built without regard for cost, rare woods such as mahogany and walnut were used for paneling. Furnishings were of fine workmanship, while, to satisfy Mrs. Farrar's love of dark red, most of the hangings were of that color. The walls were covered not with paper but with brocades and tapestries. The kitchen was in the basement, assuring a cool dining room during summer when cooking was still being done on a heat-radiating coal stove. A dumbwaiter transported food from there to the first floor.[34] Trefts and Farrar were joined together by other bonds than business. They married sisters. Trefts wed Evangeline Siver, and Farrar married Alvira Siver in 1856. Each sister each had one daughter, Evadne Trefts and Anna M. Farrar. These cousins in turn married brothers; Evadne married William H. Holloway and Anna in 1874 married John A. Holloway. The John Holloways lived at #506 until John's death in 1890. The patriarch, Chillion himself, had no time for clubs or sports or world travel. He lived a monotonous life, "never took a prolonged rest or vacation," and never sought public office "as his concentration on his industrial projects occupied both his mind and time." He died in 1907. His funeral was a mélange of Masonic ritual and Episcopal rite, conducted at home by Rev. Cameron J. Davis. Farrar's widow lived there until her death. Her granddaughter, Mrs. Nisbet Grammer, the former Evadne Holloway, who had been born at #506, resided there until 1916 when it was sold to the Knights of Columbus. They built an addition to the rear with gymnasium, swimming pool, and steam baths.[35] The roughly contemporaneous erection of the gigantic new cathedral on Delaware and West Utica was, along with what some Protestants referred to as the Catholic Club, a statement by Buffalo's Catholics that they were now a presence to be reckoned with on the Avenue which had hitherto been a WASP bastion.

8.15 ❦ Roswell Park, *PBHS*, 22 (1918), facing p. 91.

From the mid-1880s until his death in 1914 #510 was the home of the world-famous Roswell Park, a doctor who made surgery much safer than it had been.(8.15) He was born in 1852, in Pomfret, Connecticut, son of Rev. Roswell Park, West Point graduate, Episcopal priest, and college president. Educated at private

34 *CE*, April 27, 1952.
35 *Ibid.*

schools in Pomfret, the son received his B.A. in 1872 from Racine College in Wisconsin, founded by his father, and an M.A. from there in 1875. He served a year's residence at Mercy Hospital in Chicago and then at Cook County Hospital before becoming assistant surgeon at the Illinois State Eye and Ear Infirmary in 1876. He was physician to the Chicago Orphan Asylum in 1878, demonstrator of anatomy at the Women's Medical College of Chicago in 1879, and adjunct professor at Northwestern Medical School the same year. In 1880 he married Martha Durkee of Chicago, by whom he had two sons, Roswell and Julian.[36] Next year, he became attending surgeon at Michael Reese Hospital and in 1882 lectured on surgery at the Rush Medical College, experiences which determined him to specialize in surgery:

> During 1883 he spent several months in Europe studying surgery and, on his return, accepted an appointment as professor of surgery in the School of Medicine of the University of Buffalo as well as surgeon in chief at Buffalo General Hospital. He remained in Buffalo for the rest of his life, becoming one of the predominant surgeons in the United States.
>
> In a period in which modern surgery was developing, Park helped it advance by introducing to American medicine new discoveries in bacteriology and in applying the antiseptic techniques developed by Joseph Lister. He also helped popularize the discoveries in pathology of Rudolf Virchow and others and helped to disseminate new ideas about contagion introduced by Louis Pasteur and Robert Koch.[37]

Pasteur's discovery that most diseases were caused by germs is the most important in medical history and one of the foundations of modern medicine.[38] Horton complained that "for some reason American surgeons had been backward in comprehending and applying Lord's Lister's antiseptic techniques for surgical operations:"[39]

> Park's specialty, surgical pathology, became the subject of most of his papers and a topic on which he often lectured. He also edited and largely wrote a two-volume textbook, *Surgery by American Authors* (1896) and in 1907 published his most significant work, *The Principles and Practice of Modern Surgery* (1907). During his later years, he became particularly interested in cancer and wrote many papers on the subject. This led to his founding of the Gratwick Laboratory in 1898 for the study of malignant tumors. Park managed in 1911 to get New York State to take over the laboratory, which was then renamed the New York State Institute for the Study of Malignant Diseases (in 1946 it became known as the Roswell Park Memorial Institute, a leading center for research into the diagnoses and treatment of cancer).[40]

Dr. Park arrived in Buffalo in 1883. Number 510, designed by E. B. Green as an office-residence, was completed by 1886:

> The southern half of the house, built as Dr. Park's residence, is one-half story higher than the northern section intended for offices. In the office section, in addition to his office, waiting room and medical laboratory, was Dr. Park's medical library, one of the most complete private collections of its kind in Western New York. The first floor of the resi-

36 Hill, *op. cit.*, 4:357.
37 Vern L. Bullough, "Park, Roswell," *ANB*, 17:6.
38 *Rene J. Duros*, "Pasteur, Louis," *Encyclopedia Americana*, 21:516.
39 Horton, *op. cit.*, 1:262.
40 Bullough, *ibid.*

> dence comprised a large reception hall, living room, dining room, kitchen and maids' quarters. The second floor is divided into sleeping rooms and bathrooms.
>
> Preserved at the Buffalo Historical Society Museum is the telephone that was installed in the home of Dr. Park in 1879, one of the first residential telephones in this city. The house also was one of the first of the local homes to be lighted with electricity.[41]
>
> Number 484 in its early days was much more than a doctor's office. Although the house itself has changed little in nearly 70 years, the entire neighborhood has altered. Julian Park, dean of the College of Arts and Sciences at UB, and son of the late Dr. Roswell Park, recalls, as one of the joys of his boyhood, the friendly and interesting neighbors surrounding his father's home. Among them he mentions the late Dr. Peter Cornell and his talented daughter, Katherine, now a foremost American actress; Edward A. Kent, architect, designer of the first Unitarian Church; Dr. Lucien Howe, eminent oculist; Montgomery Gerrans [manager of the Iroquois Hotel], still remembered for his geniality as host; the family of Chillion Farrar, and his son-in-law, John Holloway; Mr. and Mrs. Bryant Glenny, the latter founder of the Franklin School and of the School of Pedagogy of the University of Buffalo, forerunner of the School of Education.
>
> During Dr. Park's ownership, leaders of the medical profession, both past and present, were made welcome there. The long list included William and Charles Mayo, founders of the celebrated Mayo Clinic; Sir William Osler, eminent surgeon of London, Eng; George W. Crile of Cleveland, famed for thyroid gland surgery; Maurice Richardson of Boston, and William W. Welch of Johns Hopkins. At frequent dinners for his students, Dr. Park entertained the men who have become Buffalo's foremost physicians and surgeons.[42]

Dr. Park's connection with President McKinley's death is discussed in Chapter 15.[43]

Park published 170 books and articles, was editor of the *Weekly Medical Review* and associate editor of the *Annals of Surgery*. He had been president of the Medical Society of New York and of the American Surgical Association. An accomplished lecturer, storyteller, and pianist, he strove to make Buffalo a center of good musical performances.[44] He died suddenly of heart failure in 1914 at sixty-two. His funeral was held at Trinity, and the body was cremated.[45]

After Dr. Park's death, his house was bought by his friend and one-time associate, Clayton Milo Brown, who would maintain an office there for the next forty years. Brown was born in Hermitage, New York, in 1871, attended Warsaw High and Hamilton (Ontario) Collegiate Institute, and graduated from U.B.'s medical school in 1896. He was a general practitioner until 1907 when he studied ear nose and throat diseases at Vienna. That year he married Evelyn Haines by whom he had two daughters. After a second year at Vienna in 1914 he returned to become professor of rhinolaryngology at U.B. He was attending otolaryngologist at Buffalo General, chief of service in rhinolaryngology at Children's Hospital, and consultant otolaryngologist and chief of staff in rhinolaryngology at Meyer Memorial. Brown was a member of Westminster, a diplomate of the American Board of Otolaryngologists, a fellow of the American Medical Association, and a member of the American College of Surgeons. Late in life, he resigned from practice but continued as a consultant. His wife

41 H. Katherine Smith, "Surgeon's Home Still Aids Science," *CE*, May 11, 1952.
42 *Ibid.*
43 See Chapter 15, Footnotes 6-8.
44 Bullough, *ibid.*
45 *Courier*, February 16, 1914.

told a reporter in 1952 that "the location of the house is convenient; but we have no neighbors. We live sandwiched between the Knights of Columbus and buildings converted to commercial uses;" but she had to admit that "so well constructed is the house that residents rarely are disturbed by sounds from neighboring buildings." Brown died in 1954 at eighty-two.[46]

Above 8.16 ❦ Number 514 Delaware in 1870. *PBHS*, 16(1912), 425. In 1870 Thomas Cary Welch was five years old. The householder was his mother, Maria M. Welch.
Below 8.17 ❦ Samuel M. Welch, Welch, *Home History*, frontispiece.

During the 1870s and 1880s Maria Mead Welch, widow of Thomas Cary Welch, presided over a household at #514 consisting of herself and three children, the oldest of whom, Samuel Mead, was born in 1851.(8.16) Her father had been a Congregational minister at Gorham, Maine, where she was born in 1828. She came to teach school in Buffalo in 1848 where she met her future husband, then a lawyer. However, he died in 1864 while traveling in hope of regaining his health. Samuel was then thirteen and forced to leave school to earn a living. For several years he worked for an uncle, also named Samuel M. Welch, of #271 Delaware(8.17), a dealer in hides and leather. This Samuel was not a particularly rich man but was a charter member of the Buffalo Club in 1867. For two years Samuel Mead Welch was a reporter and later assistant city editor of the *Morning Express*, and for another was traveling passenger agent for the Western New York and Pennsylvania Railroad. In the autumn of 1874 he began to read law in the office of Daniel Lockwood who would vigorously promote the young man's career. Lockwood was elected district attorney in November and on January 1, 1875, appointed Welch his clerk, a position he held until admitted to the bar in 1877. Welch was appointed district attorney to succeed Charles W. Goodyear in 1877 and held that office until January 1, 1878. President Cleveland wanted to appoint Welch Deputy Collector of the Port of New York, but Welch preferred to continue practicing law. Shortly afterwards Lockwood, then United States Attorney for the Northern District of New York, named Welch his assistant, a position he filled until October 1, 1889. (Republican Benjamin Harrison had defeated Cleveland in the presidential

46 *BEN*, March 20, 1954.

election of 1888.) In December 1894 Welch was again appointed Assistant United States Attorney, (Cleveland had defeated Harrison in 1892) a position Welch held until November 1897 (McKinley had defeated Bryan in 1896.)

Welch's consuming interest, however, was neither law, politics, family — he never married — but the military. When only seven he drilled a company of boys on the village green at Gorham where he spent the summer at his grandmother's. In 1861 he joined Lansing's Zouaves, a juvenile unit that lasted for three years and drilled in the backyard of Henry Lansing's estate on Delaware and Johnson Place. In 1877 he enlisted as a private in the Buffalo City Guard, an organization to which his father had belonged. That summer he saw action in the railroad strike that hit several major cities across the nation. In May 1879 he was commissioned first lieutenant in the 65th Regiment, NYNG, one of Buffalo's two infantry regiments. A month later he was made captain, in 1882 Major, in 1883 lieutenant colonel, and colonel in 1887. (It was at this time that the Welches moved from #514 Delaware.) In August 1892 another dangerous railroad labor disturbance broke out in Buffalo, and Governor Roswell Flower called out half the Guard to protect key points along the city's rail network. Colonel Welch's 65th was sent to the Lehigh Valley's shop and yards on Dingens Street in East Buffalo. Governor Flower commissioned Welch brigadier general by brevet in 1894 and made him acting inspector general of the state. During the Spanish-American War about ninety percent (624) of the men of his 65th volunteered for federal service. With Welch in command they entrained for the front on May 1, 1898, to the roar of thousands lined up along Main Street, but never got past Camp Alger in Virginia. As Teddy Roosevelt lamented, "There wasn't enough war to go around."

In 1904 Welch was commissioned major general by brevet and in 1911 was appointed Brigadier General in command of the 4th Brigade (Western New York.) He campaigned tirelessly for a new armory, and the Connecticut Street Armory, opened in January 1907, one of the largest in the world, was the result. Welch retired in 1915, having reached the mandatory age of sixty-four. On the eve of American participation in World War I he became an apostle of military preparedness, lecturing on the subject throughout the city. For several years he roomed at the Saturn Club, of which he was a member. He was also a member of the Army and Navy Clubs of New York City and Washington, the Sons of the Revolution, the Military Order of the Spanish American War. Colleagues regarded him as the father of the state's military law code. He died of heart failure in his sixty-eighth year at his home in Johnson Park in 1919. His funeral was at Trinity of which he had been a member since his boyhood, superintendent of the Sunday school 1871-1881, and vestryman 1877-1881.[47]

In the late 1880s the Welch house was torn down and a larger brick and stone building erected in its place and was listed thereafter as #512. Architect and first occupant was Edward Austin Kent, son

47 *Times*, November 24, 1919; Warren, *op. cit.*, p. 11.

of Henry Kent of Flint & Kent, and Harriet Kent, formerly of #274 Delaware. Edward Kent was born in 1854 in Bangor, Maine. He grew up in Buffalo and attended Professor Briggs' Classical School. Having earned a degree in civil engineering in 1875 at Yale's Sheffield School, he studied architecture at the *Ecole des Beaux Arts* in Paris where H. H. Richardson, Louis Sullivan, and Richard M. Hunt had studied. After further study in England, Kent returned in 1877 to the United States where he went to work in the office of Syracuse architect Joseph S. Silsbee, where, Austin Fox suggests, Kent came in contact with the Arts and Crafts Movement that was to flourish in Central and Western New York. In 1886 Kent helped organize the Buffalo Society of Architects and was elected its first secretary. In 1890 it became the Buffalo chapter of that society of which Kent was three times president. "About this time," Fox states, "he also designed an imposing early Queen Anne-style brick mansion at #512 Delaware for the Kent family." He also designed the domed Temple Beth Zion at #609 Delaware and, his masterpiece, the Unitarian-Universalist English gothic church at Elmwood and West Ferry. He was the only Buffalonian aboard the *Titanic* when she sank in the North Atlantic after striking an iceberg on the night of April 14, 1912. Before the end, he had brought several women from their cabins to the main deck and to the tragically inadequate supply of lifeboats.[48] It was to #512 that Albert J. Wright moved after Kent's death in 1912 and remained until his own in 1940.

At #522 in 1870 lived Thomas Chester, a native of Bedfordshire, England, where he was born in 1813, learned the miller's trade, and in the mid-1830s came to America where he went to work in the Erie Mills. About 1849 with partner Thomas Thornton he bought the Globe Mills in Black Rock and in 1868 erected the National Mills on Erie Street. A member of Delaware Avenue Baptist and of the Young Men's Association, he died at seventy-one in 1883.[49] His widow Mary lived on at #522 for several years.

She was followed at #522 for a few years by publisher, Edward H. Butler. Since his name is most closely associated #672 Delaware which he bought in 1908, treatment of his life and his son's will be postponed until chapter 10. In 1912 Doctor Lucien Howe, formerly of #183 Delaware, moved up the Avenue to #522 where he had a house erected designed by English architects.

> The architecture suggests French Renaissance, with touches from other lands. One approaches the house by a flight of stone steps leading to a small porch from which granite pillars rise. These are adorned with capitals reminiscent of the Corinthian design. As one faces the heavy oaken double front doors, a rounded tower rises three stories on the left. From above the porch rises a second tower, four stories in height. High on the right is a triangular bay window. The roof is divided into peaks and gables. From it rise several chimneys that served the many fireplaces of the mansion. The contrasting gray stone is inlaid in the brick in orate design.
>
> Through great panes of beveled plate glass set in the ample front door, one can look into the entrance hall. The interior woodwork is of mahogany, cherry, and ebony. In the

48 Austin M. Fox, "Buffalo Architect, Edward Kent: *Titanic* Hero," *Buffalo Spree*, Summer, 1984, 40-41.
49 *CA*, February 19, 1884.

8.18 **Abraham Altman, Warren,** ***op. cit.*****, p. 30.**

mahogany-paneled drawing-room, to the right of the entrance hall, is a great fireplace surmounted by a carved mantel. From the mantel, a beautiful mirror rises to the ceiling. The woodwork of the library is of ebony. Its ceiling is ornamented with an oval handpainted design of angels done in gold. The walls are covered with tapestries and rich brocades that endure, virtually unchanged for decades. First floor rooms included a solarium, dining-room, kitchen, and Dr. Howe's offices and laboratories, and waiting rooms. The upper stories were divided into sleeping rooms, living rooms [Mrs. Howes's luxurious with antique mahogany and silver], and servants' quarters.

Dr. Howe gave a gift of $250,000 [$4,357,500 in 1997 dollars] to Harvard Medical School to create a laboratory for ophthalmological research. In 1926, at the age of 78, he left Buffalo to direct that laboratory. He died two years later at Belmont, Mass. [on December 17, 1928.][50]

Harriet Harrington bought #522 in 1926 and had it divided into one-room lodgings and small apartments.

Numbers 526 and 528 constituted a double house. In 1880 the former was home to William B. Sirret, French-born county treasurer. In 1890 it was the home of Henry Altman, of Altman & Company, men's clothiers. He was the son of Abraham Altman, one of the pioneer Jews in Buffalo.(8.18) Born in Wurttemberg in 1811, Abraham and his brother Julius founded the Buffalo company upon moving from Rochester after the Panic of 1857. His was the highest income reported by Buffalo Jews in 1863. After the Civil War he was one of the organizers of Third National, widely known as "the immigrants' bank," and was its president for fifteen years. He was also an organizer of the Charity Organization Society in 1879. Selig Adler writes that "Altman was the one Jew to pierce the social barrier (he was president of the Buffalo Club in 1880) and the Altman family has been among the Buffalo gentry ever since." In 1880 he was living at #767 Delaware on the corner of Delaware and Summer. He was interested in Reform Judaism, but his wife, who Adler suggests was "socially ambitious," late in life turned Episcopalian.[51] Financial reverses darkened his last days, and his son David was killed by a fall from his horse while playing polo in Delaware Park. Abraham had moved to #147 North Street by the time he died in 1888.[52] He had two other sons associated with him in the garment business, Isaac and Julius. In 1890 Henry Altman was resident at #526, apparently the first inhabitant of that house. Ten years later it was occupied by a Canadian-born doctor, Herbert Mickle, and in 1905 by a roofer. Thereafter it served as a boarding house.

The other half of the double house was occupied in 1880 by Moses Robertson, manager of Gilbert's Starch Works on Exchange Street, who also dabbled in real estate. He, his wife, and their two oldest

50 *CE*, May 25, 1952.
51 Adler, *op. cit.*, pp. 37, 82, 107; White, *op. cit.*, I:409, 844.
52 Warren, *op. cit.*, p. 30-31.

daughters had been born in Virginia, and later moved to England, where the two youngest children were born. The Robertsons had two servant girls. Four years later, after the family had moved out of the city, #528 became the residence of another real estate agent, Edward P. Hollister. By the next centry it had been turned into a boarding house.

Buffalo's three-term mayor, Philip Becker(8.19), ended his days at #534 Delaware.(8.20) He had been born in Oberotterbach in the Bavarian Rhineland in 1830, came to America in 1847, and headed for Buffalo where he worked for seven years in various businesses. With $400 of his own and $2,000 borrowed he opened a delicatessen on Main near Court. The business, Philip Becker & Company, grew rapidly into one of the largest wholesale groceries in Western New York. In 1869 he founded and was first president of the German Insurance Company and in 1896 donned the same hats in the case of the Buffalo Commercial Insurance Company. At the beginning of the 1890s, about the time he moved into #534, he retired to spend his last days in peace. There he died in 1898.[53]

Above 8.19 ❦ Philip Becker, *Buffalo und Sein Deutschtum*, p. 81.
Below 8.20 ❦ Music Hall, *PBHS*, 16 (1912), p. 188.

Becker played an important role in the public life of his adopted city. As

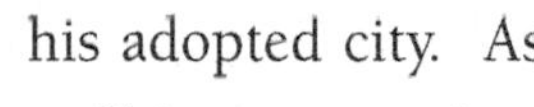

8.21 ❦ George B. Gates, Smith, *op. cit.*, II, facing p. 24.

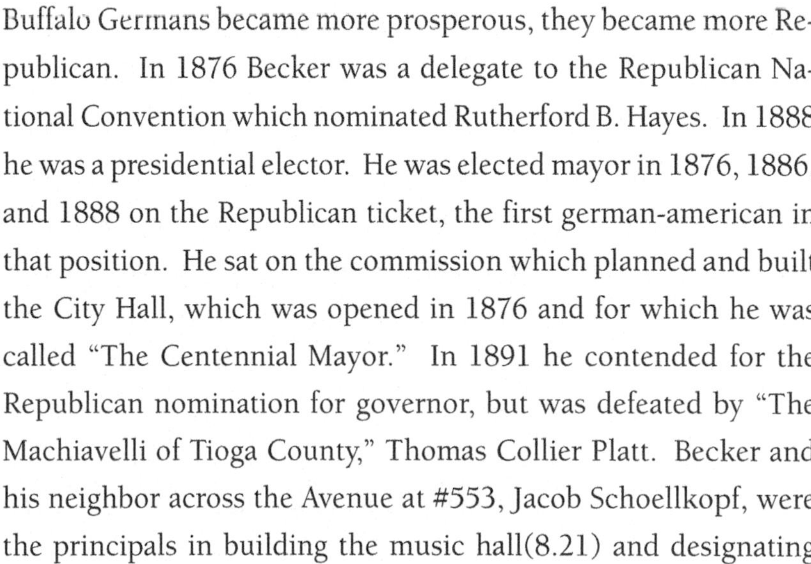

Buffalo Germans became more prosperous, they became more Republican. In 1876 Becker was a delegate to the Republican National Convention which nominated Rutherford B. Hayes. In 1888 he was a presidential elector. He was elected mayor in 1876, 1886, and 1888 on the Republican ticket, the first german-american in that position. He sat on the commission which planned and built the City Hall, which was opened in 1876 and for which he was called "The Centennial Mayor." In 1891 he contended for the Republican nomination for governor, but was defeated by "The Machiavelli of Tioga County," Thomas Collier Platt. Becker and his neighbor across the Avenue at #553, Jacob Schoellkopf, were the principals in building the music hall(8.21) and designating

53 *Buffalo und Sein Deutschtum* (Buffalo: German American Historical and Biographical Society, 1911-1912), pp. 80-82.

Above 8.22 ❦ University Club, exterior, BHS.
Right 8.23 ❦ Same, interior, BHS.

Buffalo as the site of the great 1883 German Sangerfest. In 1856 he married Sarah Goetz, an Alsatian, who lived into her eighties at #534.[54]

The house at Delaware and Allen, #546 new style, which had been built in 1835 for Sextus Shearer was briefly in 1849 the Sacred Heart Academy for young Catholic ladies. Subsequent owners were Joseph Christopher, Hiram Niles, S. N. Derrick, Stephen D. Caldwell, president of the Union Steamboat Line, and about 1880, George B. Gates,(8.22) a native of Gorham, Ontario County, New York, where he was born in 1812. At fourteen, after public school, he came to Buffalo and started as a factory hand in the foundry of Wilkeson & Beals. For several years he was Deputy Marshal for the Northern District of New York. Later he entered the sleeping car business, then in its infancy, establishing Gates' South Shore Line, over the Lake Shore Railroad, which extended first to Cleveland and then to Chicago. His cars were built according to the Woodruff patent, the exclusive right to the use of which he had been assigned by the inventor in 1858. The name was changed when the Lake Shore and the Wagner sleeping car line of the New York Central were merged, but Gates remained a major stockholder in the consolidation. He was vice-president and a director of the Bank of Buffalo from its start. In 1876 he was chosen vice president and general manger of the Buffalo, New York & Philadelphia railroad, positions he head for he rest of his life. He was also president of the Kendall & Eldred Railroad, and vice-president of the Olean, Bradford & Warren Railroad, two short lines serving Bradford. For many years he was one of Buffalo's water commissioners and regarded as chiefly responsible for the successful operation of the city's water works. His clubs were the Buffalo and the Falconwood. In 1832 he married Sarah Galligan of Buffalo. They had ten children but only three

54 *Ibid*; White, *op. cit.*, 2:27; Horton, *op. cit.*, 1:235

8.24 ❦ Delaware and Allen Street, 1884, BHS. Note the single track horsecar line along Allen Street crossing Delaware. The steeple far up the Avenue is that of Westminster Presbyterian. Note also the thick shade leafage of the elm trees, which at this date are rather thin. The house in the foreground is #560, the next up #564. Traffic on Delaware Avenue in the '80s does not seem to have been a problem.

survived to adulthood, of whom one became the wife of William Hamlin of #1058 Delaware, the other the wife of Charles Pardee of #938 Delaware. Gates died at sixty-eight in 1880. His widow was still living there in the 1890s.[55]

Numbers #536 and #546 were the site of yet another Delaware Avenue men's club:

> The establishment in Buffalo of a university club had been a dream of the Rev. Dr. Walter Clarke, pastor of the First Presbyterian Church from 1861 to 1871; and his son, the Rev. Samuel T. Clarke, had been an advocate of such an institution, but nothing was effected until the autumn of 1894, when William Burnet Wright, Jr., Sherman S. Jewett, and Lewis Stockton took up the matter actively. Sheldon T. Viele, who became the Club's first president, was early impressed into the movement and played a very important part in its inception. The club possesses a postal card calling for a meeting November 20, 1894, at the Buffalo Club, to take into consideration the establishment of such an institution, and on December 18th the organization was effected. The house, 884 Main street, just above Virginia, was rented and formally opened on March 1, 1895. Three years later, October 16, 1897, the club moved to 295 Delaware avenue, the former home of Postmaster General Wilson Shannon Bissell. In April, 1903,the first steps were taken towards building a clubhouse. The property at the corner of Allen and Delaware was purchased, the cornerstone of the present four-story building laid on October 24th, and the dedication occurring a

55 Smith, *op. cit.*, 2:23-25; John H. White, *The American Railroad Passenger Car* (Baltimore: Johns Hopkins Press, 1979),1:215, 232, 235.

> year later, on October 19, 1904.(8.23, 24) President Taft visited the club the same evening. The erection of this fine edifice was largely due to John J. Albright and William H. Glenny, the latter being president of the club at the time.[56]

(On October 19, 1904, William Howard Taft was Theodore Roosevelt's Secretary of War. His election to the presidency was four years away.) The University Club was much more boarder-oriented than the Buffalo Club. Thus the former had thirty-five boarders in 1915, twenty-nine in 1920, and twenty-nine in l925; while for the same years the count for the Buffalo Club was five, five, and seven.

Across Allen Street Hiram Niles, partner in an insurance company, had occupied the corner house in 1859.(8.24) Twenty-one years later in the same "handsome brown brick home" at #560 Delaware lived a successor to Niles, James Denison Sawyer, a grain merchant who branched out into grain storage and transport. Grandson of a veteran of Bunker Hill, he was born in Windham, Connecticut, in 1813, came to Buffalo in 1840, and married Charlotte Field. A 1906 writer saluted him as "one of the founders of the industrial and commercial Buffalo of today." He was a founder and trustee of the National Savings Bank, president of White's Bank, vice-president of the Mutual Gaslight, and vice president of the Western Insurance. A charter member of the Buffalo Historical Society and of the Young Men's Association, he served as president of Buffalo General and trustee of Forest Lawn. Until 1868 he was a member of First Presbyterian, after which he joined Westminster, of which he became an elder. He died at #560 in 1881 at sixty-seven. He had two daughters, Elizabeth and Ida. Elizabeth married George W. Parkhurst, a lawyer, and they continued to live in the corner house until Parkhurst died sometime after 1900. Their son married the sister of Ansley Wilcox of #641 Delaware.[57] Elizabeth Parkhurst lived at #560 until after 1905 and died in 1921.[58]

8.25 ❦ Joseph Pillsbury Dudley, Warren, *op. cit.*, p. 42.

The first recorded inhabitant of #564 was Joseph Pillsbury Dudley,(8.25) who had been born in Candia, New Hampshire, in 1832. After a public school education, he entered Pembroke Academy from which he graduated in 1852. In 1854 he married Mary Underhill of Concord, Massachuchusetts, and in 1858 came to Buffalo. The oil industry in America had begun with the well drilled under the supervision of "Colonel" E. L. Drake in Oil Creek, near Titusville, Pennsylvania on August 27, 1859. Dudley engaged in oil refining in Buffalo 1861-1882 as Dudley & Company. He then sold out to Standard Oil and became Standard's man in Buffalo. He was a trustee of the Erie County Savings Bank, a director of the American Exchange and Hydraulic Banks, and a director of the Ellicott Square Company, "now [1898] erecting the greatest office

56 Hill, *op. cit.*, 1:710.
57 *M&FH*, 1:117-120; *BEN*, January 14, 1920.
58 *CA*, May 5, 1923.

8.26 ❦ Charles Sumner Jones, *Men of Buffalo*, p. 381.

building in the world". He was vice president and treasurer of the Lafayette Street Presbyterian Church Society, a member and one-term president of the Country Club, and a member of Liberal, Falconwood, and Otowaga clubs. His wife died in 1891, by which time the Dudleys had moved up the Avenue to #827 on the corner of Barker Street. He died in 1907.[59]

Follwing Dudley in the 1890s #564 was Doctor Charles Sumner Jones(8.26), his wife, daughter, and three domestics, two of them middle-aged Irish women. Jones had been born in Middlesex, New York, in 1858, graduated from Cornell in 1884, and received his medical degree from U.B. in 1888, after which he did graduate work in Vienna, Paris, and London. In 1889 he began to practice medicine in Buffalo and in 1893 married Emma Pratt of an old Buffalo family. He was on the staff of Children's Hospital 1894-1907 and had sat on the advisory committee on building that hospital. During the first decade of the new century, however, the Joneses had moved up the Avenue to a new house at #695 Delaware. Thereafter brief tenure by several families followed until #564 had become a rooming house.[60]

Number 566 was the home of Doctor Herman Mynter from the mid-1890s until his death in 1903. He had been born in Karebaek, Denmark, in 1845, son of a Lutheran clergyman. He received his early education from private tutors, entered the University of Copenhagen in 1865, and received his M.D. in 1871. He continued his medical education at hospitals and clinics in Copenhagen, before serving briefly as a surgeon in the Danish navy. Coming to the United States in 1875 he elected to practice in Buffalo:

> He was one of the pioneer advocates of the knife for appendicitis, and was one of the first generally to introduce the operation in his practice here, his success being largely responsible for the acceptance of the treatment by the profession. He was also the first to introduce plaster jackets in this city, and early rising to the position of an authority in both medicine and surgery, was widely sought in consultation as well as in his private practice. An achievement which endeared him to the people of this adopted city, and which will long be remembered among them, has gone down in history. During the Spanish American War he went to Virginia as special envoy, to bring back a number of Buffalo soldiers who were desperately ill with typhoid fever. He accomplished his mission without the loss of a single life, and the gratitude of the people was as deep as it was spontaneous. His death [on January 23, 1903] cut short a brilliantly useful career, when he was still at the zenith of his powers.[61]

In 1877 Mynter married Minnie Booker Hoyt of Buffalo, who died some years later leaving two

59 *Men of New York*, 1:28-29.
60 *BEN*, November 16, 1927.
61 Hill, *op. cit.*, 3:9.

children, Agnes who graduated from Smith College, and Emily, who graduated from Vassar. His second wife was the socially prominent (D.A.R., Twentieth Century Club) Harriet Buell of Buffalo who long survived him, residing until at least 1920 at #566.[62]

Since coming to Buffalo in 1869 Stephen M. Clement was associated with three houses on Delaware Avenue, #568, #737, and #786. He had been born in Manlius in 1823. After a common school education he went to work in a grocery store, first as a clerk, then on his own. He did not take up his life work, banking, until he was thirty, when he sold his store and became cashier of a private bank in Fredonia. In 1854 he organized the Fredonia Bank and became its president. But his future belonged to the Queen City of the Lakes, where in 1850 the Marine Bank, the second bank of discount and deposit in the city, had been organized. The year Clement came to Buffalo he became a stockholder in Marine, shortly afterwards cashier, and in 1881 its sixth president, a position he held until his death in 1892. While he successfully evaded the social club whirl, Clement served as president of the board of managers of the State Normal School, and was president of the Orphan Asylum and Buffalo General. He was also a very active member of the Presbyterian Church of which he had become a member at twenty-two and ruling elder in 1855. He represented his church at presbyteries, synods, and general assemblies and was one of the founders of Auburn Theological. In 1851 he had married Sarah E. Leonard of De Witt. They had four children, but only one survived, Stephen M. Clement, Jr., who had been born in Fredonia in 1869.[63] Clement did not remain long at #568, but moved up to #737 during the mid-1870s.

Successors to the Clements at #568 in the 1880s were Samuel M. Wheeler, banker and oil producer in the Bradford, Pennsylvania area, and his family. Buffalo was not located in the oil fields but was well situated for disbursing streams of black gold which had suddenly become so important to the nationl economy. The next recorded resident at #568 was Harvey Gaylord, who had been born in Saginaw, Michigan, in 1872, and received his M.D. from the University of Pennsylvania in 1893. After graduate studies at Johns Hopkins, he married Bessie May Ketchum of Saginaw, and studied and later lectured on pathology in Goettingen, Germany, where he coauthored a book with his mentor, Ludwig Aschoff, on pathological history, a subject to which he would devote his life. An English version appeared in Philadelphia in 1901. Gaylord resided for a few years beginning in 1899 when he was instructor in pathology at U.B. at #568, with time out in 1903 for research on cancer in Copenhagen. In 1909 he was elected president of the American Association for Cancer research. On his return he received $60,000 from Mrs. William Gratwick (#776 Delaware) for a cancer laboratory, one of the first in America to use radium, which was completed in 1910. He also wrote *Carcinoma of the Thyroid in the Salminoid Fishes,* which was published by the U.S. Government Printing Office in 1914. During World War I he was a major in the Army Medical Corps and later a surgeon with the

62 *Ibid.*
63 *CA*, September 29, 1892.

99th Division. After the war the Gaylords lived in Eggertsville, during which time Gaylord again returned to Europe to investigate "deep X-Ray theory." A member of the Buffalo and Park Clubs, he had a nervous breakdown in 1925 and died at the sanitarium in Watkins in 1927.[64] The last family to have resided at #568 was that of Edward Rounds who was there *circa* 1915-1920. He was assistant manager of the Pierce-Arrow plant on Elmwood.

Number 570 and #568 were each half-houses. During the '70s and 80's Cornelia Bentley, her daughter and son-in-law, William Sage, and family lived there, though without servants during the 1880s. Sage, a lithographer, was able to retire at forty-five. He was succeeded by William G. Winslow, a grain commission merchant and lake shipping executive, who had come to Buffalo from Cleveland as a young man. He and his family lived there from the 1880s into the first decade of the new century. He belonged to the Buffalo Club and Trinity. He died in 1910 at age sixty-five, having retired some five years earlier.[65] Burt J. McGrath, his wife and two children lived at #570 in 1915; Dr. Burton Maycock followed five years later. In the 1930s #570 housed several doctors offices.

William G. Boardman, another lithographer, lived with his family at #576 in 1870. Theodore D. Barnum, resided there briefly in the early 1880s. Previously he had lived with his father, Stephen O. Barnum, a variety store proprietor, two doors up the Avenue; but Theodore later moved back to his father's at #584. During the late 1890s Carl T. Chester, an attorney with offices in the Ellicott Square Building, occupied #576. Carl had died by 1900 when his widow Lucy, and their son Carlton, resided there with two domestics. Next occupant of #576 was James How, who had been born in Brooklyn in 1876. In 1901 he came to Buffalo as manager of the Hartford Rubber Company, soon taken over by United States Rubber. In April How married Fanny Barnum Keating, an alumna of Buffalo Seminary and of Miss Porter's, Farmington, Connecticut, and widow of Langdon Keating. Fanny was the eldest daughter of the late Theodore Barnum. Her marriage took place at the extremely fashionable Grace Episcopal Church on Broadway and Tenth Street in New York. Afterwards the couple moved into #576, and James How became manager of Barnum's. By her first husband Fanny had a son, Theodore Barnum Keating, who was brought up by the Hows and eventually became president of the firm.[66] In the late 1920s the Hows moved to Saint Catherine's Court where Fanny died in 1932. She had been a member of Westminster, and the Garrett, Twentieth Century, and Country clubs. Her husband, who had been president of the Philharmonic Orchestra Society 1943-1946, later moved to Pinehurst, North Carolina, where he remarried and died in 1953.[67]

Number 578 was the home in 1870 of John W. Dickson, a thirty-three year old insurance agent, two young children, and two domestics. In 1880 the father was out of the picture, and his wife, Josephine, kept house for three children and employed two domestics. In 1890 she and her twenty-

64 *BEN*, November 16, 1927.
65 *BEN*, September 19. 1910.
66 *Times*, June 10, 1928.
67 *BEN*, December 1, 1953.

8.27 Barnum House, #584 Delaware, BHS.

one year old son William lived there alone. The Dicksons were followed in 1905 by George Holden Selkirk, seventy-five year old secretary of Buffalo's Park Commission, his wife, and two sons, one of whom was a title searcher, the other a lawyer. George had been born on Franklin Street in 1835. Educated in public schools, he went to Florence, Italy, to study to be a sculptor.[68] When news came that the Civil War had broken out, he immediately returned home and enlisted for three years as a First Lieutenant in the 49th Regiment of Infantry in 1861. The 49th participated in the Peninsular Campaign, and in the Battles of Antietam and Fredericksburg in 1862, in the Gettysburg Campaign in 1863, the Battle of the Wilderness in 1864, and in the final assault on Petersburg in 1865. He was wounded in action at Spotsylvania Courthouse in 1864, promoted to Major in 1865, and mustered out with his regiment as a Lieutenant Colonel.[69] In 1869 he married Emily S. Peabody by whom he had two sons and a daughter. He was part owner of the *Express* when Mark Twain and Joseph N. Larned were editors, and later formed a printing establishment, Selkirk & Carrell, on East Swan Street. With his splendid war record, Selkirk was named secretary to the Buffalo Parks Department in 1888, where he soon became known as "the dean," and *circa* 1895 began his thirty-year residence at #578 Delaware. He died there in 1925[70] and his widow, now seventy-nine, lived on there for a short time with an unmarried son and daughter. By 1931 the double house at #578 was well into its downward spiral.

By way of establishing some kind of a record, the house at #584 (new style) was inhabited by the same family from 1857 until at least 1910, fifty-two years (8.27). Stephen Ostrom Barnum had been born in Utica in 1816. Having attended the academy there, he worked at the post office until his father Ezra made him a partner in Barnum's Bazaar, which trafficked in what were called "Yankee notions," an all embracing term including knicknacks, gifts, and toys that were particularly in demand at Christmas time. In 1841 Stephen married Elizabeth Chatfield of Utica. In 1845 he came to Buffalo and at twenty-nine opened a similar store at #265 Main. At first Stephen and his wife lived in a frame house on Washington Street near the store. Later they moved to a better location on East Eagle Street. But in 1857 Stephen built a new house on Delaware, then out in the country, where Barnums would reside well into the next century. At different times Stephen was a director of Western Transportation, the American Exchange Bank, and the Empire Salt Works at Warsaw. In 1860 Stephen, then forty-four, and his wife, forty-two, had five children, Theodore eighteen, Frederick

68 *Courier*, January 25, 1925.
69 Phisterer, *op. cit.*, 3:2378, 2379, 2380, 2381, 2383, 2391.
70 *Courier*, May 19, 1925.

fifteen, Henry thirteen, Fanny ten, and Franklin five. They also had a German-born domestic and an English coachman. Stephen attempted to take in partners, before Theodore grew into the business. One of these partners, Julius P. Wahl, instituted a proceeding, Wahl *vs.* Barnum, which occupied the time and talents and filled the pockets of local attorneys Franklin D. Locke, John G. Milburn, George Lewis, and Adelbert Moot, and took nineteen years to settle. When Theodore, who had been born in Utica in 1842, was ready, Stephen made him partner, and the firm was thereafter known as Barnum & Son. After Theodore married Sarah Avery of Cleveland in the late 1860s, they lived at #584 for several years and had three children, Fanny, Stephana, and Evelyn. Burr thought that "Mrs. Theodore Barnum and her husband were among the delightful entertainers of the eighties and their beautiful daughters were charming additions to the society of the younger element."[71] Theodore maintained his own household at #567 during the 1870s and 1880s, but during the 1890s he had moved back. Stephen O. Barnum died in 1899 at eighty-three, and his son Theodore a year later in 1900, broken in spirit, it was thought, by the death in close order of his father and of his nineteen year old daughter Evelyn. His wife Sarah was still living at #584 at age seventy in 1910, but by 1915 it had become the home of Frank F. Henry, a miller, who was soon to move up the Avenue to finer quarters at #864. Henry was followed in 1920 by Charles L. Couch, a coal company president, his wife, their seventeen-year old son, and two maids. But in 1925 the Barnums, in a sense, were back. Ralph Huntington Sidway was born in Buffalo in 1877, the son of Franklin Sidway and Charlotte Spaulding, the daughter of Buffalo's Civil War congressman, Elbridge Gerry Spaulding. Ralph attended the Heathcote School and the Lawrenceville School in New Jersey. He did not attend college, though one brother, Frank Saint John Sidway, graduated from U.B. law in 1894, and another, Clarence graduated from Cornell with a degree in mechanical engineering in 1897. This difference was of a piece with their subsequent careers. Ralph's first business concern was to work with his attorney brother Frank to manage the real estate holdings of their family. Ralph and Frank also became officials of Robertson-Cataract Electric which manufactured electrical equipment. Ralph was also president of Lighting Fixture on West Chippewa Street. In 1908, he married Stephana Barnum, Theodore's daughter. They had one son, Ralph, Jr.[72]

8.28 ❦ Ralph Sidway house, #589, photographed by autor, 1999.

The elder Ralph Sidway was primarily a sportsman. He joined the Buffalo Launch Club in 1902, soon after its inception, and was commodore 1922-1927. His fleet of hydroplane speedboats were all named *Arab,* and aboard *Arab IV* he won the speedboat championship of

71 *Men of New York*, 1:144-145; *Times*, June 10, 1928; *CE*, November 13, 1957.
72 Hill, *op., cit.*, 3;73; 4:461-462;

the Great Lakes. At his death at fifty-two in 1936, it was noted that he had been a good horseman, an excellent marksman, and the owner of a prizewinning kennel of English Setters.[73] Sustaining Ralph's lifestyle was solid inherited wealth. A year after his and Stephana's marriage, they moved into a spanking new mansion at #589 Delaware(8.28)

> The house is substantially built from the basement with walls of hewn rock to the tiled roof. To enter, one passes beneath a porte cochere through a side door. Mounting a few stairs, one arrives in the library. All first floor rooms are heavily paneled in oak. The broad oaken stairway rising to the second floor is ornate with carved balustrade and newel posts. The ceiling of the living room is beamed. These massive beams are joined to the walls with decorative carved shields adorned with stars and stripes suggestive of our flag. A great white stone fireplace contrasts with the dark oaken woodwork of the living room. The dining room is done in golden oak, the walls tapestried above the paneling. The pilasters are carved with fruit and flowers.
>
> The bright solarium affords pleasant relief from the more formal room. In Mr. Sidway's day, a den, a veritable sportsman's paradise of hunting trophies, guns, cups won in speed-boat races, and photographs of polo players occupied the room that was later used by Dr. Eckel as an office. Throughout all the rooms of the first floor, design suggestive of the Gothic arch blends with the Tudor architecture. The second floor with its many windows suggests a second solarium. A recreation room occupies most of the third floor, above which is an ample attic.[74]

Ralph and Stephana sold #589 and moved across the Avenue to her old home at #584 in the early 1920s. They were going from a modern home to one built in 1857. Ralph's sportsmanship may have come at a price.

Number #586, was occupied in the early 1870s by James M. Willett, junior partner in the law firm of Laning, Folsom & Willett, whose career is succinctly summed up by White:

> James M. Willett studied and practiced law in Batavia and was there admitted to the bar in 1855. He was elected district attorney of Genesee county in 1859 and acquired an excellent reputation. After a brilliant war career, he settled in Buffalo in 1870 and formed a partnership with Albert P. Laning, which continued until Colonel Willett's death in 1877 at the early age of forty-five years.[75]

Willett had signed up with the rank of major, due to his civic standing, at Lockport in 1862 for three years in an infantry regiment which was quickly converted to the 8th Regiment of Artillery. His unit saw action toward the end of the war in the Richmond-Petersburg theater. He had been wounded in action at Cold Harbor on June 3, 1864, and emerged from the war a Colonel.[76] Willett's widow Helen stayed on for about a decade at #586 with her son Porter, before being succeeded in 1884 by Clarence L. Bryant, son of John C. Bryant, founder in 1854 of what became Bryant & Stratton's Business College. Clarence could be found off and on at #586 for about a dozen years until 1897 when he permanently moved to #591 just across the Avenue. Clarence was born in Amherst, Ohio, in 1851, was brought to Buffalo by his parents in 1854, attended Central High and, of course, Bryant's

73 *CE*, December 12, 1936.
74 *CE*, September 28, 1952.
75 White, *op. cit.*, 1:708.
76 Phisterer, *op. cit.*, 2:1402, 1407.

Business College. His wife was Helen Willett's daughter, Pauline. By 1891, however, the Bryants had moved across the Avenue to #591 where Clarence lived for most of the rest of his life. With the death of his father in 1901, he became principal of the college, a post he held until 1926. A member of the Buffalo Club and of Trinity, he died at eighty in 1931.[77] He was followed in the late 1890s at #586 by two widowed sisters, Mary Day and Ida Havens, the latter of whom survived at #586 until thelate 1920s when in her late seventies she enjoyed the ministrations of a nurse and two Irish-born domestics.

The mansion at #596 Delaware had been built in 1876 by Townsend Davis, partner in the insurance firm of Smith & Townsend. The Townsend Davises had three children, one of whom, Emily, married Robert K. Root, whose mansion was located at North and Delaware, a few doors above where she had been born and raised. Burr described Davis's house as:

> A handsome home on the same side of the street and in the same block [as his father's.] It is a red brick and sandstone dwelling with a hall through the center and a mansard roof. This also became a great social center, for both Mr. and Mrs. Townsend Davis were famous for their hospitality, and there was a little theater on the third floor where some clever amateur performances were given by some of the gifted members of the social set. Both Mr. and Mrs. Townsend Davis were accomplished in this line. The annual New Year's Day reception which Mr. and Mrs. Davis held, was one of the notable events of the winter season. Delaware avenue was crowded with smart equipages and throngs of handsomely attired women with their escorts filed in and out during the receiving hours.[78]

Townsend Davis had been born in Buffalo 1867, attended private schools, and graduated from Harvard in 1888. He returned to Buffalo and became junior member in the insurance firm of Smith & Davis.[79] Townsend died in the late 1890s. His widow, the former Anna C. Kowlton, and her son, H. Townsend Davis, lived there during the first decade of the new century.

Frederick B. Ussher, stepson of General George Field and a wealthy businessman, married Marie Winslow also of Delaware Avenue and resided at #596 during World War I and the 1920s, well supplied with domestic service. For the last thirty years of its existence the dated mansion provided living and office space for a husband-wife team of doctors, Roswell and Enid Brown. When it was razed in 1963 by Benderson to make way for an office building, it was the last house on the block.[80]

The first resident at #600 Delaware appears in 1880 in the person of Edward W. Eames, "one of the ablest and largest capitalists in the city." He had begun his career in the grain business but later simply "managed his private affairs" from an office in the White Building. He had been a charter member of the Merchants' Exchange and once its president. He belonged to the Buffalo Club and to Westminster. He was about seventy years old when he died in 1909. Follwing him at #600 in the

77 *BEN*, October 30, 1931.
78 *CE*, May 17, 1928.
79 White, *op. cit.*, 2:389.
80 *CE, ibid.*

1890s was Willis Chapin, partner in the law firm, Viele & Chapin. He was also a director of the Fidelity Trust and of the Fine Arts. Shortly after 1910 Chapin and family moved to a grand new mansion up the Avenue at #1205. Meanwhile, back at #600, the new owner was George Alfred Forman, son of George Van Syckel Forman, an oil man who had made good in the oil fields of northwestern Pennsylvania and had come to Buffalo in 1891. George Alfred, an oil man himself, had been born about 1876. With paternal assistance he organized the Southwestern Petroleum Company in 1900, and by 1915 was residing at #600 with his wife and three year old son.[81]

The first residents of #610 were William H. Davis of Smith & Davis, insurance brokers, and his wife Emily, parents of Townsend Davis of #596. For a few years after the marriage of their daughter Mary and George H. Dunbar, whose father was proprietor of the Eagle Iron Works on Perry Street, the William Davises and the Dunbars lived together in what Kate Burr described as "a fascinating rambling red brick structure with entrance at one side and double bay windows in front." By 1900, however, Dunbar had built his own house at #618 just above his in-laws.

Dexter Rumsey's third wife, Susan Fiske, was the daughter of Frank and Charlotte Fiske who had lived at #199 Delaware until the neighborhood had begun to deteriorate. Susan arranged for their moving up to #610, which had been occupied since the death of Emily Davis at the beginning of the century by the family of Charles Burnett. Fiske died in 1914 and his wife in 1922, after which their place was taken by their son Manson, vice-president of an insurance firm, and his German-born wife Fanny. Smith describes interior changes made by successive mistresses of #610:

> Mrs. Frank W. Fiske furnished the drawing-room in mid-Victorian style. Her daughter-in-law, Mrs. Manson Fiske, preferred a livelier atmosphere. She transformed the once formal drawing-room into a bit of old Spain. Carpet, upholstery and hangings were of crimson. Antique Spanish carvings in bas-relief, colored in black and gold, adorned the walls. Furnishings included exquisitely carved old Spanish chests. These were brought from Spain by the late Isabel Ross, Buffalo dealer in antiques.
>
> Above the great fireplace was a mantel of rich black marble, selected in New York City by Gertrude Watson [daughter of Stephen R. V. Watson, formerly of #388]. A valuable pier mirror rose to the ceiling. Before that mirror, Mrs. Manson Fiske and daughter Susan, now Mrs. John Surdam, stood to welcome guests to the latter's debut into Buffalo society. On that festive occasion, the fireplace was banked with vari-colored gift flowers. The flowers contrasted beautifully with the garlands and festoons of evergreen used in decoration. Since the debut was in December, Yuletide decorations were in order. A large Christmas tree on the veranda greeted arriving guests. Other candle-lighted trees shed soft light on guests and shone through the great bay windows. In addition to the two in the drawing room, there are bay windows in the hall, library and dining room.
>
> The library opens into the living room so that, for large social functions, the two can be used as one room. This is a convenient arrangement for the International Institute [which acquired the house in 1942 after Manson Fiske's death on September 21, 1939, at age

81 *Times*, June 24, 1924; *Courier*, June 5, 1926.

sixty- three.] Mrs. Manson Fiske furnished her library in lacquer red. Curtains were of velvet of that color, with matching carpet. On the carved old desk in the library stood an antique student lamp with Meisen shades. Antique candelabra added to the dignity of the room. The woodwork was of ebony; the fireplace, like that of the drawing-room, are black marble.

Lacquer-red velvet carpet, like that of the library, covered the halls and the broad, graceful stairway from first to third floor. Along the stairway were marble urns of ivy and red satin Chinese hangings embroidered in gold. In a niche at the turn of the stairs stood a large vase always filled with fresh flowers.

The master bedroom, which spanned the front of the second floor, was a reproduction of the Empire Period. Susan's room, [the Fiskes' daughter] furnished with French imports, was done in pink and turquoise. It was lighted by crystal chandeliers. One guest room was done in green and gold, another in early American period furniture.

The third floor was occupied by the staff of servants [usually three] who assured easy and comfortable living in the mansion. The garden famed for its beautiful flowers during the Summer, was the favorite winter play spot of the many friends of Susan's childhood. In cold weather the gardener used to flood the garden for skating. Susan's attractive play house was spacious. It stood in the cooling shade of a great oak tree. The little house was covered by climbing roses. Chintz curtains hung at the windows. In the evening, electric lights shone through the glass panes. One approached the front door across a veranda. The play house was furnished simply and comfortably. About the table in the dining room stood rush-bottom chairs. Especially popular with children was its roof garden, attractive with flower boxes filled with plants.[82]

George Dunbar did not long remain at #618. (All houses from #618 to North were built on the site of the earlier cemetery.) Dunbar was followed at #618 in 1900 by George Bush, an investor, and in the 1920s by Thomas F. Cooke, a New York City native who graduated in mechanical engineering from Columbia and came to Buffalo in 1905 to teach physics at U.B. In 1928 he and companions crossed the Atlantic in twenty-five days in a fifty-six foot ketch. In 1915 #622 was the residence of John Woodard, a state supreme court judge, his wife, and daughter. A year later he had taken a room at the Buffalo Club. Thereafter #622 was the home and office of Edgar R. McGuire, M.D., who had earlier resided further down the Avenue at #430. McGuire had been born in Mount Forest, Ontario, in 1877. Educated in Canada, he came to America, and after a year teaching public school entered the medical department at U.B. from which he graduated in 1900. He interned at Emergency and Buffalo General, and later became assistant to Roswell Park. He was assistant surgeon at Buffalo General 1903 — 1909 and then attending surgeon. In 1917 he was named professor of surgery at U.B. The author of

8.29 ❦ W. Caryl Ely, *M&FH*, II, facing p. 58.

82 *CE*, June 8, 1952.

about thirty articles chiefly on cranial and abdominal surgery, he was also member of the Buffalo, Saturn, Squash, Country, and Wanakah clubs. In 1921 he married Mildred Francis and they had two children, Edgar and Mildred.[83] Mildred was listed as the householder at #622 in 1931.

The first inhabitant of #628 was Henry Box, a native Briton and capitalist in 1900. He did not remain here long, but was soon followed by W. Carl Ely. (8.29) The first of that name had come to America from England and settled in Lyme, Connecticut, in 1651. Many of W. Carl Ely's ancestors fought in the colonial wars and in the Revolution. Sumner Ely, his grandfather, came from Lyme to Middlefield, Otsego County, in 1810, where he practiced medicine and at one time was president of the New York State Medical Society. He represented Otsego County in the assembly and senate. Later W. Carl's father, William H. Ely, also represented Otsego in the assembly. Carl was born in Middlefield in 1856, and was educated at the common schools there and at Cornell. He read law at East Worcester and was admitted to the bar at Ithaca in 1882. In 1885 he moved to Niagara Falls and formed the firm of Ely, Dudley & Cohn. During his early years Ely was a general practitioner but later functioned chiefly as counsel for manufacturing, railway, and business enterprises. In 1890 he abandoned the law almost completely and concentrated on electric railways. While he resided at the Falls, his business involvement was extensive:

> He was one of the original incorporators of the Niagara Falls Power Company and was a Trustee and local counsel of that company from its formation until 1899. He was actively engaged in forming and building the Buffalo & Niagara Falls Electric Railway and was the first President of that company. He was also actively concerned in the building of the Buffalo & Lockport and the Lockport & Olcott Railways, and was the first President of the Buffalo & Lockport Railway. He was counsel of the Niagara Falls & Clifton Suspension Bridge Company and one of the incorporators of the Lewiston & Queenstown Suspension Bridge Companies, builders of the suspension bridge between Lewiston, N.Y., and Queenstown, Canada. He was also one of the founders and is now a trustee of the Niagara County Savings Bank in Niagara Falls, and had much to do with the formation of the Carter-Crume Company, Limited, and William A. Rogers, Limited, and is now a Director of these companies, large and successful manufacturing enterprises at Niagara Falls. He was treasurer and active in the management of a large irrigation enterprise in the State of Washington, which constructed about 70 miles of irrigating canals in the valleys of the Yakima and Columbia Rivers.
>
> In the Fall of 1898 and the Spring of 1899 Mr. Ely was active in forming a plan of combining into one system the electric railroads in and between Buffalo, Niagara Falls, Tonawanda, Lockport, and adjoining towns and uniting them with Niagara Falls Park & River Railway on the Canadian side by means of the Steel Arch Bridge at Niagara Falls and the Suspension Bridge between Lewiston and Queenston, thus forming the great scenic route at Niagara.[84]

The scheme was successful, though the River Route was not included, and the result was the International Railway Corporation — the I.R.C. of happy memory — which came into existence in

83 Hill, *op. cit.* 4:433.
84 *M&FH*, 2:58-62.

8.30 ❦ 650 Delaware Avenue. Homes in Buffalo scrapbook, Buffalo Public Library, Lafayette Square, F129 B8B6925, vol. 2.

1902 as the merger of numerous streetcar routes in Buffalo and Niagara Falls and two interurbans between the two cities. With this, Ely gave up the practice of law altogether to become president of the I.R.C. and moved from the Falls to #626 Delaware Avenue. He served in this capacity until 1905 when he and his associates branched out into electric railways and public utilities in the Ohio Valley, including the very successful Steubenville East Liverpool & Beaver Valley Traction Company, which was not abandoned until 1939. From 1904 until 1906 Ely was president of the American Street & Interurban Railway Association.

In addition to his ancestral interest in politics, Ely as a railroad president needed friends, including himself, at the seats of government. After his removal to Niagara Falls, he served as village attorney, and in 1891 was nominated by the Republicans for justice of the supreme court. From 1893 until 1896 he was treasurer of the Democratic State Committee. His position also explains the astounding number of local associations to which he belonged: the Sons of the American Revolution, the Society of Colonial Wars, the Buffalo Historical Society, the Niagara Frontier Landmarks Association, the Niagara Club of Niagara Falls, and the Buffalo, Ellicott, Country, Transportation, and Automobile clubs of Buffalo. He was also a director of the Manufacturers & Traders National Bank and of the Fidelity Trust Company of Buffalo. In 1884 he had married Grace Keller of Cobleskill, a colonial dame herself, with six lines of descent from the *Mayflower*. Ely died suddenly on a visit to New York in 1922. His only child, Marion Caryl Ely, a Buffalo Seminary alumna, married Elbridge G. Spaulding of Buffalo.[85]

By 1920 Charles Wood, a factory owner, had moved into #626 and resided there during the roaring twenties and into the early thirties, with three maids in the house and a chauffeur and family in the rear. Dr. Augustus Hoxsie of #138 Delaware had married Anna Poole in 1868, and when he died in 1885 she married his associate, Dr. Joseph Tottenham Cook. The new couple lived on at #138 with Anna's daughter, also Anna, until 1893 when they moved up the Avenue to a house they had built at #638. The Cooks were well off since in 1905 the doctor, his wife, and stepdaughter enjoyed the services of three domestics in the house and a chauffeur and his family in the back. At that time Joseph was forty-nine, his wife sixty-six, and the stepdaughter thirty-five. Joseph died in 1915, and his widow, then seventy-five, and her daughter still lived on the Avenue. During the 1920s another doctor, Lee Masten Francis, was established there, but by 1931 the place had become the Polish Consulate.

85 *Ibid*; Horton, *op. cit.*, 3:77-79; George W. Holden and John F. Due, *The Electric Interurban Railways in America* (Stanford, California: Stanford University Press, 1960), p. 271.

8.31 ❦ Robert Keating Root, *Men of Buffalo*, p. 30.

A genuinely modern mansion was #650, home of Robert Keating Root, designed by McKim Mead and White and built on the southwest corner of Delaware and North in 1896.(8.30) This colonial revival bore a strong resemblance to that of George Eastman on East Avenue in Rochester, designed by the same firm.[87] Root was born in Buffalo in 1866, the son of Robert Keating, scion of an Anglo-Irish family long established in Wexford. Keating came to America in 1854 and to Buffalo the next year where he spent eleven years with [S. S.] Jewett & [Francis H.] Root, stove manufacturers. He then formed a partnership with Jewett's son, Henry C., which under the name Root & Jewett set up tanneries in Olean and Port Allegany, which sold out to the leather trust in 1892. Keating then moved into banking. He was a director of the Third National Bank, secretary of Standard Savings and Loan Association, and vice-president of Buffalo Savings. In 1888 he married his then boss's daughter, Caroline W. Root, by whom he had one child, Robert Keating, mentioned above.(8.32) When Caroline died in 1866, possibly in childbirth, Caroline's father, who wished an heir to perpetuate the family name, adopted him under the name Robert Keating Root.[87]

Robert K. Root dabbled in banking, starting from the top. He had been a director and member of the executive committee of the Bank of Buffalo and became vice-president of that institution when it merged with Marine Trust at which time he became a member of the board of Marine. He had also been a director of the Market Bank, a trustee of the Fidelity Trust, of the Commonwealth Trust of New York, and of the Ellicott Square Company. He was the eponym of and chief investor in the Root Building in downtown Buffalo. His business acumen was expended chiefly in managing the Root estate much of which was invested in real property. In 1888 he married Emily J. Davis, the daughter of the Townsend Davises of #596 Delaware. Emily died in 1917 and Robert never married again, so that the perpetuation of the Root name had not gone very far. Next year Root served overseas as a captain in the Red Cross during World War I. His *sociabilite'* embraced both Buffalo and New York. He had been dean of the Saturn Club and president of the Country Club. He belonged to the Buffalo Club, and to the Union League and the Strollers Club of New York. He died in Miami in 1923 at fifty-seven of pneumonia supposedly contracted while surf-bathing. He had taken several companions from Buffalo aboard his yacht for two weeks of fishing.[88] He was buried from his home, Rev. Cameron J. Davis of Trinity presiding. Root was followed by William A. Morgan who resided at #650 briefly, after which it was vacant for several years. It was demolished in 1935 and replaced with a Howard Johnson's.

86 *Buffalo Architecture*, p. 275; *Grand American Avenue*, pp. 52-53.
87 *M&FH*, 1:195-196.
88 *BEN*, December 3, 1923.

CHAPTER

9 VIRGINIA TO NORTH: *East Side*

The map for this chapter also is figure 8.1. Figures 9.1,2, and 3 show houses on the northeast corner of Delaware and Allen at three different periods beginning in the 1890s. Concerning these houses Buffalo's architectural guide states:

> This block of neoclassical row houses is unique in Buffalo, for its grandeur and continuity of design. Most homeowners wealthy enough to afford houses of this class preferred to build detached dwellings, and the popularity of terrace housing common to seaboard cities did not survive here after 1850. Collectively called the Midway because the block was half the distance on Delaware Avenue between Niagara Square and Forest Lawn Cemetery [actually, Gates Circle], the houses were erected individually over a period of years beginning in the late 1880s on the site of the former Cornell Lead Works. The firms of Green and Wicks (477 Delaware) and Marling and Johnson (479 and 483 Delaware) were among the architects responsible for the designs. Built mostly by business and professional people, the Midway was the clearest expression in Buffalo of the genteel spirit and nostalgia for tradition that informed national taste during the so-called American Renaissance of the 1890s.[1]

Above 9.1 ❦ The Midway, author's collection.
Middle 9.2 ❦ The Midway, BHS.
Below 9.3 ❦ The Midway, *Buffalo Architecture: A Guide*, p. 134.

Concerning these houses, another architectural study notes:

> Across the street, where the Cornell family business (8.2) once operated, are eleven extraordinary structures. Rowhouses became popular features of urban streetscapes in the late nineteenth century, and Buffalo boasts a number of fine examples of the genre, but

1 *Buffalo Architecture*, p. 135.

> seldom do rowhouses anywhere display the amazing diversity and wealth of feature demonstrated in these examples built in 1893-1895. Their styles include Georgian Revival (No. 477), Renaissance Revival (Nos. 475, 479), Colonial Revival (Nos. 481, 491), Classical elements (Nos. 483, 497), Queen Anne styling (Nos. 483, 493), Richardson Romanesque (Nos. 487-489, 499), and Sullivanesque elements (No. 497), indicating the influence of Louis Sullivan, the renowned architect, whose own work is exemplified locally in the Guaranty Building.[2]

Kowsky also makes a final general comment on the Midway:

> [Edward B.] Green [1855-1930] and [William C.] Wicks [1854-1919] were also chosen by Henry M. Birge, the owner of a well-known wallpaper company, to be the architects of his residence at 477 Delaware. The Birge house, erected between 1889 and 1895, is part of a distinguished row of dwellings known as the Midway, so called because of its location halfway between Niagara Square and Delaware Park. In a city that overwhelmingly preferred detached dwellings, the Midway evolved house-by-house according to strict covenants that governed height and design. All the houses are in some version of neoclassical design; in their totality they create the most urbane streetscape in the city.[3]

1870 (2)

VIRGINIA STREET

469 Cornell White Lead Co.

511 Cornelius S. Cooper's Marble Works

523 Henry G. White

1880

VIRGINIA STREET

469 Cornell White Lead Co.

511 James Noonan 34 England boathouse owner
Bridget Noonan 32 Ireland *ux.*
<u>Maggie Noonan</u> 1 NY daughter
Leonora Sterling 41 NY
Grace Sterling 11 NY daughter school

Hamilton Campbell 23 NY butler
Nora Campbell 24 NY *ux.*
Nora Campbell 1 NY daughter
Willie Camppbell 5 mos. NY son
Nellie Maddigan 20 NY sister-in-law

519 George C. Laverack 35 NY retail grocer
Mary Laverack 32 NY *ux.*
Belle Laverack 4 NY daughter school
Gertrude Laverack 4 NY daughter
Howard Laverack 3 NY son
<u>William Laverack</u> 1 NY son
J. H. Courigg 32 NY clerk
Katie Quinn 20 Ireland
Ellen Burns 40 Ireland

523 Frederick W. Bartlett 54 Mass.
Adela F. H. Bartlett 54 Canada *ux.*
Frederick Bartlett 14 NY son school
Hettie A. Hill 21 Canada niece
<u>Florence A. Hill</u> 7 Michigan grandniece
Hamilton Green 50 Mass.
Jemina Hill 21 NY
Katie Bauer 17 Germany

2 *A Field Guide to the Architecture and History of Allentown* (Buffalo: Allentown Association, 1987), p. 15.
3 Cigliano, *op. cit.*, p. 54.

ALLEN STREET End of Block

567 William H. Peabody 34 druggist
Elizabeth Peabody 33 *ux.*
William H. Peabody Jr. 2 mos.

585 William C. Newman 32 NY
treasurer Akron Cement Co.
Orrea Newman 30 NY *ux.*
Mary David 18 Ireland

591 S. K. Jones

609 Isaac Holloway 48 NY stone dealer
Mary Holloway 44 England *ux.*
John Holloway 20 NY paving foreman
William Holloway 18 NY school
Julia Holloway 18 NY school
Allen Holloway 4 NY school
Annie Betz 23 Prussia

615 James N. Scatcherd

535 Richard Callahan livery stable operator

537 Callahan's livery stable

ALLEN STREET End of Block

567 William H. Peabody 45 Conn. retired
Elizabeth Peabody 41 NY *ux.*
William H. Peabody Jr. 11 NY son
Lizzie Peabody 8 NY daughter
Charles Peabody 4 NY son
Mary A. Purdy 28 Canada sister-in-law
Kate Phelps 28 Canada
Emma Phillips 25 Canada

575 Oliver Swift 40 Mass. hardware manufacturer
Lucy Swift 35 Mass. *ux.*
Frank A. Swift 1 NY son
Caroline Jannuch 32 Prussia
Blanche Glenthing 18 England

581 Myron Crittenden 58 Mass. produce dealer
Alphena Crittenden 53 Mass. *ux.*
Rosella E. Crittenden Mass. daughter
Charles G. Crittenden 16 NY son school
Lucy R. Crittenden 34 Mass. sister
teacher B. Female Academy
Mary A. Clark 21 Canada
Annie Haller 29 Canada

585 Marshall Smith 38 NY house builder
Edmund Akroyd 17 NY step-son plasterer
Charles Akroyd 14 NY
Lydia Garber 24 NY

591 James Sabinack 35 NY
Harry A. Sabinack 12 NY son
Julia Dwyer 39 Ireland

595 *Olive Baptist Mission*

597 John Quinlan 58 Ireland carpenter

609 Isaac Holloway 58 England stone dealer
Mary A. Holloway 53 England *ux.*
Julia Holloway 23 NY daughter
Allen I. Holloway 13 NY son school
Sarah Denica 38 NY

615 James N. Scatcherd 54 Canada lumber dealer
Annie Scatcherd 44 Canada *ux.*
Emily L. Scatcherd Canada
Archibald Scatcherd 13 NY

621 William Powell 53 Wales wholesale grocer
Annie Powell 52 Wales *ux.*
William T. Powell 27 NY son clerk
Annie Powell 24 NY daughter
Frank L. Powell 17 NY school
Charles E. Powell 14 NY son school
Katie Graham 30 NY

623 William A. Wilkes 51 England
scrap iron merchant
Ellen Wilkes 43 England
Arthur Wilkes 23 Canada East
commercial traveler
Oliver Wilkes 21 NY
Ellen Wilkes 19 NY
Susan Wilkes 16 NY school
Jessie Wilkes 13 NY school
William Wilkes 11 NY school
Grant Wilkes 6 NY
? Wilkes 4 NY
Edward Wilkes 1 NY
Minnie Rosenbach 19 Prussia

623 Amanda Hoffman 57 NY housekeeper
Alice Hoffman 14 NY daughter
Mary Hoffman 27 NY daughter
Helen Sherr NY 24

641 Albert P. Laning

641 Albert P. Laning 62 NY attorney
Esther Laning 58 NY *ux.*
Helen Laning 26 NY daughter
Elizabeth Brennan 25 Ireland

661 Jason Parker

661 Edward Stevenson 74 NY
retired real estate agent
Amelia Stevenson 75 Vermont *ux.*
Amelia Stevenson 30 NY niece
Mary Burke 32 Ireland
Mary Maddigan 32 Ireland

NORTH STREET ❦ End of Block

NORTH STREET ❦ End of Block

1891

VIRGINIA STREET

469 Cornell White Lead Co.

1900

VIRGINIA STREET

469 Floyd S. Crego M.D. 44 NY
Katherine C. Crego 44 Ohio *ux.*
Richard Crego 13 NY son school
George Crego 5 NY son school
Mary McIntyre 24 Pa.
Minnie Laspere Canada

471 Ernest Wende M.D. 45 NY
Frances Wende 45 NY *ux.*
Flavilla Wende 12 NY daughter school
Margaret Wende 8 NY daughter school
Hamilton Wende 7 NY son school
Nora Hunt 25 Ireland

475 John Strootman 52 NY shoe manufacturer
Elizabeth Strootman 49 NY sister
Joseph Strootman 34 New Hampshire clerk
Gerhart Strootman 33 NY brother clerk
Phillipina Leis 27 Germany

477 Henry Birge 47 NY wall paper manufacturer
Fanny Birge 42 Illinois *ux.*
Mary Kelleher 40 Ireland
Charlotte Doyle 34 Canada

483 Albert Wright 42 NY banker
Gertrude Wright 40 Conn. *ux.*
Albert B. Wright 20 NY son school
Alfred Park Wright 19 NY son
Gertrude Wright 15 NY daughter
Ann Louisa Wright 10 NY daughter
Minnie Kennedy 22 NY
Magdalene Robinson 27 Canada
Mary Sheehan 35 NY
Margaret Higgins 36 NY

487 Harry Yates 30 NY general manager
BR&P Iron & Coal Co.
Mary Yates 28 NY *ux.*
Teresa Yates 6 NY daughter school
Walter Yates 4 NY son
Virginia Yates 3 NY daughter
Catherine Cariston 60 NY nurse
Mary Jones 30 Canada
Theresa Wilson 27 England

491 Charles M. Morse 46 NY mechanical engineer
Kathleen Morse NY *ux.*

493 Herman Hayd M.D. 42 Canada
Clinton Bidwell 30 Canada merchant
Margaret Stevens 30 Canada
Eileen McCarthy 28 Ireland

Phillip Cassidy 24 Canada coachman
Ada Cassidy 23 Germany *ux.*
Burt Cassidy 21 Canada bank trotter

497 William C. Cornwell 48 NY president City Bank
Agnes Gerlarot 35 NY

499 Jacob Schoellkopf 41 NY chemicals
Wilma Schoellkopf 36 NY *ux.*
Jacob Schoellkopf 17 NY son school
Ruth Schoellkopf 6 mos. daughter
Emil Silbers 40 Germany butler
Dora Silbers 43 Germany
Marnie Silbers 10 NY school
Bertha Conscer 27 Germany

501 John Gordon 59 Michigan transportation agent
Elizabeth Gordon 53 NY *ux.*
Robert G. Gordon 22 Maine son
Maria Heavey 23 Ireland
Nellie Carney 23 Ireland

503 Edwin Fleming 52 Indiana journalist
Harriet Fleming 40 Michigan *ux.*
Bessie McFadden 25 Canada

511 Joseph G. Monroe Buffalo Arms Co.	
519 George E. Laverack wholesale drugs & groceries	519 George E. Laverack 55 NY Mary R. Laverack 45 *ux.* Howard Laverack 23 son William H. Laverack 21 son Belle R. Laverack 25 daughter
	523 Elmer G. Starr M.D. 38 Michigan Elsie Starr 32 NY *ux.* Doris Starr 6 NY daughter Kelvin Starr 1 NY son Fannie McLaughlin 24 Ireland Margaret Cronwell 30 NY
	525 James W. Putnam M.D. 40 NY Caroline Putnam 30 NY *ux.* Osborne Putnam 11 NY son school John Putnam 7 NY son school Roger Putnam 2 NY son Sarah Kane 40 Ireland Mary O'Donnell 27 Ireland Ella Smith 22 NY
535 Charles W. Miller coach omnibus & baggage express	
537 Alfred Schoellkopf sheepskin linings	537 Alfred Schoellkopf 40 NY tannery prorietor Emily Schoellkopf 30 NY *ux.* Lucie Schoellkopf 4 NY daughter William Schoellkopf 2 NY son Emily Schoellkopf 10 mos. daughter Louise Mahoney 25 NY Miriam Williams 27 NY Margaret Gross 22 Germany
553 Jacob F. Schoellkopf S & Mathews millers	553 Christiana Schoellkopf 76 Germany widow Hans Schmidt 30 Germany son-in-law tannery Helen Schmidt 28 NY daughter Hans Schmidt 5 NY grandson Walter Schmidt 2 NY grandson Mary Kehoe 30 NY Lilia Smith 22 NY Freda Schaefer 19 NY Sophia Burkhardt 25 Germany
ALLEN STREET ❦ End of Block	ALLEN STREET ❦ End of Block
567 William H. Peabody	567 Elizabeth M. Peabody 62 NY widow William H. Peabody 30 NY son attorney Eliza P. Peabody 28 NY daughter Charles M. Peabody 23 NY son real estate agent Henrietta G. Peabody 22 France daughter-in-law Marian Purdy 53 NY sister Minnie Rast 50 NY Margaret Conley 33 Pa.

575 Oliver F. Swift Buffalo Register Works

581 Julius Altman Altman & Co.

591 Clarence Bryant

595 *Delaware Avenue Baptist Church*

609 *Temple Beth Zion*

615 Seward Cary

625 Isadore Michael

641 Ansley Wilcox attorney

661 Amelia Stevenson

581 John C. Nagel

591 Clarence L. Bryant 48 Ohio
business college president
Pauline W. Bryant 38 NY *ux.*
Russell W. Bryant 16 NY son school
Ruth W. Bryant 11 NY daughter
Dorothy W. Bryant 9 NY daughter
Elizabeth Hudson 22 Canada

595 Twentieth Century Club
Frank Ethridge 47 NY janitor

609 *Temple Beth Zion*

615 Seward Cary 38 NY capitalist
Emily S. Cary 38 NY *ux.*
Eleanor Cary 12 NY daughter
Phoebe Cary 12 NY daughter
Trumbull Cary 6 NY son
John S. Cary 2 NY son
Jane Cary 1 NY daughter
Annie Kelley 38 Ireland
Sarah Kelley 28 Ireland
Mary Manarey 44 Canada
Annie Cross 22 Canada

621 Heathcote School

623 Lester Wheeler 57 NY principal
Heathcote School
Genevive Wheeler 50 Mass. *ux.*
Maxwell Wheeler 26 NY son attorney
Christine Wheeler 23 NY teacher
Heathcote School
Maggie Gorman 20 Ireland
Norah McKettrick 38 Canada

625 Isadore Michael 53 NY landlord
Elizabeth Michael 43 NY *ux.*
Louise Michael 10 NY daughter
Maurice Michael 8 NY son
Frances Michael 7 NY daughter
Annie Reilly 24 Ireland
Annie Cary 40 NY

641 Ansley Wilcox 44 Georgia attorney
Grace Wilcox 42 NY *ux.*
Cornelia Wilcox 19 NY daughter school
Frances Wilcox 12 daughter school
Mary G. Welsh 28 Canada
Teresa Fogarty 23 Ireland

661 Amelia Stephenson 50 NY

Georgiana Thorne 23 NY niece
Mary Maddigan 50 New York

Edward Kieley 31 NY coachman
Lizzie Keiley 31 NY *ux.*
Edward Kieley 2 NY son

NORTH STREET End of Block

1905

VIRGINIA STREET

469 Floyd S. Crego M.D. 49 NY
Kate Crego 42 *ux.*
Floyd Crego 18 son Lawrenceville
Richard Crego 10 son school
George Crego 8 son school
George W. Reynolds 21 medical student
Ida Reynolds 28 *ux.*

471 Ernest Wende M.D 51 NY
Frances Wende 50
Margaret Wende 12 daughter school
Hamilton Wende 12 son school
Flavilla Wende 17 daughter school
Samuel J. Cutler 84 England boarder

475 John Strootman 57 shoe manufacturer
Paul Strootman 37 brother
Elizabeth Strootman 57 sister
Kate Strootman 45 sister
Bertha Strootman 17 niece
Ada Taylor

477 Mrs. Francis M. Walcott 52
Katie Koon 38 Germany
Albert Balthazard 30 France

479 William C. Krauss M.D. 42 mental disease
Clara R. Kraus 39 *ux.*
Alma Krauss 10 daughter school
William Krauss 3 son
Kate Stevenson 23 Canada

481 Bernard Bartow M.D. surgeon
Frances Bartow 50 *ux.*
Barbara Richter 34 Germany
Lottie Bell 29

483 Pendennis White 45 lumber dealer
Virginia White 43 *ux.*
Miss Virginia Kent White 20
Dorothy White 12 daughter

NORTH STREET End of Block

1915

VIRGINIA STREET

469 Alice Halliday 44
Frank Halliday 27 son
president music roll company

471 Grover Wende M.D. 47
David Wende 27 son school
Elizabeth Welch 51

475 John Strootman 65 president Strootman Shoe Co.
Paul G. Strootman 45 brother vice-president
Kate Strootman sister
Louise Smith 66

477 Kathryn Horton 63
Alice Kelly 50 Ireland
? Ganshoner 35 Canada
Lillian McGregor 40 Canada

479 Theodore Wright M.D. 34 Canada
Martha Wright 34 *ux.*
Gertrude Wright 1 daughter
Theodore Wright Jr. 5 son
Frances Nowak 23

481 Edward H. Goetz 54 wholesale grocer
Mary P. Goetz 52 *ux.*
Mary E. Goetz 26 daughter

483 Maud Polley 44
Raymond Polley 22 son school
Cyrus Polley 14 son school
Margaret Polley 18 daughter school
Lois Oyer 32

489 T. Guilford Smith 65 manager Carnegie Steel
Mary Smith 60 *ux.*

491 Richard B Lyman 47 stock broker
Mary S. Lyman 45 *ux.*
Vreeland Lyman 22 son Snow Pump Works
Duane S. Lyman 19 school
Dehli Quinlan 24
Nina Burchart 25 Canada

493 Herman Hayd M.D. 47 Canada
Jean Terry 24 Canada niece boarder
Olive McCarthy 30
Margaret Fitzpatrick 28 Canada

497 Charles J. Spaulding 58 manager Lafayette Hotel
Cynthia A. Spaulding 54 *ux.*
Mabel Spaulding 17 daughter
Anna Wadel 19

499 Jacob F. Schoellkopf Jr. 46 chemicals
Wilma Schoellkopf 50 Germany *ux.*
Frederick Schoellkopf 24 tannery
Jacob Schoellkopf 22 son Cornell
Ruth Schoellkopf 5 daughter
Esther Schoellkopf 3 daughter

501 John H. Porter 31 vice-president steel plant
Gertrude S. Porter 30 *ux.*
Sidney S. Porter 23 brother bookkeeper
steel plant
Eleanor Schroeder 25
Anna Saegner 20 Germany

503 Albert Wright 25 NY stock broker
Lucie Wright 22 *ux.*
Mary Sullivan 30
Marie Shanahan 23 Canada

513 Henry M. Gerans 52 NY proprietor
Iroquois Hotel
Maude Gerans 44 *ux.*
Gertrude Gerans 18 NY daughter school
Orpha Gerans 13 NY daughter school
Mary Carney 24 Ireland
Annie Laughlin 23

487 Allan A. James M.D.
Mary H. James 49 *ux.*
Elizabeth Wells 48
Anna Povluetika Bohemnia

489 Chauncey Smith M.D. 45
Mary Smith 75 mother housekeeper
Charlotte Willoughby 60 aunt
Alice Horan 28 Ireland
Alice Fobul

491 Arthur C. Kugel M.D. 45
Jean Kugel 45 *ux.*
Leomart Kugel 22 son school
Helen Kugel 7 daughter school

493 Herman Hayd M.D. 57 Canada
Jean Terry 32 Canada niece
Ellen Murphy 42 Ireland
Nora O'Connor 26 Ireland

497 Walter Gaston 65 Electric Furnace Co.
Mary Gaston 48 *ux.*
Nellie Foster 25 Germany

499 Jacob Schoellkopf NY 58 president chemical co.
Wilma Schoellkopf 53 *ux.*
Ruth Schoellkopf 15 daughter school
Esther Schoellkopf 13 daughter school
Rose Boger 32 Germany
Marie Sibileus 25 cook
Barbara Mandel 22 germany
Leditta Apotoski 28 Poland

501 Stephen Howell M.D. 43
Jean H. Howell 53 sister housekeeper
Frances Beckman 24

503 Bernard Bartow M.D. 65
Fanny Bartow 64 *ux.*
Margaret Carroll 52 cook
Margaret Carroll 12 school

513 Adele Blood 26 actress
Augusta Wilson 28

519 George E. Laverack 60 NY retired
Mary R. Laverack 50 *ux.*
Belle R. Laverack 30 daughter
Howard Laverack 28 son
William H. Laverack 26 son
Jean Laverack daughter school teacher
John C. Cowing 57 retired boarder
George Reynolds 30 medical student boarder
Kate Dineen 27 Ireland
Nellie Clark 20 Ireland
Anne Durkin 29 Ireland

519 George E. Laverack 69
Belle Laverack 43
Joseph Schreiber 26 Pierce Arrow management
Mary O'Gorman 23 Ireland
Mary Clark 30 Ireland

523 Elmer Starr M.D. 42 occulist
Elsie Starr 36 *ux.*
Doris Starr 11 daughter school
Sylvia Starr 2 weeks daughter
Ada D. Boger 19
Carrie Berg 17 Germany

523 Elmer Starr M.D. 53
Elsie Starr 46 *ux.*
Doris Starr 21 daughter school
Sylvia Starr 10 daughter school
Alice Klein 20
Gladys Pound 19

525 James W. Putnam M.D. 42 occulist
Caroline Putnam 40 *ux.*
James O. Putnam Jr. 15 son school
John Putnam 12 son school
Roger Putnam 8 son school
Sarah Meredith 40
Mary ? 18

525 James W. Putnam M.D. 54
Caroline Putnam 47 *ux.*
John Putnam 23 school
Roger Putnam 17 son school
James O. Putnam Jr. 25 son
American Radiator Co.
Mary R. Putnam 26 *ux.*
Sarah Meredith 50
Agnes Jordan 22 Ireland

531 Leonard Burgweger 53 Germany brewer
Lena Burgweger 49 *ux.*
Henry Burgweger son Cornell
Kate Elting 25

531 Leonard Burgweger 63 Germany brewer
Lena Burgweger 59 *ux.*
Ella Elting 24
Kate Elting 35

537 Mrs. Alfred P. Schoellkopf 35
Lucy Schoellkopf 9 daughter school
William Graebe Schoellkopf 8 son school
Emily Schoellkopf 5 daughter
Mrs. Mary Bald 56 boarder
Marie Leahy 16 Ireland
Ezra ? 26 Germany

553 Hans Schmidt 50 Germany president tannery co.
Helen Schmidt 45 *ux.*
Walter Schmidt 17 son school
Elsie Schmidt 14 daughter school
Mary L. Schmidt 9 daughter school
William Russ 19 Germany butler
Sophie Russ Germany cook
? Schrectenferger 19 Germany
Mary Brown 40 nurse
Mary Brown daughter
Kiety Walisyk 32 Poland

ALLEN STREET ❦ End of Block

ALLEN STREET ❦ End of Block

567 Elizabeth M. Peabody 67
William H. Peabody 28 son real estate agent
Henrietta G. Peabody 26 France daughter-in-law
Elizabeth Peabody 3 granddaughter
Anita Peabody 1 granddaughter
Marion Purdy 57
Minni Rast 60

575 Jane B. Welch 37
Stewart Welch 9 son
Elizabeth Welch 5 daughter
Helen Crawford 26 Ireland
Mary Tyrell 40 Ireland

581 Frank W. Hinkel M.D. 48 throat and ear surgery
Kate A. Hinkel 48 *ux.*
Edith W. Hinkel 19 daughter college
Allen W. Hinkel son 17 college
Francis Hoffman 60 Germany
Anna Fitzpatrick 46 Canada

591 Clarence L. Bryant 53 president business school
Pauline W. Bryant 43 *ux.*
Russell W. Bryant 21 son college
Ruth Bryant 16 daughter school
Dorothy Bryant 14 daughter school
Emma Lanigan 35
Bridget Leary 15 Ireland

595 Twentieth Century Club

609 *Temple Beth Zion*

615 Seward Cary 43 NY retired
Emily Cary 43 *ux.*
Eleanor Cary 17 daughter Briar Cliff Manor
Phoebe Cary 15 daughter school
Trumbull Cary 12 son school
John S. Cary 7 son school
Anne Kelly 40 Ireland
Sarah Kelley 38 Ireland
Nora Coughlin 24 Ireland
Minnie Raehill 38
Anna Turner 24
Walter Dutton coachman

623 Heathcote School
Lester Wheeler 56 principal
Genevive Wheeler 50 *ux.*
Maxwell S. Wheeler 31 son attorney
Gertrude Wheeler 30 daughter-in-law
Christine Wheeler 27 daughter
Anna Foran 22

567 William A. Peabody 38 real estate
Margaret Cummings 24
Mary Gallagher 41

575 Lee M. Francis M.D. 38
Ethel Francis 35 *ux.*
Lee M. Francis Jr. 8 son school
Ethel Gwyne Francis 2 daughter
Elena Smith 30
Margaret Retter 50 Germany
Edith McCabe 22

581 Frank W. Henkel M.D. 57
Kate Henkel 55 *ux.*
Emma Wolf 19 Germany
Olive Collis 30 England

591 Clarence L. Bryant 63 business school
Pauline W. Bryant 54 *ux.*
Ruth Bryant 26 daughter
Bridget Lanahan 26 Ireland housekeeper
Teresa Sullivan 26 Ireland

595 Twentieth Century Club

609 *Temple Beth Zion*

615 Albert Sikes 40 manufacturer Sikes Chair Co.
Jean Sikes 40 *ux.*
Robert Sikes 24 son
Edwina Sikes 19 daughter
Glendine Taylor 30
Mary Sullivan 18

623 Lester Wheeler 67 teacher
Genevive Wheeler 60 *ux.*
Christine Wheeler 38 teacher

625 Isadore Michael 59 capitalist
Elizabeth Michael 47 *ux.*
Louisa Michael 15 daughter school
Maurice Michael 13 son school
Frances Michael 12 daughter school
Anna Holmayer 58 Germany
Margaret Fleming 29 Canada
Mary McCarthy 34
Anna Shanahan 28 Canada

William Bennet 31 England coachman
Mary Bennet 36 England *ux.*
Maud Bennet 8 England daughter

641 Ansley Wilcox 49 Georgia
Grace R. Wilcox 50 *ux.*
Frances Wilcox 17 daughter
Mary Crawford 27 Ireland
Margaret Barton 25 Ireland
Hannah Flynn 25 Ireland
Annie Weigent 54
Talbert Scarlett 52 coachman

661 Amelia Stevenson 55
Mary Clancy 19
Nellie McCloskey

James Damon 48 coachman
Mary Damon 29 *ux.*
Frances Damon 5 daughter

NORTH STREET ❦ End of Block

625 Isadore Michael 65 real estate
Elizabeth Michael 60 *ux.*
Louise Michael 25 daughter
Frances Michael 22 daughter
Morris Michael 23 son

641 Ansley Wilcox 54 attorney
Grace Wilcox 60 *ux.*
Frances Farnscome 50 Canada
Ella Hunt 36 Ireland
Nellie Fitzgerald 38 Ireland
Isabella Mc ? 36 Ireland
Sarah McCarthy 30 Ireland
Mary Elliott 55 Ireland
Emma Fischer 46 personal maid

661 Amelia Stevenson 70
Octavia Thurston 54 England lodger
Kate Coughlin 27 Ireland
Rose Laughlin 52 Canada

NORTH STREET ❦ End of Block

1920

VIRGINIA STREET

469 Alice Halliday 56 NY widow
Frank Halliday 37 NY son
president insurance company
Joanna Kearney 28 NY

471 F. Grover Wende M.D. 52 NY
David F. Wende 22 NY son
Susan Wende 32 NY niece clerk
Alice Heiniman 22 NY

475 John Strootman 70 NY shoe manufacturer
Kate Strootman 60 NY sister
Gerhard Strootman 52 NY brother
shoe manufacturer

477 Katherine Horton 68 NY
Laura Pair 49 England
Margaret McCormick 47 Canada

1925

VIRGINIA STREET

471 Grover W. Wende M.D. 56
David Wende 25 son medical student
Julia B. Trotter 23 lodger

475 John Strootman 75 retired
Garrett Strootman 54 brother attorney
Catherine Strootman 62 Germany sister
Bertha J. Strootman 35 niece attorney
Antoinette Lamke 26 cousin

477 Katherine Horton 85

479 Hector Tennent 38 Scotland
apartment superintendent
Maria Tennent 31 England *ux.*
Rebecca Tennent 4 NY daughter
7 families

481 Mary F. Goetz 57 Canada
Mary E. Goetz 30 NY daughter dress designer

483 Maude B. Polley 40 NY
Ray Polley 26 NY son electrical engineer
Cyrus Polley 18 NY son
Laura Pryer 36 NY

487 Allan A. Jones M.D. 58 Canada
Mary H. Jones 56 Canada *ux.*
Justin Jones 20 Canada nephew

489 Mary S. Smith 80 NY widow
Chauncey P. Smith M.D. 31 NY son
Mary Horan 28 Ireland cook
Alice E. Fay 36 NY

491 Arthur R. Kugel M.D. 49 Illinois
Jeanette S. Kugel 49 NY *ux.*
Leonard S. Kugel 27 NY son secretary
Chamber of Commerce
Rebecca Kugel 19 NY daughter
Helen Kugel 12 NY daughter
Arthur Craig Kugel 9 mos. son

493 Herman E. Hayd M.D. 61 Canada
Jean Terry 36 Canada niece
Mary Meigan 48 Ireland
Mary Griffin 30 Ireland

George Hardy 25 NY chauffeur
Frieda Hardy 20 NY *ux.*

497 Stella Lowry 57 NY
Lillie B. Lowry 54 NY sister

499 Jacob T. Schoellkopf 62 NY
Niagara Falls Power Co.
Hilda Schoellkopf 59 Germany *ux.*
Ruth W. Schoellkopf 21 NY daughter
Esther Schoellkopf 19 NY daughter
Rose Boger 38 Germany
Marie Baumgarten 39 Alsace
Louise Stefani 32 Galicia

501 Stephen Howell M.D. 65 NY
Jean Howell 60 NY sister
Fanny Gaffney 35 NY

479 Apartments
Paul J Trudell 30 Germany university professor
Louise Trudell 40 Germany *ux.*
Ruth E. Trudell 5 daughter
Arthur Trudell 5 son
6 residents
1 servant

481 Raymond Brown 50 insurance agent
Alice Brown 49 *ux.*
Norman Brown 22 son college
George W. Flynn 70 father-in-law

483 Carl Tompkins M.D. 52
Ruth J. Tompkins 42 *ux.*
Carlotta Tompkins 13 daughter school

487 Rooming house
Bessie Miller 38 proprietor
7 roomers

489 Guilford Smith 84 retired
Chauncey P. Smith M.D. 54 son
Alvania Worth 45 Germany nurse

493 Herman Hayd M.D. 66 Canada
Mary Frank 40 cook
Margaret Tomlinson 40 Canada

499 Leo B. Englehart 47 artist
Caroline E. Pullitizer 40 sister housekeeper
Muriel Pullitizer 5 niece
Thomas B. Englehart 18 Mexico school
? Van Winke 27 lodger school teacher

501 Bruce S. Wright 46 clergy
Marguerite S. Wright 41 *ux.*
Harriet S. Wright 16 daughter

503 Bernard Bartow M.D. 70 Michigan
Jeanette Bartow 68 Mass. *ux.*
Mary Foran 27 Canada

513 Henry P. Burgard 58 NY contractor
Jean Burgard 38 NY *ux.*
Peter Burgard 6 NY son
Jane Burgard 5 NY daughter
Mary Crown 37 Ireland cook
William Crown 38 England
Lillian Maltby 20 NY

519 George E. Laverack 74 NY
Belle E. Laverack 47 NY daughter writer
Joseph B. Schrier 32 France salesman
Mary Gorham 36 Ireland
Sarah Farrell 40 England

523 Elmer G. Starr M.D. 57 Michigan
Elsie Starr 51 NY *ux.*
Sylvia Starr 14 NY daughter
Nina Cammarata 18 NY

525 James W. Putnam M.D. 59 NY
Caroline Putnam 55 NY *ux.*
John G. Putnam 27 NY son clerk
Roger W. Putnam 22 NY salesman
Sarah Meredith 60 NY

531 Leonhardt Burgweger 68 Germany owner Iroquois Brewery
Lena Burgweger 55 NY *ux.*
Henry Burgweger 40 son
Katherine Esting 30 NY
Adele George 24 NY

537 Emily R. Schoellkopf 47 NY widow
Emily C. Schoellkopf 20 NY daughter
William G. Schoellkopf 23 NY son
John Casa Aequia 25 France son-in-law
Lucia Casa Aequia 40 NY daughter
Lucey W. Wallace 40 Canada
Margaret Marlkey 57 Canada

ALLEN STREET ❦ End of Block

567 Eliza M. Peabody NY widow
Barbara Hainsworth 28 Alsace

575 Albert E. Woehnert M.D. 51 NY
Annie M. Woehnert 57 Conn. *ux.*
Emily Woehnert 21 NY daughter
Nancy Woehnert 17 NY daughter
Marion Woehnert 15 NY daughter
Nora Fennell 24 Ireland
Agnes Sharkey 38 Ireland

503 Sarah L. Truscott 69
Nora J. Mercer 68
Joyce Percy 54 nurse

523 Elmer G. Starr M.D 63
Sylvia E. Starr 20 daughter school

525 James W. Putnam M.D. 64
Caroline Putnam 60 *ux.*
Anna Neville 58 Ireland cook
Abbie Kenealy 22 Ireland

553 Rooming house
28 lodgers

ALLEN STREET ❦ End of Block

567 Rooming house
29 residents

575 Theodore Wright M.D.
Natalie C. Wright 47 *ux.*
Gertrude Wright 15 daughter school
Theodore Wright Jr. 12 son school
Frances Nowak

589 Ralph H. Sidway 35 NY executive electric co.
Stephana Sidway NY 36 *ux.*
Ralph Hunt Sidway 6 NY son
Annie Wayland 37 Prussia
Mary Engert 39 Baden

591 Clarence L. Bryant 62 Ohio business school
Pauline W. Bryant 52 NY *ux.*
Ruth Bryant 30 NY daughter
Anna Baker 48 Ireland
Nellie Sheehan 21 Ireland

595 Twentieth Century Club

605 *Temple Beth Zion*

615 Walter Steele 54 Missouri osteopath
Catherine Steele 47 Missouri *ux.*
Esther Davenport 76 Pa. widow lodger
society editor *BEN*
Ophelia Turner 41
Ben Turner 13 NY son

623 Apartments
12 families

625 Isadore Michael 73 NY capitalist
Elizabeth Michael 63 NY *ux.*
Louise Michael 29 NY daughter concert manager
Sidney Michael 28 NY son
Fannie Lewis 68 NY aunt
Catherine Callen 42 NY
Catherine McSweeney 40 NY

641 Ansley Wilcox 64 Georgia attorney
Grace Rumsey Wilcox 65 NY *ux.*
Frances Farnscome 56 Canada companion
Emma Fisher 51 NY
Ellen Hunt 37 Ireland cook
Joseph G. Hartman 35 NY chauffeur
Nellie Donovan 26 Ireland
Mary Ecriaich 26 Austria

661 Amelia Stevenson 75 NY
Catherine Haspel 32 NY
Elizabeth O'Connor 27 Ireland cook
Louise Genake 38 NY

NORTH STREET ❦ End of Block

581 Claus P. Myer 51 store manager
Emily M. Myer 38 *ux.*

589 John L. Eckel M.D. 45
Bernice Eckel 47 *ux.*
Eleanor D. Long 72 mother-in-law

591 Roberta Bennie 51 housekeeper
10 boarders

595 Twentieth Century Club

605 *Temple Beth Zion*

615 Catherine Steele 49 housekeeper
3 lodgers
1 servant

623 Rooming house
29 roomers

625 Isadore Michael 78 NY
Elizabeth Michael 68 *ux.*
Louise Michael 34 daughter shop proprietor
Sidney M. Michael 32 son salesman
Frances Lewis 71 sister-in-law
Helen Normaly 24 Ireland waitress
Mary Gormley 26 Ireland chambermaid
Nellie Hurley 52 Ireland cook

641 Ansley Wilcox 69 attorney
Grace Wilcox 70 *ux.*
Emma Fisher 55
Alice Keanis 50 cook
Genevieve Klein 19 kitchen maid
Kate Dawson 35 England

661 Amelia Stevenson 80
Catherine Brennan 23 Ireland waitress
Catherine Coyle 50 Ireland cook

James J. Damon 48 chauffeur
Mary Damon 50 *ux.*
Bart Pratt 27 machinist
Frances Pratt 27 *ux.*

NORTH STREET ❦ End of Block

The house on the northeast corner of Virginia and Delaware, #469, (since demolished), was first inhabited in the 1890s by Dr. Floyd Crego, an alienist. The east side of Delaware between Virginia and Allen was becoming a doctor's row. Of twenty houses there in 1895, nine were doctors' home-offices. Dr. A. C. Kugel had followed Crego at #469 by 1910, and was followed in 1915 by Alice Halliday and her son Frank, president of a music roll company and later of an insurance agency. They carried on without domestics into the early 1930s.

The next house, #471, was owned by the same family for thirty-five years. Its first inhabitant, dating from the late 1890s, was Dr. Ernest Wende, nationally celebrated health commissioner of Buffalo, who was born in Mill Grove, son of Bernard and Susan Kirk Wende, in 1853. Graduating from Central High in 1874, he taught school for two years and then began to study medicine, which took his next twelve years. He received an M.D. from U.B. in 1878, attended Columbia's College of Physicians and Surgeons and the University of Pennsylvania from which he graduated in 1884, and received a B.S. in 1885. Meanwhile he had married Frances Cutler of Omaha in 1881. In 1885-1886 he studied in Vienna and Berlin, specializing in diseases of the skin and in microscopy under Virchow and Koch. German pathologist Rudolph Virchow established the basis of cellular pathology through his belief that the source of the disease was within cells; while Richard Koch was the founder of medical bacteriology who proved that TB and anthrax are caused by bacteria.[4] Dr. Wende returned to Buffalo in 1886 and in 1890 was appointed health commissioner by Mayor Bishop. Under Wende's administration the city's death rate fell sharply.

> Formerly records of contagious diseases were made by mail at the convenience of the attending physician: Now all such cases must be reported immediately by telephone. Thereupon the health office, open at all hours day and night, will dispatch a man to inspect the premises, attach placards to the house, and adopt such other sanitary precautions as may be advisable. To guard against the pollution of the city water, daily bacteriological and chemical examinations are made. One of the first results of this system was to close forever an emergency inlet which was formerly used in times of low water, and which sometimes let sewage into the public mains. Over half the wells were found on examination to contain water charged with germ life, and were accordingly filled up. The periodical visitation of the public schools and annual vaccination of the pupils minimizes the danger of epidemics in the schools. All police stations, fire-department quarters, and schoolhouses are minutely inspected at stated intervals to ensure hygienic conditions.
>
> The inspection and purification of the milk supply of Buffalo involved a difficult piece of organization. The banishment of cow barns from thickly peopled districts and the compulsory observance by milk producers of regulations designed to reduce the risks of mothers and children were at last effected: and now a record is kept of every milkman, so that any diseases on his route ascribable to impure milk may lead to investigation and appropriate punishment. Another feature of the Wende administration that abolishes disease by preventing its birth may be found in the system of inspecting supplies of vegetables, meats, and the like, at markets and produce houses. Frozen oranges, rotten

4 *Encyclopedia Americana*, 9:168; 16:558.

> bananas, and other dangerous food have frequently been condemned. Tenement houses, minor hotels, and lodging places are often visited, lest infectious diseases take root and spread undetected. A vast amount of sickness has doubtless been headed off by municipal supervision of plumbing and drainage. No plumbing can now be done unless plans therefore are first filed and approved by experts; and no householder need pay for his plumbing until the completed work is passed upon by inspectors and accepted.[5]

Wende was professor of diseases of the skin at U.B. and of botany and microscopy in the College of Pharmacy. He was health commissioner for two terms, 1891-1901 and 1906 until his death in 1910. His brother, Dr. Grover Wende, and his son David moved into #471 in 1910 and lived there during the 1920s.

Number 475 was the long-time residence, beginning in the 1890s, of John Strootman's family. He was the son of Herman, a Frenchman who had come to Buffalo about 1840 where he became a boot and shoemaker, specializing in footwear for the deformed. He stuck to the old hand-bench methods. In Buffalo he married Katherine Rohr, of a prominent Alsatian family, whose uncle had commanded the personal cavalry guard of Napoleon I. John was born in Buffalo in 1851 and learned his trade from his father for whom he worked until 1872 when he had saved up enough to set himself up in business, employing at first fifteen men. Concentrating on ladies, misses, and children's shoes and selling directly to dealers in half the nation's forty-eight states, he could soon afford a four story factory on Genesee Street with 400 employees. He also became an expert on foot ailments. As nation-wide competition began to erode profits, he invested in two gold and silver mines in Colorado, which proved to be disappointments. A man of splendid physique, six-feet two inches tall, he never married. Sisters and brothers regularly lived with him, but by 1925 his factory had closed and John had retired. In 1931, however, he listed himself at age eighty as engaged in "foot easing."[6]

Number 477 had been built in 1895 by George Kingsley Birge whom Dunn calls "Buffalo's great carmaker." In 1880 George N. Pierce was making bird cages and refrigerators on Hanover Street. In 1891 he moved into bicycles and then cars. At this point Birge and some friends bought into Pierce's business, which in 1890 Birge reorganized and brought in Scottish engineer David Fergusson. Reliance on steam power was abandoned, and in 1900 a gas-powered *Motorette* was placed on the market. Two years later the company was making its own engines and a year after that was selling the fifteen horsepower *Arrow* and the twenty-four horsepower *Great Arrow*. In a fit of pique, Pierce withdrew from management in 1908. Publicity after victory in a 1908 cross-country race caused sales to climb, and in 1909 the company was renamed Pierce-Arrow, with Birge and associates as chief officers. When he retired in 1917 he withdrew half of his shares, which came to to $7,000,000. By this time he had also made a success of the Birge wallpaper company.[7] George Birge did not stay long at #477. By 1897 his brother Henry was living there with his wife and two domestics, and had

5 *Men of New York*, 1:288-289.
6 Hill, *op. cit.*, 3:170-171; *Men of New York*, 1:318-320.
7 Walter Dunn, *op. cit.*, p. 35.

become manager in the family's wallpaper business. He was plagued by ill health and died at forty-five in 1904. He traveled extensively in India and elsewhere in Asia and had amassed a collection of art treasures.[8]

9.4 Mrs. John Miller Horton, Horton, *op. cit.*, 1:407.

Following Henry Birge at #477 were Peter A. Porter, of an old Buffalo family, and in 1905 Mrs. Frances Wolcott. Before 1910 came Mrs. John Miller Horton, *nee* Katharine Lorenz Pratt(9.4), daughter of Pascal Pratt and sister of Samuel Pratt, whose widow had sold #388 Delaware to the Buffalo Club in 1887.

John Horton and his wife were probably more conscious of their alleged ancient and honorable lineage than any other of Buffalo's elite. John told Henry Hill that an ancestor had come to America in the mid-1650s, that the name went back to twelfth century France, and that "many soldiers of the Continental army bore the name of Horton and served with honor and distinction in the struggle for the independence of the Colonies." Horton was born in Mellenville, New York, in 1840. Educated at Claverack High and in Albany, he came to Buffalo in 1862, where in 1869, he married the daughter of an iron monger with a huge plant and smelting furnaces at Black Rock, in which Horton soon rose to junior partner:

> A great lover of books, an eager patron of music and art, he took unbounded delight in the lore and the treasures of the great centers of European culture, where, with his wife, several years were spent in the enjoyment of foreign travel. An expression of his tastes in this regard was his pleasure in and encouragement of his wife's studies in music, while in Europe, under the best vocal masters obtainable, and this at a time when the masters of music in Europe formed a most notable group.[9]

Though twenty-one when Fort Sumter was fired upon and celebrated by Hill as "preeminently a loyal and faithful American," Horton managed like many of his class to avoid military service during the Civil War. He belonged to the Buffalo Club and Trinity Episcopal. In 1902 he died at home at #736 Main Street.[10]

Horton's wife was born in 1842 and vied with her husband in tracing her family back to a lord of the manor in the twelfth century. Before 1910 she acquired #477 Delaware from which she promoted her career as the Daughter *par excellence* of the American Revolution. The Buffalo D.A.R. had been

8 *BEN*, August 5, 1904.
9 Hill, *op. cit.*, 4:362.
10 *Ibid.*

organized in 1892 and Katharine Pratt Horton became its second regent. Horton, who disliked the organization, called it:

> ...the hereditary college of priestesses of the cult of the nation. It commemorated historic events; it set monuments on historic sites, in its solemnities it practiced genuflections to the symbols and trophies of the state. The atmosphere of its social intercourse was the mingled fragrance of bouquets on mahogany tables and of tea poured into fragile china from old silver.[11]

E. Digby Baltzell, a social historian, writes:

> The whole movement [to form associations limited to older immigrants from Northern and Western Europe] was, of course, intimately bound up with anti-immigrant and anti-Semitic sentiments. Thus a leader of the D.A.R. saw a real danger in "our being absorbed by the different nationalities among us," and a president-general of the Sons of the American Revolution reported that: "Not until the state of civilization reached the point where we had a great many foreigners in our land...were our patriotic societies successful." The Daughters of the American Revolution was indeed extremely successful. Founded in 1890, it had 397 chapters in 38 states by 1897. That the anti-immigrant reaction was most prevalent in the urban East, however, was attested to by the fact that the Daughters made slow headway in the West and South and had a vast majority of its chapters in New York and Massachusetts.[12]

The Daughters believed that exposure to the mysteries of the Revolution would Americanize the waves of non-WASP immigrants which had swamped America's cities in the late nineteenth and early twentieth centuries, and never heard of Lexington and Concord or even of Gettysburg. Of her flag-waving, Hill, who seems to have been mesmerized by her, wrote:

> Mrs. Horton is regent of Buffalo Chapter, Daughters of the American Revolution, and under her leadership the chapter has more than trebled its membership, now registering 712 members, which places this chapter in the lead in membership in New York State, and the second largest in the national order. Through Mrs. Horton's leadership the Buffalo Chapter was the pioneer in the national society in the instituting of Americanization as a branch of their work. She has been indefatigable in keeping the interest high in this field. In Buffalo each week during the winter months the chapter gives an illustrated lecture, at a cost of $300, to the present-day pioneers from every country so they can learn citizenship in the "Land of Opportunity." Regular chapter meetings are held each month, where noted speakers discuss current events, and the best artists are employed for the musical program, three to five hundred members and guests usually attending. One instance involving exhaustive research work was the placing of one hundred and thirty bronze markers on graves of Revolutionary patriots, and flowers and flags are placed on each Memorial Day on every soldier grave in Buffalo.[13]

Katharine also enjoyed national notoriety. At the Pan-American Exposition in 1901 she chaired the Reception and Entertainment Women's Committee, presided at the Great Flag Day mass meeting of the Daughters' national society, belonged to the Women's National Board of the Louisiana Purchase Exposition in 1904, was named by the mayor to represent Buffalo at the Panama-Pacific Expo-

11 Horton, *op. cit.*, 1:294.

12 E. Digby Baltzell, "The Social Defenses of the Rich," in *The Private Side of American History*, Thomas R. Frazier, ed., (New York: Harcourt Brace Jovanovich, 1975) pp. 82-83.

13 Hall, *op. cit.*, 4:363.

sition in 1915, served on the reception committee and presented flowers to the Queen of Belgium when she and King Albert visited Buffalo after World War I, and was chairman of the Women's Committee for the Tercentenary Celebration of the Landing of the Pilgrims in 1920. She and John had been well fixed financially and she resided in Europe for ten years, and so was received warmly in European courts. She was a delegate to the Peace Congress at Stockholm and Geneva, and spoke before the noted men of science and representatives of European parliaments assembled to deliberate on establishing world peace. She was chairman of the national committee for the correct use of the American flag of which Mrs. Warren G. Harding was the honorary chairman.[14] After several years of physical and mental decline, Katherine died at her home in 1931. By a will signed in 1929 she had left the bulk of her $400,000 estate ($6,972,000 in 1997 dollars) to a sister, Annie P. Chittenden, and to Frank B. Steele of Washington D.C. who had drawn up the will in which he was named executor. Subscribing witnesses were Ganson Depew and Rev. Charles Stewart, pastor of North Presbyterian. Steele had been associated with his benefactress in D.A.R. business in Washington. Katherine's other surviving sister, Melissa Fryer of #681 Delaware, who was not mentioned in the will, and Pascal P. Jones of #695 Delaware, a nephew who was down for a mere $2,000, hired an attorney, Frank G. Raichle, to argue duress and mental incapacity on the part of the testatrix. Stewart and Depew declared that at the signing, "Mrs. Horton was rational but not mentally normal" and added that she "was not under duress," but they also admitted they were in her presence "only a short time."[15] She also willed #477 to the D.A.R. on condition that the words "Buffalo Chapter" would be changed to "Katherine Pratt Horton Chapter," which was accordingly done.[16]

9.5 ❦ Harlow C. Curtiss, *Deutschtum im Buffalo*, p. 163.

Attorney Harlow C. Curtiss(9.5) was the first resident of #479 where he could be found in 1897 with his wife and a staff of domestics headed up by a butler and a coachman. He was born in Utica in 1858 and when three was brought to Buffalo. There he attended public grammar schools and Central High. After studying law at Trinity College, Hartford, he toured Germany for a year where he acquired a love for the country, its people, and its language.[17] Dr. William Krauss, an expert in mental diseases, had his home and office at #479 in 1905. He died in 1909 in New York just off the boat from an unsuccessful trip to Europe to recover his health.[18] Ten years later, another physician, Theodore Wright, had located there with his family. By 1920, however, the address had become an

14 *Ibid.*
15 *Times*, October 15, 1931; *Courier*, December 17, 1931.
16 *Courier*, December 16, 1931.

9.6 ✥ Pendennis White, *Buffalo Club*, p. 51.

apartment house, with a Scottish immigrant and family superintending the affairs of seven families. Next door north at #481 Dr. Bernard Bartow, a fifty-year old surgeon, lived with his wife and two domestics in 1905. He had been born in Flint, Michigan, in 1858, came to Buffalo as a young man, and graduated as an orthopedic surgeon, one of the first in America, from the medical department of U.B. where he was professor for a time. Chief of orthopedic services at Buffalo General, he loved children and was especially successful in treating them. He had been active in founding Children's Hospital in 1892 and was its first surgeon. By 1915 he had moved up the block to #503 where he died in 1920.[19] His wife, the former Fanny Howe of Boston, was also a founder of Children's and served on its board of directors for forty years. She also organized the Visiting Nurses Association. She died at the Lenox in 1932.[20] Dr. Bartow was succeeded at #481 by a wholesale grocer and later in the 1920s by an insurance agent. By the 1930s the place had become a rooming house.

Albert Wright, the blind broker, had resided at #483 Delaware in 1900 before moving into the Cornell house across the Avenue. His oldest son, Albert B. Wright, would soon become a stockbroker himself and live in 1905 at #503 on the Midway. Albert, the father, was followed at #483 by Pendennis White(9.6), president of the Buffalo Club in 1904:

> White was born in Albany but lived in Buffalo most of his life. He became a top leader in the lumber industry, then at its peak, heading the firm of White, Gratwick and Mitchell. An outstanding personality, he was killed in a traffic accident on Hertel Avenue the night of May 31, 1906, at age 46. Riding in the touring car of his friend, Edwin A. Bell [#430 Delaware], they were returning from the Buffalo Country Club [on the corner of Bailey and Main Street] of which White was a director. Bell was driving west and swerved to pass a west-bound trolley car on the left. Too late, Bell saw an east-bound trolley-car approaching, tried to swerve behind the east-bound car, but not quickly enough. White got the full impact of the trolley which hurled him forty feet. No one else was injured.[21]

The Cyrus Polleys followed the Whites at #483. Cyrus was manager of the Niagara Hotel, treasurer and manger of the Silver Lake Ice Company, and treasurer of Iroquois Salt. After he died his widow and children carried on into the early 1920s when Dr. Carl Tompkins, wife Ruth, and a thirteen-year old daughter replaced them. Since Tompkins had no domestics the house was far from crowded. By 1931 it housed the offices of several doctors.

From its completion in 1893 until 1897 #487 was the home of Rev. Thomas Roberts Slicer, pastor

17 *Buffalo und sein Deutschtum*, (Buffalo: German-American Historical and Biogaphical Society, 1911-1912), p. 163.
18 *Express*, September 26, 1909.
19 *Ibid*, May 30, 1920.
20 *CE*, June 26, 1932.
21 Warren, *op. cit.*, p. 51.

of the First Unitarian Church of Our Father, which from 1880 until 1906 was located on the west side of Delaware below Huron.(5.21) Slicer was born in 1847 in Washington, D.C., son of Rev. Henry Slicer, Methodist minister, presiding elder, and for eight years chaplain of the United States Senate. Thomas attended public schools in Baltimore and Baltimore City College, and graduated D.D. from Brown. He entered the Methodist Episcopal ministry after college and during the next ten years held pastorates in Maryland, Colorado, and New York. Before defecting to the Unitarians in 1881 he was pastor of the Park Congregational Church in Brooklyn. An ardent civil service reformer, he was an ally of George William Curtis, editor of *Harper's Weekly*. At Buffalo, Slicer's congregation contained forty-eight lawyers including Adelbert Moot, John G. Milburn, Ansley Wilcox, and Sherman Rogers. Slicer left Buffalo for All Souls Church in New York where his sermons, usually on social and political questions, were taken down by reporters, and widely circulated. He died in New York in 1916.[22]

9.7 ❦ **Harry Yates, Wilner,*op.cit.*, III, facing 228.**

In 1900 #487 briefly became the home of Harry Yates(9.7), a successful industrialist. Harry was born in Rochester in 1869, son of Arthur G. Yates, who for nineteen years before his death in 1909 was president of the Buffalo, Rochester & Pittsburgh Railway, a north-south Y-shaped soft coal hauler. In fact, he got into railroads by way of coal. Son Harry was educated in the public and private schools of Rochester but gladly put aside his books to join his father in the coal, ice, and railroad business. In 1892 he came to Buffalo as president of the Buffalo Ice Company and after three years was appointed general agent of the Rochester & Pittsburgh Coal & Iron Company, another family firm, a position he held 1895-1907. Next he was vice-president of the Buffalo Union Furnace Company until it was sold in 1920. Before leaving Rochester he married Mary Teresa Duffy, a Catholic girl, whose father owned the Duffy Malt Whiskey Company, and Harry converted to her faith. He belonged to the Buffalo, Country, Park, and Buffalo Athletic clubs, and to the Genesee Valley and the Bankers Club of New York. His avocation was a 3,000-acre dairy and stock farm

9.8 ❦ **Harry Yates home, #1243 Delaware, BHS.**

22 *NYT*, May 30, 1916; *Christian Register*, August 1917.

in Orchard Park which boasted two famed herds — 200 head of Holstein-Friesian and 250 head of Aberdeen Angus. In Orchard Park he had other extensive real estate holdings. By 1905 he had moved up the Avenue to a comfortable but hardly grand home at #1243 Delaware(9.8), where he listed himself as "hotel proprietor," i.e., of the Lafayette. He lived there with his wife and four children and one domestic. Later he moved to the farm in Orchard Park. Yates died in 1956.[23]

Following Yates at #487 by 1925 was Doctor Allen A. Jones, who had been born in 1864, at Maitland, in Ontario. After primary and secondary education in Canada, he came to Buffalo where he graduated from U.B.'s medical department in 1889. He interned at Buffalo General and made further studies in internal medicine in Berlin, Vienna, and Paris. In 1898 he became adjunct professor of medicine at U.B. and rose to full professor, retiring in 1929. He had been secretary of the American Medical Association, 1897-1898, and supervised interns and residents while he was attending physician at Buffalo General and Meyer Memorial. He was president of the American Gastro-Enterological Association 1929-1932, a vestryman at Saint Paul's, and a senior member of Saturn and the Country Club. At his retirement dinner he recounted that the involvement of his family with medicine began with his great grandfather, a surgeon with General John Burgoyne's army. Doctor Jones died in 1950.[24]

T. Guilford Smith, a steel plant manager and the first occupant of #489 in 1893, was born in Philadelphia in 1838. Educated there at Central High and at Rensselaer Polytechnic, he worked as a civil engineer on the Philadelphia & Reading Railroad 1861-1865, was general manager of the Philadelphia Sugar Refinery 1866 -1869, secretary of the Union Iron Company of Buffalo 1873-1878, sales agent for the Philadelphia & Reading Coal and Iron Company 1878-1892, and sales agent for Carnegie Steel from 1889 until his death in 1912. His wife was Mary Ives of Lansingburg, New York.[25] She and their son Chauncy, who had become a doctor, lived at #489 into the 1920s.

The first occupant of #491 was Charles Miller Morse, whose first American ancestor, Samuel Morse, emigrated to New England in 1635. Charles' great grandfather, David Morse, had fought in the Revolution. David's grandson, also called David, came to Buffalo, opened a dry goods store, and died in 1908, having been identified with the Erie County Savings bank for eighteen years.[26] In 1845 David married Elizabeth G. Miller of Buffalo. They had four children, of whom Charles Morse, born in Buffalo in 1854, was the only boy. He attended private schools and Professor Briggs' Classical School and spent two years studying mechanical engineering at Yale's Scientific School. Upon graduation he worked on the survey for the Buffalo & Jamestown Railroad, and for the federal survey of the area along Lakes Erie and Ontario:

23 *HNF*, 3:228-229; *BEN*, December 30, 1939; February 11,1956.
24 Ibid., June 19, 1950
25 *Men of New York*, 1:175-176.
26 *M&FH*, 1:376-377.

> About 1874 he entered the Brooks Locomotive Works at Dunkirk, there serving an apprenticeship in the machinist's trade. He then entered the employ of the Erie Railroad Company in the motive power department at Susquehanna, Pa. Beginning as a journeyman machinist, he became a draughtsman, and later locomotive inspector in charge of repair shop construction work. In 1881 he became Superintendent of the Crown Point Iron Company, at Crown Point, N.Y., and in 1881 located in New York City, where for several years he successfully carried on the private practice of engineering.[27]

In 1889 Morse returned to Buffalo where he married Kathleen Edgar of Easton, Pennsylvania. He opened an office for general engineering in the Erie County Bank Building and rose to Commissioner of the Department of Public Works of the city and head of the Municipal Bureau of Engineering. Death came in 1921.

Morse did not live at #491 long since by 1905 it was the home of Richard B. Lyman, a stock broker, his wife, and two grown children, the youngest of whom became the architect of the Saturn Club at #977 Delaware.[28] The Lymans were there in 1910 but by 1915 they had given way to Doctor Arthur C. Kugel, who was followed in 1925 by Doctor John G. Stowe and family. By the start of the 1930s #491's owners had turned it into a rooming house.

Herman Hayd, a bachelor, resided at #493 from the mid-1890s to the mid-1930s. At his retirement he composed an autobiography of which he had fifty copies printed for his friends:

> It begins with his birth in Brantford, Ont., June 11, 1858 and gives a vivid picture of the life of a small boy of that period, with his battles and business ventures and being indentured for two years with a Brantford dentist. It is this experience that gave him his desire to follow the medical profession.
>
> "I chose to be a doctor, perhaps because of the halo I placed around our family doctors in my small town," Dr. Hayd writes. "They were the chosen friends, guides and counsellors of our people as well as their physicians, because many of them filled positions of trust differently from other men, wore dark clothes, perhaps a frock coat and a top hat. They drove fine horses, in fact for me, a young boy, the practice of medicine had a glorified future."
>
> And so young Hayd entered McGill University and upon graduation went to London "to walk" the big hospitals. His experiences in London and later in Vienna, where he saw the great medical men of that early day in action, make highly interesting reading to the layman as well as to the professional man. Lister and his work in antiseptics were just beginning to revolutionize the practice of surgery. After study in Vienna, Dr. Hayd returned to London and took up "locum tenens" work, which consisted of taking care of a doctor's practice while he was on a holiday. This gave him the first actual experience on his own.
>
> It was during Christmas week in 1882 that Dr. Hayd came to Buffalo armed with letters of introduction to Dr. Miles [read Bradley] Goodyear, father of the late Charles W. and Frank H. Goodyear, and he hung out his first shingle at 9 Niagara street. One of his early experiences was caring for those injured in the Hotel Richmond fire.

27 *Ibid.*, 379-380.
28 *Forty Years*, p.103

Running throughout Dr. Hayd's story of his early days in Buffalo are names of men and women who contributed much to the business and social life. He writes happily of the first horses he acquired and of his first White steamer. The ownership of horses and automobiles overlapped only a short time, for, as he writes: "after a few years the automobile was a very common vehicle and the streets were very slippery when it rained and from the oil that leaked out of the machines my sure-footed animal slipped on the pavement and fell and I with him. I was not hurt, nor was he, but I gave up riding.

In 1891 he went again to Europe for more study and attended the clinics of Paris and Berlin. Upon returning to Buffalo he joined the staff of Deaconesses Hospital, where he served brilliantly for many years.

Much of the volume is devoted to descriptions of his travels to all the countries of Europe and the Near East, to South America and the Pacific islands. "When I was 70 years of age," writes Dr. Hayd in closing, "I ended a very busy career and at a time when I think I was able to do my best work, with good eyesight, a wide experience, excellent judgment and steady hands. No doubt I could have carried on with a large following, but I was satisfied. I had labored long enough and had given about all that was expected of me to my profession and I desired leisure and time to read other literature than medicine and surgery and wanted opportunities for travel."

"However, I continued to keep an office hour and those who consulted me and needed surgical attention I sent to other surgeons whom I thought were best qualified to care for them. Now, when I look in retrospect, I can truthfully say I loved the practice of my profession and in measure satisfied my ambitions. I gladly gave up my operative work to the young men who were starting where we men left off and who, because of our labors, were better able to continue the beneficent practice of surgery and with the improvements and special instruments which science and the arts have provided, a better understanding will be made possible to find the causes, the signs and the symptoms of disease and its successful treatment."[29]

Doctor Hayd died at #493 in March 1944.

William C. Cornwell, president of The City Bank, which had been organized in 1893, had lived in East Aurora in 1897, but by 1900 found it more convenient to move to #497 Delaware. Five years later it was the home of Charles J. Spaulding, manager of the Lafayette. In 1912 it became the home of sixty-two year old Walter Gaston who had come to Buffalo as head of the Electric Furnace Company. He had been born in Somerville, New Jersey, in 1850 and graduated from Princeton in 1872. Fresh from college, he went to work for the Taylor Iron & Steel Company, Highbridge, New Jersey, and became general manager of the Hazard Wire Rope Company of Wilkes-Barre, Pennsylvania. Ten years later he went with the Manganese Steel Safe Company in New York and stayed there until 1912 when he formed his own plant and furnaces, manufacturing ferro-silicon, which he later merged with Union Carbide. In 1922 he retired to fishing and travel by which time he resided at #1125 Delaware. He died there in 1927.[30] Stella Lowrey and her sister Lilly followed Gaston at #497 and Stella was still there in 1935.

29 *CE*, November 30, 1941.
30 *BEN*, October 3, 1927

9.9 ❦ Number 499 and Midway houses to the south, author's collection.

The northernmost house on the Midway was #499(9.9), the residence from 1893 until the end of the century of Bryant B. Glenny, son of William Glenny, founder and proprietor of a wholesale and retail crockery and glassware store on Main Street. From at least 1900 it was the home of Jacob Frederick Schoellkopf, II, until the early 1920s. Thereafter it became briefly the residence of an artist and some relatives and after that during the 1930s of Mrs. Lucy S. Wright. The first three generations of the Schoellkopf family were immensely influential in the economic development of Western New York, and four of them maintained homes on the Avenue, three on the east side of this block between Virginia and Allen.(9.10) The patriarch of the Buffalo Schoellkopfs was Jacob Frederick(9.11), born in Kirchheim unter Teck, Wurttemberg, in 1819. His father and grandfather had been tanners, so, at age fourteen, after attending local schools, the boy was apprenticed to his father for five years, during which he learned the family trade. There followed two years at a mercantile house in Stuttgart after which he emigrated to America, realizing that as a younger son he could never inherit the family business. In 1841 at twenty-two he arrived in New York where he worked for two years and learned English. With an $800 loan from his father he came to Buffalo in 1844 and opened a leather store on Mohawk Street. That year he bought a tannery at White's Corners in Hamburg and in 1846 opened another for sheepskins in Buffalo. In 1848 he became interested in a tannery in Milwaukee and in 1850 in another in Chicago which he operated until 1856. In 1853 he built a tannery in North Evans and ran it for twenty years.[31]

```
Jacob Frederick Schoellkopf  I #553
11/15/1819-9/15/1899
Germany     Buffalo
Sophie Christiane Duerr 1848
12/2/1827-10/13/1903

     Henry Schoellkopf
     12/22/1848-2/27/1880
     Buffalo    Jacksonville Fla.
     Emily Vogel 1874

     Louis Schoellkopf
     3/25/1855-7/21/1901
     Buffalo   Buffalo
     Myra Horton 5/18/1881

     Arthur Schoellkopf
     6/13/1856-1913
     Buffalo  Florida
     Jessie Gluck 10/13/1880
     4/19/1856-5/11/1928
     Niagara Falls  New York

     Jacob F. Schoellkopf II #499
     2/27/1858-9/9/1942
     Buffalo   Lakeview
     Wilma Spring 1882
     4/1/1882-9/16/1938
     Stuttgart  Lakeview

     Alfred P. Schoellkopf #537
     7/1/1860-10/12/1901
     Buffalo    Buffalo
     Emily R. Graebe 4/12/1894
     3/15/1869-3/15/1951
     Rochester   Buffalo

          William Graebe Schoellkopf #1275
          10/9/1896-12/27/1977
          Niagara Falls
          Elizabeth Peabody 10/10/1922
          3/14/1901-
          Niagara Falls

     Carl Phillip Hugo Schoellkopf
     7/6/1862-2/24/1928
     Buffalo  New York City
     (1)Emily F. Annette 9/18/1890
     (2)Irene

     Helen Schoellkopf #553
     1870-6/3/1962
     Buffalo  Buffalo
     Hans Schmidt 2/1/1893
     1865-12/29/1930
     Hanover   Derby
```

9.10 ❦ Delaware Avenue Schoellkopfs.

Looking for new fields to conquer, he turned to milling. In 1857 he built the North Buffalo Flouring Mills, in 1871 he purchased the Frontier Mills, and two years later he built large flouring mills and a brewery at Niagara Falls. He knew nothing about milling but relied on George B. Mathews(9.12) who had been in the business for a decade. "The story of Mr.

31 *M&FH*, 1:127; Horton, *op. cit.*, 3:66-67.

9.11 Jacob Frederick Schoellkopf I, *M&FH*, I, facing p. 127.

Mathews' career is the story of milling in the United States over a fifty-year period," writes Horton. "It is, incidentally, the story of Buffalo's growth and advancement as an industrial city." Mathews, later master of an elegant mansion at #830 Delaware, was born in Almond, Allegany County in 1847. After grammar school he had intended to enter college but with the outbreak of the Civil War became a clerk in the provost marshal's office. After the war he accepted an employment offer from the management of a flour milling company in Elmira. Milling and selling flour were then local industries. Mathews led the movement for change. Rochester, the Flour City, on the Falls of the Genesee had been the milling center of the nation, but Mathews preferred Buffalo which was at the end of wheat shipments then moving down the Lakes in millions of bushels a year. In 1870 he got a job in the office of L. Enos & Company where he learned the commercial side of the business. When the Thornton & Chester Milling Company decided to abandon its Frontier Mill, Mathews persuaded Jacob F. Schoellkopf to take it over. The result was encouraging and operations soon extended beyond the Queen City:

> In 1877 Mr. Schoellkopf took over the bankrupt power development at Niagara Falls, and at that juncture convinced Mr. Mathews of the feasibility of building a 1,000 barrel [a day] flour mill along the Schoellkopf Canal. The new mill made a consistent profit thereafter except during the first year. It was not long until Schoellkopf and Mathews developed the greatest capacity to be found in any mill in this area and successfully met Minneapolis competition. By the end of the nineteenth century the firm controlled a capacity of about 4,000 barrels daily, doing a particularly large business in New England.[32]

9.12 George Brewster Mathews, Horton, *op. cit.*, III, facing p. 92.

Schoellkopf was in demand as director of large corporations in which he had invested. He was vice-president of the Buffalo, New York & Philadelphia Railroad and of the Third National Bank of Buffalo, a director of White's Bank, the German-American Bank, and of other financial institutions in Buffalo and Niagara Falls. He was director and president of the Citizens Gas Company and a trustee of Buffalo General.

In 1848 he had married a girl from Stuttgart, Christiana

32 Horton, *ibid.* pp. 92-93.
33 *M&FH*, 1:127-130

9. 13 ❦ Jacob F. Schoellkopf home, #553 Delaware, BHS. Note gaslight.

Duerr, who had come to America a year before her future husband. They had six sons and one daughter, all born in Buffalo, who reached adulthood: Henry, born in 1848; Louis, born in 1855; Arthur, born in 1856; Jacob Frederick, born in 1858; Alfred P., born in 1860; Carl Phillip Hugo, born in 1862; and Helen, born in 1870. Four died in infancy.[33] In the 1850s the family lived at #137 (old style) Ellicott; in the late 1860s and 1870s at #486 Franklin on the southwest corner of that street and Allen; by 1882 they had reached #553 Delaware on the southeast corner of Allen. Number 553 was a gingerbread house, extending deep along Allen.(9.13) Here the Schoellkopfs entertained lavishly.

Henry, the eldest of Jacob's sons, attended local schools and then started a family tradition of study in Germany but left early and came home to work with his father. In 1870 father and son formed the tanning firm of J. F. Schoellkopf & Son. Seven years later Henry and brother Louis struck out on their own as J. F. Schoellkopf's Sons, which lasted until Henry's death in 1880, in Florida. In 1874 he had married Emily Vogel. Their daughter Elsie married Karl Von Rumohr, an officer in the German Army, stationed in Schwerin, and moved there with him.[34]

Until he was ten Louis attended local private schools. Then he went to Germany for four years of study. Back in Buffalo, he had private tutors, Saint Joseph's Institute, and practical training at Bryant & Stratton Business College. After Henry died, Louis and brother Alfred reorganized the tanning firm. In 1881 Louis married Myra Horton. Their son Walter entered the diplomatic service. Louis belonged to the Ellicott and Westminster clubs, and the Orpheus Singing Society. He and Myra attended Westminster. He died at #48 Oakland Place in 1901.[35]

It was Arthur, Jacob' s third son(9.14), who assisted his father in adding electric power to the family's tanning and milling operations. He had undergone an education almost identical to that of his older brother Louis — local private schools, four years in Germany, Saint Joseph's Institute, and a course at Bryant and Stratton's. With book learning behind him, he started to work at the mills owned by Thornton & Chester but later by Schoellkopf & Mathews, and in 1877 became part owner of the Niagara Flouring Mills. Next year he and his father organized the Niagara Falls Hydraulic Power and Manufacturing Company to develop the Hydraulic Canal and to furnish waterpower for the area mills. The establishment of this company began the development of Niagara Falls as a center

34 *Ibid.*, 131-132.
35 *Ibid.*, 132-134.
36 Horton, *op. cit.*, 3:67.

of electric power production. Arthur was president of the Power City Bank, a director of the Bank of Niagara, president of the Cliff Paper Company, and in March 1896 mayor of Niagara Falls. He was active in the Masons and the Elks, belonged to the Ellicott Club, and was a member and trustee of First Presbyterian of Niagara Falls. He married Jessie Gluck of Niagara Falls in 1880 and died in 1913. His interests at the Falls were carried on by his son, Paul Arthur Schoelkopf, who graduated from Cornell in 1906:

> He at once engaged in business with his father in manufacturing enterprises, and became connected with his various interests, hydraulic and electric power, paper manufacturing, flour milling, proving himself a master of each and in all displaying the abilities of the real operator and practical business manager, and is now accounted among the men of large affairs in the city.[36]

9. 14 Arthur Schoellkopf, *Town Tidings*, March, 1931.

Paul Arthur Schoellkopf died at Lewiston Heights in 1947.

The fourth son(9.15) of Jacob F. Schoellkopf, named after his father, attended the local public schools and Saint Joseph's, and then went for seven years of study at Munich and at Stuttgart where he specialized in chemistry, graduating from the Polytechnic College there in 1880. His return to Buffalo was different from that of his brethren:

> His chemical studies had directed his attention to the subject of coal tar dyes, and he had arrived at the conclusion that the American market offered a great field for these products. The outcome was the establishment [in 1880] of the Schoellkopf Aniline and Chemical works, which were founded by Mr. Schoellkopf shortly after his return to Buffalo and which constitute the most extensive plant of the kind on the continent, the business being operated by the Schoellkopf, Hartford & Hanna Company, of which Mr. Schoellkopf is President. The enterprise has $3,000,000 capital, employs 350 men and pays $15,000 monthly in wages. The plant embraces about thirty-six acres of land, including thirty brick buildings. It has superb shipping facilities and possesses unequaled special equipment.[37]

In 1918 Schoellkopf Aniline merged with National Aniline and Jacob later retired, regarded by many as the founder of the aniline color industry in the nation. Mark Goldman writes:

> Not only the German institutions but individuals too were able to thrive during the [First World] War. Some profited enormously. Prior to 1914 most of the coal tar dyes used in America were imported from Germany. Following the Allied blockade of Germany, Americans began to turn to domestic dye makers. None benefited more from this turn of events then the Schoellkopf's National Aniline and Chemical Company. National Aniline got even bigger during the war as coal dyes were used increasingly for the manufacture of high explosives and poison gases.[38]

It was also in 1900 that Jacob became connected with the family's Hydraulic Power Company in

37 *M&FH*, 1:137.
38 Mark Goldman, *op. cit.*, p. 200.
39 *Ibid.*, 1:136-138; *Buffalo Times*, October 10, 1924;

Above 9.15 ❦ Jacob F. Schoellkopf II, *M&FH*, I, facing p. 136.
Below 9.16 ❦ Alfred P. Schoellkopf II, *M&FH*, I, facing p. 138.

Niagara Falls, which merged in 1917 with the Niagara Falls Power Company, then considered by the *Buffalo Times* "the largest hydro-electric power company in the world." In a fourth change of business base by the family, Jacob became president of Schoellkopf, Hutton and Pomeroy, a brokerage firm on Niagara Square. His clubs were Buffalo, B.A.C., and Wanakah. This Jacob F. Schoellkopf, who had previously resided at the old family home on #486 Franklin, removed to #499 Delaware in the late 1890s where he remained until the early 1920s. In 1882 he had married Wilma Spring of Stuttgart, whom he had met while studying in the Fatherland. By 1905 his menage consisted in himself, his wife, twenty-four year old son Frederick working at the family tannery, Jacob, age twenty-two, at Cornell, and Ruth and Esther, daughters aged five and three respectively. That year there were no live-in servants. Jacob Schoellkopf, II, died at his estate on the Lake Shore Road in 1942.[39] His only son, Jacob F. Schoellkopf, III, graduated from Cornell, after which he attended the University of Strasburg where he obtained a doctorate in chemistry. Returning home, he became secretary of Schoellkopf Aniline and benefited from the growth of that industry in America during the First World War. When Schoellkopf was merged into National Aniline, he became vice-president, which he remained until the fall of 1919 when he became vice-president of Schoellkopf, Hutton & Pomeroy, his father's brokerage. In 1907 Jacob, III, married Olive Abbott of Corning.[40] He died in 1952.

The fifth son of Jacob F. Schoellkopf, I, and third of his family to own a home on Delaware was Alfred P.(9.16) Educated at local public schools and Saint Joseph's, he married Emily Graebe in 1894 and was associated with his father in his sheepskin tannery on Mississippi Street. He was a director of the Niagara Falls Hydraulic Power and Manufacturing Company. He resided at #537 Delaware(9.17), next to his father, and died at forty-one in 1901,

40 *Town Tidings*, August 1931.

leaving three children, Lucy, Emily, and William. Widow Emily lived on until at least 1920 in this large house.

9.17 ❦ Numbers 531, 537, and 553 Delaware Avenue, BHS. The sign in the window of #531 reads, "Automobile: Home Office, Exchange Mutual Insurance Company." The Avenue has yet to be widened at this point.

The youngest male of the second generation Schoellkopfs was Hugo.(9.18) He was educated in the grammar and public schools of Buffalo and in 1877 went to Germany to study chemistry at Stuttgart and Berlin. Returning to Buffalo he joined his father in the aniline end of the family enterprises and for years was the leading figure in the aniline dye industry. He was also vice-chairman of the Niagara Falls Power Company, later the Buffalo Niagara & Eastern Power Company, and of Marine Trust. He belonged to the Niagara Falls Country Club, the Country Club of Buffalo, the Buffalo Club, the Masons, and the Elks. In 1890 he married Emily F. Annette of Fort Lee, New Jersey, by whom he had one son, Alfred Hugo, born in 1893. The Hugo Schoellkopfs resided at West Ferry Street.

Emily Annette Scholellkopf died young, and it was through Hugo's second wife, a flapper, that notoriety descended upon the staid family. Shortly after the stock market crash which ended the Roaring Twenties, in which as F. Scott Fitzgerald had written, "a new generation had grown up which found all Gods dead, all wars fought, all faiths in man shaken,"[41] this item appeared in the *Buffalo Times*:

> Barrie Carman, one time jester to the court of King Broadway is dead. Death overtook the dashing dancing master, artist and former escort — and for a brief time, husband — of the wealthy Irene Schoellkopf, last Saturday in South Carolina as he was on his way to Florida's winter resorts. He died from an acute heart attack. He was 37.
>
> In the days when Carman catered to the whims of the excitement craving Broadway playboys with his acting, painting and clowning, and [as] a professional dancer, his companionship was much in demand by the ladies. Mrs. Schoellkopf, then the wife of a Buffalo millionaire, first met Carman in one of these gay circles. They met at a tea dance and Mrs. Schoellkopf decided that Carmen would make an ideal companion. With her husband's consent, she engaged him as her escort to enable her to follow the noisy pursuit of the [Great] White Way. Bedecked with half [a] million dollars worth of jewels, Mrs. Schoellkopf and Carman soon became familiar figures, together at the night clubs and cabarets. Schoellkopf, as per agreement, was paying all of the bills.
>
> Carman gave a New Year's party for Mrs. Schoellkopf at his apartment in 1923. There was a fight and Mrs. Schoellkopf rushed into the hallway, only to be seized by three men, dragged into another apartment and robbed of $300,000 worth of gems. Carman was

41 F. Scott Fitzgerald, *This Side of Paradise*, (New York: Charles Scribner's Sons, 1920), p. 282.

9.18 Hugo Schoellkopf, *Town Tidings*, *ibid.*

accused of complicity in the robbery by police, but Mrs. Schoellkopf and her husband firmly asserted their belief that he was innocent and he was released.

The two traveled together in Europe, first with Mr. Schoellkopf but later alone when the husband was called home on business. Then the Schoellkopfs separated and were divorced in Paris in 1926. Mrs. Schoellkopf and Carman were then secretly married in Honolulu in 1927. Their wedding bliss lasted only four months, however, and they seperated [*sic*] in an argument over a payment of part of a $100,000 nuptial gift the bride was to make to her husband.

They were divorced in Chicago the same year that Barrie Carmen became less prominent on Broadway. He took up oil panting for a while but then turned to his old life, dancing for a livelihood. Mrs. Schoellkopf's stolen jewels were nearly all returned to her. John W. Mahan, who bought the gems for $40,000, became afflicted with paralysis and believed the illness was the result of a course [*sic*] on the gems. A part of the jewels were [*sic*] found in a fruit jar in Denver, and Mahan aided police in recovering the remainder of them before he died.[42]

Irene visited the funeral home on Broadway where Carman was waked and draped his casket with a blanket of white carnations and a card inscribed "Irene." Hugo had died two years before in the Lenox Hill Hospital in New York. Irene visited him on his deathbed and they were reconciled. His funeral was conducted by Rev. Samuel Holmes of Westminster. The bulk of his estate, estimated at $10,000,000, was left to his only son.[43]

The patriarch of the clan Schoellkopf died at #553 in 1899. With her daughter Helen, his widow Christiana continued there until her death in October 1903. Helen had married Hans Schmidt and with their three children stayed on at #553 until 1918 when they moved to a grand estate in Derby on Lake Erie. Hans was born in Hanover, Germany, in 1865. At seventeen he came to Buffalo and became a salesman for J. F. Schoellkopf & Company. In 1891 he was made partner, in 1893 he married the boss' daughter, and in 1901 he became president. Hans loved music, played the cello, and was president of the Buffalo Philharmonic Society. He was also active in the electric power industry as director of the Niagara Falls Power Company. In 1925 he was elected to the first board of directors of the Buffalo Niagara & Eastern Power Company. A member of Westminster, he died in 1930 at Derby. The estate was sold to the Saint Columban Layman's Retreat League in 1947. Helen moved to the Westbrook and died at the Niagara Lutheran Home on Hager Street in 1962 at ninety-two.[44]

42 *Times*, January 14, 1930.
43 *CE*, January 15, 1930; *BEN*, February 24, 1928; *Syracuse Post-Standard*, February 25, 1928.
44 *Times*, December 29, 1930.

At #531 was the home since the 1890s of another stalwart Buffalo German, Leonhardt Burgweger, president of the Iroquois Brewing Company. Across the Avenue at #534 lived ex-Mayor Philip Becker and later his widow Sarah. During the 1920s #553 served as a rooming house for as many as twenty-nine lodgers. In the 1930s it was known as the Stratford Hotel.

Midway houses ended at #499. Above that houses were numbered from #501 to #553 at the intersection of Allen Street. Residing at #501 from 1894 until his death at age fifty-nine in 1901, was John Gordon, who throughout his life was involved with transportation. At age eighteen he went to work for the Michigan Central in his hometown, Detroit. Seven years later, he turned to the Great Lakes and was a purser for the Ward Line. In 1868 he went on his own and bought three boats, all of which were lost within a year, so he returned to the Ward Line and served as its agent at Duluth at the head of the Lakes. Another stint on his own proved unsuccessful, so, still at Duluth, he hired on as agent for the Lake Superior Transit Company. He soon moved to Chicago where he became agent for the Anchor Line, but in 1889 came to Buffalo and put together the Northern Steamship Company which he seems to have renamed the Union Transfer Company, which he sold in 1896 to organize a Chicago-Buffalo line of passenger ships. He died without succeeding in his last venture.[45] During his last year on earth he lived with his wife Elizabeth, one son, and two young Irish female domestics.

After Gordon's death #501 became the home of John H. Porter, vice-president of Buffalo Steel. He was succeeded *circa* 1915 by Stephen Yates Howell, M.D., once president of the Buffalo Academy of Medicine and a Fellow of the Royal College of Physicians and Surgeons in London. In the early 1920s the house was the "splendid parsonage" the Delaware Avenue Methodist Church purchased for its, Pastor Bruce S. Wright.(9.19)

9.19 ❦ Rev. Bruce S. Wright, *Wilner*, III, facing p. 198.
9.20 ❦ Henry Montgomery Gerrans, *Municipality of Buffalo*, III, facing p. 150.

45 *Express*, January 13, 1901.

Wright was born at Eldred, Pennsylvania, in 1879, and was taken by his parents when two years old to Jamestown where he attended public schools and later was employed by the Jamestown Worsted Mills for two years. He then entered the preparatory department of Allegheny College at Meadville, Pennsylvania, and graduated from the college proper with a B.A. in 1905. Meanwhile, having decided on the ministry, he preached during his college years. Ordained by authority of the Erie Conference of the Methodist Episcopal Church in September 1905, he served as pastor at Fredonia, New York, Erie, Pennsylvania, and Manila in the Philippines. After two years at Trinity Church in Albany, he was called by Asbury-Delaware Methodist Episcopal on Delaware and Tupper in the fall of 1920. Author of nine volumes on religious subjects, he was also active socially, as a Mason, a member of the Buffalo Club, the Y.M.C.A., and the Buffalo Society of Natural Sciences. In 1907 he married Margarette Armstrong, a native of Sligo, Pennsylvania, who became socially active in Buffalo where she was president of the Erie County League of Women Voters. In 1931 the Wrights had two daughters at Goucher in Baltimore and a son at Nichols. By then they had moved to #80 West Tupper Street and also had a twenty-acre summer home, Wright Wood, near Kane, Pennsylvania. Wright died in November 1942.[46]

Edwin Fleming, a journalist who came to Buffalo in 1897 in advance of the 1901 Pan-American Exposition, resided at #503. After Fleming came Albert Wright, a stockbroker, and son of Albert J. Wright, the blind stockbroker, who at the time was living across the Avenue at #484 but was soon to move up to #512 Delaware. Next door to Wright at #503 was Bernard Bartow, M.D., mentioned above as residing at #481. He died in 1920, but his wife lived on there until at least 1926.

Houselots from #511 north were located above the Cornell White Lead Company land. During the 1860s #511 was the site of Cornelius Coopers' Marble Works. In 1880 James Noonan, a native of England and a boathouse owner, presided over an entourage of ten people. In 1891 Joseph C. Monroe of the Buffalo Arms Company lived there. During the late 1890s and the first decade of the twentieth century it was the home of one of Buffalo's most colorful personalities, Henry Montgomery Gerrans(9.20), whose power base for thirty-four years was the Iroquois Hotel on Lafayette Square(9.21), "the focal point of the city's social and political interests and of its outstanding visitors in every field."

Gerrans was born in 1853 at Dunkirk, the son of James Gerrans, a hotelier who had also operated hostelries in Detroit and in Akron, Ohio. After attending public schools, he left home and came to Buffalo, where he got a job as clerk with the Erie Railroad at $30 a month. By twenty he was cashier and chief clerk at $3,200 a year. In 1875 he signed contract to supply rails for the Northern Pacific Railroad, America's second transcontinental. The manager of the Buffalo branch of a stock broker-

46 *HNF*, 3:198-199; *Times*, December 29, 1930.

9.21 ❦ The Iroquois Hotel, Lafayette Square, 1889-1923. Author's collection.

age, sensing the young man's abilities, persuaded him to enter the same business. He joined the manager's office in 1883 and, as he often said, "made a little money and lost a little more." Foreseeing the demise of kerosene lamps and expecting a demand for gas for both heat and light, in 1884 he became a salesman traveling across the Northeast for Seaman's Gas Burners. The owner of a Boston hotel bought one, which was installed improperly and nearly burned down the ballroom. Chastened by this fiasco, Gerrans returned to Buffalo, in 1885 married Maude Murray whom he had won away from a prominent lawyer, and entered a new field, coal, becoming a salesman for the firm of Bell, Lewis & Yates. His luck changed and he was very successful — but very bored — and when opportunity knocked he answered. The Buffalo Public Library was erecting a new hotel, the Iroquois, to replace the Hotel Richmond, which had burned down one night in 1887. Hotel revenues supported the library. One of the finest hotels in the nation, the supposedly fireproof Iroquois opened on August 3, 1889. With his friend, William E. Woolley, Gerrans formed a company, of which he was secretary-treasurer, which leased the hotel from the library. Monty's experience, personality, and affability made the venture a success from the start. He ran his kitchen with an iron but epicurean hand, turning up every morning at 5:00 A.M. to select fresh vegetables. He charmed locals and visiting celebrities alike, including "Gentleman Jim" Corbett, E. H. Sothern, Julia Marlowe, John Drew, and George M. Cohan. To many out-of-towners Buffalo meant "Monty" Gerrans. A business partner of Colonel William ("Wild Bill") Cody in building a failed irrigation canal near Cody in northwestern Wyoming, he continued for years to maintain a hunting lodge there and, in partnership with George Bleistein of #438 Delaware and Bert Rumsey, a trading post. In his salad days he played golf in the eighties, was the epitome of physical fitness, and served as steward at Saratoga and Fort Erie. He was also on the board of directors of Hialeah, though he never owned a horse or bet on a horse race. Socially Gerrans was one of the city's best-known men. He was a member of the Buffalo, Country, Park, and Saturn clubs, and was a 32nd degree Mason. An all-night poker player, he would walk away from a table without collecting his winnings. He was no wet but no drunk either. He smoked the strongest cigars, one of which he always had in hand, seldom shaved himself, doted on loud red neckties, usually sported brown or gray suits with a soft hat to match, which he wore with the brim snapped down. He was a close family man and saw to it that his three daughters received the best education available in America and Europe. Though he and E. M. Statler were competitors, they were great friends. With his new caravansary on Niagara Square under construction, Statler convinced Monty to close down the Iroquois. Statler purchased it in 1923 and turned it into an office building which in 1927 he renamed the Gerrans Building. Gerrans retired from the hotel business — for a while — and functioned as vice-president of a realty company. His beloved wife died in 1924. Thereafter he frequently visited his married daughters in Rye, New York, and South Carolina, usually by air. In 1926 the owner of the Hotel Touraine persuaded Gerrans to become manager and president of the hotel. He moved into the Touraine and died there at age eighty-six in 1939.[47]

9.22 ❦ William Laverack. author's collection.

An actress, Adele Blood, was living at #503 in 1915. She was followed in the 1920s by Henry P. Burgard, eponym of Burgard Vocational High School on Kensington. The son of Peter Rinck Burgard, Henry was born in the Walden-Bailey district of Buffalo and educated at public schools and Central High. He began his career as an insurance agent but switched to construction, building South Park Avenue from the city line to Hamburg and miles of sidewalks within city limits. During the creation of the New York State Barge Canal he built the twelve mile stretch between Oswego and Fulton which involved constructing locks, floodgates, and two dams. He donated five and a half acres on Kensington east of Fillmore for a vocational school, which explains his claim to local immortality. He died in 1933.[48]

9.23 ❦ George E. Laverack, *M&FH*, I, 193.

William Laverack(9.22) of #212 Delaware, was an English immigrant. He married Mary Radcliffe. Their son, George Edward Laverack(9.23), a long-time resident at #523, was born in 1845:

> In 1864, when only nineteen, he became his father's partner in the wholesale drug and grocery trade. He remained continuously with his father until the latter's death, and for several years had practically the entire charge of the business. On the death of the elder Mr. Laverack in 1888, George E. Laverack bought the interest of J. L. Hunsicker as well as that of the Laverack estate, and became sole proprietor, and conducted the business until 1900. During the years of his control he

47 *BEN*, May 15, 1939; *Times*, May 14, 1939.
48 *The Craftsman*, June, 1933. The Burgard yearbook.
49 *M&FH*, 1:193-194.

9.24 ❦ Number 525 Delaware, author's collection.

developed the business greatly, making it one of the largest houses in its line between New York and Chicago, being known throughout New York State, the Middle West and Pennsylvania.[49]

George lived at #519 in the 1870s and died there in 1924. He was a member of the Chamber of Commerce and of its predecessor, the Merchants' Exchange, the Buffalo Historical Society, the Fine Arts, the Society of Natural Sciences, and the Buffalo Club. He was one of the founders of the Country Club and its president for three years. He was married to Mary Rumrill and had two sons and three daughters.[50]

Number 523 was occupied by Henry G. White, a house and boat painter, in 1872. Living there in 1880 was Frederic W. Bartlett, M.D., and his two sons. Bartlett, a *Mayflower* descendant, had been born in Kingston, Massachusetts in 1826. He attended Bridgewater Normal School, was principal of Lafayette Academy in Georgia, practiced journalism in Georgia and Massachusetts, and graduated from the New York Medical College in 1854. That year he married Adelea Hunter, daughter of Dr. James H. Hunter, a promoter of legislative reform in Upper Canada 1837-1838. Bartlett came to Buffalo in 1855 where he practiced medicine at #523 until his death in 1897. His son was George Hunter Bartlett of #1083 Delaware.[51]

Following Bartlett at #523 was Doctor Edgar G. Starr, professor of opthalmology at U.B. and pioneer in the use of X-ray and other medical photographic methods for dealing with diseases of the eye. He took the first photograph of the back and other interior portions of the eye and was among the first to obain successful x-ray photographs through opaque objects. He left #523 in the late 1920s and moved to Pasadena where he died in 1938.[52]

Number 525 was tall rectangular brick structure(9.24) built in the late 1890s for Doctor James Wright Putnam, a nationally known neurologist and psychiatrist.(9.25) Born in Fredonia in 1860, son of James Osborne Putnam, an American (Know-Nothing) Party state senator 1854-1855, Lincoln elector, and consul at Le Havre, France, 1861-1865.

9.25 ❦ James Wright Putnam, *Men of Buffalo*, p. 388.

50 *BEN*, March 3, 1924.
51 *Men of New York*, 2:11D.

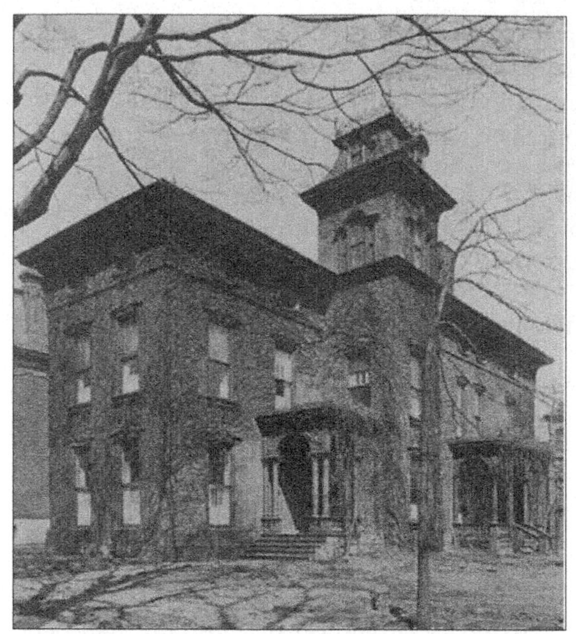
9.26 Number 567 Delaware, *PBHS*, 26(1922), np.

James spent his early years there and returned to Buffalo speaking only French. He soon picked up English, attended public schools and Central High, and graduated M.D. from U.B. in 1882. Meanwhile his father was serving as minister to Belgium by appointment from President Hayes, and on his return became chancellor of U.B., an honorific post. The son, Doctor Putnam, practiced in Buffalo for a time and went back to Europe for graduate study at Berlin, Vienna, Paris, and London. In 1889 on his return from Europe he married Caroline Moore Graves and began a thirty-year teaching association with U.B. He wrote books on neurology and psychology and was neurologist at the United States Marine, City, General, and Erie County hospitals. During World War I he was surgeon in the Army Medical Corps. Afterwards, he became neuro-psychologist at the United States Public Health Service and consultant at Providence Retreat. He was still resident at #525 in 1931. On the social side, he was one of the thirteen charter members of Saturn Club. He died in 1938 at age seventy-eight.[53]

The first house on Delaware north above Allen was #567. It faced Allen, and its grounds stretched to Franklin.(9.26). It was built in 1869 by William Huntington Peabody, a Connecticut-born druggist. Peabodys lived here for fifty-four years until 1923. William H. Peabody, Jr., grew up here, became an attorney, and died in 1927 at sixty-two. His brother Charles and his French-born wife, Henrietta Oldmixon, also lived here for some years with their two children. Charles had been born in Buffalo in 1877, attended Nichols, and in 1923 formed a realty company in partnership with William G. Schoellkopf.[54] The elder William Peabody's widow lived here after her husband died in 1898 at sixty-two. She died in 1923, after which the big house was demolished to make way for the Avenue Apartments.

9.27 Number 581 Delaware, photo by author, 1999.

Above #567 there lived during the 1880s Oliver Swift, a Massachusetts-born hardware manufacturer,

52 *CE*, April 11, 1931.
53 Smith, *op. cit.*, 2:68; *CE*, March 24, 1938.

9.28 ❦ Number 591 Delaware, photo by author, 1999.

his wife Lucy, their son Frank, and the usual complement of domestics, until at least 1910. There followed in succession the families of three doctors, Lee M. Francis, Albert E. Woenhnert, and Theodore Wright, all of whom were abundantly supplied with domestics.

Like many earlier houses on the Avenue #581 was a square box-like structure two and a half stories high topped with a captain's walk, a New England import.(9.27) Myron Crittenden, a grain dealer, lived there in the 1880s, followed through the 1890s by Julius Altman, brother of Abraham Altman of #526 Delaware. John C. Nagel resided at #581 1900-1901 after which he disappears from the records. Frank Hinkel, M.D., followed from 1905 to World War I, after which the house's days as a private home were numbered.

The original #585 was a plain structure dating from the late sixties, which housed workingmen and their families. But the grand house shown in figure 8.28 was built for Ralph H. Sidway and wife, the former Stephana Barnum, in which they lived from 1908 until the early 1920s. When the Sidways moved back across the Avenue to Stephana's former home at #576, their place was taken by Doctor John L. Eckel, who was born in Perrysburg, Ohio, in 1880, graduated from U.B. Medical School in 1907, and interned at East Manhattan State Hospital in New York. In 1911 he worked at the University of Berlin on mental diseases. Returning to Buffalo in 1913 he resumed private practice and became professor of neurology and psychiatry at U.B. During the First World War he served as a captain in the medical corps in both Buffalo and Washington, after which he returned to Berlin in 1926 for more research. He read papers before medical groups in Texas, South America, and Europe. Forty articles of his were published in learned journals throughout Europe and America. Back from the war in 1919 he married Bernice Long, an accomplished violinist. He died at the bedside of a patient in 1935 and was buried from Immaculate Conception Church in Buffalo.[55]

Number 591(9.28), like #585, was originally the site of a home for workers connected with nearby contractors. In 1897, however, it had become the mansion with an impressive colonnaded portico of Clarence L. Bryant of Bryant & Stratton's Business College. Bryant lived there into the 1920s, and died in 1927, by which time it had become a rooming house.

54 *Times*, June 15, 1923.
55 *Courier*, November 28, 1935.

9.29 ❦ Number 595 Delaware, Olivet Chapel and the first Delaware Avenue Baptist Church, *PBHS*, 16 (1912), 104.

The roots of the Delaware Avenue Baptist Church at #961 lay in the Olivet Chapel, a Sunday school organized in 1874 for the children of ex-members of the two Baptist Churches on Washington Street who had moved away from downtown toward the North Street. (See figure 6.9 where these two churches are listed as #2 and #4.) A small brick carpenter shop at #595 Delaware was modified for a school by adding a hall to the rear. The site had formerly been occupied by the officers' quarters of the Poinsett Barracks. As early as September 1874 services for adults were held at the school, and demands were being made for a full-blown establishment. The result was the Olivet Baptist Church, organized in 1882 which erected a $30,000 building known as the Delaware Avenue Baptist Church.(9.29)

The Baptists remained at #595 for only eleven years yielding place in to the Twentieth Century Club. This had developed out of the Graduates Association of the Buffalo Seminary, whose president, Charlotte Mulligan, learning that the church property was for sale, secured approval for the issuance of bonds to members to raise the $35,000 asking price for the church. She believed that the chapter house of the Graduates Association in Johnson Park was inadequate. The costs involved in purchase and conversion caused the suggestion to open membership in the association to non-graduates, which generated some opposition. The solution was to set up a separate club, The Twentieth Century Club, to which the deed to the church property, which had been delivered to the alumnae association, was in turn transferred on May 1, 1894, and $8,101.55 was spent on entirely changing the church at the back of the property into an assembly hall with a silver and terra cotta Gothic interior. It was a bad time to be spending money since the effects of the Panic of 1893, the fifth such financial disaster to strike the nation in the nineteenth century, would last until 1897. Karen J. Blair observes that the club "initially required the astronomical entrance fee of $500.00 ($8,715 in 1997 dollars) in addition to heavy annual dues."[56] But the club historian stressed the ambience of its acquisition:

> Located centrally, the property was in what was probably the most beautiful section of the city. Imposing mansions on Delaware Avenue, constructed in an era of carved marble and stone, echoed with the gaiety of fairs, balls, debuts. There were cotillions and masques and musicals. The ladies were magnificent in velvet and satin and lace and brocade. Jew-

56 Karen J. Blair, "Education and Reform in Buffalo Women's Club, 1876-1914," *Urban Education* (Beverly Hills, Sage Publications, 1984), 18, #4, 453.
57 Evelyn Hawes, *The Twentieth Century Club of Buffalo: Seventy-Five Years* (1969).

eled tiaras, necklaces, bracelets gleamed under soft lights.[57]

Within months officials of the club arranged to erect a bona fide clubhouse in front of the converted church provided the expense would not exceed $42,000 ($732,060 in 1997 dollars.) Work began on October 8, 1895, the architects being Green & Wicks. An optimistic report with an engraved picture in the *Commercial* saluted the opening of the new facility on November 4, 1896.

9.30 Views of the Twentieth Century Club, Hawes, *op. cit.*

> This new club house for women is one of the handsomest, if not the handsomest, in the country. The exterior architecture is of the Italian renaissance style. The building is 78 feet wide and 96 feet deep. The first story is of Indiana limestone and the rest of the structure of pressed brick, of a warm red tone, with a cornice of terra cotta. The ionic pillars across the front of the second story are of blue marble. The entrance gates, on either side of the club house are of wrought iron, and the windows of the top story are covered with iron grills of very artistic design.
>
> But the interior of the beautiful building fairly beggars description. Entering through the main doorway, the doors of which are massive black oak, the visitor enters a large square vestibule, which is finished entirely with white marble. Back of the vestibule is the lower court, also of white marble... To the left of the lower court a beautiful wide stairway leads to the second floor. This stairway is of marble, wrought iron and mahogany, the rich glow of which harmonizes with the marble and the iron...All the doors opening into the lower court are of plate glass. All the finishings are of white marble or of white wood...Up the stairway one enters the grand court, which is 35 feet square, with a ceiling 14 feet high, running to a height of 19 feet into the skylight of leaded glass . . . Every room on the second floor of the club house opens into this court through plate glass doors. In front of it, with windows opening upon the loggia, is the conversation room,

> finished in black oak. North...the coffee room. South...is the library...A musician's gallery, screened by white lattice is at the left of the grand court. Just back of the grand court is the music room, 29 by 35 feet, lighted from above by windows of leaded glass. This room is an artistic triumph...has a coned ceiling. It is wainscoted nine feet high. Back of the coffee room is the kitchen, to be used in connection with the coffee room alone.
>
> The third story of the building contains the servants quarters, which are large and convenient, including ample toilet room, the musicians' rooms, two in number, fitted with lockers, three large studios and two magnificent rooms fronting on Delaware Avenue of which the Graduates Association of the Buffalo Seminary has taken a five years lease for one day a week.[58](9.30)

By 1904 it was clear that the seating capacity of the Assembly Hall was too small and the few exits and aisles unsafe. The converted church was demolished and a hall was erected with a seating capacity of 576 on the ground floor and 150 in the gallery. A gymnasium, pool, showers, and a hot room were added. At a cost of $50,000 the addition was opened on November 1905.

Isaac Holloway, an English-born stone dealer had resided at #609 since the 1860s, when the area was given over to contractors. His lot and the next south at #599 were acquired in May 1889 by the Beth Zion congregation for $27,000. According to Adler there were three segments of Buffalo Jewry in the 1890s: the Orthodox, consisting of new immigrants from Eastern Europe who worshiped on the lower east side synagogues; the more liberal traditionalists who were already tending toward Conservatives; and the old German group and their associates at Beth Zion, whose synagogue was on Niagara Square. Adler writes:

> The new location was excellent. It was not too far from the downtown area, and yet was near where many Jews lived in the fast-growing West Side. The plans for the new Temple were received from the architect, Edward A. Kent in July 1889. The building was to cost about $50,000 in addition to the cost of the land.
>
> The cornerstone of the new Temple was laid on October 29, 1889, and the congregation accepted the gift of a perpetual light from its patriarchal vice-president, Leopold Warner. On Sunday, September 7, 1890, pews were auctioned off to the highest bidders to finance the new structure. The sale was conducted by Henry Weill who was then president. At this time Beth Zion had 112 members who bought, so a newspaper reported, the amazing total of $60,000 worth of pews. The choicest benches brought as much as $1,000 each.
>
> The building which has been considerably changed in the course of seventy years, was con-

9.31 ❦ Number 609 Delaware Avenue, Old Temple Beth Zion, Dunn, *Erie County*, n.p., towards the end.

58 *Ibid.*

structed according to no definite type of synagogue architecture because none existed at the time. To avoid marked resemblance to Christian churches, the architects tried to make the synagogue look oriental, thereby hoping, no doubt, to give it a Jewish look. Consequently, Beth Zion was built with a large central Byzantine dome. *The Buffalo Courier* called it "a bit of Constantinople designed in Buffalo," and the *Evening News* reported: "...it is low in proportion and wanders in an oriental way along the west side of the dome."(9.31)

In the decade between the dedication of the Delaware Avenue Temple and the end of the century, Beth Zion seems to have been in the doldrums. Although some of the newer immigrants, who had succeeded financially joined, nothing was done seriously to encourage growth. The whole spirit of the congregation was that of a closed corporation. At the same time, immigration from Hohenzollern Germany had virtually ceased and the natural increase of the original families was not sufficient to keep Beth Zion vibrant and expanding. For real growth, the Temple had to await the present century when new blood would be recruited from the sturdy sons and daughters of the East side masses.[59]

About 1870 a wealthy Canadian by the name of Beemer had built on a high elevation at #615 Delaware a large red brick house with a south wing and mansard roof. The builder went broke and returned to London, Ontario, within a year. Another Canadian, James Newton Scatcherd, purchased the house and remodeled it. The son of a longtime member of the British Parliament, he had been born in 1824, at Wyton, Ontario, was educated in local schools, and in 1852 came to Buffalo as agent of a Canadian lumber outfit with an office and yard on Elk Street. In 1855 he married Annie Belton of Fairfield, Ontario, whose father was also in the lumber business. Lumber trade boomed during the Civil War, and by the 1870s Scatcherd, specializing in expensive hard woods, was one of the principal lumber dealers in the United States. The only public office he ever held was a four-year term as Chairman of Buffalo's Board of Water Commissioners. He was a founder and a trustee of the Delaware Avenue Methodist Episcopal Church and was very generous in bequests to Buffalo General. He died in 1885 and was survived by a son, John Newton Scatcherd, and a daughter, Emily, the wife of sportsman Seward Cary. After the senior Scatcherd's death, the Carys moved into #615 and stayed until about 1905 when they moved to Hempstead, Long Island.[60] Albert Sikes, president of the Sikes Chair Company succeeded the Carys and remained for about a decade. Doctor William Steele, an osteopath, was the next householder, but his wife was there alone by 1926, reduced to taking in boarders.

In 1870 William A. Wilkes, an English-born scrap iron dealer, resided at #621 with his forty-three year old wife Ellen and nine children ranging in ages from Arthur, a twenty-three year old traveling salesman, to Edward, a year old infant. By 1880 their place had been taken by William Powell, a wholesale grocer, and family. At the same time Mrs. Alice Hoffman lived next door at #623 with her two grown unmarried daughters. The three ladies had been conducting a kindergarten on the pre-

59 Ader and Connolly, *op.cit.*, pp. 211-213.
60 *M&FH*, 1:201-202; *Courier*, February 11, 1927; *CE*, October 30, 1934.
61 Smith, *op. cit.*, 2:324.

Heathcote School,
621 and 623 Delaware Ave.

Prepares boys for College, Scientific Schools or Business.

Has representatives in Cornell, Harvard, Hobart, Johns Hopkins, Massachusetts Institute of Technology, Rochester, Sheffield Scientific School, Troy Polytechnic, Tufts, Williams, and Yale.

Has prepared a large number of our most successful young business men.

LESTER WHEELER, A. M., L. H. D.,
HEAD-MASTER AND PROPRIETOR.

623 Delaware Avenue.

mises since 1876 with Alice as principal and her daughters as teachers.[61] Living with them also was Lester Wheeler, his wife, and his lawyer son Maxwell. Wheeler had been born in Waterloo, New York, in 1848 and came to Buffalo in 1874 at the invitation of Bishop Coxe to set up a school. A building was acquired on the corner of Pearl and Genesee Streets for the Heathcote School, a private institution under the patronage of the Episcopal Church. In 1877 Wheeler purchased the school from the trustees; by the eighties the Hoffmans and their kindergarten were gone; and by the late nineties Wheeler had acquired the adjacent property at #621 to accommodate increased numbers. Figure 9.32 shows that Heathcote was a college preparatory school. The same figure also shows the colleges parents of Buffalo's elite wished their sons to attend. The emphasis on scientific schools bears note. Early in the next century the school was closed, and by 1920 the property was sold and made a rooming house. Wheeler continued, however, tutoring boys for college on an individual basis. A member of Saint Paul's for over fifty years, he died in 1927.[62]

Above 9.32 ❦ Advertisement for the Heathcote School.
Below 9.33 ❦ Wilcox Mansion, Buffalo Public Library, Lafayette Square, local history section, Special Collections, vertical file.

Number #625 was the home of Isadore Michael and family from its building in the late 1880s until Isadore's death in 1931. He was born in New York in 1864. His parents moved to Buffalo shortly thereafter where he attended P.S. 10 on Delaware Avenue and Central High. As a young man he worked in the freight department of the New York Central and was a leading figure in the formation of the first freight pool in Buffalo. He managed investments for members of the British nobility and bought up large tracts of land along the Niagara between Buffalo and Tonawanda. He was a life-long Republican and a Unitarian. His wife was Elizabeth Perry Sweet. They had three children, Louise, Maurice, and Frances. Of these only Frances married, becoming Mrs. Seymour Olmsted.

The best-known and the most historic of Delaware Avenue mansions is the Wilcox house on #641(9.33), which was a reconstruction of the officers' quarters at Fort Poinsett.(9.34) Across the

62 *Times*, November 11, 1926.

river in what was then Upper Canada disaffected elements led by William Lyon Mackenzie started an armed rebellion on December 5, 1837, as some 800 radicals marched on Toronto but were easily dispersed. Mackenzie and a handful of die-hards, abetted by some self-styled American freedom fighters, sought refuge on Navy Island in the Niagara and threatened invasion. On December 29, Colonel Alan McNab, Canadian commander at Chippewa, struck first, sending a detail to destroy the steamer *Caroline,* which docked at Navy Island in the course of ferrying recruits and supplies to Mackenzie and his American accomplices. About midnight the detail came aboard, shot dead an American named Amos Durfee, fired the ship, cut her loose, and sent her flaming down the river.[63] Hot-headed Americans, especially along the Canadian boundary, wished to make common cause with the Navy Islanders, which would have assured war with Great Britain in the midst of a serious depression. President Van Buren sent a strong protest to Great Britain but also dispatched General Winfield Scott to the frontier to order the Islanders to disband. They did and the crisis passed — for a time. In the fall of 1840 another arose with the arrest of Alexander McLeod, a British subject who was indicted for the murder of Durfee. The British government demanded his release on the grounds that the attack on the *Caroline* was a public act and that those who took part in it did so in obedience to a legal order. Van Buren refused to comply with this demand, and the Supreme Court of New York refused to treat the case as deserving of special consideration. McLeod was ordered to stand trial. This second crisis passed in October 1841 when he came up with an alibi and was acquitted. In the Webster-Ashburton Treaty of 1842 Her Majesty's government expressed regrets that an immediate apology had not been made for the attack on the *Caroline.*[64]

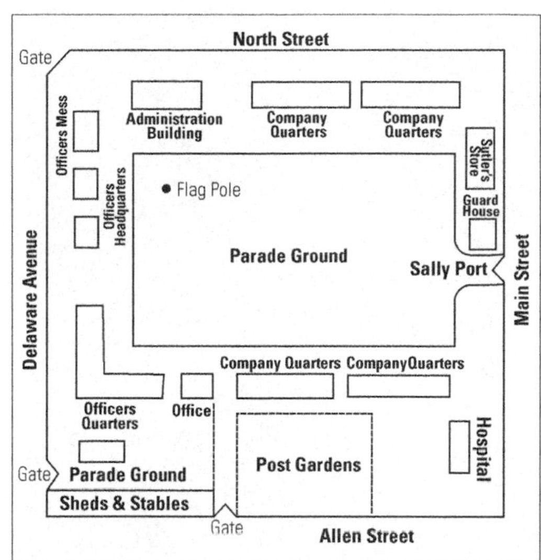

9.34 Poinsett Barracks, *Buffalo Spree*, Summer 1990, p. 53.

The upshot of the affair was the dispatch in the spring of 1838 of three companies of United States Artillery to establish a garrison, more to prevent locals from embroiling the United States with Great Britain than to dissuade Canadians from invading. The block known as Walden Hill, bounded by Delaware, Allen, Main, and North Streets, was leased from Ebenezer Walden. Design and construction of the garrison was done by the United States Army Engineers under the direction of Winfield Scott Hancock, who would distinguish himself at Fredericksburg, Chancellorsville, and Gettysburg, and nearly won the presidency in 1880. Following the wrap-up of the Seminole War in Florida in 1842 an infantry regiment was sent to Fort Poinsett (named after Secretary of War, Joel R. Poinsett)

63 P. A. Buckner, "Rebellions of 1837," *The Canadian Encyclopedia* (Edmonton: Hurtig Publishers, 1985), 3:1550-1551; Horton, *op. cit.*, 1:76-78.
64 *Ibid.*

9.35 ❦ General Bennett Riley, *ibid.*

under Colonel Bennett Riley(9.35) of whom Austin Fox wrote:

> Riley [born in 1787] was one of the great American career soldiers of the first half of the nineteenth century, one of the real heroes of the Winning of the West, the prototype for the ultimate John Wayne Western epic, the quintessential American frontier soldier.
>
> As a young army ensign of rifles, Riley had fought in the War of 1812 in three New York State engagements along the St. Lawrence frontier: at Sackett's Harbor, La Cole's Mill, and Plattsburg. His lifetime career records show that he was several times brevetted for valor to the next higher officer rank. Committed to an army career, he early on fought Indians in the Dakota Territory, in the Black Hawk Wars in Illinois, in the Southwest along the Santa Fe Trail, and in Florida against the Seminoles.
>
> Following the cessation of hostilities with the Seminoles, Riley (now a colonel) was ordered to Buffalo with his 2nd U.S. Infantry regiment, arriving in June 1842 to occupy the newly constructed Federal Poinsett Barracks, bounded by Delaware, Allen, Main and North. He was to protect the Niagara Frontier during the unsettling rebellion in Canada known as the Patriot's War.
>
> His wife and children with him, Riley spent a three-year tour of duty (1842-1845) in Buffalo before he and his men were ordered to duty at the Mexican border just prior to the outbreak of the Mexican War.
>
> The three years in Buffalo were among the happiest Riley and his family had ever known. He and his family, along with his officers and men were welcomed, entertained and honored. Five of his officers married Buffalo young women. He resolved to settle here when he retired from the army.
>
> Accordingly, after serving as military governor of California during the parlous Gold Rush days of '49, calling for and organizing the first free elections there in September of '49 at Monterey, and turning over the reins of government to the elected officials, he made plans to return to Buffalo. For reasons of health, and eligible for retirement, he declined orders to the Rio Grande and set sail with his wife, Arabella, and their five children for New York. The passage around Cape Horn to New York took five months.
>
> Arriving at the Exchange Street Station in Buffalo in 1850 by train from New York, General Riley and his family were met by a crowd of officials and well-wishers, who gave them a band-playing ovation, with a military parade and reception following.
>
> The family settled in a large comfortable frame house at 1238 Main Street, across from Northampton. Riley called the house, affectionately, "Soldier's Retreat." The site is now occupied by the former Bishop Timon High School gymnasium. Nearby Riley Street, the first street south of Northampton on the east side of Main, was cut through a few years after the General returned. It is of course named after him [as is Fort Riley in Kansas].[65]

65 Austin Fox, "The Portrait on the Wall: Who was Gen. Bennett Riley?" *Buffalo Spree*, 24: #3, Summer 1990, pp. 52-53.
66 Richard B. Morris, ed., *Encyclopedia of American History* (New York: Harper & Row, 1965), p. 473.
67 Clifford R. Williams, "The Discovery of the Buffalo Barracks," *Buffalo Irish Times*, v. 7, #6, December 1998.
68 *Times*, October 17, 1928.

9.36 ❦ Some Poinsett Barracks alumni, *Battles and Leaders of the Civil War* (New York: Thomas Yosellof Inc., 1956); Major-General Samuel P. Heintzelman U.S.A., 2:222; Lieutenant-General John C. Pemberton, C.S.A., 3:474; Major-General John Sedgwick, U.S.A., 4:92; Major General William F. Barry, U.S.A., 2:542; Major-General Henry J. Hunt, U.S.A., 2:320.

The portrait of Riley in figure 9.35, done in what Horton called "the grand manner of the late eighteenth century of a Reynolds, a Raeburn, or a Benjamin West," is by Buffalo artist Lars Sellstedt. Riley died in Buffalo in 1853, and the family is buried in Forest Lawn.

Enlisted men were not welcomed or entertained by Buffalo's elite. A researcher for the *Buffalo Irish Times* has found that most of the ranks were Irish, hardly surprising since, though Catholic Irish immigration to America reached its peak only after the great famine of 1846, it had started as early as the 1820s.[66] Living conditions for the ranks at the fort were deplorable. Hundreds deserted and about a dozen died. At one point early on the men had to sleep four in a bunk.[67]

Some of the officers at Poinsett later fought in the Civil War: Lieutenant-General John C. Pemberton, C.S.A., surrendered Vicksburg to General Grant July 4, 1863; Major General Samuel P. Heintzelman, U.S.A., fought gallantly in the Mexican War and on the frontier, less so as one of General George B. McClellan's corps commanders in the Peninsula Campaign in 1862; Major General John Sedgwick, U.S.A., was killed at Spotsylvania in the Wilderness Campaign in 1864; Major-General William F. Barry, Chief of Artillery defending Washington 1862-1865; and Major-General Henry J. Hunt, chief of artillery for the Army of the Potomac.(9.36)

When the fort was abandoned in the late 1840s the former officers' quarters became the property of Joseph Griffiths Masten, who was born in 1809, educated in local schools, read law, and was admitted to the bar as a young man. He was elected mayor of Buffalo in 1843 and again in 1845, was recorder from 1848-1854, and from 1856 until his death in 1871, was chief judge of the superior court.[68] By the 1870s #641 had become the home of Albert Pierce Laning of the law firm of Laning, Folsom & Willett. Laning was born in Allegany County in 1817. He practiced law there 1845-1855 when he came to Buffalo and for twenty-five years was one of the city's most successful litigants. He was elected to the assembly in 1857 and in 1874 to the state senate, succeeding John H. Ganson of #262 Delaware who had died that year. For a brief period Laning had been a law partner of Cleveland

69 Nevins, *Cleveland*, p. 53.
70 *Ibid.*

when the later formed the law firm of Laning, Cleveland & Folsom in 1869, but in 1870 Cleveland took a leave to serve as sheriff of Erie County.[69] Having sat in both houses of the legislature, Laning was an important Democratic figure in Western New York. His ability and prominence attracted the New York Central and other railroads to avail themselves of his services. As Nevins writes, "He was one of a new race of corporation attorneys just springing in to prominence after the war."[70] Laning died in 1880 at #641 Delaware.

The *Express* for May 21, 1901, carried this notice of the death of Laning's successor at #641, Frederick A. Bell:

> Mr. Bell, who was about 55 years old, was a millionaire. He was a prominent figure in Buffalo's business and social circles for years. He was a fine looking, well built man, who would attract attention in any group of men. He had a courteous manner that won him hosts of friends. Business was his forte. He had rare ability in that line and his judgment seldom proved to be faulty. His advice was often sought by capitalists. Mr. Bell was interested especially in bituminous coal, lumber and grain-elevating business and he probably had as comprehensive a grasp of those three industries as many men who have devoted a lifetime to each.
>
> Mr. Bell spent his early life in Rochester, where his father was a prominent citizen of large means. While still in Rochester the younger Mr. Bell became interested in the bituminous-coal business in Pennsylvania. About 1878 he came to this city as the head of the firm of Bell, Lewis & Yates. The George H. Lewis of this city, his brother-in-law, was a junior member of he firm. Mr. Yates was a Rochester man. This firm, during its eight-year existence in Buffalo, became a strong factor in the bituminous-coal industry of Pennsylvania. Among the many mines it operated was the Soldiers' Run at Reynoldsville, well known to all coalmen. The firm did an immense business. Finally, in 1894, it was absorbed by the Buffalo Rochester & Pittsburg Railroad. Mr. Bell decided to retire from active business life about the time of this transaction. He spent a good deal of his time abroad during the succeeding two years, and in 1898 bought a home at Madison N.J. He lived there summers and spent the winters in New York. Mr. Bell was at one time president of the Buffalo Elevating Company. He was a large stockholder and a director in it at the time of his death.[71]

Two days after this appeared, Buffalonians learned that Bell had been married twenty years earlier in Bloomington, Illinois, to Mrs. Mary Gridley Bruce, daughter of the late General Asabel Gridley, one of the richest men in central Illinois. The marriage was unhappy and each party had sought a divorce, but in different jurisdictions. At issue was not the estate, which the *Express* estimated at $25,000,000, but back alimony at $5,000 a year for twenty years. The case finally reached the United States Supreme Court, which seems to have decided in favor of Mary Gridley.[72] During the 1870s the portico was shifted from the east end of the building where it faced the parade grounds to the west end where it faced Delaware Avenue.

Bell did not reside long at #641 since he was followed there by Ansley Wilcox in 1883.(9.37)

71 *Express*, May 21, 1900.

9.37 Ansley Wilcox, *HNF*, 3:61.

Wilcox, son of a Connecticut-born cotton broker and a descendant of one of the founders of Hartford, was born in Summerville, Georgia, outside Atlanta, in 1856. The family evaded the ravages of Sherman's marauders and were settled safely in New Haven by the end of the war. Ansley attended Hopkins Grammar School and graduated from Yale in 1874 at eighteen[!] After a year at Oxford and the usual reading law in the office of a mentor, he married Cornelia Rumsey, daughter of Dexter and Mary Coburn Rumsey, in 1878. He began his legal career in Buffalo in 1882 as a partner in Crowley, Movius & Wilcox.[73] The Movius was Edward Hallam who had himself married a Rumsey and lived at #334 Delaware in the Rumsey compound. Much of Ansley's work at the time consisted in assisting Movius with the legal problems connected with bringing the ill-fated New York West Shore & Buffalo Railroad across Erie County and into Buffalo. By 1880 the Wilcoxes were in residence at #675 on the northeast corner of Delaware and North, which was purchased for the newlyweds by Cornelia's father. Cornelia died in 1880, leaving one child Nina. In 1883 Wilcox married his first wife's sister, Mary Grace Rumsey, and moved into #641, which had also been purchased by Dexter Rumsey in his daughter's name. Mary Grace had been born in Buffalo in 1854. She was educated at the Buffalo Seminary and the Farmington school in Connecticut.

Mabel Ganson wrote a bitter account of these marital transactions:

> Nina Wilcox is one of those whose destiny and mine have been linked together from the earliest days. My connection with her began when, as they told me, my father [Charles Ganson] fell in love with her mother. But he married my mother [Sara Cook] and she married Ansley Wilcox and Nina and I were the outcome. Nina was born in our house on the corner of North and Delaware, and my Grandfather Cook bought that house from her family and gave it to my mother when I was a year or two old. So I was moved into the nursery Nina had occupied there, and her parents moved two doors down the street into the fine old brick house with the high Doric columns. It was always painted grey and the columns were white.
>
> Nina's mother had died in giving birth to her. Ansley Wilcox was quite helpless with that infant, and what Nina told me seems entirely credible: that her mother's sister Grace took the baby and devoted herself to it and in that way won Ansley, whose red-haired child so needed a mother. They were married quite soon and then the warmth that Grace Rumsey had shown for the little thing died quite away. I think she hated it as soon as she was married, and Nina has sometimes felt she has never stopped hating her.[74]

72 *Ibid.*, May 25, 1900.
73 *HNF*, 3:60-61.
74 Luhan, *op. cit.*, pp. 82-83.

Tales of family life behind the walls of a Delaware Avenue mansion are hard to come by, hence even jaundiced views have their value. Thus Mabel continued:

> But there was a good hour in the day for Nina. That was when her father came home at night. While he was dressing for dinner, Nina and I would go up to his room and he would joke with her in his awkward way and then he would "drop" us. Nina loved that. Her father would hold her high up in the air and drop her flat on her back on the bed till it creaked. She would come to life and queer excited gawps and shrieks would rise out of her and burst on the air. I loved it too — it was thrilling and dangerous to us.
>
> Then we would wait in the sitting room while Mr. and Mrs. Wilcox ate a silent meal, for we were allowed to be with the grown-ups for a little while after their dinner. They would return and sit in two big chairs in the subdued atmosphere of that loveless house. They did not laugh or joke either with us or with each other. It was as though they suffered us — not gladly, but because it was the custom to have the children after dinner. We acted like gawks then. We put on Mr. Wilcox's hats and coats and made a "procession," the stiff bowlers coming down over our eyes to our noses and giving out a faint, sweet smell of bay rum from their leather hatbands. We trailed round and round, Frances bringing up the rear, singing and shouting a series of hoots and howls that kept time to our marching step, feeling secure under the bowlers hats; in fact, quite hidden from sight, we felt free to let off our inner feelings and they came from us in the queerest noises. Something like damned souls, I think it must have been. We were doing it to and for the ones who made us feel as we did. It was a most ironical entertainment.
>
> After we had done this for a short time, varying it by a re-arrangement and a reshuffling of the disguises that we supposed those masculine properties constituted in the eyes of the couple who endured us politely, one with a faint satirical smile, the other with a clumsy assumption of interest — you know, "Dear me! What have we got here?" — the mother one would lift an eyebrow at the peaceful clock that ticked on the chimneypiece and say in that cold drawl: "Well, children, I think you may be excused for tonight." And then she would stretch out her hand toward Frances and murmur: "Good night, my little girl. Good night, Francie." And the father one would pat Nina kindly on her shoulder and she would kiss them each, while I from the door, waiting, would drop an impatient good night, and we'd all run across the hall to the nursery. Here Mary Ann or one of our girls would be talking to Norah (that awful nurse of theirs) while she waited to take me home — all perspiring from being muffled up in those heavy dark coats and hat, and breathless from the queer rush of expression we had just had. That was known as "the children's hour."[75]

In 1892 Crowley Movius & Wilcox was dissolved in favor of Wilcox & Miner, which lasted until 1903 when Wilcox & Bull was formed, followed in 1910 by Wilcox & Van Allen, which lasted until 1917. Though highly regarded as a corporation lawyer, Wilcox gave most of his time to advisory law. In 1877 he was one of the organizers of the Buffalo Charity Organization. From 1882 until 1885 he was consul for the commission named by Governor Cleveland to acquire land for a New York State Reservation along the Niagara, and he was commissioner of that reservation 1910-1917. In 1884 he deserted the Republican party's nominee, James G. Blaine, and supported Cleveland for the presi-

75 *Ibid*, pp. 86-88.

dency. He served as professor of medical jurisprudence at U.B. 1885-1906. In Rogers *vs.* City of Buffalo he established the constitutionality of the state's civil service law which promoted merit promotion rather than political pull in the conduct of the civil service. After 1917 he devoted his time to a few old clients, to handling estates, and to civic and philanthropic activities. Like Frederick Almy of #427 Delaware, Wilcox was a progressive, concerned with adjusting civic mechanisms to produce structural political change. He developed a plan of holding local elections in odd numbered years (national elections were on even numbered years) "in order to free municipal government from politics," an impossible goal. He belonged to a committee created in 1913 to examine the public health law of the state, which resulted in a new health law. He aided in creating the National Civil Service Reform League, which promoted civil service examinations and merit promotions. It was fitting that when progressivism in the shape of Theodore Roosevelt assumed the presidency on September 14, 1901, it happened at the home of Ansley Wilcox.

A brochure entitled *The House and it History* contains this account of subsequent developments at the site:

> Previous owners had by this time built a frame addition at the rear and a brick coach house nearby. By 1901 Wilcox had further improved the property. A Buffalo architect, George Cary, rebuilt the addition and remodeled the interior. The remodeling did not affect the interior of the original part, except for the two first floor parlors, which were made into a large library. The house was transformed into a stately mansion, flavored with both Greek Revival and Adamesque styles, and seasoned with the eclecticism of the 19th century.

Wilcox belonged to the Century Association, the City Club, and St. Andrew's Golf Club in New York, and to the Buffalo, Country, Athletic, Park, Wanakah, Saturn, and University clubs of Buffalo. He died on New Year's Day 1930. His wife followed him in October 1933. In light of Mabel Ganson's observations, it bears mention that in her will Mrs. Wilcox provided that the residue of her estate after all bequests had been paid was willed to son-in-law, Thomas Cooke of #618 Delaware, the husband of Frances, with this provision: "I make this gift (all furniture, silverware, etc.) to my daughter, Frances, expressing the wish that she will give my husband's daughter, Nina, and her children, a generous share of my effects."[76]

After the Wilcoxes' deaths, a drive to raise funds to support a Roosevelt memorial failed. The site was sold for use as a restaurant. In the 1960s a campaign to save the landmark succeeded, thanks largely to Liberty Bank, which bought the place until it was declared a national site. Beginning in the autumn of 1970 it was restored through the cooperation of the Theodore Roosevelt Inaugural Foundation, the Buffalo and Erie County Historical Society, the Junior League, Erie County, New York State, and the National Park Service. It was dedicated and opened to the public on September 14,

76 *CE*, October 22, 1933; *BEN*, November 1, 1933.

9.38 ❦ Number 661 Delaware, BHS.

1971, the seventieth anniversary of the first Roosevelt's inauguration.

The last mansion covered in this chapter is #661(9.38), in 1870 the home of Jason Parker, a fifty-six year old Vermont-born grain dealer, partner in the firm of Parker & Newhall, with offices on the waterfront. The rest of the family consisted of Jason's wife, Jane Youngblood Parker, their two children, Jason aged fourteen, Charles aged eleven, and an elderly relative of Jane. The household also contained two maids and a coachman. Burr remembered that "this beautiful old house was then in its prime, and the handsomely kept grounds were ornamented with statues and striking casts, iron casts of lions and other fanciful works of art after the fashion of that period." Tending the grounds was usually one of the tasks of the coachman.[77]

Jason Parker, Sr., died in the late seventies, and his widow sold #661 to Edward Stevenson(7.10), who had been residing at #262 Delaware. Stevenson, in turn, sold #262 to James M. Ganson. Stevenson, now old, his wife Amelia and a niece, also named Amelia, resided at #661 in 1880. He and his wife had died by the time Mabel was seven or eight. In her following entry Mary Ann was a servant of the Gansons:

> Sometimes Mary Ann and I would go for walks in the afternoon — along Delaware Avenue, where the men would be racing in their cutters in the winter or a few people driving in open carriages in the summer. Sometimes Mary Ann would stop to call upon someone she knew in one of the neighbours' kitchens and the cook would give me a cake and I would sit and munch it while they gossiped. Often she took me across the street [North] to Miss Stevenson's.
>
> Miss Stevenson was a tall, thin old maid who looked to me like a "Canada fly," a narrow, blonde, moth-like pest we used to have in clouds around our gas jets in the summer time. She lived in a hoary old grey stone house that was modeled upon the English Tudor mansion, [#611 is definitely not Tudor] and it had a great deal of somber, heavy atmosphere in it, and I liked it quite well. It was thick and brooding and quiet. No one lived there except Miss Stevenson and her servants and her parrot who sat in the kitchen window.[78]

In 1925 Amelia Stevenson, then eighty, was living alone at #661 with an Irish-born waitress and cook. In the back was a chauffeur with his family.

77 *CE*, September 5, 1926.
78 Luhan, *op. cit.*, p.43

CHAPTER

10 NORTH TO BRYANT: *West Side*

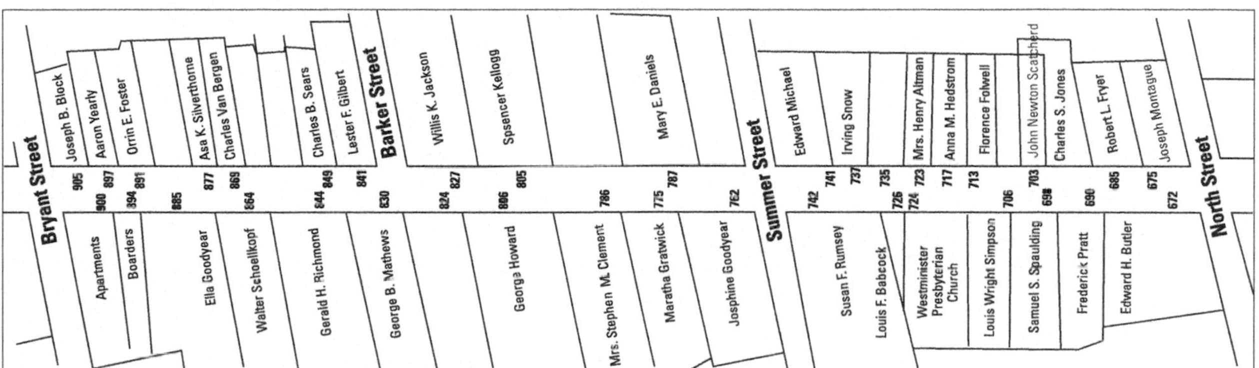

10.1 North to Bryant, 1915 Century atlas.

The base date of the map(10.1) for this chapter is 1915. This enables it to embrace more of the larger and better-known mansions than those below North. Those above North also tended to be situated on larger plots, and employed more domestics with domiciles of their own on the grounds.

WEST SIDE, Delaware Ave.

1870		1880	
	NORTH STREET		NORTH STREET
672	Sophia Rumsey	672	Harriet Metcalf 48 NY James Metcalf 21 NY son Frank Metcalf 14 NY son George Metcalf 8 NY son
698	Valorus Hodge 70 NY builder Emaline Hodge 63 NY *ux.* Julia Hodge 31 NY Dwight Hodge 26 NY boarder George Belner 21 NY hostler Eliza Corcoran 19 Ireland	698	Sherman S. Rogers
706	James C. Brown 58 NY attorney Margaret Brown 49 NY *ux.* Fanny Brown 14 NY school Allen Brown 10 NY school Walter Brown 9 NY school Nellie Brown 8 NY Lizzie Kolbrenner 17		
724	*Westminster Presbyterian Church*	724	*Westminster Presbyterian Church*

726 Erskine White 37 NY clergyman
Eliza White 33 NY *ux.*
Nelson White 9 NY school
? White 8 NY school
Edith White 6 NY school
Helen White 3 NY school
Mary Brown 25 NY
Maggie Megan 23 NY

742 Dexter P. Rumsey 43 NY leather manufacturer
Mary Rumsey 34 NY *ux.*
Mary Rumsey 15 NY
Ellen Crocker 14 NY school
Sarah Gleason 22 Ireland
Margaret Smith 20 Ireland

William Barnaby 73 England gardener
Hannah Barnaby 31 Ireland *ux.*
Mary Barnaby 11 months NY

SUMMER STREET ❦ End of Block

786 Erastus S. Prosser NY 59 retired manufacturer
Lucy Prosser NY *ux.*
Anna Prosser 22 NY at home
Ann Kelly 27 Ireland
Lizzie Maguire 26 Ireland
Ann Norman 25 Ireland

806 George Howard 60 Vermont
leather manufacturer
Amelia Howard 45 NY *ux.*
Frank Howard 16 NY school
Anna Howard 14 NY school
George Howard 9 NY school
Agnes Burchard 34 Canada West
Louise Meyer 19 Baden
Jodie Black 25 Canada West

John Newbury 28 England coachman
Joseph Cleary 40 England gardener

726 T. Ralston Smith 50 Tennessee
pastor Westminster
Harriet Smith 49 Tennessee *ux.*
Frederick Smith 21 NY son
Mamie Wilson 23 NY
Lena Zadaga 21 Hamburg wife

742 Dexter P. Rumsey 53 NY
Mary Rumsey 40 NY *ux.*
Mary Grace Rumsey 25 daughter
Elizabeth Doyle 40 NY
Elizabeth Ryan 35 Ireland

SUMMER STREET ❦ End of Block

762 Myron P. Bush 59 NY retired leather merchant
Margaret Bush 57 NY *ux.*
Margaret Bush 20 NY daughter
George Bush 17 son school
Harriet Jackson 30 NY cousin
Kate Brown 23 NY
Margaret Lynch 28 NY
Arthur Muffang 17 Ireland

786 Erastus Prosser 72 NY retired merchant
Anna Prosser 33 NY daughter
Andy Wellski 25 Poland coachman
Julie Travers 20 Canada
Mary Mink 26 NY

806 George Howard 69 Vermont
retired leather merchant
Emeline Howard 55 NY *ux.*
Frank Howard NY 26 son leather merchant
George R. Howard 19 NY school
Miles Hassan 30 NY
Bertha Seling 34 Prussia
Jennie Holman 31 England

John Sidon 30 Belgium coachman
Eliza Sidon 34 NY *ux.*
Mary Sidon 2 months NY

844 Levi Allen 68 NY retired banker
Kate Allen 30 Ireland *ux.*
Annie Donovan 28 Ireland
Patrick Killcoyne 20 NY gardener

864 Socrates Squier 72 Mass. retired manufacturer
Esther Squier 70 Conn. *ux.*
Agnes Squier 32 Mass. boarder
Henry Squier 31 flour mills
Matilda Bruch 17 NY
Iraniana Harley 43 Ireland
Robert Groomer 40 Mass.

874 Fred Jones 52 NY ship builder
Cordelia Jones 40 NY *ux.*
Benjamin Jones 21 NY bookkeeper
Carrie Jones 23 NY
Frank Jones 12 NY school
Leonard Jones 9 NY school
Ellen Bercarde 19 Canada West
Lizzie Doyle 21 NY

BRYANT STREET ❦ End of Block

844 Jewett M. Richmond 49 NY grain merchant
Geraldine Richmond 40 NY *ux.*
Jewett M. Richmond, Jr. 8 NY son
John M. Richmond 7 NY son
Lillian Richmond 6 NY daughter
Irving Richmond 4 NY son
Gerald Richmond 2 NY son
Edward Richmond 7 months NY son
Eliza McLain 40 nurse Canada
Frances Corrigan 17 Ireland
Mary Devine 55 England nurse
Betsey Devine 80 Vermont mother of Mary
Alonzo Richmond 59 NY
Lena Gorman 23 Ireland

Joseph Siler 35 Baden coachman
Mary Siler 36 Baden *ux.*
Mary L. Siler 9 NY daughter school
Lola Siler 7 NY daughter
Anna Siler 5 NY daughter
Edward Siler 4 NY son

864 Socrates Squier 82 Mass. retired merchant
Agnes Squier 32 Mass. daughter
Gertrude Talcott 35 Mass. daughter
Frank Talcott 16 NY grandson school
Lena Talcott 12 NY granddaughter school
Matilda Silman 35 Canada

Americus Haley (negro) 50 Virginia coachman
Sophia Haley (negro) 35 Virginia *ux.*
Benny Haley (negro) 5 Virginia school

Joseph Castler 26 NY coachman
Mariah Castler 22 NY *ux.*
John Castler 2 NY son

874 George Van Vleck 44 NY oil producer
Mina Van Vleck 35 NY *ux.*
Grace Van Vleck 13 NY daughter school
Martha Van Vleck 11 NY daughter school
Mary Van Vleck 9 NY daughter school
Jeanette Van Vleck 5 NY daughter school
George Van Vleck 2 NY son
Baby Van Vleck 11 months NY son
Mary Mills 56 England nurse
Margaret McMahon 23 NY
Amelia Farmer 22 NY

James Roy 26 France coachman
Kate Fitten 25 Ireland

894 Daniel Castle 64 NY jeweler
Frances Castle 42 NY *ux.*
Mary Castle 21 NY daughter school
Mary Johnson 21 NY
Jessie Ward 42 NY

BRYANT STREET ❦ End of Block

1891

NORTH STREET

672 Daniel O'Day president National Gas Fuel Co.
Daniel O'Day Jr. student
Charles O'Day secretary Snow Steam Pump Co.

698 Sherman S. Rogers Rogers Locke & Milburn
Robert C. Rogers attorney

706 Harrison D. Folinsbee real estate

724 *Westminster Presbyterian Church*

726 William H. Alexander artist
Arthur Alexander
Henry H. Hale
Frank E. Wood

742 Dexter P. Rumsey leather manufacturer

SUMMER STREET ❦ End of Block

1900

NORTH STREET

672 George L. Williams
Annie Williams
Martha T. Williams

690 Charles H. Williams 52 NY real estate
Emma Williams 50 NY *ux.*
Jennie Williams 32 daughter
Florence Kennedy 24 Canada
Elizabeth McMullan Canada 24
Julie Snyder 32 Prussia
Mary Pender 30 NY cook

George Monroe 42 Scotland coachman
Margaret Monroe 28 Scotland *ux.*
George Monroe 13 NY son school
Charles Monroe 12 NY son
Gordon Monroe 5 NY son
Margaret Monroe 1 NY daughter

706 Oscar Harries M.D. 41 NY
Jennie Harries 41 NY *ux.*
William Harries 7 NY son school
Frances Leitten 22 NY

724 *Westminister Presbyterian Church*
Frederick Spencer (black) 48
Maryland janitor
Mary A. Spencer 68 Maryland mother

726 Frederick E. Wood 40 NY auditor
Helen Wood 40 NY *ux.*
Harry J. Wood 9 NY son school
Alfred Wood 5 NY son
Sarah A. Nye 69 Conn. mother
Henry Hale 72 Conn. retired
Hilda Dawson 30 Germany
Lucy Pergrine 30 England

742 Dexter Rumsey 73 NY retired
Susan Rumsey 43 NY *ux.*
Ruth Rumsey 9 NY daughter school
Frances Cagney 55 Ireland
Katherine Wusterburg 22 Germany
Julia Donovan 40 Canada
Josephine Wood 30 Canada

William Brown 49 Germany coachman
Margaret Brown 59 Ireland *ux.*
Nellie B. Brown 25 NY clerk
William P. Brown 24 NY clerk
George C. Brown 20 NY clerk
Francis J. Brown 20 NY clerk

SUMMER STREET ❦ End of Block

762 Mrs. Myron P. Bush
George H. Bush

786 Augustus F. Tripp

806 Mrs. George Howard
Philetus C. Fuller gardener

830 George B. Mathews miller
C. H. Modisette
William Johnson coachman

844 Rev. Henry A. Adam rector St. Paul's

864 Frank S. Talcott attorney
Gertrude S. Talcott

874 George H. Van Vleck oil
Martha Van Vleck

894 Hascal L. Taylor president Union Oil Co
John Coleman coachman
Edward Maloney coachman

900 Harriman W. Lee Lee Holland & Co.

BRYANT STREET End of Block

762 Myron P. Bush attorney
John W. Bush attorney

776 F. C. Gratwick attorney
Martha Gratwick *ux.*

786 Augustus F. Tripp

806 Mr. George Howard

830 George B. Mathews
Schoellkopf & Mathews millers

844 Mrs. Jewett M. Richmond
John H. Richmond president
US Aerating Fountain Co.

894 Emory G. Taylor

900 James H. Lee Lee Holland & Co.

BRYANT STREET End of Block

1905

NORTH STREET

672 George L. Williams 60
Fannie Williams 58 *ux.*
Martha Williams 29 daughter
Annie Swift 35 Ireland

690 Charles H. Williams 62 capitalist
Emma Williams 60 *ux.*
Jeanie Williams 39 daughter
Charlotte Street 27 England
Eden Coleman 25 Ireland
Elizabeth Kelly 34 Canada
Austere Paky 25 Russia

George Monroe 48 Scotland coachman
Margaret Monroe 33 Scotland *ux.*
George Monroe 19 son groom
Charles Monroe 17 son groom
Gordon Monroe 10 son school
Margaret Monroe 6 daughter

1915

NORTH STREET

672 Edward H. Butler 38 publisher
Katherine Butler 35 *ux.*
Ernest Warne 45 butler
Michael Moritz 40 chauffeur

690 Frederick Pratt 64
Jennie Pratt 42

George Monroe 58 coachman
Margaret Monroe 45 *ux.*
Margaret Monroe 16 daughter

698 Samuel Spaulding 55 capitalist
Anna Spaulding 40 *ux.*
Eldridge Spaulding 20 school
Samuel Spaulding 18 bank clerk
Charlotte Spaulding 16 daughter

William McKay 35 Scotland coachman
Anna McKay *ux.*
Mary McKay 2 daughter

706 Oscar L. Harries MD 46
Jeanie Harries 46 *ux.*
William Harries 19 son college

724 *Westminster Presbyterian Church*
Frederick Spencer (black) 54 sexton
Mary W. Spencer 76 mother
Clara Peake 34 sister
Emma Johnson 32 boarder

726 Robert S. Weed 31 clothing
Mary Weed 27 *ux.*
Kate Dearhue 24 England

742 Dexter P. Rumsey 78
Susan Rumsey 48 *ux.*
Ruth Rumsey 14 school
Dexter Rumsey 12 son school
Julia Donovan 42 Canada
Margaret Wall 26 Wales
Mary McMahon 29 Ireland
Mary Schidell 19

SUMMER STREET ❦ End of Block

776 Martha Gratwick 60
Fredericka Gratwick 31 daughter
Margaret Smith 55
Mary Niblett 29 England
Bridget Haley 46
Mary Foley 43 Ireland

698 Samuel S. Spaulding 63
Jennie Spaulding 57 *ux.*
Katherine Constantine 60 cook
Mary Stuart 43 waitress
Helen Barker 24 upstairs maid
Mary Franck 27 upstairs maid

William McKae 50 chauffeur
Elizabeth McKae 40 *ux.*
Mary McKae 15 daughter school

724 *Westminster Presbyterian Church*

726 Louis F. Babcock 38 attorney
Georgia Babcock 42 *ux.*
Frances Babcock daughter school
Harriet Babcock 6 daughter
James Babcock 5 son
Helen McParland 23 Ireland waitress
Jennie Taba 36 nursemaid
Christine Mensbackle 38 cook

742 Susan Rumsey 58
Dexter Rumsey 21 son college
Mary McMahon 28 Ireland
Annie Mahaney 30 Ireland
Kathleen F. Ferdinand 38

SUMMER STREET ❦ End of Block

762 Josephine Goodyear 64
Frank Goodyear 22 son clerk
Anna Curran 52 lady's maid
Margaret Culligan 49 cook
Cecilia Wagner 45 parlor maid
Fannie McLaughlin 45 housemaid
Alfred Lewis 19 footman
Mary Charlton 25 kitchen maid

776 Martha Gratwick 70
Margaret Smith 60
Minnie Clancy 40 Canada cook
Charlotte Zyork 35 Sweden
Emma Jagow

786 Augustus Tripp 82 retired
Emma Frost 51 daughter
Lowell C. Frost 22 grandson school
Edith McMahon 36 Canada nurse
Julia Blygh 47
Frances Armstrong 41 Canada
Edgar Hopkins 52 coachman

806 George R. Howard 44 safe manufacturer
Mary Howard 43 *ux.*
Geraldine Howard 20 daughter
Alice Howard 17 daughter
Ethel Howard 14 daughter school
Sarah Griffin 43 sister-in-law
Carrie Riley 37 nurse
Lizzie Griffin 43
Katie Finnerty 27
Margaret Walsh 27
Mary Tighe 46

Robert Stuart 31 Ireland coachman
Anne Stuart 28 Ireland *ux.*
Juliano Weiger 30 gardener
Matthew Jones 46 gardener
Rosa Jones 42 *ux.*
Matthew Jones Jr. 15 son school
Catherine Jones 10 daughter school
Celia Jones 8 daughter school

824 George V. Forman 63 banker
Martha Forman 63 *ux.*
Henry Donovan 36 Ireland
Mary Hughes 26 Ireland
Lydia Bugman 29 Sweden

Harry L. Reed 35 England gardener
Alexander Crespin England coachman

830 George B. Mathews 50 milling
Jennie Mathews 48 *ux.*
Annie Collins 40
Sarah McCarrick 34 Ireland

John Rose 45 Ireland coachman
Mary Rose 46 Ireland *ux.*
William Rose 21 son plumber
James Rose 18 son electrician
Francis Rose 13 son school
Edward Rose 11 son school
Mary Rose 7 daughter school

786 Mrs. Stephen M. Clement 50
Marion Clement 23 daughter
Harold Clement 26 son sales
Stewart Clement 20 college
Merrell Clement 29 English teacher
Margaret M. Healey 35 Ireland parlor maid
Esther McCaffrey 40 upstairs maid
Rose Wibba 50 cook
Mary Meason 35 Scotland upstairs maid

Frank Hirsh 48 chauffeur
Elizabeth Hirsh 30 Germany *ux.*
Edward Hirsh 15 son school
Frances Hirsh 17 daughter school

806 George R. Howard 53 capitalist
Isabella Howard 52 *ux.*
Ethel Howard 22 daughter
Theodore Clark 26 son-in-law insurance
Aline Clark 27 daughter
Jessie Murphy 35 waitress
Mary Tighe 45 cook
Minnie Conrad 35 upstairs maid
Nora Fitzgerald 30 parlor maid
Katherine Smith 20 assistant cook

Louis Mischoff 33 chauffeur
Margaret T. Mischoff 32 *ux.*
Louis M. Mischoff 7 son school

Matthew J. Jones 56 gardener
Rosa Jones 52 *ux.*
Walter F. Jones 25 son chauffeur
Celia Jones 18 daughter telegraph operator
Katherine Jones 20 daughter

824 George V. Forman 75 oil producer
Martha Forman 73 *ux.*
Mary Hayes 30 upstairs maid
Mary Donovan 35 housekeeper
Jennie Jefferey 35 Scotland cook

Wilfred Jones 49 England gardener
Anne Jones 44 Germany *ux.*
Wilfred H. Jones 8 son school
George M. Jones 6 son

830 George B. Mathews 67
Jennie Mathews 65 *ux.*
Katherine Taylor 38 seamstress
Grace Kelsey 35 waitress

Frank W. Amey 46 England gardener
Emily A. Amey 30 *ux.*
Mary A. Amey 30 daughter school

844 Geraldine Richmond 60
John R. Richmond 31 son
Gerald H. Richmond 28 son
Lillian Richmond 25 daughter
Edward S. Richmond 22 son
Isabelle Fox 35 housekeeper
Lizzie Marion 40
Margaret Fuery

Hiram Owen 43 Ireland coachman
Ellen Owen 29 Canada *ux.*
William Owen 9 son school
Sara Owen 75 Ireland mother-in-law
Margaret Owen 38 Ireland stenographer

864 William Silverthorne 37 lumber merchant
Julia B. Silverthorne 31 *ux.*
Alice Silverthorne 6 daughter
Elizabeth Meeker 40
Johanna Sullivan 40
Margaret O'Mara 38
Helen Fiegel 23

888 Charles W. Goodyear 58
Ella Goodyear 51 *ux.*
Esther Goodyear 23
Charles W. Goodyear 18 Yale
Bradley Goodyear 19 Yale
Margaret Butcher 22 Canada
Mary Heaney 82 Ireland
Lena Schoenel 22
Martha Morningstar 24 Canada
William Octerberg 30 Sweden butler

894 James Frank Aldrich 51
Marsha Aldrich 42 *ux.*
Martha Aldrich 22 daughter
Anna Aldrich 2 daughter
Franklin Aldrich 6 months son
Nellie Barry 28 Ireland
Mary A. Dowd 28
Lillie McDonnell 21 Canada

900 James H. Lee 82 retired
Lucretia Lee 79 *ux.*
Cora Lee 32 daughter
Emelia Gilles 24 Canada
Anna M. Fasnacht 21
Arthur Poole 44 gardener
Michael Meyer 39 coachman

BRYANT STREET ❦ End of Block

844 Gerald H. Richmond 37 real estate
Edward S. Richmond 35 brother
Geraldine H. Richmond 71 mother
Lillian Richmond 40 sister
Ella Billingsley 35 waitress
Jane Crawford 35 cook
Sarah Riley 35 upstairs maid
Mary Coss 42 nurse
Charles Scott 53 gardener

864 Walter Schoellkopf 32 capitalist
Anna Schoellkopf 30 *ux.*
Horton Schoellkopf 4 son
Fanny Dunigan 70 Ireland cook
Lillie Brown 24 waitress
Elsie Kelly 28 waitress
Bertha Smith 34 lady's maid
Frances von Hatten 36 governess

888 Ella Goodyear 60
Frances Schmalzl 43 cook
Margaret Archibald 27 waitress
Katherine Flynn 31 waitress
Katherine Collins 47 laundress
Clare Sweading upstairs maid

Andrew Barton 50 chauffeur
Carrie Barton 43 *ux.*
Mildred Barton 16 daughter school
Andrew Barton 10 son school
Howard Barton 8 son school

894 Elsie Mckay 44
7 boarders 2 servants

BRYANT STREET ❦ End of Block

1920

NORTH STREET

672 Edward H. Butler 36 NY publisher
Kate R. Butler 31 Georgia *ux.*
Jennie Rothwell 29 Ireland
Margaret Callinan 58 Pa.
Ernestine Lennier 34 France
Ella Murray 39 Ireland
Joan S. Anderson 32 Alsace
Frances Darlicka 29 Poland

690 Frederick Pratt 71 NY capitalist
Jennie Pratt 51 NY *ux.*
Edward Gollett 32 England butler
Mabel A. Lore 30 England
Mary Nelson 33 Scotland
Wladislaw Wastka 35 Poland butler
Julia O'Keefe 28 Ireland
Elizabeth Conlin 27 Ireland

698 Samuel S. Spaulding 70 NY
Annie W. Spaulding 66 NY *ux.*
Agnes E. McMillan 27 Scotland
Minnie W. Paine 28 England
Kate F. Considine 69 Ireland
Elizabeth Efferton 17 NY

William McKay 51 Scotland chauffeur
Elizabeth M. McKay 49 NY *ux.*
Mary M. McKay 18 NY daughter

724 *Westminster Presbyterian Church*

726 Louis F. Babcock 51 NY attorney
Georgiana Babcock 49 NY *ux.*
Frances Babcock 17 NY daughter
John G. Babcock 14 NY son
Harriet Babcock 10 NY daughter
James L. Babcock 8 NY son
Doretta Gast 61 NY
Margaret McPartland 20 Ireland
Mary Hasey 50 Ireland

742 Susan Rumsey 63 NY widow
Ruth R. Donovan 28 NY daughter
William J. Donovan 36 NY attorney son-in-law
David R. Donovan 4 NY
Patricia Donovan 2 NY grandaugher
Mary McMahon 35 Ireland
Annie Mullaney 37 Ireland
Mary Serrasses 47 France
Isabella B. Anderson 26 Scotland

1925

NORTH STREET

672 Edward H. Butler 42 *News* publisher
Kate R. Butler 30 *ux.*
Kate R. Butler 4 daughter
Ernestine Lanning 40 France personal maid
Lucy Beal 23 nurse
Jessie McKenzie 40 Scotland housemaid
Annie Harbison 24 Ireland housemaid
Minnie Nordine 35 Sweden housemaid
Godfrey Selen ward Sweden school

690 Mrs. Frederick L. (Jennie) Pratt 56
widow
May Nelson 37 Ireland maid
Salome Baldwin 45 cook
Mae Wissler 34 Canada nurse
Ann Donohue 31 Ireland maid
Elizabeth Blake 30 Scotland maid

724 *Westminster Presbyterian Church*
Charles Hearn 52 England sexton
Ellen Hearn 50 England *ux.*
Henry J. Hearn 26 salesman

742 Susan Rumsey

Elizabeth J. Bird 48 England
Katherine Manies 25 Pa.

William Brown 68 NY gardener
William Brown Jr. 44 NY son chauffeur
Frank J. Brown 42 NY auto plant
Ellen Congreve 45 daughter
Chester M. Congreve 34 son-in-law traveling salesman

SUMMER STREET ❦ End of Block

SUMMER STREET ❦ End of Block

762 Frank H. Goodyear 28 NY stockbroker
Dorothy Goodyear 23 NY *ux.*
Dorothy N. Goodyear 3 NY daughter
Frank J. Goodyear 1 NY son
Hannah Kelly 17 NY
Jessie MacKenzie 28 Scotland
Vida Reed 15 NY
Alice Bulpitt 38 England
Anna Curan 57 Canada
Edward More 35 England butler

762 Frank Goodyear 32 lumber
Dorothy K. Goodyear 28 *ux.*
Dorothy K. Goodyear 5 daughter school
Frank H. Goodyear III 6 son school
Marjorie Goodyear 8 daughter school
Robert M. Goodyear 1 month son
Mary Coon 40 nurse
Marion Stevenson 26 nurse
Hilda Buckheit 19 nurse
Juenne Gandry 35 France personal maid
Louise Fletcher 31 England maid
Margaret Scannell 30 Ireland maid
Ida Vetch 40 kitchen maid
Nettie Harris 32 Scotland maid

786 Stephen M. Clement 58 NY banker
Caroline Clement *ux.*
Mary McConville 28 Ireland
Nora Haley 36 Ireland
Ida George 41 NY
Mary Neeson 40 Scotland
Katie Coule 45 Ireland
Esther McCafferty 40 Pa.
Margaret Haley 45 Ireland

Stephen Clement 32 NY
Jean Clement 31 NY *ux.*
Carolyn Clement 3 Conn. daughter
Patricia Clement 2 Washington D.C. daughter

Frank W. Hirsch 53 NY chauffeur
Katherine Hirsch 44 Germany *ux.*
Frances C. Hirsch 21 NY daughter
Edward K. Hirsch 21 NY son banker

786 Caroline Clement 70
Ida Demerly 40 Canada cook
Esther McCafferty 45 Ireland
Mary Radcliffe 25 Ireland
Nora Malone 40 Ireland
Nora Malone 40 Ireland
Mary Neeson 45 Scotland

806 Grace M. Knox 56 widow
Seymour H. Knox 21 NY son
Marjorie Knox 19 NY daughter
Frederick Taylor 41 England butler
Bertha Daigler 54 NY
Lucy Kranfeld 54 NY
Florence Stengel 41 NY
Beatrice Taylor 33 England
Mary Miller 38 NY

806 Grace Knox 62 widow
Marjorie Knox 25 daughter
James Coombs 35 England butler
Marie Coombs 32 France
Bertha Daigler 60 cook
Lucy Kranchfield 60 maid
Mary Broadbent 21

830 George B. Mathews 73 NY
Jennie Mathews 54 NY *ux.*
Catherine Tangher 40 NY
Sarah Campbell 43 Michigan
Margaret Campbell 40 England

Frank Amey 51 England gardener
Emily Amey 32 England *ux.*
Alice Amey 12 NY daughter
Emily Amey 3 NY daughter

844 Thomas B. Lockwood 46 NY attorney
Marion B. Lockwood 37 NY *ux.*
Winifred Farry 38 Ireland
Maria Coughlin 45 Ireland
Anna Ball 37 Ireland

Edward Becker 45 NY chauffeur
Matilda Becker 44 NY *ux.*

864 Daniel Good 58 Indiana
Sara E. Good 52 Pa. *ux.*
Elizabeth Good 22 Pa. daughter
Margaret J. Good 16 Illinois daughter
Charles Dickson 40 NY chauffeur
Carrie Dickson 38
Thomas Dickson 29
Frances H. Smallbrick 24 NY
John E. Jowett 41 England butler
Mary Kennedy 27 Ireland

William Barclay 42 Scotland gardener
Georgiana Barclay 34 Scotland *ux.*
Christina Barclay 16 Scotland
daughter telephone operator
Alice Barclay 15 Scotland
Pearl Barclay 11 NY daughter
Robert Wilson 23 Scotland
brother-in-law auto repairs
John Baird 30 Ireland hostler

824 Oliver F. Cabana

George Pitman 60 England gardener
Ida Pitman 60 Canada *ux.*
Louis Pitman 38 England son chauffeur
Arthur Pitman 35 England son auto mechanic
Elsie Truman 30 England daughter
Fred Truman 30 England son-in-law housework
Margaret Pitman 20 Canada housework
Donald Pitman 11 grandson school
Marion Pitman 2 granddaughter

830 George B. Mathews 78 retired
Jenny Mathews 60 *ux.*
Sarah Campbell 31 Canada
Frieda Carson 60 Sweden cook

Frank W. Amey 56 England gardener
Emily Amey 44 England *ux.*
Emily Amey 17 daughter school
Alice F. Amey 8 daughter

844 Thomas B. Lockwood 52 attorney
Marion Lockwood 38 ux.
Maria Coughlin 50 Ireland
Anna Brie 40 Ireland
Fanny Winifred 58 Ireland

Edmund Sherrick 45 houseman
Hattie Sherrick 44 *ux.*
Frank Sherrick 80 father elevator operator
La Verne Sherrick 23 son auto mechanic
Mildred Sherrick 20 daughter teacher
Viola Bower 23 daughter
Arthur Bower 25 son-in-law auto mechanic

864 Sara E. Good 56 widow
Raymond A. Van Clief 22 son-in-law
Margaret Van Clief 33 daughter
Daniel G. Van Clief 3 grandson
Marion Taylor 28 Canada nurse
John E. Jowett 45 England butler
Minnie Malyn 48 England
Phoebe Johnson 29
Anna McGregor 60 Canada
Anna Elias 49 Gerfmany cook
Anna Stlang 22 Germany

888 Ellen Conger Goodyear 66 NY widow
Charles G. White 55 NY cousin
Clara Smeading 65 NY
Nora Sheehan 42 Ireland
Mary J. Gallery 44 NY
Mary Volkrat 30 NY
Margaret Archbold 37 England

William J. Pufpaff 54 Germany gardener
Mary Pufpaff 55 Germany *ux.*
Clarence Pufpaff 22 NY son chauffeur

Andrew Barten 55 NY chauffeur
Carrie Barten 51 NY *ux.*
Mildred Barten 22 NY daughter shop keeper
Howard Barten 12 NY

900 Apartments

BRYANT STREET ❦ End of Block

888 Ellen Conger Goodyear 70 NY widow
Charles C. White 62 cousin
importer of orientalia
Nora Sheehan 47 Ireland cook
Mary Volkosh 35
Nora O'Connor 34 Ireland
Mollie O'Brien 20 Ireland
Anna Campbell 45 Scotland

Andrew Barton 60 chauffeur
Carrie Barton 56 *ux.*
Andrew Barton 20 son school
Howard Barton 18 son

Fred Duncan 40 Ireland gardener
Elizabeth Duncan 42 *ux.*
Florence Duncan 3 daughter

Charles Dickenson 42 Scotland chauffeur
Eleanor P. Dickenson 45 England *ux.*
Thomas Dickenson 15 son school

894 Bradley Goodyear 39 attorney
Jeanette B. Goodyear 34 *ux.*
Bradley Goodyear Jr. 13 son school
Fanny Goodyear 10 daughter school
Thomas Goodyear 7 son school
Rose Goerbing 31
Elsie Genet 26 cook
Cassie Creton 45 Ireland

900 Apartments

BRYANT STREET ❦ End of Block

The first occupant of red brick #672(6.20) at Delaware and North was Aaron Rumsey. Figure 10.2 is a panoramic sketch of Delaware south of that corner by an artist from the tower of Westminster. The house in center foreground is that of Valorous Hodge at #698 and that with the cupola directly south is Rumsey's. The forested area below is the cemetery on the southwest corner of North and Delaware, which was abandoned in the early 1890s. Halfway down Delaware is the Cornell White Lead Company factory, which was superseded by the Midway. The earliest date for the sketch can be deduced from the building with the large roof southwest of the cemetery, the armory of the 74th Regiment, NYNG, later the Elmwood Music Hall, built in 1875. The sketch was probably made sometime between 1875 and 1890. The famous Delaware Avenue elms are young. South on the east side of the Avenue are the Fryer and Ganson houses; across North are the Stevenson house and the Wilcox mansion. The steeple below the White Lead factory belongs to Asbury Methodist on Tupper. On the waterfront are grain elevators, the bases of Buffalo's early economy and of the wealth of many Avenue residents.

Aaron Rumsey died at #672 in 1864. His wife Sophia lived there until her death in 1870. James H. Metcalfe, of Metcalfe & Cushing, pork packers, became the owner of this fine estate, held by his heirs until purchased by Daniel O'Day in 1881.[1] O'Day, the first Irish-Catholic mansion owner on the Avenue, was born in County Clare in 1844.[2] Next year began the Great Hunger,[3] which is why the O'Days came to America in 1845:

10.2 ❦ Delaware Avenue in the 1880s: looking south from Westminster Presbyterian Church, author's collection.

> O'Day had passed through a harsh school of experience. Born in County Clare but brought to America as a small child, he had grown up in Cattaraugus County, N.Y. At fifteen he had abandoned his father's farm for the freight yards of Buffalo, and working there throughout the Civil War years had thoroughly mastered freight handling. At twenty-one, in 1865, he went to Titusville, and soon joined the Empire Transportation Company, then newly organized as a fast-freight feeder of the Pennsylvania Railroad. His chief duties were the movement of cars and solicitation of freight. He found that the post-war oil boom had thrown service into a state of chaos; all the shippers wanted transportation at the same time, and the car shortage became frightful. O'Day introduced system and order, and met all demands promptly. After leaving the Empire, he was hired by Bostwick & Tilford in 1870 to handle their large oil shipments from the Regions. This firm had a close alliance with the Erie, monopolizing most of its oil business. Soon after joining its employ, O'Day was summoned to New York by Jay Gould, president of the Erie; for Gould believed that the Empire Transportation Company and its protector the Pennsylvania Railroad were getting altogether too much of the oil traffic, and wished O'Day to intervene. The tall, broad shouldered young man, taking charge despite the hostility of the general manager, went to work with immediate success, and practically living on the rails for a month, diverted much of the current oil freight to the Erie lines. During the South Improvement war, he and Joseph Seep remained inflexibly loyal to Bostwick. Denounced by mass meetings, threatened with mob violence, subjected to every cajolery and blandishment, they refused to yield an inch, and their iron nerve finally extorted an unwilling admiration. Bostwick had strongly recommended O'Day to Rockefeller as the right man to buildup the company's pipe line system.[4]

In 1891 O'Day moved to New York where he had a town house at West 72nd Street. His summer house at Deal was one of the showplaces of the North Jersey Shore. He had been married twice, once to Louise Newell of Boston, who died in 1890, leaving fourteen children; the second time in 1892 to Mary Page who with one son survived her husband, who died at sixty-two in October 1906 on the Bay of Biscay at the home of a daughter where he had gone to regain his health which he had ruined in acquiring wealth.[5]

1 *Times*, October 2, 1928.
2 *Men of New York*, 1:60-61; *Express*, September 14, 1906.
3 Cecil Woodham-Smith, *The Great Hunger, Ireland, 1845-1849* (London: G. Hamilton, 1962), chapter 1.
4 Allan Nevins, *John D. Rockefeller: The Heroic Age of American Enterprise* (New York: Charles Scribner's Sons, 2 vols. 1940), 1:441.
5 *Express, ibid.*

Mother Church went all out for O'Day's funeral. His body was brought to New York where a service was held at his parish, Blessed Sacrament, in the presence of John D. Rockefeller, father and son, and high officials of Standard Oil on October 15. John Cardinal Farley, Archbishop of New York, presided. Fifty boys and girls from a Catholic orphanage, of which O'Day had been a benefactor, sang. A special on the Central brought the body, family, and other mourners to Buffalo where a requiem mass was sung before thousands at Saint Joseph's Cathedral. Celebrant was the rector, Rev. John D. Biden, who had grown up with O'Day in Ireland. Bishop Charles Colton presided. Burial was at Holy Cross Cemetery in Lackawanna. A reporter wrote that "there was not another carriage to be found in all of the livery stables of the city aside from those in the procession."[6]

O'Day was vice president of the National Transit Company, a pipeline operation, and president of the Northwestern Ohio Natural Gas Company, the Atlantic Coast Realty Company, Buffalo General Electric, Buffalo Natural Gas Company, and National Fuel Gas. His directorships in and around New York City were too numerous to mention. His estate was estimated at $12 to $15 million.[7]

Mabel Ganson wrote:

> On all sides of us were the large houses of the people we knew. Opposite was Daniel O'Day's house. There were about ten daughters in that Irishman's family and they moved out of it and went to New York to live quite early, before I got to know them. They have married and are all over Europe — those who did not die. Mary Forman's father made money in oil and came to Buffalo and, tearing to pieces the old red-brick O'Day house, he fashioned it over, and he bought oil paintings and expensive furniture. He lived there ten years and then, only two blocks farther up the street, he built a large cream-coloured brick house with white columns supporting a porch in front and the Formans moved into it. People with great ease and money, labor being then so cheap, built and lived in several houses in their lifetime, in and out of several huge many-roomed houses.[8]

Above 10.3 ❦ George L. Williams, *Men of Buffalo*, p. 36.
Below 10.4 ❦ Charles H. Williams, *ibid*, p. 37.

6 *BEN*, October 16, 1906; *Courier*, October 17, 1906.
7 *NYT*, September 14, 1906; *Commercial*, October 23, 1906.
8 Luhan, *op. cit.*, p. 23.
9 Goodyear, *op. cit.*, pp. 147-148.

George V. Forman and O'Day had similar careers:

10.5 Vanderbilt Mansion, Hyde Park, NY, McKim, Meade & White, *The Architecture of McKim Mead & White* (New York, Dover Publications, 1990), front cover.

> Grandfather Forman graduated from Princeton in 1861 at the age of 19, then practiced law and went into the pottery business in Trenton. Before he had reached the age of 27 he was lured by the attractions of the infant petroleum industry and moved to Oil City, Pennsylvania. Here in the course of about ten years he amassed a fortune in oil, was the first president of the famous Oil Exchange at Oil City, was president of a bank, and by 1879 had moved to Olean, New York. For over a dozen years in Olean, he was its first citizen, contributing generously to a number of charities. Then in October 1891 the family moved permanently to Buffalo, with their four children, Howard Arter, George Alfred (called Fred), Lawrence Carter, and Mary. Howard and Fred, particularly the latter, made money in the oil business, while Lawrence died of peritonitis in 1901 at the age of 23. In 1892 Grandfather was the leading organizer and the first president of the Fidelity Trust Company, which later merged with the M and T National Bank to form the M and T Trust Company. He died in Buffalo on October 10, 1922.[9]

The Formans remained at #672 only four not ten years (as Mable Ganson wrote) until 1895 when it was sold to George Lombard Williams.(10.3) His brother, Charles Howard Williams(10.4), bought the adjoining lot at #690. They were sons of Gibson T. Williams, a banker and industrialist. They once owned what was reputedly the largest tannery in the United States in Salamanca but sold it and concentrated on investing. To design their homes they engaged Stanford White of McKim, Meade & White. White had started under H. H. Richardson, the hallmark of whose style was massive stone walls. By 1885, however, White had gone classical. Two Delaware Avenue examples of Richardsonian style are the Gratwick house at #776 Delaware(10.29) and the Delaware Avenue Baptist Church.(12.4) White's Vanderbilt mansion on the Hudson at Hyde Park(10.5) is reminiscent of Williams' mansion(10.6):

10.6 Number 672 Delaware, exterior and interior views (seen on page 346), *Western New York Heritage*, Fall, 1998, front cover.

> White submitted designs for the George Williams house in 1895, after he had completed the details and construction had started on the Charles Williams house on the property just to the north...The design work was completed and construction started in 1896. ...The building took three years to finish and the construction cost [George] Williams $171,877, an

10.6 continued, *ibid.*

astonishing sum of money in those times. Charles Williams had paid $66,700 to build the house next door. The most easily recognizable external details of the larger building are the Corinthian columns and portico on the south side, and the main entrance and port cochere on the north side. While the stately elegance associated with the so-called American Renaissance is obvious from the exterior, the interior design and decorative touches are memorable. Many are the result of work by skilled craftsmen and artisans from Europe, are unique, extraordinary, and even after nearly a hundred years, still awesome and breathtakingly beautiful.

The great golden and crystal chandelier is still hanging three stories into the foyer; it is monumental and it still casts a majestic glow over the proceedings below. The marble floors, woodwork and the museum-quality wood carvings are obvious points of interest, as are the fireplaces and the spacious rooms.[10]

George and Annie Williams moved into their palace in 1899. On September 6, 1901, they were to host a dinner party for President McKinley after his visit to the Pan-American Exposition of which Williams was treasurer. Their house was the obvious setting for an event to which the elite of Buffalo were invited. But the president was shot at the exposition by an anarchist, dinner was called off, and McKinley died on September 14. In 1908 Williams sold his mansion to Edward Hubert Butler(10.7) who had been living at #522 Delaware. Williams moved to New York in 1909 where he died in 1918 in his apartment on Central Park West.

Butler was born in Leroy in 1850. He was educated in the public schools and by private tutors. As a teenager he worked for the *Leroy Gazette*, then moved to Scranton, where he was city editor first of the *Scranton Times*, then of the *Post*. At twenty-two he took his savings to Buffalo and in 1873 came out with his own paper, the *Buffalo Sunday News*,

10 Dick Hirsch, "Buffalo's Forgotten Mansion Builder," *Western New York Heritage Magazine*, v. 2, #2, Fall, 1998, pp. 5-15.

Above 10.7 ❦ Edward Hubert Butler, *M&FH*, 1:114.
Below 10.8 ❦ E.H. Butler, Jr., Horton, 3:218.

which was a success. On October 11, 1880, his weekday paper, the *Buffalo Evening News,* came out and sold more than 7,000 copies on the street alone. It cost only a cent, whereas most contemporary dailies cost two or three cents. Circulation boomed to 20,000, and soon the *News* enjoyed the largest circulation of any paper between New York and Chicago. Butler was given to leading crusades, including discipline at the Elmira Reformatory, enlargement of the Erie Canal, and a new building for the State Normal School in Buffalo. He was an original member of the Grade Crossing Commission and continued on it for twenty-six years. He never ran for public office but was a dominant figure in the state G.O.P. His wife was Mary E. Barber of Pittston, Pennsylvania, who died in 1893. Two children survived their father, one of whom, Edward H. Butler, Jr.(10.8), succeeded when Edward, I, died in 1914.[11]

The younger Butler was born in Buffalo in 1883, educated at Nichols and the Hill School in Pottstown, Pennsylvania, and graduated from Yale in 1907. A Republican like his father, he was a Presbyterian, and a member of the Buffalo, Saturn, University, Athletic, and Country clubs in Buffalo, and the Yale Club in New York. In 1909 he married Kate M. Robinson and by her had two children, Edward Hubert born in 1914 who died young, and Kate Robinson born in 1921.[12] Butler, the publisher, died in 1956 and was succeeded as president by his widow. In 1971 she became both president and publisher. She died in 1974.[13]

10.9 ❦ Number 690 Deleware, author's collection.

Charles Williams of #690 Delaware(10.9) died in 1909. In 1906 his daughter Jeannie married Frederick Lorenz Pratt, son of Pascal Pratt. Frederick was the brother of Mrs. John M. Horton of #477 Delaware. At the time of the Pratt-

11 *M&FH*, 1:115-117; Horton, *op. cit.*, 3:218-219.
12 Horton, *ibid.*
13 *NYT*, August 5, 1974.

Williams wedding, the groom was fifty-six and his bride thirty-eight. Jennie loved show:

> The first floor of the mansion was a bower of American beauty roses. The prie-dieu in the large reception hall at which the marriage ceremony took place, with the Rev. Cameron J. Davis, later Bishop Davis, officiating, was covered with these flowers. They also festooned the entire room and dining-room, lending color and fragrance. The bride wore white point appliqué and Irish lace over white satin, her veil hanging from a coronet of orange blossoms to the hem of her skirt. Her bridal bouquet was of orchids and lilies of the valley. Her jewels, rare and exquisite pearls, diamonds and Indian emeralds, merited lengthy description by a contemporary chronicler of the wedding.[14]

The groom had been born in Buffalo in 1849 and graduated from Columbia. He was a director of the M&T Bank, thanks to his brother-in-law, Robert L. Fryer, president, and belonged to the Buffalo and Saturn clubs, but does not seem to have done much regular work either before or after marriage.[15] After Charles Williams' death the childless Pratts moved into #690:

> Mrs. Pratt's unforget[t]able "gold room" on the left as one enters the front door, was decorated by Jansen of Paris. With its ceiling and wall panels of 22-carat gold, rustling taffeta hangings of light blue, and imported Louis XV furniture, it was a veritable gem of a room. For her home, Mrs. Pratt collected objects of art from Europe and the Orient. Among them were such famous paintings as The Apostles, by Justus Von Ghent; Giovanni Bellini's Flight into Egypt, works of Sir Peter Lely and Roselli, French paintings dating back to the 18th century, rare porcelains, exquisitely-wrought silver dishes and bric-a-brac, mineral carvings including rose quartz and rock crystal. Oriental rugs and hangings of finest workmanship, and furniture created of rare woods, gilded or carved, and upholstered with rich soft materials.[16]

Frederick Pratt died in 1922, but that did not diminish Jeannie's love of extravaganzas:

> Unique and exotic was the Oriental ball at which Mrs. Pratt was hostess on January 29, 1926. Flowers and colored lights transfor[m]ed her home into a tropical setting in the midst of snowclad Buffalo. The large enclosed porch was canopied in purple and gold. The table was adorned with orchids and mimosa. At midnight the Royal Marimba Orchestra and a Spanish dancer in colorful costume entertained the guests. Attired as a Persian princess in a rose, white and silver costume ornamented with ropes of pearls and a high headdress of black and white plumes, Mrs. Pratt stood picturesquely at the foot of the broad staircase to receive her guests. Every guest, in costume of brilliant hue, added to the ornamentation of the gala scene.[17]

The widow may have been competing with her sister-in-law in collecting celebrities:

> In that Delaware Ave. mansion, royalty, nobility and eminent American statesmen were entertained. They included the Prince and Princess of Hesse, the French Duke of Previse, former U.S. Secretary of State Frank Billings Kellogg, Gov. and Mrs. Slaton of Georgia, national leaders of France, Metropolitan opera prima donnas and other concert artists heard in recital by Mrs. Pratt's friends in her large drawing room, and celebrated French authors brought to this city by Mrs. Pratt to address the French-speaking population. The Duke of Previse crossed the Atlantic to visit Mrs. Pratt in appreciation of her reconstruction, following World War I, of the Town Hall of Sens, his home community.[18]

14 *CE*, January 20, 1952.
15 *Courier*, May 13, 1922.
16 *CE, ibid.*
17 *Ibid.*
18 *Ibid.*

10.10 Number 125 North, *Grand American Avenue*, p. 52.

Nothing about the mansion had been done on the cheap:

> The dining room, with gold rose and turquoise woodwork, boasts a safe the size of a modern closet, presumably for storage of silver and gold service. Upstairs, some of the bedrooms have room-size closets with built-in drawers and cupboards. The service portions of the house were only slightly less elegant. Both the butler's pantry and the kitchen at the rear of the house have ceilings and much wall space covered with 5 inch white and Delft blue ceramic tile in a lacy pattern.
>
> Walnut and mahogany paneling and beams abound in the house along with delicate brass doorknobs and window lifts. In the mahogany rooms, however, there are crystal doorknobs. Doors three inches thick, brass chains instead of slash cords, intricately inlaid floors and walls 18 inches thick attest to the original solidity of the construction.[19]

In 1920 Pratt and wife managed this operation with a butler and six servants. They also had an estate on the Lake Shore Road.[20] They spent much of their time abroad and Jeannie did so even after his death. The 1930's Depression was hard on her since, "she lost most of her fortune."[21] However she held out at #690 until 1938, when the city seized the property for back taxes, and she decamped for the Gates Circle Apartments. She died in 1949 at eighty-one and a memorial service was held at Christ Chapel.[22]

The mansion stood idle for three years during which it lost most of its plumbing and electrical fixtures through theft, and ivy overgrew the once luxuriant garden. In 1941 the house was made a G.A.R. Memorial. Fifteen groups of veterans, auxiliaries, and other patriotic clubs, held about twenty meetings a month there. In the carriage house an auditorium and card playing facilities were built for the Disabled War Veterans of America. The mansion has been restored as an office building like its sister structure at #672. There were two other Stanford White houses near Delaware and North, the Root house at #650 Delaware(8.29) and the Metcalfe house at #125 North(10.10), concerning which latter structure Kowsky writes:

> But despite the power of Richardson's example, his architecture, as well as the picturesque styles of the 1870s and 1880s, gave way to the rising tide of neoclassicism that nearly overwhelmed national taste during the last decade of the nineteenth century. Chief among the practitioners of this imperious display was the New York City firm of McKim, Mead & White. In 1882 the young office received its first commission in Buffalo, the Erzalia Metcalf house, located just west of Delaware Avenue on North Street. It may have been socialite Frances Wolcott (*nee* Metcalfe) who asked the firm to design the dwelling for her mother, for Frances associated with the writers and artists — including White, John La Farge, Augustus Saint-Gaudens, Stanford White, and Charles McKim — who

19 *Ibid*, May 27, 1955.
20 *CE*, March 27, 1929.
21 *CE*, March 8, 1935.
22 *CE*, August 19, 1949.

10.11 ❦ Sherman Skinner Rogers, Smith, *op. cit.*, II, facing p. 128.

clustered around Mariana Griswold Van Rensselaer in New York. The brick, stone, and shingle Colonial Revival house was a masterpiece of the partners' early period and surpassed in originality their more well known neoclassical works. Its demolition in 1982 for a parking lot was a grievous loss to the city.[23]

The house in the foreground of figure 10.2 belonged to Valorus Hodge who was living there as early as 1860. He was a builder and during the 1860s and early 1870s had an office and yard on the undeveloped east side of Delaware above Allen. The Hodge house was torn down in 1877 and a home built for Sherman Skinner Rogers(10.11), a native of Bath where he was born in 1830, the son of Gustavus Rogers, an ex-New Englander, and Susan A. Campbell of Scottish ancestry. At sixteen Rogers began reading law in the offices of attorneys in Bath. In 1851 at twenty-one he formed a partnership with his uncle, Robert Campbell, quondam lieutenant governor, and Charles W. Campbell of Bath, which lasted until 1854 when Rogers left for Buffalo. There he married Christina Cameron Davenport of Bath and became a partner of another uncle, Henry W. Rogers of #314 Delaware, and Dennis Bowen to form Rogers, Bowen & Rogers. Franklin Locke of #344 Delaware was later admitted to what became Bowen, Rogers & Locke. Bowen died in 1877, but the name was perpetuated until 1883 when John Milburn and Charles Wheeler were admitted, the result being Rogers, Locke & Milburn. A Democrat before the Civil War, Rogers turned Republican after Fort Sumter and was elected state senator in 1875. He ran for lieutenant governor in 1876 but lost. He was president of the Reform Association in Buffalo and of the trustees of Calvary Presbyterian.[24]

On #698 the saccharine Anglophile, Jane Burleigh, wrote:

> As I loitered along Delaware Ave., and paused a moment by the house where the Rogers once lived, (three doors above North St., on the western side), its dignified, conservative outlines conjured back the brilliance and serenity of a family which had the assurance that life is worthy of being lived with earnestness and grace.
>
> Sherman S. Rogers and his wife...were people of note in Bath, from whence they came to Buffalo. They were very dignified, very conservative, and it was natural that they should build a home that would adequately express their dominant qualities, and for which they could have a feeling of the deepest and most satisfying sort. I have always thought of this house as Tudor, but it may be Queen Anne; anyway, it is like a fine old English manor, reduced to the scale of a city dwelling. The gables, the tiled roofs, the beautiful chimneys, reminiscent of the soft richness of rose red and tawny-brown of a water-color in the Kensington Museum.(10.12)

23 Cigliano *et alii*, *op. cit.*, p. 52.
24 Smith, *op. cit.*, 2:79-80.

> Distinctly a period house, and never changed, a faint scent of lavender seemed to breathe from waxed floors, from china bowls and vases, and from busts on marble tables. The chairs and sofas were such as Fanny Burney and Walpole's Miss Berrys might have sat upon a hundred years before; of the sumptuous books which filled with their glimmer of color and gilded calf, the many shelves in the long drawing-room. Very few were too modern; and there was a legend woven about a huge Chinese jar, which stood on the floor, holding relics of ancestral rose-leaves. There were many portraits – proud judges and stately dames, and a pastel of a young woman in a turban, in the full regard of whose melting and melancholy eyes floated all the romance that troubled the days of Byron.

10.12 ❦ Number 698 Delaware, BHS.

> On all sides were traces of devotion to art and literature. Art, indeed, was represented by such fragments as three quarters of a century ago, men of taste used to bring from Europe; but the oaken library contained a collection whose character suggested that they had been gotten together by one remarkable man — a scholar as well as a lover of staid luxury. The sunny dining room shone with burnished mahogany and gleaming Georgian silver.

> A rather aloof, yet genial, host Sherman Rogers of the famous law firm of Rogers Locke and Milburn could not forbear twinkling when he told how his guest, Lord Coleridge, chief justice of England, after eating many of the "buckwheat biscuits" he had asked for, turned to his daughter and remarked: "They're not as nasty as they look, Mary!"

> Nevertheless, I like the insolent English, Mr. Rogers would add. He might have been an Englishman himself, with his side-burns, his ruddy color, and his erect carriage.[25]

The Rogers had two girls and a boy, Fanny, Lydia, and Robert Cameron. Fanny married Charles MacVeagh, son of Isaac MacVeagh, minister to Turkey in 1870, Attorney General during Garfield's administration, and ambassador to Italy 1893-1895. Charles graduated from Harvard in 1881, practiced corporation law in New York, and was ambassador to Japan 1925-1929.[26] The son, Robert Rogers, was born in 1862, graduated from Yale in 1883, traveled, attended Harvard Law, and returned to Buffalo to work in his father's law firm. But he disliked law and took up poetry and fiction. He wrote occasionally for the *Buffalo Courier* and *Harper's Weekly*. On the advice of Charles Stedman, a literary critic, Rogers was picked to write the "Pan American Ode." He is also believed to have written the poem, "My Rosary," which was translated into twenty languages, put to music, sold 4,000,000 copies, and became one of the favorite songs of Madame Schumann-Heink, a world-famous contralto. He left Buffalo in the late 1890s, moved to Santa Barbara where he married a rich widow, and died in 1912 of an unsuccessful appendectomy.[27]

25 *Times*, June 11, 1936.
26 *Concise Dictionary of American Biography*, p. 626.
27 *Ibid.*, June 11. 1936; *CE*, May 14, 1954; *Who Was Who in America*, 2:1052.

10.13 ❦ Westminster Presbyterian, author's collection.

Successor to Rogers at #698 was Samuel Strong Spaulding, son of Civil War congressman, Elbridge Spaulding. Samuel and his wife, the former Annie Watson, had previously resided at #472 Delaware, once Mark Twain's house. Number 706 was a small house on a small building lot between the Rogers-Spaulding house and Westminster. Its first occupant during the 1850s was James W. Davoch, a laborer. His widow was still there in 1870, after which James C. Brown, attorney, and family moved in, followed in the 1880s by Aldrich Allen, and in the 1890s by H. D. Folinsbee, a realtor. Late in the decade Oscar L. Harries, a realtor, took up residence there. By 1905 he was billing himself as a medical doctor. The last residents of this home were the family of Louis Wright Simpson, who had been born in Saginaw, Michigan in 1874, came to Buffalo at ten with his parents, graduated from Cornell in 1896, studied law at U.B., and was admitted to the bar in 1898. After ten years practicing law he joined R. W. Goode & Company, realtors, and became vice-president before leaving for California, where he died at Pasadena in 1931.

The angel of Westminster(10.13) was Jesse Ketchum, who had been born in Spencertown, New York, where he spent his early years as an apprentice tanner. In 1799 he went to York (later Toronto) where he and his brother started a tanning business. Later they did the same in Buffalo. Jesse had made enough money by 1832 to retire, but stayed in York until coming to Buffalo in 1845 where he soon became a wealthy property owner. That year he purchased a lot for a church on Delaware near North. Two years later as a first step in establishing a parish he built a small brick chapel which failed to attract worshipers and the chapel had to be closed. Undeterred, he built a manse next to the chapel, hoping to attract a minister. He even offered to pay $800 a year until a regular congregation came into being. Rev. John Jermain Porter took up the offer and by August 1850 services were again being held in the chapel.

However it was not until April 11, 1853, that the Westminster Presbyterian Society was incorporated, the charter members of which consisted of ten persons dismissed from First Church and thirty from other Presbyterian churches. With membership growing, the chapel was enlarged in 1855. This was a temporary solution, and the original chapel was demolished and a cornerstone laid for a church in August 1858. The first service in the new building was held on September 20, 1859.

> Constructed of Milwaukee brick, with a limestone foundation and trim, the Italianite [*sic*] building, as it appears today, is basically the same as when first dedicated in 1859. In

10.14 ❦ Louis L. Babcock, *M&FH*, II, facing p. 9.

1902, the congregation embarked upon a major renovation of it. At that time the west (rear) wall was removed and extended thirty feet, adding an extra window on both the north and south wall of the nave and allowing for greater seating capacity in the auditorium. The original flat roof was replaced with the current pitched one and the arched windows of the tower were replaced by the present rectangular ones. With Tiffany Glass and Decorating in charge of the interior renovations, electrical light fixtures and ten new windows were installed. At this time, the building was painted in colors similar to those reapplied during the 1933 renovation.

In 1930, Westminster began to replace the Tiffany windows installed during the 1902 renovation. Designed in the Gothic revival style, the current windows are similar to those found in European churches dating from the 12th and 13th centuries. The twenty-three memorial windows were designed by four prominent American artists: Henry Lee Willett studios, Philadelphia[,] and Wilbur Burnham, Charles Connick and Joseph Reynolds of Boston. Among the highlights of the collection is the "Praise" window by the Willett studios. Installed in 1967, it features notable 20th century musicians and contains a small panel depicting Schroeder of 'Peanuts' cartoon fame. The last remaining Tiffany window can be seen in the Delaware Avenue entrance to the building.[28]

North of the church in figure 10.13 can be seen part of the roof and front of #726, the manse built by Ketchum in 1849. The first two occupants were ministers, Rev. Erskine White in the 1860s and 1870s and Rev. T. Ralston Smith in the 1880s. After the church had provided its pastor with more ample living quarters, the ex-manse housed first an artist, then an auditor, and finally a clothing salesman until the First World War when a resident appeared more like the usual inhabitants of the Avenue. Louis Locke Babcock(10.14), was born in Gowanda in 1868. He attended public school, Gowanda Academy, and Professor Briggs' Classical School. At eighteen he began reading law in the office of a Gowanda firm, and two years later came to Buffalo to study law with Rogers, Locke & Milburn. Admitted to the bar in 1890, he became managing clerk and worked with Milburn until he moved to New York. Thereafter the firm was known as Rogers, Locke & Babcock. In 1896 he wed Georgia Woodin of Gowanda and they had four children. Corporate law was his specialty and he lectured on negligence law at U.B; but the military was his avocation. In January 1890 at twenty-two he enlisted as a private in Company G of the 65th Regiment, NYNG. During the Spanish-American War he raised a company for the 65th and as a captain commanded the unit March-November 1898. They never got to Cuba but spent a bad summer in an unhealthy camp in Virginia. In 1903 he was made a major and attached to the staff of the commander of the 4th Brigade, NYNG. Though he

28 Napora, *op. cit.*, pp. 57-58; Hill, *op. cit.*, 2:582.

Above 10.15 ❦ Looking north from Delaware and Summer, circa 1890, author's collection.
Middle 10.16 ❦ Looking north from Delaware and Summer, circa 1890, author's collection.
Below 10.17 ❦ Number 762 Delaware, BHS.

retired from the guard in 1913, Governor Whitman appointed him to organize a 5,000-man brigade to replace the regular guard units in Western New York that had been sent overseas during World War I. Governor Theodore Roosevelt had appointed Babcock to a two year-term as member of the Board of Managers of the State Industrial School at Rochester. He was a member of the U.B. Council and counsel for the university, executive secretary of the Erie County Bar, Dean of Saturn in 1905, and member of the Country, Buffalo, and Genesee Valley clubs. He was long identified with Westminster. An amateur historian and member of the Buffalo Historical Society, he wrote a book on the siege of Fort Erie in the War of 1812 and a manual on riot duty for the guard. In his later years, he was of counsel for Hodgson, Russ, Andrews, Woods & Goodyear. His property was reacquired by Westminster in 1956. The pastor, Dr. Albert J. Butzer, would not reveal the price, but said that the property had been sold to the Babcock family in 1916 and that "General Babcock and the church had a gentleman's agreement that we be notified should the house be offered for sale. Recently we were informed of this and a mutually agreeable price was reached." The church took occupancy in June, and the general, at eighty-seven and confined to the house, moved with his two daughters to an apartment on West Ferry where he died on November 5.[29]

The story of #742, the Dexter Rumsey house on the southeast corner of Delaware and Summer, has been told in chapter 6. At this point began a block of the most outstanding mansions on the Avenue. Figures 10.15 and 10.16 are two views looking north from Delaware and Summer about 1890.

29 Hill, *op. cit.*, 4:411-412; Horton, *op. cit.*, 3:404-405; Warren, *op. cit.*, p.96; *BEN*, March 14, 1956.

The first house on this corner, #762(10.17), was built in 1859-1860 for Myron P. Bush(10.18), scion of a family that had come to America from Germany in the eighteenth century. It was designed by J. D. Towle, a Boston architect who also was responsible for the design of Bronson Rumsey's mansion on #330 Delaware(6.27) and George Howard's at #806(10.34):

> Myron P. Bush was president [of the Buffalo Club] for 1875, the first native of the Niagara Frontier to hold the office. He was born in Clarence in October, 1819, the son of a tanner. At age twenty-five, he formed a partnership with George Howard, Bush & Howard, sole leather dealers. Their success was such that both men retired from active business after eight years, permitting sons of each to continue the business. In later life, Bush helped develop several railroads, was once president of the Hannibal & St Joseph [in Missouri]. He was partner in a New York brokerage firm, president of the Marine Bank, and a director of the Manufacturers & Traders Bank. He not only helped found the Buffalo Club but also the Buffalo Driving Park Association, a group of horse enthusiasts of great importance in that day.[30]

Above 10.18 ❦ Myron P. Bush, Warren, *op. cit.*, p. 28.
Below 10.19 ❦ Grounds of #762, *PBHS*, 16(1912), p. 431.

The Bush residence stood on five and a quarter acres, well designed and maintained.(10.19) Bush and his wife, Margaret Westervelt, had a daughter and two sons, John and George. John Westervelt Bush(10.20) was born in 1844. When his education was over, he joined his father in Bush & Howard. The senior Bush died in 1885. His son took over the firm and retained it until 1887, when he sold out to George Howard and retired. John resided at #742 until it was sold in 1903 and the house was torn down to make room for one of the Avenue's grand but short-lived mansions. Bush then moved to Lincoln Parkway, part of Delaware's irredenta. He died there in 1924 at seventy-nine.[31]

10.20 ❦ John Westervelt Bush, *HNF*, 3:381.

30 Warren, *op.* cit., p, 28.
31 Hill, *op. cit.*, 3:462; *HNF*, 3:380-386; *PBHS*, 16(1912), p. 433.

Above 10.21 ❦ Number 762 Delaware, BHS.
Middle 10.22 ❦ Number 762 Delaware, *Ibid.*
Below 10.23 ❦ Number 762 Delaware, *Ibid.*, p. 203.

The grand mansion at #762 of which three views are given in figures 10.21, 22, and 23 was that of Frank Henry Goodyear.(10.24) As with the Rumseys, genealogy must precede history here, since the Goodyears were an equally important family. Their progenitor was Dr. Jabez Bradley Goodyear, born in 1816, in Sempronius, New York. He dropped the Jabez at the time of his marriage. His first occupation was that of tailor. In his mid-twenties he spent two years traveling through the South, supporting himself by his trade before returning to New York, where he was induced by his uncle, Dr. Miles Goodyear, president of the Cortland County Medical Society, to start practicing medicine as early as 1843. Jabez graduated from Geneva Medical College in 1845 and married Esther Permelia Kinne. She had been born in Cortland in 1822 of New England stock, including an ancestor, who, in the best tradition of earnest Puritans, had come to America via Leyden, Holland, in 1635. They lived in Virgil but moved to a farm near Cortland where their two sons were born, Charles Waterhouse in 1846 and Frank Henry in 1849.[32]

Frank was a standard nineteenth century tycoon. Soon after his birth, his family moved to Holland in Erie County. As a boy he worked at Root & Keating's tannery as did brother Charles. Frank attended the district school and East Aurora Academy when his father was practicing medicine there. Later Frank taught in the district school. He then went to Looneyville in Alden as a bookkeeper for Robert Looney, a native of the Island of Man, who ran a farm, sawmill, general store, and feed and grain business and also owned vast timberlands in Pennsylvania. In 1871 Frank married the boss' daughter, twenty-year old Josephine. Next year her father died. Frank had already moved to Buffalo where he set up a coal and lumber business with help from the ubiquitous Elbridge Spaulding. Frank had arranged that Josephine's share in her father's estate should be timberlands. He threw himself into the lumber business, setting up several mills in his

32 Goodyear, *op., cit.*, pp. 1-23. I have taken almost everything about Frank and Charles Goodyear and their descendants from this work. George was Charles' grandson, and he eschewed filiopietism.

33 *Ibid.*, pp. 48-56.

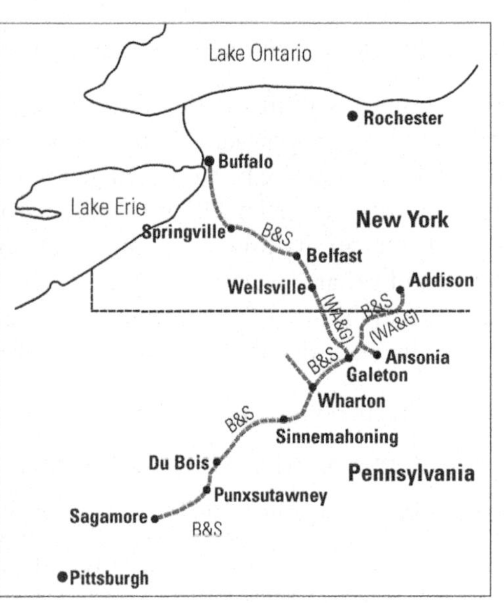

Above Left 10.24 ❦ Frank Henry Goodyear, *M&FH*, I, facing p. 102.
Above Right 10.25 ❦ Buffalo & Susquehanna Railroad, Drury, *op. cit.*, p. 44.
Middle 10.26 ❦ Buffalo & Susquehanna Iron Company, Paul Pietrak, *The Buffalo & Susquehanna Railroad* (North Boston, New York: Paul Pietrak, 1967), p. 60.
Below 10.27 ❦ The *Frank H. Goodyear*, *Ibid.*, p. 59. The private car on deck was Frank Goodyear's.

timberlands along the Western New York & Pennsylvania to Buffalo. In 1884 he bought more land in Potter County and built a sawmill at a town he renamed Austin, which became headquarters of his empire. He initiated temporary railroads, called tramways, to carry logs to his mills instead of floating them down on streams. His frantic pace brought on a nervous breakdown, during which he induced Charles to form F. H. & C. W. Goodyear and took a European rest cure. The story of their joint activities is that of two brothers who did not get along.[33]

The Achilles' heel of the Goodyear empire was Frank's decision to expand the railroads servicing his sawmills into an interstate road, the Buffalo & Susquehanna(10.25), to link his mills and the coal mines in western Pennsylvania with the Buffalo & Susquehanna Iron Company which the Goodyears had formed in 1902 to operate blast furnaces south of Buffalo on Lake Erie.(10.26) Two freighters, the *Frank H. Goodyear* and the *S. M. Clement*, were built to carry ore from the company's mines in Minnesota and Michigan down to Buffalo.(10.27) This was ver-

34 George H. Drury, *The Historical Guide to North American Railroads* (Waukesha, Wisconsin: Kalmbach Publishing Company, 1985), pp. 36-37.

tical integration, but it duplicated existing services with an inefficient railroad:

> In 1906 the Goodyears built the Buffalo & Susquehanna Railroad from Wellsville to Buffalo, nearly 90 miles. A year later Frank Goodyear died; his brother Charles died in 1911, and the Goodyear empire began to fall apart. The expense of constructing the line to Buffalo began to cause financial difficulty, and the road laid aside plans to extend its line to Pittsburgh and relocate its line to eliminate the four switcbacks over the mountains between Galeton and Wharton. The Buffalo & Susquehanna Railway leased the Buffalo & Susquehanna Railroad, but that didn't forestall receivership. After a brief period of operation as the Wellsville & Buffalo, the Buffalo extension was scrapped in 1916.[34]

More successful were Frank's ventures in Louisiana where in 1901 he acquired a large tract of white pine. Next year the Great Southern Lumber Company was formed with Frank as president and Charles vice-president. They had invested $9 million in 300,000 acres in Louisiana and Mississippi along the Pearl River. In 1905 a town site was selected along the Bogue Lusa Creek, a tributary of the Pearl, and a town christened Bogalusa was built with shops, offices, a bank, and separate black and white residential sections, all centered on a sawmill. The ninety mile New Orleans Great Northern Railroad was created to connect Bogalusa with the national network. Frank died of Bright's disease in 1907, shortly after moving into his new home at #672 Delaware. He had not gotten much physical exercise and though only five feet eight, he weighed 220 pounds, a victim of overeating. His absorbing interest was business and he had a keen business sense. His estate was worth $10,000,000. The family chronicler wrote:

> He had a quick, eager, incisive mind and was irascibly impatient with the plodder... He was forever making notes and even at a formal dinner there was a pad and pencil beside his place. Often he could not read the notes he had made ...He was never really happy. The only thing he enjoyed was success that needed constant increase and he died looking failure in the face, the failure of his pet project, the Buffalo and Susquehanna Railway. He was the head of every enterprise with which he was connected, all of them, but the one, greatly successful. He told me that if a man was successful in six out of ten enterprises he was himself a success and seven out of ten made him an extraordinary success, but when it came to his own case he needed ten out of ten.[35]

Shortly after his death the panic of 1907 struck. Town and railroad building stopped. The sawmill had been completed, but did not go into operation until late 1908. But though the effects of the panic lingered, the decision to start up proved sound. It was the largest sawmill in the world.

Frank's money-making left him little time for other activities. President Cleveland appointed him in 1886 to examine federal land granted to the Northern Pacific Railroad. He was Park Commissioner of Buffalo, president of the Buffalo Club in 1903, and director of three local concerns: Marine Bank, Rogers Brown Iron Company, and United States Leather, a customer for the bark from his sawmills. His clubs were the Lawyers' and Manhattan clubs of New York, the Buffalo, Country, Ellicott, Falconwood, and Liberal clubs of Buffalo, and the Jekyll Club of Jekyll Island, Georgia.[36]

35 Goodyear, *op. cit.*, p. 52.
36 *Ibid.*, p. 51.
37 *CA*, October 18, 1915.

Frank's mansion at #762, modeled on a house on the Champs-Elysees in Paris, was completed in 1906. By then his three daughters, Grace who married Ganson Depew, Josephine who married George M. Sicard, and Florence who married George O. Wagner, had left home. Frank had resided briefly at #443 Delaware when he came to Buffalo in 1872. Thereafter he lived in succession at #652 Main, #671 Main, and #267 North. His wife Josephine, a retiring soul, died at sixty-four in October 1915 of the effects of a heart attack at the Exchange Street Station. She was remembered as the benefactress of the convalescent home for children named after her in Williamsville.[37]

Grace, the eldest of Frank and Josephine's children, had been born in 1872. In 1894 she married Ganson Depew who had been born in 1862 and was everybody's choice for Mr. Nice Guy. He was the nephew of Chauncey Depew, president of the New York Central and Senator from New York 1900-1911. Admitted to the bar in 1887, Ganson deserted the law to work for his father-in-law and became manager of Goodyear Lumber, vice-president of Buffalo & Susquehanna Coal, and assistant to the president of the Buffalo & Susquehanna Railway. Early in their marriage, Esther contracted tuberculosis. Ganson took her to St. Moritz in Switzerland to nurse her back to health. There they spent five years. But Esther neglected her health and was unfaithful. They returned to Buffalo, lived with Aunt Ella Goodyear at #888, and were divorced in 1909. Esther moved to Colorado, built a beautiful home there, married again, divorced again, and died of tuberculosis in 1914.[38]

Frank Goodyear's second daughter, Josephine, born in 1874, married George Montgomery Sicard in 1900. The Sicards came from Utica where George was born in 1872. His uncle, George J. Sicard, was a partner of Cleveland, Bissell & Sicard, and later of Frank's brother Charles in Bissell, Sicard & Goodyear. George Sicard attended Utica Academy, graduated from Yale in 1894, received his law degree from N.Y.U. in 1895, and came to Buffalo where he began practice with Moot, Sprague & Brownell. After marriage he went to work for Frank's lumber and railroad companies. Josephine, his wife, died in 1904. Soon afterwards Sicard, who had not gotten along with his father-in-law, resigned from his companies and moved to Pelham Manor where he lived the last thirty years of his life.[39]

10.28 ❦ Florence Goodyear & Children, *op. cit.*, p. 291.

Florence(10.28), Frank Goodyear's third daughter, attended Saint Margaret's School in Buffalo and finishing school in New York. Back in Buffalo she married in 1902

38 Goodyear, *op. cit.*, pp. 247-248.
39 *Ibid.*, pp. 255-256.

George Olds Wagner, a Cornell alumnus and a civil engineer. They had two daughters but their marriage did not last. They were divorced in Paris 1907. Two years later she married Charles M. Daniels. In 1913 Josephine and Daniels built an elaborate house on eleven square miles at Sabbatis in the Adirondacks, on which they built a nine-hole golf course and a hunting lodge. Here they lived most of the year save for three winter months in Buffalo. In 1921 they bought the house at #787 Delaware where Daniels' grandfather, Judge Charles Daniels, had lived until his death in 1897 and his wife until her's in 1917. The Daniels had the house remodeled, and it was their Buffalo home until 1931 when it was razed. The Sabattis house was Florence's main residence until 1937 when all save the lodge and five square miles were sold. Soon afterwards she moved to Chapin Parkway. Florence and Daniels were divorced in 1942. She was a fine bridge and golf player, a member of the Garret Club, and the Valley Country Club and Town Club in Santa Barbara. She was also president of the Josephine Goodyear Home in Williamsville. She died in Buffalo in 1958.[40]

Frank H. Goodyear, Jr., was born in Buffalo in 1891. He graduated from the Pawling School and attended Yale with the class of 1916, but never graduated. He had married Dorothy Virginia Knox in 1915. They began their married life in the home on Delaware and Summer which had been left to him by his mother along with the cottage on Jekyll Island. In 1917 he enlisted in the Naval Aviation Service with the unit formed by his sister Grace's first husband, Ganson Depew. After training at Buffalo, Frank was commissioned an ensign and stationed at Pensacola at the Armistice. Returning to Buffalo in 1919, he formed with other wealthy Buffalonians an agency for Goodyear (no relation) tires and Ward La France trucks. In 1921 he and Hamilton Wende organized a company which acquired exclusive rights to sell Texaco products in Western New York through a string of service stations. In 1927 the company's name was changed to the Goodyear-Wende Oil Company. Positions inherited from his father were vice-president and director of the Great Southern Lumber Company, vice-president and director of the New Orleans Great Northern Railway, director of the Gulf Mobile & Northern Railroad, of Marine Trust, and of the Bogalusa Paper company. He was a member of the Automobile, Country, Athletic, Park, and Tennis & Squash clubs in Buffalo, the Niagara Falls and East Aurora country clubs, the Yale and Racket & Tennis Club in New York, and the Jekyll Island Club. He was a fine athlete, particularly at polo and squash, and was an excellent bridge player. He and Dorothy had four children, Dorothy Knox, Frank H., III, Marjorie Knox, and Robert H.[41]

Frank altered the stables behind #762 for an indoor tennis and squash court and a large second floor room for parties. The adjacent garage held a dozen cars. Frank and Dorothy also built a country house in East Aurora on land previously owned by her father. In the late 1920s they built a more spacious English style country house with stables on North Davis Road three miles from their original house which they turned over to Dorothy's brother, Seymour Knox, II. The new house,

40 *Ibid.*, pp. 258-259.
41 *Ibid.*, p. 262.

"Crag Burn," on manicured grounds and a smaller house where their youngest son Robert lived, were set on 113 acres on the west side of Davis Road. The large trees lining the driveway had been brought up on flat cars from Bogalusa. The stables and other buildings, plus a polo field and miles of wooded bridle paths, were located on 222 acres on the same side of Davis Road.[42]

Frank enjoyed yachting and had built several large yachts, all named *Poule d'Eau*. The last and largest was a magnificent vessel, 122 feet long, with two 300-horsepower diesel engines. It blew up off their winter home on Jekyll Island in 1929, only hours after Frank and his guests had left. The engineer was killed. Worse was to come.[43] The *Buffalo* News for October 14, 1930, announced: **F.H. GOODYEAR DIES IN MOTOR ACCIDENT: Millionaire Financier Injured Fatally When Car Crashes Against Tree in Transit road – Wife, Three Friends Hurt.** Goodyear, with his wife and two weekend guests, was driving his Rolls-Royce north on Transit between Broadway and Genesee on the way to a dinner engagement in North Tonawanda. He tried to pass a slower moving car, but collided with a southbound car that suddenly appeared on the scene. Goodyear's car left the road, went into a ditch, hit a tree, and turned over. Sheriff Charles Freiberg declined to take action on the conflicting stories offered by riders in the three cars involved.[44]

Dorothy extricated herself from the overturned car, called for help, and a group of men levered the Rolls away from the tree and tilted it so that Goodyear could be removed. He had suffered a broken neck, a crushed chest, a broken leg, and had lost consciousness. An Emergency Hospital ambulance brought him (he died en route) and his wife, who had wrenched her shoulder, to the hospital.[45] An odd development was the discovery of an automatic pistol beside Goodyear's body. A deputy sheriff opined that it had been catapulted from the door pocket of the car. It turned out that Goodyear was a special deputy.

A year later Goodyear's widow married Edmund Pendleton Rogers, a widower, of New York and Westbury, Long Island, a native of Hyde Park, New York, the son of Archibald Rogers who had been prominent in Standard Oil in its early days. Edmund was the most enduring of Franklin Roosevelt's childhood friends.[46] Edmund and Dorothy lived for a time in East Aurora but mostly in New York City, Long Island, and Aiken, South Carolina. After Frank's death the mansion at #762, which had cost $500,000 ($8,715,000 in 1997 dollars) to build, remained empty.[47] Mansions were a drag on the market during the Depression. Descriptions of its razing hint at what it had been like:

> The main rooms of the house are unusually large and are connected with spacious corridors set in marble. The living room is paneled with carved mahogany and its great fireplace is of marble. Adjoining the living room are a hall with an organ and a reception room only slightly smaller than the living room. On the second floor are six large bedrooms, each with a marble fireplace. The stone, like many of the furnishings, was collected by the elder Mr. Goodyear from all parts of the world.[48]

42 *Ibid.*, pp. 263-264.
43 *Ibid.*
44 *BEN*, October 14, 1930.
45 *Times*, October 14 , 1930.
46 Kenneth S. Davis, *FDR: The Beckoning of Destiny, 1882-1928*, (New York: G. P. Putnam's Sons, 1972), p. 66.
47 Goodyear, *op. cit.*, p. 265.
48 *BEN*, October 10, 1938.

10.29 ❦ Number 776 Delaware, BHS.

Every piece of marble, ornamental iron, rich woodwork and stone which went into the making of the palatial structure when it was built in 1902 [read 1906] has been sold. Every fragment of pillars and archways, which were fashioned into the famous marble hall of the mansion has been carefully numbered to be removed and delivered to its new owner.

Magnificent chandeliers already have been removed, as has the library paneling carved of black walnut, and the beautiful marble mantlepiece. One of the first things to be removed was the electric elevator. Before the day was over, most of the fixtures had been removed from the room, including stately mirrors and massive oak doors.[49]

After Rogers died in 1966, his widow found that the house and grounds in East Aurora, on Long Island, and at Aiken, all with large staffs of servants, were too expensive to maintain. Dorothy Wykoff and Robert Goodyear, Dorothy Goodyear Rogers's oldest daughter and youngest son, determined on a golf course and housing development on North Davis Road. Of 330 acres 190 were set aside for a course, and 140 acres for home sites. The stables became the clubhouse. The course, designed by Robert Trent Jones, was completed in 1971. Dorothy Knox Goodyear Rogers died at Aiken in 1980, at eighty-four.[50]

Lumber baron William H. Gratwick(7.12) had resided briefly in the 1870s at #414, the Second Empire masterpiece at Delaware and Edward. Gratwick in the early 1880s had hired H. H. Richardson to design a house further up the Avenue at #776. The result was not Second Empire:(10.29)

> As well as being the time of the Queen Anne movement, the decade of the 1880s saw Richardson's star rise to its apogee. Buffalo had given him his first truly important commission, the Buffalo State Hospital of 1870, and the city became the location of his last work, the Delaware Avenue mansion of William Gratwick. Commissioned only two months before Richardson's death [1886], the building was completed by Shepley, Rutan & Coolidge. Photographs taken when the house was new revealed that the exterior faithfully followed Richardson's intentions. The interior, however, may have been more heavily decorated than Richardson would have liked — if the [John J.] Glessner house [in Chicago] is any guide. The acres of luxurious furnishings must have reflected Gratwick's notion of how a wealthy individual should live. Self made, Gratwick had gained his fortune in lake shipping and in lumbering. His house, which he himself had few years to enjoy, was undoubtedly intended to crown his success, and it is not known if he chose Richardson as his artist for any other reason than his golden reputation. Tragically for American architecture, the massive dwelling came down within thirty years of its construction.[51]

Gratwick's daughter Mildred was a childhood friend of Mabel Ganson who recalled that "Mildred lived in a massive house made up of square blocks of granite two blocks above us on Delaware," and that "her father was a dapper little man who always wore a silk hat over his square-cut head. He had

49 *CE*, October 11, 1938.
50 Goodyear, *op. cit.*, p. 265.
51 Chigliano, *op. cit.*, pp. 51-52.

Above 10.30 ❦ Number 786 Delaware, BHS.
Below 10.31 ❦ Erastus S. Prosser, *Times*, July 23, 1882.

a bright, specious smile and he swaggered a bit as he walked up and down Delaware dressed in his frock coat." His wife "always dressed in black, I think in memory of a little girl who died. She was a pale-faced ugly woman with the long bending stride like a camel that short-waisted women with long legs sometimes have, and the amiably haughty smile of a camel." Of Mildred, Ganson wrote:

> She was a small-boned, lanky girl with brown hair and blue eyes, whose best point as far as looks went lay in her large white teeth. And the care of this — the brushings three times a day, the constant business with waxed silk, and the rinsings with lime-water — amounted to a ritual. Dot, her good fat nurse, her mother, and she seemed constantly to be dancing attendance upon those teeth. And besides that, there was a great deal of fussing over her slinky brown hair, up in the sunny dressing-room that opened off her bedroom with its twin beds for [her sister] Dot and herself that were hung with the finest white muslin over pale blue silk. Sitting before a mirror that hung between the two windows, Mildred had her hair "dressed" several times a day by her black-robed mother, who twisted and rolled the fine colourless hair around her ears and then braided it behind and tied red or dark blue ribbons on it. Mrs. Gratwick had a curious smile on her face as they did this — it was as though only she knew how precious and how beautiful her daughter was, how exquisite those locks she tenderly brushed, how incomparably winning, adorable and rare was the whole creature to whom she ministered.[52]

The Gratwick mansion was torn down in 1919. It was not replaced. The site was divided between the Goodyear property on the south and the Clement property on the north.[53]

Burr remembered the original mansion at #786 as:

> ...an imposing brown brick mansion of picturesque architecture, presenting a broad front to the street, with a main part and wings on either side, and the inevitable cupola on top. This house up to the very time it was razed to the ground to make way for the William H. Gratwick home and the S. M. Clement mansion, was considered by local and visiting architects as one of the most beautiful specimens of architecture in Buffalo.(10.30) It was the home of E. S. Prosser, one of the city's wealthy and prominent citizens, and the grounds were always perfectly kept, with ornamental flower beds to give a brilliant color effect.[54]

52 Luhan, *op. cit.*, pp. 99-101.
53 *PBHS*, 24(1920), p. 38.
54 *Courier*, June 28, 1927.

Erastus Sabinus Prosser(10.31), who lived there in the 1850s, was born in Westerloo, New York, in 1809, son of a country doctor. Erastus attended school for two or three years and at thirteen hired out to a farmer for the summer at four dollars a month. That fall he took the Erie Canal as far as it then went, which was Rochester, and despite his own deficient education taught school for two years at nearby Clarkson. After the canal was completed to Buffalo in 1825, he got a job on a canal boat and in three years had worked his way up to captain and half-owner of *The Lion of Brockport*. He next was employed as a clerk in a grocery store in Brockport and, aided by outside trade and speculation, amassed $3,000. In 1834 he married Lucy Wilber of Monroe County and had four children, a son and three daughters. Returning to Albany, he clerked for Dows & Cary, forwarders, impressed his employers, and at the end of a year, having set aside another $4,000, became a partner in Dows, Carey & Prosser. In 1854 he came to Buffalo and with other entrepreneur secured a stock of 1,500 animals, mostly mules, monopolizing this end of the canal transportation business. With two partners he built two steam-powered canal boats, the first such craft with any prospect of success. He owned the Prosser Block at West Seneca and Pearl where the Manufacturers & Traders Bank had its offices. In politics Prosser started as a Free-Soil Democrat and "went with the great body of Democratic Free-soilers into the Philadelphia convention that organized the Republican party and nominated Col. Charles Fremont for President" in 1856. In 1858 he was elected to the state senate and remained there until 1862. He was also elected to the 1866 state constitutional convention. In senate and convention he promoted the interests of the state's canals. During the 1860s he was vice-president of the International Bank and associated with Mayor William Fargo in many enterprises and in the 1870s he bought a big cement plant in nearby Akron. In religion Prosser moved from his ancestral Quakerism through Presbyterianism to rationalism and contributed to the Unitarian Church of Our Father.[55] He died in 1888, at seventy-eight.

That he may have died happier than many of his contemporary millionaires is suggested by the following item:

> AGED MILLIONAIRE WEDS: But the romance in the life of Miss Anastasia Finnegan was far more than Buffalo has experienced in the forty or more years since it culminated in her marriage with the aged ex-Senator Erastus S. Prosser, then residing at No. 786 Delaware Avenue.
>
> Miss Finnegan, tall, 'nice looking," was fashionable in her attire and one of the cleverest of our teachers. She resided with her widowed mother and sister, Mary, also a teacher in South Division Street and at that time Miss Anastasia was teaching at No. 12 in Spruce Street. But later she became department principal at No. 718 under Dr. Fullerton's principalship, and not far from the luxurious home of the very aged capitalist.
>
> In his daily walks the aged Mr. Prosser frequently encountered the smiling and rosy-cheeked teacher, Miss Finnegan and her many charms, of person, manners and character,

55 *Times*, July 23, 1882.

> won the old gentleman's heart. Well past the septuagenary period of life, Mr. Prosser's friends and relatives sought to break up the increasing friendship between the susceptible teacher and her aged admirer, but in vain, for shortly after a brief courtship, they were married and the fair bride went to preside as mistress of the Prosser mansion, in between the mansion of William H. Gratwick and that of Mrs. George Howard.
>
> Near neighbors of Mr. and Mrs. Prosser were such well-known Buffalonians as Dexter P. Rumsey, Myron P. Bush, George B. Mathews, Hascal L. Taylor, George H. Van Vleck and Jewett M. Richmond. In later years the Prosser mansion was occupied by Augustus P. Tripp and family.
>
> PROSSER INCOMPETENT? Strong efforts were made to have the courts decide that the marriage was void, that the aged bridegroom was senile and incompetent, etc. Mr. Prosser did not long survive this contest and when he died he made ample provisions for his young widow, as well as for his own blood relations.
>
> Mr. Prosser's young widow gave much of her newly acquired means to charity and then completed the sensational episode in her life by retiring to the seclusion and comforts of a well-known home for the aged. She paid for a suite of rooms therein, for both herself and her sister Mary and there they spent the remainder of their days.[56]

Prosser's successor at #786 was Augustus Franklin Tripp, son of poor farmers in New Haven, Vermont, where he was born in 1822. He went west in the early 1840s. He gave Buffalo a quick look and moved on via lake steamer to Painesville, Ohio, where he repaired the machinery of an oil drill, and then pushed on to Cleveland where he got a job in the office of the Cuyahoga Steam Furnace Company. In 1847, having married Mary M. Steele of Painesville, he retraced his steps to Buffalo where he got a job with John D. Shepard & Company, a steam engine works. In 1849 this company passed out of existence and Tripp returned to Ohio where he established a firm with his brothers-in-law, Steele Brothers & Tripp. He also formed a firm in Buffalo under the name of A. F. Tripp & Company. The partnership with his in-laws was dissolved in 1852, and Tripp entered the employ of Sidney Shepard & Company. He started as a clerk and bookkeeper but had acquired such a grasp of the business that he advanced rapidly and in five years he had become a partner. He stayed forty years with this concern whose tinware and house-furnishings were shipped worldwide. A widower, Tripp in 1868 married Caroline Brown of Chelsea, Massachusetts. He loved music and was for a time president of the Buffalo Music Association. Due to ill health he retired about 1897 and died at age eighty-five in 1908, an elder of First Presbyterian.[57]

After Tripp's death his house was sold to Stephen Merrell Clement, Jr.(10.32), who demolished it and erected in 1910 a great house(10.33) such as Henry-Russell Hitchcock had in mind when he wrote: "An alternative to the academic classical manner of McKim, Mead and White was an equally academic and archeological style based on the English medieval manor house."[58] The purchaser's father, Stephen Merrell Clement, had been born in 1825, in Manlius, was educated in the district

56 *Times*, January 29, 1929.

schools, and at sixteen began clerking in a grocery store before going into business for himself. In 1850 he moved to Fredonia where he was employed in H. Miner's bank. From this developed the Fredonia National Bank of which Clement was cashier, then manager, and in 1867 president. In 1851 he had married Sarah Leonard of DeWitt by whom he had four sons. Meanwhile he had come to Buffalo in 1869, and while still with the Fredonia Bank, became cashier of the Marine Bank of Buffalo of which he was made president in 1861 when he resigned his position in Fredonia. Now a part of the city's power structure, he built a three-story brick mansion with a mansard roof at #737 Delaware, one door down from Summer. He had become a Presbyterian at twenty two-, a ruling elder in 1885, and represented Westminister at presbyteries, synods, and general assemblies. A founder of Auburn Theological Seminary, he was president of the board of the State Normal School, the Buffalo Orphan Asylum, and Buffalo General. He belonged to no clubs and died at sixty-seven in 1892.

Above 10.32 ❦ Stephen M. Clement,Jr., *Men of Buffalo*, p. 22.
Below 10.33 ❦ Number 786 Delaware, Mark H. Hubbell, *Buffalo the City Beautiful* (Buffalo: Buffalo Truth Press, 1931), p. 11.

Stephen M. Clement, Jr.,(10.32) had been born in Fredonia in 1859. He attended the district school and Buffalo State Normal School. Graduating from Yale in 1882, he spent a year in travel abroad and began his career as assistant cashier in his father's bank in Buffalo upon returning home. Next year he was promoted to cashier and still later treasurer. In 1884 he married Caroline Tripp, daughter of Augustus Tripp of #786 Delaware. Three years after his father's death Stephen Celement was considered very conservative and very successful. In 1902 he took out a federal charter and Marine became Marine National. He was also responsible for the impressive Marine Bank building on Main and Exchange Streets. Association with Frank Goodyear explains Clement's directorships in the Great Southern Lumber Company and the New Orleans & Great Northern Railroad. He was also president of the Buffalo Steamship Corporation, the Buffalo Clearing House, the Merchant's National Bank at Dunkirk, and the Bank of North America of New York, and a director of the Ontario Power Company. He died of heart disease in 1913 at Atlantic City, where he had gone to recover from a long stay at

57 *CA*, January 24, 1908.

Johns Hopkins Hospital in Baltimore. Though nominally president of Marine until his death, he had not functioned as such for months. Like his father he had been a devout Presbyterian, very generous in supporting foreign missions. He was also a benefactor of the Y.M.C.A., and a trustee and treasurer of the Buffalo Orphan Asylum. His clubs were Ellicott, Buffalo, Saturn, Country, University, and University in New York. In 1910 he had began construction of a new $300,000 ($5,229,000 in 1997 dollars) mansion(10.33) on the site of his wife's childhood home at #786 but lived in it only a short time. At the beginning of 1913, in view of his probable death, he sold almost all his holdings in Marine National to Seymour Knox and John Albright. This meant that his sons' careers would not be as his had been. Like many Delaware Avenue widows, Caroline Clement long outlived her husband, in her case by twenty-eight years. In 1914 she donated land for the Westminster parish house (of which her son Stephen Clement, III, was selected as architect) and endowed a chair of Christian Methods at the Yale Divinity School. She had belonged to Westminster since 1876. All her sons fought in World War I. She opened a summer camp for poor children at Angola, belonged to the U.B. Council, served on the board of State Teachers College, was a trustee of Buffalo General, and president of the Twentieth Century Club. In 1941 she donated her home, #786, to the Red Cross. She died at age eighty-one in 1943.[60]

Above 10.34 ❦ Number 806 Delaware, *PBHS* 22 (1918), *post* p. 437.
Below 10.35 ❦ George Howard, Smith, *op. cit.*, II, facing p. 512.

The careers of many Delaware Avenue residents were cases of rags to riches, none more so than that of the first to live at #806(10.34), George Howard(10.35), who was born in Charlotte, Vermont, in 1810. His father John was a tanner and worked a 200-acre farm. George attended school in winter and farmed in the summer, weather permitting. Otherwise he worked in his father's tannery. His formal education was over by the time he was thirteen. When George was eighteen, his father went bankrupt. Vermont allowed imprisonment for debt, so John Howard fled to the Holland Purchase where he somehow acquired rights to 115 acres near Westfield. In the spring of 1828 he went west with one son to locate the farm. They cleared off a few acres of

58 *Buffalo Architecture*, p. 147.
59 *Express*, September 30, 1892.
60 White, *op. cit.*, 2:66; *Express*, March 27, 1913; *Who Was Who in America*, 1897-1942, p. 230. *NYT*, March 2, December 30, 1943.

forest, planted crops, built a log cabin, and next year brought out the rest of his family. They came via the Erie Canal and schooner to Westfield where John met them and drove them to his farm on a cart hauled by a yoke of oxen. Father and sons cleared trees from about a hundred acres and planted crops. George found this back-breaking work and he resolved to become a sailor. In 1831 he went to Buffalo and signed on as a seaman at $12 a month. Sailing proved no better than farming. He jumped ship at Westfield and went home.

In 1832 George started work at Aaron Rumsey's Westfield tannery for fifteen months at $100, seeing this as putting the finishing touches on his skills. After six months Rumsey agreed to let Howard go to Buffalo as foreman at Rumsey's tannery there. Rumsey went broke; nevertheless he and his ex-foreman survived to form Rumsey & Howard in 1838. This lasted several years until in 1844 Howard entered partnership with Myron P. Bush with a tannery on Chicago Street, which made substantial and increasing profits. In the early 1880s the sons of both partners succeeded to the business.[61]

George Howard was married three times: in 1835 to Ellen Martin of Warsaw, who died in 1846; in 1848 to Louise Corley of Ithaca, who died in 1851; and in 1852 to Amelia Flagler of Lockport who produced an heir, George Rumsey Howard. She died in 1902. Her husband George had died in 1888. Several Howard children died in infancy. In 1870 George's mansion housed himself, Amelia, his forty-five year old wife, and three children, Frank sixteen, Anna fourteen, and George nine. They were waited on by three servants, an English coachman, and an English gardener:

> Though a business man of strenuous activity, Mr. Howard knew how to enjoy recreation. At one period of his life he made an extended foreign tour, visiting all important points in England and on the Continent. Among his favorite diversions were yachting and lake fishing. He was a noted yachtsman, being the owner of the famous steam yacht "Orizaba," which after Mr. Howard's death was purchased by the late Dexter P. Rumsey.[62]

10.36 George Rumsey Howard, *M&FH*, I, facing p. 56.

For George Rumsey Howard(10.36), a rich man's son, there would be no starving time. Born in Buffalo in 1861 he completed his education at Professor Briggs' Classical School. No college for George either. His first business experience was as a clerk in Bush & Howard where he quickly became a partner, continuing as such until two years after his father's death. In 1890, at twenty-nine, he disposed of his share in

61 Smith, *op. cit.*, 2:32-34.
62 *M&FH*, 1:56-58.

the business and embarked upon the sea of finance. He was a trustee of Erie County Savings and director of the Cary Safe Company. His clubs were Country, Ellicott, and Park. He was director of the Y.M.C.A. and trustee of Westminster, Buffalo General, and Forest Lawn. In 1882 he married Isabella, daughter of John B. Griffin, president of the Queen City Milling Company. Howard died at his Tudor Place home in 1933 at seventy-two.[63]

10.37 ❦ Seymour H. Knox, I, Hill, *op. cit.*, III, facing p. 79.

Howard's mansion was acquired by Mrs. Seymour Knox who had it razed in 1916 with a modern replacement in mind. Of Scots-Irish ancestry, Seymour Horace Knox(10.37) was born in 1861 in Russell, Saint Lawrence County, New York, the son of James Horace Knox, a farmer, and his wife, the former Jane E. McBrier. James' grandfather had fought in the Revolution. The first of these Knoxes in America, William, came to Massachusetts from Belfast in 1737. Seymour attended the district school and at fifteen, though he had never gone to high school, began to teach school himself. At seventeen he moved to Hart, Michigan, where for a few years he worked as a salesclerk. Then he left for Reading where in partnership with his first cousin, Frank W. Woolworth, he opened a five-and-ten-cent store which failed. Unfazed, young Knox established the same kind of operation in Newark, New Jersey. This succeeded, but Knox once again sold out and with Woolworth formed Woolworth & Knox in Erie. With success here, Knox came to Buffalo in 1890 where he opened two stores, one on Main, the other on William Street, to be known as S. H. Knox. Woolworth expanded his empire by using partners to organize single outlets. Thus he could minimize his own outlay. In 1912, however, he merged his rivals, including S. H. Knox, into a company, which in time boasted 596 stores worldwide. Its headquarters were in the Woolworth Building, a $13 million skyscraper on lower Broadway in New York built in 1913. The new company, F. W. Woolworth, was capitalized at $65 million. Besides his large holdings in this gigantic venture, Knox was made first vice-president. He had also become a heavy player in the affairs of Marine National by purchasing Stephen Clement's interest in 1913.

Knox was married in June 1890, the year he came to Buffalo:

> Mrs. Knox was the former Grace Millard of Detroit, the daughter of Charles and Sarah Avery Millard. ...To some of her friends, Mrs. Knox confided the story of her romance with the young man with whom she was to rise to riches. She recalled to these friends that a trip to Buffalo brought about her meeting with Mr. Knox. She was one of a party of girls

63 *Ibid.*, p. 59; *BEN*, June 16, 1933.

10.38 ❦ #1049 Delaware, author's collection.

who came here on a short vacation, one of the girls knew Mr. Knox and he entertained the group.

Especially attracted to Grace Millard, he saw her frequently during her stay here and it wasn't long after the visit that they were married in Detroit and returned here to make their home. Her parents followed, arriving here shortly before Mr. Knox opened his first Buffalo store in the old Palace Arcade near Lafayette Square in the early 1880s [read 1890s.][64]

The newlyweds' first home was #414 Porter Avenue; by 1896 they were at #467 Linwood; and in 1904 the city directory listed them at #1049 Delaware.(10.38) The 1905 census describes this household:

> Seymour H. Knox 44, Grace Knox 40 wife, Dorothy Knox 9 daughter at school, Seymour Knox 7 son at school, Marjorie Knox 5 daughter at school; domestics were Bertha Dengler 40 maid, Florence Heath 40 maid [and over the stable] Damon Sherman coachman, Kate Damon 25 wife.

The oldest of the Knox children, Gracia, born in 1893, died in infancy; the second, Dorothy Virginia, married Frank Goodyear, and then Edmund Rogers; the third, Marjorie, married J. Hazard Campbell, and after his death Benjamin Klopp, and died in 1980; and the fourth, Seymour H. Knox, II, born in 1898, married Helen Northrup. Seymour Knox, I, died in 1915, at fifty-four. In 1918 his widow moved from the baronial house her husband had built in 1904 into a magnificent mansion at #806.(10.39)

At Mrs. Seymour Knox's death in 1936, a writer reminisced on a life style which was hardly affected by the Depression:

> Since the new Knox residence at 806 Delaware was opened in 1918 many of the social functions of the city were held there; celebrations of holidays, particularly the Christmas season, were gala occasions in the Delaware avenue mansion. Mrs. Knox's principal joy was her many friends. She seldom wanted to be alone — her great desire was to be surrounded by her intimates and her children and grandchildren. Christmas time at the huge avenue mansion was always particularly happy time for her children, Seymour Knox Jr., Mrs. J. Hazard Campbell and Mrs. Edmund P. Rogers of New York City and Buffalo, made a point of returning home for the festive celebration at which were present also Mrs. Knox Jr., Mr.

10.39 ❦ Number 806 Delaware, *City Beautiful*, p. 206.

Campbell and Mr. Rogers and their children.

Her children have always been close by. Mr. & Mrs. Campbell living with her; Mrs. Rogers owning a home two doors away at Summer street and Delaware avenue and living there until the time of the death of her husband, Frank H. Goodyear, and her son and his wife live in Oakland place. Mrs. Knox's magnificent summer place in East Aurora has in the last few years become the rendezvous for her children. As each one married, she built a charming home on the land for the couple and the original home has become the guest house. Mrs. Rogers, who has made her home in New York City since 1931, joins them here each year.

Mrs. Knox had a track of her own and fine stables in East Aurora. Her love of fine horses was fostered by her husband and for some time she had been vitally interested in the polo team headed by her son, Seymour. When an English team came over last year to play against them, Mrs. Knox entertained for the poloists.

At the time of the Peace Bridge opening ten years ago, Mrs. Knox had a large luncheon in her Delaware avenue home and among the notable guests were Vice President Charles G. Dawes, Premier and Mrs. Stanley Baldwin of England, and Secretary of State and Mrs. Frank B. Kellogg. When Lady Burley of England was in town as the guest of Mrs. Norman E. Mack, Mrs. Knox entertained for the out of-of-town guests. Mr. Knox's entertainments were not so much for out-of-town people, however, as much as they were for her many Buffalo friends. The ballroom, with mirrors lining the walls and ceiling is only one of the sumptuously furnished rooms in the large house. The drawing room, library and living rooms of the home, furnished in Empire style with much gilt framework and red brocaded upholstery, combine stateliness with comfortable hominess. Crystal chandeliers reflect the lights in each room.

Travel was balm for Mrs. Knox after the death of her husband and she was heard to remark recently, "If I were 45 today, there would not be a place in the world that I wouldn't see." She has motored all over Europe, traveled in the Orient and over this continent. She has a particular fondness for Pasadena, Cal. Her charities were extensive but she preferred to keep them quiet.[65]

Doctor Albert Butzer and Bishop Cameron J. Davis conducted funeral services for Grace Knox at #806. Burial was beside her husband in the family mausoleum at Forest Lawn.

In 1927 Marjorie Knox married J. Hazard Campbell, born in 1900 in Providence, Rhode Island, a descendant of Oliver Hazard Perry, the victor at the Battle of Lake Erie in the War of 1812. Campbell was cruise director for a steamship line and met Marjorie aboard ship. They wed at the end of the cruise and returned to Buffalo where they lived at #806 and at Willardshire Road next to the East Aurora estate of Seymour Knox, II. Campbell went to work at Marine, now a family bank. When Marine Union Investors was formed with Seymour as president in 1929 Campbell joined the firm. A few years later, he became associated with Dann, Wickwire & Company, a brokerage with which he remained for five years, leaving in 1935. From then until his death he devoted his time to riding, hunting, fishing, and other outdoor sports. On August 23, 1938, Campbell and Lieutenant Com-

64 *BEN*, August 31, 1936.
65 This passage is a conflation of obituaries of Mrs. Knox on August 31, 1936, in the *News* and the *Courier*.
66 *BEN*, August 24, 1938; *CE*, August 23, 1938.

Above 10.40 ❦ Seymour H. Knox, Jr., courtesy of Mike Vogel of the *News*.
Below 10.41 ❦ Number 57 Oakland, Seymour H. Knox, Jr., *City Beautiful*, p. 207.

mander Frank Hawks, a famous speed flyer, were killed in a crash just after take-off in a small plane made by a company of which Hawks was vice-president and for which he was seeking Campbell's backing. The tragedy was witnessed from Edmund Rogers' polo field by Marjorie and two of their children. Hazard was the second son-in-law of Seymour Knox, I, to have died violently.[66]

The widowed Marjorie returned to her former home at #806. In 1948 she married Benjamin Klopp, Buffalo native, Lafayette High graduate, World War I veteran, and partner in Phillips Brothers Basket Company. He was also associated with Niagara Falls Power Company and Sterling Engine. His first wife, who died in 1948, was Else Schmidt, niece of power company president Jacob Schoellkopf. The Klopps lived at #806 until Marjorie's death in 1971. Then Benjamin moved to Florida where he had wintered since 1957. An ardent clubman, he had been a director of the Canoe Club, and president of the Niagara Falls and the Wanakah Country clubs, and a member of Saturn, Buffalo, and Derby Hunt clubs in New York and the Naples Yacht Club and the Royal Poinciana Club of Naples. He died in Naples in 1972 at seventy-three.[67]

Seymour H. Knox, II(10.40), was born in Buffalo in 1898. He attended Nichols and the Hotchkiss School in Connecticut. Graduating from Yale in 1920 he needed merely to fold into the family business. Since college he was identified with Marine Trust, of which he became director in 1921, vice-president in 1926, and chairman 1943-1970, when construction began on Marine's thirty-eight story building straddling lower Main Street. He joined the F. W. Woolworth board in 1926 and was chairman from 1943 until reaching the mandatory retirement age forty-five years later in 1971. At various times he was director of the New York Central and of Penn-Central when it went bankrupt in 1970, American Steamship Company, Hewitt-Robins, and Niagara Share. Like his father, who had bred champion trotters and pacers at his rambling East Aurora estate, the son, known as "Shorty" was a polo enthusiast. He led his Aurora team to the United States Championship in 1932 and later won a tournament in Europe and toured South America. His ranking as a seven-goal handicap player

67 *BEN*, April 27, 1972.
68 *Ibid*, September 27, 1990; *NYT*, September 28, 1990.

was one of his proudest boasts. He was a top squash player and invited the best to compete with him at East Aurora where he raised Angus Aberdeen cattle.[68] His clubs included Buffalo Country, East Aurora Country, Park, Buffalo Tennis and Squash, and Yale.

Abandoning polo in the 1960s, Knox turned toward art. Conger Goodyear had talked him into pouring millions into avant guard works and donating them to public art museums. In the 1950s, with the advice of Gordon Smith, director of the Albright, Knox began buying for the gallery the works, then modestly priced, of Abstract Expressionist painters. In 1961 the Albright became the Albright-Knox. Knox encouraged younger artists as well as "old masters" of modern art like Picasso, Gauguin, and Giacometti. He was also a major benefactor of U.B., a longtime member of its council, and its chairman 1949-1969.[69]

In 1923 Seymour H. Knox, II, married Helen Northrup, born in Buffalo in 1902, daughter of Louis G. and Sara E. Northrup of Buffalo. Helen graduated from Lafayette High and the Albright Art School in Buffalo. It was a marriage of likes since Helen loved horses, was an accomplished rider prominent in the Genesee Valley Hunt, played excellent tennis, and shared her husband's passion for the arts. The newlyweds moved into the recently completed mansion behind #806 on #57 Oakland Place.(10.41) They had two sons, Seymour H., III, born in Buffalo in 1926, and Northrup, born in Buffalo in 1928. Both grew up at #57 Oakland, though the family owned a summer home in East Aurora and a winter retreat in Aiken, South Carolina. They followed the example of their father in business, sports, the arts, and community service. Together they brought the Sabres hockey team to Buffalo in 1969. Helen Knox died in 1971, Seymour, III, in 1990, and Northrup in 1998.[70]

When Marjorie Klopp died in 1971, #806 went on the market. The total destruction of the Montefiore's Club in 1969 made officers think of #806 as a replacement. They approached Seymour Knox, II, and intimated that for a reduced price they would be glad to rechristen the club Montefiore-Knox. He brushed the hint aside but sold the building anyway.[71] The club went bankrupt in 1977.[72] The need to build athletic facilities and a furnace house had overtaxed club revenues. Previously #806 Delaware and #57 Oakland had been heated by the same unit, which with the sale went with #57 Oakland. In 1978 three companies acquired three Avenue mansions as quality corporate headquarters. Number 690 Delaware, the old Pratt place, went to Niagara Trading, #806 was sold to Computer Task Group, and #891, the Orin Foster mansion, was obtained by De Rose Food Brokers. A *Courier-Express* writer noted that "all three houses were built with rich, expensive materials which are not commonly used today," and pointed out that, "the imported marbles and hardwoods of these homes could only be acquired now — if at all — at a price many times the original cost."[73] These purchases pleased a scarcely revolutionary local group whose slogan was "Save the Mansions!" Later

69 *Ibid.*
70 *BEN*, December 7, 1971; May 23, 1996; August 2, 1998.
71 Interview with Mr. George M. Martin, May 29, 2002. Mr. Martin's sister was the private secretary of Seymour H. Knox.
72 *BEN*, January 27, 1976.
73 *CE*, August 25, 1978.

10.42 ❦ Number 824 Delaware, BHS.

a *News* writer recalled that "Dr. Charles Battista in 1974 prevented IBM from demolishing three buildings on the 800 block of Delaware Avenue to erect what the writer described as "a god-awful piece of garbage to stick in the middle of a pristine block."[74]

George Forman, by 1895 living at #824(10.42), had four children. His oldest son, Howard Arter Forman, born in 1870, came to Buffalo where in 1892 he married Georgia Green of Lockport. Georgia had been born in 1871 and graduated from Miss Masters School at Dobbs Ferry. Howard, vice-president of Eastern Petroleum of which his father was president, and Georgia lived for some years on North Street. During the World War I he was Federal Fuel Administrator for Buffalo. After the war he and Georgia separated and by the early 1920s he had moved to Lexington, Kentucky, where he died in 1931.[75] He left his wife well situated since in 1928 she moved into an exquisite modern mansion at #77 Oakland Place behind her ex-father-in-law, George Forman.(10.43) She traveled widely through Europe and the Orient, amassing a fine collection of Japanese and Chinese *objets d'art*. Two years before her death in 1955 she moved after twenty-five years on Oakland into *The Campanile*.[76] Number #77 Oakland was sold to the Catholic diocese of Buffalo in 1955 for an episcopal residence. A third Forman mansion in Buffalo was that of George Forman's second son, George Alfred, at #1260 where his widow was residing in the early 1930s.(10.44) George Forman's daughter Mary married Conger Goodyear of the #888 Delaware Goodyears.

Above 10.43 ❦ Number 77 Oakland Place, *City Beautiful*, p. 8.
Below 10.44 ❦ Number 1260 Delaware, *City Beautiful*, p. 45.

George V. Forman died in 1922.[77] He was succeeded at #824 by Oliver F. Cabana, who was born of French-Canadian ancestry in Island Point, Vermont, in 1865, one of ten children of Oliver Cabana, the village blacksmith, and his wife Edmire De Rainville. At fourteen he came to live with relatives in Buffalo where, after studying bookkeeping at Bryant & Stratton, he went to work for a tanning

74 *BEN*, July 3, 1999.
75 *CE*, November 1, 1931.
76 *BEN*, June 25, 1955.
77 *Express*, October 11, 1922.

and belt manufacturing firm. Six years later he sank his savings of $480 in a belt fastener and mender invented by his half-brother. He then bought out the brother's interest and formed the Buffalo Specialty Company, later Liquid Veneer, whose products became very popular. In 1886 he married Isabelle Josephine Pilliard of Buffalo in the French Church at Clinton and Washington. He then got into gold mining, hospitals, oil producing, cattle raising, and banking, and was director of thirty-five companies and a member of numerous societies and clubs.[78]

Cabana used his wealth to become a power in the Democratic Party. He bankrolled banquets for visiting sachems and during the Smith-Hoover presidential election wrote Al a check for $25,000, besides spending locally $26,000 ($888,930 in 1997 dollars.) During the 1930s he gave more than $100,000 to Democratic causes besides making good on $27,000 worth of notes signed by party leaders. Cabana was an original Roosevelt-for-president man. For his second inaugural as governor in January 1931, Roosevelt summoned him to Albany and deputized him to clean house in Erie County. This made William H. Fitzpatrick, off-and-on County Democratic boss for thirty years, unhappy, but Cabana put down a Fitzpatrick revolt in the primaries. In the general election Democrats not only won the city clerk's office and captured the common council but for the first time in memory gained a one-man majority on the Board of Supervisors. It was a Democratic year anyway, but Cabana claimed credit for the win. This was the zenith of his political career. Shortly before the election he resigned the chairmanship and appointed George Zimmerman in his stead. Cabana expected to remain the power behind the throne, but Zimmerman was his own man, and Cabana was out.[79] He died in 1938. His friend, Archbishop Thomas J. Walsh of Newark, formerly of Buffalo, came back to celebrate the funeral Mass. The widow, Isabella, stayed at #824 until her death at ninety-two in 1953.[80] A daughter lived there until 1960 when the house was vacant for two years until it became a child care center.

Number 840 Delaware was the home of George B. Mathews(9.11) who came to Buffalo in 1870 and whose career was intertwined with that of Jacob F. Schoellkopf who provided the money and Mathews the know-how in the creation of Schoellkopf & Mathews, millers. For twenty years Mathews and his wife, the former Jenny Rebecca Modisette, daughter of a Le Roy minister, lived in a small brownstone cottage at #830, which had been the home of a former mayor, Jonathan Scoville. The Mathews continued to live there until their mansion on the site was completed in 1901. Jenny was interested in music and was a member of the Twentieth Century, the Garret, and the Country clubs. An able pianist, she financed the studies of young musicians of talent. She and her husband also enjoyed horseback riding. George donated $1 million toward building of the Michigan Avenue Y.M.C.A. to make social and athletic facilities available to young black men. He also gave generously to the Booker T. Washington Foundation. At his death at ninety-five in 1942, Mathews was the

78 *CE*, January 22, 1938.
79 *Times*, July 14. 1934.
80 *BEN*, December 15, 1953.

oldest member of both the Union League in New York and the Buffalo Club. Jenny died in the winter of 1950-1951, after which the house, "among the last of the Delaware Ave. homes to remain a private residence," was sold to the Children's Aid Society and the Society for the Prevention of Cruelty to Children as a home for from sixteen to twenty boys and girls six to twelve with serious emotional problems:

> The 16-room Mathews home is smaller than its neighboring Delaware Ave. mansions. In elegance, comfort and convenience, it equals any mansion on the avenue. The walls of the library, which occupies the entire front of the first floor, are covered with rich green brocaded velvet. The dark green marble fireplace of that room is exquisitely carved as are the extensive oaken bookcases that line two walls. Leaded windows add to the attractiveness of the library. Between two bookcases is a recess built to fit exactly a rare painting Mr. and Mrs. Mathews brought from France several years ago. Special lighting was installed to reveal its artistry.
>
> The carved woodwork of reception hall and dining-room is white. Most walls of first floor rooms are covered with rare English materials. This same wall covering, in red, surmounts the paneling of the wall along the graceful staircase. The balustrade is of wrought-iron toped by a mahogany rail. The dining room retains its original spacious buffet and is equipped with small tables, at which the children will eat their meals, supervised by members of the staff.
>
> Overlooking the garden is a solarium, floored with mosaics of marble. This will serve as a bright school- room, with plants to add color. The window frames of that room are of attractive wrought-iron. The enclosed porch, heated for winter use, will serve as a pleasant bad-weather room for the girls.
>
> Outdoor play in the large yard, extending nearly to Oakland Pl., will be encouraged. In the basement, boys will find workshops and other indoor equipment for games and creative work. The ample kitchen has been newly redecorated in a gay primrose yellow. Two spacious pantries make up the first floor rooms. Second-story sleeping rooms are large enough to accommodate four children each. Every room has its dressing-room and bath, with capacious clothes closets. There are cupboards with enclosed shelves and drawers extending from floor to ceiling.
>
> Bathrooms are done in white marble. In the front bedroom which was occupied by Mrs. Mathews is a small safe for her jewelry. This is one of three safes in the house. In a pantry is a large one for silver. The third is in the small first floor room that was Mr. Mathew's den. A second story sitting-room is bright and inviting with convenient bookcases. Two third floor sleeping rooms will be used for boys. Others will be occupied by one staff member and by the cook and other members of the domestic staff.[81]

10.45 ❦ Number 844 Delaware Avenue, BHS.

81 *CE*, October 12, 1952.

Above 10.46 ❦ Jewett Melvin Richmond, Smith, *City of Buffalo*, facing p. 230.
Below 10.47 ❦ Thomas B. Lockwood, *PBHS*, 30 (1930), following p. 22.

Levi Allen was living at #193 Delaware in 1880. Ten years earlier he was residing up the Avenue at #844. Since he had built several houses on the Avenue, including Aaron Rumsey's at Summer and Delaware(6.20) which Allen then lived in before selling it to Rumsey in 1860, it is probable that Allen then built for himself the Victorian house at nearby #844.(10.45) From 1873 on #844's owner was Jewett Melvin Richmond(10.46), a *Mayflower* descendant. His grandfather Josiah fought in the Revolution and moved west after the war to Barnard, Vermont. Josiah's son Anson fought in the War of 1812, after which he married Betsy Melvin and moved on to Salina, near the present Syracuse, where he manufactured salt until his death in 1834. Anson's son, Jewett Melvin, born in Onondaga County in 1830, received a common school education and at sixteen began to clerk in a store in Liverpool. In 1854 he formed a partnership with two older brothers and a former employer as manufacturers and dealers in salt and flour. Business prospered and during the next six years they extended operations to Salina, Syracuse, Oswego, Buffalo, and Chicago. In 1860 Jewett severed relations with this firm and, with cousin Henry Richmond of #348 Delaware, formed J. M. Richmond & Company which engaged in the grain storage, commission, and elevator business in Buffalo. In 1863 this firm was dissolved, Jewett spent a year abroad, and on his return formed a new firm under the old name which lasted until 1881.

During his business career in Buffalo Jewett engaged in several enterprises. He was a director of the Buffalo & Jamestown Railroad and president 1871-1875. During the depression after the Panic of 1873 the B&J went bankrupt. Nevertheless, Richmond was director of its reincarnation, the Buffalo & Southwestern. He was president of the Buffalo Mutual Gaslight Company and of the Marine Bank 1867-1869. For fourteen years he was vice-president and director of the Buffalo Savings Bank and at his death was president. He also engaged in many civic and social activities. He was a founder of the Buffalo Club and a member of the Country Club, but his favorite

10.48 ❦ Number 844 Delaware as remodeled by Thomas Lockwood, author's collection, 1999.

club was Falconwood on Grand Island. He was a member and president of the Board of Trade, a member of the Buffalo Historical Society, the Society of Natural Sciences, the Fine Arts Academy, and the Young Men's Association, so detested by Mark Twain. While he was president of the Buffalo Library Association the main library was built at Lafayette Square. Richmond Avenue was named after him.[82]

In 1870 Richmond wed Geraldine Hull Rudderow of New York. Three years later he bought #844 from Levi Allen. By 1880 it housed a sizeable contingent: Jewett and wife, six children ranging in age from seven months to eight years, a staff of six domestics including two baby nurses, and over the stables a Baden-born coachman, his wife, and four young children. The main house was destroyed by fire in 1887 and rebuilt next year. Richmond died in 1899 at sixty-eight.[83]

Geraldine, Richmond's widow, lived on at #844, at first with several of her children, until the time of the First World War. By 1920 it had become the home of Thomas Brown Lockwood(10.47), born in Buffalo in 1873, son of Daniel Newton Lockwood, District Attorney of Erie County 1874-1877, member of the 45th Congress 1877-1879, United States Attorney for the Northern District of New York 1886-1889, member of the 52nd and 53rd Congresses 1891-1895, and unsuccessful candidate for lieutenant governor in 1894.[84] His son, Thomas Lockwood, graduated from Yale in 1895 and studied law at the U.B. and Cornell law schools. His first wife was Marion Birge, his second Mildred F. McGuire. He was admitted to the bar in 1897 and began to practice law in his father's firm, though as time passed he lost interest in law and turned to other activities. He was Buffalo's Commissioner of Parks 1906-1916, chairman of the campaign committee of the Erie County Democracy in 1912 and in 1914 ran unsuccessfully for lieutenant governor. He was a director of the M&T Bank 1912-1918. In 1918 he remodeled his house(10.48). A bibliophile who lived with books, he saw to it that the library was the largest room in the house. The library gave on to Lockwood's study, its walls lined with autographed photographs of friends and authors of his favorite books. Christopher Morley, a frequent visitor, made it under both headings. Photos of Mark Twain, Thackeray, and Emile Zola occupied places of honor. In 1935 Lockwood gave his famous collection of rare books to U.B. along with $500,000 for which he became the eponym of Lockwood Hall and in 1942 he received the university's Chancellor's Medal. His clubs were the Buffalo, of which he was president in 1935, and the Country Club. After a four year illness, he died at #844 in 1947, at seventy-four.[85]

82 Hill, *op. cit.*, 3:139-140; *BEN*, June 6, 1952.
83 *Ibid; BEN*, June 1, 1952.
84 *Biographical Directory of Congress*, pp. 1383-1384.
85 *Who Was Who in America*, 2:327; Warren, *op. cit.*, pp. 98-99. Warren is incorrect when he states that Lockwood ran for governor of New York in 1916.

10.49 ❦ Number 864 Delaware, *City Beautiful*, p. 28.

Beginning in the late 1860s #864 was home to a shifting coalition of Squiers, Talcotts, and associates until the end of the nineteenth century. Massachusetts-born Socrates Squier, who bought the yellow wooden gothic building about 1870 and resided there into the 1880s, manufactured plantation machinery. Frank Talcott, his son in-law, an attorney, was there in 1890. Harlow Curtiss, attorney and realtor, bought the house in the early 1900s, tore it down, and replaced it with an impressive red brick three-story building. By 1905 lumberman William E. Silverthorne was on the scene and added a music room wing which noticeably enlarged the mansion.(10.49) He was followed in 1906 by William Horton Schoellkopf, grandson of "King" Jacob. William had been born in Buffalo to Louis and Myra Lee Horton Schoellkopf in 1882. He attended Nichols, Masten Park High, Cascadilla School in Ithaca, and Penn Military College (four prep schools), and graduated from Cornell with an engineering degree in 1906. He then became an executive in the family's Niagara Falls Power Company and manager of the large estate of his father who had died in 1901. As a result Walter became a director in many Western New York firms. He married Anna G. Johnson of New Orleans in 1908. In 1915 his household consisted of himself, his wife, and one son, four-year old Horton Schoellkopf. The family was well supplied with domestic help: a cook, two waitresses, a lady's maid, and a governess. That year as Woodrow Wilson's America drifted toward war, Walter left Buffalo for officers training school at Madison Barracks. After the Armistice, he left the army a major in the 27th Division and entered the diplomatic service, starting as third secretary at the American Embassy in Paris. There followed postings to Panama, Bucharest, Vienna, and finally, during the Spanish Civil War, Madrid. He resigned from the diplomatic service and moved to Baltimore where his wife died in 1952. Walter died at seventy-two in Chevy Chase, Maryland, in 1955, where his last four years were spent in a wheelchair. He kept open the Buffalo connection, retaining memberships in Buffalo, Saturn, Ellicott, and Country clubs. He was buried from Westminster.[86]

10. 50 ❦ Daniel Good, Hill, *op. cit.*, III, facing p. 9.

Sometime partner of Seymour Knox, I, was the next resident of #864, Daniel Good(10.50), who was born in Indi-

86 *BEN*, September 5, 1940; July 16, 1955.

10.51 ❦ Frank F. Henry, Warren, *op. cit.*, p. 92.

ana in 1862. He opened a five-and-ten-cent store in Fort Wayne, which was so successful that he moved to Chicago to take charge of Siebert & Good which under Good's direction developed a chain of stores in and about the Windy City. Their flagship store at State and Monroe Streets did the most business of any store of its kind in the nation. In 1905 this chain was consolidated with the chain Knox had developed back east, and Good came to Buffalo to assist Knox with the consolidation. With the merger of Knox's chain with Frank Woolworth's in 1912, Good retired from the business but remained a director of the new chain. He also conducted a small investment firm. He was in poor health the last few years of his life and died at his summer home in Crescent Beach, Ontario, in 1922. Before his health failed he was a prominent member of the Park, Buffalo, Ellicott, Country, Wanakah, and Lake Shore Hunt clubs. He was also an active member of North Presbyterian.[87] His wife Sara lived on at #864 with her daughter Margaret Van Clief, her husband Raymond Van Clief, and their three-year old son, a family outnumbered by seven domestics.

Number 864 had been bought in 1929 before the Crash by Frank Forrest Henry(10.51) for $200,000. He had been born on the Indian Ocean in 1870, aboard the barque *Lizzie A. Williams*, of which his father was captain. He was educated in the public schools of Thomaston, Maine, and graduated from Old Academy in 1887. That year he came to Buffalo and got a job with the Lehigh Valley Transportation Company's grain fleet. In five years he became assistant general manager. In 1893 he opened the Buffalo office of the Washburn-Crosby Milling Company and was vice-president when it merged with General Mills in 1928 and became president and later chairman of General Mills. In 1898 he married Grace Davis by whom he had two children.[88] General Mills had a major impact on the area's economy:

> In 1949 Buffalo mills turned out 10 million pounds of flour a day, to which should be added a considerable weight and value of foodstuffs used in agriculture. The giant among the seven major companies was General Mills, organized around the Washburn-Crosby Company in 1928. It had better than a third of Buffalo's capacity, elevators to hold six million barrels, a thousand employees, a cereal plant that wrapped half a million pounds a day, and a machine shop which had been enticed into war work and now made household appliances.[89]

87 *Express*, July 14, 1922.
88 *HNF*, 3:26-27; Warren, *op. cit.*, p. 28; *BEN*, February 23, 1961.
89 Dunn, *op. cit.*, p. 224.

The Henrys moved into #864 in 1929 and remained for ten years. Unable to sell the huge house in 1938, Frank let the city repossess it for back taxes.[90] It continued to be a white elephant for the city for years.[91] Meanwhile Henry moved up the Avenue to a smaller place at #1131. He had served on the board of the Great Northern and the Buffalo Rochester & Pittsburgh Railways, and the M&T Bank. He was a Mason, and belonged to the Country Club of Buffalo, the Niagara Falls Country Club, and the Buffalo Club, of which two latter clubs he served as president. He was also president of Forest Lawn. He was a trustee of the Erie County Savings Bank and of the Buffalo Orphan Asylum. In 1951 he retired from General Mills and died in 1961 in a nursing home at ninety-one.[92]

Earliest mention of a house on future #874 Delaware occurred in 1847 when Henry W. Rogers, an attorney who would later reside at #314 Delaware, built a frame structure about 100 feet from what was called Delaware Extended and moved there from Black Rock. In 1849 he sold it to George Truscott, a broker, who enlarged the house but he too lived in it but briefly. Meanwhile Truscott used the place on Delaware Extended as a country seat, with a corps of English gardeners to keep the grounds in park like shape. The house boasted a huge basement with a wine cellar, a compartment for vegetables, another for preserves, and a big summer kitchen with a brick Dutch oven below stairs. Caroline Stevens, the daughter of Captain Frederick N. Jones, who bought the house and grounds in 1855, wrote:

> I can remember our cook baking bread in this oven, also roasting turkeys for our Thanksgiving parties, when the upstairs stoves were in use. This mansion had 22 rooms, eleven of which were bedrooms...The place was called 'Thornbush' on account of a row of thorn trees lining the drive way on one side, there being an osage orange hedge on the other, into which we used to tumble from our ponies backs. The estate included five acres and there were hundreds of cherry, pear and apple trees, from which the barrels were filled and distributed to the orphan asylum and poor families. There was a smoke house and a huge ice house, filled every winter, and the cellars and larders always overflowed with good things.[93]

Captain Jones, on his father's side of Welsh descent and on his mother's English, was born in Essex, New England, in 1814. When he was nine the family moved to Black River, now Lorain, Ohio, where his father worked at shipbuilding. At twelve Frederick was apprenticed to his father's trade, and his first work was on the schooner *Marie Antoinette* at Sandusky, Ohio. At nineteen he modeled, drafted, and built the schooner *Jacob A. Barker*, at Monroe, Michigan. After building several vessels at Black River and acquiring the title captain from having commanded his own boat, *Lexington,* he came to Buffalo where in 1843 he married Cordelia, sister of William Hodge of #938 Delaware. He opened a shipyard on Ganson Street where he built the propeller *Pocahontas*, the schooners *Watts and Sherman*, and other craft both sail and steam. In 1855 he moved from Cold Spring to what would become #874 Delaware and in 1866 transferred his shipyard to Tonawanda

90 *CE*, October 23, 1938.
91 *CE*, June 24, 1944; *BEN*, May 4, 1946.
92 *HNF, loc. cit*; Warren, *loc cit*.

where he built numerous schooners, steamboats, and tugs. During his career he had built 103 vessels. In 1878 he sold his Delaware Avenue house and moved to Hodge Street. A devout Christian he was a deacon then an elder for over twenty-five years at Westminster. He died in 1883 at sixty-nine.[94]

Jones' grantee was George Van Vleck, an oil dealer, whose household in 1880 consisted of himself, his wife, six children and five domestics. In 1884 he had his house razed and replaced by a brick mansion.(10.52) The second house did not last long, since it was in turn purchased as the site for a truly elegant mansion.[95] This was the home at #888 Delaware(10.53) of Charles W. Goodyear(10.54), elder brother of Frank, whose equally striking mansion was on the same block at #762. Charles was born in Cortland and attended academies in Cortland, Wyoming, and East Aurora, before coming to Buffalo in 1868 where he read law in the office of Laning & Mills. Admitted to the bar, Goodyear attracted the favorable attention of Daniel Lockwood, who on election as District Attorney in 1874 named Charles Assistant District Attorney and upon election to Congress in 1876 appointed him to finish Lockwood's term as District Attorney. In 1877 Goodyear returned to private practice. When Cleveland was elected governor in 1883, he retired from the law firm of Cleveland, Bissell & Sicard, which became Bissell, Sicard & Goodyear. In 1877 he stepped in when brother Frank suffered a nervous breakdown and called for help in running the Goodyear empire.[96]

Above 10.52 ❦ Number 874 Delaware, George H. Van Vleck's 1884 Queen Ann, Buffalo State College. Middle, Below 10.53 ❦ Number 888 Delaware, 2 views, *City Beautiful*, pp. 12-14.

In 1876, Charles was married to Ella Portia Conger, who had been born in Collins Center in 1853, by Dr. Albert Tracy Chester, head of the Female Academy. The Congers had moved from Danby, Vermont, early in the century. Ella's father,

93 *Times*, March 8, 1911.
94 *Times* , March 7, 9, 1911.
95 *Ibid.*, March 8, 1911.
96 *M&FH*, 1:98-102.

Anson Griffith Conger, was a banker and a member of the legislature, the first citizen of Collins Center. Ella attended Miss Nardin's and the Female Academy. Upon graduation she worked as a bookkeeper for her father. She was interested in singing, and traveled to New York, Brooklyn, and Washington for lessons.[97] In 1879 the Goodyears moved to a new house on #723 Delaware across from Westminster, a gift from Anson. Here their children grew up.[98]

10.54 ❦ Charles Waterhouse Goodyear, *M&FH*, I, facing p. 98.

In the summer of 1904 Charles Goodyear contended for the Democratic nomination for governor. He had the support of William J. Connors, owner of the *Courier* and the *Enquirer*, respectively the largest morning and evening Democratic papers in Western New York. He was opposed by Norman E. Mack, owner of the *Evening and Sunday Times* and Democratic National Committeeman from New York, who was an ally of the state Democratic boss and former United States Senator, David B. Hill. A staunch supporter of Goodyear was Charles Francis Murphy, boss of Tammany Hall. Goodyear clubs sprang up, thousands of Goodyear buttons appeared, and campaign headquarters were opened on Ellicott Square. Charles himself was lukewarm and declined the nomination at Frank's urging.[99]

Charles died in Buffalo in 1911. Ella survived him by twenty-nine years, dying in Buffalo in 1940 at eighty-six:

> She loved to entertain. The garden and lawn of her house were lush and extensive, and here she was accustomed to give large garden parties. Perhaps the zenith in her entertainments was when King Albert of Belgium, Queen Elizabeth, and crown Prince Leopold were her guests, during their stay in Buffalo in 1919.[100]

Ella had been raised a Methodist Episcopalian, turned Presbyterian upon her marriage, but joined a species of Christian Science after a successful operation for cancer in 1905. She started holding bible classes at #888 attended sometimes by over a hundred people. These classes continued until 1934. None of the family participated. She read the bible over and over and quoted texts at the family, but they failed to share her piety. In 1913 she published *The Journey of Jesus*, which went through three editions. None of her family ever seems to have read it.[101]

Charles and Ella had four children, Conger, born in 1877; Esther Permelia born in 1881; Charles W., Jr., born in 1883; and Bradley in 1885. By the new century, Conger wrote:

97 Goodyear, *op. cit.*, pp. 41-44.
98 *Ibid.*, p. 42.
99 *Ibid.*, pp. 266-270.
100 *Ibid.*, p. 44.
101 *Ibid.*, pp. 43-44.

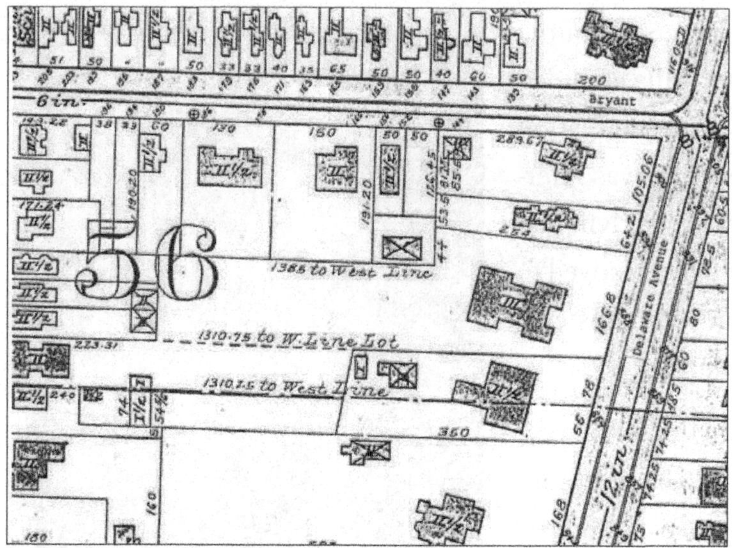

10.55 ❦ Goodyear compound at Delaware and Bryant, Century Atlas Co., *op. cit.*, I, plate 26.

> ...723 had become too cramped for our expanding egos. Father bought the Van Vleck property just a block up the avenue at 888. Edward B. Green was employed as architect and the new house was completed in the fall of 1903.(10.55)...It was built of Portland brick and stone in the style of the French Renaissance. As you entered there was a marble foyer, with a cloak room on the right and marble steps ahead leading to a large hall, that never seemed to be used much, although it contained a pipe organ and a piano. There was a large stone relief over the fireplace by Karl Bitter. On the left of the entrance to the hall was a reception room, used even less, with silk wall coverings and tapestry-covered furniture. In the middle was a bronze and marble round table, one of two, we were told, belonging to the Tsar of Russia. Opposite the entrance to the reception room was the staircase, to the second story, with a study opening on the first landing.
>
> Beyond the hall was the library, a large room done in Circassian walnut, with velvet wall coverings, used also in the hall. To the right of the hall were the dining room and breakfast room with mahogany woodwork. Near the cloak room, on a slightly lower level was a billiard room and in the back hall a lift to the cellar and top floors. The four master bedrooms and two morning rooms on the second floor were all large, done in mahogany. Esther had one of the morning rooms and her bedroom on this floor. Charles and Bradley and I were on the third floor. As heir apparent I had also a library and dressing room and, of course, we each had a bathroom. The servants' rooms were over the service wing. Down the drive was a new stable with an entrance on Bryant street. Besides the long lawn in the rear there was an orchard and a vegetable garden with a tennis court adjoining. The Buffalo papers called the house a palace. It was very comfortable and livable. We all enjoyed it, and as we married and built our own houses we put then all on adjoining land.

Everything about the mansion was big. Above the marble fireplace in the main hall was a six-foot marble relief called *Life* which had taken first prize at the Saint Louis Exposition. Weighing two tons, it rested on a foundation extending to the cellar. The kitchen boasted a stove with an overhanging metal hood and an electric refrigerator large enough to hold a side of beef. The graceful main staircase with a wrought iron balustrade and an oak handrail spiraled through three of five floors. A heavy iron chain dropped forty feet through the well and from it hung a polychrome chandelier. The main floor was supported by steel "I" beams resting on giant stone pillars. On the beams was a two-inch layer of concrete which undergirded a rough wood flooring and the hardwood. It was built like

102 *BEN*, February 4, 1942.

a factory floor.[102]

Starting at six Conger Goodyear attended a private school on Virginia Street. Five years later he entered the State Normal School, of which his father was a trustee, and graduated in 1892, followed by a year at Central High. He spent a year at Nichols, during which he played quarterback and broke his collarbone. He disported himself with other children of his class in Rumsey Park. Graduating from Yale in 1899, he spent a summer in Europe in assorted escapades before returning home and going to work at Uncle Frank's lumber business in Pennsylvania. In the fall of 1903 the whole family moved into #888 where as eldest son he was installed in the biggest and best suite on the third floor which had not only a bed and bathroom but a dressing room and a twenty-five foot long library with furniture to match. Late in 1903 he traveled with a party which included Mary Forman, his intended, aboard *Yakima,* the private car of Daniel Lamont, politician, investor in street and steam railways, and private secretary of President Cleveland. During the trip Mary assented and the two were married in 1904. Ella wanted her children around her and got Charles to buy a house in the rear at #160 Bryant which the newlyweds had torn down and in 1908 built a brick house with a red tiled roof. In 1912 a west wing was added, with a library and garden room downstairs and two bedrooms and a dressing room on the second.

> The house was spacious and comfortable, with a large central hall, large living room, large library, garden room, dining room pantry, kitchen, etc. on the first floor, about eight bedrooms and six bathrooms on the second floor, and servants' quarters on the third floor. We thought it luxurious. The grounds, too, were spacious, with an elaborate sunken garden with stone walls. The property was surrounded on all sides by family.[103]

With the deaths of Frank in 1907 and Charles in 1911, Conger, who had worked in both the Pennsylvania and Louisiana operations, found his executive duties too much. His conduct of the southern companies was unsatisfactory and so he quit. Even before America's entry into the war, he was an ardent disciple of "Preparedness," and trained troops in America. When as a major he finally arrived in France in October 1918 the war was almost over. Because of his supposed expertise in coal distribution, he was placed in charge of this sector of the post-war reconstruction agency under Herbert Hoover, U. S. Food Commissioner. Conger returned to America in 1919 and resumed his duties with the Louisiana operation. He also widened his interest in modern art, which had been whetted by his succeeding his father on the board of the Albright in 1911 and by his visit to the Armory Show in New York in 1913. He and Mary separated in 1928. She ended up in New York where she remarried in 1942 and died in 1973 at ninety-three. Conger also moved to New York where he remarried in 1950. He died in a new age style house in Wheatley Hills on Long Island in 1964.[104]

103 Goodyear, *op. cit.*, pp. 142-143.
104 *Ibid., passim.*

10.56 ❦ Esther Goodyear Watson, *Goodyear, op. cit.*, p. 285.

Number 180 Bryant was the start of a Goodyear family compound. Esther(10.56), the second oldest child, had been sent in 1897 to Saint Timothy's School at Catonsville, Maryland. Next year she transferred to a school at Bryn Mawr. In 1910 she married Arnold Beach Watson, son of Henry Watson of #622 Delaware, street railway and Bell Telephone president. Arnold was an 1898 graduate of Yale's Sheffield Scientific School. Thereafter he worked for Bell Telephone for a decade and as a broker for another ten. After his return from World War I, during which he was a captain in the Red Cross, he became vice-president of M&T National Bank, but retired when that bank merged with Fidelity Trust to form M&T Trust Company in 1925. In 1913 Arnold and Esther moved into a brick and stone house at #180 Bryant Street, next to Conger's, on land which had been given to them by Esther's mother, Ella.(10.55) It was a better house than #160, and Arnold could afford it since both his parents had recently died and he was their only heir. The couple lived there quietly and happily for the rest of their lives and their children grew up in a functional family. Arnold was largely responsible for the formation of the Buffalo Tennis & Squash Club in 1915 and its first president, serving until 1924. He was also president of the Country Club 1926-1927 when it moved from Main and Bailey to Williamsville, and was treasurer of Buffalo General 1911-1952. The Watsons owned two summer houses in succession in the Adirondacks. The second, Green Bay Camp, which they bought 1927, was an elaborate affair on Upper Saranac Lake. Esther was active in the Garret Club and on the board at Children's Hospital of which she served as treasurer for several years. She was an avid horsewoman, so in 1925 Arnold bought a farm on Main Street, Clarence, where she could keep and ride her string of horses. He died of a heart attack in 1953 and Esther of lung cancer in 1955.[105]

Charles Goodyear, Jr., second son of Charles and Ella, attended Nichols, the Hill School, and Yale, class of 1906. In 1908 he married Grace Rumsey, youngest daughter of Laurence Dana and Jennie Cary Rumsey of #1 Park Place and later #330 Delaware. After their marriage the newlyweds moved to Bogalusa, center of the Goodyear operations in Louisiana and lived there for two years. Grace hated the place and came home for the birth of her first child, Charles W. Goodyear, III, in 1909. They returned to Buffalo permanently in 1910 because of Grace's insistence. By 1912 they had moved to #123 Oakland Place which bordered on #888. This house was undoubtedly a gift of Ella.

105 *Ibid.*, pp. 215-219.

Here they lived for about twelve years until 1924 when the property at #190 Bryant, owned by Ella and occupied by Charles' brother Bradley from 1912 to 1915, was turned over to Charles, who had it torn down and, with Duane S. Lyman as architect, built a Tudor mansion next to his sister Esther Watson. Besides this house, they had a summer home on River Road built in 1917 amid beautiful gardens overlooking the Niagara north of Lewiston next to Grace's sister, Gertrude Rumsey Smith. Younger Goodyears entertained there often. After Charles and Grace's divorce, she got this house as part of the settlement, and lived there or in an apartment in Buffalo until her death.[106]

The marriage between Charles Goodyear and Grace started to go sour in 1925. He spent too much time with Marion Perkins Spaulding, wife of his friend Stephen Spaulding. The common interest was ostensibly horseback riding, particularly at the Watson farm in Clarence. By the early 1930s matters had come to a head. Marion left her husband and both Marion and Charles got divorces and were married in 1935. A large part of Buffalo society disapproved of this affair and the pair was banned from some social circles. Arnold Watson had forbidden them entrance to his house as early as 1932. Charles moved from Bryant and built a large house at #4985 Sheridan Drive and he and Marion moved in after their marriage. They sold it in 1954 and moved to the Westbrook Hotel, where they were living when she died in 1960. He died in 1967. For forty years he had belonged to the Country Club. He also belonged to the Saturn, Park, Buffalo, B.A.C., Buffalo Tennis and Squash, and East Aurora Hunt clubs.

After graduation in 1906 Charles Goodyear, Jr., had gone to Bogalusa where he spent four years as assistant general manager. When Conger was forced out of the operation, Charles returned to Buffalo where he worked or invested in several companies which were not very successful. During World War I he went overseas like Arnold Watson, with the Red Cross. When Conger resumed his relationship with Great Southern Lumber, Charles did so too as first vice president. In 1925 he became first vice-president of Bogalusa Paper. From then until 1937 he participated in all the major decisions of both companies. In 1935 he organized the Bogalusa Tung Oil Company, which planted 6,000 tung trees and by 1939 was one of the biggest producers of tung oil in America. He spent a great deal of time in Bogalusa and wrote a book entitled *Bogalusa Story*. He even built a house there where he lived on his many visits, nearer the larger house of his son, Charles, III, who had gone to work for the Bogalusa Paper Company after graduating from Yale in 1931, and who his father hoped would take over the Bogalusa operation. After Charles, III, married Mary Thompson in 1932 they moved there and became social and civic leaders. He was even president of the Bogalusa Country Club. He died there in 1968.[107]

106 *Ibid.*, p. 224.
107 *Ibid.*, p. 227.

10.57 ❦ Bradley Goodyear, *op. cit.*, p. 287.

Bradley Goodyear(10.57) was the youngest son of Charles Goodyear, Jr. The boy's early education was as his father's had been, Nichols, Hill School, and Yale, 1907. From there he went to Harvard Law where he graduated second in his class in 1910. Thereupon he became managing clerk for Kenefick, Cooke, Mitchell & Bass. Two years later he teamed up with William J. Donovan in Donovan & Goodyear which they combined with John Lord O'Brian and Chauncey J. Hamlin to form the firm of O'Brian, Hamlin, Donovan & Goodyear, which was dissolved when its three youngest members marched off to World War I. Bradley was the most active participant of the Goodyears in the war. In February 1916 he joined the NYNG as First Lieutenant and was assigned to the 65th Regiment of Infantry, which was mustered into federal service in August. The next month he was promoted to captain and sent to the Texas-Mexican Border with the 3rd NYNG Field Artillery where he served until March 1917. Mustered out, he reenlisted in August as a captain, serving until November as an instructor at Fort Sill, Oklahoma. He left Fort Sill and was assigned to the 106th Field Artillery at Camp Wadsworth, South Carolina, until May 1918 when his regiment was sent overseas for the rest of the war. He participated in the Meuse-Argonne offensive and became a major on November 3, 1918. Ultimately he was made commanding officer of the regiment which he led up Main Street in the Welcome Home parade in Buffalo in 1919. He and Donovan resumed their law partnership which Bradley dissolved immediately upon learning of Donovan's notorious raids on the clubs of Buffalo's elite. In fact, Bradley practically withdrew from practicing and eventually from the social life of the city. He kept an office in downtown for a while and continued as director of the Great Southern Lumber Company and Bogalusa Paper. In 1920 he had bought 100 acres of land on Lake Otsego in Central New York as a summer home and moved there permanently in 1931.[108]

10.58 ❦ Arthur Douglas Bissell, Hill, *op. cit.*, III, facing p. 13.

In 1910, Bradley had married Elizabeth Jeanette Bissell, who was born in 1886 on the corner of what would become

108 *Ibid.*, pp. 228-231.

Delaware and Hodge Avenues, #950 new style. Her father was Daniel B. Castle, a jeweler. Fanny Castle, her mother, was an alumna of the Buffalo Seminary and the Pratt Institute in Brooklyn. In 1874 she married Arthur Douglass Bissell(10.58), eldest son of John and Isabella Jeanette Halley Bissell who lived in a brownstone mansion at #1058 on the southwest corner of Delaware and Butler Street (later Lexington Avenue.) Following their marriage, Arthur and Fanny occupied a small house at #1081 Delaware across from her former home at #950. After the death of Daniel Castle in 1883 and a brief occupancy by attorney Thaddeus Davis, Castle's former home at #950 was bought by Arthur D. Bissell, so that Fanny Castle Bissell now lived in the house in which she had been born and married and her mother had been born, married, and died. Arthur Bissell was born in New London, Oneida County, in 1844 and came with his family to Buffalo at age six. He was educated in public schools, a prep boarding school at Clinton, and Yale, graduating in 1867. He spent seventeen years in the shipping business on the Erie Canal, which was still the chief route from the grain fields of the Mid-West to the east coast. With friend Grover Cleveland in the White House, Bissell was appointed Collector of the Port of Buffalo. An organizer of the People's Bank which opened in 1899, he was vice-president until 1903 when he became president. He was also connected with Federal Telephone, later absorbed by Bell.[109]

Until they moved to Lake Otsego, Bradley and Jeanette almost always lived in the family compound. In 1912, two years after they were married, they moved to #190 Bryant and in 1916 to #894 Delaware, next door to #888. Oddly enough, #894 had been the home of Daniel Castle, Fanny's father, at the end of the 1870s until his death in 1883. Number 894 was torn down in 1934 after the move to the Finger Lakes. There Bradley lived the life of a country squire, enjoying games and sports, first tennis, boating, and golf, later croquet, canasta, and bridge. The Goodyears traveled extensively. He refused to have his medical problems treated. Finally he agreed to be taken to a hospital in Cooperstown where he died in 1959.[110] Jeanette died in 1983 at ninety-three.

Explaining why the four children of Charles W. Goodyear, Sr., never seemed to want for money, George Goodyear wrote:

> By the time they moved to 888 the family was financially secure. Neither the parents nor the four young ever afterwards suffered from any degree of want. The fortune accumulated by their uncle and father insured this. Conger once said that he had never wanted anything that he couldn't afford to buy. Perhaps there is some exaggeration in this statement, but it does indicate the security to which they were accustomed, and which lasted all their lives. Furthermore, none of them married into poor families. Finally, all of them had sense enough not to live beyond their means, and astuteness enough to hang onto and add to their inheritance. Thus the Great Depression of the thirties had little impact upon them — they all avoided the pitfall of speculating with borrowed money.[111]

109 Hill, *op. cit.*, 3:13-14.
110 Goodyear, *op. cit.*, p. 233.
111 *Ibid.*, p. 135.
112 *M&FH*, 2:358-359; *Times*, November 14, 1909.

10.59 ❦ **Number 900 Delaware, a brick Queen Anne, SCNYAB.**

They may not have married poor but the eight third generation Goodyears obtained five divorces, which at the time was high. Grace, Conger, and Charles obtained one each, and Florence two, which comes to 62.5%.

The first resident of #894 was Hascal L. Taylor, president of Union Oil Company. He died in 1894 and was succeeded by Emory G. Taylor in 1900. James F. Aldrich, his wife, children, and three domestics followed in 1905. By 1915 the place had become a boarding house but it was returned to residential status with the coming of Bradley Goodyear who lived there throughout the 1920s.

The striking house on the southwest corner of Delaware and Bryant, #900(10.59), was built for James Howe Lee(10.60), a lumberman in 1881. He was born in Warsaw, New York, in 1822. His Connecticut-born father, Oliver, had moved to Genesse County in 1814 and settled at Westfield in 1824. He moved in 1828 to Silver Creek where he was a farmer, proprietor of a general store, banker, and freight fowarder. He and his wife had fifteen children 1815-1835. In 1841 he came to Buffalo and opened the Oliver Lee Bank. His son James attended grammar school at Silver Creek and Fredonia Academy. At eighteen he left school to clerk at his father's store for two or three years. When his father moved to Buffalo, James and his brother Charles took over the store which prospered for fifteen years. In 1856 he married Lucretia Clark from Silver Creek and moved to Buffalo with brother Franklin and engaged in government contracting. Later with his brother-in-law, Franklin N. Holland, and Henry Montgomery, Lee organized Lee, Holland & Company, which bought 6,000 acres of timberland in Michigan. By 1881 the company had built a lumber yard and planning mill on Wilkeson Street, which became the largest lumbering operation in Buffalo. James Lee retired in 1900 but continued as an investor and as vice-president and trustee of the Erie County Savings Bank and died in 1907.[112] His widow stayed at #900 but by 1920 it had been replaced by an apartment house.

10.60 ❦ **James H. Lee, *M&FH*, I, facing p. 358.**

CHAPTER

11 NORTH TO BRYANT: *East Side*

The map for this chapter is figure 10.1. The base date is again 1915 for reasons given at the start of the last chapter.

1870

NORTH STREET

675 Jerome Pierce 40 NY
Mary Pierce 36 Mass. *ux.*
Mary Pierce 6 NY
Anna Pierce 4 NY
Lucy Sand 30 Mass. at home
Ann Mooney 28 Ireland
Bridget Brown 21 NY
Kate Brown 13 NY
George Pratt 18 NY coachman

685 Frederick Squier 37 Conn. retired manufacturer
Ellen Squier 34 NY *ux.*
Kate Oalts 30 England
John Smith 20 NY gardener

1880

NORTH STREET

675 Ansley Wilcox 24 NY attorney
Cornelia Wilcox 28 *ux.*
Mary Niles 26 NY
May Niles

685 Louis Arend 43 NY dry goods merchant
Mary Arend 29 NY *ux.*
Richard Smith 40 Virginia coachman
Mary O'Brien 30 Ireland cook

703 John N. Scatcherd Jr. 23 NY lumber merchant
Mary Scatcherd 21 California *ux.*
Emma Wood 19 California sister-in-law
Kate Peter 23 Austria
Peter Dann 23 Canada coachman

723 Charles Goodyear 33 NY attorney
Ella Goodyear 26 NY *ux.*
Anson Goodyear 2 NY
Louisa Nemo 29 Baden
Anna Rief 21 NY

735 John Trefts 55 Ohio iron merchant
Angeline Trefts 45 NY *ux.*
Eva Holloway 22 NY daughter at home
Ann Mackey 25 Ireland
Nellie Mackey 10 Ireland

737 Stephen M. Clement 55 NY banker
Sarah Clement 55 NY *ux.*
Stephen M. Clement 19 NY son school
Harry Ogle 46 Canada boarder
Emma Mole 40 England

Sarah Masters 42 Ireland housekeeper
George Masters 15 Ireland son stable boy
Agnes Masters 8 NY daughter school
John Masters 5 NY son school
Clara Masters 4 NY daughter

SUMMER STREET

805 Charles Forbush 45 Mass
boot and shoe manufacturer
Caroline Forbush 40 Mass. *ux.*
Florence Forbush 16 NY school
Henry Sommers 24 England hostler

827 Albert S. Stevens 53 New Hampshire attorney
Sarah Stevens 37 NY *ux.*
Albert Stevens 15 NY school
Cora Stevens 14 NY school
Anna Stevens 6 NY school
Prudence Jones 23 England

BARKER STREET

841 Noyes Darrow 71 Vermont retired merchant
Mary Darrow 69 NY *ux.*
Charles Darrow 33 NY clerk in store
Fanny Allen 17 NY at home
Celia Johson 22 Louisiana

849 Catherine Bartow 45 Michigan
Charles Bartow 27 Michigan at home
Kate Bartow 25 Michigan at home
John Bartow 24 Michigan clerk in store
Louis Bartow 22 clerk in store
Bernard Bartow 20 Michigan
Grace Bartow 16 NY school
Bridget Barrett Ireland

SUMMER STREET

767 Abraham Altman 60 NY president
3rd National Bank
Clara Altman 39 NY *ux.*
Cornelia Altman 19 NY daughter at home
Eliza Mesmer 23 NY
Mary Showhacker 40 NY

Thomas Butt 35 NY
Agnes Butt *ux.*
George Butt 2 NY son

795 Leonidas Doty 67 Conn. banker
Sabina Doty 54 Mass. *ux.*
Florence Doty 17 Mass. daughter at home
Mary Hesse 22 Batavia
Elizabeth McComack 25 Ireland

805 Jonathan Forbush 55 Mass.
boot and shoe manufacturer
Susan Forbush 52 Mass. *ux.*
Florence Forbush 16 NY at home
Grace Forbush 7 NY

827 Joseph P. Dudley 46 New Hampshire oil producer
Mary Dudley 43 NY *ux.*
Mary Underhill 20 NY niece at home
Mary Metzger 23 Wurtemburg
John Kebler 24 Saxony coachman

BARKER STREET

841 Noyes Darrow 80 Vermont retired merchant
Mary Darrow 79 NY *ux.*
Charles Darrow 44 NY son paper hanger
Bessie Darrow 6 NY granddaughter
Carrie Darrow 5 NY granddaughter
John Swanenburg 60 England gardener
Sarah Fleishammer 26 Austria
Ellen Donnell 30 Ireland

857 Norris Morey 40 NY attorney
Annita Morey 37 Ohio *ux.*
Bella Morey 5 NY daughter
Joseph Morey 3 NY son
Nellie Williams 19 Ohio sister-in-law
Nellie Sullivan 19 Ireland

869	Charles Baylis 60 England produce merchant Lucy J. Baylis 42 Vermont *ux.* Alma Rice 70 Vermont boarder Frank Baylis 18 NY Louisa Brooks 40 housekeeper Susan Sautenschlager 20 Prussia	869	Charles Baylis 70 England retired Lucy Baylis 52 Vermont *ux.* Mary McNeal 17 Scotland
891	Henry C. Bryant 40 NY nurseryman Lucy Bryant 38 NY *ux.* Susan Bryant 13 NY school Vincent Bryant 10 NY school Henry Bryant 4 NY	891	Henry C. Bryant 50 NY retired merchant Lucy Bryant 45 NY *ux.* Julia Bryant 15 NY school Julia Bryant 13 NY daughter at home Harper Bryant 21 NY son at home Vincent Bryant 18 NY son Harry Bryant 13 NY son Amy Bensenger 35 NY
905	Price Matteson 33 NY attorney Frances Matteson 30 NY *ux.* Hattie Matteson 4 NY Bessie Matteson 2 NY Fanny Matteson 1 NY Alexander Brown 57 NY boarder Hattie Brown 50 NY boarder Dora Smith 19 NY	905	Price Matteson 41 NY attorney Frances Matteson 39 NY *ux.* Hattie Matteson 14 NY daughter Bessie Matteson 12 NY daughter Fanny Matteson 10 NY daughter Brooks Matteson 4 NY son Harriet Brown 61 NY mother-in-law Nellie Dalton 19 NY
	BRYANT STREET ❦ End of Block		BRYANT STREET ❦ End of Block
	1891		**1900**
	NORTH STREET		NORTH STREET
675	Charles F. Ganson	675	Charles Ganson 44 NY Sarah Ganson 47 NY *ux.* Mabel Ganson 21 NY daughter Annie Gavigan 32 Ireland Susan Hoard 35 Ireland Dora Brown 25 NY Hanna McCarthy 48 Ohio
685	Herbert C. Williams manager Bank of Commerce	685	Robert Fryer 52 NY banker Melissa Fryer 46 NY *ux.* Livingston Fryer 12 NY son school Margaret Fryer 6 NY daughter school Mary Marooney 31 NY Kate Nugent 36 NY Lizzie Hall NY George Henry Smith 51 England coachman Nettie Smith 35 NY *ux.* Mary K. Smith 20 NY daughter
703	John N. Scatcherd S&S Lumber 471 Louisiana Charles Arr coachman Robert Shields coachman	703	John N. Scatcherd 42 NY lumber dealer Mary E. Scatcherd 41 California *ux.* Margaret Scatcherd 25 California Madeleine Scatcherd 19 NY daughter James N. Scatcherd 42 NY cousin insurance agent

Margaret Scatcherd 25 Canada cousin
Robert Scatcherd 31 Canada insurance agent
Rosie Kelly 37 Ireland
Mary Meehan 30 Ireland
Sarah Taylor 27 Canada
Maggie Watt 29 NY
Charles Orr 27 NY coachman

713 Bainbridge Folwell M.D.
Patrick Kane coachman

713 Florence Folwell 40 NY widow
Bainbridge Folwell 15 NY son school
Kate Burke 31 Ireland
Norah Clark 19 Canada
Mary Chase 25 Canada

717 Eric L. Hedstrom coal and pig iron
17 White Building
William Smith coachman

717 Anna Hedstrom 62 Pennsylvania widow
Charlotte Brown 33 Canada
Hannah Callahan 27 Ireland
Patrick Kane 27 Ireland

Charles Farg 27 England coachman
Martha Farg 22 Canada *ux.*
Arthur Farg 2 NY son

723 Charles W. Goodyear
Ella Goodyear

723 Charles W. Goodyear 53 NY vice-president
Buffalo & Susquehanna
Ella Goodyear 46 NY *ux.*
Bradley Goodyear 14 son school
Anna McHattie 29 Scotland
Mary Leachy 30 NY
Minnie Miessner 20 NY

Andrew Barton 45 NY coachman
Carrie Barton 32 NY *ux.*
Genevieve Barton 7 NY daughter school
Mildred Barton 3 NY daughter

735 John Trefts

735 John Trefts 76 Ohio iron works
Angeline Trefts 58 NY *ux.*
Evadne Trefts 36 NY
Rose Fox NY
Mary Davis 21 Ireland

737 Stephen M. Clement president Marine Bank
220 Main

737 Stephen M. Clement 40 NY banker
Caroline J. Clement 38 NY *ux.*
Norman F. Clement 15 NY son school
Stephen M. Clement Jr. 12 NY son school
Harold J. Clement 9 NY son school
Marian Clement 8 NY daughter school
Clement M. Cochrane 20 Persia ward Yale
Sarah Huston 35 Canada
Theresa McGowan 22 Canada
Annette Koescher 21 Germany
Ada Stolka 35 NY
William Gorst 41 England coachman
Annie Gorst 32 Ireland *ux.*

SUMMER STREET

787 Charles Daniels judge superior court

795 Mrs. Leonidas Doty

805 Jonathan C. Forbush F. & Brown
boot and shoe manufacturers 105 Main

827 Joseph P. Dudley Star Oil Co.
Swan and Washington
William Miller coachman

BARKER STREET

841 Andrew C. W. O'Brien druggist 35 West Eagle

849 Charles M. Underhill manager
J. Langdon Coal Co.

741 Edward Michael 45 attorney
Celia Michael 40 *ux.*
Clara Michael 13 daughter school
Edwine Michael 11 daughter school
Jeanette Michael 10 daughter school

SUMMER STREET

787 Mary Daniels 61 NY widow
Nellie Cary 38 Ireland
Margaret Foran 32 Scotland

William Webster Canada coachman
Lizzie Webster 38 Pennsylvania *ux.*
Gertrude Webster 13 NY daughter
Grace Webster 12 NY daughter school
Mary J. Webster 11 NY daughter school
Charles D. Webster 9 NY son school
Walter A. Webster 4 NY
William J. Webster 1 NY

795 Mrs. Leonidas Doty 64 Mass. widow
Katherine Hewitt 36 NY
Jane Palmer 30 Canada
John Grill 32 coachman

805 Mrs. Jonathan Forbush 74 Mass. widow
Grace Forbush 26 NY daughter
Grace A. Touchenbrot 19 Canada
Lizzie Goetz 28 Canada cook

827 Joseph P. Dudley 67 New Hampshire oil producer
Mary J. Dudley 39 niece
Annie Bedford 28 Wales
Weatherby Ingram 42 Conn.
Howard Turner 40 NY coachman
Minnie Turner 39 NY *ux.*

BARKER STREET

841 William B. Hoyt 42 NY attorney
Esther Hoyt 35 NY *ux.*
Josephine B. Hoyt 11 NY daughter school
Esther L. Hoyt 10 daughter school
Abeline H. Hoyt 8 NY daughter school
Hilda Hoyt 6 NY
John Hoyt 2 NY son
Katherine Laffaly 32 NY
Bertha Miller 25 Holland
Mary Lynch 40 NY
Mary Vespser 28 Ireland

849 Charles M. Underhill 60 NY coal dealer
Anna P. Underhill 60 NY *ux.*
Irving S. Underhill 34 NY son
Augustus Underhill NY 32 son
Bertha P. Underhill 35 NY daughter
Bella C. White 48 Canada
Margaret Lynch 22 Canada

857 George C. Beals 47 Board of Trade
George Beals 14 White Building

869 William H. Orcutt 44 Mass. attorney
Leafie S. Orcutt

877 George S. Donaldson Collingwood & D. cut stone
John Donaldson
William E. Donaldson bookkeeper
Erie County Savings Bank

891 Mrs. Henry Bryant
Henry Bryant stenographer

BRYANT STREET ❦ End of Block

1905

NORTH STREET

675 Sarah Ganson 49 NY
Mary E. Leahy 43
Annie Sullivan 36
Hannah McCarthy 51

685 Robert L. Fryer 58 banker
Melissa Pratt Fryer 50 *ux.*
Pascal Fryer 20 son student
Livingston Fryer 17 son
Margarita Fryer 7 daughter
Margaret Nugent 32 cook

857 Willis K. Morgan 44 Illinois furniture dealer
Nellie F. Morgan 44 NY *ux.*
Darwin E. Morgan 70 Illinois father
Katherine Austin 50 NY sister
Margaret J. Wilson 24 Canada

869 William W. Sloan 61 Ireland retired
Elsie M. Sloan 62 Ohio *ux.*
Leafie Orcutt 25 NY daughter widow
Anne McAuliffe 24 NY
Clara Ahearn 25 NY

877 John Donaldson 74 Ireland retired
William E. Donaldson 32 NY son invalid
Agnes Geary 37 Canada
Luther Miller 35 Germany coachman

897 Deborah Jewett 78 NY widow
Mildred Rand 28 Maryland niece
Anna Smith 28 Ireland
Margaret Scanlon 39 Ireland

Aaron Yenky NY 36 coachman
Mary Yenky NY 26 *ux.*
Lottie Yenky 1 NY daughter
Henry Corah 21 NY brother machinist

905 Joseph Block 49 Germany broker
Elizabeth Block 49 NY *ux.*
Cornelle Block 24 NY daughter
Henry Block 22 NY son
Arthur Block 15 NY son school
Edgar Block 12 NY son school
Edwin Block 9 NY son school
Louisa Schreiber 20 Germany
Emma Niederman 63 Canada
Mary Lafarge 29 NY

BRYANT STREET ❦ End of Block

1915

NORTH STREET

675 Joseph Montague 68
Sarah Montague 61 *ux.*
Katherine Clark 50 housekeeper

685 Robert L. Fryer 68 banker
Melissa Fryer 57 *ux.*
Livingston Fryer 27 son bank clerk
Pascal Fryer 32 son
Kathleen Nugent 40 cook
Helen Walsh 35 upstairs maid

Flora McLeod waitress

Charles McSorley 43 Ireland coachman
Elizabeth Hill 38 servant
Suzanne Hat 38 Switzerland servant

695 Charles Sumner Jones 44 M.D.
Emma Jones 43 *ux.*
Pascal Jones 10 son school
Julia Sullivan 38 Ireland

Michael Miller 31 coachman
Bertha Miller 30 Germany *ux.*
Gladys Miller 8 daughter school

703 John N. Scatcherd 47 lumber merchant
Mary E. Scatcherd 45 *ux.*
John N. Scatcherd 20 son
Madeline Scatcherd 24 daughter
Margaret Connell 25 Ireland
Margaret Gleason 34 Ireland
Kate Horan 47 Ireland

713 Florence Folwell 57
Bainbridge Folwell 20 son
Katherine Crawford 21 Ireland
Katie Burke 35 Ireland

William Thomson 50 England coachman
Libby Thomson 45 England *ux.*

717 Anna Hedstrom 67
Charlotte Brown 39 Canada
Anna Crew 35 Canada

723 William Connors 40 publisher
Mary A. Connors 31 *ux.*
Mary M. Connors 20 daughter school
Katherine Connors 18 school
Peter Connors 17 son school
Alice Connors 9 daughter
William Connors 8 son school
Ruth Connors 2 daughter

737 Stephen M. Clement 45 banker
Caroline J. Clement 43 *ux.*
Norman P. Clement 20 Yale
Stephen M. J. Clement 17 son
  Hill School Pottstown
Harold Clement 15 son
Marion Clement 13 daughter
Stuart H. Clement 10 school
Sophia Haley 60

Frances Greene 24 upstairs maid
Matilda Moll 24 kitchen maid

695 Charles Sumner Jones 58 M.D.
Pascal Jones 20 son school
Violet Wissler 44 housekeeper
Katherine McGraw 23 Ireland upstairs maid
Minie McMann 24 Ireland waitress
Emma Weih 40 Germany cook

Michael Miller 43 chauffeur
Bertha Miller 42 Germany
Gladys Miller 18 daughter school

703 John Newton Scatcherd 57 lumber
John N. Scatcherd Jr. 30 son sales
Edith Scatcherd 23 daughter-in-law
Julia Manley 19 Ireland waitress
Margaret Gleason 35 cook

713 Florence Folwell 65
Annie Leary 23 Ireland waitress
Nellie Moriarity 28 cook

Walter Holland 25 chauffeur
Mary Holland 26 *ux.*
Walter Holland 4 son
George Gastall 28 brother-in-law janitor
Margaret Gastall 25 sister

717 Anna M. Hedstrom 70
Charlotte Brown 43 Canada maid
Josephine Clark 35 cook

741 Edward Michael 50 attorney
Celia Michael 50 *ux.*
Clara Michael 18 daughter school
Edwine Michael daughter 16
Jeanette Michael daughter
Ethel Tee 22
Ida Bachman 22
Hellie Leise 22
Mary Thomson 39 Canada
Louise Hoffman 85
Henry Hughes 40 coachman

SUMMER STREET

787 Mary E. Daniels 70
Margaret Dolan 33 Scotland
Delia Dolan 35 Scotland
Louis Deuter 38 gardener

William Webster 40 Canada coachman
Lizzie Webster 43 *ux.*
Gertrude Webster 19 daughter
Grace Webster 18 daughter
Mary E. Webster 16 daughter
Charles Webster 12 school
Walter Webster 9 school
William Webster

795 Selena A. Doty widow 74
Katherine Hewitt 38
Anna Comer 38
Lucy Hoffel 15
Ferdinand Grill 31

805 Spencer Kellogg 52 oil merchant
Jane Kellogg 50 *ux.*
Howard Kellogg 24 son oil merchant
Gertrude M. Kellogg 22 daughter
Ruth Kellogg 15 daughter school
Doris Kellogg 11 daughter school
Thirga James 35 England housekeeper
Mary Murphy 25 Ireland
Alice Kelly 30
Charlotte Moran 45 Canada
Kitty Riley 25 Ireland

William McGee 44 Ireland coachman
Katherine McGee 45 *ux.*
Jerome McGee 21 son
Maria McGee 15 daughter school
Lee McGee 9 son school

827 Joseph P. Dudley 72
Sarah Dudley 39 *ux.*
Sarah J. Dudley 40 niece
Mary McGarvey 36
Elizabeth Cuffe 35 Ireland
Howard Turner 45 coachman

741 Edward Michael 60 attorney
Celia Michael 54 ux.
Clara Michael 28 daughter
Edwine Michael 26 daughter
Jeanette Michael 25 daughter
Anna Langfield 52 Ireland cook
Nora Horan 27 upstairs maid
Martha Zembie 25 Scotland waitress
Katherine McTaggert 26 waitress

SUMMER STREET

787 Mary E. Daniels 80
Margaret Dolan 43 Scotland waitress
Delia Dolan 45 Scotland cook

William Webster 50 Canada chauffeur
Elizabeth Webster 53 *ux.*
Charles D. Webster 22 son inspector
Walter Webster 19 son office clerk
William J. Webster 17 son school
Grace Webster 27 daughter dressmaker

805 Spencer Kellogg 65 linseed oil
Jane Kellogg 60 *ux.*
Ruth Kellogg 29 daughter
Doris Kellog 24 daughter
Donald Kellogg 20 son school

827 Willis K. Jackson 55 lumber
Annette Jackson 41 *ux.*
Kitty McCloud 30 Scotland cook
Sophie Goress 32 upstairs maid

George Burbank 45 chauffeur
Margaret Burbank 40 *ux.*

BARKER STREET

841 William B. Hoyt 40 attorney
Esther L. Hoyt 37 *ux.*
Josephine Hoyt 16 daughter
Esther Hoyt 15 school
Alberine Hoyt 13 school
Hilda Hoyt 11 school
John Hoyt 7 school
Frederick Margeret 33 Germany
Katherine Lafferty
Louise Sullivan 30 Canada

849 Charles W. Sears 34 attorney
Florence G. Sears 32 *ux.*
Winifred McDermott 20 Ireland
Mary M. ________ Ireland

857 *The Morey Flats*
Robert B Cox 48
Fraicke D. Cox 46 *ux.*
Clara R Allen
Constance Allen 12 daughter school
Ann E. Meldrum 70 Scotland
Florence Meldrum 26 daughter
Katherine Crocker 22
Lena Ashley 37

869 Eugene A. Goerger 55 president German Bank
Charlotte Goerger 51 *ux.*
Nattelie Goerger 24 daughter
Francis Goerger 21 school
Thomas Thompson 78 Ireland father-in-law
Mary Allisondinger 27

877 Douglas Gibson 65
Anna M. Gibson 62 *ux.*
Ellen Brennan 27 Ireland
Albert Elwell 54 coachman

BARKER STREET

841 Lester F. Gilbert 30 attorney
Josephine Gilbert 30 *ux.*
Frederick Gilbert 3 son
Grace Staffel 23
Molly Kuhn 27

849 Charles S. Sears 44 attorney
Florence G. Sears 42 *ux*
Nellie Kelleher 24 Ireland
Katie Kelleher 22 Ireland

857 Jacob Brecht 63 Germany janitor
Louise Brecht 64 *ux.*
Julia C. Clark 45
Louise Clark 25 daughter
John D. Clark 23 son school
George D. Clark 18 son school
Lillian Berg 27

869 Charles Van Bergen 46 France M.D.
Amelia Van Bergen 44 *ux.*
Frank S. Thorn 74 father-in-law
Albert Balthazard 39 France
Helen O'Halloran 27 Ireland
Marie Preece 33 England
Minnie Schrader 48 Denmark

Herbert Taylor 35 England
Lillian Taylor 32 England
Kenneth Taylor 2 England son
Marion Taylor 10 daughter

877 Asa K. Silverthorne 50 lumber
Mattie F. Silverthorne 48 *ux.*
Mary Shelby 25 Canada
Belle Beeman 30

William Judson 23 chauffeur
Anna M. Judson 21 *ux.*
Louise Judson 55 France mother

891 Orin E. Foster 75 medical supplies
Emily L. Foster 60 Canada *ux.*
Helen Foster 29 daughter
Mary McMahon 39 Ireland
Margaret McMahon 39 Ireland
Mabel Kennedy 24
Ebert Fredericka Germany

897 Deborah Jewett 83
Louise Jewett 18 daughter *illegible* Germany
Susana Hayes 39
illegible 39 Ireland
illegible 38 Ireland
Margaret Scanlon 38 Ireland

905 Joseph Block 53 Germany president Citizens Bank
Henry J. Block 27 son banker
Arthur J. Block 20 son Cornell

Henry J. Brock 34 wholesale clothing
Camille B. Brock 28 *ux.*
Elizabeth Brock 3 daughter
Hannah Brock 1 daughter
Mary Le Fevre 24
Bertha Le Fevre 20
Emma Hunter 28 Ireland

BRYANT STREET ❦ End of Block

George E. Fillmore 38 chauffeur
Mabel E. R. Fillmore 34 *ux.*

Aaron Yearly 55 gardener

905 Joseph B. Black 54 Germany banker
Blanche Black 52 *ux.*
Edgar N. Black 26 son clerk
Adrian Black 21 son school
Rose N. Priebe 30
Hannah Schumacker 25 Germany
Louise Schumacker 39

BRYANT STREET ❦ End of Block

1920

NORTH STREET

675 Joseph Montague 44 Mass. vice-president power company
Sarah Montague 50 NY *ux.*
Catherine Clark 53

685 Robert L. Fryer 55 NY
Livingston Fryer 30 son banker
Alfred Lewis 23 England
Ellen Welsh 60 Mass.
Rosine Knopske 53 Germany
Nora Moffat 57 Canada

695 Charles Sumner Jones 61 NY M.D.
Pascal P. Jones 25 NY
Violetta M. Wissler 34 Canada nurse
Alice Geiger 20 NY
Mattie Dority 45 NY

Michael Miller 47 NY chauffeur
Bertha Miller 47 Germany *ux.*

703 Morris S. Tremaine 58 Kansas machine manufacturer
Maude M. Tremaine 44 NY *ux.*
Laurence Tremaine 17 NY son
James G. Tremaine 14 NY son
Sarah B. Rogers 68 England housekeeper
Katherine Foley 28 Ireland

1925

NORTH STREET

675 *The Westbrook*
106 residents

685 Melissa P. Fryer 72 widow
Pascal Pratt Jones 36 son
Livingston Fryer 28 son
Catherine Fryer 24 daughter
Ellen Welsh 72 housekeeper
Nora Moffat 60 Canada cook
Rosine Knoehke 58 Russia maid

695 Charles Sumner Jones 66 M.D.
Pascal Pratt Jones 30 son agriculturalist
Matilda Perrin 22 maid
Salome Baldwin 45 cook
Mae Wissler 34 Canada nurse

703 Morris Tremaine 52 manufacturer
Marie Tremaine 49 *ux.*
Laurence Tremaine 23 son
James Tremaine 19 son student
Nellie Hedley 40 cook
Delia Breen 23 Ireland maid

713 Florence Folwell 69 NY widow
Nora O'Keefe 62 Ireland
Margaret Donovan 28 Ireland

Walter P. Holland 35 England chauffeur
Mary E. Holland 38 England *ux.*
Walter G. Holland 9 NY son

717 Anna Hedstrom 83 Pennsylvania widow
Lena Huck Canada 37
Charlotte Brown 54 Canada

723 Boarding house
Cornelia N. Burtis proprietor
52 boarders

735 Albert W. Starke 46 Illinois manager steel plant
Jessica V. Starke 46 NY *ux.*
George A Reyolds 24 NY relation
Laura M. Reynolds

737 Irving Snow 58 NY M.D.
Violette Snow 36 NY *ux.*
Mildred Snow 2 NY daughter
Julia Snow 1 NY daughter
Joanna Smith 62 NY
Elsie McGregor 25 Scotland
Harriet Hill 22 NY

741 Edward Michael 68 NY M.D.
Celia B. Michael 16 NY *ux.*
Clara Michael 32 NY daughter
Edwine Michael 30 NY daughter
Jeanette Michael 27 NY daughter
Katherine Sommerville 32 NY

SUMMER STREET

713 Mr. Bainbridge Folwell

Walter P. Holland 46 England chauffeur
Mary Holland 43 England *ux.*
Walter Holland 14 son school

717 Anna M. Hedstrom 88 widow
Charlotte Brown 58 Canada housekeeper

735 Apartments
10 residents

737 Irving Snow 64 M.D.
Violette P. Snow 42 *ux.*
Mildred P. Snow 6 daughter
Julia M. Snow 6 daughter
Bertha Shad 23 nurse
Margaret Breen 22 Ireland

741 Edward Michael 75 attorney
Celia Michael 70 *ux.*
Clara Michael 36 daughter
Edwine Michael 34 daughter
Jeanette Michael 32 daughter
Frances McAuliffe 38 Canada seamstress
Julia Senkow 55 Poland cook
Margaret McCarthy 30 maid
Elizabth Farrell 40 maid
Belinda Quinn 20 Scotland
Blanche Waite 50 laundress

SUMMER STREET

787 Charles M. Daniels 39 proprietor fox farm
Florence Daniels 35 *ux.*
Grace W. Daniels 19 daughter
Goodyear Daniels 15 son school
Christine Reeve 3 England
Marian Shuman 30 Austria
Margaret Mitchell 25 Ireland
Elizabeth Simon 3 Austria cook
Arletta Ridley 50 nurse
Louis Deuter 53 gardener
Emma Pilaosher 35 laundress

George Roughead 46 chauffeur
Lillian Roughead 30 *ux.*

805 Spencer Kellogg 68 NY linseed oil
Jane M. Kellogg 66 NY *ux.*
Doris Kellogg 27 NY daughter
Mary Jarrell 34 Canada
Mary Mugero 20 Ireland
Ferdinand Phillips 20 Germany
Charles Steen 56 Germany
Anna Evans 34 Ireland
Annie Donaldson 57 Canada
William Mahar 36 NY
A. Barrell 48 Germany

827 Willis K. Jackson 58 Wisconsin lumber
Annette Jackson 58 NY *ux.*
Margaret Reilly 37 Ireland
Hekla Palmquist 32 Sweeden
Sophia Goers 30 NY

BARKER STREET

849 Charles B. Sears 49 NY supreme court judge
Florence Sears 46 Conn. *ux.*
Katherine Kelleher 26 Ireland
Nellie Kelleher 26 Ireland

857 Apartments 7 families

869 Charles Van Bergen 50 France M.D.
Amelia Van Bergen 48 Ohio *ux.*
Kate Simon 50 NY
Mary O'Connor 21 Ireland
Delia Kelly 27 Ireland

Henry H. Taylor 39 England gardener
Lillian Taylor 37 England *ux.*
Marion Taylor 14 England daughter
Kenneth Taylor 6 NY son

795 Richard Wilhelm 55
Alice Wilhelm 55 *ux.*

Arthur J. Dearlove 50 England gardener
Elizabeth Dearlove 50 *ux.*

805 Jane M. Kellogg 71 widow
Charles T. Neale son-in-law steel salesman
Doris K. Neale 33 daughter
Spencer K. Neale 3 grandson
Margaret Neale 2 granddaughter
Angelica Neale 3 months granddaughter
Lizzie Clark 40 nurse
Charles Stein houseman
Ferdinand Phillip 26 Germany butler
Elizabeth Phillip 28 Germany nurse
Mary Griffin 36 Irleand
Vera Wood 42 cook

Henry Thobaben 40 Germany
Dagmar Thobaben 40 *ux.*
Henry Thobaben 9 son
Alfred Thobaben 9 son
Grace Thobaben 3 daughter

827 Willis K. Jackson 65 lumber
Annette Jackson 63 *ux.*
Nellie A. Coles 42 England
Marie Jagg 29 Germany
Vera Derkowitz 20 Hungary

BARKER STREET

849 Charles B. Sears 54 judge supreme court
Florence Sears 51 *ux.*

John Carney 36 gardener
Emma Carney 35 Canada *ux.*
Mary Carney 9 daughter school

857 Apartments 25 residents

Herbert Taylor 45 England gardener
Lillian Taylor 43 England *ux.*
Marion Taylor 20 England daughter
Robert Kenneth 12 son

877 Asa K. Silverthorn 54 Iowa lumber merchant
Mattie Silverthorn 52 NY *ux.*
Mary L. Shelby 47 Canada
Harry F. Brewer 31 NY chauffeur
Blanche G. Brewer 27 NY *ux.*
Vernon Brewer 1 NY son

891 Orin E. Foster 79 NY
Emily L. Foster 75 Canada *ux.*
Emma R. Clout 52 England
Margaret C. McMahon 46 Ireland
Mary M. McMahon 35 Ireland

George E. Fillmore 43 NY chauffeur
Mabel E. Fillmore 36 Canada *ux.*
Harry L. Dickson 27 Canada brother-in-law auto mechanic

897 William M. Decker 64 NY glass manufacturer
Elizabeth Decker 59 *ux.*
Dorothy S. Decker 30 NY
Margaret E. *illeg.* 8 NY granddaughter
Grace Victor 30 NY
Alice F. Coates 63 Pennsylvania

905 Arthur J. Block 34 NY jeweler
Annie K. Block 33 Ohio *ux.*
Henrietta Block 7 NY daughter
Joseph Block 2 NY son
Edgar Block 67 NY jeweler
Joseph Block 67 Germany father
Florence Metcalfe 38 NY
Gladys Bukowski 24 NY

877 Theodore Wickwire 74 retired
Emma Wickwire 70 *ux.*
Jessie MacDougal 45 Scotland
Blanche Cherkauer 32 England
Margaret Callanan 64 cook

George Rathbon 46 Canada chauffeur
Margaret Rathbon 35 Ireland *ux.*
Anna Marie Rathbon 6 daughter school

891 Orin E. Foster 85 chemist
Emily Foster 78 Canada *ux.*
Helen Foster 30 daughter
Sarah Facknal 40 England cook
Mary McMahon 40 Ireland maid
Margaret McMahon 51 Ireland

George Fillmore 50 chauffeur
Mabel E. Fillmore 45 Canada *ux.*

897 William M. Decker 69 NY bottle company
Margaret Decker 64 *ux.*
Mary E. Hodge 57 England
Abigail Hill 46 cook

905 Rooming house

The house at North and Delaware was occupied in 1870 by Jerome Pierce, his wife, three children, three servants, and an eighteen-year old coachman. Pierce's body was found one night in the mid-1870s floating in the Ohio Slip near his sawmill. The house was empty until Dexter Rumsey bought it in view of the marriage of daughter Cornelia to Ansley Wilcox in January 1878.[1] By 1883 Wilcox and his second wife had moved to #641 Delaware, and #675(11.1) was the home of Charles F. Ganson(11.2), son of

11.1 ❦ Where Mabel Ganson grew up, Number 675 Delaware, BHS.

1 *CE*, March 16, 1933, p. 8.

11.2 ❦ Charles Ganson and Sara Cook Ganson, Hahn, *op. cit.*, following p. 116.

James M. Ganson, a banker, and his wife Nancy. Charles was highly neurotic. Trained in the law, he never practiced and spent his days in a downtown office, doing nobody knew what. His wife was Sara Cook(11.2), a lively woman, daughter of a banker from Bath who moved to New York and built a mansion on 5th Avenue across from the Metropolitan Museum of Art. Mabel Ganson believed her parents' marriage had been arranged because both fathers were very wealthy. Charles' hobby was flags and he had designed his own. He flew it whenever Sara visited her parents. When she returned he lowered it to half-mast. When he couldn't stand it at #675 he would retreat to mother's who was always glad to see him.[2] Mabel, fortunately her parents' only child, was born in 1879. Figure 11.3 shows her at three points in her youth. Her memories of "Our Town" were, like herself, strong on feeling if not always accuracy:

> In 1880 Buffalo was a cosy town. At least it was for those who formed the nucleus in the centre of it, that central part made up of Delaware Avenue and the avenues parallel to it and the cross-streets that intersected the privileged area. This fashionable part of Buffalo, where one knew practically everyone one met on the street, was only a small portion of it, but seemed to us to be the only real Buffalo. On the other side of Main Street where all the stores were, it was just an outer wilderness.
>
> Our instinctive feeling towards the East Side was one of contempt that had something inimical in it. Charlotte Becker made one of her jokes about the beautiful Reinhardt girls whose German father came to live in our part of town when they began to grow up. Because they had lived on the East Side, everybody snickered at Charlotte's remark that the Reinhardt girls didn't "come out" like other girls — they just "came over."
>
> The western limit of our life in Buffalo was Lake Erie, though hardly any one we knew lived on the lake front or even considered it very interesting or important. The life in Buffalo went on away from it. We weren't conscious that it was there.
>
> Delaware Avenue ran downhill till it came to the business part of the town and branched off into streets with horse-cars on them; and it ran slightly uphill to the park and the cemetery, and to the country club [where Nottingham Terrace is now] where we used to go

2 Emily Hahn, *Mabel: A Biography of Mabel Dodge Luhan* (Boston: Houghton Mifflin Company, 1977), p. 4.

> when we were old enough to want what was found there. All up and down both sides of our streets grew many beautiful trees. They grew while we grew ourselves until now [1933] they make the city all shady and cool in the hot summer days. Before I left Buffalo, thirty years ago, the trees almost met overhead on Delaware Avenue.[3]

Years later Buffalo had come to seem a winter wonderland:

> In the winter there was always plenty of snow and good sleighing, and on the bright sunny afternoons that were so frequent then, many ladies would go driving in sleighs with great buffalo and bearskin robes under them and hanging over the back of the sleighs and over their knees. The coachmen were hidden in buffalo coats, caps, and gloves. The little boys and girls used to hitch sleds to the runners of their family sleighs or catch rides from any one they could fasten to, single sleds and sometimes long bob-sleds.

> It was the custom for hard-faced men unknown to us all to come over from the East Side, or from the other part of town, and drive fast-trotting horses up and down the avenue from Ferry Street, six blocks up and ending below North Street, where our house was. They sat in the center of small spidery cutters upholstered in bright-red plush and raced each other down the hill, two and three abreast. There were fine horses in Buffalo in those days, and a good deal of betting on these races went on among the coarse-voiced strange drivers. They raced from two o'clock until it grew dark and the man who lighted the street gas lamps began to prick the dusk with yellow flames; then the street grew gradually empty and the sharp sound of silver sleigh bells became fainter and fainter in the darkening evening. In the winter time there was never any sound on our streets except of people's voices and the bells, and these were muffled by

Top left 11.3 ❦ Mabel Ganson at sixteen, 1895; Bottom left ❦ as a debutante, aged eighteen; Bottom right ❦ and at twenty-one, 1900. Hahn, *op. cit.*, following p. 116.

3 Luhan, *op. cit.*, p. 12.

> the snow — plenty of coming and going of the family sleighs and people walking and children playing. But after dark the streets we knew were mostly empty except for an occasional figure passing in the silence and everybody was at home.[4]

Mabel hated the repression that had become a mark of Buffalo and advocated focusing on feelings and imagination. She professed to believe that failure to adopt this liberating outlook had produced havoc along the Delaware of her youth:

> At the same hour in all the houses a maid would be seen pulling down the window-shades in the front of the house and lighting the gas, and presently they glowed within, safely sheltering their privacies and their curious reserves. For almost every house held a family with some strange deviation in it, and they all tried to dissemble their individual peculiarities. Each house held its own secret, helpless shame.
>
> Within the narrow limitation of life in Buffalo, where the occupations were so unvaried and the imaginations so little fed, there came to be many queer characters and people with curious ways. Although everybody knew everybody else and all there was to know about everybody else, yet by a kind of mutual agreement they all pretended to ignore each other's inward life. People never talked to each other except of outward things, but about each other they exchanged many conjectures. There was hardly any real intimacy between friends, and people had no confidence in each other. To their neighbours or to their families, they only talked of other people's feelings. Inside the house or outside, no one ever talked about how she felt. Her own pain and fear — she just felt and buried it. Life flowed on in an apparently commonplace way until, once in a while, something happened. Donald White would be found hanging to the gas fixture in his bedroom, naked except for a pair of white gloves; Caroline Thompson would suddenly be seen no more among her friends and her mother would not mention her absence. But people would whisper: "They say they had to take her out to the Insane Asylum" and she would never be seen again. It would not be long before she was forgotten by everyone except perhaps her parents, who seemed to go on as they always had, though their faces changed almost unnoticeably from the hidden grief.[5]

Lavish dinner parties at home were a major part of the Delaware Avenue social whirl. Mabel described one such feast when her parents believed she was asleep in her second floor room:

> Quiet as a mouse, I crept on through the still rooms to the dining-room. There stood the long table covered with flashing glass and silver, every kind of wine and water glass, three or four of them at each place, and four or five knives and forks. Dozens of small silver dishes filled with candy and sweetmeats covered the lace center-piece, and in the middle of the table a huge silver bowl was filled to overflowing with pink roses. Oh, the sight and smell of a dinner party! How my heart contracts as I write of my first one!
>
> The loaded table stood in the subdued light of the room, glistening and portentous, like a sumptuous altar before the god descends upon it. I heard the maids in the pantry conversing in the low, serious voices that the occasion produced in them. Such a party was always a severe ordeal for them all in the kitchen. Twelve guests and nearly twelve courses of food, dozens and dozens of delicate glasses to be cared for, dozens and dozens of costly china places; and all these dishes to be served promptly without a break in the rhythm - one thing followed another smoothly, inevitably. The wine bottles standing in rows ready

4 *Ibid.*, pp. 12-13; Goodyear, *op cit.*, p. 139.
5 *Ibid.*, pp. 13-14.

to be uncorked, for every glass must always be full; the accessories ready waiting at the side; the crackers and cheeses and jellies and sauces, the pickles and sauces and olives and relishes. My mother had her own contribution to the usual inconsequential food. After the last sweet ice and cake or hot dark dessert was delivered and removed, she always ended her ritualistic dinner with what she called a savoury, if I remember aright. Some crisp celery or some bitter cool thing; it's gone from me now just what it was. Only the feeling remains, the contrast after the thick, murky, delicious, cloying dinner.[6]

Her reactions to her nearby school were predictable:

> Spring days when the ground in our yards grew moist and soft and stringy and when the air was full of the sweet rich smell of the manure on the lower beds, and the trees began to show buds — and then to have to go to school! Into the close, overwarm rooms across the street to St. Margaret's. How I hated it! But a new freedom came with the spring; then one could run and make a dash over the way to our home and into the kitchen and in a jiffy grab up a handful of cookies from the tin cake box and back again, hair flying — breathless and wild.[7]

She didn't remember learning a single thing at this school she attended until she was sixteen. For her, "school meant only one thing,...people and one's feelings about them and the shifting, changing relationships one had with them." Each one "had her own flavour and quality to be savoured and assimilated or rejected." Miss Tuck's eyes "looked as though they hurt her — as though what she saw with them hurt her." Mabel developed a crush on Miss Moore and would beg, borrow, or steal pennies in order to buy a rose every day and present her beloved with it. Mabel's reward was that "all day, through school, I could see the stem of the rose tucked into Miss Moore's breast between the buttons of her shirtwaist." Miss Clark, the art teacher, was "tall and puritanical. She wore white shirtwaists on her flat torso, and corduroy skirts." But she adored beauty and so Mabel liked her.[8]

Mary Rockwell has written that while working-class girls could escape to dance halls, elite girls of the late Victorian Era seldom broke loose from the watchful gaze of chaperons:

> A breach in behavior was known instantly and provided gossip giving reason for a girl to be excluded from social circles. Buffalo socialite and memorialist Mabel Dodge Luhan's experience provides a powerful example. Luhan eloped with a young man named Karl Evans in 1901. An heir to a considerable fortune from his family's steamship company, he was, for some unknown reason considered unsuitable for Mabel. Her father expressly forbid [sic] her to see him: "I won't have you carrying on with that Evans boy. He's no good. If I catch you speaking to him again, I'll lock you up." Her father's dictum seemed to strengthen her resolve and she declared herself engaged to him. According to her memoirs, Karl tricked her into marriage on the pretense of showing her his summer home in Canada. She and Karl setup housekeeping on the sly, affording a small house on Bryant St. by selling some of Mabel's jewelry. Once her parents knew her situation, they had no choice but to accept it, and her mother immediately planned a lavish church wedding to legitimate the union.

6 *Ibid.*, pp. 75-76.
7 *Ibid.*, p. 235.
8 *Ibid.*, pp. 235-248.

> It seems that Luhan suffered from stepping outside her prescribed role, however. Her father would not attend her formal wedding ceremony. Her mother tried to cover up the embarrassment as best she could. The quick birth of her first child and the unfortunate death of Evans in a hunting accident led Luhan to a nervous breakdown. Her mother sent her off to Europe for a "change" but partially to avoid the ostracism of Buffalo society. Defiance of the rules of society led to exclusion and, in this case, a self-imposed exile.[9]

Rockwell's reading of Mabel's frequently opaque memoirs gives at least a partial explanation for her bitterness toward her native city and its inhabitants. Another reason her mother sent her to Europe was the scandalous and almost public affair she carried with her married gynecologist, Dr. John Parmenter. In 1904 she met and married architect Edwin Dodge in Paris and moved with him to Florence, where with her mother's money she bought a Medicean villa that the Dodges reconstructed. Mabel also collected famous guests to grace a salon she ran there. She returned to the United States, settled in New York's Washington Square, and separated from her husband because he stood between her and "reality." A sympathetic cultural historian writes:

> In the [Greenwich] Village she established one of the most successful salons in U.S. history, incorporating the diverse social, artistic, and political rebellions of the time and attempting to direct them through her liberated life force. Her openness to the ideas and issues that played out before her in her living room — birth control, woman suffrage, peace, socialism, anarchism, postimpressionism, psychoanalysis — allowed her to taste and influence rich and variegated slices of the intellectual and cultural life of her times and to meet and learn from such luminaries as Walter Lippmann, Emma Goldman, Lincoln Steffens, and Margaret Sanger.[10]

11.4 The Westbrook, Cigliano *et alii*, *op.cit.*, p. 62.

Mabel raised funds for the Armory Show, the first major exhibition of postimpressionist art in the United States. A third and final phase of her search for whatever it was she was searching for worked itself out among the Pueblo Indians of Taos in New Mexico whose culture she thought embodied "timeless and stable values that offered what twentieth century society was not able to." In the end she "was responsible for helping to purvey the myth of the exotic Indian 'other,' a romantic construct that has more to do with the needs of the dispossessed Anglo elite than with the real lives and needs of America's native peoples."[11] Here too she picked up

9 Mary Rich Rockwell, "Early Marriage Patterns in the Pan American Era," *Buffalo Spree*, January-February 2001, pp. 50-55.
10 "Luhan, Mabel Dodge," Lois Palken Rudnick, *ANB*, 14:112.
11 *Ibid.*, p. 113.

her last husband, Antonio Luhan, a Pueblo Indian, who gave her syphilis. George Goodyear called Mabel "an avid man hunter," who had been in her youth "pretty and attractive", but later she, "grew to look more and more like a squaw, and a rather dirty one at that." She died in Taos in 1962.[12]

Meanwhile back in Buffalo Charles Ganson died, and Sara married retired Admiral Reeder, an alcoholic, and then Joseph E. Montague, general manager of Buffalo & Niagara Falls Electric Light & Power, director of the Power City Bank, member of the Niagara Falls Country Club, and crusader to abolish tuberculosis, probably the husband she had in mind all along. They lived 1915-1925 at #675 Delaware and then moved since the Westbrook(11.4) was built at #675 in the mid-1920s. Montague died in 1939, Sarah having expired several years before.[13] Mabel merited inclusion in both the 1932 *Dictionary of American Biography* and the 1999 *American National Biography.*

At #685, above Jerome Pierce's in 1870, was the home of Connecticut-born Frederick Squier, his wife and two domestics, one a gardener. Squier was well off since he retired from manufacturing at thirty-four. Ten years later Louis F. W. Arend resided there. He was the proprietor of Arend & Morgan, dry goods, carpets, and upholstery, at #259 Main Street, next to Flint & Kent. Arend was followed in short order by Renel H. Thayer, tanks and cisterns, and in the late 1880s by Herbert C. Williams, manager of the Bank of Commerce. At the start of the 1890s James Tillinghast(11.5) appeared at #685 and built a red brick gothic pile(11.6) befitting one who had had reached the highest rung in the operations of the Central.[14]

11.5 ❦ James Tillinghast, Smith, *op. cit..*, II, facing p. 94.

Parton Tillinghast of Sussex, the first of his family in America, had fought in Cromwell's army and came to Rhode Island with Roger Williams in 1645. Gideon Tillinghast, James' father, had built power looms at Walpole, Rhode Island. He moved to Cooperstown, New York, where he oversaw the installation of the first power looms in that state at Little Falls. James was born in Cooperstown in 1822, learned about machinery without an apprenticeship, worked in country stores, graduated into lake shipping, returned to his father's machine shop

11.6 ❦ Number 685 Delaware Avenue, BHS.

12 Goodyear, *op.cit.*, p. 139.
13 *CE*, November 27, 1939; Hahn, *op. cit.*, pp. 173.
14 Katherine Smith, *CE*, March 10, 1952.

and foundry in 1846, and in 1851 turned to railroads at the start of what was to be an expansive decade for that industry. He began with the Rome & Watertown as superintendent of motive power and assistant general superintendent. In 1856 he transferred to the Northern Railroad of Canada (Toronto to Collingwood.) Here he managed lake steamer connections Collingwood-Chicago and Toronto-Oswego. In 1862 he joined with Captain Robert Montgomery of #1217 Delaware and E. B. Ward of Detroit to run steamboats between Goderich and Port Huron — Lake Huron ports respectively of the Buffalo & Lake Huron Railroad and the Grand Trunk — and Chicago. Since these two roads served Buffalo, Tillinghast briefly made Buffalo his headquarters. But he soon liquidated his steamboat interest to become superintendent of motive power on the Michigan Southern at Elkhart, Indiana. In July 1864 he was persuaded by an old friend to return to Buffalo as assistant general superintendent in charge of the mechanical department of the Buffalo & Erie. In 1865 Dean Richmond, president of the Buffalo & Erie and the New York Central, appointed Tillinghast general superintendent of the latter road's Western Division. In 1867, Vanderbilt, having just secured control of the Central, made a tour of inspection, during which he met Tillinghast and they became fast friends. Vanderbilt died in 1877, but Tillinghast continued as general superintendent of the road until 1881, when he became personal assistant to the Commodore's son, William.

> More and more Buffalo became a focal point of Central operations. Superintendent Burrows' office was moved there from Rochester and General Superintendent Tillinghast now spent most of his time there, as he became increasingly involved in the affairs of the Canada Southern and the Wagner [Sleeping] Car Company, both of which centered largely at Buffalo.[15]

Tillinghast's earlier house in Buffalo had been at #138 Swan Street, which he had bought from his friend, George Gates, president of the Gates Sleeping Car Company, who had moved into a house at #546 Delaware.[16]

Tillinghast died in 1898. His successor at #685 was Robert Livingston Fryer, great grandson of Chancellor Robert Livingston (1746-1813), member of the Continental Congress, prominent on the committee which drafted New York's constitution, and minister to France who grasped the opportunity of securing Louisiana from Napoleon. Livingston was also an agriculturalist and a backer of Robert Fulton of Clermont fame. Robert Fryer was born in Albany in 1848, son of William and Margaretta Livingston Fryer, and had to make his own way in the world. He became a partner in the lumber business with William Gratwick, later of #414 and still later #776 Delaware. The company owned vast timberlands in Louisiana and Michigan and yards in North Tonawanda. In 1882 Fryer married Melissa Dodge Pratt, daughter of Pascal P. Pratt, and the Fryers moved to Albany where Robert was still in business. Two years later they transferred to Buffalo. Fryer became vice-president of M&T in 1884 when his father-in-law, who in 1856 had been a founder and vice-president, became

15 Edward Hungerford, *Men and Iron: The History of the New York Central* (New York: Thomas Y. Crowell Company, 1938), p. 303.
16 Smith, *op. cit.*, 2:92-97; *Men of New York*, 1:84.

president and his son-in-law succeeded him as vice-president. When Pratt retired in 1901, Fryer became president. He was also president of Fidelity Trust of which Pratt had also been a founder and which was to be merged with M&T in 1925 to form the M&T Trust. Fryer was a director of the Pennsylvania Railroad, the I.R.C., the Commercial Bank of Albany, vice-president of Buffalo Gas, and a warden of Trinity. He was active in the Sons of the American Revolution, the Society of Colonial Wars, the Holland Society of New York, the Metropolitan and Bankers' clubs of New York, and the Fort Orange Club of Albany. Locally he belonged to the Buffalo, Saturn, Country, and Ellicott clubs. His only sister was the wife of Daniel Manning of Albany, Cleveland's Secretary of the Treasury in 1885. Fryer died in 1915 at sixty-seven. His widow, a son Livingston, his wife Catherine Appleton, and two more of his sons lived at #685 Delaware until Melissa's death in 1932 at seventy-eight. After his mother's death, Livingston and family remained in the mansion until it was sold for a medical center in 1948.[17] He had graduated from Harvard in 1910, served during World War I in the Norton-Harjes Ambulance Corps in France, and was commissioned an artillery officer. For a time he was director of the Albright Art Gallery, but he and his wife spent much of their time at their chateau at Arapajon, near Paris. For having given land to that village for a school, he was elected to the Legion of Honor. He belonged to the usual clubs in Buffalo and to the Racquet & Tennis, Union League, Polo, and Travelers clubs in New York as well as in the Cercle Inter Allies. He died in Buffalo in 1960 at seventy-seven.[18]

In 1915 Boston architects remodeled #685:

> As one entered the house and stood in the central hall, the spacious living room was on the right, with the exquisite French drawing room on the left. Behind the French drawing room was the music room, and behind the living room the dining room in which 50 or more guests could be seated comfortably.
>
> The large living room is comfortably remembered by Buffalonians for its exquisitely carved mantel surmounting a large fireplace and the three rare Beauvais tapestries created in the 17th Century. It was furnished with sofas, chairs and tables designed and produced by master craftsmen of Europe. The oak paneling of the dining room also was hand carved. The room, known as the French drawing room, across the hall from the living room, was a virtual replica of a drawing room of the Lyse [read Elysee] palace occupied by the president of France. The furniture gilded and upholstered in rich tapestry, appeared golden. The tables were inlaid with tulip wood, rosewood and other woods in ornate design.
>
> Among the portraits that adorned the walls was a self portrait by the French artist, Vigee le Brun, and a likeness of Livingston Fryer as a boy, by William H. Chase. Paintings by Sir Thomas Lawrence contributed to the charm of that room. Other portraits that graced the walls of the mansion were those of Mrs. Robert Livingston Fryer, and Mrs. Frederick L. Pratt by de Laszlo who painted likeness[es] of the late King George VI of England and his wife Elizabeth before the monarch ascended the throne. This music room, its walls covered with a soft, green silken material, provided a lovely background for

17 *Times*, April 3, 1917; *BEN*, May 21, 1932; Horton, *op. cit.*, 1:411.
18 *NYT*, June 26, 1960.

the delightful music heard there.

The second floor was divided into eight attractive sleeping rooms with five baths. The T-shaped garden, carefully tended for nearly a century, was a delight to the Fryers and their friends during the entire Summer season. Today that onetime garden is a parking lot. Behind the house stands a one-time barn, later a garage. Today that building houses the Guidance Center of Buffalo, maintained by Community Chest funds.[19]

11.7 ❦ **Number 695 Delaware Avenue, BHS.**

The Fryers dearly loved a lord and often entertained present and past members, invariably second string, of European royalty. Robert Fryer had a theater and a ballroom on the third floor and an elevator to whisk guests and actors up from basement dressing rooms. The mansion had been constructed so solidly that rooms were virtually soundproofed. Livingston Fryer cultivated stage performers and among guests at #685 were Elsie Janis, Katherine Cornell, Ina Claire, Leland Hayward, Gilbert Miller, Fritzi Scheff, Madeleine Carroll, and Margaret Sullivan.[20] Melissa Fryer's younger sister Emma had married Doctor Charles Jones, dean of U.B's. medical department. Early in the 1900s the Joneses moved into #695, a modern brick building next to the Fryers(11.7). Doctor Jones died at sixty-nine in 1927.[21]

11.8 ❦ **John Newton Scatcherd, *M&FH*, 1:202.**

The house, part of which is visible to the left of 11.7, was #703, built about 1880 by lumber baron John Newton Scatcherd(11.8), son of James Newton Scatcherd, who had resided at #615 and died in 1885. Thereafter #615 became the home of Seward Cary who had married the elder Scatcherd's daughter Emily. The younger Scatcherd had been born to money and was a power in the wholesale lumber world. Born on Perry Street in 1857, he attended public schools and Professor Briggs' Classical School and graduated from Helmuth College in London, Ontario, in 1872, after which he joined his father's lumber firm then known as Scatcherd & Belton. In 1879 he was made partner in what became Scatcherd & Son. On his father's death in 1885 John carried on the business which became one of the largest hardwood lumber concerns in the nation.

19 *CE*, March 30, 1952.
20 *Ibid.*
21 *BEN*, November 16, 1927.

He was also president of the Batavia & New York Woodworking Company, manufacturers of fine interior finishing. He helped found the National Wholesale Lumber Exchange and was its president for years. Closer to home he was president of the Merchant's Exchange, chairman of the Buffalo Terminal Commission, for four years president of the Bank of Buffalo, president of the Buffalo Club in 1897, chairman of the executive committee of the Pan-American Exposition, and a superior polo player. He was a projector of the Ellicott Square Company and president 1894-1906. He was a director of the Buffalo Railway Company and its successor, the I.R.C. In 1897 he ran for mayor against Conrad Diehl and lost. John was president of the Country Club and a member of the Ellicott and Park clubs. In 1879 he married Mary Wood, who died in 1914; in August 1917 he married Loris Horton and died shortly thereafter.[22]

Mabel Ganson loved to visit the Scatcherd's which was three houses above hers. She found it "very small and ordinary on the outside but [it] had a strong particular charm within." There were two girls there, Dorothy and Madeleine, "like beautiful Dresden china figures in their bowery rooms. Everything about them was feminine and dainty." As for the parents, Mabel wrote:

11.9 ❦ Morris Sawyer Tremaine, Warren, *op. cit.*, p. 91.

> Mr. Scatcherd was a charming, stout, red-faced man with a small turned-up nose and curly hair. A real English country squire of a man. Mrs. Scatcherd was beautiful in all her forms but had no colour. Her body was full-breasted, with large sleek hips, and her waist and arms were slender. Her face was very sensitive and thin; she was one of those small-headed women with fine unpadded features and feathery dark hair brushed straight back and wound about her head.[23]

About 1889 when Mabel was ten Emily Wood, Mrs. Scatcherd's sister, came to live at #703. She had spent years in Paris, smoked cigarettes, and dressed like a man in her room. The girls, including now a third Scatcherd girl, Emily, were fascinated by her. Every day Aunty Em took Dorothy and Emily up Delaware in a buggy, past the Country Club, over the Belt Line which circled the city, and out to the fields and woods:

> And then ...one day [in October 1894]... I can hardly write it down! It shattered our neighbourhood. A train ran along the level crossing just as they were passing — and drove into them and killed them all three: Dorothy and Emily and Aunty E. The engine-driver said over and over that he blew his whistle until it was almost in their ears and yet they paid no attention. He could not make them stop, nor could he stop his train. It happened under his eyes.

22 Warren, *op. cit.*, pp. 46-47; *Courier*, September 24, 1917; February 11, 1927.
23 Luhan, *op. cit.*, p. 198.

> Madeline grew very quiet in the weeks after this. She sat all day long in the chair in the sitting-room window and read Walter Scott. She was silent and motionless. In the spring she began to twitch and shake and they called it St. Vitus's Dance and she grew as restless and nervous as before she had been contained. Mrs. Scatcherd's face became like a mask as she sat always sewing in her bedroom window. Mr. Scatcherd stayed away more and more from the dismal house. It was never the same again.[24]

Morris Sawyer Tremaine(11.9), another lumber executive, followed Scatcherd at #703 at the time of the First World War. Tremaine had been born in 1871, at Fort Dodge, Kansas, son of Dr. William Tremaine, a surgeon in the Union Army during the Civil War who had stayed on in the Army. In 1881 he came east to Buffalo where he practiced medicine until his death in 1898. Morris was educated at P.S. 14 on Franklin Street and attended the Buffalo Normal School, followed by a course in the Upper Canadian College at Toronto. At seventeen he started work as a tally boy for Holland, Graves & Montgomery, wholesale lumber, was promoted to inspector; and at twenty-one became a salesman and then manager of a branch office in New York. In 1897 he was made partner in Montgomery Brothers; in 1903 he reorganized the Toledo Fire & Marine Insurance Company and became its president; in 1905 he organized and became president of the National Lumber Insurance Company of Buffalo. In 1914 he entered into an association with J. G. Wilson Corporation, manufacturers of rolling steel doors, and was elected its president in 1916. He was elected president of Smith Fassett & Company of North Tonawanda, another wholesale lumber company, and was a director of the National Wholesale Lumber Dealers Association. The King Sewing Machine Company, which he had organized and which employed 1,100 men, was later sold to Sears & Roebuck. During World War I he was a member of Buffalo's first Red Cross Committee and vice-chairman of the second. On January 1, 1927 he became Comptroller of New York, the first of seven terms in which he established a reputation

Top 11.10 ❦ Number 703 Delaware Avenue, *CE*, April 25, 1943.
Bottom 11.11 ❦ Number 713 Delaware Avenue, Cigliano *et alii*, *op. cit.*, p. 49.

24 *Ibid.*, pp. 205-206.

for ability and integrity in managing the state's money and heading the Department of Audit and Control. He was an Episcopalian, president of the Buffalo Club in 1927, and belonged to the Country, Saturn, and Canoe clubs. He died of a heart ailment in Albany in 1941.[25] During the Second World War his son leased #703 to an entrepreneur who converted it to a multiple dwelling for war workers(11.10)[26]

The Bainbridge Follwell house at #713 Delaware(11.11) was an example of a style that was very popular toward the end of the nineteenth century and that has been warmly endorsed by Kowsky:

> If architects and clients in Buffalo tended to shy away from the high seriousness of Victorian Gothic, both welcomed the warm and relaxed atmosphere for living that the Queen Anne style evoked. Buffalo, with its nearby sources of timber, is a city that in its older quarters possesses many fine examples of this "free classic" style that was popular through the 1890s. No architecture more perfectly expressed the nineteenth-century notion of domesticity than these warmly textured, broad-roofed, generously proportioned dwellings. Many of these structures were erected by speculative builders, men who most often got their designs from pattern books and trade magazines. On Delaware Avenue, however, there were constructed a number of architect-designed Queen Anne houses. James Lyman Silsbee, who for a time had an office in Buffalo before moving to Chicago, designed at least three strikingly picturesque Queen Anne houses here. The large stone and shingle dwelling he built around 1884 for Mrs. Bainbridge Folwell at 713 Delaware attracted international attention when two photographs of it appeared in L'Architecture Americaine, a portfolio of architectural views by the New York City Photographer Albert Levy that was published in Paris in 1886. The steep roofs, slender chimneys, banks of windows, and delicate low-relief decoration in gables showed Silsbee's consummate mastery of this free-ranging style.[27]

Top 11.12 ❦ Number 735 Delaware, earlier view, Buffalo State College.
Bottom 11.13 ❦ Number 735 Delaware, later view, BHS.

25 Warren, *op. cit.*, p. 91; *HNF*, 2:323-315.
26 *CE*, April 25, 1943.
27 Cigliano *et alii*, *op. cit.*, pp. 49-50.

Mahlon Bainbridge Folwell was born in Romulus, New York, in 1841. He graduated from Hobart in 1861 and studied medicine in Geneva. In 1862 he enlisted in the 50th Regiment New York Volunteers as a hospital orderly. He soon made First Lieutenant and later captain and served throughout the war. His last campaign was under General Phil Sheridan in the Shenandoah Valley in the spring of 1865. After the war he came to Buffalo and studied under Dr. Cornelius Wykoff, also a Romulus native. Folwell graduated from the Medical Department of U.B. in 1867 as a general practitioner and specialist in children's diseases. He was an attending physician at the Buffalo Orphan Asylum and a consultant at Buffalo General as well as Professor of the Diseases of Children at U.B. A member of the Liberal, Buffalo, University, and Saturn clubs, he was a vestryman of Trinity. His wife Florence was the daughter of Leonidas Doty. Dr. Folwell died in 1895 at fifty-four. After his death an adjunct building at Children's Hospital was named after him. Florence continued to live at #713 until the mid 1920s.[28]

Eric L. Hedstrom, a Scandanavian-born coal and iron dealer, appeared at #717 Delaware in 1884. He was the father of Arthur Hedstrom of #498 Delaware. By 1900 Eric had died and his widow Anna was living alone at #717 with three servants and a coachman and family in the carriage house. She was still there at eighty-seven in 1925. Shortly thereafter the house was demolished and replaced by the Hotel Fairfax.

Number 723 Delaware was the seat 1879-1903 of the Charles Goodyear, Sr., family before they moved across the Avenue to #888. Their place at #723 was taken by William J. Connors, a colorful entrepreneur and publisher who by 1915 had erected a granite mansion at Delaware and West Ferry. With his departure, #723 became a boarding house which in 1920 sheltered a clientele of fifty-two presided over by Mrs. Cornelia Burtis, ex-manager of the Castle Inn on Niagara Square. In 1880 the Queen Anne house at #735 Delaware(11.12 and 11.13) was home to John Trefts who had come to Buffalo in 1845 and became a partner of Chillion Farrar of #506 Delaware. By 1900 Anna, John Trefts' widow, was still living at #735. In 1920 it was the residence of a steel plant manager, but by 1925 it had become a "converted multiple residence."

Number 735 remained empty for a few years, but during the 1920s it was the home of Dr. Irvin Miller Snow who had been born in Buffalo in 1860. On his father's side he was descended from veterans of the Revolution. His mother, Julia Miller, a Quaker, attended Miss Porter's School in Connecticut. She was an intimate of Abigail Fillmore and authoress of children's stories which appeared in Harper's and of two books of essays entitled *Afternoons and Memories of Old Buffalo*. Her husband Irving graduated from P.S. 14 and Central High and attended the University of Rochester. He graduated from the medical department of U.B. in 1881 and took special studies in Vienna and

28 *M&FH*, 2:194.

Top 11.14 ❦ Number 741 Delaware, *Buffalo Magazine*, 1896.
Bottom 11.15 ❦ Number 741, another view, BHS.

London. From 1889 until 1916 he was Clinical Professor of Diseases of Children at U.B. and served on the staffs of City, Buffalo General, and Children's. He was a founder of the Buffalo Fresh Air Mission, interested in improving the quality of the local milk supply. The author of numerous essays in professional journals on children's diseases, he promoted civic improvements including clearing streets of overhead wires and planting trees along streets and highways. He was a member of Trinity and the Saturn and Rotary clubs. The Snows had a country residence at Owasco Lake near Auburn. In 1914 Snow married Violetta Pierce, a member of the Garret Club.[29] The doctor died in 1932.

At Delaware and Summer stood a massive thirty-three room stone mansion built 1892-1893 for Edward Michael. Its designer was H. P. Rinn, a Boston architect. Though facing Summer, it bore a Delaware Avenue number, #741.(11.14,15) The heavy glass main doors of #741, ornamented with wrought iron, opened into a large foyer, where the eye was carried upwards by a circular staircase. Off this front entrance, the drawing room sported gilt-ornamentation on charcoal-colored walls. All first floor rooms were finished in carved oak paneling, stained a dark tone. Each room had a fireplace and marble or carved oak trim. On the second floor there was a maze of bedrooms, with connecting dressing rooms each with a fireplace, and baths. Owner of this fortress, Edward Michael(11.16), was born on the site of the future Hotel Lafayette in 1850. His father owned and managed the American Hotel, now site of Main Place Mall. At the hotel Abraham Lincoln rested during his trip from Springfield, Illinois, to his inauguration in 1861. Edward played leapfrog with the President-elect's two boys, Willie and Tad, in which their father joined. Edward attended P.S. 10 and Central High, read law in the offices of Talcott & Clark, was admitted to the bar in 1871, and practiced law for twenty-five years. After his father died in 1885, his son abandoned the law to manage his father's estate. Michael was an avid steam yacht operator on the Lakes and along the Atlantic Coast. He was also a Unitarian and a

29 Hill, *op. cit.*, 4:355.

11.16 Edward Michael, Attorney at Law, *Men of Buffalo*, p. 347.

bibliophile. But, though he had not attended college, his favorite project was U.B. where for forty years he chaired the buildings and ground committee. He worked with Chancellor Charles Norton to acquire the campus on Main and Bailey, and designed all the buildings until he resigned from the committee in 1947. In 1885 he married Celia Blake who died in 1934. They had three daughters, Clara, Edwine, and Jeanette. This ménage was served in 1925 by six domestics: a cook, three maids, a seamstress, and a laundress. Michael had owned a summer home in Derby since 1886; when he sold #741 in 1934, after his wife's death, father and daughters moved to a new forty-room home called "Hickoryhurst" at Derby. Michael died there at 101 in 1951.[30]

In 1937 Michael leased #741 to Florence Radder who opened a restaurant there and named it "Kipling's If." In 1946 he sold the property to Joseph Savaree who opened the "Stonecroft Restaurant," and also rented rooms. "Stonecroft" sometimes served as many as 2,000 meals a day according to Mrs. Savaree who recalled, "I can remember times when 12 and 13 wedding receptions would be going on at one time in different rooms of the old house. Some of them would start with wedding breakfasts and continue all day through luncheon, dinner, and midnight supper." Number 741 was sold in 1954 to Nelson Barrett who sold it to the Exchange Mutual Insurance Company as an office building site.[31]

Across Summer Street on the northeast corner stood at #767 the mansion of Abraham Altman, a Second Empire masterpiece by architect George Allison, an exponent of this style who had designed the Sternberg house at #414 Delaware in 1869.[32] Altman was born in Wurttemberg, Germany, and came to America with his family as a young man. He and brother Julius started in Buffalo, moved east to Rochester, then reversed themselves and in the hard times after the Panic of 1857 returned to Buffalo where they founded the clothing firm of A. Altman & Company and helped found the Third National Bank of which Abraham became president in 1869. In 1880 he was president of the Buffalo Club. His wife, the former Clara Abrams, was socially ambitious. Abraham espoused reform Judaism and gave $1,000 toward the purchase of a site on Niagara Street for Beth Zion:

30 *Buffalo Business*, March, 1949; BEN, September 2, 1950; October 24,1951; Carl Sandburg, *Abraham Lincoln: The War Years* (New York: Harcourt, Brace & Company, 1936), 1:52.
31 CE, January 8, 1956.

11.17 ❦ **Number 787 Delaware, *PBHS* 30(1930), n.p.**

A local tradition states that Altman met and gave some assistance to the notorious Jay Gould while the latter was a surveyor, and that Gould later lent Altman the money to invest in the funding of the Third National bank. This bank, unlike other American banks of the period, was not owned and run by old Yankee families. Rather it was run by immigrants, some of whom seem to have been German Jews. Altman served as its president for a dozen years.

Altman, in addition to his banking and clothing interests, engaged, according to records in the County Clerk's office, in many real estate dealings throughout the city. In 1881, broken in spirit by the accidental death of his son David in a fall from a horse while playing polo in Delaware Park two years before, Abraham Altman resigned from the bank. This seems to have been the turning point in his career, for his fortune declined from then until his death [in 1888]. Despite his former high social and economic position, he died almost penniless. In his last days he sold tailor's trimmings and worked for the clothing firm of Levey & Co., although he still lived in his palatial Delaware Avenue home.[33]

No residents are listed at #767 for the 1890s or 1900s and the lot was empty in 1915. It is now the site of the Jewish Center.

Charles A. Daniels, lawyer, judge, and congressman, was the first resident of #787 Delaware.(11.17) He was born of poor Welch parents in 1825, in New York. His father was a shoemaker and his son learned that trade. Hoping to better their lot, the family moved to Toledo where both parents died. Alone at seventeen, Charles decided to return to New York, but passing through Canandaigua he heard attorney Mark Sibley arguing a case and resolved to become a lawyer. Desiring to acquire a traditional education first, he studied the classics while plying his trade, came to Buffalo in 1842, and read law in the offices of Clinton & Nichols and then of Eli Cook, an ex-mayor of Buffalo. Daniels passed the bar in 1847 and was Cook's partner until 1850. In 1863 Daniels was appointed by Governor Seymour to the state supreme court to fill the vacancy caused by the death of Judge James Hoyt. In November he was elected to serve the rest of Hoyt's term, which lasted until 1869 when he was elected to a full term. In 1873 Governor John Dix appointed Daniels associate justice of the General Term, First Department. Governor Cornell reappointed him in 1880. Having reached the age limit for judges in 1891, Daniels retired, and was elected to Congress as a Republican for the 33rd District in 1892, reelected in 1894, and died in 1897.[34] He was married twice; first to one of the Porter girls from Niagara Falls, by whom he had two sons, Charles H. Daniels, a New York lawyer, and Thomas

32 Cigliano *et alii, op. cit.*, p. 45.
33 Adler, *op. cit.*, pp. 107-108.
34 White, *op. cit.*, 2:25-26; *Express*, September, 1888.

11.18 ❦ Number 795 Delaware, BHS.

Porter Daniels of Dayton, Ohio; and second to Mary King, the widow of Laurens Enos. Mary survived Judge Daniels by almost twenty years.[35] In 1915 she lived alone there with two middle-aged female domestics. In the ample converted stable out back lived her long-time chauffeur, his wife, and four children, three of whom were adults with outside employment. Mary Daniels died at #787 in 1917 at about seventy-one. Florence Goodyear, daughter of Frank of #762 Delaware, and her second husband, Charles Daniels, bought #787 in 1921, and lived there until 1931 when it was razed. It too became part of the Jewish Center. Daniels was a renowned swimmer:

> He introduced the Australian crawl to the United States, was unbeaten in the 1904 Olympic games, and held many American and world swimming records, including the 100-yard free style record from 1906 to 1913. In his obituary he was called "the Johnny Weissmuller of his day." In golf, he played in the 70s, and once held the world's record for most holes played in one day, over 200 on his own Sabbatis course. Also at Sabbatis he maintained a farm for the raising of silver foxes.[36]

The Victorian red-brick mansion at #795 Delaware — two stories high with a mansard roof, an enormous hall through the center featuring a spiral staircase, a ballroom on the third with a raised stage, mantels of Carrara marble and intricate woodwork throughout(11.18) — was built in 1872 by David Bell, a Scotsman, who came to America in 1836 and in 1843 to Buffalo. He settled there and assembled a foundry, machine shop, and shipbuilding yard where about 1862 he launched the first iron-hulled vessel to sail the Lakes. A crowd of the curious gathered on the docks expecting to see it sink immediately; instead it knifed through the waters and headed out into the Lake, creating a sensation along Central Wharf. Bell also built several revenue cutters for the federal government and a pleasure steam launch, the *Idaho*. The Bell Locomotive Works in 1866 built four stationary engines that were monsters for their time, each weighing thirty tons and costing $25,000 ($435,750 in 1997 dollars.)[37]

Toward the end of the 1870s Bell's house was sold to Leonidas Doty, a *Mayflower* descendant and grandson of a veteran of the Revolution. Leonidas was born in 1803 on a farm in Greene County, New York. When he was nine his family moved to Attica where he attended public school and at twenty went to work in the Attica Mills. Then he rented a farm next to his father's for a year at the end of which he paid off his debts and moved to Michigan intending to settle there. However he

35 *Courier*, January 11, 1917.
36 Goodyear, *op. cit.*, p. 261.
37 *BEN*, January 28, 1956.

returned to Attica and bought a grocery store, which made money for the next twenty years. With adequate capital, he opened a private bank in Attica in partnership with Dean Richmond. Doty was soon able to buy Richmond out and moved the bank to Batavia. In 1876 he bought Bell's residence and four years later sold his interest in the Batavia bank and retired. By his wife, Lydia Holbrooke, Doty had two daughters, Alice and Florence. He died in Buffalo in 1888. His widow survived on Delaware until about 1912. During the First World War it was a Red Cross center. [38]

11.19 ❦ Number 805, BHS. To the right can be seen the port cochere of #795.

The last resident at #795 was the multi-millionaire "glue king of America," Richard Wilhelm, born in Rothenburg, Germany, in 1856. He came to America in 1884 and gradually acquired a monopoly on glue making in the United States, with factories in California, Pennsylvania, Wisconsin, and Gowanda. The holding company which enabled him to do this was Peter Cooper Corporations. The Wilhelms lived at #795 in the 1920s, but the house was often empty as they spent much of their time at their estate in Gowanda where Wilhelm died in 1940. His widow lived almost exclusively in Gowanda and the mansion was demolished in 1956.[39]

11.20 ❦ Spencer Kellog, Horton, *op. cit.*, III, facing p. 1.

In the late 1860s what was to become #805 Delaware was occupied by Charles Forbush. Ten years later he had been supplanted there by Jonathan Chester Forbush. Since both were Massachusetts-born boot and shoe manufacturers they were probably brothers or at least cousins. The house was a square wooden box topped by a cupola, without any distinctive character.(11.19) Jonathan had been born in Grafton, Massachusetts, in 1825. He worked on his father's farm, and attended district schools and the high schools in Worcester and Hopkinton. His business career began with three years working for his uncle, Calvin Forbush, a shoe factory owner. A partnership with Nathaniel Brown to manufacture shoes under the name of Forbush & Brown followed. The factory burned down in 1853 and the partners moved to Buffalo and engaged in the same work.

38 *M&FH*, 2:240-242.
39 *Times*, October 14, 1930; NYT, August 6, 1940.

11.21 ❦ Number 805 Delaware, BHS.

In 1848 Jonathan married Susan Flagg, like himself a member of an old New England family. Brown died in 1883, but Forbush carried on until his death in Buffalo in 1901.

The next resident at #805 Delaware was Spencer Kellogg(11.20), who had the Forbush house razed and replaced with a splendid red-brick Georgian mansion with Doric columns which was completed in 1905 at a cost of $500,000.(11.21) Kellogg was born in West Galway, New York, in 1851. He graduated from the Gloversville Seminary and was also privately tutored. In 1875 he married Jane Morris, by whom he had three children, Martha, Howard, and Spencer. After his marriage he was engaged briefly in banking in Des Moines. But he moved to Buffalo in 1879 where he founded a linseed oil business, which became Spencer Kellogg & Sons. Flax seed from which this oil is made could easily be brought from the Midwest and North Central States via the Lakes to Buffalo for processing and distribution to eastern markets. He also became a grain elevator operator, a manufacturer of brooms and brushes, paints and varnishes, white lead, iron and steel, and vegetable oils. Kellogg & Sons became the largest of its kind in the world, with plants and offices throughout the United States and Europe.[40] In 1910 on the death of Colonel Barnard, owner of the Sizer mansion on Niagara Square, Spencer Kellogg & Sons bought the house, expanded it, and made it company headquarters.(4.9)

At first the new #805 housed Spencer, fifty-two, his fifty-year old wife Jane, and four children: Howard twenty-four, Gertrude twenty-two, Ruth fifteen, and Dorris eleven. There were five domestics, the majority Irish girls, and in the back an Irish coachman and family. In 1952, when the Kelloggs had long decamped, a reporter recalled the glories of the mansion, not all of them gone:

> Before beginning construction of the Kellogg home, architects for the firm of Green & Wicks and plaster workers from Marcott & Co., New York, interior decorators, were sent to Europe to observe various aspects of French and Italian architecture and art for adaptation to the mansion. Throughout its building only the finest materials were used. Fireplaces were of imported marble, balustrades of artistic wrought iron, lighting features of hammered bronze, wrought iron, crystal and gold, doors of solid mahogany, door knobs of cut glass; and the gold leaf ornamentation in the ceiling was very costly. Built into this one-time home are the basement theater, ...an art gallery and the beautiful music room in which more than a hundred persons can be seated without crowding.

40 Horton, *op. cit.*, 2:1-2.

> Mr. Kellogg collected paintings and other objects of art from many distant countries. One of his favorite paintings was a Thomas Moran landscape. The gold andirons, harmonizing with the color scheme of the mahogany and gold library, came from Egypt. Carved gilded chairs of the reception hall were created in Austria. A table, topped with hand-tooled leather, is of Italian workmanship.
>
> Above the heavy wrought iron door of the mansion are curving windows suggestive of the Palladian design. Passing through the marble vestibule, one comes into the spacious entrance hall with marble fireplace ornate with Italian carving. The two front rooms are the drawing room and music room with library and dining room behind them. A bright loggia, with a blue Della Robia [read Robbia] Christ Child contrasting attractively with the dark walnut of the ceiling, overlooks the garden in the rear. There too, is the ballroom, scene of delightful social functions at which Mr. and Mrs. Kellogg were hosts.
>
> The art gallery is equipped with lighting designed to display paintings to advantage. Bedrooms are spacious and all bathrooms are in marble. Fixtures, including showers, are plated in gold.
>
> The rooms of the first floor are virtually as they were when Mr. Kellogg lived there. In the reception hall, the crimson hangings and upholstery and the crimson velvet carpet have been replaced. The French blue damask covered walls of the drawing room, with its ample fireplace of cream-colored marble surmounted by a gold-framed arched mirror, are impressive. In the ivory and gold music room, the consoles of rare veined marble, selected by Mr. Kellogg, remain.[41]

Spencer Kellogg had a summer home, "Lochevan," in Derby. After his death in 1922, son Howard, who had made this his regular home and had become executive vice-president of the family firm, became president. Spencer Kellogg's widow remained at #805 for a few years until it was sold to the Town Club, a woman's group founded in 1926, which moved into its new quarters the next year.[42] It had served as a private home for a mere dozen years.

11.22 ❦ Number 827 Delaware, *PBHS*, 16 (1912), 435.

By the 1920s the exodus from Delaware Avenue to not merely suburbia but exurbia, Derby, Orchard Park, and East Aurora, had become pronounced. For a small metropolis like Buffalo exurbia was not that far away, and could be easily reached over recently paved roads. The auto had changed everything. Motorized bustle was infecting the Avenue. Boarding houses were cropping up even above North Street along with two high-rise aristocratic apartment houses, the Westbrook at North, and the Campanile at Bryant.

On the southeast corner of Delaware and Bryant in 1866 at #827(11.22) lived Frederick P. Stevens who

41 CE, November 5, 1952.
42 *Ibid.*

Above 11.23 ❦ Joseph P. Dudley, Warren, *op. cit.*, p.42.
Below 11.24 ❦ Willis K. Jackson, *M&FH*, II, facing p. 139.

came to Buffalo from New Hampshire already a lawyer in 1833. He was an early Master in Chancery and functioned as such until January 1845 when he was appointed First Judge under the Constitution of 1846. He practiced but little at the bar, was elected mayor in 1856, and assemblyman in 1863.[43] He was followed by Joseph P. Dudley(11.23), who had been born in Candia, New Hampshire, in 1832, and attended public schools and Pembroke Academy. In 1854 he married Mary Underhill of Concord, Massachusetts. By 1858 he was operating an iron foundry in Buffalo, but, with Colonel E. L. Drake's oil strike in northwestern Pennsylvania next year, Dudley headed for the oil fields, set up a refinery, and became a top man in petroleum when his Empire Oil merged with Standard Oil in 1882. Thereafter he was general manager of Standard's vast interests in Western New York. He was also trustee of the Erie County Savings Bank, director of the American Exchange, the Hydraulic Bank, and of the company which built the Ellicott Square Building. He was vice-president and treasurer of the Lafayette Street Presbyterian Church Society and moderator of the church's music program. He was president of the Buffalo Club in 1894, his term of office being bracketed by that of two Delaware Avenue stalwarts, Ansley Wilcox of #641 and John Milburn of #1168. Dudley was also vice-president of the Ellicott Club, a director of Falconwood, and a member of the Country Club. He died in 1907 at his home on Delaware Avenue.[44]

Succeeding to Dudley on the corner was Willis K. Jackson(11.24), born in Edgerton, Wisconsin, in 1862, son of Alanson and Susan Jackson. He came with his parents to Buffalo at age six, attended public school, and after graduation from high school got a job with the tugboat association at Central Wharf. Realizing his educational deficiencies, he spent two winters at Professor Herman Polley's Practical School, studying commercial subjects and higher math. At twenty-five he went to work in the cooperage firm of Thomas Tindle, whose daughter he married in 1886, after which the firm became Tindle &

43 Smith, *op. cit.*, 2:467.
44 *Men of New York*, 1:28-29.

Jackson. With headquarters in Buffalo and mills in Michigan, Tindle & Jackson was doing $1.5 million business annually by 1900.[45]

11.25 ❦ Number 827 Delaware, BHS.

About 1914 Jackson had the old Dudley house demolished and replaced with a state of the art brick and steel mansion, three stories high, with twenty rooms and six baths on a plot 150 feet on Delaware and 357 feet on Barker. The heating plant, one of the first in the city, was located in the apartment-garage in the rear.(11.25) The north side of the Kellogg mansion can be seen to the right. Mrs. Jackson died in 1941 and her husband in 1942 at eighty-one. The house was occupied by John M. Prophet and wife, son-in-law, and daughter of the Jacksons, until December 1943. It was bought by the Buffalo Bible School in 1944.[46]

In the end, the entire eastside of Delaware from Summer to Barker was taken over by the Jewish Community Center(#787) and Temple Beth Zion(#805). The first Beth Zion on #599 Delaware burned down in 1961. A second was built at #805 Delaware on simple modern lines and dedicated in 1967.(11.26) Architect Max Abramowitz saw the ten-sided marble exterior as symbolic of the ten commandments reaching to heaven.

11.26 ❦ Number 805 Delaware, Temple Beth Zion, Dunn, *op. cit.*, n.p.

A house on the northeast corner of Delaware and Barker dating from at least 1860 was the home of Thomas Stocking from Massachusetts, who had a single domestic, Anna William, a black. Next occupant, Noyes Darrow, another Yankee, had run a livery stable in Buffalo before it became a city in 1832. Later he became a merchant and builder of luxury apartments, and probably built his own which in the late 1860s was numbered 841.(11.27) Burr recalled him as "a very handsome old man with white hair and something that suggested the men of Colonial days." She remembered a "little

45 *M&FH*, 2:138-139; *CE*, May 26, 1944.

11.27 ❦ Number 841 Delaware, *City Beautiful*, p. 94.

rubber ball that danced merrily up and down in the fountain that stood in the front yard" of his house which was "a lovely old home with a hall through the center and rooms with bay windows on either side."[47] Andrew O'Brien, a druggist, lived briefly at #841 in the early 1890s, but 1896-1912 it was the home of William B. Hoyt(11.28) who had been born in East Aurora in 1858, son of Doctor Horace and Josephine Ballard Hoyt. William attended Aurora Academy, Central High, and graduated from Cornell in 1881. As a collegian he had been a prize-winning speaker, manager of the college monthly, editor of the weekly, and a founder of the Cornell *Daily Sun*. He returned to Buffalo, read law in the offices of Humphrey & Lockwood, was admitted to the bar in 1883, and began practice with Humphrey, Lockwood & Hoyt, which underwent several changes in nomenclature over the years. In 1887 he married Esther Lapham Hill, daughter of Doctor John D. Hill of #192 Delaware. The newlyweds lived with the Hills for a few years. Among Hoyt's clients were New York Central, Pierce Arrow, Aetna Life, and M. Birge & Son. From 1886 to 1889 he was Assistant U.S. Attorney for the Northern District of New York. In 1894 Richard Olney, Cleveland's Attorney General, appointed Hoyt counsel to the United States Interstate Commerce Commission for New York and Ohio. For six years he was a director of the Buffalo Club, for five a trustee of Cornell, and for three curator of the Buffalo Library. He was also a trustee of the Albright, Nichols, and the Buffalo Law Library. Hoyt died in 1915 after an unsuccessful appendectomy.[48] For a short period his daughter Josephine and her husband Lester F. Gilbert, an attorney, lived at #841. Gilbert was born in New Haven, graduated from Harvard in 1908, joined Hoyt's law firm in 1911, and in World War I was a captain in the army. Afterwards he was associated with the North Buffalo Foundry and McNaughton Realty. He was president of the Country Club and a member of the Harvard Clubs of New York and Buffalo. He died in 1945.[49]

11.28 ❦ William Ballard Hoyt, *M&FH*, II, facing p. 37.

46 *CE, ibid.*
47 *Courier,* May 23, 1927.
48 *M&FH*, 2:38-39; *NYT*, June 12, 1915; Warren, *op. cit.*, p. 56.
49 *BEN*, March 14, 1945.

11.29 ❦ W. Dunn, *op. cit.*, p. 35.

Gilbert was followed until 1923 by Edwin Ross Thomas, who was born in Webster, Westmoreland County, Pennsylvania, in 1850. Having disposed of his auto and bicycle interests in Toronto, he came to Buffalo in 1898, where he manufactured motorcycles at Broadway and Elm. Demand forced him to move to larger quarters at #1200 Niagara where in 1904 he turned to cars. His first proved a success when an employee "achieved the remarkable record of climbing Delaware Avenue hill on the high gear, the first car ever to have had this distinction." Model 22, the six cylinder Thomas Flyer, came out in 1905.(11.29) At the auto show where it was featured the whole next year's production was sold out. The Flyer won the international race from New York to Paris via Siberia in which European cars also participated. Thomas sold out in 1923 and left to form the Chalmers Automobile Company of Detroit. He traveled widely, but Buffalo was his home base for many years. His summer home was at Niagara-on-the-Lake in Canada. He died in Buffalo in 1936.[50]

The last family at #841 was that of Judge Daniel Joseph Kenefick. He was born in 1863 to Michael and Mary O'Connell Kenefick, natives of Ireland where they were married. They came to America in the 1850s and settled in the friendly environs of the First Ward. Daniel attended public school and graduated from Central High, read law in the office of Crowley & Movius, and was admitted to the bar in 1884. On New Year's Day 1886 he became assistant in the City Corporation Counsel's office, a post he resigned to become second district attorney under George Quimby 1887-1892. When Quimby resigned in 1894, Governor Roswell Flower appointed Kenefick to fill the unexpired term. The same year, Kenefick received the Republican nomination for district attorney and won by a big majority. In 1897 he was reelected and served until his appointment to the Supreme Court the next year to fill the unexpired term of the late Hamilton Ward. In 1899 Kenefick was nominated by the Republicans for Supreme Court and was elected to a fourteen-year term from which he resigned in November 1906 to return to private practice. He was a partner in the firm of Kenefick, Cooke, Mitchell, Bass & Letchworth, which, under changing names, had been in existence since 1834 and once included Cleveland as a member. In 1926 Kenefick was chosen chairman of a committee to draft a new city charter which abolished the commission form of government and replaced it with a strong mayor and a common council of fifteen members. Of Kenefick's handiwork Horton writes: "One of the best things about the instrument was that it made the Mayor the responsible head of the administration and gave him powers commensurate with his responsibility."[51] The charter was adopted

50 Homes in Buffalo & Vicinity, local history section, *B&ECPL*, 1:37.
51 Horton, *op. cit.*, 1:407.

11.30 ❦ Number 849, BHS.

in a special election in 1927. In 1891 Kenefick married Mayse Germain; they had two sons, Daniel and Theodore. Both became lawyers in Buffalo. Theodore married Mary Goodyear, Conger's daughter, in 1928. That year Judge Kenefick's wife died. He died in 1949 at eighty-six.[52]

Judge Kenefick's favorite room had been the library on the first floor. It was paneled in oak and its floor-to-ceiling bookcases contained the many books he had collected on a wide range of subjects. The second floor bedroom he occupied ran the width of the house and commanded an excellent view of the Avenue. His home office with a large worktable was on the third floor. He had been chairman of Buffalo's Board of Education, the City Planning Commission, the finance committee of U.B., and the Annual Catholic Charities Appeal. He was president of the state bar association in 1928 and for years sat on its Commission on the Administration of Justice. He was also a member of the board of trustees of Grosvenor Library and Buffalo State Teachers College. Number 841 later housed some of the clerical faculty of Bishop Fallon High School, which enjoyed but a brief existence.

One of the least impressive Delaware Avenue houses was located at #849, a two-story wooden arrangement with a silo-like structure on the front known as The Cistern.(11.30) During the 1870s and 1890s it was the home of Doctor Bernard S. Bartow, resident physician at the Erie County Almshouse, then on the grounds of U.B.'s future Main Street campus. A decade later it had become the residence of Charles Munson Underhill(11.31), a descendant of Captain John Underhill (1597-1672), the stormy petrel of Massachusetts' early days. Charles was born in Red Creek, Wayne County, New York, in 1839. He graduated in 1860 from Genesee Wesleyan College in Lima, New York, in 1860. For several years he was professor of Latin and mathematics at Falley Seminary in Fulton. From 1868 until 1870 he was general sales agent of the Anthracite Coal Association at Rochester, composed of the Lackawanna and Lehigh Valley railroads, and the J. Langdon and the Pittston

11.31 ❦ Charles M. Underhill, Wilner, *op. cit.*, IV, facing p. 168.

52 *Ibid;* Wilner, *op. cit.*, 4:421-422; W. Dunn, *op. cit.*, pp. 268-269; *NYT*, December 27, 1949.

11.32 ❦ Charles B. Sears, Warren, *op. cit.*, p. 102.

& Elmira coal companies. In 1870 he came to Buffalo where he continued in the same capacity until 1886 when the association was dissolved. He then became western manager of J. Langdon & Company of Elmira. Leaving this company in 1893, Underhill struck out on his own as a coal salesman until 1907. In 1862 he married Anna Price, an 1860 graduate of Genesee Wesleyan. They had three children. Underhill was the first superintendent of the Delaware Avenue Methodist Episcopal Church Sunday school, but later, because he admired its pastor, Dr. Samuel Holmes, he joined Westminster. Underhill died at eighty-five in 1924.[53]

A judge's judge, Charles B. Sears(11.32), moved from #443 Delaware where he had resided in 1900 to #849 sometime before 1905 and remained there until his death. He was born in Brooklyn in 1870, attended Adelphi, and graduated from Yale in 1892. He received his law degree in 1895 and moved to Buffalo to practice law, starting at Rogers, Locke & Babcock, and to lecture at the U.B. law school. He received an interim appointment in January 1917 to the State Supreme Court from Governor Charles Whitman, and in November 1917 was elected for a fourteen-year term, and was reelected in 1931. In 1929 Governor Franklin Roosevelt appointed him presiding judge of the Appellate Division, Fourth Department, and in 1932 made the appointment last for the rest of Sears' term on the court. In 1940 Governor Lehman appointed him to the state's highest tribunal, the Court of Appeals. On becoming seventy in 1940 Sears retired and became an official referee. In 1915 and again in 1938 he was a delegate to the State Constitutional Convention. He chaired the State War Council on Discrimination in Employment 1941-1946. In 1947 he was a judge at the Nuremberg trials of Germany's World War II leaders.

Judge Sears was married twice; first in 1896 to Florence Gilbert who died in 1939. His second wife, whom he married in 1946, was Mary Vanderpoel of Albany. He was vice-chairman of the U.B. Council, president of the Buffalo Philharmonic Society and of the Albright, and trustee of the Buffalo Joint Charities and the Community Chest. During 1915-1916 he had been president of the Erie County Bar. Long a vestryman at Trinity, he belonged to the Buffalo Club of which he had been president in 1938, and to the University Club in New York, and the Genesee Valley Club in Rochester. He died in 1950 at eighty.[54]

Number 857 in 1880 was the home of attorney Norris Morey followed in 1890 by George C. Beals and by 1900 by Willis K. Morgan, treasurer of the D. E. Morgan & Son furniture store on Main Street.

53 Wilner, *op. cit.*, 4:168-175.
54 *NYT*, December 18, 1950.

Shortly thereafter #857 was divided into apartments, known as The Morey Flats. The next house north, future #869, had been the home during the 1860s of Charles Bayliss, an English-born gardener, later a produce merchant. In the early 1880s it was bought and torn down by William W. Sloan, who built a fine residence there "which after a trip abroad was luxuriously furnished with furniture draperies and bric-a-brac from foreign countries." Sloan had been born in Ballymena, County Antrim, Ireland in 1831. He came to America in 1848 and set up a malt house on Van Rensselaer Street in Buffalo. Business boomed and in 1860 he purchased the Charles Norton house on Franklin Street. With the profits of his flourishing malt house he became a financier, a trustee of the Merchants Exchange and the Buffalo Savings Bank, a director of the Buffalo & Niagara Falls Electric Light & Power Company, the People's Bank, and the Hydraulic Bank, and trustee and member of the Buffalo Club for over thirty years. His daughter Leafie attended a finishing school in New York. The girl was a fine singer and a protege of Charlotte Mulligan of the Twentieth Century Club. In 1889 Leafie married Judge William H. Orcutt, Harvard 1869, of Cleveland who resigned his judgeship, moved to Buffalo, practiced law, and lived nearby at #37 Hodge Avenue. However Orcutt died at fifty in 1898 and by 1900 his twenty-five year old widow had moved back to #869. William Sloan died there in 1901.[55] The next family at #869 was that of Eugene A. Goerger, president of the German Bank. During the 1920s Charles Van Bergen, a French-born physician, resided there followed in the 1930s by the Daniel Streeters.

In 1891 George S. Donaldson of Collingwood & Davidson, dealers in cut stone, resided at #877 Delaware, a two and a half story frame house. Ten years later Irish-born John Donaldson, seventy-one and retired, resided there with an invalid son William. The turn of the century saw Douglas Gibson and his wife with an Irish serving girl and a coachman there. Next resident, Asa Silverthorne, was the defendant in the longest trial in the history of the local federal district court. He was born on a farm in Iowa in 1878. At eighteen he headed for Chicago to learn the lumber business from two uncles. He spent three years learning, then moved to Tonawanda, a major lumber port since logs floated down the lakes were transshipped above the Falls by rail or canal. There he opened a subsidiary of his uncles' firm but soon bought them out and went into business with his brother. In 1911 he was accused of defrauding a railroad but the case was dismissed. In December 1920 the case against him of defrauding the government came to an end. Once again the charge concerned railroads, but during World War I and until 1920 railroads were run by the federal government. Putting in the evidence took nine weeks, and Silverthorne was exonerated. It was said that he made and lost two fortunes. He died at fifty-three in 1921.[56] His successor at #877 was Theodore Wickwire whose father was a farmer in Cortland where Theodore was born in 1851. He and brother Chester pioneered in steel wire and wire cloths. He moved his operation to Buffalo around 1896 where he

55 *Times*, December 17, 1909; *Men of New York*, 1:170.
56 *Courier*, February 10, 1921.

11.33 ❦ Orin E. Foster, Wilner, *op. cit.*, 4:4.

erected three blast furnaces along River Road to supply material for his plant now known as Wickwire-Spencer. In 1878 he married Emma Woodmancy by whom he had four children, including Theodore, Jr., who followed his father in business and lived until 1923 at #1217 Delaware. Theodore, Sr., died in 1926 at seventy-five.[57]

Future #891 was the home since at least the late 1850s of Henry C. Bryant, a nurseryman, and probably the eponym of Bryant Street. His widow was still living there in 1891 and by 1897 had moved to #1094 Delaware. By 1905 #891 had been purchased by Orin Foster(11.33), who had the original house razed and a gray stone mansion erected.(11.34) Foster was born on a farm in Colden in 1840. When he was six, his family moved to Whitby, Ontario, where he attended rural schools and the academy at Newcastle. He farmed until he was twenty-eight when he hit the road with a horse-drawn wagon hawking patent medicines throughout eastern Canada for a Toronto drug firm for eight years for $400 a year. In 1876, with partners T. Milburn of Toronto and W. G. Greenwood of Saint Catherine's, Foster established a factory in Buffalo to manufacture medicines to which the partners had patents. In the early years Foster continued on the road as a salesman, promoting his wares by way of signed local testimonials. In 1885 Foster-Milburn obtained the right to Doan's Kidney pills, which proved the most profitable of the company's products. Foster McClellan Company was then formed to handle foreign business. In 1876 Foster had married Emily Lazier. They had three children. Shortly before his death at eighty-eight in 1928, Orin and wife, who had a country home on the Lake Shore Road in Wanakah, moved to Tudor Place. The main object of his charity was U.B. for which he had a building built in 1920 called Foster Hall. In 1926 he gave the university a permanent endowment of $100,000. He worshipped at Westminster and was a member of Buffalo, Saturn, Wanakah, and Buffalo Athletic clubs. He had been president of Foster Milburn, Foster McClelland, Foster Bolt Nut Company, chairman of the board of the Union Insurance Company of Buffalo, and director of Marine Trust and the Sterling

11.34 ❦ Number 891 Delaware, *City Beautiful*, p.61.

57 *Courier*, August 21, 1926; *BEN*, October, 27, 1960.

Engine. He was a trustee of U.B., the Albright, and Community Fund.[58]

Sherman Skinner Jewett of #256 Delaware, the ironmonger and longtime president of the Bank of Buffalo, had died in 1897. His widow Deborah had moved up to #897 by 1900, where she lived with a niece, two Irish girls, and a coachman with the usual family in the rear. She died about 1915 in her eighties and was followed there by William F. Decker, a glass manufacturer, whose daughter Margaret was living there in 1931.

First resident at #905 on Delaware and Bryant was Price Matteson, an attorney. He had been born in Darien in 1840, and attended the district school and Darien Academy. He came to Buffalo in 1855, was admitted to the bar in 1861, and married Frances Brown in 1865. He was supervisor for a year and city attorney 1878-1879. He was a Mason and a member of the Delaware Avenue Methodist Episcopal Church. Fond of the country, he took summers off and spent them in Darien. He died in 1901.

Concerning a later resident at #905 in 1900 Adler writes:

> In the case of Joseph B. Block (1851-1927), success in the jewelry business led to banking enterprise. As we have already noted Abraham Altman [of #767 Delaware] had invaded this field early, and Block was to become the second outstanding Jewish banker of Buffalo. Born in Ihringen, he received a good education in Germany and France before emigrating to the United States. Block was attracted to Buffalo by the other immigrants from Baden, and he arrived here at the age of twenty. He first entered the wholesale jewelry business, but soon drifted to real estate, for the county clerk's records reveal that he acquired considerable holdings in the early eighties. It was in this field that he probably built his fortune.
>
> Block founded the Citizens Bank of Buffalo in 1890 at William and Spencer Streets. It is said that his success in banking could partially be attributed to the fact that, with a bank on William Street, he enjoyed the confidence and the respect of the newer Jews who huddled in this neighborhood. Block's bank was the first on the East Side, and he remained as president until it merged with the Black Rock Bank to become the Citizens Commercial Trust Company. In 1923, it merged with the Marine Trust Company as the William Street branch. Block became a member of the board of directors of the Marine Trust Company. He was also a member of the Buffalo Board of Trade and a treasurer of the Buffalo Clearing House. He was very active in civic and Jewish affairs. He lived in a grand house at 905 Delaware Avenue and at that time was said to be the only Jew in Buffalo to have a home on that fashionable boulevard. [Altman was living at #767 in 1870.] Block Street in Buffalo was named for him.[59]

By 1920 Joseph's son Arthur resided at his father's former home:

> Mr. Arthur J. Block (b.1885) was graduated from Cornell University and for a time was engaged in the clothing business. Later, in conjunction with his brother Edgar, he bought control of the retail jewelry firm of T. C. Tanke, Inc., reputed to be one of the largest stores of its kind in the country.[60]

58 Wilner, *op. cit.*, 4:4.
59 Adler, *op. cit.*, pp. 175-176.
60 *Ibid.*, p. 352.

CHAPTER

12 BRYANT TO WEST FERRY: *East Side*

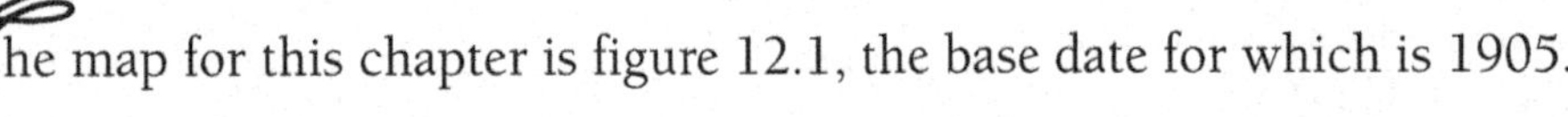

The map for this chapter is figure 12.1, the base date for which is 1905.

1870

BRYANT STREET

957 Isaac Jones 57 NY retired mechanic
Lavinia Jones 53 NY *ux.*
Lavinia Jones 22 NY at home
Lizzie Jones 19 NY at home
Adin Swan 70 male boarder
Anna Swan 70 female boarder

961 Warren Granger 54 NY land agent
Mary Granger 48 NY *ux.*
Sophie Granger 21 NY at home
Walter Granger 15 NY school
Anna Granger 13 NY school
Ellen McLaughlin 26 Ireland

1880

BRYANT STREET

925 Porter Lee 30 NY banker
Jennie Lee 25 NY *ux.*
John Lee 4 NY son
Hubert Lee 2 NY son
Parker Lee 6 months son
Jennie Connell 23 Scotland
Nora Sullivan 40 Ireland
Thomas Butler 18 Ireland

939 *Public School* #16

949 Stewart Swan 60 NY police court officer
Mary Swan 57 NY *ux.*
Bella Swan 18 NY daughter
Kate Lyons 60 Ireland
Mary Swaglet 18 Austria cook

957 Moritz Block 46 Baden cloak manufacturer
Fanny Block 37 Baden *ux.*
Carrie Block 13 NY daughter
Herman Block 8 NY son
Eugene Block 7 NY son
Carrie Beck 16 NY
Anna Swaglet 19 Austria

961 Warren Granger 64 NY real estate agent
Mary Granger 58 Conn. *ux.*
May Granger 36 NY daughter-in-law
Virginia Granger 34 daughter in-law
Walter Granger 24 NY son
Harrison Granger 32 son bookkeeper
Ann Maloney 21 Ireland

973 DeLancy D. Benson 43 NY art dealer
Julia Benson 46 Tenn. *ux.*
George Benson 20 NY law student
Emma Benson 11 NY daughter
Mary Benson 8 NY daughter
Eliza Fellows 47 Tenn. sister-in-law at home
Hattie Fellows niece
Eliza Fellows niece
Clara Gurteen 15 Belgium
Minnie Riffield 15 Hesse-Darmstadt

997 Thomas Wilkinson 45 England grocer
Margaret Wilkinson 42 NY *ux.*
Nettie Wilkinson 21 NY at home
Albert Wilkinson 12 NY school
Jane Gardner 70 NY boarder
Charlotte Smith 19 Ireland

WEST UTICA STREET

1013 E. J. Newman 52 NY cement manufacturer
Lucinda Newman 51 NY *ux.*
Judson Newman 22 NY office clerk
Florence Newman 22 NY at home
Mary Wright 19 Prussia

1023 William Morehouse 52 NY store clerk
Mary Morehouse 50 NY *ux.*
Nellie Morehouse 14 NY school
William Morehouse 8 NY school
Abigail Phelps 87 Mass. boarder
Rhoda Lightholz 44 NY public school teacher
Anna Osborne 21 seamstress
Eliza Kriss 20 Saxony

1069 Henry Hearne 42 England candy manufacturer
Elizabeth Hearne 38 England *ux.*
George Hearne 6 months NY
Julia Hearne 9 NY school
Henry Hearne 14 NY school
Alfred Hearne 6 NY school
Charlotte Cord 20 Baden
William Wood 19 NY

1081 John Bissell 62 NY transportation agent
Isabella Bissell 57 NY *ux.*
Arthur D. Bissell 26 NY bookkeeper
Wilson Shannon Bissell 22 NY law student

993 Alfred W. Haines 34 NY lumber merchant
Emaline Haines 30 NY *ux.*
Harrison Haines 10 NY son
William W. Haines 7 months NY son
Kate Smith 17 Ireland nurse
Ida Oppenheimer 22 Baden

WEST UTICA STREET

1013 Edmund J. Newman 63 NY merchant
Lucinda Newman 60 NY *ux.*
Judson Newman 31 NY son merchant
Flora Newman 22 Pa. daughter-in-law
Edmund Newman 1 NY grandson
Florence Newman 29 daughter
Lizzie Hazzard 29 NY
A. Tyler 19 NY

1023 Edmund S. Ralph 51 England S. O. Barnum
Malvina Ralph 45 Conn. *ux.*
Ida M. Ralph NY 26 daughter
Augusta B. Ralph NY 22 daughter
Benjamin C. Ralph 20 NY son bank clerk
Edna Ralph 18 NY daughter
Everrett S. Ralph 15 NY school
Mary Ralph 10 NY daughter
Reuben S. Ralph 10 NY son
Frank de Vaux Ralph 13 NY son

1069 Thomas C. Reilly 71 Ireland druggist
George O'Bryan 30 Canada nephew
Mary F. O'Bryan 20 Canada niece
Lizzie E. O'Bryan 25 Canada niece
Marian Johnson 18 Canada grandniece
May Hefner 30 Ireland
John Cheseria 20 NY
Alfred Cassel 47 NY

1081 Arthur D. Bissell 35 NY vessel owner
Fannie Bissell 27 NY *ux.*
Fannie Bissell 5 NY daughter school
Mary E. Bissell 8 NY daughter
Howard Bissell 4 NY son
Sophia Weber 19 NY
Barbara Weber 19 NY

1103 James H. Goldsborough 35 Maryland oil producer
Helen Goldsborough 25 Washington D.C. *ux.*
Gertrude Goldsborough 9 Pa. daughter
Martin Goldsborough 7 Pa. son

Willie Goldsborough 5 NY son
Randolph Goldsborough 3 NY son
Sylvia Bartelman 25 NY
Julia Fleming 20 NY

1119 George S. Potter 33 NY attorney
Frances Potter 33 NY *ux.*
Delevan Potter 5 NY son
Meredith Potter 3 NY son
Roderick Potter 8 months son
Maria Williams 68 mother-in-law
Mary G. Williams 29 Vermont son-in-law
Robert Pershars 17 NY

WEST FERRY STREET ❦ End of Block

1891

BRYANT STREET

925 Henry C. Gould 41 secretary Gould Coupler Co. vp Gould Air Brake Co.

939 *Public School #16*

973 Charles H. Donaldson

993 Alfred Haines Haines & Co. 45 NY lumber 225 Erie St.
George R. Haines *ibid.*

WEST UTICA STREET

WEST FERRY STREET ❦ End of Block

1900

BRYANT STREET

925 Daniel McIntosh 40 NY attorney
Grace McIntosh 36 NY *ux.*
Gould McIntosh 5 NY son
Donald McIntosh 3 NY son
Ella Gould 68 NY boarder
Leona White 40 NY
Jennie Hude 24 NY

James Farrell 33 England coachman
Mary Farrell 32 England *ux.*
Bertha Farrell 6 Canada daughter
Arthur Hearne 19 NY boarder
Henry Smith 31 NY boarder
John Bacon 40 NY boarder

939 *Public School #16*

949 Hugh Montgomery 50 NY
Harry F. Montgomery 26 NY attorney
Alice Lalaney 30 Ireland

961 *Delaware Avenue Baptist Church*

WEST UTICA STREET

1013 William C. Newman 60 NY flour & cement
Orrid Newman 59 NY *ux.*
Harry F. Shuttleworth 41 NY son-in-law miller
Anna J. Shuttleworth 34 NY *ux.*
Frederick J. Newman 17 NY nephew school
Florence A. Newman NY 49 sister
Delia B. McCarthy 24 Ireland
Mary A. McCarthy 21 Ireland

1025 Rt. Rev. Stephen Vincent Ryan bishop of Buffalo
Rev. James F. McGloin rector

1025 James E. Quigley 49 Canada bishop of Buffalo
Nora Minehan 27 NY

Chapel of the Blessed Sacrament

1035 Cicero J. Hamlin pres. American Glucose Co. 19 W. Swan
Charles Johnson coachman

1035 Cicero Hamlin 80 Mass. retired
Susan Hamlin 78 NY *ux.*
Sarah Frazier 34 NY housekeeper
Mary J. Lillis 28 Ireland
Nellie O'Leary 35 Ohio
Mary R. Gantzer 34 NY
Ella Traynor 27 Pa.

James Wilson 35 Ireland gardener
Margaret Wilson 31 Ireland *ux.*
Elizabeth Wilson 2 NY daughter
Margaret Wilson 10 months daughter
Wilson Wilson 34 Ireland brother takes care of rabbits
Annie E. McNeal 12 Ireland niece school

1065 George E. Moore hats & furs 327 Main

1069 Wilson S. Bissell 52 NY attorney
Louise B. Bissell 33 NY *ux.*
Margaret H. Bissell 8 NY daughter
Emma Muzik 27 Ohio
Lydia Harrison 26 Kansas

1081 Edmund Fish White & Fish 56 Niagara St.

1081 Frank S. McGraw 39 NY broker
Nellie A. McGraw 41 NY *ux.*
John McGraw 9 Michigan son school
Sears McGraw 5 NY son
Bridget Keough 24 NY
Sarah E. Cronin 33 Canada nurse

1083 George Bartlett 35 estate manager
Alice Bartlett 32 NY *ux.*
Virginia E. Bartlett 5 daughter school

1083 George Bartlett 44 NY estate manager
Alice Bartlett 41 NY *ux.*
Virginia E. Bartlett 14 NY daughter school
Evans E. Bartlett 9 NY school
Addie H. Bartlett Canada mother
Harriet M. Wall 26 Canada
Eleanor Mary Ryan 31 Ireland

1089 Austin Roe Preston attorney 14 Court St.

1089 Joseph G. Dudley 31 Minn. attorney
Caroline Dudley 30 Indiana *ux.*
Dorothy Dudley 2 NY daughter
Lena Fink 18 NY
Ella Ash 25 Ireland

1093 Loran L. Lewis Jr. attorney Lewis Moot & Lewis 14 Court St.

1093 Loran L. Lewis Jr. 35 NY attorney
Anna Lewis 36 NY *ux.*
Loran Lewis III 10 NY son school
Lorraine Lewis 9 NY daughter school
Elizabeth M. Lewis 2 NY school
Sarah C. Browne 40 NY daughter-in-law
Sophia Fink 19 NY

1103 Edward W. Hatch judge supreme court
Charles S. Hatch Peck Hammond Peck & Hatch
105 Franklin
Michael Kennedy coachman

1105 Alonzo R. James treasurer Century
Milling Co. 33 Board of Trade

1105 Alonzo R. James 58 Ohio vp Niagara Mill Co.
Sarah E. James 58 Mass. *ux.*
Grace E. James 18 Mass. daughter
Elsa James 18 Mass. daughter
Sarah McNichols 30 Canada

1109 William Jebb 42 NY manufacturer
Anna Jebb 36 NY *ux.*
Frances M. Jebb 11 NY daughter school
Katherine Jebb 7 NY daughter
William Jebb Jr. 3 NY
Martha E. Luther 23 Germany
Sophia Dudunhoffer 43 Conn.
Sophia Bilirager 19 NY
Ann Hartley 37 Canada

1115 James A. Roberts 53 Maine attorney
Martha D. Roberts 26 Maine *ux.*
Joseph B. Roberts 26 Maine bakery manager
Amelia M. Roberts 18 daughter school
Minnie A. Clancy 33 Canada
Minnie M. Cavanaugh 20 Ireland

1119 George S. Potter attorney
Williams & Potter 220 Main

1119 George S. Potter 53 NY attorney
Frances Potter 53 NY *ux.*
Meredith Potter 22 NY son
Kenneth Potter 18 NY son
George Potter 10 NY son
Maria L. Williams 87 Vermont mother-in-law
Mary Williams 50 NY sister-in-law
Mary Dryden 30 England

1125 Henry C. French commission merchant
agent Union Steamboat Co. 50 Main

1125 Henry C. French 55 NY president
Union Transit Co.
Eva J. French 50 NY *ux.*
Henry C. French Jr. 24 NY son manager
Thomas B. French 22 NY son
secretary and treasurer
Washington B. French 19 NY son school
Jean P. French 17 NY daughter school
Albert A. French NY 15 son school
John B. French 10 NY son school
Jeremiah Burgess NY butler
Alfred Burton 35 England butler

1131 Charles B. Germain attorney clerk US District
Court P.O. Building

1131 Charles B. Germain 55 NY attorney
Mary Germain 39 Ohio *ux.*
Annie E. Germain 11 NY daughter school
Edward B. Germain 9 NY school

WEST FERRY STREET ❦ End of Block

1905

BRYANT STREET

925 Daniel McIntosh 45 attorney
Grace McIntosh 40 *ux.*
Gould McIntosh 10 son school
Donald McIntosh 8 son school
Ella M. Gould 75 mother-in-law
Mazie McCullough 24
Elizabeth Matthews 58 Canada nurse

939 *Public School #16*

949 Susan Montgomery 52
Harry E. Montgomery 31 son attorney
Hannah Sullivan 30 Ireland

959 Eben McNair 55 banker
Lena McNair 50 *ux.*
Augustus McNair 18 son clerk
Lawrence N. McNair Annapolis
Pauline McNair 13 daughter school
Augustus ? 38 Germany cook
Walter Dems 20 coachman

961 *Delaware Avenue Baptist Church*

973 Mary Donaldson 70
Agnes B. Donaldson 32 daughter
Susan J. Turner 40 daughter widow
Charles H. Turner 45 manager
Hattie Fogelsanger 30
Mary Fogelsanger 25

993 Thomas A. Ritson
Mary Ritson 53 *ux.*
Mary Ritson 13 daughter
Douglas Ritson 22 son clerk
C. A. Ritson nephew clerk
Mary Archer 28 Ireland

997 Harry J. Fellows 38 music teacher
H. Fellows 31 *ux.*
Margaret Fellows 12 daughter school
Clara Fuchs 19

WEST UTICA STREET

1025 Charles H. Colton 50 bishop of Buffalo

Blessed Sacrament Chapel

1035 Susan Hamlin 84
Minnie Lutz 33 cook
Isabella Steward 38 Canada
Anna Callon 29

WEST FERRY STREET ❦ End of Block

1915

BRYANT STREET

925 Daniel McIntosh 56 attorney
Grace G. McIntosh 50 *ux.*
Donald McIntosh 18 son

939 *Public School #16*

949 Harry E. Montgomery 41 attorney
Jane Montgomery 37 *ux.*
Nellie Jewett 38

959 Joseph Devine 48 manufacturer
Blanche H. Devine 39 *ux.*
Charles P. Devine 24 son manufacturer
Graham Devine 11 son school
Evelyn Devine 8 daughter
Julia Rademacher 40
Caroline Szczepaniec 25 Poland

961 *Delaware Avenue Baptist Church*

973 Mary Donaldson 78
Susan J. Turner 49 daughter
Charles Donaldson 58 son
Walter J. Donaldson 50 son clerk
Agnes B. Donaldson 44 daughter
Josephine Hielback 30 Germany
May Welsch 48 nurse

993 Elizabeth Eagan 56
Julia Litwin 32 Austria

997 Ralph J. Quale 58 gas manufacturer
Corrinne H. Quale 58 *ux.*
James H. Quale 32 son garage business
Julia Snow 23 Indian

WEST UTICA STREET

Saint Joseph's Cathedral

1035 Josephine B. Colton 50
Katherine Bingham 14 niece
Helen Bingham 13 niece

May Binglace 42
Ella Trainor 36

James Whelan 40 gardener
Margaret Whelan 37 *ux.*
Catherine Whelan 5 daughter
William J. Whelan 2 son
Anna McNeil 17 niece stenographer
Kathy McCarthy boarder

1045 Seymour H. Knox
Grace Knox 40 *ux.*
Dorothy Knox 9 daughter school
Marjorie Knox 5 daughter school
Bertha Denler 40 maid
Florence Heath 40

Damon Sherman 27 coachman
Kate Sherman 25 *ux.*

1069 Frederick H. Stevens 46 financier
Katie B. Stevens 45 *ux.*
Kathleen B. Stevens 20 daughter
Gretchen B. Stevens 13 daughter school
Sarah D. Clifton 46 boarder
Frank C. Taylor 25 England butler

Peter Walker 40 Scotland coachman
Edith Walker 40 *ux.*
Drier Walker 13 son school
John Atken 28 Scotland coachman

George Smith 34 gardener
Eliza Smith 28 *ux.*

1081 Frank S. McGraw 43 broker
Nellie McGraw 40 *ux.*
John McGraw 15 son school
Seares McGraw 10 son school
Beatrice Kloneet 27
Anna McHatties 28
Sarah Cronin 35 Canada

1083 G. Hunter Bartlett MD 49
Alice M. Bartlett 46 *ux.*
Virginia Evans Bartlett 18 school
Evans E. Bartlett 15 school
Eliza Briskee 28 Canada
Harriet Brown 31

1085 Austin R. Preston 43

Bridget Coughlin 24
Theresa Heavey 30 Ireland

1045 Grace Knox 48
Dorothy V. Knox 18 daughter school
Seymour H. Knox 16 son school
Marjorie Knox 14 daughter school
Fred C. Taylor 35 England butler
Beatrice Taylor 25 *ux.*
Lucy Krenichfeld 48
Bertha Daigler 48
Margaret Reilly 39 Ireland
Helen Lambkin 19

Damon Sherman 37 chauffeur
Katherine Sherman 34 *ux.*
Grace Sherman 7 daughter

1069 Fred H. Stevens 56
Hattie Stevens 55 *ux.*
Walter Chard son-in-law
Thomas Chard grandson
George Allen son-in-law
Gretchen Allen 23 daughter
Elizabeth Allen granddaughter

George C. Smith 44 gardener
Elizabeth M. Smith 40 *ux.* Canada
George S. Smith 2 son

1081 Frank S. McGraw 53
Nellie McGraw 50 *ux.*

1083 George H. Bartlett 58 estate manager
Alice M. Bartlett 57 *ux.*
Virginia E. Bartlett 30 daughter
Evans E. Bartlett 25 son school
Clara Lutz 30
Anna M. Lanim 21

Charlotte R. Preston 18 daughter school
Louise Preston 17 daughter school
Sarah W. Preston 15 daughter school
Austin R. Preston 10 son school
Rebecca R. Preston 70
Eliza Wellwood 50
Julia Brown 20 Poland

1093 Loran L. Lewis Jr. 40 attorney
Anna B. Lewis 39 *ux.*
Loran L. Lewis III 15 student
Lorraine Lewis 12 daughter school
Elizabeth M. Lewis 7 daughter school
Sarah C. Brown 44 sister-in-law
Agnes Sullivan 30 nurse
Delia Gennam 24 Ireland waitress
Annie Hopkins 35 cook

1103 Susan Butts 32
Dorothy Butts 6 daughter school
Margaret Butts 5 daughter school
Eliza Caldince 28 Canada
Margaret Pechere 38

1105 Alonzo R. James vp Niagara Falls Milling Co.
Sarah James 63 *ux.*
Elsa James 23 daughter Wellesley
Nora McCarthy 28 Ireland
Ella Black 40

1109 William T. Jebb 43 retired
Ann Jebb 38 *ux.*
Frances Jebb 16 daughter school
Kathryn Jebb 12 daughter school
William Jebb 8 son school
Delia Garvey 38
Bessie McIntyre 28
Alice Camino 30

1119 George S. Potter 52 attorney
Frances Potter 52 *ux.*
Meredith Potter 30 attorney
Roderick Potter 25 bank clerk
Kenneth Potter 23 clerk
George Potter 18 school

1089 E. R. Thomas

1093 Loran L. Lewis Jr. 50 attorney
Anna B. Lewis 51 *ux.*
Loran L. Lewis III 25 son
Lorraine Lewis 22 daughter
Elizabeth M. Lewis 17 daughter school
Sarah C. Browne 55 sister-in-law
Caroline Ryan 58 Germany
Louise Smith 35
Margaret Walsh 36

1103 Henry J. Jacobs 55 England president Buffalo Lounge Co.
Harriet Jacobs 46 *ux.*
John L. Fisher 24 son-in-law builder
Harriet J. Fisher 22 daughter
Bertha Walters 21

1105 Sarah E. James 73
Elsa D. James daughter
Sarah Mahoney 24 Ireland
Elizabeth Marooney 19

1109 John Clawson 50 president Clawson Wilson Co.
Frances P. Clawson 48 *ux.*
Hamilton P. Clawson 22 son school
Emma Franklin 31
Freda Lamprecht 29 Germany
Hanna A. Pray 71 companion

1115 Daniel Good 53
Sarah E. Good 52 *ux.*
John E. Jewett 37 England
Mary Toohey 40
Frances Smobrek 24 Germany
Hilda Clout 20 England
Mabel Smith 21

Charles Dickison Scotland chauffeur
Elena Dickison 37 *ux.*
Thomas Dickison 5 son

1119 Nelson S. Taylor 32 lumber dealer
Mary C. Taylor 31 *ux.*
Verona Demerly 30
Minnie Burkhart 65 Germany

Maria Williams 95 mother
Mary H. Potter 48 sister
Maggie Baumgarten 28 Germany
Margaret George 30 nurse

1125 Agnes Demarest 73
Daniel Streeter 21 nephew Harvard
Edward J. Streeter 13 nephew student
Frank H. Barton 44 nephew
Eliza Pier 23
Helen Daley 40
Agnes Cummings 42 Ireland
Theresa More 58

1131 Elgood Channing Lufkin 41 manager Snow Steam Pump Works
Lula Lufkin 36 *ux.*
Florence Lufkin 14 daughter
Chauncy Lufkin 12 son school
Elgood Lufkin Jr. 3 son
Rachael Moulton 66 mother-in-law
Katherine Burger 34 Germany

Frank Estiner 37 coachman
Mary Estiner 41 *ux.*
Edward Estiner 11 son school
Alice Estiner 9 daughter school
Mabel Estiner 7 daughter school

WEST FERRY STREET ❦ End of Block

1125 Agnes Demarest 83
Edward Streeter nephew 23 newspaper writer
Mary F. Daly 58
Helen Daly 50
Elizabeth Pier 53

1131 Edward L. Koons 53 banker
Anna H. Koons 50 *ux.*
Dorothy Koons 23 daughter
Louise Koons 22 daughter
Clara Krohn 35
Mary Winski Austro-Poland
Sheldon Knight 28 chauffeur
Addie Knight 29 Canada *ux.*

1141 Apartments
6 families

1149 Apartments
6 families

WEST FERRY STREET ❦ End of Block

1920

BRYANT STREET

925 Daniel McIntosh 60 NY attorney
Grace G. McIntosh 55 NY

939 *Public School* #16

949 Henry Mulford MD 53 Ohio
Maude Mulford 43 NY *ux.*
Paul Mulford 16 NY son
Ruth Mulford 11 NY daughter
Hugh Mulford 9 NY son

957 Joseph P. Devine 53 Pa. machinery manufacturer
Blanche Devine 45 NY *ux.*
Evelyn Devine 12 daughter
Graham Devine 15 son
Margaret Sullivan 28 Pa.
Rhoda Burne 23 NY

961 *Delaware Avenue Baptist Church*

1925

BRYANT STREET

Campanile Apartments

939 *Public School* #16

949 Henry Mulford MD 58 Ohio
Maude Mulford 49 NY *ux.*
Montgomery Mulford 22 son literary pursuits
Ruth Mulford 17 daughter school
Hugh M. Mulford 14 son school

957 James P. Devine 57 Pa. manufacturer
Blanche Devine 50 NY *ux.*
Graham Devine 20 son manufacturer
Evelyn Devine 18 daughter school
Elizabeth Barnett 45

961 *Delaware Avenue Baptist Church*

973 Charles J. Donaldson 62 NY
Walter J. Donaldson 48 NY brother
Agnes B. Donaldson 48 NY sister
Anna D. Hopkins 60 NY sister
Josephine Heilbach 33 Baden

993 Howard Smith 47 NY grain merchant
Juliette A. Smith 42 NY *ux.*
Alan R. Ferguson 47 Maryland boarder
Constance L. Ferguson 42 Tenn. boarder
Robert C. Ferguson 5 Illinois boarder
Gladys N. Jansen 22 Canada

WEST UTICA STREET

1025 *Saint Joseph's Cathedral*

1035 William Turner 55 Ireland bishop of Buffalo
Catherine Connelly 42 Ireland
Mary McKenna 23 Ireland
Harold J. Fitzpatrick 25 NY

1045 William H. Donner 55 Ohio president Donner Steel
Dora B. Donner 35 Pa. *ux.*
Joseph W. Donner 25 Pa. son steel co.
Dorothy R. Donner 16 Pa. daughter
Katherine N. Donner 15 Pa. daughter
William H. Donner 9 Pa. son
Dora B. Donner 7 Pa. daughter

1069 Frank B. Baird 61 Ohio Union Furnace Co. executive
Flora C. Baird 35 Arkansas *ux.*
Frank B. Baird 17 Michigan son
Cameron Baird 14 Texas son
William C. Baird 12 NY son
Catherine Constantine 38 Ireland
Mary Appleton 40 Canada
Margaret McCullough 35 Ireland
Jessie B. Oliver 56 Canada
Margaret Fitzsimons 48 NY nurse

William Calder 39 Scotland chauffeur
Mary A. Calder 35 Scotland *ux.*
Mae Calder 16 Scotland daughter
Nellie Calder 13 Scotland daughter

1081 Frank S. McGraw 57 NY WNY Water Company executive
Nellie A. McGraw 60 NY *ux.*
John A. McGraw 24 NY bonds
Julia M. Kearney 26 Ireland
Anna M. Lynch 35 NY
Amelia Laufenberger 38 NY

977 Saturn Club

993 Howard J. Smith 50 NY Palace Theatre
Juliette A. Smith 45 NY *ux.*
Elizabeth McDermott 45 cook

997 Ralph Quale 67 director
Connie Quale 65 *ux.*
Leone Martini 25

WEST UTICA STREET

1025 *Saint Joseph's Cathedral*

1035 William Turner 59 Ireland bishop of Buffalo
Catherine Connolly 49 Ireland
Theresa Connolly 46 Ireland

1069 Frank B. Baird 72 Ohio
Flora Baird 48 *ux.*
Jessie Oliver 60 nurse
Margaret McCullough 42 Ireland waitress
Anne Langford 62 Canada cook
Catherine Considine 45 Ireland upstairs maid

William Calder 45 Scotland chauffeur
Mary Calder 44 Scotland *ux.*
Mae Calder 21 daughter Scotland
Nellie Calder 19 Scotland stenographer

1081 Frank S. McGraw 62 NY
Catherine Talty 25 Ireland downstairs maid
Mary Hannon 50
Elizabeth Goetz 45 Canada cook

1083 G. Hunter Bartlett 62 NY estate manager
Alice E. Bartlett 60 NY *ux.*
G. Raynolds Stearns MD 30 NY son-in-law
Virginia B. Stearns 20 NY daughter
Frances Butkiewicz 35 Poland

1103 Joseph P. Burke MD 46 NY
Evelyn Burke 40 NY *ux.*
John Burke 16 NY son
Eleanor L. Burke 10 NY daughter
Joseph Burke 9 NY son
Kevin Burke 8 NY son
Mary E. Burke 6 NY daughter
Ann Burke 5 NY daughter
Edward Burke 3 NY son
Thomas Burke 3 NY son
Emily Burke 37 England
Nora Dolan 40

1105 Sarah James 77 Mass. widow
Dora Egritz 30 Austria
Anna Stack 31 Ireland

1109 John L. Clawson

1115 Charles M. Daniels 34 NY fox ranching
Florence Daniels 35 NY *ux.*
Florence Daniels 16 NY daughter
Grace Daniels 14 NY daughter
Frank H. Daniels 10 NY son
Catherine Mullens 40 Ireland
Arletta Ridley 44 Ohio nurse
Agnes Gordon NY
Mary Smith 20 NY
Leon Cousin 50 France
Lynn Brooks 16 NY
Catherine McGeever Ireland

Ross E. Smith 29 Pa. chauffeur
W. A. Smith 25 NY *ux.*
Jennie Smith 10 months NY daughter

1119 James D. Warren 40 NY newspaper
Eleanor Warren 35 NY *ux.*
James D. Warren Jr. 9 NY son
Grace B. Sewell 22 England
Leah Brownlow 27 Scotland

1083 G. Hunter Bartlett 68 NY estate manager
Alice Evans Bartlett 66 NY *ux.*
Raynolds Stearns Jr. 39 NY partner attorney
Virginia Stearns 39 daughter
Martha Palmer

1089 John G. Wickster 68 insurance
Josephine Wickster 68 *ux.*
Della Keating 32 Ireland

1093 Henry Adsit Bull 52 attorney
Mary S. Bull
Julia Connolly 38 cook
Katherine Kelly 34 Ireland

1103 Joseph P. Burke MD 51 NY
Evelyn M. Burke 46 NY *ux.*
Joseph Burke 15 son school
Kevin Burke 14 NY son school
Thomas Burke 9 son school
Edward Burke 9 son school
Eleanor Burke 19 daughter school
Elizabeth Burke 16 NY daughter
Annie Burke 10 daughter school

1105 Albert H. Garvin MD 46
Elsa Jane Garvin 43 *ux.*
Delia Rowen 23 Ireland
Katherine Piltez 60

1109 John L. Clawson 58 merchant
Jane Clawson 32 *ux.*
Anna McCarthy 26 Ireland
Elizabeth Hatt 28

1115 Harry Thorpe Vars secretary-treasurer
Foster-Milburn

1119 James D. Warren 45 auto sales
Eleanor Warren 40 *ux.*
James D. Warren Jr. 15 school
Rose Harding 60 Ireland

1125 Walter Gaston 70 NJ manufacturer
Mary L. Gaston 53 Delaware *ux.*
Clare L. Nesselbaum 27 Germany
Elizabeth H. Smith 30 NY

Louis C. Heim 59 NY chauffeur

1131 Edward L. Koons 58 NY real estate
Anna H. Koons 55 NY *ux.*
Dorothy Koons 22 NY daughter
Clara Krohn 40 NY

Sheldon G. Knight 33 NY chauffeur
Addie Knight *ux.*
George S. Knight 9 NY son
Ferdinand E. Knight son
George W. Sharf 33 England nephew

1141 Apartments
6 families

1149 Apartments
7 families

WEST FERRY STREET ❦ End of Block

1125 Walter Gaston 71 steel manufacturer
Mary Gaston 55 *ux.*
Matida Weinholz 45 nurse

1131 Leonard A. Yerkes 44 manufacturer
Helen G. Yerkes 40 *ux.*
Leonard Yerkes 16 son school
William Yerkes 13 son school
Evelyn Yerkes 18 daughter school
Lisa Yerkes 14 daughter school
Jane Yerkes 8 daughter school
Marie Doherty 24 Ireland
Fredericka Ebert 55 cook
Christine Miller 30

1141 Apartments
6 families

WEST FERRY STREET ❦ End of Block

The frame houses on the eastside of Delaware between Bryant and Utica were plain edifices. The first building on the corner was not even a house but a planing mill built by John R. Monroe from Lancashire, where he learned carpentering. In 1850 he married Ann Stewardson and with wife, sister, and father, came to America and settled in Buffalo. They resided first on Carroll Street whence they had an unobstructed view of Lake Erie. Monroe started in business on his own in 1852 and in 1854 moved to the future West Delavan, then farmland, where he built a horse-powered planing mill, which was moved to Delaware and Bryant in 1864. From then until 1889 he was a contractor, putting up homes rather than business blocks. He was president 1876-1879 of the Builders Exchange of which he had been a founder, and was its treasurer 1885-1888. He was a Mason, a charter member of Westminster, and a trustee from 1886 until his death. In 1872 he built Hope Chapel, a Westminster mission at Richmond and Utica where he taught Sunday school. Ann Monroe died in 1907 and John in 1916.[1]

1 *Express*, January 4, 1916.

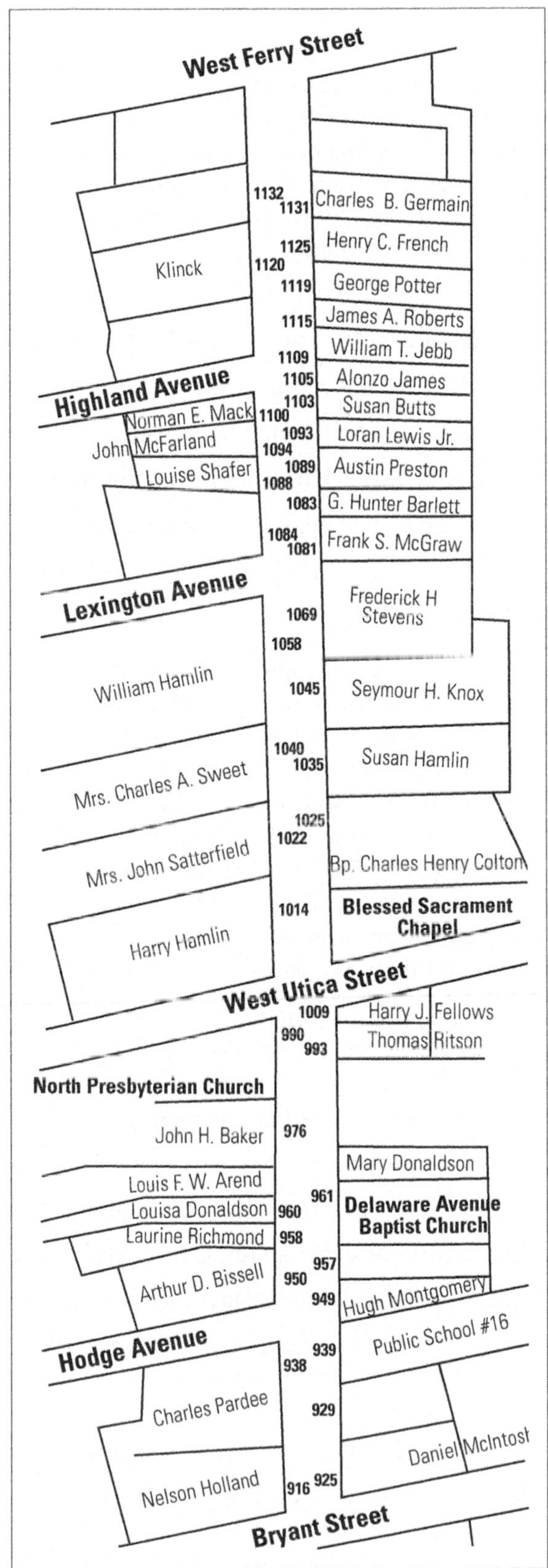

12.1 ❦ Bryant to West Ferry, 1905.

The gothic house at #925(12.2) was built in the mid-1870s, probably by Monroe, for R. Porter Lee who had been born in Buffalo in 1850 and lived there over fifty years. He was an accountant and cashier at the First National Bank. In 1874 he married Jennie Blanchard and they lived at #925 until 1883. They had bought a summer home at Elma, which grew into a mansion after Porter retired. There they celebrated their golden wedding anniversary, attended by some of the Buffalo elite who motored out for the event. Lee died in 1924.[2]

12.2 ❦ Number 925 Delaware, *PBHS*, 30(1930), np.

Charles Albert Gould and family superseded the Lees at #925. He had been born in Batavia in 1849 but came to Buffalo as a young man. He was a staunch Republican and was rewarded by appointment as Deputy Postmaster in 1878 and Collector of Customs for the Port of Buffalo by President Arthur. With the return of the Democracy to the White House in 1885 Gould needed a new job. The historian of American

2 *Courier*, October 31, 1924.

railroad rolling stock explains:

> Gould was not a mechanic, but he had the knack of recognizing marketable items for the railway supply trade. He bought into the steam forge business in 1884 and began to turn out car couplers. Several years later he acquired the rights to the platform and vestibule patented by Thomas A. Bissell of the Wagner Car Company. Next he opened a steel plant in the Midwest, and he built a giant factory for the production of car parts, locating it next to the New York Central shops at Depew, New York (near Buffalo). When electric car lighting came in Gould began to manufacture batteries.[3]

Meanwhile Gould had moved to a luxury apartment at #270 Park Avenue in New York. He also had an estate at Port Chester and two more on Long Island. An avid sportsman and yachtsman, the "Commodore" was wont to entertain old Buffalo friends aboard his yacht. He was president of the American Yacht Club and a member of the New York Yacht Club, the Union League, the Sons of the American Revolution, and the Society of Colonial Wars. In 1921 he began investing in New York real estate through Gould Realty Company. He died in 1926, worth over $10 million.[4] When his property was auctioned, his heirs got an additional $6,714,000.[5]

> Following his removal to New York the Delaware avenue house became the home of Mr. and Mrs. Daniel McIntosh, the latter being a sister of Commodore Gould. The McIntosh family lived there for many years [1900-1925]. Once more the house was empty after the death of Mrs. McIntosh. Then it was leased by Mrs. Frank Penfold, wife of the noted American artist, who came back to Buffalo after a long residence abroad. Mrs. Penfold was one of the famous beauties of her time and as Jenny Wells, was sister of Elizabeth Wells, daughter of the late Mr. and Mrs. Chandler J. Wells, [and] was a leading belle in society. At the never to be forgotten ball given in the old Buffalo Club, that stood at the north west corner of Delaware avenue and West Chippewa street, the royal guest of honor, the Grand Duke Alexis of Russia, selected Miss Wells as his partner in the royal quadrille.
>
> Mrs. Penfold only lived in the Gould house for a short time and died there. Once more the house was without a tenant. Then a few years before his death, Commodore Gould came back for occasional visits to his former home, but after his death the house was deserted, and soon its place will be filled by a building that will be a distinct ornament to the avenue [the Campanile.][6]

Daniel McIntosh was an attorney, born in Buffalo in 1859 of parents from Ulster. His oldest son was named Gould, and Ella Gould, mother of Commodore Gould and his sister, Grace McIntosh, lived with the McIntoshes at #925. Gould threw much legal work his brother-in-law's way by having him assemble land in Depew for the vast shops of Gould Coupler and the Central in the 1890s. Daniel died at sixty-six in 1927.[7]

Above #925 on a plot going back to Linwood was P.S. 16. At #957 was one of the oldest houses on the Avenue. It had been built before the Civil War by Isaac Jones, who lived there with wife, children, and in-laws:

> Originally, it was a straight up and down white frame house with [a] square cupola on

3 White, *American Railroad Passenger Car*, 2:651.
4 *BEN*, January 6, 1926; *Times*, October 20, 1914.
5 *Courier*, November 19, 1927.
6 *Courier*, February 21, 1929.
7 *Times*, September 8, 1927.

> top and ornate walks leading up to the house with beds of tulips, daffodils and bleeding hearts lending color to the lawn. Mr. and Mrs. Jones lived there for many years and then the property was purchased by the late Moritz Block. After some years it was the home of the late Eben O. McNair, and now [1926] it is the Devine home, the last owners having remodeled it within and without.(12.3) Next door [at #949] is the property which the late Stewart E. Swan purchased from his sister, Mrs. Isaac A. Jones, and upon which he erected the present square frame house directly next door to public school No. 16. The next owner was Hugh Montgomery and now his daughter, who married Dr. Henry Mulford, lives there.[8]

In 1860 Isaac Jones was a forty-year old commission merchant on Central Wharf. Moritz Block, a cloak manufacturer from Baden, was probably Jewish though not mentioned by Adler among the many Blocks from there who were early Jewish emigrants to Buffalo. Eben McNair, a banker, lived at #957 1905-1910. In 1905 Eben's son Lawrence was a midshipman at Annapolis. Joseph P. Devine resided at #957 1915-1928.(12.3) He was born in Philadelphia in 1865 and came to Buffalo in 1896 where he established J. P. Devine & Company, a machine manufacturing firm. He also held patents on apparatus for drying materials and foodstuffs. He belonged to the Buffalo Club, the American Society of Mechanical Engineers, and the Japanese Society of America. He died at sixty-three in 1928,[9] and was followed at #957 by Doctor Ray A. Edson.

12.3 ❦ Number 957 Delaware, taken by author, spring 1999.

Stewart Elisha Swan had been born near Albany in 1820. He came to Buffalo with his family in 1848 and with his father and a brother set up Swan & Sons, commission merchants, on Central Wharf. In 1863 he was working for J. M. Matthews, commission merchants. In the 1880s he was a police court officer residing at #949. After a long retirement he died in 1909.[10] Harry Earl Montgomery, with his parents Hugh and Susan, moved into #949 in the mid-1890s. Hugh ran a wallpaper and window shade store on Main Street and died in 1899. Harry died 1915. The Montgomerys were followed by Dr. Henry J. Mulford, born in Toledo in 1867. A graduate of the U.B. medical department in 1889, Mulford did postgraduate work in otolaryngology (eye, ear, nose, and throat) in Columbia's College of Physicians and Surgeons. Later he became professor of otolaryngology at U.B. In 1891 he and Doctors Frank Abbott and Benjamin Grove incorporated the Buffalo Eye, Ear, and Throat Hospital. Mulford also attended at Children's Hospital, the Crippled Children's Guild, Meyer Memorial, and the University Dispensary. He wrote extensively on tonsillectomy and child care. He died in 1958 at ninety-one. He seems not to have belonged to any church or club.[11]

8 *Courier*, May 30, 1926.
9 *PBHS*, 30(1930), 276.
10 *BEN*, August 11, 1909.
11 *BEN*, November 6, 1941; *Courier*, July 20, 1958; Hill, *op. cit.*, 4:229-230.

Since the 1850s what was to become #961 was the home of Warren Granger, Jr., the grandson of Erastus Granger, who had been sent to Buffalo in 1803 by President Jefferson. Erastus and his brother Gideon were natives of Suffield, Connecticut, who, while surveying frontier lands in Virginia, met Jefferson, came to admire him, and campaigned for him in the election of 1800. Gideon was Postmaster General 1801-1814. He had his brother Erastus made postmaster of Buffalo Creek and Collector of Customs and Indian Agent in Buffalo. Gideon settled in Canandaigua in 1816 and died there in 1826. Erastus remained in Buffalo and in 1804-1806 built a stone mansion near the present Main Street gate of Forest Lawn. In this house surrounded by an extensive farm, was born in 1817 Warren Granger, Jr., who became a real estate agent. One of the local organizers of the Republican Party, he built during the 1850s a house at future #961 Delaware. An ad in the 1875 City Directory read: "Warren Granger, Land Office and Real Estate and fire insurance agency; rents collected, taxes paid, bonds and mortgages negotiated." He died in 1888.[12] Warren Granger, III, enlisted in the 100th New York Infantry in September 1861, was captured at Strawberry Plains, Virginia, in 1864, but paroled early next year. He was mustered out a colonel by brevet in 1865.[13]

Olivet Baptist at #595 Delaware by 1883 had become known as the Delaware Avenue Baptist Church. In fall 1893 members, seeking larger quarters, bought the former Granger property at #961. The former church at #595 was sold to the Twentieth Century Club in 1894 for $30,000. During construction in winter 1894-1895, Sunday services were held at Beth Zion. The $122,500 church was dedicated during a week of ceremonies beginning in December 1895. The Richardson Romanesque edifice(12.4), which Horton called "hesitantly gothic,"[14] (the rounded arch is definitely not gothic) was designed by an architect who was a member of the congregation, John H. Coxhead. Neo-classical details were added and supplemented by some of the finest mosaics in the city. Those above the pulpit contained a million pieces of tile. The building was vaulted and crowned with an art glass dome.[15] Horton opined that this "church with its somber stone walls and it 202-foot spire made an impression of both dignity and size and added to the architectural interest of the town's most fashionable street."[16] The first pastor at the new location was Dr. O. P. Gifford who

12.4 ❦ Number 961 Delaware, Delaware Avenue Baptist Church, Dunn, *op. cit.*, np.

12 *Courier*, January 8, 1931.
13 Phisterer, *op. cit.*, 4:3166.
14 Horton, *op. cit.*, 1:249.
15 Napora, *Houses of Worship*, p. 68.
16 Horton, *op. cit.*, 1:249.

12.5 ❦ Number 977 Delaware, the Saturn Club, exterior. *Forty Years*, p. 109.

resigned in 1907 after twelve years. He had joined most other local Protestant divines in calling for the defeat of William Jennings Bryant during the lively election campaign of 1896. Gifford was succeeded by Dr. Carl D. Case, pastor for eleven years, followed by Rev. Arthur H. Gordon. In 1920 the church had over a thousand members. It was always noted for its excellent music programs.[17]

In 1880 #973 Delaware was the home of Delancy Benson, an art dealer, who in 1868 had opened a store on Main below Seneca. He died in 1889, and his store was taken over by his son George. Succeeding Delancy at #973 in 1890 was Charles H. Donaldson, a coal dealer. After Saturn had purchased the vacant lot at #977 in March 1920, an extra fifty feet were acquired the next month which caused the club to abut upon the Baptist church. Razing the Donaldson house followed. Figures 12.5 and 12.6 show the results in Tudor of club member Duane Lyman's architectural skill.

12.6 ❦ Saturn Club, interior: *ibid.*, grill, p. 127; billiard room, p. 135.

The two houses north of the club were frame structures on small lots. Alfred W. Haines, a lumberman, lived at #993 through the 1880s and 1890s and died in Rochester in 1903. His line of business at the foot of Erie Street explains why he had been a leading promoter of the New York State Barge Canal, since water transport has an affinity for lumber. At the turn of the century he was followed by the assistant man-

17 *Times*, February 28, 1925.
22 Donohue, *op. cit.*, pp. 35-36.

12.7 ❦ Number 1013 Delaware Avenue, *PBHS*, 16 (1912), 434.

ager of the American Express Company, Thomas A. Ritson. During the second and third decades of the twentieth century #993 was the home of Howard J. Smith who was born in Elmira 1872. He came to Buffalo with his family at six, attended the University of Rochester, and entered the grain business with the Western [Grain] Elevating Association where he remained for twenty-five years. In 1925 he became assistant superintendent of Linde Air Products. He was a Mason and a deacon of the North Presbyterian across the Avenue. He died in 1931.[18]

Thomas Wilkeson, a grocer, lived in the little house on the corner of Delaware and West Utica in 1870. About 1880 it was the home of Annie Farnham, art teacher at Buffalo Seminary. Burr called her "a gifted artist, who later moved to California."[19] Circa 1900 another artist, music teacher Harry J. Fellows, was there with his family. From 1910 until the early 1930s #997 was occupied by Ralph Quale, whose jobs signaled the arrival of a new century, since he was a sports promoter and sold cars.[20]

12.8 ❦ Bishop Stephen V. Ryan, the first Catholic bishop to reside on Delaware Avenue, White, *op. cit.*, 1:368.

On the next house up the Avenue(12.7) Burr wrote in 1930:

> Years ago, there stood at the northeast corner of Delaware avenue and West Utica street, an immense square white house with a verandah across the front, and that sat well back from the street. The roof was surmounted by a square cupola and on the southern side were bay windows. There were spacious grounds and the usual flower beds that graced the velvety lawn after the fashion of the period. It was one of the most imposing homes on the avenue, and was built by the late Edward J. Newman, who with his family resided there for many years.[21]

Two generations of Newmans, Edward J. and William C. and their families, had lived at #1013. The father was in the cement business, and the son somehow mixed flour dealing with cement. North of the Newmans at #1025 was a plain house, occupied in 1870 by William Morehouse, a

18 *BEN*, March 12, 1931.
19 *Times*, February 24, 1930.
20 *BEN*, January 25, 1932.
21 *Times*, February 24, 1930.

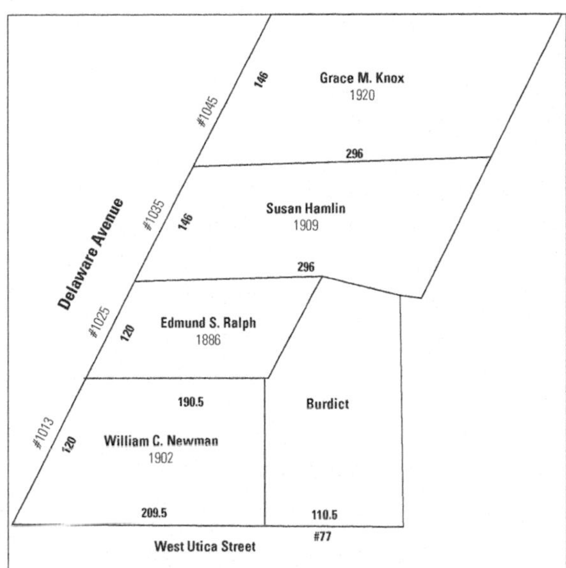

12.9 ❦ Grantors of properties for the new cathedral and bishop's residence.

12.10 ❦ Episcopal residence, #1025 Delaware, and the Chapel of the Blessed Sacrament, before they were moved northward in 1911. Fred A. McGill, *Right Reverend Charles Henry Colton: A Character Sketch of the Fourth Bishop of Buffalo* (Buffalo Catholic Publication Company, 1903), p. 49.

clerk, followed by Edmund Ralph. Between them they had only one domestic. Matters changed in the winter of 1886-1887 when Bishop Stephen V. Ryan(12.8) was on vacation in California. The episcopal residence on Franklin was now directly across from the Terrace Station as well as surrounded by factories.(3.15) With him away, the diocese purchased the Morehouse-Ralph house(12.9) and replaced it with an episcopal palace pleasing to tastes of the mauve decade but to later eyes a grotesque conflation of gothic and Queen Anne. In a corner of the plot the Chapel of the Blessed Sacrament(12.10) was built with Rev. James McGloin in charge. The idea was that this would become a regular parish church. Some laymen suggested "selling the cathedral site for development and constructing a new cathedral elsewhere."[22]

12.11 ❦ Bishop James Edward Quigley, *ibid.*, p. 36.

Bishop Ryan took no steps toward a new cathedral. His successor(12.11), James Edward Quigley (1897-1903), acquired the Newman property at #1013 in 1902. The News quoted McGloin as saying that the cathedral would be "of imposing dimensions," and that plans would "insure a superb example of church architecture." The day before, however, the *Express* had him saying that building was "not going to take place right away" and that "we haven't even thought what sort of a building it will be."[23]

22 *Ibid.*
23 *Express*, February 2, 1902; *Courier*, February 3, 1902.

Concerning Quigley an historian writes:

> Later in 1879 Quigley returned to the diocese of Buffalo and was appointed pastor of St. Vincent's Parish in Attica, New York. In 1884 he was made rector of St. Joseph's Church, the diocesan cathedral, and in 1886 he became pastor of St. Bridget's Parish, a working-class neighborhood in Buffalo where a great number of dockworkers lived. In 1897 he was consecrated bishop of Buffalo. His most noteworthy accomplishment in this capacity came in 1899, when he played a crucial role in settling a major strike by the local longshoremen's union over working conditions. After the State Board of Mediation and Arbitration failed to bring the two parties to terms and the dispute threatened to drag on interminably, Quigley began attending the meetings of the strikers, many of whom he knew personally from St. Bridget's. He vowed to support their cause until their employers promised to make suitable concessions regarding hours, safety, and pay. His involvement marked the first time that a U.S. bishop took a prominent prolabor stand and resulted in the amicable settlement of the strike ten days later.
>
> In 1903 Quigley was appointed archbishop of Chicago, Illinois, at the time a hotbed of labor unrest and social upheaval. Chicago was a center for the newly founded Socialist Party, which was attracting the attention if not loyalty of a growing number of working people. Although he continued to support the efforts of trade unionists to secure a better standard of living for themselves and their families, he vigorously opposed any alliance between the labor movement and the party because he believed that socialism denied both the existence of God and the right of private property.[24]

12.12 ❦ Bishop Charles Henry Colton, *ibid.*, p. 8.

Next resident of #1025 Delaware was Bishop Charles Henry Colton (1903-1915), born of immigrant Irish parents in New York in 1848.(12.12) He attended Saint Francis Xavier College in Manhattan, leaving in 1872 for Saint Joseph's Seminary in Troy where he was ordained in 1876 and assigned as curate to a large working-class parish in Manhattan, Saint Stephen's, where the pastor, Dr. Edward McGlynn, had become involved in what was then called "The Social Question." Neither a close student nor a great orator, he was still in demand in Catholic circles. He had fallen under the influence of Henry George whose panacea for the problems of poverty and unemployment to which modern industrial civilization had given rise was the Single Tax on land. When McGlynn began campaigning for George for mayor of New York in 1886, Michael Augustine Corrigan, Archbishop of New York, ordered him to stop. When McGlynn refused, Corrigan removed him from Saint Stephen's and installed Colton, whose success in restoring order in a tense situation assured his rise to chancellor, chief financial officer of the diocese, and then Bishop of Buffalo in 1903.[25]

24 Charles W. Cary, Jr., "Quigley, James Edward," *ANB*, 18:32-33.
25 *NYT*, May 1, 1915; Dominic Scibilia, "McGlynn, Edward," *ibid.*, 15:59-61.

Now under Colton, McGloin felt surer of himself, announcing in late 1906 the arrival of plans from Rome for a $500,000 cathedral ($8,715,000 in 1997 dollars) seating 1,500 people.[26] In January 1907 the *Express* reported that some priests were objecting to "a cathedral on that corner," saying that it would be "a large and costly structure and there may not be a congregation large enough to support it."[27] Trimming his sails, McGloin said that "there will be no cathedral church at least for the present." A year later, however, a huge parade of 25,000 marched up Delaware from Niagara Square to Utica Street where a vast throng, not seen in Buffalo since the sound money march of 1896, heard a speech about the future cathedral by John Cardinal Farley, Archbishop of New York.[28] The Delaware-Utica site was enlarged next year when the diocese purchased the home of the late Cicero Hamlin at #1035 Delaware from his widow Susan for $70,000.[29]

Hamlin had been born in Columbia County, New York, in 1818, the youngest of ten children of a Methodist minister. In 1836 Cicero moved to East Aurora where he kept a dry goods store. In 1842 he married Susan Ford and in 1846 they came to Buffalo where he set up a dry goods store at #252 Main Street. In 1860 he joined Mendsen & Company, carpets and house furnishings, which was renamed Hamlin & Mendsen, which kept expanding its line of house furnishings. Meanwhile he was investing in real estate which was sure to rise in value with the rapid growth of mid-nineteenth century Buffalo. In 1874 he became president of American Grape Sugar, later merged into the American Glucose, which in 1888 employed over 2,500 workers in Buffalo.[30] It was sold to the glucose combine in 1897. Since glucose was the base of Cicero's considerable fortune and that of his sons, Harry and William, and his grandson, Chauncey, all residents of Delaware Avenue, the following is a brief account of this commodity:

> Glucose is the most common of the naturally occurring sugars. It is also known as dextrose or grape sugar. In men and other animals heat and energy needs for muscular activity, chemical syntheses, and other energy-requiring processes are obtained from the breakdown of glucose...Glucose is used in the manufacture of candy and other foods. It is used as a preservative because the high concentration of sugar inhibits the growth of bacteria.[31]

In 1868 Cicero Hamlin was the was the chief promoter of Driving Park which occupied a rectangle bounded by Jefferson, Puffer, (later Northland), Humboldt Parkway, and East Ferry Streets.[32] Cicero and Susan lived at #1035 from the late 1880s until his death there 1905. He had retired from the turf in October 1900. His widow died in 1909, at Palm Beach.[33]

Enough land had been assembled to accommodate the cathedral and the bishop's mansion. In 1898, the year of the parade, both Buffalo and the Catholic Church seemed to be on a roll. It appeared fitting, therefore, for Catholics, who were absent from the city's beginnings, to stake a claim to preeminence on Buffalo's most fashionable street, even as their coreligionists in New York, having by

26 *Courier*, March 6, 1906.
27 *Express*, January 14, 1907.
28 *Ibid.*, September 15, 1908.
29 *Ibid.*, March 2, 1909.
30 *Ibid.*, September, 1888.
31 Peter O. Esper, "Glucose," *Encyclopedia Americana*, 12:817-818.
32 Horton, *op. cit.*, 1:300.
33 *BEN*, September 24, 1963.

1879 taken over the government of their city, completed the move of their cathedral from downtown on Mott Street to the heartland of fashion and the Four Hundred on Fifth Avenue. Both groups of Catholics were riding the crest of a wave of what later would be wryly termed triumphalism.

12.13 ❦ Moving Bishop Colton's house 200 feet to the north, April 1911. Kindness of Msgr. Walter Kern, former archivist, diocese of Buffalo. Knox Mansion to the left.

The 1908 parade may have been a bit premature. The planned dimensions of the cathedral were such as to make more space necessary. Accordingly, Bishop Colton's house was moved north 200 feet onto the former Hamlin place at #1035(12.13) by Gus Britt, uncle of the future Monsignor Britt, rector of the old cathedral. The building at the extreme left in 12.13 is the mansion at #1049 of Mrs. Seymour Knox, I,(10.38) who moved from there in 1918 to a grander home at #806.(10.39) She rented #1049 to William H. Donner, the steel king, who with his family was there when the federal census taker came around in 1920.

Donner was born in Columbus, Indiana, in 1864. He attended public schools and Hanover College. At thirty he organized National Tinplate at Anderson, Indiana, of which he became treasurer. With this venture a success, he formed another tinplate plant, in Monessen, Pennsylvania. Donner, like Andrew Carnegie an organizer rather than a steel maker, sold both these companies to American Tinplate, which became one of the original units of United States Steel. By thirty-five Donner had made a fortune. In 1889 he organized Union Steel south of Pittsburgh on the Monongahela River which he called Donora after himself. In 1907 Donner merged Union with Sharon Steel. The same year he was named a receiver of Westinghouse Company of Pittsburgh. Because of his heavy investments, he was elected president of Cambria Steel in 1911, and later was chosen chairman of the board of directors of Pennsylvania Steel Company which merged with Bethlehem. On the lookout for challenges, he came to New York because he saw defects he believed he could remedy in New York Steel. He bought it in 1915 and renamed it Donner Steel. It became one of the biggest pro-

12.14 ❦ Bishop William Turner, Wilner, *op. cit.*, III, facing p. 198.

ducers of carbon and alloy steel in the world. He resigned in 1929 and moved to Villanova outside Philadelphia where he lived until 1937 when he moved to Switzerland for a time following a dispute with the government over income taxes. He spent the last twenty years of his life funding agencies fighting cancer which had killed his son, Joseph Donner. Donner Steel on Abbott Road in Buffalo was a precursor of the better-known Republic Steel. Donner was a Republican and a Presbyterian, and a member of these clubs: Union League, Rittenhouse, Buffalo, and Philadelphia Country. He died in 1953.[34] He could not have lived at #1094 past 1922 since, as the historian of the diocese writes, "The Bishop continued to dwell in the Delaware Avenue house until the Spring of 1922 when the magnificent Knox home, adjoining his property, was purchased for an episcopal residence. After a visit to Rome, Bishop Turner(12.14) moved into his new house in September 1922."[35] This may be taken as an obituary of the place:

> A quite modern residence, adjoining the new St. Joseph's Cathedral at Delaware and Utica streets — known as the Bishop's House, was taken down within the past year. It was a somewhat costly house of brick and brownstone, but its architecture did not harmonize with the white marble cathedral adjoining, or with the beautiful residence at the north which had been acquired by the Diocese as the Episcopal residence. The older house, which was built by the late Bishop Colton [false] was apparently sacrificed in the interests of beauty. Its site is now a well-kept lawn, and its removal has added greatly to the charm of one of Buffalo's most charming neighborhood.[36]

Meanwhile the cornerstone of the new cathedral had been laid on June 9, 1912. It was to be dominated by two towers, each 260 feet high(12.15), the width across the nave was to be 100 feet, and through the transepts 150 feet.[37] The designer was Aristides Leonori of Rome, "an architect of much experience and of great sympathy and the spirit of fine ecclesiastical architecture." His knowledge of the destructive power of Buffalo winters was less profound. Just before the work was finished, Bishop Colton died on May 5, 1915. Nonetheless his funeral was held there and his body laid to rest in a marble sarchophagus in the sanctuary.

12.15 ❦ Saint Joseph's New Cathedral, front view, *Commercial*, November 14, 1910.

34 *BEN*, November 4, 1953; Dunn, *op. cit.*, p.33.
35 Donohue, *op.cit.*, p. 146.
36 *PBHS*, 26(1922), 418.

In Colton's vision one of the glories of the cathedral, placed on a promontory higher than almost anywhere else in the city, was the forty-five bell carillon which Bishop Timon had purchased at the Paris Exposition in 1855, sparing nothing to make his cathedral a magnificent setting for the splendors of the Roman liturgy to be performed within, which would impress non-Catholics. The huge carillon would dothe same thing for those outside. The largest bell was 4,000 lbs., the smallest twenty-five. The whole cost $25,000 ($435,000 in 1997 dollars). It was the largest carillon in America at the time. Unfortunatly, only one of Timon's twin bell towers was completed. Structural problems militated against a second. The carillon was consecrated early in Bishop Ryan's time and installed in the single tower, but the arrangement proved unwieldly, and the bells were removed and stored against a better day. Colton saw the triumphal twin 260-foot towers at Delaware and Utica as proclaiming the message on Sundays and feast days to the surrounding city. Unfortunately, when the bells were installed and rung once or twice it became clear that they had to be removed since their percussions endangered the safety of the towers. The bells were stored in the basement and the towers razed. Bob Ripley's syndicated feature "Believe It or Not" described this cathedral with its belfry in the basement. One by one the bells were stolen, so that when Rev. Paul Juenker was made rector and checked out the basement he discovered that only four had survived. The largest ended up in Forest Lawn where it reposes today near the Delaware Avenue gate.[38]

The next occupant of the see was Dennis Dougherty, who went from Nueva Segovia in the Philippines for which he was consecrated 1903, to Jaro in the Philippines, to which he was transferred in 1908, to Buffalo, to which he was transferred December 1915, to Philadelphia to which he was promoted in 1918.[39] His successor was William Turner (1919-1936), who was born in Killmalloch, County Limerick in 1871, attended national schools and the Jesuit college in Limerick, received a B.A. from the Royal University of Ireland in 1888 and an S.T.D. from the North American College in Rome in 1893. That year he was ordained and at the behest of Archbishop John Ireland of Saint Paul Turner taught philosophy at the Saint Paul seminary. In 1906 he became chairman of the philosophy department and librarian at Catholic University in Washington. He wrote two textbooks on scholastic philosophy, *History of Philosophy* in 1903 and *Lessons in Logic* in 1911. He was editor of the *American Ecclesiastical Re-*

12.16 ❦ The last Catholic bishop to reside on Delaware Avenue, Joseph A. Burke, *Azuwur*, (Canisius College Yearbook 1959), p. 4.

37 *Express*, November 13, 1910.

38 Telephone conversation with Monsignor Paul Juenker, July 30, 2002. The source for Bishop Timon's motivation in constructing such a grand cathedral with bells in the circumstances of 1855 is an ms. biography by the late Leonard Riforgiato in the Buffalo diocesan archives which I read some years ago. The story of the bells' consecration and installation in Ryan's time is in Charles G. Deuther, *Life and Times of the Rt. Rev. John Timon, D.D.* (Buffalo: published by the author, 1870), pp 323-333, which also gives the original number of bells as forty-five.

39 *The Official Catholic Directory Anno Domini 2000* (New Providence, N.J. P. J. Kennedy & Sons, 1999), p. 174.

view 1914-1919 and assistant editor of the *Catholic Historical Review* 1915-1918. In 1919 he became Bishop of Buffalo where he combined charitable institutions, organized the diocesan Catholic Charities, and promoted Saint Vincent de Paul Societies to help the poor. He died in 1936.

Turner's two immediate successors lived at #1049 Delaware, John A. Duffy (1937-1944), who was made honorary member of the Buffalo Club in 1939,[40] and John F. O'Hara, ex-president of Notre Dame (1945-1951.) The experience of O'Hara's successor, Joseph A. Burke(12.16), was reminiscent of that of Stephen Ryan who found that the trains on the Central kept him awake and moved uptown. Burke became bishop in 1952 and found the traffic on the Avenue too noisy. So he retreated to the tasteful ex-Forman mansion on Oakland Place.(10.41) Two entrepreneurs failed to make a go of #1049 as a luxury office building, sisters at Cathedral School lived there, and finally it became the rectory for the clergy of Blessed Sacrament.[41]

Meanwhile the cathedral was deteriorating alarmingly. Five years after it opened major repairs were needed. North and south transepts had been rebuilt in 1924-1925 at a cost of over $100,000 ($1,143,000 in 1997 dollars.) The twin steeples were removed in 1927-1928 at a cost of $72,000, and other repairs over the years totaled about $700,000, (over $12 million in 1997 dollars.) Large chunks of ceiling plaster had begun to fall, and several sections of pews had to be roped off. The exterior marble facing had not been properly bonded to the brick wall behind it, and gradually pulled away from it, causing in places a gap of several inches. Bishop Edward D. Head said that the cathedral was the "victim of bad design or bad construction." Miss Kathryn Summers, daughter of a general contractor for the cathedral, recalled, "I remember the heartache my father had about the unwarranted complaints about the cathedral. He maintained until his last day that it wasn't his fault; that he built to specifications." She blamed the Roman architect. Bishop Head appointed a large committee of pastors of major churches in the diocese and successful contractors and businessmen both Catholic and non-Catholic so that the decision to raze

Above and Below 12.17 ❦ Two versions of Number 1069 Delaware Avenue, *City Beautiful*, p. 26.

40 Warren, *op. cit.*, p. 102.
41 Conversation with Msgr. Paul R. Jeunker, *ibid.*

the monster would not be seen as his alone. After an eight-month study it was found that it would cost more than $2.2 million to restore the building, that annual maintenance would be about $30,000, and that the cost of a new cathedral would be even more prohibitive. The building, whose long-time deterioration caused its builder "a lifetime of heartache," was razed, and its furnishings were sold by the wreckers in partial payment for the $250,000 the job was estimated to cost. Bishop Colton's remains were reentombed at Saint Joseph's on Franklin Street. On his original tomb was an inscription which had cited the cathedral as "his crowning glory." On the site was erected an apartment complex, Timon Towers.[42]

Henry Hearne, an English-born wholesale confectioner built a house with a mansard roof at #1069 in the late 1860s.(12.17) Subsequent owners made additions, but preserved and extended the original mansard roof. Hearne was followed in 1880 by Thomas C. Reilly, an Irish-born druggist with his sister's children and the usual complement of servants. Two years later it had become the home of George E. More, a hatter and furrier at #327 Main Street. More had been born in Bungay, Suffolk, England, in 1849, attended the village school, worked for a grocer in Norfolk, and in 1870 took up an elder brother's invitation to join him in the grocery business in Brooklyn. Disappointed by his lack of progress, More had decided by 1872 to return to England, but first visited a cousin in Buffalo, Harry Smith, who had been conducting a Main Street haberdashery. More changed his mind. In 1879 he married Clara Stanton, a niece of druggist Thomas Reilly. In 1882 More bought out Smith's interest, began investing in downtown properties, and moved briefly into #1069. His wife Clara died, and he married Emma Louise Cole, whom he had known in England. He resided at #1069 but a short time, since in 1884 it had become the home of Sheriff Harry H. Koch.(12.18) Koch had been born in Williamsville of Pennsylvania Dutch ancestry in 1841. His father ran a store and sawmill and served as deputy sheriff, constable, and collector of internal revenue. He was among the many Whigs who because of their abolitionism joined the new Republican Party in the 1850s. Harry worked in his father's store and graduated from the Williamsville Classical School at seventeen, after which he put in three years at his father's sawmill. He then went to Buffalo where he attended Bryant & Stratton. While there he worked with W. S. Abbott, shoe store proprietor, as salesman and bookkeeper. In 1861 he taught district school in Amherst, re-

12. 18 ❦ Harry H. Koch, Biographical Sketches and Portraits of 100 Buffalonians, Buffalo and Erie County Public Library, Lafayette Square, pp. 92-93.

42 *CE*, November 26, 1975.

turning to Buffalo in 1862 to spend three years in the employ of T. C. Fields who owned three shoe stores. In 1865 Koch entered the employ of another shoe dealer, E. Neff, who took him into partnership. In October 1868 Koch sold his interest in the business to his partner and the following year started a store of his own. The business prospered and the store was enlarged from time to time, so that by 1880 he was proprietor of a large boot and shoe store at #480 Main Street. He was an active Republican and had been elected alderman of the 10th Ward in 1861. In 1882 he was nominated for sheriff and was elected by a majority of over 4,000, serving a three-year term which ended January 1, 1888. A country boy, he owned a stock farm in Amherst, which ran some of the finest Jersey cows in the county. In December 1865 he had married Hattie N. Coe of Williamsville by whom he had two sons, Harry and Carlton.[43]

Koch's life seemed so ordinary that most Buffalonians were shocked when they read in the papers one cold day in January 1887 that he had had committed suicide by hanging himself from a rafter in the attic of his #1069 Delaware Avenue home. He had his coachman drive him to a doctor's office only to find the doctor away. He dismissed the man and somehow returned home unnoticed by anyone.

> During the last few days of his life, his mind ran incessantly on religious subjects. He also acted very strangely at his boot and shoe store on Main street, at times following his clerks around and asking irrelevant questions. He would start to leave, getting into his buggy, and then leaping out again and re-entering the store, apparently without aim or object. He had devoted much time lately to the establishment of the boot and shoe factory on Hickory street, for the wholesale branch of his trade. It is thought probable that this unusual application might have aided to develop his mental disorder. His general business affairs were in good shape.[44]

12.19 ❦ Wilson Shannon Bissell, *PBHS*, 7 (1904), facing p. 488.

Koch's widow lived at #1069 for two more years, after which it became for a short time the residence of Meyer Geismer and his son-in-law Isadore H. Falk. Geismer was among the German-Jewish immigrants who settled in Buffalo after the Civil War. Born in Ihringen in 1842, he came to Buffalo where he became a cattle dealer, like his ancestors in Baden. He met and married Matilda, daughter of fellow cattle dealer, Emanuel Straus, also a Bavarian. Eventually Geismer abandoned his cattle and entered the clothing business on Pearl Street. His daughter Carrie married the contractor, Isadore H. Falk(1865-1942), who had also started off as a cattle dealer but became a clothier in

43 *"Biographical Sketches of 100 Prominent Buffalonians,"* pp. 92-93, Local History Section, Buffalo Public Library, Lafayette Square.
44 *CA*, January 26, 1887.

partnership with his father-in-law. Isadore's father had been Rabbi Samson Falk of Beth Zion, the first real Reform rabbi in Buffalo. Adler writes that "Falk was the first Jewish clergyman in Buffalo with enough savoir faire and western secular education to represent the Jews before the general population and make an impression." Isadore, the rabbi's son, "joined the Klondike gold rush of 1897, drilled oil in Oklahoma, and returned to Buffalo to found a contracting firm that built bridges and highways in New York and neighboring Pennsylvania."[45] All this was after his short stay at #1069 Delaware.

The first generation of the Delaware Avenue Bissells was represented by John, born about 1814, who came to Buffalo from New London, Oneida County, New York, with his wife, the former Jeanette Halley, and their two sons, Arthur Douglass Bissell (10.58), born in 1844, and Wilson Shannon Bissell, born in 1847(12.19). John engaged in transporting grain on the canal under the aegis of Bissell Transportation Company. In 1870 the family resided at #1081. Arthur, then twenty-six, had attended public schools in Buffalo, spent three years at a boarding school in Clinton, New York, graduated from Yale in 1867, and worked with his father in Bissell Transportation. Wilson, twenty-two in 1870, attended the Hopkins Grammar School in New Haven, graduated from Yale in 1869, where he was elected to Skull and Bones, and read law under Laning, Cleveland & Folsom. This account of Wilson Bissell's career was probably composed by Frank H. Severance:

> In 1870 when Mr. Cleveland was elected sheriff of Erie County, the law firm became Laning, Folsom & Willett, and Mr. Bissell was head clerk until 1872, when he was invited to a partnership with Lyman K. Bass. Later, Mr. Cleveland joined the firm, which became Bass, Cleveland & Bissell, and continued until Mr. Bass removed to Colorado. Mr. Cleveland and Mr. Bissell continued in partnership until Mr. Cleveland was elected Mayor of Buffalo, in 1881; then Mr. Geo. J. Sicard was admitted, the firm becoming Cleveland, Bissell & Sicard. This firm was attorney for the Lehigh Valley Railroad, when that road was brought to Buffalo, and for other large corporations. When, in 1882 Mr. Cleveland was elected Governor of New York State, Mr. Charles W. Goodyear entered the firm and remained until 1887, when he went into the lumber business. Mr. Bissell's firm became counsel for the Buffalo & Susquehanna Railroad, and the Buffalo & Susquehanna Iron Co., both Goodyear interests. After Mr. Goodyear's withdrawal, the firm became Bissell, Sicard, Brundage & Bissell, the Hon. Frank Brundage and Herbert P. Bissell being admitted. In 1894 Judge Brundage withdrew and Martin Carey entered the firm, and in 1896 Mr. Herbert P. Bissell left it, Walter P. Cooke being admitted, the firm name becoming Bissell, Carey & Cooke.
>
> A coincidence worthy of note is, that Millard Fillmore, a former President of the United States; Nathan K. Hall, former Postmaster General and a United States District Judge, and Grover Cleveland occupied at different times the same offices, subsequently rented by Mr. Bissell. Mr. Bissell became President Cleveland's Postmaster General in 1893. He was a staunch Democrat, and a good organizer. He served at the head of the Post Office Department for two years, his administration being marked by practical business ability, an excellent conception of the needs of the department, and a careful effort to introduce

45 Adler, *op. cit.*, pp. 137, 145-146, 176.

> reforms where needed. But there was much about the position that was irksome to him, and the persistency and pettiness of politicians and place-hunters greatly harassed him. Against the wishes of his associates in the Cabinet, and of the President, Mr. Bissell resigned his portfolio and returned to the practice of the profession which he loved, in Buffalo. In 1884 he had served as Presidential elector at large on the Democratic ticket; and in 1891 Governor David B. Hill appointed him member of the commission which revised the judiciary article of the State Constitution.
>
> In his practice, Mr. Bissell was a counselor, not a pleader before juries. He rarely appeared in court, and the only speech he is known to have made was at a dinner given for Grover Cleveland by the Cleveland Democracy of Buffalo in May, 1891. But in his chosen line of practice, Mr. Bissell was probably the peer of any one who ever belonged to the Bar of Buffalo, and very many important interests were successfully committed to his care. He was a member of the directorate of the Lehigh & Lake Erie Railroad Co., the Lehigh Valley Railroad Co., the Lehigh & New York Railroad Co., the Lehigh Valley Railroad Co., the Lehigh & New York Railroad Co., the Elmira, Cortland & Northern Railroad Co., the Canastota Northern Railroad Co., the Elmira Transfer Railway Co., the Canal Railway Co., and the Pioneer Real Estate Co. He regarded life insurance as a judicious investment, and at the time his death carried policies aggregating $80,000. He was a member of the old City Club, of the Buffalo, Country, and Ellicott Clubs, and of the University Club of New York. He was a trustee of Yale University, and in 1892 succeeded the Hon. James O. Putnam as chancellor of the University of Buffalo. At one time he was president of the Young Men's Association, and a vestryman of Trinity Episcopal Church.[46]

The author was padding the list of railroads of which Bissell was a director. They were all non-operating subsidiaries of the Lehigh Valley whose chief consul Bissell was.

Bissell had managed Cleveland's campaign for governor in 1882 and expected a reward when his friend reached the White House in 1885. Allan Nevins, Cleveland's biographer, recalls:

> Bissell wished a seat in the cabinet, but there were two New Yorkers there already. He then asked to be made a consul general in London — the fees of $40,000 making this the most lucrative of all government offices. He was tired and needed a change, he wrote, the money would be useful and his family would enjoy London Society! For good reason Cleveland again refused although he offered Bissell several other positions.[47]

Bissell did get to join the cabinet as Postmaster General during Cleveland's second administration. Nevins' judgment of Bissell's handling this job is positive: "Bissell also showed great capacity and stood loyally by civil service reform. He could sit sturdily in his office and repel the assaults of the politicians day after day, and when several candidates appeared for any office, he was all ready decided in favor of the best man.[48] Another estimate of Bissell in the cabinet was equally positive:

> At the end of two years, Bissell, as recorded by [Champ] Clark [Democratic congressman from Missouri], had become one of the most popular members of the cabinet and one of the most respected. His only rival in cabinet popularity was Daniel S. Lamont, who had served as private secretary during the first Cleveland term and was then secretary of the navy. Bissell, remarked Clark in conclusion, would never have inspired enthusiastic devotion, but he expresses the belief [that] if he had served out his full term of four years, he

46 *PBHS*, 7(1904), 488-490.
47 Nevins, *Cleveland*, pp. 238-239, 513.
48 *Ibid.*, p. 513.

would have rivaled his New York colleague, Dan Lamont.

> Although Clark, an unbiased observer, testifies as to Bissell's substantial success and increasing popularity in the most laborious and difficult position in the cabinet, the distribution of the vast amount of postal patronage, the job of office holding became irksome to Bissell. At the end of two years he insisted on retiring and resumed his large practice. Undoubtedly Bissell was a great aid to Cleveland during the latter's activities in law and in the mayor's office. But the relationship seems not to have continued in the last years.[49]

Bissell was president of the Buffalo Club for three years 1888-1890. Before his marriage in 1889 he had roomed in various homes along the Avenue, including the Trubee at #414. He and his wife moved into #295 Delaware where they remained until they purchased #1069 which Bissell during his stay from 1898 until 1903 enlarged to where it contained eight rooms on the first floor and thirteen bedrooms and ten baths on the second and third.[50] Bissell died in 1903 at fifty-five. He was buried from Trinity on October 9th, the Rev. Cameron Davis presiding.

Next resident at the big house was Frederick H. Stevens, a native of Canandaigua. He began his business career as a merchant in Fredonia and then got a job at Brooks Locomotive in nearby Dunkirk. He married Ida Brooks of Dunkirk, a member of the family that owned the company, and rose to director and eventually president. When Brooks was taken over by American Locomotive in 1901 Stevens became a director of that company and described himself as a "financier." He was a member of the Saturn and Buffalo clubs. A few years before his death he acquired a summer home in Pasadena and a winter home in his native village. He died in 1931 in Pasadena.[51]

12.20 ❦ Frank B. Baird, Warren, *op. cit.*, p. 57.

Of Frank Burkett Baird(12.20), president of the Buffalo Club in 1914 and next householder at #1069, the club historian writes:

> Baird was an outstanding community leader in the tradition of [William G.] Fargo [of Wells Fargo fame]. He was born in Marietta, Ohio, November 24, 1852, and came to Buffalo in 1888. A peerless organizer with extraordinary powers of persuasion, his initial interests were in iron, steel and coke, first organizing the Tonawanda Iron & Steel Company. He later organized three other firms in the same fields, put them together in 1900 as the Buffalo Union Furnace Company, operated by Hanna Furnace Company of Cleveland under management contract. A director of banks, railroads, and iron, steel and coke properties, he was best known for his civic interests, notably as "the father of the Peace Bridge," constructed by the Buffalo & Fort Erie Public Bridge Company, an organization he put together out of diverse American and Canadian interests. He pre-

49 *CE*, October 6, 1929.
50 *BEN*, October 21, 1952; Warren, *op. cit.*, p. 38.
51 *BEN*, January 24, 1931.

> sided at the opening ceremonies, August 7, 1927, and introduced the Prince of Wales, Vice President Charles G. Dawes, and Stanley Baldwin, prime minister of England, among others. A former president of the Buffalo Chamber of Commerce, he led the First World War I charity drive, that for relief of the Belgians. He helped develop Millard Fillmore Hospital and Albright Art Gallery. In the fall of 1939, he suffered a fall, fractured a hip, and died November 15th.[52]

Baird's widow, the former Flora Cameron, and two sons, Frank B., Jr., and William Cameron, lived at #1069 until 1957 when it was bought by the Catholic diocese of Buffalo. She retired to a two-story suite in the Campanile at #925 Delaware. The property is now the site of the Catholic Academy of West Buffalo. A third son, Cameron, who grew up at #1069, attended the Franklin and the Nichols schools in Buffalo, graduated from Williams in 1926, and did advanced studies at the Harvard Business School in 1927. He was associated 1914-1919 with the Hanna Furnace Company of Cleveland and in 1930 joined Buffalo Pipe Foundry as its president. He was also head of the music department at U.B., where he donated what became known as Baird Hall. He married Jane Dugan of Buffalo in 1937 and they had four children.[53] He died in 1961.

After the Arthur Bissells had vacated #1081 in the mid 1880s to move back to Jeanette's old home on the west side of Delaware, the house was acquired by Edmund P. Fish who arranged loans and brokered securities. In 1891 Frank Sears McGraw had become, among other things, Fish's partner and the owner of Fish's house. McGraw had been born in Dryden near Ithaca in 1871. He attended the Ithaca Free Academy and Cornell, leaving in 1884 before graduation to engage in the lumber business in Michigan. In 1891 he moved back to Buffalo where he got into water supply. In 1900 the Western New York Water was founded to distribute water to suburban areas with McGraw as vice president and general manager. The venture was a success and in 1909 it merged with Depew & Lake Erie Water, with McGraw as president. In 1931 he became chairman of the board. When a Buffalo chapter of the American Red Cross was erected in 1916 McGraw became its president, a position he held until his death. He was also a trustee of Buffalo General, a director of People's Bank, and a member of Saturn, the Buffalo Club, and the Country Club. McGraw and his wife, the former Nellie Ainsworth, were the parents of two sons. McGraw's hobby was horses. In the 1890s he was among the prominent citizens who raced their trotters on Richmond Avenue and he was saddened when the horse gave

12.21 ❦ "Doctor" G. Hunter Bartlett, *PBHS*, 30 (1930), following page 22.

52 Warren, *op. cit.*, pp. 57-58.
53 Horton, *op. cit.*, 3:437; Dunn, *op. cit.*, p. 401.

way to the motor car. He died at seventy in 1931.

12.22 ❦ Interior view of # 1083. Olaf, William Shelgren, Jr., "Buffalo Homes," in *Adventures in Western New York History*, vol. xvi., Buffalo and Erie County Historical Society, p. 11.

The first resident at #1083 was George Hunter Bartlett (12.21), son of Frederic W. Bartlett, a doctor who lived and practiced at #523 Delaware until his death in 1897. George Bartlett's mother was the former Alice Hunter, daughter of a Canadian doctor and political activist, James H. Hunter. G. Hunter Bartlett was born in Buffalo in 1856. He attended the Heathcote School, graduated from Yale's Sheffield Scientific School in 1879, and from the medical department of U.B. in 1883. On April 18 that year in Saint Paul's Cathedral he married Alice Mary Evans, daughter of Charles W. Evans, of #468 Delaware, grain elevator owner and descendant of Joseph Ellicott. Though he always used the title "Doctor," G. Hunter never practiced medicine. Instead he managed his father-in-law's grain elevators. After Evans died in 1889 Bartlett administered Evans' estate and became director of the Western [Grain] Elevating Co. In 1889 the Bartletts moved into a house(12.22) they had built that year at #1083 Delaware.[54]

G. Hunter and Alice were well matched since they were both interested in history, particularly that of their own ancestors. He wrote several articles, the latest of which, "Andrew and Joseph Ellicott and the Plans of the City of Washington and the Village of Buffalo," appeared in volume xxvi of the *Publications of the Buffalo Historical Society* in 1922. The doctor was also an accomplished photographer. The Buffalo Camera Club of which he was first president originated at his house in 1889. His other hobby was wood and metalworking, and he patented several inventions, one of which was a fusible link used by his father in his medical practice and later developed for fire prevention equipment. Hunter was a founder of York Hall, the Yale chapter of Chi Phi fraternity. His memberships included the Saturn and University clubs, the Sons of the American Revolution, the Society of Colonial Wars, and the Society of Mayflower Descendants. G. Hunter Bartlett died at home after an illness of two years in 1931.

12.23 ❦ G. Raynolds Stearns, Jr. Wilner, *op. cit.*, 3:469.

54 *Times*, November 9, 1931.

His widow died there in 1936.[55] The Hunter Bartletts had two children, Virginia Evans Bartlett and Evans E. Bartlett.

Virginia Bartlett, an alumna of Saint Margaret's, Buffalo Seminary, and Smith, married G. Raynolds Stearns, Jr.(12.23), in 1917. The groom, a native Buffalonian, was the son of Doctor George R. and Jennie Raynolds Stearns. He attended public school, Lafayette High, Columbia, class of 1913, and Columbia Law School. During World War I he joined Troop 1 of the New York Cavalry and was sent to Camp Travis in Texas. Discharged as a first lieutenant at the beginning of 1919, he returned to Buffalo where the Stearns moved in with their parents at #1083. They were still there in 1940, but by 1948 he was living at the University Club, and #1083 had become a doctors' office building when Stearns died at seventy-nine in 1968.

Seven families occupied #1089 between the late 1880s and early 1930s when it too had become a doctors' office building. A young attorney, Austin Roe Preston, resided there in the early 1890s. By 1893 it had become the home of Robert L. Fosburgh who had come to Buffalo from Saint Louis as secretary and treasurer of Eastern Elevator. When the company was sold he engaged briefly in general contracting on a large scale. His daughter May graduated from the Buffalo Seminary in 1895. In July 1900 the family moved to Pittsfield, Massachusetts, where the father had undertaken a $250,000 contract.[56] On August 20, 1900, at about two o'clock in the morning May was shot in the chest and died instantly. At first burglars who had been seen running away were blamed, but later the grand jury indicted Robert Fosburgh, Mary's brother, whose July 1901 trial lasted six days at the end of which the judge directed the jury to find the accused innocent. The only evidence was that the victim was shot with a thirty-eight caliber revolver and Robert owned such a gun. Loran Lewis, Jr., of #1093 Delaware, an attorney and recently a next door neighbor of the Fosburghs, attended the trial daily.[57]

12.24 ❦ **Joseph G. Dudley, Warren, *op. cit.*, p. 102.**

After the Fosburghs at #1089 was Joseph G. Dudley (12.24) an attorney, who resided there with his wife, daughter, and two domestics *circa* 1900. Dudley descended from Thomas Dudley who had come to Massachusetts aboard the *Arbella* in 1630, served as Winthrop's deputy governor in 1630, and was elected governor himself for four more terms. Joseph Dudley was born in Winona, Minnesota, in 1869, son of a Congregational minister, Joseph F. Dudley, who served parishes in Winona and Eau Claire, Minnesota, and

55 BEN, November 9, 1931.
56 *Express*, August 26, 1900.
57 *Ibid.*, July 27, 1901.

Fargo, North Dakota. The son grew up in Eau Claire, received his A.B. from Beloit College in Wisconsin in 1892, spent a year at Harvard Law, and came to Buffalo in 1893 at the urging of his cousin, Joseph P. Dudley of #564, later #827 Delaware, president of Empire Oil. Joseph Dudley clerked for Ansley Wilcox, was admitted to the bar in 1895, formed a partnership with Judge Frank Brundage which lasted until Brundage died, and in 1917 formed another partnership known as Dudley, Stowe, & Sawyer. In 1896, Dudley married Caroline Moon. Their daughter Dorothy married Daniel J. Kenefick, Jr., of #841 Delaware. In a rare venture into politics, Dudley campaigned to elect John Lord O'Brian mayor, whose opponent, Louis Fuhrmann, won. Dudley held the longest continuous membership in the Country Club, fifty-four years. He was a long-time director of Manufacturers & Traders Trust, dean of Saturn in 1900, and in 1939 president of the Buffalo Club, of which he was a member for fifty years. He was the last resident of Delaware to have been club president. A lawyer for fifty-four years, he died at eighty in 1949.[58]

12.25 ❦ Albert F. Laub, Hill, *op. cit.*, III, facing p. 289.

Austin Roe Preston returned to #1089 in 1905. He was followed by Albert F. Laub(12.25), a third generation tanner, who resided there 1909-1912. Albert's grandfather George was born in Hesse-Darmstadt in 1795, came to America in 1831, and settled in Hamburg where he worked at farming and lumbering. He used the bark of the trees he cut for curing leather and set up his first tannery in Eden in 1846. In 1858 he retired and moved to Buffalo where he spent thirty-two years, dying in 1890 at ninety-five. George Laub had three sons, Adam, Frederick, and George. George, Jr., was born in Hamburg in 1837. After public school, he went to work for four years in his father's tannery, before entering into a partnership with his two brothers in a tannery in Abbott's Corners. This was dissolved in 1864, and George, Jr., formed one with G. Frederick Zeller of Buffalo which lasted until 1889 when George entered another with his father known as George Laub & Son. The other two sons later joined up, the father retired a second time, died in 1905, and the boys formed George Laub's Sons. George, Jr., married Bertha Schaller of Saxony and they had three sons, George C., Albert F., and Charles J. Albert, born in Buffalo in 1870, attended public schools and spent three years at Cornell, returning to become a partner in the family business. In 1898 he married Clara Hoffman of Buffalo. He was vice president of the Tanners' Council of America, and of Nichols' board of trustees. His clubs were Buffalo, Country, Wanakah, Park, and Ellicott. While his father and

58 "Dudley, Thomas," *DAB*, 5:484-485; *CE*, September 14, 1949; Warren, *op. cit.*, p.102.

12.26 ❦ John G. Wickser, *PBHS*, 30(1930), facing p. 20.

grandfather were German Evangelicals, Albert belonged to Westminster. In 1912 he moved to a new mansion on #1272 Delaware.(15.11) He died at fifty-one in 1921.[59]

Beginning in 1912 Edwin R. Thomas of Thomas Flyer fame made #1089 his home for three years before moving to #841. John G. Wickser(12.26) was the last regular householder at #1089, residing there from about 1920 until his death in 1928. He had been born in Buffalo in 1856, son of Jacob Wickser and his wife, the former Eva C. Becker. He attended public school and Central High and then went to work for the Buffalo German Insurance Company. In 1876 he severed ties with this company and organized Becker & Wickser, saddlers and harness makers, as a junior partner of his Uncle Philip of #534 Delaware. In 1896 he became associated with the Philip Becker Company, wholesale groceries, one of Buffalo's largest and best-known mercantile concerns. An ardent Republican, Wickser did not seek public office and refused to run for mayor or governor. He was, however, treasurer of New York 1903-1904. He was chairman of the state prison commissioners in 1905, during World War I, he sat on the district draft board of appeals, and was an effective advocate of the Peace Bridge. Wickser was married twice, first in 1886 to Katherine Houck of Buffalo, then in 1918 to Josephine Wilhelm Hard.[60]

In 1891 #1093 Delaware was the residence of Loran L. Lewis, Jr.,(12.27) born in Buffalo in 1864, son of Loran L. Lewis, a native of Auburn, who had read law in the office of William H. Seward. The elder Lewis, who died in 1916, had been a state senator and for thirteen years a state supreme court judge. His son graduated from Williams in 1887 and from U.B. law school in 1889. That year he married Anna M. Browne of Albany. He served as city attorney in 1893, resigning to have more time for his growing legal practice. He had also been president of the Erie County Bar, secretary of the State Bar, president of the board of trustees of the Buffalo Orphan Asylum, and three-term president of the University Club. His sister was the wife of attor-

12.27 ❦ Loran L. Lewis, Jr., *PBHS*, 17(1913), xix.

59 *M&FH*, 2:221-223; Hill, *op. cit.*, 4:289; Horton, 3:262-263.
60 *PBHS*, 30(1930), 268.

ney Austin Roe Preston of #1069 Delaware. By 1920 Loran Lewis had moved to #107 Oakland Place. After an illness of five years he died at sixty-five in 1930. His long-time friend, Dr. Samuel Holmes of Westminster, conducted the funeral.[61]

Following Lewis at #1093 in 1923 was Henry Adsit Bull, born in Buffalo in 1873. His father was Henry Bull and his grandfather, Jabez Bull of #6 Delaware, a leather merchant and president of Western Savings Bank. Henry Bull attended P.S. 14, the Heathcote School, and Harvard, class of 1895. He was a captain during Spanish American War but does not appear to have left the States. His wife was the former Mary Stewart. Bull was an instructor at the U.B. law school 1903-1906, and a law partner of Ansley Wilcox. A Republican, he was an avid supporter of Theodore Roosevelt, and broke with the G.O.P. and voted Bull Moose in 1912. Bull was a Mason and a devout member of Trinity Church where he chaired the Committee on the State of the Church of the Western New York Diocese of the Episcopal Church. In 1920 he was living at #1171 Delaware and in 1933 moved to Columbia Road in Wanakah where he practiced law, relying on the telephone. There he was injured in a car accident, from the results of which he died in April 1956, having been a lawyer for over fifty years.[62]

At #1103 Delaware north of Loran Lewis there lived in 1880 James H. Goldsborough, a Maryland-born oil man. He was followed during the next decade by Edward Wingate Hatch who had been born in Friendship in Allegany County November in 1852. His grandfather had fought in the Revolution and his father had fought and died in the Civil War. Goldsborough attended public school and worked as a blacksmith. He read law in the offices of an attorney in Attica and while clerking in the post office from 1872 to 1876, when he was admitted to the bar. He practiced law in Buffalo 1876-1886, including five years as District Attorney of Erie County 1881-1886. He sat 1887-1895 on the Superior Court of Buffalo. However he was appointed by Governor Morton appellate judge for the Second Department for five years at the beginning of 1896. Hatch died on 1924 long after he had moved from #1103.[63] At that address in 1905 lived Susan Butts, age thirty-two and probably a widow, with two young children. In 1925 it was the home of Henry J. Jacobs, English-born president of the Buffalo Lounge Company, with his wife, daughter, son-in-law, and a single domestic. By 1920 it was the residence of forty-six year old Doctor Joseph P. Burke, a nationally known surgeon, his wife, eight children, and two domestics. Burke had been born in 1873, on Louisiana Street in the First Ward. His parents were John Burke, a building contractor, and the former Elizabeth Murphy. His was educated at Saint Bridget's parochial school, Saint Joseph's Collegiate Institute, Manhattan, class of 1893, and the U.B. medical school from which he graduated in 1896. In 1901 he married Evelyn Mooney, and they had five sons and four daughters. Burke opened an office on South Division Street where he practiced medicine for two years. There followed a year of postgraduate training at the Vienna General Hospital in Austria, after which he returned to Buffalo and joined the staff of Emer-

61 *BEN*, January 4, 1930.
62 *CE*, April 30, 1956.

gency Hospital for a year. In 1905 he again opened his own office where until 1910 he specialized in obstetrics. In 1910 he spent six months studying surgery at the University of Chicago's medical school. In 1916 he became chief of staff at Sisters but left to join the army in 1918 as a major. After six months at Camp Jackson, Columbia, South Carolina, he was mustered out at Christmas 1918. He returned to his practice in Buffalo and to his prewar job as chief of staff at Sisters. In 1921 he spoke to an international medical congress at Carlsbad. In 1929 he again went to Vienna where his son, Doctor John Burke, was studying nose and throat surgery. Back in Buffalo he opened Central Park Clinic, but had to retire due to illness in 1930 after having performed thousands of operations. He died in 1934.[64]

Alonzo R. James, secretary of Century Milling and later vice president of the Niagara Falls Milling, resided at #1105 in 1891. He had been born in Chillicothe, Ohio, in 1843 but as a boy moved to Western Massachusetts with his father and thence to Boston where he was initiated into the mysteries of milling. He married Sarah O'Donnell of Chelsea, Massachusetts. They had two sons and a daughter, Margaret, an alumna of Wellesley. A resident of Buffalo for over twenty years and president of the Chamber of Commerce, Alonzo James died on in 1908 at sixty-five.[65] His widow lived on at #1105 until at least 1920 when she was seventy-seven. She was alone but enjoyed the ministrations of two domestics.

By 1925 #1105 was the home of Albert H. Garvin who had been born in Joliet, Illinois, and graduated from the Yale Medical School in 1903. He decided early on to specialize in tuberculosis, and went to Raybrook Sanitarium in the Adirondacks, the first state supported TB facility. Within a year he had been named superintendent, a post he held until 1919 when he left to study the effects of the World War I on French civilians. From there he returned to America to supervise the construction of the Detroit Sanitarium where he was superintendent until 1923 when he came to Buffalo. In 1928 he became president of the TB Association, formed to unify the efforts of local groups fighting the disease. This led to improvements in Meyer Memorial, the J. N. Adam Memorial Hospital in Perrysburg, and the Black Rock Clinic. He was president for twenty-three years until his death in 1951.[66]

12.28 ❦ John L. Clawson, Warren, *op. cit.*, p. 81.

William T. Jebb, who lived at #1109 in the 1900s, was born in Buffalo in 1857 on the site of the third Buffalo Club.

63 Men of New York, 1:249-250.

64 *BEN*, December 14, 1934.

65 *Commercial*, July 9, 1908.

66 *BEN*, December 20, 1950.

At different times he was a manufacturer, a promoter, and a capitalist. He was quite successful since he had taken early retirement by forty-three. He died at sixty-nine in 1926.[67]

About John L. Clawson(12.28), 1917 president of the Buffalo Club who followed Jebb at #1109, the club historian writes:

> At this time, Clawson was president of the well-entrenched wholesale dry-goods firm of Clawson & Wilson Company. He was born in Campbell, Steuben County, on March 17, 1865, and came to Buffalo in 1891. He was first associated with a manufacturer of men's clothing, but soon found a partner in James P. Wilson. Aside from business — he was also a longtime director of the Marine Bank — he was well known as a collector of rare books, autographs, and manuscript[s]. The collection was sold before his death on November 27, 1933, in Doctors' Hospital, New York City, where he had lived his last two years. Twice married, he long lived at 1109 Delaware Avenue.[68]

Daniel Good, a sometime partner of Seymour Knox in the five and-ten-cent-store business was living at #864 Delaware prior to his death in 1922. However in 1915 he had been briefly at #1115 Delaware(12.29). Later, it was the winter home of the former Florence Goodyear and her second husband, Charles Daniels, before they acquired Daniel's grandfather's house at #787.

12.29 ❦ Number 1115 Delaware, photo by author, spring 1999.

In the early 1920s #1115 was the home of Harry Thorpe Vars, born in 1864, in Port Colborne. He came to Buffalo where he rose to secretary-treasurer of Foster-Milburn, the patent medicine company of Orin Foster of #891 Delaware. Vars was also secretary of Foster McClelland, secretary of Sterling Engine, director of the Union Fire Insurance, president of the Main Street Association, and past president of the Buffalo Advertising Club. He was a Republican, a member of Westminster, and a world traveler. On a trip to Japan he met with an accident from the effects of which he died in Kobe in February 1926.[69]

Vars' son Addison succeeded his father at #1115. Addison had attended Elmwood, Nichols, Phillips Andover, and Yale's Sheffield Scientific School. In April 1917 he enlisted in the naval reserve, and after sea duty as a petty officer was commissioned an ensign in June 1918. He married Cadis Lindsley, a Texas girl, in New York. Back in Buffalo he became associated with the E. P. Remington Advertising Agency. He incorporated the company in 1925, became president, and in 1927 changed the name to Addison Vars, Inc., with offices in Buffalo, Rochester, and New York. As befitted an advertising man,

67 *Courier*, June 27, 1926.
68 Warren, *op. cit.*, p. 81.
69 *BEN*, July 14, 1951.

Addison Vars belonged to a record twenty-two social clubs in Buffalo, Rochester, and New York. Like his father, he was a Republican and a member of Westminster.[70] His monument is the four-story Art Decco Vars Building at #344-352 Delaware designed by Bley & Lyman.

At #1119 from the 1880s until about 1905 resided attorney George S. Potter. He was born in Gowanda in 1847, attended school until he was fourteen, and somehow managed to enlist as a regimental clerk with the 10th New York Cavalry. After a short time in uniform he was invalided home and came to Buffalo. He read law at various times, passed the bar, lectured on law at Cornell, became senior member of Potter & Wright, and belonged to the Buffalo and Saturn clubs. He spent the last seven years of his life in archeological research in Rome. He died at his home in 1923.[71]

Next at #1119 by 1915 was Nelson S. Taylor, a lumber dealer, who lived there a few years and died elsewhere in 1952. The next resident, James D. Warren, was a recapitulation of Western New York history. His great-grandfather, Orsamus Warren, one of the pioneers of the area, settled in Bennington in what became Wyoming County. At twenty-three he moved to Wales Hollow and opened the first store there. In 1827 he moved to Clarence, where he farmed and set up another general store. His son, James D. Warren, was born in 1823. When the family moved to Clarence, James was two. As a boy he attended school and helped his father on the farm and at the store. While still a minor he made a tour of the ante-bellum South and spent about a year at Natchez. Back in Clarence he served several terms as Supervisor. In 1854 at thirty-one he was elected to a three-year term as County Treasurer and then became Clerk of the Board of Supervisors. In 1861 Warren together with Joseph Wheeler and Joseph Candee purchased the *Commercial Advertiser*, and Warren settled down to his life work as newspaper publisher. In 1862 Wheeler and Warren bought out Candee's interest and admitted James N. Matthews to the firm that, with Wheeler's retirement in 1864, became Matthews & Warren. In 1877 Warren bought out Matthews and became sole proprietor and publisher of the *Commercial*, which became the leading Republican paper in Western New York. Warren served regularly as member of the state central committee and delegate to state and national nominating conventions. He was also president of White's Bank.[72] He died 1886, and control of the *Commercial* passed to his son Orsamus who died in 1892. The James D. Warren who resided at #1119 from about 1910 until the First World War was Orsamus' only son. Born in Buffalo in 1879, James attended the Hill School, Pottstown, Pennsylvania, and married Eleanor Bissell, daughter of People's Bank president, Arthur Bissell, and the former Fanny Castle of #950 Delaware. This made Warren the brother-in-law of Bradley Goodyear. During the second decade of the twentieth century the Warrens resided at #1275 Delaware just south of Lafayette. James controlled the *Commercial* for twenty-one years until 1926 when it was sold. Meanwhile he moved to #1119 Delaware and joined the investment firm of J. C. Dann & Co. for which he worked for eighteen years. He was also a trustee of Western

70 Wilner, *op. cit.*, 4:296-299.
71 *BEN*, February, 28, 1923.
72 Smith, *op. cit.*, 2:110.

12.30 ❦ Number 1125 Delaware, photo by author, spring 1999.

Savings. He enjoyed his numerous trips to Europe, sometimes staying only a week. The Warrens had a home at Bay Beach in Canada, and James belonged to Cherry Hill, the Canoe Club, and Saturn. On a cold night in November 1938 he and Elizabeth were involved in a two-car accident at Starin and Parkside. Both were hurled from their car and Elizabeth was mortally injured.[73] Her husband survived and died in 1944.[74]

Henry C. French resided at #1125(12.30) from about 1884 until 1900. He was born in Buffalo about 1848, educated in public school, and manufactured hoops and staves. Much canal freight was transported in barrels, so this led him to canal boating, which in turn led him to lake-borne commerce. He organized and was the sole head of Union Transit, which soon had offices in nearly every city on the Lakes. In 1902 he moved to Pasadena where he had a grand mansion built, leaving three sons in charge of business. In 1904 the whole family went west and Union was dissolved. In his younger days French was an avid sportsman, active in several game societies. Every fall he led a hunting party to northern Minnesota. Over the years he had amassed large holdings in downtown Buffalo properties. He died in Pasadena in 1912, survived by his wife, the former Eva Shattuck of Buffalo.[75]

Under the eye of their grandaunt, Agnes Demarest, brothers Daniel Willard Streeter and Edward Streeter, moved into #1125 after the departure of the Frenches. Daniel had been born in 1883 in Highland Park, Illinois. He attended the Hill School and Harvard where he majored in mining and graduated in 1907. He began his career with Buffalo Weaving and Belting. In 1908 he married Gertrude Norton and moved away from #1125. That year he was made treasurer of the company of which he was to be president 1917-1922. The *News,* which had hailed him as "Buffalo's #1 Citizen," said:

> Mr. Streeter was a tremendously successful business executive as well as an explorer, big-game hunter, and author before he entered civic life. He rehabilitated Buffalo's Civil Service system after it fell into disrepute during the city affairs investigation of the late 1930s. During World War II, he headed six of Buffalo's seven bond drives, raising nearly $1 billion for the war effort. To spur Boy Scout troops in one house-to-house canvas, he offered as prizes six Nandi tribal hunting spears from his African safaris. The seventh and final war-loan drive he ushered in with a big "Here's Your Infantry" show in civic stadium

73 *CE*, November 15, 1938.
74 *BEN*, September 16, 1944.
75 *CA*, July 11, 1912.

May 14, 1945.

Mr. Streeter was city comptroller for eight months in 1947, named by unanimous vote of the Common Council to succeed George W. Wanamaker, who had moved to County Hall to head the newly created Sales Tax Division. In a typical move, he also directed the Community Chest campaign that year. He said that he'd agreed to accept the arduous posts months before he was called to the comptroller job, and he didn't want "to let the organization down."

Daniel Streeter helped explore Greenland's icy wastes in 1926 as a member of the American Museum of Science's expedition headed by Capt. Bob Bartlett, who had been Admiral Robert F. Peary's skipper on his successful dash to the North Pole. At one time Mr. Streeter was shipwrecked 700 miles from the North Pole at the northern tip of Baffin's Bay. He finally got back to camp - bringing two polar bear cubs as pets. The experience resulted in a book, An Ar[c]tic Rodeo, published in 1928. In between, Mr. Streeter sandwiched a half-dozen pack animal trips through out-of-the-way parts of the American West.

The onset of the depression brought Mr. Streeter into Buffalo's civic life. He began by supervising the "Man-a-Block" relief scheme in 1931. For five years he headed the succession of alphabetically named relief agencies here. He considered his task completed when the County Welfare Board was reorganized in 1938 to include city relief on a permanent, professionally operated basis.

During the depression, Mr. Streeter resumed his business activities as vice president of Niagara Share Corp. He owned and operated Gredag Inc., of Niagara Falls, distributor of industrial greases and lubricants, during World War II. Mr. Streeter at various times also had been a director of McCall Corp., magazine publishers, a director for more than 15 years of Schoellkopf, Hutton, & Pomeroy, investment bankers, part owner of Buffalo Wholesale Hardware Co., and a trustee for 17 years of Erie County Savings Bank.

Daniel Willard Streeter suffered a fatal heart attack in the Saturn Club, on July 27, 1964. He was seventy-nine years old.[76]

Edward Streeter, Daniel's younger brother, was born in 1891. During his youth in Buffalo he was an avid reader and wrote fiction before he was ten. He edited the school newspaper and his class yearbook at Pomfret School in Connecticut, and at Harvard was editor of the *Lampoon* and scenarist for the Hasty Pudding performance. Graduating in 1914 he became a reporter for the *Buffalo Express*. He was among the young Buffalo bluebloods William Donovan induced to join Troop I, First Cavalry, 27th Division, and saw active duty on the Mexican border in 1916. A series of mock serious letters composed by Streeter purporting to have been written by a commonsensical but barely literate private from Mexico and later from France to his girlfriend were published as *Dere Mable: Love Letters from a Rookie*, which sold over 750,000 copies. It was a forerunner of *See Here, Private Hargrove!* during World War II. After the first war Streeter returned to Buffalo where in 1919 he married Charlotte Warren. They had four children.[77] Streeter also had an interesting post-war life:

He sought a career as a professional writer, but with initially disappointing results. His efforts to produce material as a house author for *Collier's* magazine culminated in his

76 *BEN*, July 28, 1964.

77 Ray Arthur Swanson, "Streeter, Edward," *ANB*, 21:23-24. Swanson states that "during his childhood in Buffalo, New York, Streeter made considerable use of his affluent parents' extensive library." I could find no mention of Harvey B. Streeter and wife in the Buffalo city directories 1891-1915.

publication of a short story in, not *Collier's*, but the *Saturday Evening Post*, and in his getting locked into short-story writing against his preference for other forms of narrative.

Although he eventually gained substantial writer's earnings beyond *Dere Mable*, it was as a banker that Streeter gained a financially secure life. He found a position with Bankers Trust Company in New York and served as assistant vice president from 1921 to 1929. From 1929 to 1930 he was a partner at Blake Brothers on the New York Stock Exchange. In 1931 he became vice president of the Fifth Avenue Bank, which later merged with the Bank of New York. During the depression of the 1930s he briefly revived his "Dere Mable" letters for, and contributed articles to *Redbook* magazine.[78]

In 1938 his *Daily Except Sundays or, What Every Commuter Should Know* was published by Simon & Schuster. It showed the author to be a poor man's Robert Benchley. In 1949 Simon & Schuster published Streeter's masterpiece, *Father of the Bride*, which became the book for the hit movie of the same name starring Spencer Tracy. After Streeter retired from the bank in 1956, he wrote three novels, none of which equaled in sales or acclaim his earlier works. A member of New York society, he belonged to the Century Association, the Harvard Club, the Coffee House Club, and the Union Club. He was also 1965-1971 on Harvard's board of overseers. He died in New York in 1976.[79]

The earliest resident at #1131 was Charles B. Germain, scion of family which came to the area before the War of 1812. He was born in Buffalo in 1844, graduated from Hamilton College in 1866, read law in the office of Laning & Miller, passed the bar in 1868, and practiced law until he became judge of the United States District Court in 1884. In 1881 he had married Mary J. Beggs of Cleveland. He belonged to the Buffalo and Falconwood clubs and to the Trinity vestry. His son, Edward B. Germain, was president of Dunlop Tire.[80] Charles Germain died in 1926.

By 1900 Elgood Channing Lufkin was resident at #1131(12.31). He had been born in Springfield, Massachusetts, in 1864, and attended high school in Titusville where his father had gone seeking oil. After graduating from M.I.T. in 1886, Elwood worked as an engineer at Holly Manufacturing in Lockport until 1889. From then until 1895 he was chief engineer of Independent Pipe Line, Lima, Ohio. Meanwhile in 1890 he had married Lula Moulton of Emporia, Kansas. From 1895 until 1908 he was general manager of the Snow Steam Pump Works on the corner of Snow and Roesser Avenues in Buffalo. In 1909 he went to Houston and became vice president of the Texas Company, an oil-drilling firm. In 1901 an oil strike in Spindeltop had marked the beginning of an

12.31 ❦ Number 1131 Delaware, taken by author, spring 1999.

78 *Ibid.*
79 *Ibid.*
80 *Times*, August 3, 1924.

oil boom there. Lufkin was getting into Texas oil on the ground floor. In 1911 he was made president of the Texas Company of New York. He became president of the latter 1913-1920, right through World War I. During the war he was a member of the sub committee on oil and metals of the Council of National Defense. During his presidency his company's name became Texaco. From 1920 until 1926 when he retired Lufkin was chairman of the board and of its executive committee. Republican, Protestant, and a Mason, he died at his estate in Rye, New York, in 1935.[81]

After Lufkin's departure for Texas until the early 1920s #1131 was the home of Edward L. Koons, who had been born circa 1862, attended P.S. 13 and Central High where he was a schoolmate of Francis Folsom, future wife of Grover Cleveland. Koons read law in the offices of William H. Glenney and married Anna Hengerer, daughter of Hengerer's founder. Koons and his brother Henry bought up East Side land and quickly resold it, invested the profits in gold mines in Ontario and merged them into Sylvanite Gold Mines of which Edward was president. They managed Grover Cleveland's successful mayoral campaign and were prominent in the local end of his campaign for governor and later president. Edward founded and was president of Abstract Title and Mortgage, director for over fifty years of Buffalo Insurance, first vice president of the Buffalo Savings, and in 1920 president of the Chamber of Commerce. He was a member of the Church of the Redeemer (Lutheran), and of the Automobile, Country, Buffalo Athletic clubs, and for forty-five years of the Buffalo Club. Koons died at eighty-four in the Park Lane Apartments in 1946.[82]

Leonard A. Yerkes, a manufacturer, his wife Helen, and five children lived at #1131 in 1925, with three live-in servants. By 1931 it had become the home of Doctor George T. Mosley, formerly of #202 Delaware. He died in 1935 and his wife Isabelle continued there for a short time. For many years the southeast corner of West Ferry and Delaware was vacant. However by 1912 it had become the site of two brick and stone luxury apartment houses, #1141 called Hill-Crest, and shortly thereafter #1149, called Del-Nord. They were only three stories high and contained only two apartments on each floor for a total of six, ground was left open for lawns and gardens, and most of the families made the annual *Buffalo Blue Book*. For example, Henry Adsit Bull, who in 1915 would be residing at #1093 Delaware, was to be found in 1912 at #1141; George Rumsey Howard, who grew up at #806 Delaware lived at #1141 in 1916.

81 *CE*, October 9, 1935; *Who Was Who in America*, 1:753; *International Directory of Company Histories* (Chicago and London: Saint James Press, 54 + vols.1988), 4:551.
82 *CE*, February 25, 1946.

CHAPTER

13 BRYANT TO FERRY: *West Side*

The map for this chapter is figure 12.1. The base date of this map is 1905 as it was in chapter 12.

1870

BRYANT STREET

928 Henry H. Otis 36 NY bookseller
Persico Otis 37 NY *ux.*
Charles Otis 19 NY school
William Otis 8 NY school
Eliza Perrini 17 NY school

938 William Hodge 65 NY retired farmer
Arletta Hodge 53 NY *ux.*
William Hodge 19 at home
Willard Hodge 17 NY school
Patience Hodge 17 NY school
Patience Hodge 76 Mass.
Kate Swan NY

HODGE AVENUE

950 Daniel B. Castle 55 Conn. jeweler
Fanny Castle 53 NY *ux.*
Thomas Castle 22 NY store clerk
Fanny Castle 18 NY at home
Mary Castle 11 NY school
Kate Sade 28 NY boarder
Jonathan Mackey 21 NY coachman

980 James M. Johnson 43 Maine proprietor *Courier*
Aloisa Johnson 36 NY *ux.*
Mabelle Johnson 14 NY school
Mary Barnes 17 Canada West

1880

BRYANT STREET

928 Henry Otis 46 NY bookseller
Teresa Otis 47 NY *ux.*
Charles Otis 20 NY clerk
Willis Otis 19 NY clerk
Margaret Mullen 35 NY

HODGE AVENUE

950 Thaddeus Davis 47 NY attorney
Anna Davis 34 NY *ux.*
Henry Davis 25 son law student
Mary Davis 20 daughter at home
George Davis 17 NY son school
Morris Davis 18 NY son school
John Davis 13 NY son school
Bridget Fitzpatrick 40 Ireland
Mary O'Brien 25 Ireland
George Cleaver 40 England coachman

958 Willard Brown 34 NY lumber dealer
Emma Brown 34 NY *ux.*
Lillia Brown 10 NY daughter school
Helen Brown 8 NY daughter school
Arthur Brown 6 NY son school
Harry Brown 4 NY
Hattie Bryler 71 NY mother-in-law
Hanna Roach 40 Ireland
Henry Cross 22 Ireland coachman

978 George Haines 46 NY lumber dealer
Helen Haines 36 NY *ux.*

980 Sarah Becker 51 NY teacher
Anson Pierce 19 NY nephew bookkeeper
Jerome Pierce 17 NY nephew
Tammy Pierce 15 NY niece school

Mary Kaner 22 NY

990 Edward J. Dann 38 NY bank secretary
Jane Dann 30 NY *ux.*
Edward Dann 6 NY school
Walter Dann 5 NY son
Hannah Webster 54 boarder
Elizabeth Jones 19 England
Frances Barrows 20 NY

WEST UTICA STREET

1022 Callista Phelps 48 Illinois housekeeper
Marie Phelps 21 NY at home
Calvin Phelps 19 NY school
Andrew Stolzer 33 Prussia
Bridget Sheehan 15 Ireland

1040 Sarah N. Becker 47 NY housekeeper
Mary Pierce 17 NY school
Warren Pierce 13 NY school
Cora Pierce 14 NY school
Charles Pierce 12 NY school
Anson Pierce 10 NY school
Jerome Pierce 8 NY school
Fanny Pierce 6 NY school
Grace Pierce 3 NY
Kate Ramsey 22 Canada West
Rosa Jon 21 Prussia

Grace Pierce 12 NY niece
Caroline Morris 45 NY sister at home
Margaret Patterson 16 NY
Kate Riley 41 NY housekeeper
Emma Riley 14 NY daughter school
Isaac Riley 11 NY son school
Kate Riley 9 NY daughter school
Margaret Hens 16 Ireland
Mary Hens 20 Ireland

990 Edward Dann 48 banker
Jane Dann 40 NY *ux.*
Walter Dann 14 NY son school
Edward Dann 16 NY son school
Jessie Dann 13 NY son school
Helen Stephenson 16 NY niece school
Carrie Kress 23 NY
Margaret McMullen 35 Ireland

WEST UTICA STREET

1008 W. Eugene Richmond 32 NY ship owner
Clara Richmond 30 NY *ux.*
Watsies Richmond 7 NY son school
Jennie Richmond 5 NY daughter school
Adelaide Richmond 3 NY son
Clara Richmond 1 month NY
Maggie McMahon 20 Ireland
Christina Davy 20 Ireland
Julia Duggan 14 Ireland
Tillie Coopman 38 Scotland
William Walters 26 England coachman
Richard Laverack 18 England

1022 Mrs. Calvin M. Phelps 57 NY widow
Calvin Phelps 24 NY son
Harriet Trippelet 55 Canada cook
Ellis Riley 12 Canada school
Joseph Kaufman 28 Switzerland

1040 Ray V. Pierce MD 40 NY
Mary Jane Pierce 38 Ohio *ux.*
Matthew V. Pierce 16 Pa. son school
Ida Belle Pierce 9 NY daughter school
Hugh Clay Pierce 4 NY son
Maggie Scheitel 26 NY
Bridget Larkin 21 Ireland

Charles Cassidy 38 NY coachman
Minnie Cassidy 29 NY *ux.*
Charles Cassidy 4 NY son
Samuel Cassidy 1 NY son
Mary Wade 60 NY mother-in-law

1058 William Hamlin 28 NY grape sugar manufacturer
Kate Hamlin 26 NY *ux.*.
Katie Hamlin 4 NY daughter
Mary McMahon 25 Canada

BUTLER STREET

1080 John Stephenson 35 NY jeweler
Hannah Stephenson 30 NY *ux.*
George Stephenson 11 NY school
Thomas Stephenson 10 NY school
Jennie Stephenson 8 NY school
Helen Stephenson 6 NY school
John Stephenson 5 NY school
Bessie Stephenson 2 NY
Webster Stephenson 2 months NY
Mary Hinckley 21 England
Minnie Betz 21 NY

WEST FERRY STREET ❦ End of Block

Rosa Leen 30 Ireland
Philip Jones 30 Ireland coachman
Bridget Riley 24
Bessie Sweeney 25

BUTLER STREET

1094 Augustus H. Field NY 43 milliner
Theresia Field 27 Pa. *ux.*
Lulu B. Field 7 NY daughter
Anna Paff 15 NY

1106 J. B. Holmes 72 NY planing mill proprietor
James S. Holmes 22 NY son machinist
Emma S. Holmes 26 NY daughter
Martha Armstrong 28 Canada
Eddie Cox 15 England

1120 Arioch Lapham 60 NY wholesale grocer
Sylvia Lapham 62 NY *ux.*
Ella Caroline Lapham 28 NY daughter at home
Deborah Lapham 86 NY mother-in-law
Jennie Gillies 19 NY

1132 John Wayland 43 Conn. banker
Mary Wayland 37 Conn. *ux.*
John Wayland 1 NY son
Richard Wayland 9 NY son
Fredericka Gerber 24 NY

WEST FERRY STREET ❦ End of Block

1891

BRYANT STREET

916 Nelson Holland 62 Mass. lumber

928 H. H. Otis books 288 Main
Charles C. Otis *ibid.*

938 Charles W. Pardee Penokee Lumber Company of Tonawanda

1900

BRYANT STREET

916 Nelson Holland 71 Mass. lumber
Helen Lee Holland 24 NY daughter
Grace Holland 27 NY daughter
Nelson Clarke Holland 25 NY son lumber
Ida Bundschue NY 23

938 Charles W. Pardee 49 NY banker
Georgia Pardee 42 NY *ux.*
Margaret Dawson 35 NY
Jack Forney 35 England
Sean Eaton 35 Ireland

HODGE AVENUE

950 Arthur D. Bissell vice-president Peoples Bank
2357 Washington

958 Eugenia Comstock
Marion Comstock

960 William C. R. Hazard Hazard & Arend real estate
W. E. Richmond shipowner 18 Chapin

964 L. F. W. Arend real estate 1 Austin Building

990 Edward S. Dann secretary & treasurer
National Savings Bank 308 Main
Edward W. Dann Star Oil Company
Jessie C. Dann Lee Holland Co. planing mill

WEST UTICA STREET

1014 Harry Hamlin vice president American Glucose

1022 John Satterfield president Union Oil Company
Charles Tuttle coachman

HODGE AVENUE

950 Arthur D. Bissell 56 NY bank president
Fanny Bissell 48 NY *ux.*
Howard Bissell 20 NY son school
Raymond Bissell 18 son school
Douglas Bissell 16 NY son school
Mary Eleanor Bissell 23 NY daughter
Jeanette Bissell 14 NY daughter school
Clementine Kaufer 19 Germany
Margaret Sheedy 35 NY
Emily Goergens 41 Germany

958 Lorraine Richmond 51 NY widow
John Richmond NY son clerk

960 Louise Hazard 65 NY widow
Carrie L. Hazard 46 NY daughter
William C. Hazard 27 Canada son
Agnes Hazard 25 Virginia his wife
Eugene Hazard 32 Canada cousin agent
Alberta Healey 20 NY
George Wates (black) 20 NY laborer

964 Louis F. W. Arend 63 Germany
Mary Arend 61 NY *ux.*
Margaret Learshald 24 NY
Dick Smith (black) 31 NY laborer
George Johnson 34 NY laborer

WEST UTICA STREET

1014 Harry Hamlin 44 NY retired
Grace Hamlin 42 NY *ux.*
Chauncey Hamlin 19 NY son
Bessie McIntire 36 Ireland
Mary Young 47 NY
Anna B. Sticht 31 NY
Nellie Diggins 17 Ireland
William Massie 39 Ireland coachman
Katherine Massie 40 NY *ux.*
W. Jerome Massie 10 NY son
Mary B. Massie 10 NY daughter
Leo J. Massie 4 NY son

1022 Mrs. John Satterfield 47 Pa. widow
John Satterfield 20 Pa. son
Mary Satterfield 20 Pa. daughter
Frances Achmald 21 Germany
Delia O'Day 22 Scotland
Mary Walsh 26 England
Robert Lennie 67 Scotland coachman
Barbara Lennie 34 Scotland *ux.*
Elizabeth Lennie 6 NY daughter

1040 Charles A. Sweet president Third National Bank Mrs. James G. Dickie George Brown gardener	1040 Charles A. Sweet 64 Mass. president Third National Bank Fannie Sweet 55 NY *ux.* Winifred Sweet 29 NY daughter Charlotte P. Sweet 18 NY daughter Charles A. Sweet Jr. 14 NY son Olive P. Dickie NY 70 aunt Kate Duggan 29 Ireland Margaret Riordan 24 Ireland Walter Armstrong 54 Canada coachman Mary Armstrong 55 England *ux.* Alexander Armstrong 24 Canada son Frederick Armstrong 21 NY son
1058 William Hamlin treasurer Amercan Glucose Company Richard Johnson coachman William Lee coachman	1058 William Hamlin 50 NY retired Kate Hamlin 47 NY *ux.* Sarah Hamlin 20 NY daughter Susan Hamlin 15 NY daughter school Mary Fassnacht 26 NY Katherine Miller 19 NY Mary Koerner 19 NY Katherine Sweeney 29 NY Mary Mordock 47 Africa
LEXINGTON AVENUE	LEXINGTON AVENUE
1080 Frederick J. Wheeler assistant editor *Buffalo Express*	1080 Charles Bingham 56 NY iron forge Margaret Bingham 50 England *ux.* Anna O'Connor 39 NY Maria Coleman 28 Ireland Jennie Langford 18 Ireland Bernard McCabe 28 Ireland coachman
1100 Emory F. Close attorney	1100 Norman E. Mack 44 Canada editor *Buffalo Times* Harriet Mack 26 NY *ux.* Norma E. Mack 5 NY daughter Harriet J. Mack 3 NY daughter Frances C. Taggart 47 mother-in-law William Kernahan 40 NY collector Harriet Jacobs 20 Germany Henry Edward 40 Germany coachman
HIGHLAND AVENUE	HIGHLAND AVENUE
1106 Mr. Libertus Van Bokkelen	
1120 Edward N. Cook Frank S. McGraw lumber	1120 Christian Klinck 67 Germany meat packer Albert Klinck 29 NY son clerk Alice E. Klinck 25 NY daughter Julia Pfeiffer 36 NY daughter Henry W. Pfeiffer 42 NY brother-in-law Hazel E. Pfeiffer 14 NY granddaughter Julia Stahlin 30 Germany Vera Fierschbach 29 Canada Jacob Machter 38 Germany coachman
1132 John V. Wayland secretary Buffalo Savings Bank Edward E. Wayland clerk Bank of Commerce	1132 John Wayland 63 Germany bank official Mary S. Wayland 56 Conn. *ux.*

John L. Wayland clerk Buffalo Savings Bank

WEST FERRY STREET ❦ End of Block

Edward E. Wayland 27 NY son bank clerk
James O'Rourke 57 Ireland coachman
Mary Schumacher 45 Germany
Leona Watson 26 Canada

WEST FERRY STREET ❦ End of Block

1905

BRYANT STREET

916 Nelson Holland 75 Mass. retired
Jennie Miller 40

938 Charles W. Pardee 52 financie
Georgia Pardee 47 *ux.*
Rose Whitney 35
Margaret H. ? 27
Jennie Patterson

HODGE AVENUE

950 Arthur D. Bissell 61 president Peoples Bank
Fanny Bissell 52 *ux.*
Eleanor Bissell 28 daughter
Howard Bissell 26 son
Raymond Bissell 24 son
Douglas Bissell 21 son
Jeanette Bissell 19 daughter
Lloyd Bissell 13 son school
M. Sheedy 35
L. Donovan 30
Grace Smith 28

958 Loraine Richmond 68 widow
Mary Daily 24 Ireland
S. Litzman 47 Switzerland

960 Louise Hazard 70
Carrie Hazard 45 daughter
? 45 male boarder
Leo Winkler 27 boarder
Rosa Zappender 23
Lucy Tee 26 Canada

964 Louis F. W. Arend 68 real estate
Mary L. Arend 54 *ux.*
? Groll 20

976 John H. Baker 31 real estate
Blanche Baker 25 *ux.*
Francis Baker 28 attorney
Sarah H. Baker 3 daughter
Jean Baker 2 daughter
Margaret Remen 35
Anna Hutt 29
James Wilson 42 Scotland coachman

1915

BRYANT STREET

916 Nelson Holland 86 Mass. retired
Jennie Miller 50

938 Georgia Pardee 60
Allan Pardee 9 son school
Bertha Bell 30 Canada nurse
Katherine Caufield 27
Rose Whitney 45
Charles C. Nagel 45 Germany chauffeur
Betty Nagel 53 Germany *ux.*

HODGE AVENUE

950 Arthur D. Bissell 71 banker
Fannie C. Bissell 62 *ux.*
Arthur D. Bissell Jr. 3 son Frontier Iron
Lloyd Bissell 21 son school
Elizabeth Broad 60 Canada
Maragaret Sheedy 42
Marie Leontin 42 France

958 Lorraine Richmond 78
Katherine Crawford 35 England

964 Mary L. Arend 64
Margaret Leupold 41

976 John H. Baker 42 investments
Blanche H. Baker 39 *ux.*
Sarah H. Baker 13 daughter school
Jean W. Baker 12 daughter school
John H. Baker Jr. 9 son school
Edward F. Baker 7 son school
Barbara Baker daughter 2
Katherine Eagleton 20 Ireland
Celia Goodwin 35 Ireland

990 *North Presbyterian Church*

WEST UTICA STREET

1014 Harry Hamlin 44 retired
Grace Hamlin 46 *ux.*
William Davison 20 Canada butler
Thomas Waters England 25 butler
Mary Morgan 25
Alice Nolan 25
Lizzie Connors 35 cook
Mary Grerson 30 Ireland
William Nelligan 40 coachman
Peter Grayson 24 Ireland chauffeur

1022 Mrs. John Satterfield 55
George Hanson 30 gardener
Agnes Hanson 27 *ux.*
George Hanson 4 son
Mary Hanson 2 daughter

1040 Mrs. Charles A. Sweet 50
Charles J. Sweet 19 son student
Charlotte Sweeet 22 daughter
Oliva Dickie 70 aunt
Anna More 35
Nellie Denby 42 laundress
Anna Chadwick 23 England
Thomas Chadwick 57 England coachman
Emma Chadwick 51 England *ux.*
Frank Chadwick 22 son stableman

1058 William Hamlin 45 retired
Kate Hamlin 42 *ux.*
Susan Hamlin 20 daughter
Alice Kent 40 Canada cook
Carrie Walker England waitress
Kate Onions 30 Canada parlor maid
Patrick Connelly 40 Ireland coachman
Margaret Connelly 35 Ireland *ux.*
Henry Gerard 24 coachman

LEXINGTON AVENUE

990 *North Presbyterian Church*

WEST UTICA STREET

1014 George F. Rand 48 banker
Vina S. Rand 48 *ux.*
George F. Rand Jr. 22 son school
Evelyn R. Rand 16 daughter
Gretchen Rand 13 daughter school
Calvin G. Rand 9 son
Nora Quinlivan 58 Ireland

1022 John M. Satterfield 37 banker
Rachel P. Satterfield 34 *ux.*
Elaine Satterield 13 school
John P. Satterfield 9 son
Abbey Kelleher 27 Ireland
Anna Laughlin 26
Louise Reinhart 26 Switzerland
Helen Neville 46 England
John Morgan 46 chauffeur
Mary F. Morgan 47 *ux.*
Olive F. Morgan 22 daughter nurse
Harold L. Morgan 17 son school
Grace Morgan 7 daughter

1040 George A. Mitchell 41
Sarah H. Mitchell 12 daughter school
William H. Mitchell 12 son school
Thomas W. Mitchell 12 son
Kate L. Mitchell 6 daughter
Anna Meid 34
Elizabeth Richards 34 England
Emily Nichels 38 German
Nellie Ellicott 30 Scotland
Anna J. Smith 45 nurse
Charles J. Shirley 46 chauffeur
Emma Shirley 52 *ux.*

LEXINGTON AVENUE

1080 Virginia White 50
Bessie Urqurhart 34 sister
Dorothy P. White 21 daughter
Earl McGresham 20 Canada chauffeur
Margaret Gilmore 45
Anna Williams 45 England

1084 Charles Bingham 60 retired
Margaret Bingham 55 *ux.*
Julia Conway 50
Nellie Sullivan 21 Canada
Mary McCann 40 Ireland

1088 Louise C. Schafer
Theresa A. Schafer 26 daughter

1094 John McFarland MD 30
Lena Snyder 28

1100 Norman E. Mack 48 Canada publisher
Harriet B. Mack 32 *ux.*
Norma Mack 11 daughter school
Harriet Mack 8 daughter school
Frances Taggert 55 mother-in-law
William Kernahan 50 boarder circulator

HIGHLAND AVENUE

1120 Albert Klinck 31 beef packer
Alice Klinck sister 25
Harry Pfeiffer 46 livestock dealer
Julia Klinck 40 *ux.*
Hazel Klinck 19 daughter
Elizabeth Schaab 22 Canada

1132 William M. Ramsdell 40 manager newspaper
Margaret Ramsdell 38 *ux.*
Margaret Ramsdell 10 daughter school
Grace Ramsdell 9 daughter school
Jeannie Ramsdell 5 daughter school
Grace Adam mother-in-law
Nora Wilcox 41
Gertrude Gadges 32
Susan Shutz 32 Canada
Daniel McCarthy 38 coachman

WEST FERRY STREET ❦ End of Block

1084 Harold Hunisicker 27 manufacturer
Florence Hunisicker 23 *ux.*
Alice Kohn 21

1088 Clark M. Ingham 43 broker
Anna Ingham 40 *ux.*
James Ingham 18 son school
Catherine Smalt 27
Nellie Coughlin 23 Ireland
Victor G. Kullman 30 chauffeur
Cecelia E. Kullman 27 *ux.*
Richard E. Kullman 120 days son

1094 Jacob S. Otto MD 42
Elizabeth T. Otto 41 *ux.*
Elizabeth T. Otto 4 daughter
Joanna Draber 20 Germany nursemaid

1100 Norman E. Mack 57 newspaper publisher
Harriet B. Mack 42 *ux.*
Norma E. Mack 21 daughter
Harriet T. Mack 18 daughter
Katerina Zautty 36 Hungary

HIGHLAND AVENUE

1132 William M. Ramsdell 50 newspaper publisher
Margaret Ramsdell 48 England *ux.*

1140 William Connors 55
Margaret Connors 48 *ux.*

WEST FERRY STREET ❦ End of Block

1920

BRYANT STREET

938 Georgia Pardee 64 NY widow
Allan Pardee 14 NY son
Bertha M. Bell 35 Canada nurse
Rose Whitney 47 NY
Katherine Malloy 46 Canada

1925

BRYANT STREET

938 Georgia G. Pardee 70 widow
Allan Pardee 19 son school
Marion Gemmel 50 friend high school teacher
Maude Bell 41 companion
Rose Whitney 55 housekeeper
Kate Simon 55 cook

HODGE AVENUE

950 Arthur D. Bissell 75 NY banker
Fanny Bissell 67 NY *ux.*
Arthur D. Bissell Jr. 36 NY son motor company
Howard Bissell 47 NY son
Margaret Sheedy 52 NY
Anna O'Hara 35 Ireland

958 Lorraine Richmond 82 NY widow
Mary Gallagher 26 Ireland
Nellie Callaghan 63 NY

964 Harriet Riley 57 NY widow housekeeper
Grace Riley 30 NY daughter bookkeeper
Mildred Kiernan 28 NY daughter widow
millinery shop
7 lodgers

William Hyer 43 NY housewrecker
Agnes J. Hyer 40 NY *ux.*

976 John H. Baker 48 NY stockbroker
Blanche Baker 41 NY *ux.*
Sarah Baker 18 NY daughter
Jean Baker 16 NY daughter
John Baker 14 NY son
Edward Baker 14 NY son
Barbara Baker 7 NY daughter
William Baker 2 NY son

990 *North Presbyterian Church*

WEST UTICA STREET

1014 Ellis M. Treat 47 Pa. oil & gas
George T. Treat 19 Pa. son
Ellis F. Treat 17 son
Milo F. Treat Pa. son
Louise Daykens 48 England
Josephine Galvin 42 Canada

1022 Matilda Satterfield 66 Pa. widow
John Lausch 17 Austria gardener
Lillian E. Huebsch 34 NY
Emma Mason 47 Illinois

HODGE AVENUE

950 Arthur D. Bissell 81 banker
Fanny C. Bissell 75 *ux.*
Arthur D. Bissell Jr. 41 son
Margaret Sheedy 50
Elizabeth Casey 67 cook
Christine Kuster 38

958 Charles J. Fimiani 38 contractor
Josephine Fimiani *ux.*
Jane Fimiani 9 daughter school
Mary Nagy 20

960 Samuel Angert 56 Russia auto sales
Otto Angert 30 son auto sales
Jack Angert 29 son auto sales
Henry Angert 26 son auto sales
Evelyn Levine 24 daughter
Arthur Levine 30 son-in-law auto sales
Max Kaiser 15 nephew auto sales

964 Charles Tropp 55 real estate
Mrs. Charles Tropp 54
Walter Tropp 28 son architect
Margaret Jones 27 daughter
4 lodgers

William C. Hyer 48 contractor
Agnes J. Hyer 46 *ux.*

976 John H. Baker 53 investor
Blanche H. Baker 50 *ux.*.
Sarah H. Baker 23 daughter
Jean Baker 22 daughter
John H. Baker Jr. 19 son school
Edward Baker 17 son school
Barbara Baker 12 daughter school
William W. Baker 7 son school
Daisy Dicklon 47

990 *North Presbyterian Church*

WEST UTICA STREET

1014 Chauncy Hamlin 43 retired attorney
Emily Hamlin 42 *ux.*
Chauncy J. Hamlin 20 son college
Matilda Hamlin 18 daughter school
Mary Hamlin 14 daughter school
Agnes Kells 40 England cook
Elizabeth Bryant 45 England
Katherine McIllhagga 36 Scotland
Mary MacAuley 31 Scotland

1022 Matilda Satterfield 71 Pa. widow
John Larish 22 grandson college
Demetri Larish 20 grandson college
Lillian Heback 40
Kunigunde Dingfelder 27 Germany cook

Robert Roth 30 chauffeur
Marguerite Roth 32 *ux.*
Helen Rasboahn 35

1040 George A. Mitchell 46 wholesaler
Sarah H. Mitchell 39 NY *ux.*
William H. Mitchell 18 NY son
Thomas W. Mitchell 16 NY son
Kate L. Mitchell 11 daughter
Anna Mied 39 Maryland
Jeannie Schmidt 17 Denmark
Louise Larsen 52 Denmark
Clara King 35 Vermont
Anna Smith 51 NY nurse

Charles Shirley 50 NY chauffeur
Emma Shirley 50 NY *ux.*

1040 George Mitchell 48 lumber
Sarah Mitchell 45 *ux.*
William Mitchell 24 son school
Thomas Mitchell 22 son school
Kate Mitchell 19 daughter school
Margaret Pitzar 29 Ireland
Mary Stokes 37 Ireland
Jessie Sherett 38 Scotland
Lily Plunkett 75 England

John Hoffle 43 chauffeur
Elizabeth Hoffle 43 *ux.*
Clarence Hoffle 20 son school
Kenneth Hoffle 15 son school

1058 William Hamlin 70 NY retired
Kate Hamlin 67 *ux.*
Katherine Weaver 42 Canada nurse
Jennie Hunter 32 Canada
Lilliam M. Hathier 56
Mary J. St. Leger 36 Ireland
Luise Muna 34 NY

1058 William Hamlin 78 retired
Louise K. Hamlin 72 *ux.*
Margaret Kennedy 40
Rose Brady 40
Anna McCarthy 48 Ireland
Elizabeth Baker 56 Canada

LEXINGTON AVENUE

LEXINGTON AVENUE

1080 Lloyd Bissell 27 NY auto parts executive
Dorothy P. Bissell 26 NY *ux.*
Arthur Bissell 2 NY son
Virginia L. Bissell 1 NY daughter
Virginia K. White 57 NY mother-in-law
Nellie Hurley 50 Ireland cook
Matilda Luade 28 Missouri
Rosie Bauer 23 NY
Annie Odell 50 NJ nurse

1080 Lloyd Bissell 32 merchant
Dorothy Bissell 30 *ux.*
Douglas Bissell 8 son school
Virginia Bissell 6 daughter school

1088 Clark L. Ingham 55 NY real estate
Annie Ingham 53 NY *ux.*.
James R. Ingham 23 NY son rubber company
Helen C. Ingham 21 NY daughter
Emma Larush 35 NY
Bertha Droll 47 Germany

Raymond Boller 26 NY chauffeur
Olive B. Boller 26 NY *ux.*

1088 Clark Ingham 62 real estate & insurance
Annie S. Ingham 51 *ux.*
Courtland Van Clief son-in-law
Carroll Brothers
Helen Van Clief granddaughter
Nora Fitzgerald 45 Ireland waitress
Nellie Fitzgerald 47 Ireland cook
Emma Roth 46 Canada upstairs maid

Larry V. Sykes 26 chauffeur
Victoria Sykes 24 Poland *ux.*
Gladys Sykes 3 daughter

1094 Phillip Metz 28 Nebraska *Buffalo Times*
Norma Metz 25 NY *ux.*
Margaret Mahan 38 Ireland

1094 Phillip Metz 31 publisher
Norma Metz 29 *ux.*
Phyllis Metz 3 daughter
Cecile Du Pont 21 France
Olga Halkiewicz Austria
Marie Eiser 32 cook

1100 Norman Mack 72 NY newspaper Harriet Mack 46 NY *ux.* Joseph Zautty 40 Hungary Arthur Formbly 30 NY	
HIGHLAND AVENUE	HIGHLAND AVENUE
1114 Roscoe R. Mitchell 33 NY attorney Ada B. Mitchell 32 NY *ux.* Marjorie Butler Mitchell 8 NY daughter Edward Butler Mitchell 7 NY son Charlotte Street 30 England ? Howard 24 Ireland Hilda Varinn 30 England governess Julia Lisenbar 27 NY waitress	
1120 Henry Zeller 60 NY tanner Kate Zeller 50 NY *ux.* Mary Meyer 25 NY cook Frances Hallen 25 Sweden Denis Page 65 NY gardener	1120 Henry Zeller 65 tanner Kate Zeller 55 NY *ux.* Frances Hallen 30 Sweden housekeeper Mary Mayer 31 cook
1132 William M. Ramsdell 55 NY newspaper publisher Margaret Ramsdell 53 England *ux.* Robert A. Ramsdell 21 NY son Jean S. Ramsdell 19 NY daughter Edna Volkosz 40 NY Delia Murphy 40 Ireland cook	1132 William Ramsdell 60 Margaret Ramsdell 58 *ux.* Robert Ramsdell 26 son retail merchant Caroline Walker 54 England Cary Rothenmeyer 35
1140 William J. Conners 60 NY newspaper publisher Mary Conners NY 43 *ux.* Ruth Conners 17 NY college Julia Fisher 17 NY	1140 William J. Conners Jr. 26 publisher Cora Conners 26 *ux.* William J. Conners III 3 Rita Conners 1 daughter Mary Doherty 49 housekeeper Frances Talbot 50 nurse
WEST FERRY STREET ❦ End of Block	WEST FERRY STREET ❦ End of Block

The impressive brick and sandstone Second Empire mansion(13.1) on the northwest corner of Delaware and Bryant was built in 1881 for Nelson Holland(13.2), one of Buffalo's leading lumbermen. Eighth in descent from John Holland who came to New England in 1633, Holland was born in Belchertown, Massachusetts, in 1829. With his parents he moved to Niagara Falls in 1836 and a year later to Springville where he attended public schools and Springville Academy. At eighteen he began working on his father's farm until 1850 when he moved to Buffalo where he worked briefly for his uncle, Selim Sears, and later for another lumberman, Oliver Bugbee. Sent by the latter to promote his interests at Detroit, Holland got to know the business thoroughly. In 1855 he formed a partnership with William Oakes to buy and ship lumber from Saint Clair, Michigan, at the southern end of Lake

13.1 ❦ Number 916 Delaware, SCNYAB library. For identification of this house as 2nd Empire I am indebted to Michael Tunney, S.J. of the Canisius College art department.

Huron. The partners also acquired a sawmill and purchased 6.25 square miles of Michigan pinelands. In 1862 the partnership was dissolved and Holland came to Buffalo where he bought an interest in Eaton Brown & Company's planing mill. In 1867 he married Susan Ann Clarke of Silver Creek, the sister of Lucretia Clarke, who had married James H. Lee of #900 Delaware, just across from Holland at Delaware and Bryant. In 1881 the firm of Lee Holland was set up, which soon had 250 employees turning out sashes, doors, and blinds on Wilkeson and Court Streets. Of this concern Holland's biographer wrote: "Its output was immense, and it was soon a conceded fact that Lee, Holland & Co. was the most important firm of its kind in Buffalo." Holland owned several lake vessels and was the proprietor of Standard Radiator at the end of Porter Avenue. His only son, Nelson Clarke Holland, born in Buffalo in 1875, graduated from Yale in 1899 and represented his father in New York. The father had no time for clubs but he was president of the trustees of North Presbyterian when it was on Main Street. When it moved to Utica and Delaware he joined Westminster in which he became an elder. His holdings included timberlands in several states. Managing them required much of his time away from Buffalo. He died at #916 in 1916.[1] By the 1920s the corner had become the site of The 916 Delaware Avenue Apartments.

13.2 ❦ Nelson Holland, *M&FH*, 2:130.

The lot above, #928, had been since 1869 the site of the home of Henry H. Otis, a Methodist bookseller. He was born in Rome, New York, in 1834; but when he was five the family moved to a farm in Jefferson County, where he attended school for three months during winter. In 1853 at nineteen he came to Buffalo and was made head clerk in a branch of the Methodist Book Company in the Weed Block where he remained for forty-three years. In addition, he

1 *M&FH*, 2:130-131; *CE*, February 12, 1939.

13.3 ❦ William Hodge, Smith, *op. cit.*, facing p. 156.

opened a branch store at Chautauqua on the Assembly Grounds. He was one of the principal founders of the Plymouth and the Asbury Methodist Episcopal Churches in Buffalo and for over forty years was superintendent of the city's Methodist Sunday Schools, a trustee of the Buffalo Orphan Asylum, and a prominent Mason. His wife whom he married in 1858 was active in Women's Christian Temperance Union circles. Henry belonged to no men's clubs and died at sixty-eight in 1902.[2]

Since 1856 what was to become #938 was the home of William Hodge(13.3), who when five months old had come to Buffalo with his father, William, Sr., in 1805. The father had obtained land from the Holland Land Company upon which he built a brick hotel at Main and Utica. He also began the county's first nursery. The hotel was sacked by the British in 1813, and the Hodges fled to Harris Hill. William, Jr., seems to have built his house on Delaware Street in 1856.[3] He was fifty-five in 1860, a gardener, with his wife Arletta, and three boys. In 1870 he listed himself as a "retired farmer" but by 1880 he was back in business at #55 Hodge Street around the corner from #938, surrounded by what had been Hodge land and occupied with "nursery and real estate."

> The William Hodge home...was a red brick house with [a] wing. William Hodge was one of Buffalo's representative citizens and a sort of old patriarch in the neighborhood. He had a tall, imposing figure, snowy white whiskers, and always wore black broadcloth, a silk hat and carried a gold-headed cane. It was the delight of the children of the neighborhood [to hear] when he was a boy, how he fled with his mother for safety when Buffalo was burned by the Indians. The Hodge homestead was torn down when Hodge avenue was laid out, and one Buffalo woman recalls the day when the first shovel of dirt was cast up for the new street.

Since Hodge was five months old in 1813 he must have been a precocious baby. Moreover Buffalo was torched by the British not the Indians. The eponym of Hodge Avenue, he died in 1887.

Under the next occupant of #938, Charles W. Pardee, an H. H. Richardson-style stone mansion designed by E. B. Greene was erected in 1888 on what was now the southwest corner of Delaware and Hodge.(13.4) Concerning this

13.4 ❦ Number 938 Delaware, *PBHS*, 30 (1930), n.p.

2 *BEN*, April 28, 1902; *Express*, April 28, 1902.
3 Crisfield Johnson, *Centennial History of Erie County, New York* (Buffalo: Matthews and Warren, 1876), pp. 9, 130, 194, 253, 263.

house, Francis Kowsky writes: "The Charles W. Pardee house at 938 Delaware emulated Richardson's Romanesque heaviness and rough-hewn surfaces. But its clumsy composition only served to point up by contrast with the Gratwick house(10.29) the difference between the genius of the master and failings of less-talented imitators."[4]

Charles Pardee was born in 1852 in Owego, son of Myron Pardee, a maltester. He was educated at the Pennsylvania Military College in Chester and worked for his father until 1871 when he came to Buffalo and married Georgia Gates, daughter of George B. Gates of #546 Delaware. Charles was employed by Penokee Lumber of Tonawanda and was chairman of the finance committee of the Bank of Buffalo and a founder of Commonwealth Trust and the Market Bank. He cared about hospitals and became president of Buffalo General. He was also a member of the Buffalo and Park clubs. He died in 1912. Georgia lived at #938 until the late 1920s and died in 1930 in California. Her estate was valued at $1 million ($17,430,000 in 1997 dollars.) The house was torn down in 1930, shortly after the stock market crash, probably to avoid taxes.[5] Concerning the Gates, Burr wrote:

> The recent death in California of Mrs. Charles Pardee adds one more to the long list of prominent women who in their day were leaders of society in Buffalo and whose passing recall[s] many kindly memories. For years Mr. and Mrs. Pardee resided in the handsome stone house at the southwest corner of Delaware and Hodge avenues. There was a ballroom on the third floor which was the scene of many brilliant functions, for both Mr. and Mrs. Pardee were lavish in their hospitality, and their dinner parties were always among the events of the social season. Mr. Pardee was a handsome debonair host, and came from a prominent and wealthy family in Oswego.
>
> Mrs. Pardee was before her marriage, Georgia Gates, youngest daughter of Mr. and Mrs. George Gates, who lived in a fine old home in Swan street, and later in a square grey brick mansion that stood at the southwest corner of Delaware and Allen street on the present site of the University Club. There were two other daughters in the Gates family. Kate, who married William Hamlin and resides in the beautiful stone house at the southwest corner of Delaware and Lexington avenue, and Elizabeth Gates, who never married but who was a stunning looking woman of the brunette type. After the death of her parents, she continued to reside in the family home and became deeply interested in art. She spent much time abroad, and collected many rare paintings which are now in the permanent collection at the Albright Art Gallery, including a striking portrait of herself.[6]

Number 950, new style, a red brick house with a southern wing, was the home since the late 1850s of Daniel B. Castle, a jeweler, born in Connecticut in 1815. In 1860 he resided there with his wife, three children, a boarder, and a coachman. One of the daughters, Fanny, married the boy across the street, Arthur Bissell. After Castle's death in 1883 and a short occupancy by the family of Thaddeus C. Davis, a lawyer, the Arthur Bissells bought #950 and celebrated their golden wedding there in 1924. Of their children Thomas died at twenty-two, Eleanor married James D. Warren of #1119 Delaware, Jeanette married Bradley Goodyear, Howard became president of People's Bank, and Raymond had been manager of Buffalo Telephone and was appointed postmaster by President Wil-

4 Cigliano and Landau, *op. cit.*, 51.
5 *CE*, March 18, 1912; *PBHS*, 30(1930), np.
6 *Courier*, June 14, 18, 1930.

son. The other surviving children were Arthur D., Jr., and Lloyd. Like their father, all the Bissell boys had gone to Yale. Arthur Bissell, Sr., died at #950 in 1926.[7]

North of Castle in the 1850s lived Thomas Stephenson, a jeweler and founder of a company that manufactured organs. Ten years later, his son John Curtis Stephenson(13.5), also a jeweler, born in Buffalo in 1836, had moved up the Avenue to #1080 on the corner of Butler Street and, abandoning gemmology, went back to work at his father's organ factory. In 1858 he married Hannah Joy Webster, daughter of George and Hannah Webster, who lived above Thomas Stevenson. John Stevenson died in 1906.

13.5 ❦ John Curtis Stephenson, *M&FH*, 2.270.

Willard W. Browne, a wholesale lumber dealer, resided at #958 (previously #960) in 1880, and remained there until the end of the century. Next came Lorraine Richmond, widow of Moses M. Richmond, a partner of his brother, Jewett Richmond(10.45), as grain merchants on Central Wharf. Lorraine stayed there nearly a quarter of a century until her death in 1922. She was followed by Charles J. Fimiani, probably an Italian immigrant, who in 1915 formed his own construction business and for eighteen years built scores of homes on Linwood, Chatham, Lafayette, and Goulding avenues in Buffalo, and also in West Seneca. His marriage to Josephine Corridan was performed by Bishop Colton in the chapel next to the new cathedral where Fimiani ushered for forty years and for which he had raised funds. In 1933 in the depths of the Depression he retired from house building and became a real estate appraiser. He was the first Italian-American admitted into the Buffalo Elks and the second to join the Buffalo Knights of Columbus. His country club membership was at Erie Downs. Fimiani died in 1958.[8]

In the early 1890s William Hazard, a real estate agent, and his wife Louise resided at #960. By 1900 she was a widow. In 1905 she was seventy years old and taking in boarders. Of the Russian-born family which had taken over #960 in 1925 Adler writes: "The Angert family of the automobile parts business represented Buffalo Jewry in that area and at one time they could advertise their concern as 'The World's Largest Auto Wreckers.'" He locates them "among Buffalo Jewish merchants of the more recent [i.e., post World War I] period."[9] In 1925 fifty-six year old Samuel headed up the family followed by three sons, Otto, Jack, and Henry, all auto salesmen, and Arthur Levine, his thirty year old son-in-law and fifteen year old nephew, Max Kaiser, all "auto sales." They did it all without domestics.

7 *CE*, November 14, 1926.
8 *Courier*, January 21, 1958.
9 Adler, *op. cit.*, p.351.

In 1880 forty-three year old German-born Louis F. W. Arend was conducting a dry goods, carpet, and upholstery store at #259 Main Street while residing at #685 Delaware. Eleven years later he was selling real estate in the Austin building and had moved up the Avenue to #964. He was still there in 1905 and at sixty-eight, still selling real estate. He and his wife Mary could yet be found there in 1910, but by 1915, Mary, now a widow, was living alone with a single domestic. By 1920 a complete transformation had taken place as a fifty-seven year old widow with the help of two daughters was keeping house for seven lodgers. In the former stable lived a housewrecker and his wife.

Number 980 was in 1870 the home of James M. Johnson, allegedly publisher of the *Daily Courier*, though a study of the periodical press of Buffalo makes no mention of him,[10] and in 1880 that of Sarah Becker, a schoolteacher with a passel of nieces and nephews. By 1905 it had been replaced by a larger three-story brick structure, the home of John H. Baker, who had been born in Otsego County in 1873. His father was Rev. E. Folsom Baker of Cold Spring Harbor, Long Island. John Baker graduated at seventeen from Saint Paul's, Garden City. He began his career with Atlantic Mutual Marine Insurance on Wall Street, where he remained until 1893 when he came to Buffalo, beginning as a real estate agent with William B. Cutter, #600 Ellicott Square Building. In 1902 Baker became a broker on his own but represented the New York house of Spencer Trask & Company. In 1900 he married Blanche Hutchinson, daughter of Edward, eponym of Hutchinson Technical High. About 1935 Baker moved to East Aurora. His clubs were Saturn, Wanakah, Idlewood, and Country. A trustee of the Church Home on Seventh Street and of Saint Margaret's School, he died in 1947.[11]

13.6 **Number 990 Delaware, *PBHS*, 16 (1912), 432.**

Future #990, the Victorian gothic cottage at Delaware and West Utica(13.6), was built in 1853 by George Webster.[12] He had just sold his house and property on Swan and Franklin to Bishop Timon for his cathedral complex. In 1858 John Stevenson married Hannah Joy Webster, Webster's daughter. Another daughter, Jennie, married Edward S. Dann and the couple moved into #990 after George Webster died. Dann had been born in Little Falls in 1834 and came to Buffalo at twenty with his father J. C. Dann with whom he was associated in banking. Later he worked for banks in Cincinnati, Saint Louis, and Schenectady. He even spent a year in Toledo at the head offices of the Lake Shore & Michigan Southern Railroad. In 1861 he returned to Buffalo and became a partner in the Webster family's oil refinery. By 1863 the Danns were living at #990 Delaware. At the formation of the National Savings Bank, Dann became its secretary and treasurer. He

10 Frank Severance, "The Periodical Press of Buffalo, 1811-1915," *PBHS*, 19(1915), 179-280.
11 *A History of the City of Buffalo, its men and institutions*, (Buffalo, *Buffalo Evening News*, 1908), pp.76-77; *CE*, February 4, 1947.
12 *PBHS*, 16(1912), 433.

13.7 ❦ North Presbyterian Church, #990 Delaware Avenue, BHS.

was also warden of the Church of the Ascension, treasurer of the Church Home, and a member of the standing commission of the Episcopal Diocese of Western New York. All the more remarkable then was the news which shocked Buffalo on June 22, 1892, that a visit from bank examiners four months previously had revealed that Dann had been stealing money from his bank for almost fourteen years. He was arrested on July 2, spent time in jail, but was freed on payment of $40,000 bail. He was indicted on sixteen counts of forgery, grand larceny, and embezzlement. The total amount of his defalcations came to $415,000 ($7,233,450 in 1997 dollars.) On October 2 he died at his home at age fifty-eight. No mention was made in the press of suicide.[13] His son, Edward W. Dann, was still living at #990 in the employ of Standard Oil in 1897. But change was in the offing for the corner. North Presbyterian had been organized in 1847. The name showed what was then considered north since the congregation's first church building was located on Main below Chippewa.(6.9 #22) It was dedicated in 1847, and remained there for fifty-six years until it was sold in August 1903 for $264,000 to Boston interests as a site for the Kieth Theatre.[14] In April 1904 the congregation bought the old Dana house for $60,000 from William J. Conners who had bought it as the intended locale of his new house but changed his mind.[15] The last service at the old North was held on April 17, 1904, and the cornerstone for the new was laid on July 5, 1905. Since the new English country gothic edifice(13.7) would not be ready until the winter of 1906-1907, North Presbyterian held services at the Twentieth Century Club, Beth Zion, and in the chapel of the church under construction at #990.[16] North Presbyterian lasted less than fifty years on Delaware. January 1, 1953, saw the first service there of the Annunciation Hellenic Orthodox Church. The Presbyterians had sold out for $250,000 and moved to Amherst.[17]

13.8 ❦ Number 1014 Delaware, exterior, BHS.

Henry Richmond of #348 Delaware, Dean Richmond's son, had two brothers who lived in succession at #1014, Alfred and W. Eugene. The Alfred Richmonds resided there 1871-1874, and the Eugene Richmonds 1876-1877. Alfred was a lithographer and

13 *Express*, October 9, 1892.
14 *CA*, August 15, 1903.
15 *BEN*, April 22, 1904.
16 Hill, *op. cit.*, 2:281-282.
17 *CE*, September 17, 1960.

13.9 ❦ Number 1014 Delaware, interior, BHS.

died in 1881, and Eugene was a shipowner. Burr described the place as "a charming brown frame gothic house of fascinating architecture surrounded by lovely flower gardens."[18] About 1887 it was demolished and Harry Hamlin erected the Queen Anne residence shown in figure 13.8. For an interior view of the same see figure 13.9.

Harry Hamlin was born in Buffalo in 1855, son of Cicero Hamlin and the former Susan Ford. At seventeen he entered the class of 1876 at Yale but left because of bad eyesight and engaged in the glucose business with his father and brother William, rising to vice president. In 1878 he married Grace Enos. They had one son, Chauncey, born in 1881, and two daughters, Martha and Mary. After the house was razed, Burr wrote nostalgically:

> Mr. Hamlin built this house in 1887. The dining-room never pleased him and one day in the nineties, after a polo game, he asked Mr. George Cary to look it over and finally to make it over. The result was a room which had been the delight of artists and laymen ever since. Duvine of New York designed the carvings on the fireplace, the panels, and the wonderful buffet cabinet was from Duvine. When Mr. Cary purchased it for this room, the Payne Whitneys and a Vanderbilt or two also wanted it.
>
> The ugly walls on the south were torn out, medieval archways took their place and conservatory windows filled with ferns gave the needed light. The set-in cabinet over the fireplace and all the wall spacing is the repository of priceless examples of old Chinese periods - potteries a king might envy. The Indian room, leading from the dining-room is a treasure trove of embroideries, Oriental carvings in wood brass and silver. The Indian room contains a wealth of idols - Buddhas of every size and shape and the god Good Luck must have reigned many a year.
>
> Of the main hall, built as were many of the mansions of the Victorian period, for general occupancy, is a room of which Buffalo has no duplicate. The "Trophy Room," ...is furnished with a frieze of prize ribbons won on the track by "Cogent" and "Duke," the "Abbott," and other champions of Harry Hamlin's stables. For it was "like father like son," when the youngest son of Cicero Hamlin, world-known breeder of record smashing horses, took to owning pacers and trotters and hunters which made the horse-lovers of the country sit up and take notice.
>
> Mrs. Hamlin painted in gold letters on a blue ground each winner's record with a horseshoe worn by each underneath. Portraits in oil of several of the victors hang on the walls of the trophy room. When one has owned a horse which broke a world-record twenty times or so and who won the master's cup at the New York Horse Show one perpetuates the history of these triumphs. Silver cups ceased to be a novelty they came so thick and fast. They too adorned the Trophy room.

18 *Times*, February 24, 1930.

> This story began with a marvel of a [Kenilworth] dinner. There was often something unique and original in the form of amusement for the Hamlin guests. On the occasion of a New Year's ball to usher in the century, at midnight lights were turned out, and a group of singers from the Orpheus, of which John Lund was then director, came in and sang a song to the infant year, words and music by Mr. Lund. When young Chauncey, the son of the house, and the present owner of the Hamlin home, returned from Yale for the Yuletide holidays, there were numerous parties in his honor. Mrs. Harry Hamlin had the house full of his friends, but a delightful feature, now almost obsolete was the joining of the fathers and mothers with the young people in the Christmas merriment. Chauncey's acquaintances were invited to parties, formal and informal, and Mr. and Mrs. Hamlin's friends were invited at the same time.[19]

During the hard times following the Panic of 1893 Harry went to Peoria in charge of the glucose refining plant there. Back again in Buffalo he joined his father in running Village Farm in East Aurora, the success of whose prize-winning horses was largely due to him. When polo in America was in its early days he was an enthusiastic player and a leader in coaching, "careful and skillful with the whip." After the family business was sold in 1897 he had even more time for horses. With the sale of Valley Farm shortly before the death of his father in 1905, Harry devoted himself to motoring, covering much of Central, Eastern, and Mid-Western America. On the occasion of his violent death in 1907, a writer for the *Express* observed:

> From the earliest days of automobiling as a sport Mr. Hamlin was an enthusiast, and he imported one of the first high-power French cars seen in this district. He followed the development of the machines closely and always had the fastest built.
>
> He was a very capable driver, but reckless. His mishaps were countless. He raced on many of the sea beaches. At Newport a few years ago, by his driving he forced another contestant into the serf [sic.] He was frequently defendant in suits in this city brought by pedestrians. A few years ago a woman guest was pitched out of his car, and her face disfigured for life.
>
> With his mania for speed he was a likeable man and most of the adventures told of him related to jokes he would play on unsuspecting strangers. Often speeding on the streets and avenues in the early hours of the morning he would encounter night workers and invite them to have a ride. With his new found guest safe [?] in the car it was his delight to put the machine to its highest speed.[20]

Such irresponsibility had to end in tragedy. At 3:40 P.M. June 4, 1907, Hamlin was traveling east on Main Street through Eggertsville half a mile north of the Country Club, then at Bailey and Main. At Eggertsville the road bends slightly to the right. His big Mercedes was being driven by chauffeur, T. P. Meinhard. Hamlin was in the right front seat, Tony Gavin, a Buffalo policeman attached to the Sixth Precinct, and John Harter, an employee who took care of the Hamlin automobiles, sat in the rear. The party was headed for Mugel's, a roadhouse ten miles east of Buffalo. As Hamlin's car rounded the bend it smashed into a westbound rig driven by Jacob Schaller, accompanied by a young

19 *Times*, October 19, 1927.
20 *Express*, June 5, 1907.

boy, John Heckel. It would seem that the buggy was being driven on the wrong, that is left hand side, of the road. Hamlin's chauffeur claimed that his car was being passed by two racing machines going east, which forced the horse-drawn vehicle to turn to the right where it was hit by Hamlin's car, causing a cloud of dust that obscured visibility. Witnesses in Eggertsville confirmed the cloud of dust detail. The left wheel and mudguard of the car tore off the left foreleg of the horse. The chauffeur swerved to the left, which reduced the buggy to splinters and then hit the ties of the Williamsville trolley line, which ran along the left side of Main Street. The jolt threw Hamlin out and pitched him headfirst against the farther rail, breaking his neck. He died immediately. The chauffeur could not control the car while the wreck of the buggy clung to it, but kept his head and, after contact with the ties, swung the car back onto the road, finally stopping 125 feet from the first impact. Schaller and the boy were taken by ambulance to Sister's Hospital. Gavin and Harter in the rear had their faces cut by splinters of glass from the windshield. The only damage to the auto was the breaking of the windshield, the wrenching of the axle and left forward wheel, and the smashing of the mudguard. The horse was shot. Covered by a raincoat, Hamlin's body lay in the road from 3:30 o'clock until five. A doctor found that the left side of Hamlin's chest had been crushed. There was a gash on his head from the back to the left eye. He was found to be carrying $1,115 in his wallet. Young Heckel had both legs broken and received a fracture at the base of his skull. The list of honorary pallbearers at Hamlin's funeral at Trinity conducted by Rev. Cameron Davis the next day was a roster of the Delaware Avenue elite: John J. Milburn, J. N. Scatcherd, Dr. Roswell Park, Montgomery Gerrans, George L. Williams, Dr. Charles Cary, Thomas Cary, Trumbull Cary, J. H. Metcalfe, Laurence D. Rumsey, Bronson Case Rumsey, Ansley Wilcox, George Bleistein, Harry Seymour.[21]

Chauncey Hamlin, son of the deceased and a lawyer, put together for the press an explanation of the collision that by stressing the great dust cloud exonerated the chauffeur. Chauncey had been educated at Miss Hoffman's, the Heathcote School, and Nichols, and at the Hill School in Pottstown. From there he went on to Yale where for two years he played football and, having made Phi Beta Kappa and Skull and Bones, graduated in 1903. In 1905 he graduated from U.B. law school. While in law school he married Martha, daughter of David Gray, of whom Severance wrote:

> David Gray, poet and essayist of rare refinement, gave the best working years of his life to the Courier. His connection with the paper began in 1859, as commercial reporter; in 1860 he was made associate (or city) editor and at that time acquired a quarter interest in the property. On Joseph Warren's death in 1876, Mr. Gray became editor-in-chief, in which office he served until his health failed. He sold his interest in the paper in 1884, his death occurring in 1887.[22]

Upon graduation Hamlin clerked in the offices of Rogers, Locke & Milburn. Now a married man, he moved out of #1014 and lived for several years on West Ferry before moving to Snyder in 1910.

21 *Express*, June 5, 1907.
22 Severance, *op. cit.*, p. 217.

He became a solo practitioner in 1907 and was appointed referee in bankruptcy by Federal Judge John R. Hazel. With John Lord O'Brien, then U.S. District Attorney for Western New York, Hamlin formed a partnership which included William Donovan and Bradley Goodyear. In 1910 Hamlin had organized the Buffalo Legal Aid Bureau and was its first president. A Republican, he broke with his party in 1912, became the Erie County Chairman of the Progressive (Bull Moose) Party and attended its convention in Chicago. In the presidential election that followed Erie County gave twice the votes to Roosevelt as to regular Republican, William Howard Taft. In 1914 Hamlin led the movement back to the G.O.P and was its unsuccessful candidate for lieutenant governor. In February 1916 he signed on with the 65th Infantry, NYNG. A few months later his regiment was called into federal service and assigned to Camp Whitman. There it was transformed into a heavy field artillery unit, and on August 3, 1916, he became First Lieutenant. On November 11 he was promoted to captain in command of Battery B. When the United States entered World War I in April 1917 each of the law partners except O'Brien left his lucrative law practice to join the colors. Early in 1917 Hamlin's regiment was sent to Camp Wadsworth, South Carolina, and transformed to the 106th Field Artillery. Finally in June they sailed for France where in July 1918 Hamlin was taken away from the regiment and transferred to the headquarters of the 52nd Field Artillery Brigade at Camp de Sourges and assigned the duties of brigade munitions officer. He served there until the Armistice and came back from France in April 1919 reluctant to return to the law.[23]

Number 1014 was leased 1915-1918 to George Rand, president of Marine Bank. Grace Hamlin, Harry's widow, died in 1918, and her funeral was conducted at #1014 by Rev. Cameron Davis of Trinity.[24] The house at #1014 was rented in 1919-1920 to Ellis Treat, an oil man. However by the mid-1920s Chauncey Hamlin was back at #1014. The census for 1925 shows him, a forty-three year old retired attorney, residing with his family and six domestics. A rich man, he could give himself to activities aimed at the public good. His major interest was the Buffalo Society of Natural Sciences of which he became president in 1920. That year he was appointed to the Buffalo City Planning Committee by Mayor George Buck. Hamlin had a major part in selecting the site for City Hall on Niagara Square. In 1924 President Coolidge formed the National Conference on Outdoor Recreation and made Hamlin chairman. He pushed for the creation of the Museum of Science at Humboldt Park for which he won U.B.'s Chancellor's Medal in 1931.[25] In 1927 the main house was torn down and the stable made into a home known as Barnstable.

As Chauncey Hamlin's father perished in an automobile accident, so too did Chauncey's second wife, Emily. The couple was returning in September 1933 from their summer home in the Muskoka Lake region of Ontario. Twenty miles north of Niagara Falls their car driven by Chauncey collided with a car headed in the opposite direction and overturned into a ditch. The injuries Emily suffered

23 *Express*, June 19, 1918.
24 *Ibid.*
25 *BEN*, February 24, 1931.

were not judged serious, but she died on September 25. Like her husband she was a progressive, opposed to child labor and an advocate of minimum wages laws for women, birth control to check poverty and improve the race, peace, and disarmament. She first favored then opposed Prohibition. In 1934 Hamlin married Elizabeth Wilkeson Freeman, widowed daughter of Samuel Wilkeson who had died in his home on Niagara Square in 1915. In 1940 Hamlin became local head of the Committee to Save America by Aiding the Allies at the request of its founder, William Allen White. By 1955 Barnstable had become an Elks Lodge, then a medical research center, and then burned down. It was noted then that Hamlin "now spends most of his time in New York City and California."[26]

Hamlin had been named to the board of managers of the American Association of Museums in 1915, and upon his return from World War I was made president of the council of that body, a post he kept until 1948. In 1946 he was elected president of the International Council of Museums. He was credited with the creation of Allegany State Park. He thus became a member of the New York State Council of Parks 1943-1946, serving also as chairman of the Allegany State Park Commission. He was a partner in several brokerage firms beginning in 1937 and joined the New York Stock Exchange in 1941. Locally, Hamlin was an associate member of the Buffalo Council of the Boy Scouts, president of the Buffalo Chamber Music Society, and vice chairman of the Buffalo Philharmonic Society. He died at eighty-two in Carmel, California, in 1963. He was survived by his fourth wife, Ella Gayle Hand Hamlin, a son, Chauncey, Jr., two daughters, ten grandchildren, and nine great-grandchildren.[27]

13.10 ❦ Number 1022 Delaware Avenue, BHS.

The first resident at #1022 was Calvin Phelps who lived there in the late 1860s. By 1870 he had died and his widow carried on with two children and two domestics. Widow and twenty-four year old son were still there in 1880, but by 1883 the lot had a new Queen Anne house(13.10) and a new family, that of John Satterfield(13.11), who had been born in Sharon, Pennsylvania, in 1839. He had a public school education and was set to learn the wheelwright's trade. However he enlisted as a private in the 140th Pennsylvania Volunteers, served in the Army of the Potomac throughout the Civil War from Gettysburg to Petersburg, and was present as a first lieutenant at Appomattox. After the war he got into the booming oil business in western Pennsylvania where he was

26 *CE*, April 16, 1960.
27 *NYT*, September 25, 1963.

13.11 ❦ John Satterfield, *M&FH*, 2:52.

associated with Hascal Taylor of #894 and later #1120 Delaware and later with T. S. McFarland, and George Forman of #824 Delaware. In 1875 John married Matilda Martin of Allentown and the couple lived in the Oil Regions for a few years. In 1880 he came to Buffalo as president of the Union Oil Company which merged with Standard Oil in 1892. For three years in the early 1880s the couple worked to complete the house that had been designed by Milton E. Beebe, designer of many handsome homes on the Avenue. This house boasted a long drawing room finished entirely in the finest white mahogany, a stained glass stairway window by John La Farge with a rich medieval design of acolytes with Yule candles, a third floor billiard and ballroom, an exceptionally large garage, and deep lawns and gardens extending to Atlantic Street, with tennis courts and a baseball diamond and the beautiful trees — elms planted by the Satterfields, and pear and apple trees, one of the latter a century old. In Buffalo Satterfield was director and vice president of the Third National Bank and an official of several streetcar lines that in 1902 were combined into the I.R.C. He was also an officer of the Cataract Power & Conduit Company and the Niagara Falls Power Company, and a member of Westminster. The Satterfields had two children, John Martin and Marie. The latter married an Austrian Count, grandnephew of the Empress Elizabeth. John Satterfield died in 1894.[28]

John Martin Satterfield had been born in Millerstown, Pennsylvania, in 1876. He came to Buffalo at six, attended P.S. 16 on Delaware Avenue, the Heathcote School, Lawrenceville Prep in New Jersey, and Yale's Sheffield Scientific School from which he graduated first in his class with a Ph.B. in 1898. Back in Buffalo he administered his father's large estate, especially the Boise operation which required time and travel. Subdivision and development of farm land off Main Street in Snyder and Williamsville which his father had purchased before his death was another Satterfield enterprise. He was a trustee of Fidelity Trust and first vice president and trustee of the American Savings Bank of which he had been an organizer. He also was involved with real estate in Idaho where for eight years he was president of the Boise City Irrigation and Land Company. Locally he belonged to the Chamber of Commerce, the Buffalo, Country, Saturn, University, Ellicott, Park, and Automobile clubs, and in New York to the Yale Club. He was a congregant of Trinity and was a Mason. In 1910 he married Rachel Phillips, daughter of James and Elizabeth Bartlett Phillips of Fitchburg, Massachusetts.[29] Rachel was an alumna of Miss Porter's at Farmington, studied in France and Germany, and was an excellent

28 *M&FH*, 2:51-52.
29 *Ibid.*, 53-54.

golf, tennis, violin, and contract bridge player. For twenty-five years she was on the board of the Visiting Nurses Association, and president for six. Her husband's most notable civic service concerned military aircraft and the Buffalo airport:

> In the early days of aviation back in 1908 he organized the present Aero Club of Buffalo, one of the first of its kind in the United States. Associated with him in the enterprise were such men as George Urban, the late Dr. Charles Cary and Ralph H. Sidway. This group built several workable airplanes which they tested at the risk of life and limb on a piece of property next to the Old Buffalo Country club. As the World War engulfed the major nations, Maj. Satterfield foresaw the time — which was not to come until 1917 — when the United States would be drawn into the conflict.
>
> In 1915, with the assistance of Aero club members, he organized a ground school of aviation in the 65th Armory building. Meetings were held once a week. Although the school had no official status it received assistance from both federal and state authorities. The major's right-hand man in this venture was Russell W. Bryant of the Bryant & Stratton Business School. It was at this time that Maj. Satterfield wrote what was one of the first books on military aviation. Maj. Satterfield was in France 18 months and was attached nearly all that time to the staff of Gen. John J. Pershing. His duties consisted principally of procurement of aircraft for the airmen of the line and the location and development of airfields and hangars.
>
> It was when he returned to Buffalo from France that he started the movement for the establishment of an adequate airport here. He was supported in his efforts by the Aero Club and the Buffalo Chamber of Commerce and later gained the active backing of leaders in all walks of life. Maj. Satterfield won public opinion to his side and in 1925 the City Council voted to establish a municipal flying field. Mr. Satterfield was in charge of designing and construction until the airport was completed in September 1926. Maj. Satterfield's services in the supply branch of the air service won the public commendation of Brig. Gen. William Mitchell, head of the United States army air forces in France during the World War.[30]

From his marriage until he left for France for eighteen months during World War I Major Satterfield resided at #1022 Delaware. On his return the family resided at #355 Linwood and his mother moved to #1022. "The Father of Buffalo's Airport" died in 1932 after an apparently successful operation. The funeral was at Trinity with Cameron J. Davis, bishop of Western New York, and Elmore M. McKee, rector of Trinity, officiating.[31]

13.12 ❦ Number 1040 Delaware, BHS.

Doctor Ray V. Pierce moved from #138 Delaware to #1040 (13.12) where he lived during the early 1880s and was succeeded by Charles A. Sweet. Sweet was born in Berkshire County, Massachusetts, in 1836

30 *BEN*, February 13, 1927.
31 *BEN*, February 12, 1932.

but spent his early years in the West. At nine, thrown back on his own resources, he came back east and found work as a clerk in a grocery store in Schenectady and later in the same position at Troy. In 1855 he went south for two years but reappeared in Troy engaged in freight forwarding. In 1862 he came to Buffalo where for twenty years he worked in transportation. He was quite successful since by 1881 he was president of the Third National Bank, of the Board of Trade when it entertained the United States Senate Committee on Transportation, and of the Young Men's Association. He was also member of the Grade Crossing Commission, and trustee of the Buffalo State Normal School and Buffalo General.[32] He died in 1903

By 1915 the householder at #1040 was George Armstrong Mitchell, prominent in Buffalo wholesale lumber circles for three decades. Born in 1874 in Washington, D. C., son of a minister, he came to Buffalo with his parents when his father was made pastor of First Presbyterian. He graduated from Central High in 1890 and from Princeton in 1894. He began his business career with Pratt & Letchworth, saddlery and hardware, and transferred to Union Car Company at Depew. In 1901 he, Pendennis White (#483 Delaware), and William H. Gratwick (#776 Delaware) formed White, Gratwick, & Mitchell, lumber dealers. Later he became vice president of Shredded Wheat of Niagara Falls until it was sold to National Biscuit. In 1910 he married Sarah Gates Hamlin, daughter of his neighbor, William Hamlin. In 1920 Mitchell became a trustee of First Presbyterian. He was also a dean of Saturn, and 1911-1915 president of the trustees of Nichols where Mitchell Hall is named for him. His last year at #1040 was 1925.[33]

The H. H. Richardson-style house at #1058 on the southwest corner of Butler Street (later Lexington Avenue) was for its entire existence a William Hamlin habitation:(13.13)

> The Gratwick house inspired several imitations along Delaware Avenue. Foremost among this group was the house at 1014 [read 1058] designed in 1889 by the Buffalo firm of Marling and Burdette for Harry [read William] Hamlin, vice president of the American Glucose Company. Henry Burdette had actually worked for a time in Richardson's office, and one assumes that he had the upper hand in what was a thoughtful interpretation of Richardson's principles. The carefully detailed Hamlin house, which was built of brick, echoed the refinement of surfaces of Richardson's Sever House at Harvard and the powerful masses of his Gratwick house.[34]

13.13 ❦ Number 1058 Delaware Avenue, Cigliano, *op. cit.*, p. 51.

William was the son of Cicero Hamlin of #1035 Delaware and brother of Harry of #1014. Both broth-

32 *Express*, September, 1888.
33 *CE*, May 4, 1943.
34 Cigliano and Landau, *op. cit.*, p. 51.

ers had been active, along with their father, in running American Glucose until it was sold in 1897. William's wife was Kate Gates, daughter of George Gates, the sleeping car magnate of #546 Delaware. William died in 1931 at eighty-one. His wife died in 1932. The house, a glut on the market in the Depression, stood empty until it was demolished in 1937 along with the barn where some of the famed Hamlin horses had been stabled. At that time three daughters of William and Kate Hamlin, Mrs. George A. Mitchell, Mrs. Susan Hamlin Follwell, and Mrs. Wilmot Griffiss, resided at the nearby luxury apartments at #800 West Ferry.[35]

Thomas Stephenson was a jeweler, who in 1850s had lived just north of Dan Castle. Stephenson's son John moved up to #1080 on the corner of Delaware and Butler in the mid-1860s. John was there in 1883 but next year it had become the home of Frederick J. Wheeler, assistant editor of the *Buffalo Express*. At the turn of the century and for several years afterwards it was the home of Charles Bingham, son of Robert M. Bingham of #393 Delaware, British-born proprietor of an iron forge back in 1860. Charles was born in Buffalo in 1843, attended public school and Central High, and at twenty-one entered business with his father under the name Bingham & Son. Later he was associated with Perry Taylor in Bingham & Taylor. His wife was Margaret Sudrick. However Bingham never got over the death of his only child, a seventeen year old daughter who was thrown from a horse in a Buffalo park. He was a fisherman and sportsman, and on his doctor's advice retired and moved to Florida for his wife's health. He died in 1914, leaving an estate estimated at $400,000 ($6,972,000 in 1997 dollars.)[36] He was followed at #1080 by Virginia White, her sister, and daughter, two domestics and a chauffeur. Lloyd Bissell, an auto parts executive and son of Arthur Bissell of #950 Delaware, resided at #1080 during the 1920s and early 1930s.

Mother and daughter, Louise and Theresa Schafer, were the first inhabitants of #1088 during the early twentieth century. By 1910 it had become the home of Clark Leonard Ingham and his wife, the former Annie Snell. Clark had been born at Ingham Mills, Herkimer County, in 1863. He attended public school, Little Falls Academy, and Mount Pleasant Military Academy. After clerking at a general store and in an underwear factory in Centerville, Michigan, he came to Buffalo in 1893, entered the real estate business and soon became vice president of Buffalo Realty. Between 1893 and 1900 he took a leading part in building operations. One of his major projects was the Lenox Apartments on North Street. He built and owned the Hengerer Building on the site of the Tifft House on Main Street. He promoted the formation of Frontier Telephone in 1902 and its merger with Consolidated Telephone. Ingham was also involved in building the Buffalo Rochester & Lockport Railway, a fifty-four mile high-speed line between Rochester and Lockport with rights into Buffalo on the I.R.C. which lasted 1909-1931. Two other utilities in which Ingham was concerned were gas companies in Niagara Falls and Dunkirk. He was a member of the Buffalo, Ellicott, and Country clubs, and attended

35 *BEN*, November 5, 1937.
36 *CA*, February 3, 1914.

Westminster. The Inghams were still living at #1088 in 1935.[37]

Number 1092 in 1880 was the home of Augustus H. Field. In 1905 it had become home to Dr. John McFarland, born in Petrolia, Pennsylvania, in 1876. In 1898 he graduated from Yale where he played football and was intercollegiate heavyweight wrestling champion in senior year. In 1902 he received his M.D. from Johns Hopkins. McFarland was issued one of the first licenses locally for operating steam-powered autos, an interest which led him to advocate traffic safety and to join others in founding the Judges and Police Executive Conference in 1932 of which he was chief medical advisor. He had been a member of the B.A.C. and the Canoe Club, and was an honorary member of the Lotus Bay Country Club at Farnham, where he had a summer home which became part of Evangola State Park in 1955. He died at eighty-nine in 1965, survived by his wife, the former Hazel Pfeiffer of Buffalo, a son, and two daughters. His funeral was held at Trinity.[38]

In 1910 the G. W. Olmsteads were living at #1094 and were followed there by Doctor Jacob S. Otto, a native Buffalonian, who attended P.S. 14, Central High, Princeton, class of 1895, and U.B. medical school, 1898, and practiced medicine in Buffalo for fifty years. He was captain and surgeon in the 74th Regiment NYNG 1901-1903 and for thirty-seven years until 1950 attending physician at Children's and at Meyer Memorial 1916-1937. For many years he taught medicine at U.B. Doctor Otto died in 1952.[39]

Next to occupy #1094, Phillip Metz, was son-in-law and next-door neighbor of the occupant of #1100 (13.14), Norman E. Mack (13.15.) And preceding Mack at #1100 in 1890 was Emory F. Close, an attorney. Therefore a sketch of the careers of Close and Mack will precede that of Metz. Close was born in Buffalo in 1859 of New England ancestry. His father was a ship captain on the Lakes. After public school, Emory clerked in a store and worked three years as assistant librarian at the Buffalo Public Library, a job which gave him the opportunity to study philosophy, biography, history, and English literature on his own. He also studied stenography and in 1877 entered the offices of Slocum & Thornton, official stenographers to the Eighth Judicial District of the Supreme Court for which he worked 1880-1888. In 1884 he was elected official stenographer of the state assembly, meanwhile studying law on his own. In 1885 he

13.14 ❦ Number 1100 Delaware Avenue, *City Beautiful*, p. 193.

37 *M&FH*, 2:88-89.
38 *CE*, March 15, 1965.
39 *CE*, May 5, 1952.

13. 15 ❦ Norman Edward Mack, *M&FH*, I, facing p. 308.

married Etta S. Cobb and in 1886 was admitted to the bar and formed a law partnership, Close & Fleishman, later Marcy & Close. His rise was rapid. In July 1897 President McKinley appointed him U.S. Attorney for the Northern District of New York. He had been an ardent Republican and the previous summer during the McKinley-Bryan contest led a contingent to Canton to "meet the Major." Emory Close died in 1902.[40]

Norman Edward Mack was born in West Williams, Ontario, in 1858. His parents moved to Cass City, Michigan, where his father worked as a farmer-contractor. Here Norman obtained a public school education. At thirteen he moved to the nearby village of Pontiac where he worked in stores and learned clerking. At fourteen he went to Chicago, then rising from the ashes of the previous year, 1871. There and in Detroit he had his first experience with journalism by way of selling advertising and subscriptions. In 1878 hearing that Jamestown, New York, was ripe for a local paper, he went there and started publication of the *Jamestown Sunday Gazette*. Next year he sold it at a profit and pushed on to Buffalo which had three Sunday papers struggling for existence. On September 7, 1879, the first issue of his *Buffalo Sunday Times* appeared. Colonel John B. Adams, another pioneer Buffalo publisher, suspended publication of his sheet and assumed editorial direction of the *Times*. Soon the *Sunday Herald* folded, and for a while Buffalo was down to two Sunday papers, the *Times* and the old *News*. When the *News* folded the *Times* quickly became the influential Sunday journal in Western New York. On September 13, 1883, Mack introduced the *Buffalo Evening Times*, a weekday afternoon paper. Bright and newsy, its growth was steady but not spectacular, its editor always taking the side that he thought was the most popular with the masses. Among causes for which he crusaded were clean government, free textbooks in public schools, free music in parks, shorter hours and better pay for policeman, and the abolition of overhead wires, overcrowding in public schools, and grade crossing abolition. The *Times* was a Democratic paper, supporting Cleveland for the presidency in 1884, 1888, and 1892 and in 1896 even Bryan, whom many Democrats detested. Until he retired in 1929 Mack was editor and publisher of both *Sunday* and *Evening Times*. He attended as a delegate every Democratic state and national nominating convention 1892-1912. He married Harriet Taggart of Buffalo in 1891. Among guests entertained at #1100 were Thomas Alva Edison, Alfred E. Smith, William Gibbs McAdoo, Harry Lauder, Lillian Russell, and Eleanor Roosevelt. The Macks had two daughters, Norma Emily

40 *M&FH*, 2:179.

Another interior view in the Mrs. Norma Mack Metz residence in Delaware Avenue.
A picture of one of the interiors of the Delaware Avenue home of
Mrs. Norma Mack Metz

13.16 ❦ Interior, #1094 Delaware, *City Beautiful*, p. 192.

and Harriet Taggart. The former married Phillip Metz, the latter Stuart Cary Welch. Mack was a member of the Buffalo Athletic and Country clubs, and of the National Chamber of Commerce and the National Press Club of Washington, D.C. He died in 1932.[41] His widow Harriet stayed at #1100 until her death in 1954. It remained vacant until purchased in 1958 by Benderson Development which acquired thereby the entire 281' frontage of the block on the west side of Delaware between Lexington and Highland. Benderson announced plans for a high rise, twelve to fifteen story apartment house there in the spring.[42] In anticipation of the razing, the Mack's household belongings were put on display the day before an auction. A traffic jam on Delaware resulted. Inside was a magnificent collection of silver, china, crystal, linens, and rugs the deceased widow had acquired on her world travels. Worth special mention was a gold-lined egg set with its egg-cups and spoons nestled in a silver carrier. Also shown were sparkling chandeliers and English, French, and Italian furniture. In the Red Damask Room was a collection of Staffordshire china cups from the eighteenth and nineteenth centuries.[43]

Phillip Metz, who married Norma Mack, was born in Omaha and came to Buffalo where he began his career in journalism as a reporter for his father-in-law's paper, the *Times*. After its purchase by Scripps-Howard, Phillip was briefly president and business manager, but the Metzes soon left for Omaha where Phillip joined the staff of the *Omaha Bee*. He died there in 1941.[44] Figure 13.16 gives

41 *M&FH*, 2:308-311; Wilner, *op cit.*, 3:124-130; *Who was Who*, 1:762; *CE*, September 9, 1958.
42 *BEN*, November 13, 1959.
43 *CE*, September 22, 1958.
44 *CE*, July 15, 1941.

Above 13.17 ❦ Number 1114 Delaware, two views. photograph by author in spring 1998.
Below ❦ *City Beautiful*, p. 22.

two views of the interior of his Buffalo home shortly before he and wife went west.[45]

At #1106 in 1880 before Highland Avenue had been put through to Richmond lived J. B. Holmes, a planing mill proprietor, his twenty-two year old machinist son, a twenty-six year old daughter, and two domestics. In 1886 upon the retirement of her husband, Libertus Van Bokkelen, rector of Trinity, his wife moved into #1106. He died in 1899, but the pair seem to have gone their separate ways after his retirement.

At #1114(13.17) on the northwest corner of Highland and Delaware by 1920 a handsome Second Empire mansion had been erected for Roscoe Rowland Mitchell who had been born in 1883 in Cohoes to Doctor James H. Mitchell and his wife Margaret Rowland. Roscoe had graduated from Williams College in 1904 and from Albany Law School in 1907, the year he came to Buffalo and passed the bar. There his first association was with Norton, Penny, & Sears, which handled mostly I.R.C. work. In 1914 he formed a new firm, Mitchell & Albro, but in 1917, with America at war, he devoted most of his effort to promoting successfully the First Liberty Loan. Thereafter he was named assistant of a bureau of the Federal Food Administration and sent to England and France as chairman of the Federal Food Commission. He returned to Buffalo in February 1918 and stumped the country on the need for conservation. In May he returned to France where he worked with the Red Cross. He was made chief of the French Zone Home & Hospital Services, which covered the area from Verdun to Amiens, with headquarters in Paris. He rose from first lieutenant in the Red Cross to Chief of the Aviation Service, a post he held until the Armistice. Back in Buffalo he became a member of Botsford, Lyte, Mitchell, & Albro, which had been formed in 1917. His local fame was enhanced when he won the acquittal of a man who had previously been found guilty of murdering his mother and brother. He was also made a member and secretary of the Niagara Bridge Commission, established in 1921 to build the Grand Island Bridges. He was a member of Westminster

45 *Times*, September 6, 1931.

and an astonishing number of social clubs: Buffalo, Saturn, Country, Trap & Field, Aero, Tennis & Squash, Saddle & Bridle, Erie Downs, Bath of Miami, and Everglades of Palm Beach. He died after an unsuccessful operation in 1932, survived by his wife, Ada Butler Mitchell, the daughter of Edward Butler of the *News*, a son, Edward Butler Mitchell, and a daughter, Marjorie Butler Mitchell. Mitchell's brother-in-law had to be called home for the funeral from the Republican Convention at Chicago, then engaged in pointlessly renominating Herbert Hoover for president.[46]

Succeeding Mitchell at Delaware and Highland was William C. Baird, the son of Frank B. Baird of #1069, the "Father of the Peace Bridge." William Baird was born in Buffalo in 1907. He attended Nichols, Phillips-Exeter, Williams, from which he graduated in 1929, and the Harvard Business School. In 1930 he entered the family business, Buffalo Pipe & Foundry, of which he became secretary-treasurer. At thirty-one in 1938 he became the youngest president of the Buffalo Chamber of Commerce. After his father's death, William joined the Buffalo and Fort Erie Public Bridge Authority. He was also a director of M&T. During World War II he served as a lieutenant commander in the Naval Reserve. He was a Mason and belonged to the Country and Tennis and Squash clubs. His wife was Marjorie Butler Mitchell, the daughter of Roscoe Mitchell, whom he married in 1930 and divorced in 1945. Baird died in Williamsville in 1987.[47]

In the early 1940s #1114 became the home of Kent S. McKinley who had been born in Adams, New York, came to Buffalo at ten, graduated from Dartmouth, and fought in World War I. He exhibited an early fascination with the theatre, backing and writing plays for Broadway and playing summer stock. He married Marjorie Butler Mitchell, William Baird's first wife, worked at Buffalo's Bell Aircraft plant during World War II, and after the war owned and managed Trans Studio, the area's Muzak franchise. He published his first newspaper in 1946, the *Watertown (N.Y) News* and was active in a marble firm in Bradenton, Florida, and a brokerage house in New York. In 1950 Mrs. McKinley, who had grown up there, donated #1114 to the Episcopal Diocese of Western New York to house the bishop's study, a private chapel, and diocesan offices. Then the McKinleys moved to Sarasota where Kent became a newspaper editor, a member of the state legislature, and a major figure in organizing the Republican Party in the state. The *Sarasota News*, an afternoon daily which he founded in 1954, was widely billed as the first Republican paper south of the Mason-Dixon line. McKinley numbered James C. Hagerty, press secretary to President Eisenhower, and President Nixon among his personal friends. At seventy-four McKinley died in 1972 at his summer home in Lorraine, Ontario, outside Port Colborne. He had been a member of The Players Club in New York City, the Saturn and Buffalo clubs in Buffalo, and Cherry Hill in Ontario. He also belonged to several clubs in Sarasota.[48]

46 *Courier*, June 15, 1932.
47 Horton, *op. cit.*, 3:437-438; *Who Was Who in America*, 9:17.
48 *BEN*, October 19, 1972.

Hascal Taylor, an oil man, was the first inhabitant at #1120 Delaware in 1884. He was followed by 1891 by Frank McGraw, a lumber dealer, and in 1897 by Gibson L. Douglass, vice president and manager of the Western Transportation Company. At the dawn of the new century, the owner was Christian Klinck, born in Schonenberg, Bavaria in 1833, of whom Hill wrote in 1923:

> The founder of the Christian Klinck Packing Company came to Buffalo in the 'fifties. Christian Klinck was then seventeen years old, and had learned the trade of butchering in Germany. He had only enough money to pay his railway fare to Buffalo, and so came, though it had been his intention of settling in Cincinnati. He found employment at his trade in Buffalo at a salary of six dollars a week; yet out of that amount was able to save sufficient within six years to venture into independent business. As a retail butcher he succeeded well; so well that in 1868 he was able to establish himself reasonably well in the wider branch of the meat trade - packing. Within forty years the packing establishment he founded had expanded its operations to such an extent that its plant on Depot street, South Buffalo, covered twenty-five acres and embraced twenty-five buildings. In 1906 more than 370,000 head of cattle and hogs were slaughtered in the Klinck plant; and the expansion since had been proportionate. Christian Klinck was a man of fine character, and while for thirty years he devoted himself closely to the development of his large packing business, he did, early and late in his Buffalo residence, enter into civic activities. He was an alderman in 1863, and in the 'nineties was a member of the City Council.[49]

Klinck had lived for many years on Swan Street, once the most fashionable in the city. He was the last to desert the old neighborhood which he did three years before his death in 1903.[50] His son Albert, who had followed his father into meatpacking, was still at #1120 in 1910.

13.18 ❦ Henry C. Zeller, Wilner, *op. cit.*, 3:221.

By 1920 Henry Zeller(13.18) and family had taken up residence at #1120. Henry was born 1860, in a house on Court Street, attended P.S. 13 on Oak Street, took a business course at Bryant & Stratton, and went to work with his father at Laub & Zeller, tanners. The elder Zeller had come to Buffalo from Wurttemburg. This firm was dissolved in 1888 because each partner wished to start his own business. That year Laub formed George Laub & Sons and next year Zeller formed G. F. Zeller & Sons. The Laub concern remained at #1051 Clinton while Zeller moved to Smith and Howard Streets. G. F. Zeller died in 1907 and his son succeeded him as president until 1941 when he became chairman of the board, and another son, Edward, was elected president. During Henry Zeller's thirty-four years as president the company tripled its business. In 1906 he was appointed Police Commissioner by Mayor J. N. Adam. The automobile was becoming a threat to life

49 Hill, *op, cit.*, 2:821-822.
50 *Express*, June 4, 1903.

and limb, and Zeller reacted by creating the city's first motorcycle patrol and drawing up a set of traffic rules. He zealously served his six-year term at the end of which he told Mayor Louis Fuhrman that he did not wish to be reappointed. Zeller had long been a Democrat but was also a friend of Herbert Hoover. In 1940 he opposed a third term for Franklin Roosevelt, saying, "I don't think the spending of millions has brought results." World War II was to solve the problem. Golf was among Zeller's favorite diversions. In 1927 he made a hole-in-one on the third at Wanakah. he spent several weeks in the summer hunting and fishing in the Canadian woods. He and his wife, the former Kate Lenhard, whom he married in 1884, made frequent trips to California, Hawaii, and the West Indies. He was involved in local activities, achieving an attendance record of 102 consecutive months at the Rotary Club. He was a three-term director of the Chamber of Commerce and was a director of the Buffalo Livestock Exchange and the Buffalo Tuberculosis Association, and from 1905 until his death director of the Liberty Bank and its predecessor, the German-American Bank. His memberships included the Buffalo Club for forty years, the Buffalo and the Niagara Falls Country clubs, the B.A.C., the Buffalo Society of Natural Sciences, the Society for the Prevention of Cruelty to Animals, and the Automobile Club. He and his wife celebrated their golden wedding anniversary in 1934; she died two years later. He died at eighty-two in 1942.[51]

Beginning in 1872 #1132(13.19) Delaware was the home of John Wayland, a German immigrant, who had been born in 1837. In 1852 he began as a junior clerk with the Buffalo Savings Bank. When he retired in 1902 as a cashier, he had been with the bank for a half-century. In 1863 he had been sent with the 65th Regiment, NYNG, in which he was a captain, to take part in putting down the draft riots which had broken out in New York City after Gettysburg. In 1900 he and his wife Mary could afford a coachman and two domestics. His twenty-seven year old son Edward lived at home and worked in his father's bank. The father had become an ardent horseman and a devout member of Westminster, in which he was a deacon. Poor health forced him to retire in 1902, sell his house in Buffalo, and head for Pasadena where he died in 1919.[52]

13.19 ❦ Number 1132 Delaware Avenue, photograph by author, spring, 1999.

Wayland's successor at #1132 was William M. Ramsdell, descendant of Elder William Brewster of Mayflower fame. Ramsdell's parents had come to Buffalo from New London, Connecticut. The

51 *BEN*, April 8, 1942.
52 *CA*, October 10, 1902; June 4, 1919.

father invested in the Delaware Avenue Land Company, which owned a tract between Delaware and Military, where Ramsdell Avenue recalls this arrangement. William had been born on Mariner Street in 1864, attended P.S. 36 on Cottage Street, and Central High. In 1879 while still in school he became a newspaper carrier for the *Express*. At seventeen he applied for and received an office job at the same paper at $2.50 a week, and began his ascent up the management ladder through assistant business manager, business manager, and publisher from 1909 until the 1926 merger with the *Courier*. Travel was his hobby. In 1893 he opened the first travel bureau in the state outside New York. In 1894 he married Margaret Adam, sister of Robert B. Adam of #448 Delaware. The couple had four children, one of whom became Mrs. Dexter P. Rumsey. In 1912 Ramsdall met Rudyard Kipling and family on a train stalled during a severe storm in the mountains above Bologna. The men became friends and subsequently corresponded. Ramsdell was a great lover of music, which derived from his mother who had sung in a church choir in New London. He sang as a boy in the choir of Ascension Church and later was active in the Buffalo Vocal and Philharmonic Society. He was a voracious reader, a long-time member of Wanakah, the Academy of Fine Arts, and Westminster. He died at eighty-three on New Year's Day in 1948.[53]

The granite mansion at #1140(13.20) on the southwest corner of West Ferry and Delaware was erected for self-made multimillionaire and tycoon William James ("Fingy") Conners, who was born in Buffalo in 1857, son of Peter Conners(13.21), who was born and raised in Canada and was a university graduate, and his wife, the former Mary Scanlan, a native of Ireland. Their home stood near the corner of Louisiana and South Streets in the First Ward. William attended P.S. 4 on Elk Street and then P.S. 30 on what became O'Connell Street. He earned his first money ferrying scoopers working on the elevators along Buffalo Creek and the City Canal across the Ohio Basin:

13.20 ❦ Number 1140 Delaware Avenue, photograph by author, spring, 1999.

> It was at the age of 13 that Mr. Conners began work on a lake steamboat, a connection which he afterwards expanded and retained until the day of his death. Those were rough days on the docks. His early companions were stevedores, grain shovelers, and sailors. One had to be handy with his fists in the primitive struggle for place which marked the Great Lakes ports in the early 70s.
>
> There is abundant record that Mr. Conners early became a leader among those with whom his lot was cast. It was a school that bred leaders in more than one walk of life. The Sheehans, John C., and William F., were graduates of it. So was the late Archbishop Quigley. So is former Supreme Court Justice Daniel J. Kenefick.

53 *CE*, January 2, 1948.

> Mr. Conners became a stevedore. Of keener mind than his mates he saw the possibilities of organization. There were boss scoopers who held sway in the business of unloading grain, why not a similar system among the stevedores.
>
> Mr. Conners answered the question by gradual expansion of his sphere of authority until he controlled the loading and unloading of package freight at all the important ports on the Great Lakes: Buffalo, Cleveland, Detroit, Chicago, Milwaukee, Duluth. With other business enterprises in which he later became interested he headed an army upwards of 6000 employees.[54]

13.21 ❦ William J. Conners, *M&FH*, I, facing p. 297.

There is much sweeping of facts under the rug here, a careless use of chronology, and a failure to mention intimidation of workingmen by Connors and his henchmen. The Sheehans were standard late nineteenth century Irish-American machine politicians, more adept at ballot-stuffing than good government. William C. moved to New York where he became a power in Tammany Hall. In the early 1870s James Quigley was a student at Saint Joseph's College and in 1874 began five years of study for the priesthood in Rome. As Bishop of Buffalo in 1899 his role in settling a dockers' strike was in direct opposition to that of Conners. Judge Kenefick was born in 1863, so that at the beginning of the 1870s he would have been seven years old.

Very different from the viewpoint of the *News* is that of Professor J. David Valaik, in the *Canisius College Chronicle* for February 1985:

> In the spring of 1899, 10,000 Buffalo dockworkers went on strike against the corrupting tyranny of William J. Connors. For years "Boss" Connors was the sole employer of almost every laboring man on the docks. If not chosen by a Connors henchman, you didn't work. To be paid, you went to a Connors salon, of which there were many near the docks; there you spent your hard-earned pay, or you didn't work again. It was cruel, it was degrading, but it worked, and it made Connors a rich man. The "white slaves" of the docks, as Buffalo's Catholic newspaper referred to the workers, made him a wealthy man, and seeking respectability, Connors bought newspapers, the Enquirer in 1895 and the Courier in 1897.
>
> Impressed not at all, the workers formed a union independent of Connors' control, and when locked out by his henchman, they struck not for more money, not for fewer hours, but for elementary justice. Soon the effects of the strike were felt as far west as Chicago and east to the anthracite mines in Pennsylvania, and as the strike persisted the prospect of violence increased. There were two shootings, but in spite of numerous provocations the striking workers, a very large percentage of whom were Irish, remained peaceful as their priests were urging.

54 *BEN*, October 5, 1929.

> Taking their signal from Albany, the A.F. of L. came to town and endorsed the credentials of the new, anti-Connors union. The State Board decided in their favor and a few "mysterious" businessmen from out of town visited Connors, as did from the shipping companies which had contracts with him. Then to the very forefront of the battle lines stepped Bishop James E. Quigley, who boldly championed the strikers' cause. Week after week, the Catholic Union and Times urged restraint upon the workers but pounded away at Connors as an "atrocious liar," and charged him with seeking to incite mutiny and murder. By May 23, 1899, the battle was won. Connors' power was broken, and the rights of Buffalo's workers were advanced.[55]

The most recent historian of Erie County in a garbled account of the 1890 dock strike, while conceding that Quigley's intervention was "very effective indeed," that "Conners ceased the struggle," and that "in time it became clear that the workers were victorious," also pointed out that "these gains were wiped out in spite of the growth of the labor movement, after only a few years." Grain scooping was not a skill, and workers who enjoyed gains at the time were members of skilled trade unions.[56]

Connors moved from freight handling to other fields. In 1889 he became president of the Vulcanite Asphalt Paving Company, and a year later president of Magnus Beck Brewing. He acquired extensive land holdings in South Buffalo and built whole neighborhoods. It was the period of the city's greatest population growth. Connors had concurrently been moving into newspaper publishing, probably as a prelude to politics. In 1895 he purchased a controlling interest in the *Buffalo Enquirer*. A year later he acquired complete control and modernized its printing plant with a Hoe press, equal to the best in the state. Soon circulation of the *Enquirer* tripled. At the same time he launched the *Morning Record*, an immediate success. In 1897 he bought the *Buffalo Courier* and merged it with the Record under the name of *Courier-Record*, later shortened to *Buffalo Courier*. He continued with the *Courier* until January 1925 when it was transformed into a tabloid and christened the *Daily Star*. The *Star* may not have been a success since in 1926 it was discontinued after the merger of the *Courier* and the *Express* into the *Courier-Express*, which survived until 1982. The new paper was the first in Buffalo to come out with a colored supplement and cutouts.

Long nominally a Republican, Connors threw off the mask when he bought the *Courier* and was elected chairman of the Democratic State Committee 1906. His man for governor that year was the mercurial William Randolph Hearst, whose national chain of newspapers specialized in non-news. He was defeated by the more admirable Charles Evans Hughes, but the rest of the Democratic statewide ticket won. Connors' last hurrah in politics came in 1922 when he tried to capture control of the Erie County Democracy in the interests, once again, of Hearst as candidate for governor. The Hearst-Connors forces were handily defeated by others led by former Governor Alfred E. Smith and Buffalo's own William H. Fitzpatrick.

55 J. David Valaik, "Theodore Roosevelt in Buffalo," *Canisius College Chronicle*, 15, #5, February 1985, pp. 6-7.

The waterfront had not seen its last of Connors:

> Mr. Connors was 59 years old when, in 1916, he undertook what many describe as his greatest achievement, the organization of the Great Lakes Transit Corporation, which gave him control of practically all of the railroad lake transportation interests, including the largest fleet of package freight and passenger steamships, with one exception, that ever had been assembled by a single American company on the Great Lakes. Congress having passed a law forbidding railroad lines from owning, controlling or operating water transportation lines, Mr. Conners conceived the plan of forming a corporation to take over the great fleets of steamships operated on the lakes by the railroads and which under the provisions of the act, they would be obliged to abandon. Through the organization of the Great Lakes Transit Corporation, Mr. Conners brought his stupendous plan to complete consummation [*sic*] and, as chairman of the board of that corporation, he became the head of a company controlling about 85 percent of the package freighters on the Great Lakes. . . . .
>
> It was the Panama Canal act that forced the railroads to surrender their steamship lines. At that time seven great trunk lines were operating fleets of freight and passenger boats on the lakes, among them the New York Central, Pennsylvania, Erie, Lackawanna, Rutland, and Lehigh Valley roads. The Great Lakes Transit Corporation's stock was fixed at $20,000,000 and it took over about 33 big freight boats, some passenger vessels and in addition, acquired splendid terminal facilities in any lake cities.[57]

The government's war on the railroads, which had begun in earnest under TR, had moved into high gear. The nation would be the loser.

In 1917 Connors became interested in Florida, where he had a winter home at Palm Beach. He purchased about 5,000 acres along the shore of Lake Okeechobee for a model farm. Reclamation progressed on a big scale. The land was stocked with cattle and hogs and became one of the outstanding stock farms in South Florida. In 1923 he began a fifty-mile highway around the shore of Lake Okeechobee which connected with a road out of Palm Beach. This was finished the following year and operated as a toll road by the Conners Florida Highway Company. He also contracted with the state to build the Harding Memorial Bridge across the Kissimmee River west of Lake Okeechobee which was completed in record time. Desiring more time in Florida, Conners turned over direction of his newspapers in 1919 to William J. Conners, Jr., who became the publisher. The father likewise turned over to Junior the direction of the Great Lakes Transit Corporation, the W. J. Connors Contracting Company, the George W. Jennings Lumber Company, and the William J. Connors Car Shops — the former New York Central shops in East Buffalo.

William J Conners, Sr., was married three times: in 1881 to Catherine Mahaney of Buffalo, who died leaving three children, Peter Newell, who died in 1908, Mary, who married Edwin C. Andrews, and Katherine, the wife of Francis X. Ryan of Pasadena; in 1893 Connors married Mary Alice Jordan of West Seneca, by whom he had three children, the youngest of whom was William, Jr; in March

56 W. Dunn, *op. cit.*, pp. 236-238.
57 *CE*, October 5, 1929.

1924 he married Grace Hammond who survived him. Shortly before his death Conners unveiled plans for a modern printing plant at Main and Goodell. It was completed in December 1930. Meanwhile Conners had died at seventy-two on October 5, 1929. Within two weeks the Panic of 1929 struck Wall Street followed by the Depression Decade of the 1930s. [58]

William J. Conners, Jr., had been born in 1895. He attended Nichols and Harstrom School in Norwalk, Connecticut, in preparation for Yale. In October 23, 1917, he married Corinne H. Tilford of New York. One of the first naval air units was formed at Yale, and Conners immediately joined. After the Armistice he returned to Buffalo, became head of most of his father's enterprises and continued to live in the paternal home at #1140 Delaware. He was recalled to active service in the Navy during World War II, which he spent in administrative duties in Buffalo, the Panama Canal Zone, and at Sampson Naval Training Center in New York. He was an indefatigable sportsman engaged in hunting, sailing, and deep-sea fishing. His memberships included the Saturn, Country, and Buffalo clubs, and the Anglo-American Fish & Game Club in Canada. Besides involvement in strictly family enterprises, he was a director of Marine Trust, Sterling Engine Company, Maxson-Cadillac, Dold Meat Packing, and American Shipbuilding, and was a trustee of Millard Fillmore Hospital. He died at fifty-five on in 1951 and was buried at Holy Cross Cemetery in Lackawanna. All the companies forming the Connors industrial empire, save for the Courier Express, were being dissolved at the time of his death.[59]

Number 1140 was sold to Irving Rosen, owner of United Recovery Company, a scrap-metal firm that dealt with industrial plants. He was also president of R & R Salvage Company, which worked with auto wreckers. Rose said that he intended to occupy the twenty-room house. He noted that it was built in 1908 of stone and marble. The basement contained a gaming room, two fireplaces, a swimming pool, and a gymnasium. On the first floor was a large reception room, a semicircular solarium, and a mahogany paneled dining room. There were five bedrooms and four bathrooms on the second floor, plus a large library. More bedrooms could be found on the third floor together with a stage and dressing rooms on the third. The four-car stone garage had two apartments on the second floor.[60]

58 Wilner, *op. cit.*, 473.
59 Horton, *op. cit.*, 3:165.
60 *BEN*, May 2, 1951.

CHAPTER

14 WEST FERRY STREET TO CHAPIN PLACE: *East Side*

The map for this chapter is figure map 14.1. The base date of this map is 1915 There are no side streets intersecting on the eastside, three on the west.

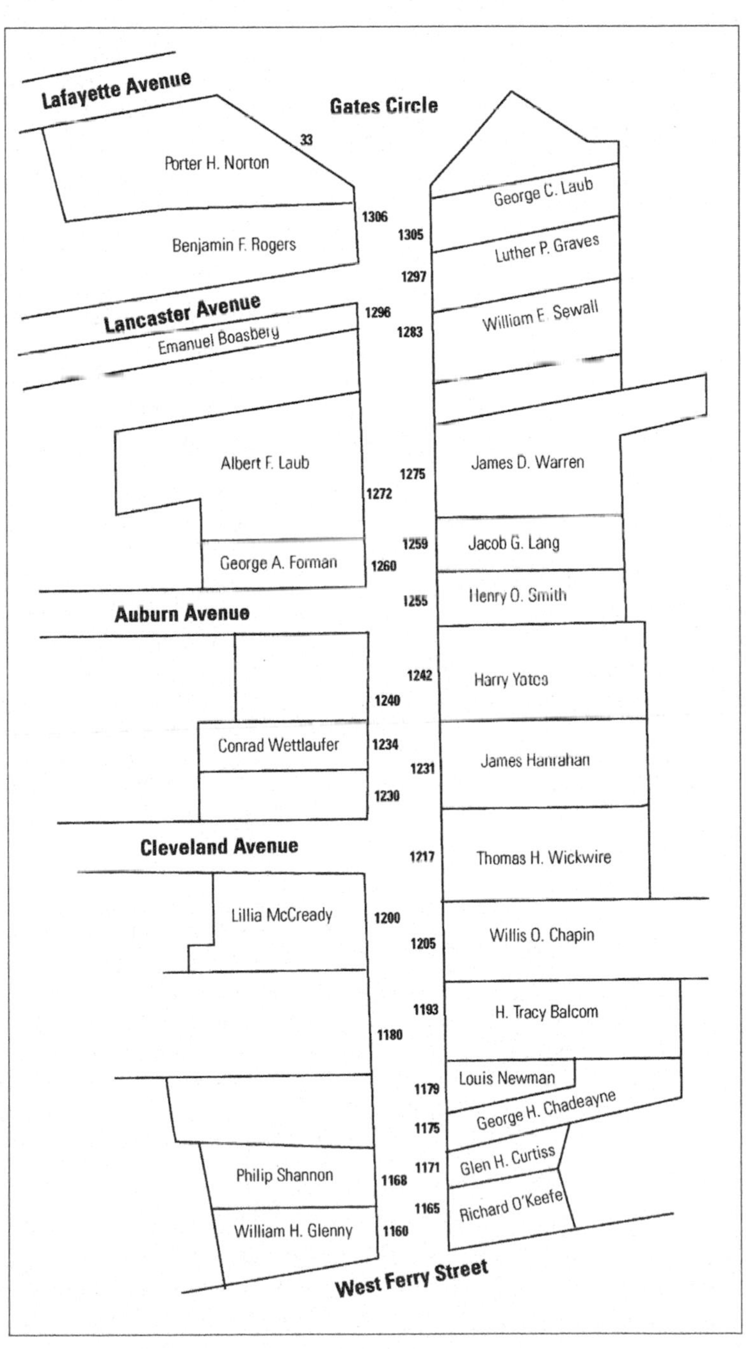

14.1 ❦ West Ferry to Gates Circle, 1915, drawn by author from 1915 Century Atlas.

1870

WEST FERRY STREET

1171 John K. Tucker 51 NY hotelier
Mary Tucker 40 *ux.*
Mary Beals 20 NY
John Smith Canada West hostler

1181 John L. Alberger 38 Maryland butcher
Mary Alberger 36 Ohio *ux.*
Alois Alberger 2 NY
Louis Alberger 6 NY school
Eliza Pauls 20 NY
Mary Oatfield 20 NY
David Thompson 29 NY hostler

1193 George Peugeot 62 France
Susan Peugeot 61 France *ux.*
Frank Peugeot 22 NY office clerk
Sonia Peugeot 22 boarder
Mary Almey 17 Prussia

1217 Robert Montgomery 50 NY ship captain
Mary Montgomery 16 NY school
Emma Montgomery 14 NY school
Susan Montgomery 13 NY school
Schuyler Montgomery 11 NY school
Irving Montgomery 10 NY school
Kate Montgomery 8 NY school
Robert Montgomery 6 NY school
Jane Sang 47 NY
Eliza Fider NY
Eliza Vollmer 16 NY

1880

WEST FERRY STREET

1171 Amelia Tucker

1181 John L. Alberger 49 Maryland retired merchant
Mary Alberger 46 Ohio *ux.*
Louis R. Alberger 16 NY son school
Allie H. Alberger 11 NY son
Henry Daw 21 NY coachman
Louisa Grundlach 22 NY

1203 Eliza S. Sisson 48 NY widow
Margaret Willis 70 NY mother
Ruth Donshee 42 NY visitor
Jennie Donshee 4 NY visitor school
Eaton Whiteman 14 NY school

1205 Courtney De Cew 32 Canada lumber dealer
Herbert De Cew 18 Canada clerk

1217 Robert Montgomery 63 Ireland vessel owner
Agnes Montgomery 42 Ohio *ux.*
Mary Montgomery 25 NY daughter
Emma Montgomery 24 NY daughter
Laura Montgomery 22 NY daughter
Kate Montgomery 18 NY daughter school
Robert Montgomery 16 NY son school
Mary Robbins 18 California
Henry Parah 15 Prussia

1243 Edward Rischman 59 Hesse-Darmstadt yeoman
Wilhelmina Rischman 50 Prussia *ux.*
Louis C. Rischman 21 NY son clerk
Edward C. Rischman 19 NY son
Mina Rischman 17 NY daughter
Nellie Rischman 14 NY daughter school
Rosa Rischman 11 NY daughter school

1277 George A. Armstrong 36 Canada carpenter
Marian Armstrong 35 Canada *ux.*
Corah Mabel Armstrong 7 NY daughter
Alfred Armstrong 4 NY son
John W. W. Armstrong 2 NY son
Val Armstrong 2 months son

1283 Edward Daw 58 England laborer
Ann Daw 49 England *ux.*
James Daw 21 NY machinist
William Daw 18 NY wagon manufacturer
Edward Daw 114 NY school
Henry Daw 11 NY school
George Daw 11 NY school

BOUCK AVENUE ❦ End of Block

1891

WEST FERRY STREET

1175 George H. Chadeayne builder

1179 Walter G. Robbins vp Buffalo Fish Co.
Frederick R. Robbins bookkeeper

1181 John L. Alberger sugar and salt machinery
Alvin Alberger

1203 Benjamin Fenton president Erie Preserving Co.

1283 Edward Daw 68 England laborer
Ann Daw 59 England *ux.*
Edmund Daw 23 NY son machinist
Henry Daw 14 NY grandson

BOUCK AVENUE ❦ End of Block

1900

WEST FERRY STREET

1165 Alice Hoffman 54 NY teacher
Mary Hoffman 46 NY sister teacher
Kathleen Haggerty 19 Ireland

1171 Edwin D. Poole 57 Mass. lumber dealer
Gertrude Poole 52 Georgia *ux.*
Harriet Poole 29 NY daughter
Gardiner Poole 24 NY son
Gardiner Manley 16 Missouri school
Norton Manley 14 Missouri school
Ida C. Smith 31 Canada

1175 George H. Chadeayne 54 NY builder
Iona Chadeayne 52 Wisconsin ux.
William C. Chadeayne 24 NY son sales
Eleanor J. Chadeayne 22 NY daughter school
Mary E. Chadeayne 18 NY son school
George D. Chadeayne 18 NY son school
Marie Hinds 30 England

Israel Dearlove 26 England coachman
Maria Dearlove 26 England *ux.*
David Williams 32 Wales boarder coachman

1179 H. Tracy Balcom 35 Ohio
Margaret Balcom 27 Kentucky *ux.*
H. Tracy Balcom 4 Pa. son
Minnie Olsen 29 Sweden maid
Susie Miller 21 Canada maid

1181 John L. Alberger 68 Maryland
mechanical engineer
Cassie Alberger 51 Ohio *ux.*
Jeannie Alberger 24 Illinois niece
Scott C. R. Alberger 20 Illinois nephew
Abby Louima NY 13

1203 Benjamin Fenton 69 NY
Julia F. Fenton 62 Pa. *ux.*
Benjamin W. Fenton 28 California son
Frances H. ? 20 NY

1217 Robert W. Jones Brinker & Jones

1231 James Hanrahan coal and wood
Thomas J. Hanrahan clerk

1243 Gustave Fleischman distiller

1275 Mrs. E. M. Lay

1283 Edmund Daw gardener

BOUCK AVENUE ❦ End of Block

1217 Robert W. Jones 69 Pa.
B.L. Jones 32 Pa. son
Candice Jones 32 NY daughter-in-law
Kathleen Jones 31 Pa. daughter
Helen Jones 24 Pa. daughter
Louise H. Elsner 34 Pa. maid
Maggie Ryan 29 NY maid

1231 James Hanrahan 57 Ireland coal dealer
Rosanna Hanrahan 50 Pa. *ux.*
James E. Hanrahan 20 NY son school
Mary F. Hanrahan NY 18 daughter school
Emmet Hanrahan 13 son school
Margaret Hanrahan 24 NY daughter
Bertha Gaffney 24 Canada

1283 Frank N. Clare 32 NY coach manufacturer
Sophie Clare 31 NY *ux.*
Margie Clare 5 NY daughter
Franklin Clare 5 NY son

1297 Luther P. Graves 38 NY lumber merchant
Nellie Graves 39 NY *ux.*
Chester Graves 15 NY school
Stanley Graves 13 NY school
Lucy Graves 21 NY school
Luther P. Graves Jr. 6 NY school
Nelson M. Graves 5 NY school
Helen Graves ? months NY
Mary Bernhardt 54 Pa. nurse
Carrie Campbell 24 Canada housemaid
Mary Glass 45 Canada cook

LAFAYETTE AVENUE ❦ End of Block

1905

WEST FERRY STREET

1171 Edward D Poole 62 lumber merchant
Helen Poole 53 *ux.*
Gardiner Poole 25 son
Hallie Poole 32 daughter teacher
Henry H. Wilcox 38 boarder publisher

1915

WEST FERRY STREET

1165 Richard C. O'Keefe 41 secretary
Chamber of Commerce
Nell O'Keefe 42 *ux.*
Richard C. O'Keefe Jr. 10 son
John B. O'Keefe 3 son
Harold Jackson 51 captain US Army
Eleanor Jackson 39 *ux.*
Flora Sackett 30
Anna Hinzman 22 nursemaid
May Darren 24 cook

1171 Glenn H. Curtiss 36 manufacturer
Lena Curtiss 35 *ux.*
Glenn H. Curtiss Jr. 2 son
Jennie Neff 57 mother-in-law
Minnie A. Hendershott 29 nursemaid

1175 George H. Chadeayne 59 builder
Clara Chadeayne 57 *ux.*
William C. Chadeayne 29 son motor builder
Eleanor Chadeayne 27 daughter
Mary E. Chadeayne 25 daughter teacher
Leo D. Chadeayne 23 son student

1179 H. Tracy Balcom 40 piano dealer
Margaret Balcom 37 *ux.*
H. Tracy Balcom Jr. 10 son school
Joseph Huber 33
Nellie Huber 33 cook

1181 John Alberger 73 pump manufacturer
Cassie M. Alberger 54 *ux.*
Jeanne Ross 29 niece
Louise Alberger 71 sister
Barbara Moer 53 Canada

1203 Benjamin Fenton 74 manager caning company
Julia Fenton 67 *ux.*
Benjamin Fenton 34 son clerk

1217 Harlow W. Bailey 40 manufacturer of machines
Florence Bailey 32 *ux.*
Harlow W. Bailey Jr. 7 son school
Phoebe A. Bailey 1 daughter
Mary O'Brien 28 Ireland
Elizabeth Neubeck 33
Anna Schatzer 18

1231 James Hanrahan 59 Ireland coal dealer
Rosanna Hanrahan 52 *ux.*
James E. Hanrahan 25 son carter
Florence Hanrahan 21 daughter
Emmet Hanrahan 19 son school
Annie Bracklett 29 Norway

1243 Harry Yates 40 hotel proprietor
Mary Yates 35 Canada *ux.*
Theresa Yates 11 daughter school

1175 George H. Chadeayne 69 real estate
Clara H. Chadeayne 67 *ux.*
Mary E. Chadeayne 35 daughter
kindergarten teacher
George D. Chadeayne 33 son builder
George A. Newman 67 caretaker
Barbara Newman 64 Germany *ux.*

1179 Louis Newman 56 Tonawanda Board & Paper
Lillian D. Newman 50 *ux.*
Lloyd D. Newman 28 son purchasing agent
Cedric A. Rebadow 25 son-in-law salesman
Anne G. Rebadow 23 daughter
Christine Custer 28
Catherine Custer 30

1193 H. Tracy Balcom 50 retired
Margaret M. Balcom 42 *ux.*
H. Tracy Balcom Jr. 19 son college
Jane R. Balcom 7 daughter school
Harriet Fogelsanger 16 cook
Lena Hornung 25
Maria Wilkinson 20

1205 Willis Chapin 54 attorney
Abbie F. Chapin 46 *ux.*
William R. Chapin 22 son student
Delia Talty 32 Ireland maid
Annie Davis 30 England waitress
Margaret Needham 50 Ireland cook

Benjamin Coulter 41 chauffeur
Minnie Coulter 43 *ux.*

1217 Theodore H. Wickwire Jr. 35 iron and steel
manufacturer
Sophie Wickwire 33 *ux.*
Theodore H. Wickwire III 8 son school
Hedge Wickwire 5 son
Harriet Stoddard 40 governess
Nellie Driscoll 53 Ireland cook
Lizzie Leary 26 Ireland waitress
Julia Beleski 35 Russian-Poland maid

1231 James Hanrahan 70 Ireland retired
Rosanna Hanrahan 64 *ux.*
Kate Scull 24 Canada

1243 Harry Yates 44 Buffalo Furnace Co.
Mary D. Yates 40 *ux.*
Theresa L. Yates 16 daughter

Virginia Yates 9 daughter school
Richard Yates 5 son
Harry Yates 2 son
Mary Dickson 30

1275 Emmett Fleming 60 secretary electrical association
Olive E. Fleming 43 *ux.*
Bryan Fleming 29 son
Sarah J. Wise 74 mother-in-law

Alois Steos 37 Germany coachman
Amelia Steos 32 *ux.*
Raymond E. Steos 7 son school
Edna M. Steos 6 daughter school
Frank A. Steos 2 daughter
Mildred R. Steos 2 daughter
Edwin W. Steos 6 months son

1297 Luther P. Graves 43 lumber dealer
Nellie W. Graves 44 *ux.*
Chester W. Graves 21 son Lawrenceville
Stanley Graves 18 son Lawrenceville
Lucy C. Graves 17 daughter student
Nelson Graves 10 son student
Helen Graves 5 daughter school
Margaret Graves 4 daughter
Louise Lack 29

Walter A. Yates 19 son
Virginia Yates 18 daughter
Richard C. Yates 14 school
Mary Yates 9 daughter school
Robert L. Yates 5 son
Mary T. Hayes 30 Ireland guest
Annie M. Morris 36 Wales
Anna Scobell 28

Andrew Wright 39 Canada chauffeur
Maria Wright 34 England *ux.*

1255 Henry O. Smith 27 Foster Milburn Company
Edna Smith 30 *ux.*
Emily L. Smith 4 daughter
Henry O. Smith Jr. 1 son
Mary O'Boyle 34 Ireland maid
Helen Fiegel 30 cook
Clara Brennan 25 nursemaid

1259 Mrs. Gerhard Lang
Jacob Gerhard Lang son

1275 James D. Warren Buffalo Commercial
James D. Warren Jr. 5 son
Hilda White 30 cook
Margaret Dray 20 nursemaid

1279 William E. Sewall 40 England landscape gardener
Winifred Sewall 20 England daughter

1297 Luther P. Graves 53 lumber dealer
Nellie W. Graves 54 *ux.*
Chester W. Graves 30 son traveling salesman
Nancy Graves 3 granddaughter
Luther P. Graves Jr. 21 son college
Nelson P. Graves 20 son college
Helen Graves 15 daughter Buffalo Seminary
Margaret Graves 14 daughter school
Genevieve Smith 22 Germany cook

Chadwick Dryden 34 England chauffeur
Elizabeth Dryden 45 Ireland *ux.*
Evelyn Dryden 14 daughter school
Edna Dryden daughter 9 school

1305 George C. Laub 45 tanner
Cora Laub 40 *ux.*
Ethel C. Laub 16 daughter Buffalo Seminary
George C. Laub Jr. 12 school

LAFAYETTE AVENUE ❦ End of Block

1920

WEST FERRY STREET

1165 Richard O'Keefe 46 Mass. business properties
Eleanor O'Keefe 49 NY *ux.*
Richard O'Keefe 14 NY son
John B. O'Keefe 7 NY son
Anna Himansen 25 NY

1171 Henry Adsit Bull 46 NY attorney
Mary Bull 43 Canada *ux.*

1175 George Chadeayne 74 NY
Clara Chadeayne 74 NY *ux.*
Mary Chadeayne 40 NY daughter
George Chadeayne 37 NY son house builder
Leah Stutzman 60 NY
George Newman 72 Germany laborer
Barbara Newman 63 Germany *ux.*

1179 Louis C. Newman 60 NJ
Lillian D. Newman 55 Michigan *ux.*
Lloyd D. Newman 30 Michigan son
Cedric Rebadow 32 NY son-in-law
Anna Rebadow 28 Indiana daughter
Elizabeth Dowd 39 Ireland
Winifred Kelly 50 Ireland

1193 Henry Tracy Balcom 54 Ohio retired
Margaret Balcom 42 Kentucky *ux.*
Henry Tracy Balcom Jr. 24 Pa. son
Jane R. Balcom 12 NY daughter
Lena Hornung 35

1205 Abby Chapin 44 NY widow
Anna Talty 26 NY housekeeper
Delia Talty 2 NY
Nora O'Connor 24 Ireland

1217 Theodore Wickwire 59 NY
Sophie Wickwire 55 NY *ux.*
Theodore Wickwire 14 NY son
Hedge Wickwire 9 NY son
Nellie Driscoll 37 NY
Anna Hurley 35 NY

1231 Nelson Taylor 39 NY lumber dealer
Mary Taylor 35 NY *ux.*

LAFAYETTE AVENUE ❦ End of Block

1925

WEST FERRY STREET

1165 Delaware Avenue Apartments

1171 Donald A. Campbell 40 manager
Hemphill Noyes & Co.
Edith Campbell 28 *ux.*
Virginia Campbell 4 daughter
Doris Campbell 2 daughter
Christine Lally 21
Julia McWilliams 36

1175 George Chadeayne 79 real estate
Eleanor Chadeayne 49 daughter
Mary Chadeayne 45 daughter
George D. Chadeayne 42 son house builder
George Newman 77 Germany caretaker
Barbara Newman 73 Austria *ux.*

1179 Louis C. Newman 66 retired
Lillian D. Newman 64 *ux.*
Lloyd Davis Newman 39 son coal dealer
Clara Johnson 19 Norway
Mary McCarthy 40 Ireland

1193 H. Tracy Balcom 60 merchant
Margaret M. Balcom 50 *ux.*
H. Tracy Balcom Jr. 29 real estate
Jane R. Balcom 17 daughter school
Harriet Fogelsanger 16 cook
Lena Hornung 40
Maria Wilkinson 20

1217 William J. Simon 43 beverage manufacturer
Florence K. Simon 43 *ux.*
Florence Louise Simon 9 daughter school
Marjorie E. Simon 7 daughter school
William K. Balcom 10 son school
Clara Paulette 29

1231 Nelson S. Taylor 43 lumber dealer
Mary C. Taylor 41 *ux.*
Nellie Coughlin 31 Ireland
Anna Sendelbeck 45 Germany cook

1243 Harry Yates 50 NY proprietor furnace company Mary Yates 48 NY *ux.* Virginia Yates 23 NY daughter Richard Yates 18 NY son Harry Yates 16 NY son Mary E. Yates 14 NY daughter Robert Yates 9 NY son Margaret Freeman 45 Ireland Elizabeth McCarthy 27 NY Christiana Neubusch NY Andrew Wright 39 Canada Maria Wright 48 England *ux.* Margaret Wright 46 Canada sister	1243 Harry Yates 53 coal dealer Mary Duffy Yates 51 *ux.* Virginia Yates 27 daughter Richard Yates 24 son Lackawanna Steel Harry Douglas Yates 22 son college Mary Elizabeth Yates 19 college Robert L. Yates 15 son high school Elizabeth McCarthy 29 Ireland Evelyn Case 19 cook Andrew Wright 49 Canada chauffeur Maria S. Wright 53 England *ux.*
1255 Henry O. Smith 36 Pa. Edna Smith 23 NY *ux.* Emily Smith 8 NY daughter Henry Smith 6 NY son Roberta Smith 3 NY daughter Thomas Talbot 40 England chauffeur Jean Cairns 27 Scotland Barbara Longado 56 Pa. Adele Hayes 43 Pa.	Dr. James E. King (City Directory, 1926)
1263 Jacob Lang 41 NY president Gerhard Lang Brewery Augusta Lang 50 NY widow Katherine Lang 49 NY sister Maria M. Lang 51 NY sister Krisgang Nichter 33 Germany Rose Wagner 50 Germany Teresia Brayer 40 NY Edward Sweitzer 28 NY chauffeur Anna Sweitzer 25 NY *ux.* Helen Sweitzer 5 NY daughter	1263 Jacob Gerhard Lang
1275 Mrs. Porter H. Norton widow	1275 William G. Schoellkopf 28 capitalist Elizabeth Schoellkopf 24 *ux.* Ann Elizabeth Schoellkopf 1 daughter William J. Schoellkopf 1 month son Mabel Styers 29 Canada Catherine Darrock 30 Canada cook Sarah Meyers 50 nursemaid Leda Racette 30 Canada nursemaid
1297 John F. Burke 54 NY oil producer Clara Burke 53 NY *ux.* Ronald Burke 30 NY son Janet Burke 18 NY daughter Hilda Burke 23 NY daughter Patrick Maddigan 35 NY Katherine Maddigan 28 NY *ux.*	1297 John F. Burke 60 oil producer Clara Burke 58 *ux.* Janet Frances Burke 22 daughter

1305 George C. Laub 52 NY tanner
Cora Laub 52 NY *ux.*
George Laub 17 NY son
Ethel Laub 22 daughter
Sophie Leffenthitt 30 Germany
Edward Hoefle 43 NY chauffeur
Jennie Hoefle 45 Germany *ux.*
Gertrude Hoefle 18 NY daughter stenographer

LAFAYETTE AVENUE ❦ End of Block

1305 George C. Laub 58 tanner
Eliza F. Laub 53 *ux.*
George A. Laub 22 son college
Katherine Deig 64 cook

Edward Hoefle 48 chauffeur
Jennie L. Hoefle 50 Gemany *ux.*
Gertrude E. Hoefle 24 daughter comptometer

LAFAYETTE AVENUE ❦ End of Block

Number 1165 was assigned to the lot on the northeast corner of Delaware and West Ferry diagonally across from the Conners' mansion at #1140. Its first recorded occupant was Frederick Krapp, a boat builder, who resided there throughout the 1890s. Around 1915 it became for about five years the abode of Richard C. O'Keefe, a farm boy from Woburn, Massachusetts. Before the turn of the nineteenth century he had established himself in the construction business in the nation's capital. In 1901, the year of the Pan American Exposition, he came to Buffalo where he joined the executive staff of the Chamber of Commerce, of which he was general secretary 1913-1917. He also became secretary of the Buffalo Retail Merchants' Association. In 1926 he returned to contracting and arranged the merger of the Builders' Exchange with the General Contracting Builders' Association. He was the spokesman for general contractors in the midst of labor controversies at a time when unionization of the building industry had taken place and he acted with great tact and success as a buffer between two sets of antagonists. During World War II he promoted a no-strike blanket agreement that avoided strikes until the late 1940s. His wife was the former Eleanor Egan and they had one son, Richard. The father died at age eighty-one in Buffalo on July 18, 1954, and was buried with a solemn high mass at Saint Joseph's Cathedral of which he was a parishoner. His club memberships were Buffalo, Country, Wanakah, and the old Park when it adjoined Delaware Park.[1] By the mid-1920s the northeast corner of West Ferry and Delaware was occupied by an apartment house which, unlike the two on the southeast corner, made no provision for a lawn but was built almost to the sidewalk.

14.2 ❦ John K. Tucker, Smith, *op. cit.*, II, facing p. 500.

Number 1171 Delaware, an unpretentious brick cottage which is still (2004) standing, was occupied in the late 1860s by John K. Tucker(14.2), proprietor of Tucker's European Hotel at Michigan and Exchange Street, directly across from the New York Central Station, and his wife Mary. Tucker

1 *BEN*, February 8, 1951; July 18,1954.

died November 11, 1878, and by 1880 Amelia Tucker was the only resident listed there in the census for that year. She was probably John and Mary's daughter. Edwin D. Poole, a wholesale lumber merchant, lived at #1171 from the mid-1890s until at least 1905. In 1910 the little house was the home of Josiah Jewett, Jr., son of Sherman S. Jewett of #256 Delaware and vice president of S. S. Jewett, manufacturer of stoves. On January 21, 1916, Josiah was killed when his automobile was hit at a grade crossing by a milk train. By that date #1171 had been serving briefly as the residence of an inventor whose contributions to aeronautics merited inclusion in both the *Dictionary of American Biography* and its successor, the *American National Biography*. Glenn Hammond Curtiss was born in Hammondsport, New York, May 21, 1878. After graduating from eighth grade in 1892, he purchased a bicycle and became a Western Union messenger boy. Soon bicycling became the center of his life and he entered races throughout Western and Central New York. In 1898 he married Lena Pearl Neff whom he met at a race. Next he designed a light but powerful engine, attached it to a bicycle, and became a motorcycle speed enthusiast. G. H. Curtiss Manufacturing Company, which produced the Hercules motorcycle, began in 1902. Its president was one of the best-known motorcycle racers of his day. In January 1907 he set a record of 136.3 miles an hour for one mile. Curtiss' engines attracted the attention of aeronautical experimenters, and in July 1907 his two-cycle engine powered the first dirigible to fly in the United States. Impressed by Curtiss's engines Alexander Graham Bell invited him to join the Aerial Experiment Association. In 1908 the first airplane trip by Curtiss in *White Wing* using Bell-conceived ailerons for lateral control proved superior to the wing warping used by the Wright brothers. Piloting a plane of his own design, Curtiss won a trophy in the first international air meet in France, and back in the States garnered the $10,000 prize offered by the *New York World*, flying 150 miles between Albany and New York City in two hours and fifty-one minutes. From exhibition flying Curtis shifted to designing planes that could land on water. In 1910 he established an aviation camp in San Diego which gave birth to an airboat which interested military and civilian buyers. A Wall Street syndicate in 1916 put together the Curtiss Aeroplane and Motor Company, which during World War I employed 18,000 workers throughout New York State and turned out 10,000 aircraft.[2] This development is what brought Curtiss to Buffalo in what the most recent historian of Erie County called "the gigantic Glenn Curtiss enterprise which was established in the great factory building on Elmwood Avenue north of Hertel."[3] In 1915 he resided at #1171 and for two years after that at #76 Lincoln Parkway. By 1920 he had left Buffalo for a career in real estate in Florida. It has been said of him that he "stands in the forefront of American aeronautical pioneers, second only to the Wright Brothers in historical significance." He died in Buffalo July 23, 1930, from complications following an appendectomy. Meanwhile #1171 had become the residence of Henry Adsit Bull, an attorney, whose career has been sketched in connection with #1093 Delaware. Bull was followed in the 1930s by Luke Ferritor, a railroad agent.

2 "Curtiss, Glenn Hammond," *ANB*, 5:904-906.
3 Dunn, *op. cit.*, p. 219.

In 1870 #1181 was the home of John L. Alberger, who had been born in Baltimore October 27, 1831. At age five he came to Buffalo with his family via steamboat and Erie Canal. The school he attended here had had Millard Fillmore as a teacher. Young Alberger also attended the Academy for Boys at Canandaigua. After graduation he went into business with his father, Job Alberger, who operated a "provision and packing plant" at Delaware Avenue and Scajaquada Creek and a meat market on the Terrace. Later they established a meat market next to the stockyards in East Buffalo. In 1870 John could still list himself as a butcher, but by 1880 he put himself down as a retired merchant, though aged only forty-nine. Actually at the time he was manufacturing machinery for processing grape sugar with his son Alvin and enjoyed the services of a coachman and another domestic. Offices were in the Ellicott Square Building. John Alberger was married twice. His first wife, Mary Ross Cleve, whom he married in 1859, died in 1890. His second wife, Cassie H. Ross, was the sister of a Civil War mayor of Buffalo. Alberger served as park commissioner during the 1870s. He was a member of Westminster Presbyterian but attended Lafayette Avenue Presbyterian after its founding in 1894. He died at #1181 on March 9, 1907.[4] During the 1880s he had sold his property to George H. Chadeayne, a housebuilder, under whom the lot was renumbered #1175 and a small lot in the northwest corner was numbered #1179. Alberger then moved into the tract directly north of his former property, but continued to list his new property (really #1193) as #1181. The original householder of #1193 was a French native, George Peugeot, proprietor of a lampshade company and inventor of the Peugeot Lamp Shade.[5] Since Chadeayne was in construction, it is probable that he was responsible for the house at #1175(14.3), a big, roomy, wooden structure.

14.3 ❦ Number 1175, BHS.

By 1925 George H. Chadeayne, aged seventy-nine, had retired from house building and settled into real estate, but his son George D. followed his father's profession and was still found at #1175 in 1925. More remarkable is that fact that another Chadeayne, William, due doubtless to having had Glenn Curtiss as a neighbor, held many motorcycle racing records and was an engineer for the Glenn Curtiss Company in Hammondsport before and during World War I.[6]

Earliest on the ground at #1179 was Walter G. Robbins who resided there from 1891 to 1897. He was proprietor of the Buffalo Fish Company. His place there had been taken by 1897 by H. Tracy Balcom, who is better remembered in connection with the

4 *BEN*, March 10, 1907.
5 *Buffalo Artists Register*, Lee F. Heacock, ed. (Buffalo: Heacock Publishing Co., 1926), p. 433.
6 *CE*, February 18, 1966.

mansion at #1205, discussion of which will be postponed until that point is reached. The next resident of #1179 was Louis C. Newman who lived there from about 1905 until 1925 when he moved his family into the Hotel Statler. Newman was born in 1857 in Hartford, Connecticut, where he spent his early boyhood. He moved with his family to Chicago but left after the Great Fire of 1871. Thrown on his own resources, he opened a dry goods store in nearby South Bend, but came to dislike selling and started two manufacturing plants, one in Kokomo, Indiana, and another in Marion, Ohio. In 1902 he came to Western New York where he organized the Tonawanda Board and Paper Company of which he became president, treasurer, and general manager. He retired in 1921 and died February 21, 1928 at age seventy-one, survived by his wife, the former Lillian Davis, a son Lloyd, and a daughter who married Cedric A. Rebadow. The Rebadows lived with the Newmans from about 1910 to 1920. The Newmans usually spent their winters at Palm Beach. Louis Newman was a Mason and a member of Wanakah, the Niagara Falls Country Club, and the Buffalo Athletic Club.[7] From 1925 until the mid-1930s #1179 was the home of Mrs. Louis Kissinger.

Above 14.4 ❦ Number 1193, BHS.
Below 14.5 ❦ Number 1205, BHS.

Numbers 1193(14.4) and 1205(14.5) were genuine mansions designed by the same architect, Charles Platt of New York City, for H. Tracy Balcom and Willis O. Chapin respectively and built in 1911. Balcom was born in Cleveland April 9, 1865, and moved to Buffalo where he entered the employ of the Utley Piano Company on Main Street. Trained as a concert pianist, he was an accomplished musician who gave piano and organ recitals at #1193. He became proprietor of the Balcom Piano Company which seems not to have been successful since he later abandoned it and opened an antique shop. In 1894 Balcom married Margaret Wiedman in Newport, Kentucky. They had one son, H. Tracy Balcom, Jr. The father was a director of the Buffalo Public Library, and a member of the Buffalo Club and the Buffalo Museum of Science. He died at age eighty-three on March 19, 1949.[8]

7 *BEN*, February 21, 1928.
8 *CE*, March 20, 1949.

The Balcom home was a Georgian mansion with a two-stories high entrance hall floored in white marble with walls paneled in white wood. The owner was a career-long collector of European *objets d'art* for which his home served as a museum. The walls of the living room were hung with Italian sixteenth century brocatello, a rare brocaded cloth. The heavily beamed ceiling was decorated with classic Italian scenes, and the furniture was also appropriately Italian. (Balcom himself painted similar scenes on the ceiling of the billiard room on the third floor.) A mammoth gothic tapestry masked the pipes of the organ on the first floor, which also boasted a renaissance mantelpiece of carved gray stone. The walls of the library were covered from floor to ceiling with cases groaning with books. The dining room walls were paneled with butternut, a wood of satin-like finish, each ornamented with a different fruit design. A loggia or solarium floored with rose-tinted tiles featured another mantelpiece, this one of chiseled marble. All first floor rooms opened through French doors onto the terrace from which stone steps led to the garden protected from the public by an eight-foot brick wall. The finest ever social function at #1193 was the wedding of Jane Reeve Balcom to Hubert L. Perry on January 5, 1935.[9]

The Balcoms resided at #1193 for twenty-six years until 1937. From then until June 1950 it belonged to Mr. and Mrs. Stuart C. Welch. Stuart had been born in Buffalo August 7, 1897, the son of Thomas Cary Welch and Jannie Augusta Baker. He attended Saint Paul's, Concord, New Hampshire, and graduated from Harvard. Thomas Welch was a prominent Buffalo attorney who after the Spanish-American War practiced in Manila in the Philippines where he died in 1927. During World War I Stuart was a First Lieutenant in the American Expeditionary Force when he was assigned to the British Royal Flying Corps, predecessor of the Royal Air Force, and was decorated by Winston Churchill, who was Secretary of State for War 1919-1921. After the war Welch returned to Harvard to study in the School of Architecture and later became an associate in the firm of local architects, Bley and Lyman, until 1926. On January 10, 1924, he married Harriet Mack, daughter of Norman E. Mack of #1100 Delaware, publisher of the *Buffalo Times* and for half a century a power in the Democratic Party. Harriet attended the Elmwood-Franklin School, and enjoyed the services of private tutors in Buffalo and later in Paris. In 1940 she organized the Buffalo Chapter of Bundles for Britain for which she received the King's Medal from George VI. In 1933 the Welches donated a chapel to the house at #1114 which the daughter of Roscoe Rowland Mitchell had donated to the Episcopal Diocese of Western New York. The Welches were undoubtedly anglophiles. During the 1930s Stuart Welch functioned as state supervisor of home reconditioning for the Home Owners Loan Corporation. Celebrities entertained by the Welches during their tenure at #1193 included Eleanor Roosevelt, Helen Hayes, Margaret Sullivan and her husband, Leland Hayward, Gracie Fields, and Joseph C. Grew, United States Ambassador to Japan at the time of Pearl Harbor. Harriet Welch died March 27,

9 *CE*, December 16, 1951.

14.6 ❦ Willis O. Chapin, *PBHS*, 17 (1913), *xii.*

1952, at #900 Delaware; her husband Stuart died on October 21, 1959, at the Park Lane.[10] In June 1951 #1193 became the Guardian Angel Day Nursery under the direction of the Felician Sisters. The facility cares for sixty-five to seventy boys and girls between the ages of two and five whose mothers are obliged to work in order to support them.[11]

A scion of one of Buffalo's very oldest families, Willis O. Chapin(14.6), a native of Royalton, just east of Lockport, was the first resident of #1205, a stone house of English architecture and Charles Platt design. The best known of the family was the Civil War casualty, Brigadier General Edward P. Chapin, for whom Chapin Parkway is named. Inherited wealth and the fact that his wife, the former Abby Flint, was the daughter of William B. Flint, a founder of the Flint & Kent department store, explain why Willis Chapin had no need for gainful employment besides being a director of the Fidelity Trust Company. He was the author of *The Masters and Masterpieces of Engraving*, which was illustrated with sixty engravings and heliogravures and was published by Harpers in 1894. He was an aesthete, devoting much of his time to the Albright Art Gallery. Experts declared that the engravings he donated to the Albright were "priceless." For more than a quarter century he was a member of the board of directors of the Fine Arts Academy, which he had also served as president. He died in Pasadena California April 7, 1917, only a few years after his mansion had been completed. His wife, a connoisseur like her husband, died at #1205 on January 7, 1931. Her son, William Flint Chapin, and his wife and daughter continued there until 1937 when it was purchased by the Hellenic Eastern Greek Orthodox Church as a cultural center for $250,000. In 1950 it was occupied by Presbyterian Homes of Western New York. Subsequently it was bought by Rich Products to house its affiliate, Healy-Schutte & Company, an advertising and marketing firm. In 1995 a huge addition was built on three levels, bringing the building's total size to 15,325 square feet.[12]

Mrs. Janet Chapin Coit, a daughter of the original owner, recalled how carefully she and her parents carried through Europe exquisite glass decorations for the mansion. These included stained glass panes from Germany for the window on the stair landing and a Louis XIV chandelier with matching wall bracket lighting fixtures from France. "Father would entrust these rare finds to no hands but ours," she remembered. "We had to carry then in and out of hotels and trains during months of travel."

10 *NYT*, March 29, 1952; October 22, 1959.
11 *CE*, July 16, 1937; December 16, 1951.
12 *BEN*, December 13, 1998.

H. Katherine Smith wrote in connection with the takeover of the mansion by the Greek Center:

> The reception hall of the former Chapin home is floored with marble. The ceiling is supported by heavy beams painted by an Italian artist. Above the fireplace is a large mantel of German workmanship. In the spacious living room, now used for activities ranging from church services to dancing parties, the mantel, imported from France, is of white marble inlaid with black. Passing through the loggia, beyond the living room, one comes out onto the terrace with its fountain ornamented with cupids, steps lead down to the large garden at the far end of which was a pool with any goldfish.
>
> In the days when it was a private residence, six servants were required to care for the house and garden. They were a cook, a waitress, an upstairs maid, a chauffeur, and two gardeners. The gardeners worked Winter and Summer; the Chapin green house was famed in Buffalo. From it came lovely chrysanthemums and flowering plants to brighten not only the mansion but the homes of relatives and friends of Mr. and Mrs. Chapin. The 7 lawns and gardens on the rear of the house extended nearly to Linwood Ave.[13]

14.7 ❦ First #1217, *BHS*.

As early as 1860 what would become #1217(14.7) was the home of Robert Montgomery, an Irish-born lake captain and later ship owner, his wife, and four American-born children. The Montgomerys lived there for at least a quarter of a century. A contemporary remembered the residence as "a rambling delightful old house, with [a] barn from which in winter time many a merry sleighing party jingled out and down the avenue." All the families that came afterwards remodeled the house to suit themselves. The Montgomerys were followed from the mid-1880s and throughout the 1890s by Robert W. Jones, a coal dealer, and in 1897 treasurer of the Niagara Falls & Lewiston Railroad. This company had built a double track trolley line from Niagara Falls to Lewiston which ran along the bottom of the gorge of the Niagara River in 1895. It was renamed the Niagara Gorge Railway in 1899. Service was provided by double-truck open cars, and the great majority of passengers were sightseers. The route was a great tourist attraction for more than thirty years, but was highly vulnerable to auto competition, and was abandoned at the end of the 1935 season.[14] By 1905 Harlow W. Bailey, a manufacturer of machines, with his wife, three young children, and three domestics resided there. They were followed in 1910 by Theodore H. Wickwire, Jr., whose father resided at #877 Delaware and about 1896 had erected blast furnaces along River Road to supply his steel wire plant. Theodore, Jr., was born in Cortland, on April 6, 1879, attended the state normal school there, and graduated from Andover in 1898 and from Yale in 1903. Shortly after graduation Theodore married Sophie Bremmer Hedge. The couple had two children, Theodore H., and Hedge. Theodore, Jr., went to work in the family business in Cortland, first as chemist, later

13 *Ibid.*
14 Hilton and Due, *Interinban Railways*, p. 319.

14.8 ❦ Second #1217, *City Beautiful*, p. 130.

as superintendent of the hearth, and assistant treasurer. He moved to Buffalo in 1907 and into #1217 Delaware. He assisted in forming Wickwire Steel Company of which he was vice president and treasurer. More mergers occurred of which the result was the formation of the Wickwire-Spencer Steel Company of which Theodore was president until June 1925. Afterwards, he moved to Narberth, Pennsylvania, and became chairman of the board of Trent, Inc., manufacturers of industrial heating equipment. His wife Sophie died in 1952. Theodore Wickwire died October 30, 1960.[15]

The next resident of a much-remodeled #1217 (14.8) was William J. Simon, Jr., whom the *News* saluted as "a sportsman and a colorful figure in the brewing industry." He was born in Buffalo October 21, 1880, graduated from Canisius High School and from Bryant & Stratton, after which he attended the Hanke Brewers Institute in Chicago and served his apprenticeship in several Milwaukee breweries. He returned to Buffalo and went to work at the brewery founded by his father, Bavarian-born William J. Simon, Sr., at Clinton and Emslie. Simon Pure brewery baseball teams won more than a dozen mini-league titles. Among the athletes over whose development Simon presided were Sibby Sisti, Buddy Rosen, and Dan Carnevali. With the coming of Prohibition, Simon opened the Copland Brewery Company in Toronto, which he sold to Labatts in 1946. The Simon brewery reopened in 1933 with William J. as president but he lost it after a year, only to win it back in a stockholders' fight in 1935. He resigned the presidency in 1956. Simon was an ardent fisherman, spending every other weekend during the summer on Lake Erie. He died at #1217 Delaware on January 14, 1958. He had been a Catholic and a member of the Master Brewers Association of America, the Rotary, Buffalo Athletic, Brookfield, and Launch clubs and the Buffalo Turn Verein.[16]

14.9 ❦ Number 1231, BHS.

Long time resident at #1231(14.9) was James Hanrahan

15 *Who Was Who in America*, 6:437; *NYT*, October 30, 1960.
16 *BEN*, January 15, 1958.

who had been born in County Clare, Ireland, in 1842, came to America at age thirteen in 1855, resolved on an education, and graduated from Central High in 1865 at age twenty-two. He became cashier for the company that laid the first pipeline between Titusville and Oil City, Pennsylvania, in the course of which he was for three years an associate of fellow Hibernian Daniel O'Day of #672 Delaware and Alexander J. Cassatt, legendary president of the Pennsylvania Railroad 1889-1906. It was in Pennsylvania that Hanrahan met his future wife Roseanna by whom he had four children. Returning to Buffalo, he became a coal dealer and banker. He was elected First Ward Supervisor, but declined to run for a second term. Under the new city charter of 1892 he was elected to the first council. He was one of the organizers of the Irish-American Bank. For years he was a trustee of the American Savings Bank and vice president at the time of his death April 18, 1920, at age seventy-seven. His sole club membership was in the Knights of Columbus.[17]

The next householder at #1231 was Nelson E. Taylor, a nationally known hardwood lumber executive and student of the life and times of George Washington. Taylor lived there during the 1920s. He was born in Buffalo August 13, 1881, the son of Frederick W. Taylor and the former Ellen Maria Mills. He attended local public schools, Central High, and Phillips Andover, after which he studied at Columbia University School of Mines. His first employment was at the Columbia National Bank. In 1904 he married Mary Crate and began his forty-year association with the Taylor and Crate Lumber Company.

The first householder listed in the 1880 census for #1243(9.8) was Edward Rischman, a native of Hesse-Darmstadt, who described himself as a yeoman. His wife Wilhelmina was from Prussia, but all their five children were born in New York. The Rischmans had no domestic servants, which may be what Rischman meant by classifying himself as a yeoman. *The City Directory* for 1880 calls him a gardener. His nineteen-year old son, Edward C., was a law student who succeeded in achieving his goal. By 1891 Gustave Fleishmann was resident at #1243. He had been born in Vienna, Austria, on March 22, 1850. He emigrated to America at age sixteen and secured employment as a marble cutter In New York City. He also attended night school at Cooper Institute taking classes in mathematics and drawing. Poor health forced him to leave the city and in 1869 he went to Cincinnati to work for a distiller and yeast manufacturing firm of which his two brothers were members. In 1877 he came to Buffalo where he engaged in distilling under the name of Frost and Company. Next year Frost resigned, and Gustave Fleishmann became a partner with another distiller, E. N. Cook. In 1893 he bought out Cook and organized the Buffalo Distilling Company, 82-86 Main Street. He was also president of the Meadville [Pennsylvania] Distilling Company and of the Frontier Elevating Company of Buffalo. He was president of the Meadville Lodge of the Elks, and, "passionately devoted to hunting," was a member of the Adirondack League. On August 24, 1880 Fleishmann married Emily

17 *Courier*, April 19, 1920.

Robertson of New York City.[18] Harry Yates, coal magnate and president of both the Buffalo Rochester and Pittsburgh Railroad and of the Lafayette Hotel, resided with his family at #1243 from the early 1900s until the mid-1920s. He had earlier resided for a brief period at #487 Delaware.

In 1910 Henry Oliver Smith, who had been born in Pittsburgh in 1882, took possession of #1255. That year he had married Emily Foster, daughter of Orin E. Foster of #891 Delaware, founder of the Foster-Milburn Company, manufacturers of patent medicines, and donor of Foster Hall on the U.B. campus. With the death of his father-in-law in 1928 Smith became president of Foster-Milburn and its subsidiary, Foster McClellan. Smith was on the board of many banking houses in the United States and of Smith Hair Pin Company, Sterling Engine, Tide Water Portland Cement, Standard Reserve of Baltimore, and the Bolt and Nut Manufacturing Company. He was a member of the Buffalo and Wanakah clubs, and past president of the Buffalo Automobile Club. Henry Smith died on June 6, 1935.[19]

By 1930 a new home(14.10) had been erected at #1255 for Dr. James E. King who had been associated with U.B. for nearly fifty years. He was born in Buffalo, the son of James E. King and the former Sarah Kendall. His education consisted in public grade school, Central High School, and U.B., followed by postgraduate medical studies in New York City, London, and Dresden. He joined the U.B. medical department in 1898, and taught anatomy, embryology, obstetrics, and gynecology before retiring. King became one of the foremost women's specialists in the United States. He was a life fellow of the American Gynecolgical Society, and its vice president in 1934. He was also fellow of the International College of Surgeons, its vice president in 1920, and president in 1938-1939. He died at age seventy-one on March 9, 1947.[20]

14.10 ❦ Number 1255, *City Beautiful*, p. 130.

When the Gerhard Lang brewery closed its doors in 1949 it was the oldest brewery in Buffalo, having been in operation for 106 years. Its founder was Gerhard Lang who had been born in Germany in 1834. In 1848 he came to America with his father Jacob, a butcher. In 1864 Gerhard married Barbara Born, the daughter of Phillip Born, a brewer, and entered partnership with him in a brewery Born had founded at Genesee and Jefferson. The partnership was dissolved in 1874, but not

18 *Men of New York*, 1:54.
19 *CE*, June 6, 1935.
20 *CE*, March 10, 1947.

14.11 ❦ **Number 1263, house and ground,** ***ibid.*****,** p. 161.

before Lang in 1870 had begun at Best and Jefferson a brewery which under his successor would become one of largest in the state outside New York City. Meanwhile a malt house had been built on the Genesee and Jefferson site. (Barley is made into malt and malt is brewed into beer.) Lang was a director of the Western Savings Bank, the German-American Bank, the People's Bank, and was president of the Erie County Natural Gas Company. In addition, he owned a horse and cattle stock farm at Delavan Avenue and the City line. Gerhard Lang died on July 14, 1892, and was buried from Saint Louis Church of which he had been a devout communicant and generous supporter. Bishop Stephen V. Ryan conducted the obsequies.[21] Lang was succeeded in the presidency of the family brewery by his son-in-law, Gerhard G. S. Miller, who died on November 3, 1915, and was in turn succeeded by his brother-in-law, Jacob Gerhard Lang. Jacob had been born in Buffalo August 10, 1871, attended Central High, and studied at the Brewers Academy in New York City. By 1914 Gerhard and his father's widow had moved into a fine new house surrounded by ample grounds at #1263 Delaware.(14.11)

He would remain there until his death on May 31, 1959, at age eighty-seven. Prohibition, which went into effect January 16, 1920, was obviously the end of the road for law-abiding brewers. Jacob Lang turned to manufacturing soft drinks, organizing Lang's Products, Inc., to which he added a creamery, bakery, and ice cream manufactory. He also became a guiding spirit in developing the former Lang farm on the East Side under the name of Lang Field, Inc. With Repeal in 1933 Lang modernized his plant and resumed brewing beer and ale. But times had changed and new brewing and marketing conditions forced him to discontinue the Gerhard Lang Brewery in 1950. Disposal of the other ventures, except for the creamery, soon followed. Like many others of the Delaware Avenue elite, Jacob Lang was an ardent horseman, breeding and racing thoroughbreds. His colt Footmark broke the track record at Fort Erie, and Kahla Dillon won the Transylvania, a race for trotters. His stables had long been in Lexington, Kentucky, but for the last few years of his life he boarded his

21 Hill, *op. cit.*, 2:826; *CA*, July 14, 1892.

horses at the Fort and at Woodbine in Canada. He had been a member of the Buffalo Club for fifty years, as well as holding memberships in the Country, Buffalo Athletic, and Woodbine and Fort Erie Turf clubs. He was also a director and honorary vice president of the Liberty Bank, a post-war reincarnation of his father's German-American Bank. Having never married, his sole survivor was a married sister.[22]

The first recorded inhabitant of #1275 was Emmett Fleming, an ex-lumber dealer, who by 1905 had developed an interest in the growing field of electricity and was the secretary of the Buffalo Electrical Association. He had no domestic servants, but did enjoy the services of a German-born coachman with a family of five children, aged seven and under. He was followed by James D. Warren who lived there for about a decade before swimming against the tide and moving southward to #1119. He was followed by Jennie Watson Norton, the widow of Porter H. Norton, formerly of #33 Gates Circle who died in 1918 and whose career will be treated at that point. She died April 6, 1922 survived by two children, one of whom became the wife of Daniel W. Streeter, the big game hunter formerly of #1125 Delaware. Next at #1275 was William Graebe Schoellkopf, the genealogy of whose prominent family, of which he was third generation, can be found in figure 9.9. He was born in Niagara Falls October 9, 1896, the only son of Alfred P. Schoellkopf and the former Emily R. Graebe. His early years were spent at his parents' home at #537 Delaware on the Midway. His father Alfred died in 1901 before William reached four years of age, and William was educated at the public schools of Rochester. He also attended the Holbrook School in Ossining, and graduated from Cornell in 1919. He returned to Buffalo and became a member in the investment firm of Schoellkopf, Hutton & Pomeroy in 1930 on 70 Niagara Street. (During the twenties it seemed as if everybody was selling stocks. Professor Irving Fisher of Yale is supposed to have announced during that decade that the nation had reached a permanent plateau of prosperity.) On October 19, 1922, William Schoellkopf married Elizabeth Peabody, and moved into #1275 Delaware. He left the brokerage and with other Buffalo associates formed Nukem Products, manufacturers of acid proof industrial cements and coatings. In 1926 he joined H. O. Babcock, a New York Stock Exchange firm, which in 1931 became Schoellkopf & Company. In the mid-1930s he moved to Chapin Parkway. Later his brokerage merged into Doolittle, Schoellkopf & Company. During World War II Schoellkopf took a leave of absence to serve as executive assistant at the Bell bomber plant in Marietta, Georgia. In 1948 he became a partner with J. F. Schoellkopf IV in a new Schoellkopf & Company, but in 1962 he returned to Doolittle. His memberships included Buffalo, Country, Wanakah, East Aurora, Saturn, and Buffalo Tennis and Squash. William Graebe Schoellkopf died on December 27, 1977, at age eighty-one.[23]

22 *BEN*, June 1, 1959.
23 Wilner, *op. cit.*, 3:455-457.

14.12 ❦ Number 1297, *CE*, June 22, 1952.

At the turn of the nineteenth century a# 1283, relatively small frame house, was occupied Frank N. Clare, a coach manufacturer, his wife, and two children. They had no servants. Neither did the next occupant, William E. Sewall, an English-born landscape gardener, whose twenty-year old daughter was also his housekeeper. Many of his neighbors had extensive lawns and gardens and no gardeners. Hence he was well situated for exercising his profession.

In 1925 H. Katherine Smith, a staff writer for the *News*, told the sad story of the next home up the Avenue:

> The mansion of Pompeian brick at 1297 Delaware Ave.(14.12), now a residence for student nurses of the Millard Fillmore Hospital, was a house of untimely death and failure during more than half century as a private home. Had it been built earlier, Nathaniel Hawthorne well might have chosen this proud dwelling for the scene of one of his novels portraying the tragic working of relentless, inescapable Fate.
>
> The late Luther P. Graves, who built the house for his family with high hope and faith in the future, died in its luxurious master bedroom at 55. Of the seven sons and daughters of Luther P. Graves, for whose home the mansion was designed and erected, only two are living today. They are Nelson M. Graves, president of the Edward J. Barcalo Manufacturing Co., and Mrs. Charles Swingley of Cincinnati. In 1917, within a few months of its builder's sudden and early death, the mansion was sold to John F. Burke, then one of Buffalo's most prosperous citizens. Mr. Burke's extensive financial interests included transportation, real estate and oil. While he and his family occupied the mansion, his son became seriously ill and his first wife died. Later the sale of the home was forced by the owner's financial reverses.
>
> In 1894, the year of its completion, the mansion was the last word in luxury and comfort. The construction was ahead of its time, for the house was fully wired long before electricity was available for home lighting. That was typical of Luther P. Graves' foresight and faith in the then new wonder of Niagara: electric power. His house probably was the first in Buffalo to be heated by a gas furnace. Back in the '90s, when a bathroom was deemed something of a luxury, the Graves home was equipped with five complete bathrooms and a lavatory. Its refrigeration facilities also were exceptional for its day. It was the only residence here equipped with an entire refrigerated room.
>
> The scope of Luther P. Graves' lumber interests was international. In Buffalo he was a partner successively in the firms of Holland, Graves & Montgomery and Graves, Manbert & George. His Canadian firm, Graves Bigwood of Toronto, controlled large lumber tracts in Ontario and extensive mills for processing white pine, spruce and hemlock. His firm's Buffalo lumber yard, planing mill and box factory was at the foot of Hertel Ave. Wide-

14.13 ❦ Jubilee Water Works, *PBHS*, 16(1912), 289.

spread lumber connections enabled Mr. Graves to import from South America mahogany for all interior woodwork of his home. For the woodwork of the reception hall, rare white mahogany was used. The large dining-room table was hewn by hand from a single mahogany log.

The front door of the Graves home opened into a hall so spacious that it always has been furnished like a living-room. Today, this hall and its counterpart on the second floor are sitting-rooms for student nurses. Other first floor rooms were, on the right, the living-room which looked out on Delaware Ave., and on the left, overlooking the pleasant garden, the library and dining-room. The latter, unique in Buffalo, was circular in shape. In the rear were the kitchen, maids' dining room, and icebox room. On the second floor, opening from the broad hall, were six sleeping rooms with four baths. Three servants' bedrooms and a bath occupied the major part of the third floor. The room dearest to the hearts of the Graves children was the third-story play room. Inspired by Luther P. Graves' familiarity with logging camps of the Canadian forests, this play room was a replica of a log cabin.

Streams that supplied the old Jubilee Water Works(14.13) flowed through the home site, and builders had to use 120 loads of earth to fill in those areas before construction could begin. In the garden a large willow tree, carefully tended and watered, flourished years after the streams disappeared.

The house was designed by the late Edward B. Greene. Interior woodwork, with elaborate hand carving, was produced by Metz & Meyer.

During the near quarter century of occupancy by the Graves family, the walls of the mansion often resounded to excellent music. Crosby Adams, pianist and founder of the music school of Ashville, N. C., was a frequent guest in the house.

Born in Niagara Falls, N.Y., Luther P. Graves was the son of a Civil War veteran. Exceptionally philanthropic, Luther P. Graves was a director of the local YMCA, the Young Men's Hotel, the Buffalo Orphan Asylum, the Buffalo General and Buffalo Homeopathic hospitals. Active for decades in North Presbyterian Church, he was president of its board of trustees, senior deacon and chairman of the building and music committees. He was a charter member of the Buffalo Canoe Club and affiliated with the Country Club and the Sons of the American Revolution.

The late John F. Burke, who bought the house in 1917 and occupied it for more than 20 years, was a leader in the development of South Buffalo. With his brother, William Burke, he developed the Kenefick, Lockwood, Whitefield section of South Buffalo. He also played a leading role in developing Cleveland Hill. He was identified prominently with two transportation lines. For more than a score of years, he acted as receiver for the Hamburg Railway coach lines, and he was organizer of the company that built the Buffalo-Dunkirk trolley line. [Actually the Buffalo & Lake Erie interurban.] In the closing years of his life, Mr. Burke became identified with oil interests in Tulsa, Okla.[24]

24 *CE*, June 22, 1952.

The east block of Delaware between West Ferry and Lafayette boasted yet a third member of a wealthy German-American family. George C. Laub, the patriarch, was born in Hesse Darmstadt in 1795 and died in Buffalo October 5, 1900 at age ninety-five. Educated in Germany, he came to America and in 1846 settled in Hamburg, where he engaged in farming and the lumber trade. To make full use of his lumber product, he employed the bark of his timber in tanning. In 1858 he retired from business and moved to Buffalo where he was a member of the German Evangelical Church. His son, George, Jr., was born March 4, 1837, in Hamburg and attended public school there. In 1854 he went to work in his father's tannery and stayed for four years. He then formed a partnership in the business at Abbott's Corners with his brothers Adam and Fred which lasted until 1865 when George, Jr., formed a new firm with G. Frederick Zeller of Buffalo. Laub & Zeller lasted until 1889 when the firm of George Laub and Son was formed, the son being George C., the eldest of the three sons of George Laub, Jr., and his wife Bertha Schaller. Two younger sons, Albert F. and Charles J. Laub, became partners later. In 1903 George Laub, the father retired, and the family firm was carried on under the name George Laub's Sons. His son, George C. Laub, born in Buffalo on August 10, 1866, and educated at Central High, married Cora Spitzmuller of Buffalo, and directed the family's tanning operations from 1921 until 1942. Meanwhile he built himself a red brick mansion at #1305 Delaware. A writer for the *Courier Express* recalled in 1952:

> In the Laub home, no expense was spared. Many of the woods and wall coverings used in its interior were imported. The living room was paneled in Circassian walnut above which the walls were covered with English tapestry with a soft shade of green predominating. The dining room was paneled in Brazilian mahogany. Its walls were adorned with a rare, attractive scenic paper.
>
> The entrance hall seemed to welcome visitors into the mansion. Broad and attractively furnished, it included an ample fireplace. The second floor hall . . . also has large fireplace. On one side of the first floor hall was a spacious living room, carpeted with an extraordinarily large Oriental rug. There stood the grand piano, especially constructed of Circassian walnut to match the paneling of the room.
>
> Across the hall from the living room were the oak-panelled smoking room, a favorite haunt of younger members of the family, and the dining room. Two sun porches have been left unchanged. From the hall of the second floor opened four sleeping rooms, three of them with adjoining baths, and a sewing room. The third floor, originally occupied by servants, equaled the lower floors in comfortable design. There too ceilings were high and excellent hard woods were used in construction.[25]

George C. Laub and his family occupied this house for forty years. In time he acquired a second home in the country at Athol Springs. His second wife was Eliza Pfeiffer. A mason and a Presbyterian, he was also a member of the Buffalo Athletic, Park, Country, and Wanakah clubs. Three years after George Laub died on February 16, 1947, the home was sold to Millard Fillmore Hospital for a nurses' residence.[26]

25 *CE*, Aprl, 20, 1952.
26 *BEN*, May 26, 1947.

14.14 ❦ Number 7 Gates Circle, *City Beautiful* p. 146.

Millard Fillmore Hospital, which was gradually to encroach upon Gates Circle and commercialize it in much the same way as long before had been the fate of Niagara Square, began as the Homeopathic Hospital in 1872. Doctor Augustus C. Hoxie, originally of #138 and later of #536 Delaware attempted to admit a patient suffering from typhoid fever to a regular hospital in the city, but was rebuffed because he was a practitioner of homeopathic medicine. Under his direction, several like-minded physicians organized the Buffalo Homeopathic Hospital which opened in October 1872 in a three-story house on Washington and South Division Streets. The permanent staff consisted of a janitor, a matron, and a nurse; half a dozen doctors were listed on its medical staff. Within two years of its opening the Homeopathic Hospital was moved into a house at Maryland and Cottage. In 1884 the house on Maryland was expanded and two neighboring houses were converted into hospital use. Three years later the nurses' training school admitted its first students. In 1911 the hospital was moved to the southeast corner of Lafayette and Linwood Avenues. The name was changed to Millard Fillmore Hospital in 1923 due to the rapid decline in the popularity of homeopathy early in the twentieth century. In 1928 east and west wings were added and in 1939 the Pavilion was built. In 1941 the Burke property at #1297 Delaware was bought with further westward expansion in mind. This brought an angry delegation of local residents protesting to the municipal zoning board. Led by Parke Wright of #7 Gates Circle(14.14) and William Palmer, #34 Gates Circle(14.15), the opponents of the projected $500,000 four-story building overlooking the circle asserted that it would "mar the beauty of the Gates Circle section and impair residential property values." Nevertheless, the building went up next year at a cost of $518,745, and seven years later six more floors were added for $1,002,872. It was also in 1949 that the Laub property at #1305 and the Wells V. Moot property at #9 Gates Circle were acquired by the hospital for more expansion. The Parke Wright property at #7 Gates Circle was acquired for the same purpose in 1953. Wright probably reasoned that the battle to preserve the character of the circle was lost anyway. He would have been right. In 1955 the three-story and basement $1,500,000 West Building, which could

14.15 ❦ Number 34 Gates Circle, *ibid* p. 34.

be expanded to eleven stories, was completed. The same year acquisition of the former William Schoellkopf estate at #1275 Delaware made possible the construction of the Delaware Avenue Medical Center.[27]

27 *BEN*, May 29, 1941; August 20, 1959.

CHAPTER

15

FERRY TO CHAPIN PLACE: *West Side*

The map for this chapter is map 14.1 as was the case for the last chapter. The base date for that figure was 1915.

1870

WEST FERRY STREET

1168 Erastus Scoville Newman & Scoville
ship chandlers

1192 George D. Teller general passenger agent
Northern Pacific Railroad
Susan Teller 44 NY *ux.*
Emma Teller 21 NY daughter
Frank Teller 17 NY son school
Susie Scott 19 Canada West

1202 Whitney A. Case 45 Canada West coppersmith
Mary A. Case 37 NY *ux.*
Edward Case 23 NY
Mary Case 20 NY daughter *ad dom.*
Elizabeth Case NY 17 daughter school
Whitney G. Case 14 NY son school
Mary Bryan 25 Ireland

1250 Philip Kissel 61 Hesse Darmstadt wire worker
Barbara Kissel 24 Hesse Darmstadt housekeeper
Gustav Kissel 21 Hesse Darmstadt wire worker
Edward Walther 20 Hesse Darmstadt
Paul Hirskorn 21 Hesse Darmstadt wire worker

1880

WEST FERRY STREET

1168 Alexander Meldrum 46 Scotland
dry goods merchant
Ann Elizabeth Meldrum 44 Mass. *ux.*
Arthur Meldrum 19 Mass. son clerk
Alfred Meldrum 14 Mass. son school
Herbert A. Meldrum 10 NY school
Lizzie Alice Meldrum 16 Mass. daughter school
Jessie Meldrum 9 NY daughter school
Florence Jean Meldrum NY daughter
Elizabeth Pollock 68 Maine cousin widow
Alexander Meldrum 60 Scotland cousin
machinist
O. M. Green 27 NY
Anna Bellgraves 24 Scotland
Sarah Hudson 30 Nova Scotia
William Garrett 27 England coachman
Thomas Fields 19 England

1192 Jacob Bergtold 45 NY farmer
Louise Bergtold 42 NY *ux.*
Harry Bergtold 14 NY son school
Alfred Bergtold 11 NY son school
Clara Bergtold 10 NY daughter
Lulu Bergtold 18 NY niece
Maggie Burghardt 19 Hesse Darmstadt
Fred Ruder 22 Prussia

1202 Whitney A. Case 56 NY coppersmith
Mary H. Case 48 *ux.*
Mary M. Case 28 NY daughter
Whitney G. Case 25 NY son coppersmith
Ellen Corah 24 NY
Lucy Corah 18 NY
Fred Smith 24 Hanover
George Smith 20 Hanover

1306 Joseph H. Lessler 49 Prussia
Betsey Lessler 36 NY *ux.*
Hannah Lessler 16 NY school
Jessie Lessler 14 NY school
Clara Lessler 12 NY school
Eva Lessler 10 NY school
Virginia Lessler 8 NY school
Aaron Lessler 6 NY school
Rose Lessler 4 NY
Kate Ludwig 22 NY
Mary Schaghtman 24 Prussia

BOUCK AVENUE ❦ End of Block

1306 Mrs. Austin A. Howard

BOUCK AVENUE ❦ End of Block

1891

WEST FERRY STREET

1168 John George Milburn

1180 C. F. Christiensen florist

1208 Whitney A. Case

1900

WEST FERRY STREET

1160 William H. Glenny 55 NY merchant
William H. Glenny 26 NY son merchant
Bryant B. Glenny NY son merchant
Charlotte M. Glenny 35 daughter-in-law
Bryant Glenny 13 NY grandson school
Anna Glenny 13 NY granddaughter school
Mary Donovan 46 NY housemaid
Kate Bollyn 30 Ireland cook

1168 John G. Milburn 48 England attorney
Patty Milburn 46 NY *ux.*
John G. Milburn Jr. 20 NY son college
Devereux Milburn 19 NY son college
Ralph Milburn 11 NY son school
Andrew Ewing 30 Illinois coachman
Laura Ellis 36 Canada housemaid
Louise Sauers 40 NY waitress
Mary Sawyer 34 NY cook

1192 Joseph T. Jones 41 oil producer
Melodia Jones 41 NY *ux.*
Joseph A. Jones 22 Pa. son
Grace Jones 19 NY daughter school
Kate Gilchrest

1208 Mary Case 68 NY widow
Elizabeth McCready 46 NY daughter
Catherine Hodnutt 30 NY housemaid
Katie Gray 35 Canada cook
Charles W. Throll 41 NY coachman
Bertha Throll 33 Switzerland *ux.*
Whitney A. Throll 3 NY son
Louise Throll 9 months NY daughter

CLEVELAND AVENUE

AUBURN AVENUE

LANCASTER AVENUE

1306 Dr. Benjamin F. Rogers

LAFAYETTE AVENUE ❦ End of Block

1905

WEST FERRY STREET

1160 William H. Glenny 61 real estate
Anna Glenny 60 *ux.*
John Annan 84 father-in-law
Lena Tant 26 Canada
Rose Harter 32
Elizabeth Arcella 25

1200 Mary H. Case 73
Elizabeth McCready 51

CLEVELAND AVENUE

AUBURN AVENUE

LANCASTER AVENUE

1306 Benjamin E. Rogers 50 MD
Mary E. Rogers 39 *ux.*
Sara P. Rogers 17 daughter
Alice A. Howard 43 sister-in-law
Albert W. Rogers 66 brother nurse
Anna Sogar 27

LEXINGTON AVENUE ❦ End of Block

LAFAYETTE AVENUE ❦ End of Block

1915

WEST FERRY STREET

1160 William H. Glenny 70
Anna H. Glenny 60 *ux.*
Richard K. Noye 44 treasurer Noye Brothers
Florence Noye 41 *ux.*
Richard Noye III 15 son
James K. Noye 10 son
Theresa Tubbridy 38 Ireland
Mary Owen 26 Ireland

1168 Phllip Mark Shannon 60 coffee grower
Henriette Shannon 48 *ux.*
Hazel Shannon 25 daughter

1200 Elizabeth McCready 60
Mrs. William Collins 63 sister
Elizabeth Halt 31
Minnie Spennikley 26
John Hillbrecht 31 chauffeur
Anna Hillbrecht 31 Germany *ux.*
John Hillbrecht 3 son school

CLEVELAND AVENUE

1234 Conrad E. Wettlaufer 40 manufacturer
Irene Wettlauffer 38 *ux.*
Taylor Wettlaufer 7 son
Gretchen Wettlaufer 5 daughter
Arthur A. Radka 45 chauffeur
Mrs. Arthur A. Radka 40 *ux.*
Arthur Radka 22 son

AUBURN AVENUE

1272 Albert Laub

LANCASTER AVENUE

LEXINGTON AVENUE ❦ End of Block

1920

WEST FERRY STREET

1160 William H. Glenny 74 NY manufacturer
Annie Glenny 71 NY *ux.*
Richard K. Noye 81 Conn. brother-in-law retired

1925

WEST FERRY STREET

1160 William H. Glenny 80 retired
Annie Glenny 78 *ux.*
Richard K. Noye 53 nephew of Annie manufacturer

Sara Noye 80 NY sister
Richard K. Noye 48 NY nephew
Noye Brothers manufacturers
Florence B. Noye 46 Mass. niece
executive secretary
Richard K. Noye 3 NY grandnephew
Keith Noye 15 NY grandnephew
Mary Fox 50 Canada cook
John Carroll 45 NY
Elsa Baines 45 NY
Harry Rankin 60 NY chauffeur
Emma Rankin 59 England *ux.*

Florence Noye 59 *ux.* secretary
Riichard K. Noye 25
James K. Noye 20 son college
Frances Kornbow 46 nurse
Mrs. Elsie Bean 60 England cook
Hannah Healey 25 Ireland
Katrina McPartland 17 Ireland

1168 George F. Rand Jr. 27 NY assistant secretary
Marine Trust
Evelyn Rand 20 NY sister teacher
Millbrook School
Gretchen Rand 18 NY sister teacher
Millbrook School
Henriette Shannon NY 54 widow
Hazel Shannon 30 Pa. daughter
Elizabeth Regan 30 Ireland

1168 Wilbur F. Groom 31 auto Oakland Motor
Company
Louise Groom 47 *ux.*
Wilhelmine Harlay 27 West Indies

1170 Charles F. Stork Holland milliner
Christel Stork 28 Holland *ux.*
Anna Grantiskt 23 Hungary

1180 Buffalo Consistory Ancient Accepted
Scottish Rite of Freemasonry

1200 Mary M. Collins 68 NY widow
Elizabeth McCready 65 widow
Catherine Hudnutt 49 NY nurse
Loretta J. Nye 38 NY nurse
Lottie Mayer 47 Alsace
Matilda Meyer 41 Alsace

James Grant 50 Scotland chauffeur
Isabella Grant 42 Scotland *ux.*
James Grant 18 Scotland son factory worker
William Grant 9 NY son
Mary Grant 14 Scotland daughter
Dorothy Grant 2 NY daughter

1200 Elizabeth McCready 71 widow
Mrs. Nellie Doyle 52 cousin
Eleanor Doyle daughter
Catherine Hudnutt 54 nurse

CLEVELAND AVENUE

CLEVELAND AVENUE

1230 William R. Huntley 46 vice president
electric company
Jennie Huntley 41 *ux.*
Charles R. Huntley 15 son high school
Caroline M. Larson 32 Denmark cook
Grace M. Winter 42

1234 Conrad E. Wettlaufer 50 Canada wholesale
hardware
Irene Taylor Wettlaufer 48 NY *ux.*
Gretchen Taylor Wettlaufer 15 NY daughter

1234 Conrad E. Wettlaufer 55 Canada merchant
Irene Taylor Wettlaufer 47 *ux.*
Gretchen Taylor Wettlaufer 20 daughter
Conrad Taylor Wettlaufer 16 son high school

Conrad Taylor Wettlaufer 11 NY son
Mary B. Rankin 48 NY secretary
Margaret Collins 34 Ireland
Anne Ryan 34 NY
Lena Mauren 60 NY cook
Frank Radka 48 Germany chauffeur
Johanna Radka 42 Germany *ux.*
Frances Radka 24 NY daughter
Benjamin Ainsworth 59 England roomer

AUBURN AVENUE

1260 George A. Forman 30+ Ohio oil producer
Lucie Forman 30+ Indiana *ux.*
George A. Forman 8 NY son
Lucie Forman 4 NY daughter
Nora Jost 20 Luxemborg
Anna Kearney 25 Ireland
Julio Retzoff 37 Poland chauffeur
Jennie Retzoff 37 NY *ux.*
Muriel Retzoff 6 NY daughter

1276 Albert Laub 49 NY tanner
Clara Laub 46 NY *ux.*
Raymond Laub 19 NY son
Herbert Laub 17 NY son
Albert H. Laub 14 NY son
Grace Laub 10 daughter
David Laub 8 son
Muriel Rotter 31 NY
Lena Frank 65 Alsace
Rose Hopper 18 NY

Henry Geigle 31 Iowa
Mabel Geigle 30 NY *ux*
Laverna Geigle 4 NY daughter

1296 Emanuel Boasberg 53 NY wholesale tobacco
Bessie Boasberg 50 Michigan *ux.*
Norman Boasberg 25 NY
Emanuel Boasberg Jr. 14 son
Edna Marshall 21 NY niece
Mary Madigan 33 Canada

LANCASTER AVENUE

1306 John Bradley 62 Vermont president
iron & steel company
Fannie Bradley 60 NY *ux.*
Helen Bradley 41 Vermont daughter
Martha Siegnian Canada
Hilda Rentoff Germany

LEXINGTON AVENUE ❦ End of Block

Mary B Rankin 53 governess
Rose Collins 40

AUBURN AVENUE

1260 George A. Forman 83 +6/2/1925
Martha Forman 78 *ux.*

1276 Clara Laub

LANCASTER AVENUE

1306 vacant

LEXINGTON AVENUE ❦ End of Block

The northwest corner of Ferry and Delaware was a vacant lot until 1897 when William H. Glenny, Jr., built a home there at #1160, having closed down the imported pottery and glassware business he had inherited from his father. The son had been born in Buffalo in 1845, graduated from Yale's Sheffield Scientific School in 1864 and entered the family business. After retirement he concentrated on his library, which was piled high with books, pamphlets, and pictures. He amassed a large collection of books and manuscripts about early Buffalo and its families. Besides membership in the Buffalo Club, Glenny was a charter member of the University Club of which he was president when its modern clubhouse (8.23) was built. For over fifty years he was a director of the Buffalo Savings Bank, chairman of the board of the Spencer Lens Company, and a director of Forest Lawn. He died at eighty-four in 1929 in Boston where he had gone to attend the weddings of two of his grandchildren.[1]

In 1926 Burr put down some disconnected thoughts about the next three houses "from an old chronicle left by the late George D. Teller, one of Buffalo's former citizens, who came here in 1839, and lived to see the city grow into great prosperity:"

> There were three houses that stood on the west side of Delaware street above Ferry street - the first two having been built by Charles and Edward Partridge who were associated together in a dry goods store and who later went to Chicago where they amassed wealth in the same business. One of their descendants, Mrs. Alfred Schoellkopf of West Ferry Street, was, before her marriage, Miss Virginia Partridge of Chicago.

15.1 ❦ Number 1168 Delaware. BHS.

> The two Partridge homes were comfortable two and a half story frame structures, built after the style of the times, and the other one [#1168] in this trio of residences was near the corner, surrounded by spacious grounds, and which is now encompassed in the home owned by Mrs. Philip Mark Shannon, and which bears historic interest, and is usually referred to as "Milburn House," owing to the fact that it was the home of John G. Milburn, the distinguished lawyer who now resides in New York, and also that it was in this house that the late President McKinley died after being shot while holding a reception in the Music Temple of the Pan-American Exposition.(15.1)

> This house was once the home of Capt. Darley, later that of a family named Scoville, and again was leased by the late Alexander Meldrum, before he built the handsome brick house in North street that is owned by William A. Rogers. The John G. Milburns lived there for some years, and in turn sold it [in 1904] to Philip Mark Shannon.

1 *Times*, February 11, 1929; *BEN*, February 11, 1929.

> Next to this house stood the two Partridge houses, and when they removed to Chicago, George D. Teller, a prominent railroad official, purchased the Charles Partridge home [#1192, later #1180], and Whitney G. Case the Edward Partridge [#1200] home.[2]

15.2 ❦ John George Milburn, Warren, *op. cit.*, p. 42.

Captain Edward Darley resided at #1168 from 1864 until 1868. Erastus Scoville of Newman & Scoville, ship chandlers, replaced the captain in 1869. However Erastus died in 1871, and his widow Esther remained there for three more years but was gone by 1875. The next resident was Alexander Meldrum, born in Kenoway, Fifeshire, Scotland, in 1833. He was apprenticed to a dry goods house in nearby Markinch. At twenty-two he emigrated to Boston where in 1859 he married Ann Elizabeth Webster, a grandniece of the godlike Daniel, and worked in a dry goods store until 1867, when he came to Buffalo with Scotsman Robert B. Adam. The result was AM&A's. Meldrum died in 1891,[3] by which time #1168 had a new occupant, John George Milburn (15.2), born near Sunderland, England, in 1851. He was educated privately and came to America at nineteen. His father was a civil engineer and wished his son to follow in his footsteps, but John settled in Batavia where he read law and passed the bar in 1874, but, since he was not a citizen, could not practice. He married Patty Stocking of Batavia in 1878. They moved to Buffalo, and John, now a citizen, became a solo practitioner. They spent a year in Denver in 1882 where John was a partner of ex-Senator Edward Wolcott, but returned to Buffalo in 1883, when the firm of [Sherman S.] Rogers, [Franklin D.] Locke & Milburn was formed. Milburn rendered important service to Buffalo as a member of the city charter revision committee and of another which adjusted the relationship of street railways and the city. He had three sons, John George, Jr., Devereux, and Ralph. John George was born in Buffalo in 1880, and Devereux in 1881:

> Milburn's rambling brick house on the corner of Delaware Avenue and Ferry Street was the cultural center of the community. When Matthew Arnold came to Buffalo, he stayed with the Milburns and was charmed by them, as his letters show. Here lived two who had learned the art of living. The book-lined library, with its log fire and cushioned comfort, the table where wit and good discourse were the accompaniment of good fare, were reflections of the warm and stimulating personalities who welcomed us there.
>
> No man of his time in Buffalo quite equaled John Milburn in grace and charm. Though no sportsman himself, he was the intimate of the hunting and polo playing crowd. In the Buffalo Club the great nights centered around him. When local pride launched the Pan-American Exposition, Milburn was made its president. McKinley died in his house. He

2 *Courier*, February 15, 1926.
3 *M&FH*, 1:242-243.

> [Milburn] loved his wine and his cigar and understood them. Before a jury as with his friends, his manner, his appeal, were fascinating. To his deliberate and cultured speech - his wit, his smile and gestures — all succumbed.
>
> Patty Stocking was a great woman of noble presence and warm generosity of spirit. She was quiet and understanding — of a quick humor and sympathy. She was delighted with her husband and her boys, but sometimes you caught apprehension in her eyes.
>
> In this atmosphere George and his brother Devereux were brought up. When they were boys, the upper part of Delaware Avenue was still unpaved. The houses were few and far between. Each stood in its own grounds and many of them had long gardens and orchards stretched behind. Two squares down the Ferry Street hill was Main Street where the East Side began and sand lot ball was in full swing. Just to the north a half hour away was the Country Club with its stables and polo fields. Here American polo was born when old Doctor Cary came back from touring Europe with his family in his coach and four. The Cary boys — Tom and Charles, George and Seward with Lawrence and Bert Rumsey, Jack Scatcherd, Harry Hamlin and Dr. Hopkins got some western cow ponies and began to knock the ball around. In a few years they sent a team to Newport and played there one of the first matches in this country.
>
> The Milburn boys rode almost as soon as they walked. They might be said to have been born with polo mallets in their hands. George had a ball bat in his other hand. His hours out of school were divided between the Country Club and the sand lots, with occasional expeditions to the Rumsey garden a mile or so down Delaware Avenue, where we could swim in the pond in summer and play hockey in winter. Bob and Pad Rumsey and Hal Movius lived around the garden and the Laverack brothers and I were the other habitues. The Milburns went to the Heathcote School but the rest of us went to Nichol's. *[sic]* Heathcote and Nichol's were bitter rivals and their annual baseball games were as furious as they were funny. George caught on his nine and was the clean-up batter.

And then there was hunting:

> Fifty miles away in the Genesee Valley Austin Wadsworth kept his pack of hounds. His house, in its wide park, faced one end of the village street and at the other was his brother Congressman Jim. Across and up and down the valley stretched their many farms. Generations of the family had lived here before them. Their tenants rode with the hounds, and their fences were post and rail. Austin was the grand seignior, keeping open house, and mounting, if needs be, the gentry from Buffalo and Batavia and Rochester. The Milburn boys were keen on hunting as they were on polo. With Craig and Jim-Sam Wadsworth, Pad Rumsey and David Gray they headed the coming generation of the Hunt.[4]

In 1896 John went to Hill School in Pottstown, Pennsylvania, followed by Devereux the next year. Here John continued to excel in athletics but not in academics. While still at the school his love for Madeleine Scatcherd of #703 Delaware began and never ended until her death thirty years later. The senior Milburn, a native of England, was an anglophile and steered his two sons to Oxford. They failed to pass the entrance exam for Magdalen College but were accepted by "the backwater of a smaller college — Lincoln," as Conger Goodyear put it. There they had a grand old time, adding rowing to their other accomplishments, meanwhile pub crawling and spending county weekends

4 Anson Conger Goodyear, *"John George Milburn, Jr., A Memoir,"* privately printed, 1938, pp. 8-10.

with their opposites in the British aristocracy, all which John described in lively letters to Madeleine. He returned to Buffalo after four years at Oxford and entered U.B. law school and his father's office. Devereux went on to Harvard.[5]

President McKinley and his wife Ida visited Buffalo in September 1901 for the Pan-American Exposition that summer, arriving on the 4th at #1168 as guests of exposition president, John Milburn. At 4:07 P.M. on the 6th McKinley was shot as he was shaking hands in front of the Temple of Music by anarchist Leon Czolgosz. The wounded president was brought to the Milburn house, where he lingered for six days, finally dying on September 14th. Meanwhile the scene in and around #1168 was chaotic.

> The Milburn house had lost the character of a private residence. The second floor was a hospital, with its waiting room occupied by Mrs. McKinley and her circle. Downstairs, there was a continuous subdued reception, graced by dignitaries and consulting physicians. The stables accommodated an improvised executive office, outfitted with a telegraph apparatus. The house next door took in the overflow of clerks and stenographers who had been summoned from Washington to handle the heavy mail. Ropes, manned by police, were stretched across Delaware Avenue to shut off the traffic. The sidewalk was patrolled by a detachment of regular infantry. On the opposite corner, a big election booth and several tents sheltered the members of the press on their twenty-four hours watch.[6]

A graduate of U.B. medical school in 1962 recently published a study of the assassination, including the role of the doctors, of which the following is a summation:

> The president's surgical team, granted heroic stature immediately following surgery, was declared incompetent by laymen and professionals alike. Nearly every historical interpretation of the McKinley era concludes that "bungled surgery" cost the nation its leader. A different explanation emerges when the medical evidence is reexamined in light of a more thorough understanding of surgical physiology. It is unlikely that [Roswell] Park or any other surgeon could have saved McKinley in 1901. Similar surgery today, however, would likely be successful. A reevaluation of the McKinley tragedy thus also provides the occasion of celebrating a century of medical progress.[7]

In 1904 the colossus at the mouth of the Hudson beckoned and Milburn joined a distinguished firm which thereupon became Carter, Ledyard, & Milburn of which Conger Goodyear writes:

> John C. Carter had recently retired from practice, the acknowledged leader of the bar of the United States. Carter was a crusader. He had been the prosecutor of Tweed, represented the United States in the arbitration of the Bering Sea sealing rights, and beat [Joseph H.] Choate in defending the constitutionality of the federal income tax. Louis Cass Ledyard was J. Pierpont Morgan's closest advisor, and trustee for many large estates.[8]

There Milburn served as legal counsel for many important organizations and institutions, including the New York Stock Exchange and the Milwaukee Memorial Fund of New York, of which he was a director. He was also a director of Barnard College and of the New York Public Library. In 1920 he

5 *Ibid.*, pp. 11, 38.

6 Margaret Leech, *In The Days of McKinley* (New York: Harper & Brothers, 1959), p. 598.

7 Jack Fisher, M.D., *Stolen Glory: the McKinley Assassination* (La Jolla, Ca: Alaman Books, 2001), blurb.

8 Anson Goodyear, *op. cit.*, p. 39. Actually, Choate beat Carter in this case, Pollock v. Farmers Loan & Trust Co., 1894.

represented railroad security holders in a case before Congress. He was president of the New York City Bar 1919-1920 and of the New York State Bar in 1924, and was on the standing committee on legal affairs for Columbia. He succeeded in getting his sons, John and Devereux, into his New York law firm. The senior Milburn's country estate, Groombridge, was located at Manhasset, Long Island. In 1922 Harvard made him an honorary Doctor of Laws. Among the many clubs to which he belonged were the Century, Knickerbocker, Union, Metropolitan, Lawyers, Downtown, and New York Yacht Club. He died suddenly at Claridges Hotel in London in 1930. His wife Patty had died two weeks before on July 25, 1930. John George Milburn, Jr., died at Roosevelt Hospital in New York on June 19, 1932, at age fifty-two of internal hemorrhaging, caused undoubtedly by a lifetime of serious injuries sustained playing polo. Madeleine had predeceased him on August 14, 1928. His club memberships in New York included the Racquet and Tennis, Knickerbocker, Downtown, and Meadow Brook. He had also maintained his membership in the Saturn Club in Buffalo. Devereux, who had risen to major in the field artillery in the First World War, died of a heart attack on the ninth tee of the Meadow Brook Club in Westbury, Long Island. His two-column obituary in the *New York Times*, which devoted but a single sentence to his legal career, saluted him as the "greatest back ever to play polo." Milburn, it was asserted, "one of the great figures in the history of American sport, was a magnetic and strong leader as well as a consummate performer; a man of forceful bold personality, quick to see new ways of doing old things; finding joy in every moment on the polo field and playing the game to the last whistle with every ounce of his strength and spirit."[9]

When he left for New York in 1904 Milburn sold #1168 to Philip Mark Shannon, son of Christopher and Martha Shannon, who was born in 1848 in Shannondale, Clarion County, Pennsylvania, a town named after his great grandfather, an emigrant from County Antrim in Ulster. At fourteen Philip had enlisted in the 62nd Pennsylvania Volunteers, and served in the Army of the Potomac until 1864 when he was wounded and honorably discharged. Thereafter he became a traveling salesman for a Pittsburgh mercantile house from which he resigned in 1868 to perform the same work for a New York firm. In 1869 he became interested in the petroleum industry at Parker's Landing, Pennsylvania, in association with Richard Jennings, a pioneer operator in the Millerstown oil field 1871-1872. In 1873 Shannon was elected burgess of Millerstown. From there he moved on to the Bradford field and to Allegany, New York. In 1881 Shannon and associates formed Melvin, Walker, Shannon & Company, which developed the profitable Shannon Mystery on the Cooper Tract in Forest County, Pennsylvania. He was mayor of Bradford in 1885, and in 1890 moved to Pittsburgh from where he managed petroleum operations in Ohio, West Virginia, Pennsylvania, Wyoming, Texas, and Alabama. In 1904 he moved to Buffalo. A member of the Duquesne, Park, Buffalo, and Birmingham, Alabama clubs, he died in Pittsburgh in 1915, survived by his wife Henriette and Hazel, a daughter.[10]

9 *NYT*, August 16, 1932.
10 *Courier*, April 26, 1915.

Henriette and Hazel stayed at #1168 under the next householder, George F. Rand, Jr., who resided there 1919-1921, before yielding it to Wilbur F. Groom, an army pilot during World War I, head of an automobile agency, and member of the usual social clubs.[11] (Groom shared the house with a Dutch-born milliner, Charles Stork, for whom an addition had been built and assigned the number #1170 Delaware.)

15.3 George Frederick Rand, Sr., Hill, *op. cit.*, III, facing p. 21.

Rand's father George Franklin Rand, Sr.,(15.#3) had leased #1014 Delaware 1915-1918 from Harry Hamlin's widow. For Rand, Jr., #1168 was a temporary arrangement while the next-door mansion, which had been started under his father at #1180 in 1919, was being built. The spacious site for this mansion, alternately listed as #1180, #1190, and #1192, had in 1870 contained the residence of George D. Teller, passenger agent for the Northern Pacific Railroad, in 1880 of Jacob Bergtold, farmer, in 1891 the home and greenhouse of C. F. Christiensen, florist, and in 1900 the residence of Joseph T. Jones, an oil producer. The elder Rand, an immensely successful banker, wanted a mansion that would end all mansions on the Avenue. It did, but he never saw it finished.

Rand, Sr., was born in Forest Home, Niagara County, in 1867, son of Calvin and Almira Long Rand. Educated at local schools and at the state normal school in Brockport, he began his banking career at sixteen as assistant cashier of the State Bank of North Tonawanda. In 1888 Rand married Vina S. Fisher in Tonawanda. They had four children, George F., Jr., Calvin, Evelyn, and Gretchen. In 1888 George Rand, Sr., at twenty-one, was elected president of the First National Bank of Tonawanda, a position he filled for ten years, resigning to become vice president of the Columbia National Bank of Buffalo. He moved to Buffalo in 1901 and a year later became president of Columbia. After a few years as president of Columbia, he was made vice president and then president of the Marine National Bank of Buffalo, when he purchased a large block of stock in it from its long-time president, Stephen M. Clement. Shortly before his death Rand was instrumental in achieving a long cherished vision by merging Bankers Trust of Buffalo, Erie Finance Corporation, and Marine National into one giant, the Marine Trust Company of Buffalo, one of the strongest financial institutions in the nation. Like many of his class, Rand was a superpatriot during World War I. After President Wilson secured a declaration of war in April 1917, Rand telegraphed him offering to equip an entire regiment at Rand's own expense. This theatrical offer was not ac-

11 *CE*, July 30. 1936.

cepted. Under Rand's direction, Marine purchased for itself and its customers $75,000,000 in Liberty Bonds, and another $75,000,000 in other government securities.

On June 11, 1916, during the bloody siege of Verdun, a section of the 137th Regiment of the French Infantry, with rifles shouldered and bayonets bared, stood ready to attack the Germans. An enemy bombardment suddenly buried the poilus on the spot, leaving only the protruding bayonets visible when Rand, on a business trip to Europe during the so-called Peace Conference of 1919, visited the battlefield. He offered to make a half million francs available to the American ambassador to France for a memorial to the bravery of the defenders of Verdun. Rand and the ambassador visited Georges Clemenceau, premier of France, who accepted the offer. Next morning Rand was killed in a plane crash at Croydon Field, England, December 11, 1919, as he flew to London on the first leg of his homeward journey. The plane crashed through trees in a thick fog and landed in a field. Rand was discovered pinned under the wing, his pilot, Lieutenant S. B. Bradley, under the other. Witnesses said Rand attempted to speak but his words were unintelligible. Death was due to a compound fracture of the skull. The pilot died two days later:

> Like several other big Buffalo businessmen, [Rand] died at the pinnacle of success in life and while building a beautiful house on the west side of Delaware near West Ferry. He was erecting a mansion near the circle and had the architects' sketch of it on display in his office and looked forward to the time when he could enter it. "...Other Buffalo men who died while building homes in the vicinity of the Rand home were S. M. Clement, the two Goodyears, and Mr. Gratwick.[12]

His children agreed to honor their father's offer. The monument was dedicated on December 8, 1920.[13]

George Franklin Rand, Jr., who was to succeed his father as president of Marine Trust, had been born in North Tonawanda in 1892, attended P.S. 16 on Delaware and Lafayette High, and graduated from the Wharton School of Commerce in 1916. That year he began his business career, obviously with Marine Trust, and in 1917 became assistant secretary. In 1917, after America entered the war, Rand, Jr., who because of a physical disability could not serve in the military, went to France with the Y.M.C.A. in which he served until the end of the war. He returned to his former job in March 1919 and in 1920 advanced to the vice-presidency in charge of branch banks. In the summer of 1921 he and a group of younger men, some of whom were sons of his father's close associates, acquired a major interest in one of Buffalo's smaller financial institutions, the Buffalo Trust Company. Rand was elected president, and by 1925 its assets had risen from $15 million to $70 million. The reason for his success was following his father's policy of opening branch banks in neighborhoods throughout the city. In 1926 Buffalo Trust merged with Marine Trust and Rand was elected president of the new company. In the fall of 1929 the Marine Midland Corporation was formed, a group of banks centered

12 *BEN*, December 12, 1919.
13 Hill, *op. cit.*, 3:20-22; Wilner, *op. cit.*, 3: 473-476.

around Marine Midland Trust of Buffalo and Marine Midland Trust of New York.

Beyond his banking activities, Rand was director of National Dairy Products, Studebaker, Pierce-Arrow, American Steamship, Cleveland & Buffalo Transit, Buffalo, Rochester & Pittsburgh Railroad, General Baking, Remington Rand, Niagara Falls Power Company, and Buffalo, Niagara & Eastern Power Company. He was also a director of the Buffalo Foundation and the Fine Arts Academy. His social club memberships were equally numerous: Buffalo, Saturn, Saddle & Bridle, Buffalo Athletic, Niagara Falls Country, University, and the Bankers Club of New York. Rounding out his memberships, he was a 33rd Degree Mason, a Republican, and a communicant of North Presbyterian. In 1920 he was living with his two unmarried sisters at the old Milburn house at #1168 Delaware. Next year the Tudor style mansion at #1180, which had been begun early in 1919, was completed and Rand and his two sisters, Evelyn and Gretchen, moved in. During his 1921 whirlwind tour of the United States as guest of the American Legion, Marshal Ferdinand Foch, commander-in-chief of the Allied armies in France, stayed at #1180 as he promised Rand at the unveiling of the memorial at Verdun. One of the highlights of the 1921 Christmas season was the debut at #1180 of Rand's sisters. Next March 28, he was married to Isabel Hadley Williams. They had three children, George F., Isabel Hadley, and Calvin Gordon.[14]

George Rand rarely took a vacation, though he made many trips to New York on business. He had a summer home, *Ravenwood*, in Niagara-on-the Lake and drove to and from work in Buffalo daily. Despite his many club memberships he rarely dined in any of them. He had a private dining room on the top floor of the 1929 Rand Building where he lunched regularly with associates.[15]

For George and his sisters, what was already being called the Rand mansion at #1180 Delaware had too many unpleasant memories. Therefore in November 1922, six months after his wedding, he offered to sell the building to the Ancient and Accepted Scottish Rite Free Masons whose clubhouse and cathedral had hitherto been on the corner of Delaware and Huron(5.21,22) for $1 million. Included in the proposal was a gift of $500,000 from Rand. A hall,

15.4 ❦ Number 1180 Delaware, Clubhouse and Consistory, north side, *Ancient Accepted Scottish Rite of Free Masonry, 38th Annual Reunion,* **1930, frontispiece.**

14 Wilner, *op. cit.*, 4:516-518.
15 *BEN*, November 19, 1942.

15.5 ❦ Number 1180 Delaware, Clubhouse and Consistory, south side, *Don't Be A Stranger*, Welcome Song of the Buffalo Consistory, 1924, cover.

the Consistory, was to be added to the rear of the mansion for another $500,000.(15.4,5) Soon Consistory came to designate the entire complex. The sale took place in 1924 and ground was broken for the addition on May 24th. The architect was Harold Jewett Cook and the contractors were Ballard I. Crooker and Townsend S. M. Carpenter. The Buffalo Trust, of which Rand was president and which merged with Marine, furnished the funds. The Consistory was dedicated in the course of a four-day program in November 29, 1925, which drew thousands of Masons across the state:

> Masons who thronged through the temple for the first time on the day of its dedication found the original home converted into a graciously-furnished clubhouse. They entered a large auditorium, on the ceiling of which the constellations were painted as seen above Buffalo the night of the groundbreaking; they climbed the wide marble staircase to the grand ballroom, lighted by special French chandeliers.
>
> Murals and woodwork depicting the history of Masonry added to the decorations of the temple; the grand staircase, and hand-wrought iron enriched the door to the lobby. Downstairs were a swimming pool, bowling alleys, huge kitchens, boilers, heating and air-conditioning equipment. No money had been spared throughout the building, and splendor marked the entire effort.[16]

Departing from Delaware, Rand moved into a house built according to his wishes 1928-1929 at a cost of $350,000 at #161 Nottingham.(15.6) There he died at fifty after a short illness on November 19, 1942. In his memory the flag over City Hall was flown at half-mast.[17] His wife died at Nottingham in 1951. After an unsuccessful attempt to give it to the city as a home for the mayor, the cottage was demolished.

16 *Ibid.*, November 25, 1925.
17 *CE*, November 22, 1942.

15.6 ❦ Number 161 Nottingham Terrace, BHS.

Nineteen-forty-two, the year George Rand died, was a bad year for Buffalo's Masons:

> Financial difficulties early beset the Masons. In [April] 1929 [five months before the Stock Market Crash] they launched a campaign among the members for $1,500,000 because the "building is unfinished, in spirit, until the building debt is cleared." Interest charges were absorbing the revenues and leaving nothing for retirement of the debt or for repairs. The campaign did not succeed.[18]

The organization began defaulting on its city and county taxes in 1934; yet in 1936 commander-in-chief, George A. Newbury, emphatically denied that the Delaware Avenue property was going to be put up for sale. "We're in pretty good shape," he insisted.[19] By 1942 the city had had enough and set a date for a tax foreclosure sale. But Newbury, an attorney, had a plan. The Consistory would bid $100,000 for the property at the sale and if it is "the successful bidder, it plans to convert the building into a Masonic Center and establish it as a tax-exempt institution." Newbury alleged that $100,000 "was about all that could be raised by subscription."[20] His gambit failed. The Delaware Avenue property was acquired by the city for $5,000 at a foreclosure sale held in the lobby of the County Hall on May 24, 1942. This sale also wiped out the mortgage, the capital of which had never been paid. Arrears dated back to 1934 and totaled about $381,000, including interest and penalties, on an assessed valuation of $444,480. Of this $287,945 was owed to the city, $90,908 to the county, and $2,381 to the Sewer Authority.[21] The Masons had pretty much of a free ride 1934-1942. However they kept the property in repair and heated in winter, and their white elephant was not something that would find many buyers either in the Depression or even in the beginning of 1942 when the outcome of World War II was not certain:

> Now the city had to sell or lease the property which was costing $14,000 a year just to heat. The Masons vacated the property at year's end in favor of new quarters in the Ancient Landmarks Lodge Temple, 318-320 Pearl Street. The former Consistory was leased to Canisius College on February 3, 1943, as living quarters for air cadets. Inspectors from the Army Air Force had approved campus buildings and the former Consistory early in 1943. The boys in uniform would march up Delaware and across Delavan to Canisius for instruction in English, geography, mathematics, history, physics, medical aid, and physical training. Flight training was at the Clarence airport. Two hundred air cadets arrived on March 1, 1943, and another 150 on April 1, bringing the total for the 22nd College Training Detachment to 350 cadets, officers, and instructors. The program was completed on May 25, 1944.[22]

18 *Ibid.*
19 *Ibid.*, January 28, 1936.
20 *Ibid.*, May 5, 1942.
21 *Ibid.*, June 25, 1942.
22 J. Clayton Murray, *"A Historical Retrospective of the Last 125 Years of Canisius College*, 1870-1995," (Buffalo: Canisius College, 1996), pp. 9-10.

With the end of the program in view, a bid of $95,000 for the Consistory was submitted for Canisius High School to the Common Council in February 1944. The school had been located on downtown Washington Street next to Saint Michael's Church since 1870. The cornerstone of the main building which had also housed a college of sorts had been laid in the spring of 1872. The rector of Canisius wrote to the Jesuit General in Rome in 1895 that "the college had been built so poorly that it required almost continual rebuilding (continua readificatione)."[23] The college was moved uptown in 1912, leaving the high school in an increasingly congested environment. Canisius' bid for the Consistory triggered other bids. The C.I.O. wanted it as union headquarters, the Army wanted to rent it for an induction center, others urged that it be made into a public school. Moreover, the Masons cannot have been happy that their once magnificent building was being acquired by Jesuits for $95,000. Nevertheless, the Common Council approved the sale to Canisius on March 8, 1944, and air cadets marched out of the Consistory for the final time on April 17, 1944.[24]

A key player in the acquisition of the Consistory by the Jesuits was George J. Evans, a graduate of St. Brigid's Parochial School in the First Ward, of Canisius High in 1915, of Canisius College in 1922, of U.B.'s law school in 1928, and president of the Common Council. He learned from his old friend, Father James Redmond, that Canisius High, of which Redmond had recently become president, was interested in a swimming pool which would cost about $25,000. A home-coming party for Father was held at the Statler with Evans as toastmaster, at which he announced a drive for the pool. Meanwhile the federal government cancelled its lease on the Consistory from the city. Evans obtained the keys from the Commissioner of Buildings and inspected the place with Father Redmond who pronounced it ideal for conversion into a school. Redmond made an offer of $95,000 to the city and the sale with Evans' guidance sailed through the Council. By an oversight the deal was made for cash, but all the prospective buyer had was $25,000 collected for the pool. Evans had this treated as a down payment and arranged a first mortgage of $75,000 for two years, to which the Council agreed. A second drive was set in motion to purchase adjacent land for grounds, classrooms, and a residence for Jesuits.[25]

From 1944 until 1948 the high school was conducted in two divisions. Junior and seniors remained downtown, sophomores and freshmen moved to #1180 Delaware. A classroom wing was added to the south side of the mansion, and the former Milburn house was acquired as a residence for the Jesuit faculty. The classroom wing had three floors with twenty-seven classrooms and laboratories. The basement had a cafeteria and kitchen that would accommodate a student body of 800 or more comfortably. The Milburn house was a rattletrap and was razed in 1957 and replaced by Frauenheim Hall, a faculty residence north of the Consistory.[26]

23 Edward T. Dunn, *"A History of Canisius College, 1870-1907,"* A Thesis submitted to the Faculty of the Department of History, Canisius College, in partial fulfillment of the requirements for the degree Master of Arts, May 1964.

24 *CE*, March 1, 5, 8, 12, 21, April 18, 1944, September 8, 1945.

25 Canisius High School archives.

26 James J. Hennessy, *"A History of Canisius High School,"* Woodstock Letters, 83(1954), 352-364.

First occupant of #1200 Delaware was Whitney A. Case who resided there at least as early as 1868. He had been born in Hammond near Ogdensburg in 1824, but moved with his parents to Watertown where the family lived for seven years. When he was eight the Cases moved to a farm on the Mohawk River across from Schenectady where Whitney attended school until he was fourteen. Then he worked on the farm until he was seventeen. His father had taken a contract for part of the work on the Genesee Valley Canal, "the wildest project of all New York's list of canal schemes."[27] Whitney accompanied his father on this construction, most likely on the section between Mount Morris and Olean, and then on his own took a contract on the Troy & Schenectady, a railroad which was completed in 1842. Exposure to railroads, the wave of the future, made him decide to become an expert in copper and sheet iron working. He apprenticed himself to a master in the craft and when time was up Case had mastered every detail of locomotive, copper, and sheet-iron work. His first wife, whom he had married in 1846, died in 1851. By his second wife, Mary Emeigh of Buffalo, he had four children who survived infancy, Edward, Mary, Elizabeth (Lillia), and Whitney G. Since Buffalo was becoming a railroad center, Whitney Case went there, worked for S. Dudley & Son, coppersmiths, and within three months had become foreman, a position he held for seven years. At the request of several railroad officials who wanted him for all their copper work, he opened a shop in 1852 on Washington Street where he was soon employing eighty men, which enabled him to afford a house on Delaware. A few years later, he took on his son, Whitney G., as a partner in what became Whitney A. Case & Son, Copper, Tin, & Sheet Iron Works.[28] The elder Case died in 1892.

Case's widow Mary and two daughters managed to keep #1200 Delaware in the family until 1926. In 1900 Mary lived there with her daughter Elizabeth whose husband, Riley Washington McCready, had died in 1894, leaving her $150,000 with instructions how it should be divided upon her death. She invested so well that at her death in 1926 her husband's estate had grown to $2,524,316 ($43,998,827 in 1997 dollars.) But the testatrix had had a mind of her own and left a will at variance with her late husband's instructions. Moreover many of the beneficiaries under his will resided in Illinois. Counsel for beneficiaries under Elizabeth's will argued that she had earned the increase by her own efforts and hence had the right to dispose of what she had earned. In all over 400 would-be beneficiaries filed claims.[29]

By 1915 Mary had died, and Elizabeth had been joined at #1200 by her sister Mary, the wife of William Collins, who had also died. The sisters enjoyed the services of two female domestics and of a German-born chauffeur who lived in the back with his family. In 1920 the sisters still lived at #1200, and two of their four domestics were nurses, but the sisters still required the services of a chauffeur. In all, a dozen people resided at #1200 in 1920. Mary had died by 1925 and Elizabeth, now alone, had invited aboard a cousin, Nellie Doyle, and the cousin's daughter, Dorothy. Only a

27 Alvin F. Harlow, *Old Towpaths: The Story of the American Canal Era* (New York: D. Appleton & Co., 1926), p. 152.

28 *Buffalo Express Extra Edition*, September, 1888.

29 *BEN*, May 24, 1928.

15.7 ❦ Number 1230 Delaware, BHS.

single domestic was left, a nurse, and Elizabeth, then over seventy, had no need of a chauffeur. In 1926, the place, which had been in the family since the 1860s, was occupied by Mr. and Mrs. Riley Washington McCready, Elizabeth's son and daughter-in-law.

The building lot on the northwest corner of Cleveland and Delaware, #1230, had long been vacant. The first householder there was William Russell Huntley, so the house(15.7) had probably been built for him. His father was Charles R. Huntley, an important figure in the Western New York electric power picture. In 1916 ground was broken for the coal-fired electric plant on River Road, which was completed shortly after his death in 1926, and was named for him. With America's involvement in World War I impending, fears surfaced that Niagara Falls power might not be enough for the demands that were going to be made upon it. Huntley presided over the 1925 merger of several power and light companies resulting in the formation of the Buffalo Niagara & Eastern Power Company.[30] His son, William R. Huntley, was born in Bradford in 1879. He spent a year at Cornell 1897-1898 and married Jannie Speer in 1907. They had one son, Charles Russell II. William was associated with his father for many years. In 1920 he was living at #1230 Delaware with his wife and son and two domestics. He was vice president of one of his father's electric power companies, succeeded to the presidency of the Buffalo Niagara & Eastern after his father's death, but resigned effective April 1, 1930, and entered the investment business. He was also a director of George Urban Milling. Clubs to which he belonged were Buffalo, Automobile, and Country.[31] The Huntleys lived at #1230 until at least 1935.

The home with the classical facade at #1234(15.8) was built in 1908 for Conrad E. Wettlaufer(15.9), who had been born in Canada in 1868, son of Conrad and Elizabeth Wettlaufer, German immigrants. The father had come to the New World in 1830. Conrad was educated in the day and night schools of Canada, worked on his father's farm and sawmill, traveled across Canada selling farm equipment, and in 1890 entered the Philadelphia Dental College, graduating in 1894. He opened an office in Buffalo where he practiced and taught in the dental department of U.B. In 1901 he married Irene Taylor, daughter of Harry Taylor, owner of H. D. Taylor Company, wholesale distributors of automotive supplies, for which Wettlaufer went to work next year, abandoning his dental practice. Given his extensive knowledge of Canada, he put together and became president of the Wettlaufer Silver Mine in South Lorraine in the Cobalt district of Canada. He was also largely instrumental in financing Sir Harry Oakes in the Lake Shore Gold Mine in 1917 of which Wettlaufer was a director and

30 *Times*, December 15, 1928; *Who Was Who in America*, 1:611.
31 *BEN*, March 28, 1930; *Who Was Who in America*, 6:205.

15.8 ❦ Number 1234 Delaware, BHS.

15.9 ❦ Conrad E. Wettlaufer, Horton, *op. cit.*, III, facing p. 392.

treasurer for five years. Sir Harry, an immensely wealthy Canadian gold mine owner, eccentric and unpopular in Canada, was the victim of an unsolved murder in Nassau, the Bahamas, in 1943.[32] Back in Buffalo Wettlaufer became a generous contributor to the Buffalo Orphan Asylum and was its president for several years. In 1916 he became president of the Buffalo Association for the Blind and in 1926 rescued the Buffalo Eye and Ear Infirmary, later the Buffalo Eye and Ear Hospital and Wettlaufer Clinic. He was a 32nd Degree Mason and belonged to the Buffalo, Country, and Niagara Falls Country clubs. For five years 1915-1920 he was chairman of the Erie County Republican Committee. The Wettlaufers presented the Girl Scouts with a farm in Erie County known as Seven Hills. Doctor Wettlaufer died in 1959 and his wife in 1963. Next year their son, Conrad Taylor Wettlaufer, sold #1234 to Pascal C. Rubino as a funeral home.[33]

By 1931 the long empty lot on the corner of Delaware and Auburn, #1240, was occupied by the Commodore Apartments. On the northwest corner at #1260, also long vacant, a large house was built in 1916 for George A. Forman, a wealthy oil man of #824 Delaware.(10.40) George was president of the Southwestern Petroleum Company which he had organized in 1901. He died of a heart attack at forty-nine in 1925, aboard the *Berengaria*, just before she docked at Plymouth, England. With his wife and two children he was preparing for a European vacation. (Figure 15.10 is a reminder that transatlantic crossings and European tours and vacations were an important away from home activity for the American elite during the first half of the twentieth century.) Southwestern Petroleum controlled installations in Oklahoma, Kentucky, Kansas, and Texas. The company was sold after Forman's death for $15 million ($261 million in 1997 dollars.)[34] His widow stayed on at #1260 until the early 1930s when the house was sold to Harry Blanchard Spaulding, grandson of Buffalo Civil War congressman, Elbridge Spaulding, and son of Edward Rich Spaulding and the

32 Daniel Frances, "*Oakes, Sir Harry, The Canadian Encyclopedia* (Edmonton, Hurting Publishers, 1985), 2:1305.
33 Horton, *op. cit.*, 3:392-293; *CE*, May 5, 1964.
34 *Express*, June 24, 1925; June 5, 1926.

former Mary Tenney Blanchard. Edward succeeded his father as president of the Farmers & Mechanics Bank. He was also president of the Buffalo Gas Light Company until 1907. Harry B. Spaulding was born in Buffalo in 1881, attended P.S. 14, prepared for college at the Thatcher School in California, and graduated from Yale in 1905. He worked for Bell Telephone for a year and was treasurer of the John R. Keim Mills until 1910 when he became treasurer of the Long Grate Bar Company, manufacturers of revolving and rocking boiler grates. In 1916 he organized the Power Efficiency Company, engineers and contractors, of which he became president. He was by inheritance a wealthy man and enjoyed a brisk social life, belonging to Saturn, the Buffalo Club, the Buffalo Tennis and Squash Club, the Lake Shore Hunt Club, and the Yale Club in New York and New Haven. His favorite sports were polo, hunting, and golf. In 1908 he married Mary L. Ramsdell, and they had one child.[35] The Spauldings were still living at #1260 in 1940.

15.10 ❦ *The Berengaria*, John Malcom Brinnin, *The Sway of the Grand Saloon: A Social History of the North Atlantic* (New York: Barnes & Noble Books, 1971), following p. 330.

A stone Tudor house(15.11) was built at #1272 for a third generation Laub, Albert(12.25), director of George F. Laub's Sons, tanners, in 1912. After his death in 1921 at fifty-one his widow Clara continued to live there until 1942 when she gave it as a memorial to her husband to the local Council of Churches of Christ in America. She died in 1957.[36] A vacant lot long lay just north of the Laub home until the late 1920s when it became the site of the 1290 Delaware Avenue Apartments. On the southwest corner of Lancaster and Delaware at #1296 there was erected about 1914 the yellow brick home of Emanuel Boasberg, a prominent Buffalo Jew. Born in Buffalo in 1865, he attended the public elementary and high schools of the city and at an early age entered the tobacco business. In 1889 he and August Keiser formed the wholesale native (i. e., Connecticut) leaf tobacco house of Keiser & Boasberg with offices at #147 Elm, which developed into one of the largest independent tobacco firms in the United States. In 1925 both partners decided, although their business was then at its peak, to abandon the enterprise in favor of travel, philanthropy, and cultural activities. Boasberg and Keiser also got into real estate with an office in the Genesee Building. Their company was reputedly one of the largest property owners in the city, with several choice downtown parcels.

35 Hill, *op. cit.*, 36-37.
36 *CE*, June 24, 1942.

15.11 ❦ Number 1272 Delaware, BHS.

With his broadening interests he found his services in demand in several areas. He was a director of Marine Trust, of the Abstract Title & Mortgage Corporation, and a trustee of a liquidating firm. He was among the earliest advocates of the Peace Bridge and, when the Buffalo & Fort Erie Public Bridge Company was incorporated, was a director. In July 1925 on his fiftieth birthday he endowed a chair of history at U.B., the first occupant of which was Julius W. Pratt, a noted historian of American Foreign Policy. A staunch supporter of the Boy Scouts, Boasberg was active in its Buffalo Council for fifteen years, during three of which he was a director. He was also an outstanding contributor and worker for the Jewish Federation for Social Service, and, as clouds gathered over Nazi Germany, was active in the United Jewish campaigns for foreign relief conducted by Buffalo Jews in 1935-1937. He died in 1937 at his summer home, Idlewood, in Lakeview, survived by his wife, the former Bessie Jandorf, and two sons, Norman, a realtor, and Emmanuel, Jr., an attorney. Rabbi Joseph L. Fink of Beth Zion, of which Boasberg had been a member, conducted his funeral. Burial was at Forest Lawn.[37]

Concerning #1306(15.12) Burr wrote in 1926:

> Way back in the late '40s and early '50s, the wealthy men of the city began building stately homes after the fashion of their time. Many of these houses are still standing, but most of them have been razed for more modern structures.
>
> Come stroll with me down the Delaware avenue of fifty years ago [1876.] At the extreme end of the avenue stood the beautiful brown square brick house with [a] hall through the center and a stained glass window in the upper hall over the veranda, that was built some years before by the late Jacob Lessler. A conservatory at the southern exposure was filled with a rare collection of plants, for Mrs. Lessler was a great lover of flowers and had the magic touch that made them blossom into beauty where others worked in vain. It was Jacob Lessler who at his own personal expense had the hill that was located on the street near his home leveled for pedestrians and drivers.[38]

Jacob Lessler was a Prussian and presided over a household which in 1870 comprised himself, his wife Betsey, seven children in ages from sixteen to four, and two domestics. Burr added that "following many years' residence there, the Lessler family was succeeded by a family named Howard and later by Dr. Rogers who married one of the Howard girls." Benjamin F. Rogers had been born near Medina in 1854 and graduated from the U.B. medical department in 1879. He returned to Medina to

37 *BEN*, June 22, 1937; Adler, *op. cit.*, p. 174.
38 *Courier*, May 30, 1926.

15.12 ❦ Number 1306 Delaware, *PBHS*, 29 (1927), 334.

practice, but after his marriage to Edna, daughter of Austin and Sarah Howard, in 1887, he moved to Buffalo. He became an oculist after postgraduate study in New York. Mrs. Rogers' sister Alice lived with the Rogers at #1306. In Dr. Rogers later years he closed his practice at the end of October and he and his wife drove to California for the winter. He died there in 1925 at seventy-two.[39]

The last inhabitants of #1306 as a private dwelling were John Bradley, a native of Manchester, Vermont, his wife, and daughter. He had been president and later chairman of the board of Pratt & Letchworth Malleable Iron & Steel Company, trustee of Erie County Savings Bank, and director of M&T.[40] He died in 1930. By the mid-1920s, the corner of Lancaster and Delaware had become the site of the six-story Gates Circle Apartments.(15.13)

At the end of the nineteenth century Delaware and Richmond Avenues were joined by a system of grass-margined parkways named after local Civil War heroes and Abraham Lincoln, their commander-in-chief. Daniel D. Bidwell and Edward P. Chapin were Buffalo's two brigadier generals and were killed in action. Before the war Bidwell had been a captain in Buffalo's 74th Regiment NYNG. When war broke out he organized the 49th Regiment, which he led during the Peninsular Campaign, Antietam, Fredericksburg, and Gettysburg. In the spring of 1864 his regiment participated in the Wilderness, Spotsylvania, and Cold Harbor. Promoted to brigadier, he was killed at the battle of Cedar Creek in Virginia October 9, 1864.[41] Chapin enlisted in the 116th New York Volunteers in 1861 as a captain but soon rose to colonel. In 1863 he was promoted to brigadier and killed leading an attack on Port Hudson on the Mississippi on May 21, 1863.[42]

15.13 ❦ Number 1306 Delaware, Gates Circle Apartments, BHS.

39 *BEN*, January 5, 1925; *Express*, January 8, 1925.
40 Warren, *op. cit.*, p. 84.
41 Hill, *op. cit.*, 1:306.
42 *Ibid.*, p. 310.

In 1902 Georgia Gates Pardee, widow of Charles Pardee of #938 Delaware and daughter of the late George Gates(8.21), the sleeping car company executive, offered to build a circle with a sunken garden and fountain surrounded by trees at the intersection of Lafayette and Delaware Avenues, hitherto Chapin Place, provided that it be renamed Gates Circle. Members of the Grand Army protested in the name of their fallen brother-in-arms. But their protest was brushed aside.[43] The project was completed in 1903.

Figure 15.14 Concluded shows the Porter Huntington Norton mansion at #33 Gates Circle in 1903. Norton was born on July 9, 1854, son of Charles D. Norton, U.B. Chancellor. Porter was educated at private schools including Professor Briggs' Classical School; after graduating he went to work for a book dealer. At seventeen he began reading law in the office of Ebenezer Sprague. Admitted to the bar in 1875 Porter soon became managing clerk in the law offices of Loran L. Lewis (#1093) and William H. Gurney, after which he became a solo practitioner. In 1880 Norton entered partnership with Henry Box which lasted until 1891 when he joined Thomas Penney and Charles Sears. For twenty-five years he was counsel for the IRC. He was a director of the Crosstown Street Railway Company, Bell Telephone, Niagara Falls Electric Railway, and the Fresh Air Mission. He was a trustee of De Veaux, vestryman of Trinity, and a member of the Sons of the American Revolution and the Society of Colonial Wars. His clubs were the Buffalo, the Ellicott, and the Country. In 1878 he married Jennie, daughter of Stephen V. R. Watson, whose house at #388 Delaware, where Jennie grew up, became the third home of the Buffalo Club. The Nortons had two children, Porter Huntington who married Gilbertine Coakley, and Gertrude Van Rensselaer who married Daniel Streeter.[44] Porter Norton, Sr., died in 1918. His wife moved across the Avenue to #1275 where she died in 1922. The mansion at #33 Gates Circle was not razed but incorporated into the Park Lane. It burned down in the early seventies.

Burleigh grew ecstatic in 1936 when describing #33:

> The house is of Pompeian brick, with cream colored pillars along the front, and on the side which faces the driveway. The interior was stuff for dreams. There was a great hall, with a fountain that trickled a drowsy little tune; an oddly shaped library, lined to the ceiling with rare books; a distinctive drawing-room and a dining room that breathed welcome. The furniture was mostly from old Spanish palaces and the portraits which Soholla pain[t]ed of the master and mistress of the house peered in inimitable fashion from gorgeous old Spanish frames.
>
> Mr. Norton, whose Uncle [read brother] Charles has gone down in local history as the first Chancellor of the University of Buffalo [He wasn't. Millard Fillmore was], was gentle, sweet-tempered, thoughtful, cheerful and charming; a broad-shouldered figure of middle height, a broad forehead, smiling eyes, and a sensitive mouth. He had a gay sense of humor, and was in love with acting. He had been a vivid member of Col. Cornell's gifted troupe of amateurs.

43 *Commercial*, February 19, 1902.
44 *M&FH*, 1:67.

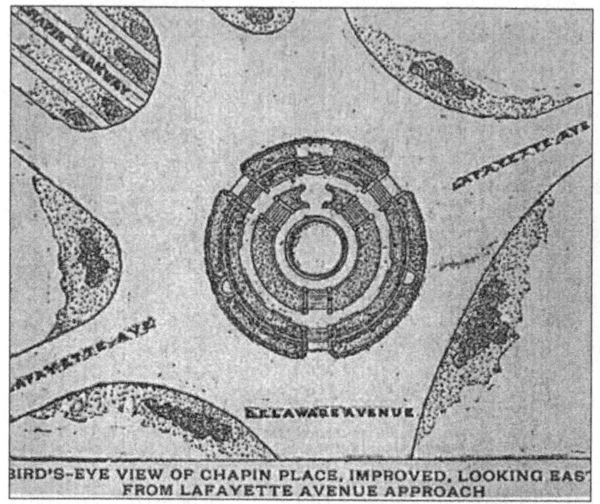

LAFAYETTE AVE
LAFAYETTE AVE
DELAWARE AVENUE
BIRD'S-EYE VIEW OF CHAPIN PLACE, IMPROVED, LOOKING EAST FROM LAFAYETTE AVENUE APPROACH

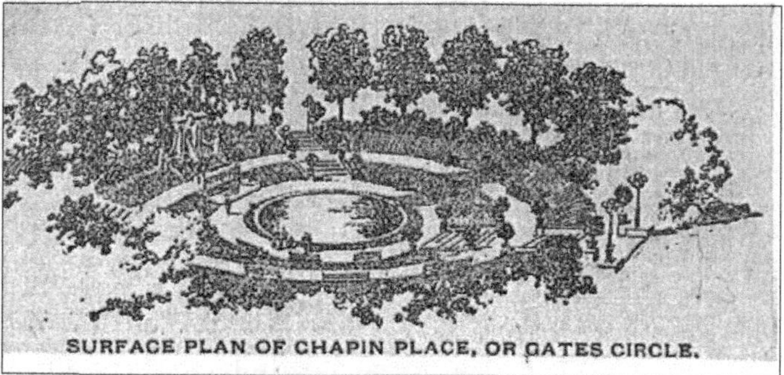

SURFACE PLAN OF CHAPIN PLACE, OR GATES CIRCLE.

SECTION OF CHAPIN PLACE, IMPROVED, LOOKING NORTH FROM DELAWARE AVENUE APPROACH; FOUNTAIN AND CASCADES IN BACKGROUND.

15.14a ❦ views of Gates Circle, *Express*, February 19, 1902; BFN. April 5, 1903.
15.14b ❦ Gates Circle under construction. William Schoellkopf mansion, #1275 Delaware, on left; Porter Norton mansion, 33 Gates Circle on right.

Mrs. Norton was born Jennie Watson, a noted patroness of music, and no mean pianist herself. Jennie Norton was slim and willowy, with sparking eyes and curly brown hair. When I recall her pretty graces and wining ways, her bountiful and vivacious hospitality, an air of the grand siecle seems to blow through them, an initiation for the younger generation into the meaning of style.

The garden of this glamorous house had an avenue of poplars, planned so that its plumy trunks looked the limit of all things. It was only right that this plaisance, carpeted with green grass, fringed with stocks and wall-flowers, and sprinkled with bird-notes, should be separated by a mist of fragrance from the world without, with which its magic had nothing in common.

> The Nortons had been much in Italy, and they loved the charm of the Tuscan gardens bordered with iris and roses, where nightingales sang in the daphne trees, and the ilexes whispered ancient legends, one always thought of these things, when one was privileged to linger in the garden, which delicately blew one a whiff of rosemary for remembrance.
>
> There were bits of Italian stone at the end of the walks; I seem to remember a satyr asleep in the sun dreaming of ghost-gardens, where little green lizards slipped through crumbling balustrades. I have forgotten much that was significant, yet after all, forgetting seems sometimes an art to be cultivated - a picture all light is as bad as one all shadow.[45]

The Norton property ran back 440 feet east from Delaware, which explains the extensive garden on the site of which the Park Lane Apartments were later built.

45 *Times*, June 13, 1936.

Appendix 1

Buffalo Club presidents who were Delaware Avenue residents.

1867-1869	Millard Fillmore, #52 Niagara Square
1864	Sherman S. Jewett, #256
1875	Myron P. Bush, #762
1876-1878	Rufus L. Howard, #251
1880	Abraham A. Altman, #767
1884	Jewett M. Richmond, #844
1886-1887	E. Carlton Sprague, #235
1888-1890	Wilson S. Bissell, #1097
1891	Dexter P. Rumsey, #742
1892	George S. Field, #452
1893	Ansley Wilcox, #641
1894	Joseph P. Dudley, #827
1895	John G. Milburn, #1168
1897	John N. Scatcherd, #703
1899	Charles W. Goodyear, #723, 888
1903	Frank H. Goodyear, #762
1904-1905	Pendennis White, #483
1908	Laurence D. Rumsey #1 Park Place
1913	William B. Hoyt, #841
1914	Frank B. Baird, #1069
1917	John L. Clawson, #1109
1920	John C. Bradley #1306
1927	Morris S. Tremaine, #703
1928	Frank F. Henry, #864, 1131
1932	Louis L. Babcock #844
1938	Charles B. Sears #849
1939	Joseph G. Dudley #1089

Appendix 2

Ivy League Colleges and Delaware Avenue residents: *attended, did not graduate

Harvard (1636)
Almy, Frederick, #427
Baird, Frank B., #1060
Baird, William C #1069
Bull, Henry A., #1093
Cary, Seward, #615
Cary, Thomas, #184
Cary, Walter, Jr., #184
Davis, Townsend, #596
Dorsheimer, William E., #438*
Fiske, Frank W. #199, 610
Fryer, Robert L., #685
Ganson, John H., #262
Gilbert, Lester F., #841
Lord, Walter D., #330
Matthews George E., #295
Norton, Charles P., #313
Rumsey, Charles C., #330
Rumsey, Dexter P., Jr., #742
Rumsey, Laurence D., #330
Streeter, Daniel, #1125
Streeter, Edward, #1125
Welch, Stuart C. #1193

Yale (1701), including
Scientific School (1861)
Austin, Stephen G., N.S.

Bartlett, G. Hunter, #1083

Beals, Pascal P., #214

Butler, Edward H., #672

Bissell, Arthur D., #1081

Bissell, Wilson S., #1081

Chester, Carl T., #112

Clement, Stephen M., #786

Conners, William J., Jr., #1140

Garvin, Albert, #1105

Goodyear, Anson C., #894

Goodyear, Bradley, #894

Goodyear, Charles W., #888

Goodyear, Frank H., #762

Glenny, William H., #1160

Hamlin, Chauncey, #1014

Hamlin, Harry, #1014

Holland, Nelson C., #916

Kent, Edward, A., #512

Knox, Seymour H., Jr., 806

Lockwood, Thomas B., #844

McFarland, John, #1092

Mixer, Frederick K., #427

Morse, Charles, #491

Rogers, Robert #698

Satterfield, John M., #1022

Spaulding, Henry B., #1260

Vars, Addison, #1115

Watson, Arnold, #622

Wickwire, Theodore D., #1217

Wilcox, Ansley, #641

Wilkeson, Samuel, 17 N.S.

Princeton (College of
New Jersey, 1746)

Otto, Jacob S. #1094

Cornell (1865)

Block, Arthur J., #905
Robert M. Codd, Jr., #369
Ely, W. Carl, #628
Hoyt, Wiliam B., #706
Huntley, William R., #1230*
Jones, Charles S., #564
Laub, Albert F. #1272*
McGraw, Frank S., #950*
Schoellkopf, III, Jacob F., #489
Schoellkopf, William G., #1272
Schoellkopf, William H. #864
Sidway, Clarence, #584
Simpson, Louis W., #70

Appendix 3

Congressmen who were residents of Delaware Avenue

Albert H. Tracy, Niagara Square, 1819-1825
Millard Fillmore, Niagara Square, Millard Fillmore, 1833-1835, 1837-1843
Ray Vaughn Pierce, #138, 1040, 1879-1880
John H. Ganson, 262, 1863-1865
William E. Dorsheimer, #438, 1883-1885
Charles A. Daniels, #787, 1893-1897

Mayors who were residents of Delaware Avenue

Ebenezer Johnson, 1832, 1834
Samuel Wilkeson, 1836
Frederick Stevens, 1856-1857
Philip Becker, 1876-1877, 1886-1889
Jonathan Scoville, 1884-1885

Delaware Avenue Residents in either the *Dictionary of American Biography* or the *American National Biography*

1. Wilson Shannon Bissell, #295, 414, 1069, *DAB*.

2. Samuel Clemens, #472, *DAB, ANB*.

3. Arthur Cleveland Coxe, #314, *DAB, ANB*.

4. Glenn H. Curtiss, #1171, *DAB, ANB*.

6. William J. Donovan, #742, *ANB*.

7. William H. Dorsheimer, #434, *DAB*.

8. Millard Fillmore, #35 Niagara Square, *DAB, ANB*.

9. Lucien Howe, #183, 522, *DAB*.

10. Mabel Dodge Luhan, #675, *ANB*.

11. Roswell Park, #510, *DAB*.

12. James Edward Quigley, #1025, *DAB, ANB*.

13. Henry Augustus Richmond, #348, *DAB*.

14. Bennett Riley, Fort Poinsett, *DAB, ANB*.

15. Charles Cary Rumsey, #1 Park Place, *DAB, ANB*.

16. Edward Streeter, #1125, *ANB*.

17. William Turner, *ANB, DNB*.

17. Samuel Wilkeson, Niagara Square, *DAB, ANB*.

Bibliography

BOOKS

Adler, Selig and Connolly, Thomas E. *From Ararat to Suburbia: The History of the Jewish Community of Buffalo.* Philadelphia: The Jewish Publication Society of America, 1960.

Ahlstrom, Sidney E. *A Religious History of the American People.* New Haven: Yale University Press, 1972.

Battles and Leaders of the Civil War. New York: Thomas Yosellof Inc. 4 vols., 1956.

Becker, William H. *Encyclopedia of American Business History.* New York: Facts on File, 1989.

Biographical Directory of the United States Congress, 1774-1989. Washington, D.C: United States Congress, Printing Office, 1989.

Blum, John M. *et al. The National Experience: A History of the United States to 1877.* New York: Harcourt Brace, 2nd ed., 1968.

Brinnin, John Malcom. *The Sway of the Grand Saloon: A Social History of the North Atlantic.* New York: Barnes & Noble Books, 1971.

Bruce, R. V., 1877: *Year of Violence.* New York: Bobbs-Merrill, 1959.

Buffalo und Sein Deutschtum. Buffalo: German American Historical and Biographical Society, 1911-1912.

Burrows, Edwin G. and Wallace, Mike. Gotham: *A History of New York City to 1898.* New York: Oxford University Press, 1999.

Canadian Encyclopedia. Edmonton: Hurtig Publishers, 3 vols., 1985.

Chazanof, William. *Joseph Ellicott and the Holland Land Company: The opening of Western New York.* Syracuse: Syracuse University Press, 1970.

Cigliano, Jan and Landau, Sara Bradford, *The Grand American Avenue, 1850-1920.* San Francisco: Pomegranate Artbooks, 1994.

Conlin, John. *Buffalo City Hall: Americanesque Masterpiece.* Buffalo: Landmark Society of the Niagara Frontier, 1993.

Cornell, Katherine. *I Wanted to Be an Actress.* New York: Random House, 1938.

The Craftsman, June 1933. The Burgard year book.

Davis, Kenneth S. *FDR: The Beckoning of Destiny, 1882-1929*. New York: G. P. Putnam's Sons, 1972.

DeMille, George E. *Saint Paul's Cathedral, Buffalo: A Brief History.* Buffalo. Hoffman Printing Co., 1960.

Derks, Scott, ed. *The Value of a Dollar: Prices and Incomes in the United States, 1860-1999.* Lakeville, Connecticut: Grey House Publishing, 1999.

Deuther, Charles. *Life and Times of the Rt. Rev. John Timon, D. D.* Buffalo, published by the author, 1870.

Dictionary of American History. New York: Charles Scribner's Sons, 1927.

Dictionary of American Biography. Dumas Malone, ed. New York: Charles Scribner's Sons. 21 vols., 1932.

Donlop, Richard. *Donovan, America's Master Spy*. New York: Rand McNally & Co., 1982.

Donohue, Thomas. *History of the Diocese of Buffalo*. Buffalo Catholic Publication Co., 1929.

Drury, George H. *The Historical Guide to North American Railroads*. Waukesha, Wisconsin: Kalmbach Publishing Co. 1985.

Dunn, Edward T. *A History of Railroads in Western New York*, 2nd ed. Buffalo: Canisius College Press, 2000.

Dunn, Walter S. *History of Erie County, 1879-1970*. Buffalo: Buffalo Historical Society, 1972.

Encyclopedia Americana. Danbury, Connecticut: Grolier Inc., 30 vols., 1998.

Encyclopedia Britannica, 11th ed. (Cambridge: University Press, 1910-1911.

Encyclopedia of Religion and Ethics. New York: Charles Scribner's Sons, 12 vols., 1962.

A Field Guide to the Architecture and History of Allentown. Buffalo: The Allentown Association, 1987.

Fisher, Dr. Jack C. *Stolen Glory: The McKinley Assassination*. La Jolla California: Alamar Books, 2001.

Fitzgerald, F. Scott. *This Side of Paradise*. New York: Charles Scribner's Sons, 1920.

Garraty, John A. and Carnes, Mark C. *American National Biography*. New York: Oxford University Press, 25 vols., 1999.

Gerber David A. *The Making of an American Pluralism: Buffalo, New York, 1826-1860.* Chicago: University of Illinois Press, 1989.

Goldman, Mark. *High Hopes: The Rise and Fall of Buffalo, New York.* Buffalo: State University of New York Press, 1983.

Goodyear, George. *Goodyear Family History.* Buffalo: privately printed, 1976-1977.

Gordon, William R. *90 Years of Buffalo Railways, 1840-1950.* Buffalo: 1970.

Hahn, Emily. *Mabel: Biography of Mabel Dodge Luhan.* Boston: Houghton Mifflin Co., 1977.

Harlow, Alvin F. *Old Towpaths: The Story of the American Canal Era.* New York: D. Appleton & Co., 1926.

Hawes, Evelyn. *The Twentieth Century Club of Buffalo: Seventy-five Years, 1984-1969.* 1969.

Hayes, Charles Wells. *The Diocese of Western New York.* Rochester. Scrantom Whetmore & Co, 1904.

Heacock, Lee F, ed. *Buffalo Artists Register.* Buffalo: Heacock Publishing Co., 1926.

Hill, Henry Wayland. *Municipality of Buffalo, New York: A History, 1720-1923.* New York: Lewis Publishing Co. 4 vols., 1923.

Historic American Buildings Survey No. NY5613, 15-Buf, Cary House. Office of Archeology and Historic Preservation, National Park Service, Department of the Interior, Washington D.C.

A History of the City of Buffalo, its men and institutions. Buffalo: Buffalo Evening News, 1908.

Holden, George W. and Due, John F. *The Electric Interurban Railways in America.* Stanford, California, Stanford University Press, 1960.

Horton, John T. *History of Northwestern New York.* New York: Lewis Publishing Co., 3 vols., 1947.

Hubbell, Mark H. *Buffalo the City Beautiful.* Buffalo: Buffalo Truth Press, 1931.

Hungerford, Edward. *Men and Iron: The History of the New York Central.* New York: Thomas Y. Crowell Co. 1938.

International Directory of Company Histories. 54 vols., Chicago and London: St. James Press, 1988-.

Johnson, Crisfield. *Centennial History of Erie County, New York. Buffalo*: Matthews and Warren, 1876.

Ketchum, William. *An Authentic and Comprehensive History of Buffalo*. Buffalo: Rockwell Baker & Hill, 1865.

Klein, Maury. *The Life and Legend of E. H. Harriman*. Chapel Hill, North Carolina: University of North Carolina Press, 2000.

Kowsky, Francis. *The Best Planned City: The Olmsted Legacy in Buffalo*. Buffalo: Buffalo State College, 1992.

__________ et al. *Buffalo Architecture: A Guide*. Cambridge, Massachusetts: MIT Press, 1981.

Larned, J. N. *A History of Buffalo*. New York: Progress of Empire State Co., 1911.

Leech, Margaret. *In the Days of McKinley*. New York: Harper and Bros., 1959.

Logal, Nelson W. *History of Old Saint Joseph's Cathedral, 1847-1947*. Buffalo: 1947.

Luhan, Mable Dodge. *Intimate Memories*. London, England: Martin Secker, 1933.

McGill, Fred. *Right Reverend Charles Henry Colton: A Character Sketch of the Fourth Bishop of Buffalo*. Buffalo Catholic Publication Company, 1903.

McKim, Meade & White. *The Architecture of McKim, Mead & White in Photographs, Plans and Elevations*. New York: Dover Publications, 1990.

McLellan, Dave and Warrick, Bill. *The Lake Shore & Michigan Southern Railway*. Polo, Illinois: Transportation Trails, 1989.

Memorial and Family History of Erie County. New York: Genealogical Publishing Co., 2 vols., 1906-1908.

Men of Buffalo. Chicago: A. N. Marquis & Co., 1902.

Men of New York. Buffalo. G. E. Matthews & Co., 2 vols., 1898.

Mixer, Mary E. *History of Trinity Church*. Buffalo: The Peter Paul Book Co., 1897.

Morris, Richard B., ed. *Encyclopedia of American History*. New York: Harper & Row, 1965.

Mowry, George E. *The Era of Theodore Roosevelt and the Birth of Modern America, 1900-1912*. New York. Harper & Row, 1958.

Murray, J. Clayton. *A Historical Retrospective of the Last 125 Years of Canisius College, 1870-1995*. Buffalo: Canisius College, 1996.

Nevins, Allan. *Grover Cleveland: A Study in Courage*. New York: Dodd, Mead & Co., 1948.

____________. *John D. Rockefeller: The Heroic Age of American Enterprise.* New York: Charles Scribner's Sons, 1948.

The New Catholic Encyclopedia: 2nd ed. New York: McGraw Hill Books, 16 vols., 2002.

New York: A Guide to the Empire State. New York: Oxford University Press, 2 vols. 1940.

The Official Catholic Directory, Anno Domini 2000. New Providence, New Jersey: P. J. Kennedy & Sons, 1999.

Phisterer, Frederick. *New York in the War of the Rebellion, 1861-1865.* 3rd ed., Albany: J. B. Lyon & Co., 6. vols., 1912.

Pierce, Ray V., M.D. *The People's Common Sense Medical Adviser in Plain English, or Medicine Simplified.* Buffalo: World's Dispensary Medical Association. 95th ed., 1918.

Pietrack, George. *The Buffalo & Susquehanna Railroad.* North Boston, New York: Paul Pietrak, 1967.

Porzelt, Paul. *The Metropolitan Club of New York.* Milan, Italy: Rizzoli International Publications Inc., 1982.

Rayback, Robert J. *Millard Fillmore: Biography of a President.* Buffalo: Henry Stewart, 1959.

Sandburg, Carl. *Abraham Lincoln: The War Years*. New York: Harcourt, Brace & Co., 4 vols. 1936.

Saturn Club. *Forty Years, 1885-1925.* Buffalo: Saturn Club, 1925.

Shaw, Ronald A. *Erie Water West: A History of the Erie Canal, 1792-1854.* Lexington, Kentucky: University of Kentucky Press, 1966.

Sherwood, Sidney G. and Bosche, John. *The Buffalo Elite Directory or Ladies Visiting List*. Buffalo: Baker Jones & Co., 1883.

Smith, H. Perry. *History of the City of Buffalo and Erie County*. Syracuse: D. Mason & Co., 2 vols., 1884.

Statistical Abstract of the United States, 1910. Washington, D.C: United States Government Printing Office, 1911.

Steele, O. G., Esq. *Memorial of the Late Walter Joy*. Buffalo: Commercial Advertiser, 1864.

Turner, Orsamus. *Pioneer History of the Holland Land Purchase of Western New York.* Buffalo: George H. Derby & Co., 1858.

Valaik, J. David *et al.* *Celebrating God's Life in Us: The Catholic Diocese of Buffalo, 1847-1947.* Buffalo: Western New York Heritage Press, 1997.

Van Ness, Cynthia. *Victorian Buffalo.* Buffalo: Western New York Wares, 1999.

Warren, Rupert. *The Buffalo Club, 1867-1992.* Buffalo: Buffalo Club, 1992.

Welch, Samuel W. *Home History: Recollections of Buffalo During the Decade from 1830-1840.* Buffalo: Peter Paul & Bro., 1891.

White, John H. *The American Railroad Passenger Car.* Baltimore: Johns Hopkins Press, 2 vols., 1979.

White, Truman C. *Our County and its People: A Descriptive Work on Erie County, New York.* Boston: The Boston History Co., 1931.

Who Was Who in America, 1897-1942; vol. 2, 1943-1950; vol. 3, 1951-1960; Chicago: A. N. Marquis Co., 1942, 1950, 1960.

Woodham-Smith, Cecil. *The Great Hunger: Ireland, 1845-1849.* London. G. Hamilton, 1962.

Wilner, Merton M. *Niagara Frontier: A Narrative and Documentary History.* Chicago: S. J. Clarke Publishing Co., 4 vols., 1931.

Articles in Journals (excluding PBHS)

Alleva, Richard, "Missing the Dark Side." *Commonweal*, 129 (February 22, 2002), 1920.

Baltzell, E. Digby. "The Social Defenses of the Rich," in *The Private Side of American History: Readings in Everyday Life.* Orlando: Harcourt, Brace Jovanovich, 2 vols., 1975, 2: 97-99.

Biederman, Patricia Ward, "Mark Twain in Buffalo." *Western New York Heritage*, Summer 2001, 73-88.

Fox, Austin M. "Buffalo Architect, Edward Kent: Titanic Hero." *Buffalo Spree*, 18 (Summer 1984), 40-41.

__________. "The Portrait on the Wall: Who was Gen. Bennett Riley?" *Buffalo Spree*, 24 (Summer, 1990), 53-53.

Hirsch, Dick. "Buffalo's Forgotten Mansion Builder." *Western New York Heritage Magazine*, 2 (Fall 1998), 5-15.

Hennessy, "A History of Canisius High School." *Woodstock Letters*, 83(1954), 352-364.

Reigstad, Tom. "Mark Twain and Buffalo." *Western New York Heritage Magazine*, 4(Fall 2000), 4-22, 48. 1989,

Rockwell, Mary Rech. "Elite Marriage Patterns in the Pan American Era." *Buffalo Spree*, 35 (January-February 2001), 50-55.

J. Valaik. "Theodore Roosevelt in Buffalo." *Canisius College Chronicle*, 15 (February, 1985), 6-7.

Williams, Clifford R. "The Discovery of the Buffalo Barracks." *Buffalo Irish Times*, December, 1998.

Articles in PBHS

Adam, Robert B. "History of the Abolition of Railroad Grade Crossings in the City of Buffalo." 8(1905), 151-254.

Barton, James L., "Early Reminiscences of Buffalo and Vicinity." 1(1879), 153-178.

"Historical Writings of Judge Samuel Wilkeson." 5 (1902), 148-150.

Hodge, William, "Buffalo Cemeteries. " 1 (1879), 49-52.

Hosmer, George W., "The Physiognomy of Buffalo." 2 (1880), 1-16.

Lord, Rev. John C., "Samuel Wilkeson." 4 (1896), 71-85.

Severance, Frank, "The Periodical Press of Buffalo, 1811-1915." 19(1915), 179-280.

________________, "The Changing Town." 29(1927), 333-349.

________________, "Historical Sketch of the Buffalo Board of Trade," 12 (1909), 271-279.

Graduate Theses

Dunn, Edward, A History of Canisius College, 1870-1907. A Thesis submitted to the Faculty of the Department of History, Canisius College, in partial fulfillment of the requirements for the degree Master of Arts, May, 1964.

Farley, James Anthony. History of the Pan-American Exposition, May 1, 1901-November 1, 1901. Master's Thesis, Department of History, Canisius College, June, 1961.

Napora, James. Houses of Worship: a guide to the religious architecture of Buffalo, New York. M. A. thesis submitted to the faculty of the State University of New York at Buffalo, 1995.

Atlases

Century Atlas Company. *The Century Atlas of Greater Buffalo*. Philadelphia: Century Atlas Company, 3 vols., 1915.

Hopkins, Griffith Morgan. *Atlas of the City of Buffalo, Erie County, New York*. Philadelphia: G. M. Hopkins Company, 1872.

________________. *Atlas of the City of Buffalo, New York*. Philadelphia: G. M. Hopkins Company, 1884.

Rayback, Robert J., ed. *Richards Atlas of New York State*. Phoenix, New York: Frank E. Richards, 1957-1959.

Newspapers

Buffalo Commercial Advertiser, Buffalo Courier, Buffalo Courier-Express, Buffalo Express Buffalo Evening, Republican,Buffalo Times, New York Times, Syracuse Post-Standard

Manuscripts

Evans Bartlett Family Papers, Buffalo Historical Society, Nottingham Terrace, Buffalo.

Index

This index is divided into four parts: Renumbering and images, House addresses, Places including estates, and Persons.

The Renumbering Index serves as a reference to the numbering system used before the renumbering of Delaware Avenue in 1867. It is an important tool to use in conjunction with the House Address Index, which index includes both pre-1867 and post-1867 house numbers for Delaware Avenue as well as other addresses from other streets. The Place Index includes the name of institutions or estate names referenced in the book. The Person Index lists each person mentioned in the book alphabetically by last name.

INDEX BY AMY MILLER
ASSISTANT LIBRARIAN
BUFFALO HISTORY MUSEUM

INDEX GUIDE

RENUMBERING AND IMAGE INDEX

The houses on Delaware Avenue underwent renumbering in 1867/1868. Below is a list of the numbers before the renumbering alongside the new (modern) number. The house numbers are in ascending order based on the post-1867 (modern) numbers. When searching the House Index (22-430 modern), be sure to reference both house numbers.

The column for image page indicates on what page a photograph, map, plan, drawing, etc. of the house appears in the book. Only addresses with a pre-1867 number change and/or an image are included in this index. For a full listing of all house numbers mentioned in the book, see the House Address Index on page 589.

Delaware Avenue

Pre-1867	Post-1867	Image page
2	22	27-28
6	26	27-28
8	28	28
10		28
12	36	28
14	38	27-28, 36
16	42	28, 36
18	44	28, 36
20	46	28
22	50	28, 58
24	60	
	64	35
	69	61
	86	62
30	89	
32	91	
34	93	
	98	39, 48
	116	71
	118	71
	137	72
47	141	72
	142	82
49	145	72
	151	72
	153	72
53	157	72
55	161	72
57	163	72
	168	83
63	169	72
68	184	90, 92, 105

Delaware Avenue

Pre-1867	Post-1867	Image page
70	190	
72	194	
	199	119
76	202	
78	210	96, 103
71	211	
80	212	
82	214	
73	217	
84	220	
86	222	
88	224	
	225	112
	227	112
	240	149
99	251	136
100	256	150
102	262	150-151
106	274	
107	265	
109	271	
111	275	
113	277	
119	285	
	295	138
121	297	
1 Park Place	300	152, 154, 156
129	305	
139	313	
130	314	
145	321	
149	329	

Delaware Avenue

Pre-1867	Post-1867	Image page
	330	154, 156, 162, 164
	331	
156	334	164
155	335	
157	339	
158	340	164
	341	142
	344	164
	348	164
	349	
167	357	215
170	358	187
169	363	
173	367	
174	368	
177	371	218-219
181	381	
185	387	
	388	188, 190
187	391	
189	393	
184	396	193
191	399	
193	405	
207	409	
	410	193
209	413	
	414	193, 197
227	415	
	423	223-225
231	427	227
234	430	
	431	227
	435	227
	438	202
	443	227, 229
	452	201
	469	231, 283
	471	283
	472	249
	475	283
	477	283
	482	254
	484	255, 255
	487	308

Delaware Avenue

Pre-1867	Post-1867	Image page
	489	308
	490	254
	491	308
	493	308
	497	308
	498	254
	499	308
	506	254
	514	263
	525	319
	531	313
	534	266
	536	268
	537	313
	546	268
	553	310, 313
	560	269
	564	269
	567	320
	581	320
	584	274
	589	275
	591	321
	595	322-323
	609	324
	641	326-327
	650	281
	661	334
	672	349-350
	675	407, 412
	685	413
	690	351
	695	416
	698	355
	703	418
	713	418
	724	356
	735	419
	741	421
	762	358-360
	776	366
	786	367, 370
	787	423
	795	424
	805	425-426, 429

HOUSE ADDRESS INDEX

This index includes both pre-1867 and post-1867 house numbers for Delaware Avenue and includes other addresses from other streets. Please refer to the Renumbering and Image Index for Delaware Avenue house numbers. The House Address Index is in alphabetical order by street, then by ascending house number.

Gates Circle

Delaware Avenue

Niagara Square

Park Place

PLACE INDEX

This index includes estates, neighborhoods, institutions, businesses, and other place names along Delaware Avenue referenced in the book. It is in alphabetical order.

PERSON INDEX

This index is alphabetical by last name, then first name. A single entry is used for a shared name without the inclusion of middle initial in the book. A woman is entered by her married name with a *See mention* from her maiden name when known.

About the Authors

EDWARD T. DUNN was born in Orange, New Jersey, in 1925, where he attended parochial grammar and high school before entering the Society of Jesus in the summer of 1943. After college at Woodstock, Maryland, he taught Latin, English, and German at Regis High School in New York City from 1950 to 1953, returning to Woodstock to study theology. Ordained in 1956, he came to Canisius College in Buffalo, New York in 1958, where he taught religion, moderated the Little Theatre, and earned a Masters degree in History in 1964. He received a Ph.D. in History from the University of Rochester in 1969. At Canisius College, Father Dunn taught courses on Colonial America, the American Revolution, the Federalist Era, the Age of Jackson, America between the Civil War and World War I, and American Railroads. He wrote *A History of Railroads in Western New York* and a *History of the Park Club*, among other books, as well as many articles. He retired from teaching in 1991, but continued to golf, ride his bicycle and cheer on the Buffalo Bills until his death in 2013.

CYNTHIA VAN NESS earned a Bachelor's degree in Art History from SUNY/Empire State College and a Masters in Library and Information Science from the University at Buffalo. Her first job upon receiving her graduate degree was at the Buffalo & Erie County Public Library, where she worked for thirteen years. Half of those years were in the Grosvenor Room, the local history and genealogy collection, where she developed research and reference expertise in the people, places, things, and history of Buffalo. She was appointed Director of Library & Archives at the Buffalo History Museum in October, 2007. On her own time, she is the author of Victorian Buffalo (1999), Quotable Buffalo (2011), and the creator of BuffaloResearch.com, a guide to researching ancestors, buildings, and companies in Buffalo.

AMY MILLER currently works at the Buffalo History Museum Research Library as the Assistant Librarian and Archivist and is a part-time professor at University at Buffalo. She earned a Masters in Library and Information Science from the University at Buffalo in December, 2011 and an Advanced Certificate in Library and Information Science in December, 2014.

Front cover photograph of The Mansion on Delaware Avenue was generously provided by **KIM SMITH PHOTO**.

CPSIA information can be obtained
at www.ICGtesting.com
Printed in the USA
BVOW09s0251290317
479448BV00004B/14/P